ANTIQUES ROADSHOW

COLLECTIBLES

20TH-CENTURY

The COMPLETE GUIDE to
COLLECTING 20TH-CENTURY TOYS,
GLASSWARE, COSTUME JEWELRY,
MEMORABILIA, CERAMICS & MORE
from the MOST-WATCHED SERIES *on* PBS®.

by CAROL PRISANT

WORKMAN PUBLISHING, NEW YORK

Antiques Roadshow is produced for PBS by WGBH/Boston.
Executive Producer for Antiques Roadshow: Peter B. Cook
Senior Producer: Marsha Bemko
Consulting Producer: Dan Farrell

Antiques Roadshow would like to thank Bonhams & Butterfields, Christie's, Doyle New York,
Skinner, Inc., Sotheby's, our independent dealers and appraisers nationwide,
and the staff and crew of the television series.

Major funding for *Antiques Roadshow* provided by the Chubb Group of Insurance Companies.
Funding also provided by public television viewers.

Antiques Roadshow Online: www.pbs.org/antiques

Library of Congress Cataloging-in-Publication Data
Prisant, Carol
Antiques Roadshow Collectibles: the complete guide to collecting 20th-century toys,
glassware, costume jewelry, memorabilia, ceramics, and more,
from the most-watched series on PBS / by Carol Prisant.
p. cm.
Includes index.
ISBN 0-7611-2887-5 — ISBN 0-7611-2822-0 (pbk. : alk. paper)
1. Art objects, European—20th century—Handbooks, manuals, etc. 2. Art objects,
American—20th century—Handbooks, manuals, etc. 3. Art objects—Collectors and collecting—
Handbooks, manuals, etc. 4. Antiques roadshow (Television program : Great Britain)
5. Antiques roadshow (Television program : U.S.) I. Title.

NK925 .P75 2003
745.1--dc21   2002034207
CIP

Workman books are available at special discounts when purchased in bulk for premiums and
sales promotions as well as for fund-raising or educational use. Special editions can also be created
to specification. For details, contract the Special Sales Director at the address below.

Workman Publishing Company, Inc.
708 Broadway
New York, NY 10003-9555
www.workman.com

Printed in the U.S.A.

First printing May 2003
10 9 8 7 6 5 4 3 2 1

For Millard, as ever
and
Barden, our son

ACKNOWLEDGMENTS

MY THANKS TO . . .

My dear friend Peter Workman, for his good sense, rectitude, and generosity.

Suzanne Rafer, who gracefully walked the knife edge of editorial diplomacy, deadlines, and compassion without a misstep.

Ann ffolliott, whose work combined empathy with intelligence and experience, and then some.

Janet Parker, whose design brought the text to life.

Beth Doty, Katherine Adzima, Robyn Schwartz, and Francine Almash, who assisted in every way possible.

The photo research team of Leora Kahn, Anne Kerman, and Aaron Clendening, and Michael Fusco for design assistance.

Sally Kovalchick, for helping to start us off.

............◆............

A special thanks to Eric Alberta—our "designated hitter"—for his thorough and very timely research, and Danny Peary, for his ninth inning "relief pitching."

............◆............

And a special thanks to Dennis Gaffney for all his work, particularly in researching and writing many of our *Antiques Roadshow* Discoveries and sidebars. His willingness, effort, and boundless enthusiasm helped to make our collectibles come alive.

............◆............

My *Antiques Roadshow* editorial board: Eric Alberta; Noel Barrett, Noel Barrett Antiques & Auctions; Leila Dunbar, Sotheby's; Rudy Franchi, The Nostalgia Factory; Tim Luke, TreasureQuest Auction Galleries; David Rago, David Rago Auctions; Gary Sohmer, Wex Rex Collectibles; and Richard Wright, Richard Wright Antiques, who, with immeasurable, unexpected, and most welcome good will made their knowledge and resources freely available to me.

The following appraisers from *Antiques Roadshow*: Caroline Ashleigh,
Nancy Druckman, Ken Farmer, Michael Flanigan, Rudy Franchi,
David Gallager, Kathleen Guzman, Reyne Haines, Riley Humler,
Daile Kaplan, Kerry Keane, Chris Kennedy, David Lackey,
Nicholas Lowry, Louise Luther, Phillip Merrill, David Rago,
Christie Romero, Rosalie Sayyah, Sig Shonholtz, Kerry Shrives,
Eric Silver, Usha Subramaniam, Arlie Sulka, and Kevin Zavian,
all of whom allowed me to cull, from their years of hard-won
knowledge and specialization, everything this book required.

◆

The staff of *Antiques Roadshow*, including Executive Producer
Peter B. Cook, Senior Producer Marsha Bemko, and Consulting
Producer Dan Farrell, for their feedback on this text, and for
allowing me to travel with their amazingly accomplished and
talented Roadshow team.

◆

WGBH Managing Director Betsy Groban and Publishing
Manager Caroline Chauncey, for their incisive comments and
for shepherding this book within WGBH.

◆

For their advice and special expertise: Anthony Annese, Steve Balkin,
Mark Bergin, Louis Bofferding, Leila Buckjune, Al "Big Time"
Daniels, Van Dexter, Andy Eskind, Bob Farino, Joe Freeman,
Jack Herbert, Fritz Karch, Jay Kennedy, Rodger Kingston, David
Mann, Frank Marciello, Nancy McClelland, Mark McDonald,
Alan Moss, J. Stewart Johnson, Keni Valenti and Jerry Weist.

◆

For sharing their collections (and expertise): Herb Barker, Barker
Animation Museum; Anthony Barnes, Rago Modern Auctions;
Caroline Birenbaum and Cristina Capello, Swann Galleries; Diane
Buckley and Louis Weber, Doyle New York; Jane H. Clarke,
Morning Glory Antiques & Jewelry; Jeffrey Ellis, for access to his
beautiful images of golf collectibles; Laura Fisher, Laura Fisher
Antique Quilts and Americana; Ron Gast, for use of his wonderful
lures, reels, and tackle; Kristin Gelder, Sotheby's; Barry Halper, for

generous access to the Barry Halper Baseball Archives (and to
Joseph Pecora, Esq., for access to Barry Halper); Dan Kubert,
American Toys; Karen Marks from Howard Greenberg Gallery;
Brian McGrath, H. Leonard Rod Company; Shari McMasters,
Kandice Cain, Patti Wallace, and Mark Harris, McMasters Harris
Auction Company; Roger Reed and Walt Reed, Illustration
House; Catherine Riedel and Anne Trodella, Skinner, Inc.; Nicole
Rivette, Toledo Museum of Art; Elissa Swanger, Phillips, de Pury
& Luxembourg; Joe and Donna Tonelli, for use of their wonderful
fishing and tackle collection Steve Whitney, for his terrific golf
card collection; and Rosemary Trietsch, for use of her beautiful
Depression glass collection.

❖

My good friend, Sanford Goldstein, for his counsel, fine
intelligence, warmth and kindness.

Robert Rufino, Roger and Doris Straus, Norma and Gordon
Smith, and Bo Niles, for their affection and care.

Carolan Workman, who is better than a sister, and certainly
funnier.

Richard and Judy Lincoff, providers of boundless long-distance
love and support.

Norah McNelis, for keeping me and my fur family clean,
well-fed, and tidy.

Barden and Catherine Prisant, always loving and always there.

And my Millard, who encouraged me in this, as he encouraged
me (with the requisite grumbling, naturally) in everything, always.

—C.L.P.

CONTENTS

Newcomb potter, page 32

Point-of-purchase display, page 33

Drink MOXIE

*Lalique
Escargot vase,
page 72*

*Mickey Mantle
bobble-head
doll, page 135*

CHAPTER SIX

FASHION AND TEXTILES 219

FASHION 220

TEXTILES 254

CHAPTER SEVEN

DOLLS AND DOLL ACCESSORIES 263

DOLLS 264

DOLLHOUSES & ACCESSORIES 293

*Fortuny textile,
page 238*

*Japanese
Smoking Robot,
page 169*

*Howdy Doody
doll, page 285*

*Watch necklace,
page 299*

*A B. B. King
guitar,
page 351*

*Salvador Dalí
pendant,
page 422*

FOREWORD

BY PETER B. COOK
Executive Producer, Antiques Roadshow

I'm a television guy, and my greatest passion in the TV business is figuring out the best ways to tell stories on the screen. What's particularly fun about that is that storytelling— writing and producing and directing and performing—for the screen is a team sport; and I'm a team sport guy. At *Antiques Roadshow,* we have a particularly talented, hardworking, and diverse team that includes over a dozen staff members, two dozen crew members, many dozens of people in all kinds of support activities, and a pool of 150 experts who contribute their time—and pay their own way—to what has been for years the most-watched primetime series on PBS.

If you ask the experts why they do it—why they take the time and take on the expense of running around the country to be part of *Antiques Roadshow,* they'll tell you it's good for their business, it's good for their professional relationships, and it's great for their psyches: There's always the chance they'll see something new, something really exciting, something they've never seen before. Every one of them is passionate about some area of collecting, some aspect of the business— and about the hunt, the thrill of the chase that inspires so many people around the United States to collect things.

Antiques Roadshow began production in the summer of 1996; I came on board as the production unit was being formed in the fall of 1995. By that time, I had a quarter century under my belt as a researcher and producer at WGBH Boston. I had worked mostly in public affairs programming: a debate program called *The Advocates,* a series called *Arabs & Israelis,* docudramas about the trials of

Alger Hiss and the triumph of Thurgood Marshall. When I joined *Antiques Roadshow*, I had just finished four years researching and developing a series about the African-American experience up to the Civil War.

For four years I was Senior Producer of the *Roadshow*, responsible for what we call the field production—basically, everything the host did and everything outside the appraisal segments that make up three-quarters of the show. Aida Moreno was the Executive Producer then; she ran a tight ship, built a well-oiled production machine, and allowed me to have all the fun, as I saw it, running around to museums and other local attractions with the host and an occasional expert while the other guys did all the work back at the Convention Center. Early in 2000, as we prepared for our fifth season, Aida moved on to new enterprises, and I took on the overall responsibility for *Antiques Roadshow*. Blessed with a terrific staff headed by now Senior Producer Marsha Bemko, I still feel that I have all the fun.

When I first started with the show, however, I didn't know a whole lot about the world of antiques and collecting. But I had grown up in a family of artists, and I had often helped my painter father build occasional tables and chairs for the family, pieces that were designed after simple American models.

I knew *Antiques Roadshow* had been a big hit in England for years and years, but I was completely unprepared for the popularity the series enjoyed as soon as our version hit the air here.

For one thing, I had no idea how many people in every part of the United States were involved—passionately involved—in collecting and trading things.

Now, that passion may not fully explain *Antiques Roadshow*'s success, at least in the ratings. The broadcast reaches millions of people who are drawn by the stories, personal anecdotes, and professional analyses, with collectors making up a significant and critical part of our audience. We receive a lot of mail from people whose passion is a certain area of collecting, and who want more than they get from most of our broadcast segments—more nuts and bolts, more inside information, more challenges to broaden and deepen their purview, so they can sharpen their skills, improve their "performance," and, let's face it, have more fun.

The way I see it, that's where our Web site comes in, that's where our newsletter comes in, and that's where a book like this comes in. Here is *Antiques Roadshow*'s chance to give something useful to those collectors who may feel, for lack of a better term, "underserved" by the television series.

Millions of Americans navigate both the well-traveled and the uncharted waters of twentieth-century collectibles, and thousands bring them to *Antiques Roadshow*. And we love their enchantment: All you have to do is spend ten minutes around the collectibles area at any of our events and you get a sense of the joy the people on both sides of the table carry with them. I know this first-hand: The appraisers, who select from thousands of collectibles brought to each *Roadshow* event, pitch their favorites to me and Marsha Bemko. Our job is narrow down the selections even further, to about fifty per event.

If collectors reveal a lot about themselves by what they choose to collect, so do the dealers and auctioneers who travel (and traffic) in the world of collectibles and memorabilia. When you read the many sidebars in this book, you'll catch a whiff of what motivates these greatly experienced professionals, what keeps them in the hunt. Their observations are often as poignant and as funny as they are perceptive and useful. It figures: Like all of us, they love talking about their passion.

At the end of the day, as the British say, that's what it's about—passion: You can't fake it, you either have it or you don't. It shows up on the screen in *Antiques Roadshow,* and you'll find that it permeates these pages.

COLLECTING 101

> "If the battered, cracked, and broken stuff our ancestors tried to get rid of now brings so much money, think what a 1954 Oldsmobile, or a 1960 Toastmaster will bring."
>
> —JOHN STEINBECK, *1962*

Steinbeck was either prescient or had a true collector's soul, for he was absolutely right about that car and that toaster. Today collectors are snapping up Danish modern furniture, Venini glass, Roseville pottery, Norman Norell dresses, Hamilton wristwatches, and toasters from the 1940s. Collectors come in all shapes and sizes, from all socioeconomic brackets, and from all parts of the country. They track down this potpourri of objects at yard sales, on the Internet, at auctions, and in shops.

ORCHERADE

OGDEN'S CIGARETTES

Previous page: Twentieth-century collectibles are as dissimilar from each other as the enthusiasts who collect them: from left, the prototype of the dining chair designed by Charles and Ray Eames; an autographed publicity photo of film star Leslie Howard; golfing great Ben Sayers on an Ogden's Cigarette card; a Carnival glass bowl manufactured by Fenton; a 1964 Yonezawa tin robot; and an advertisement for Orcherade, one of the many early soft drinks that didn't grow up to be Coke.

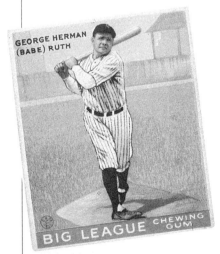

The Babe swings away on one of the several Big League Chewing Gum cards that pictured his image.

But how did "they" become "us"—a nation of collectors, in the midst of a collecting epidemic, evidence of which is the devoted weekly following *Antiques Roadshow* has enjoyed since 1997?

THE COLLECTING BUG

If you've got the collecting bug, it's more than likely that you know it. The bug insinuates itself into many aspects of your everyday existence. It makes its home in your heart and feeds on your yearnings, memories, and emotions. Once it has insinuated itself into your life, it seems to be a bug that's virtually unkillable. The usual pesticides—guilt, being the butt of long-running family jokes, insufficient funds—are ineffective. It's impervious to snow, rain, and dark of night (think of those 5 A.M. flea marketers with flashlights). Overflowing shelves and lengthy rationalizations barely slow it down. It has adapted to its difficult environment and is wholly at home in your home.

Nobody is immune. Says Peter Cook, the producer of *Antiques Roadshow,* "Every so often somebody walks into a *Roadshow* event with a collection that's been lovingly pulled together over the years. Baseball cards, vintage eyeglasses, fountain pens, snuff bottles, silver hairbrushes, fire-fighting memorabilia. It's always a great moment for our appraisers. Their excitement reveals that they aren't simply experts, they are collectors, too."

So, if all this seems to tell—more or less—the story of *your* life, you, too, have been fatally bit. You're a collector. You may even be a "born collector."

THE BORN COLLECTOR

A "born collector" is many things, most of them deeply passionate. He or she is utterly addicted to that heady blend of thrill-of-the-chase and thrill-of-discovery. He or she is someone who generally prefers that the desired object be a trifle difficult to obtain—because (and, surprisingly, studies confirm this), if it's too easy to get, it's a whole lot less interesting. A born collector's usual MO is to collect either in quantity—acquiring, for instance, every single Madame Alexander doll that's ever been manufactured—or to collect for rarity—acquiring just the rarest Madame Alexander dolls in existence. A born collector is knowledgeable about his or her subject, fiercely competitive, and willing to stand for hours in the rain waiting for tag sales to open. For all born collectors, there is never too much. The hunt is all.

THE LATENT COLLECTOR

Luckily, only some of us are born collectors. Otherwise, it would be truly a jungle out there. Compared with such unquenchable thirst, such burning passion to acquire absolutely all the Lalique perfume bottles ever manufactured or the fifteen best and rarest toy robots, the rest of us are furnishers or accumulators at best. Perhaps one of the nicest things about *Antiques Roadshow* is that it introduces us to hundreds of people like ourselves, people who already are—or soon will be—collectors.

Often, latent collectors start out as innocent heirs of their grandfather's toy cars or grandmother's dolls, things that they had loved as children. Maybe they were forbidden to play with these toys—or allowed to touch them only on special occasions. Today, these heirs have become the careful conservators of that inheritance. While many of them are a little reverential about the family "thingamajig," they have rarely been interested in even semischolarly diggings into methods of manufacture, for instance, or in tracking down makers' names. Most of them are simply curious and not too knowledgeable about values other than sentimental.

Until they visit or watch *Antiques Roadshow,* that is. Because any time a latent collector learns a little more about his grandparents' thingamajig, he starts to look around a lot more carefully. Sporting a similar thing in a shop window, he may go in to ask the price. Often, although it's pricier than imagined, he buys it to complement the one he inherited—first, because it's like the one he already owns and second, he now knows a little about it. Then he adds another and another of the same type of item to something that is suddenly on its way to becoming "The Family Collection of Thingamajigs."

Top: A visitor to the New Orleans Antiques Roadshow, *given this poster by his sister—who'd found several in the trash—exhibits his treasure: Cassandre's classic image of the ship* Normandie, *one of the best-known posters of the twentieth century. Below: An American mechanical bank in which a Japanese rickshaw man pulls a kimono-clad woman features splendid detail and artistically rendered paint.*

This 1940s acid-etched Daum Nancy glass vase, retro-style in shape, has an unusual central panel of clear glass.

From here, it's just a tiny step to purchasing a good magnifying glass; tracking down reliable reference materials; reading every book available on the subject; ransacking the Internet; attending specialty shows, flea markets, tag sales, and auctions; and always upending, touching, pinging, and turning inside out any and all examples of thingamajigs that cross his path. Now, our latent collector begins examining inner workings and condition (that's what the magnifying glass is for), searching for labels and indications of age, analyzing materials, and thereby expanding his knowledge. Excited and in love, our passive caretaker has become a full-blown collector—late blooming, perhaps, but passionate and thrilled, joining thousands of others drawn to his field by accident, or by interest, or by the object's eye appeal, or—like our collector—by nostalgia.

Unlike born collectors, this group isn't usually driven to own the "all" or the "every." The latent collector's fascination with the object of choice is grounded basically in curiosity, accident, and—all right—some smidgen of acquisitiveness. Love of collecting Mickey Mouse memorabilia, Buddy L trucks, or Norman Rockwell posters has less to do with *omnium gatherum* than it does with the latent collector's interest in this particular thing and its relevance to the social and historical past—most frequently, his own.

WHAT IS A COLLECTIBLE?

Just because someone collects something—clothes hangers, wedding cake tops, ticket stubs—doesn't make it a "collectible," and coming up with an exact definition for a "collectible" isn't easy. Even the experts disagree (see facing page).

A collectible is generally an object that is plentiful, because enough of it has to exist for a market to be made in it. A wide and enthusiastic collector base is also a prerequisite. So it has to be an object that is being purchased by more people than just your Mom and three first cousins, because the more collectors there are who are in pursuit of an item, the more collectible it is.

In addition to that plentitude of objects, and the crowd of people who want them, there needs to be at least one or two collectors who are willing to write down and share what they know about their field, thereby providing the imprimatur of scholarship.

What Are Collectibles, Anyway?

When a group of *Antiques Roadshow* collectibles experts shared their opinions of the history and meaning of the word *collectible,* it soon became clear that it was one of those things that even experts disagree about.

Eric Alberta, who is familiar with the workings of the auction salesroom, says, "My experience has been that 'collectibles' include anything the auction people don't know what to do with. It's a word that has become overused, perhaps because modern manufacturers have appropriated it." Tim Luke, also referring to his auction experiences, says, "At Christie's, where I worked in the 1990s, it was a term that made it easy to lump all the odd things together. Also, the proliferation of licensed products seemed to make it a value-added word: If you collect them, they're 'collectibles.' It's a great, convenient word, but now it probably includes too much. What else could we call it? Popular culture, maybe."

Leila Dunbar notes that although her father collected popular-culture items, such as advertising memorabilia and Disney toys, she doesn't remember hearing the word *collectibles* until the 1980s, when the first price guides using the word began to appear. Gary Sohmers, also remembering his father's collecting habits, says, "In 1960, my Dad, who collected political campaign material—he specialized in Lincoln and Kennedy campaign buttons—explained to me that such things were called collectibles.'"

Chris Kennedy agrees that the term has become a huge catchall but suggests a definition: "I think it should only be applied to objects that are both compelling and affordable." Noting that the word describes a category that needs a word to describe it, David Lackey says, "When I first heard the term, I was happy to know that a word actually existed to describe all those things that it seemed to me people really wanted to collect."

Some of the appraisers don't like to use the term, which they think has been appropriated by manufacturers and merchandisers. "*Collectibles* is not a term I like especially," says Ken Farmer. "It brings to mind all those modern companies that create and market what they like to call collectibles, and the very idea of a plate-of-the-month club kind of takes all the challenge out of the thing for me."

Noel Barrett points out that, "In the late 1960s, collectibles were things that were mostly new and that were marketed specifically to be collectible—like Christmas plates. Now, the word tends to be used for things that aren't necessarily old—Pez dispensers and McDonald's happy-meal toys, for instance. It's not really a word a serious person wants to be involved with." Rudi Franchi added, "Today, 1970s figurines and items from the Franklin Mint are tastefully and certainly more accurately described as 'cherishables,' but many Americans think of these as collectibles."

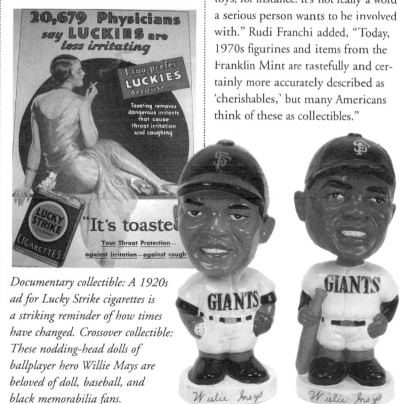

Documentary collectible: A 1920s ad for Lucky Strike cigarettes is a striking reminder of how times have changed. Crossover collectible: These nodding-head dolls of ballplayer hero Willie Mays are beloved of doll, baseball, and black memorabilia fans.

Red Goose children's shoes had a superbly graphic logo, seen here as a neon sign, but also on pens and pencils, shoe horns, banks, signs, tin whistles, calendars, tiny red "goslings" distributed as premiums—and shoes.

(As of this moment, many areas of twentieth-century collecting are so new that they are just being studied and defined. This is why collectors of certain types of fifties glass, for instance, may not yet know just how many pieces of it were actually manufactured. Nor do they begin to know how many are still in existence—hidden on the top shelves of china closets or, terrifying to the collector's soul, stockpiled by the thousands in warehouses.) We are still at the beginnings of scholarship for certain fields of twentieth-century collectibles—and just because something is less than one hundred years old doesn't mean that there is always a lot of information available about it.

Throughout this book, our definition of *collectible* is based in part on when the object was made. Things that are more than one hundred years old are legally antiques, and the term *collectibles* has come to be a convenient catchall term for many things—ceramics, furniture, glass—that are not yet old enough to be antiques. (Some collectibles, however, may never be considered antiques—baseball cards, toy robots, or fishing lures, for instance. See page 515 for a roundtable discussion of this issue.) The items featured in this book date—generally speaking—from the period between the end of World War I and about 1975. World War I provides a convenient starting point because of postwar changes in manufacturing techniques, as well as stylistic shifts that occurred in many of the categories covered in this book—furniture, glass, fashion, ceramics, and so forth. Many of these technological advances and new forces in design came about as a result of the 1925 Exposition Internationale des Arts Décoratifs Industriels et Modernes, which was held in Paris. The Exposition launched the style that was later named for it—Art Deco. The Bauhaus too, a school of art, design, and architecture in Weimar (1919–1925) and Dessau (1925–1933), Germany, gave us such important modern designers as Walter Gropius, Ludwig Mies van der Rohe, and Marcel Breuer. You will read more about the Exposition and the Bauhaus in the ensuing chapters.

The year 1975 makes a convenient ending point because it takes about twenty-five years for a collectible to begin to prove itself in the marketplace. Before an object has stood the test of at least a quarter century, the market is still too volatile to know

Pflueger, its manufacturer, claimed that this Muskill spinner bait (here, on its original card) was "a killer for muskallunge, pike, pickerel, and other large game fish."

what will be significant and have lasting desirability. Like any good rule, this one has its exceptions, as you will see below.

No one volume, naturally, can cover in detail a subject as diverse and amorphous as this one. We've chosen, therefore, to give you a brief overview of the types of collectibles that are brought most often to *Antiques Roadshow,* believing that these categories best represent the types of things that Americans own, collect, and are most interested in learning more about.

CAN A COLLECTIBLE ALSO BE AN ANTIQUE?

As previously noted, legally an antique is at least one hundred years old from the current date, but there are certainly a number of things that are usually considered collectibles but that also qualify as antiques. There are golf clubs, for instance, that are more than one hundred years old, as are Art Nouveau posters. Along with several other types of century-old objects, however, golf clubs and posters are generally placed in the collectibles category rather than in the antiques category, because their collectibility is rather a new idea. The concept of mass-manufactured items like golf clubs or posters or advertising memorabilia being something that people would want to collect in multiples is, in fact, a twentieth-century phenomenon. Posters, after all, were produced by the thousands and left out to disintegrate in the rain. Millions of advertising gizmos—all "throwaways"—were distributed nationwide. And golf clubs, like all sports equipment, are purely utilitarian. Such things, whether they were manufactured in the hundreds or just five at a time, were never intended to be anything other than useful tools of one kind or another. This, too, makes them legitimately collectible, for true collectibility is always inadvertent.

HOW IS A COLLECTIBLE CREATED?

Certainly never by intention. The modern-day manufacturer creating thousands of dolls, ceramics, or bronzes and calling them collectibles does not make them collectibles—not even by advertising such products as "limited editions" or by promising to

IS IT ART?

Some collectibles—including some of the photographs, posters, glass, and furniture discussed in this book—are recognized as being works of art.

One definition of art may be its closeness to the cutting edge. Art is always modern in its own time, fresh seeming, probably unfamiliar, and very possibly unloved or misunderstood. In every era, the truly cutting edge design will incorporate a concept without historical precedent. (Folk art, on the other hand, is always *sui generis.*)

On your way to assembling a great collection, therefore, it might help to keep in mind that some great collectibles (such as Pez dispensers and baseball cards), will never be considered works of art, but furniture, ceramics, glass, vintage clothing, and photographs are all collectibles that have been the subjects of extensive exhibitions by influential and important museums. Once that happens, formerly overlooked objects, even the most utilitarian ones, begin to be seen by others as works of art.

Indeed, if your collection of Eames furniture or Orrefors glass were an exact duplicate of the Eames and Orrefors pieces that comprise museum collections, that museum imprimatur would ultimately make your own collection more admirable and more desirable to other knowledgeable collectors of similar things.

"destroy the original mold." Such artificially created collectibles are not included in this book, because although someone might some day choose to collect them, there is really nothing to learn in studying them. They are *synthetic* collectibles, and despite the hype that surrounds them, they will never be as desirable or valuable as the collectible that springs directly from the taste and idiosyncrasies of the individual collector and our culture.

What actually does make an object collectible is a combination of several things, of which the ever-questing eye of the museum curator is perhaps among the most important. When such a scholar takes a fancy to a particular 1930s industrial designer or a 1950s couturier, then works by that person almost immediately become collectibles among the cognoscenti. When newspapers review the ensuing exhibitions, and when magazines publish articles about this next new thing, that heightened visibility serves to reinforce the perception of the thing as a collectible among a wider audience.

Curators aren't alone. Dealers are always looking for the next collectible thing, too. They have a genuine interest in the newly discovered or rediscovered, of course, but they have a commercial agenda as well. So if they have been priced out of Tiffany glass by a lack of supply combined with too much of a market demand, they turn, instead, to Loetz glass. When they're priced out of Loetz, they find carnival glass (also known as "the poor man's Tiffany"). As they buy these things from each other, which they do regularly, dealers spread the word of growing interest in a field or manufacturer. Eventually, specialized dealers appear, and the national community of dealers begins to seek out and stock what is suddenly becoming the latest trend. It wasn't until dealers began to carry fifties furniture, for example, that it became a recognized and highly sought-after collectible. The public can buy only what it is offered, after all.

Sometimes, however, collectibility begins at the other end of the spectrum—in the grass roots, so to speak—as it did with baseball cards and comic books. Kids traded these items among

The best collectibles always reflect the prevailing style of the period in which they were made. Rudi Gernreich's flower-power and kabuki-like sixties and seventies dresses are classic.

themselves, and even if they packed them away when they got older, that didn't mean they had lost interest. However, their moms, who have been known to toss, give away, or sell stuff at a yard sale, often unintentionally divest their children of treasures. As adults with discretionary income, the former traders went in search of the cards and comics they once owned. Eventually, specialty card and comic booths appeared at small local markets. In due course, an entire show was devoted to baseball cards or comics—or to toy trains, or dolls, or vintage textiles—interest in which sprang, initially, from the private passion of a few devoted enthusiasts.

Each country, of course, has its own home-grown collectibles. Americans are partial to American toys and sports memorabilia—although we do fervently collect Japanese ceramics and robots, English china, and Scandinavian and Italian glass. In Great Britain, the going price for a handkerchief printed with the portrait of a champion cricketer is $400. If such an item were to turn up in the United States, however, no one would be particularly interested in it. So if you owned that handkerchief, and if you were somehow aware of its popularity in Great Britain, you'd have to travel to England, or go on the Internet, to find a fellow enthusiast—or, for that matter, to sell it profitably.

In Depression-era America, the car in this 1934 Marx tin litho "automatic" garage was as much a rarity as the toy itself is today.

WHERE DO COLLECTIBLES COME FROM?

While not everyone owns antiques, there's probably not a household in America that doesn't have—somewhere in the cellar, attic, or toy chest—something that someone somewhere considers a collectible. Thus, the collectibles market is fed by deaccessionings from thousands of retirees and simple chucker-outers. And it follows that the more of a thing that has been accumulated, the more things for collectors there will be. Metlox dinnerware, half-dolls, Beacon camp blankets—"If your Mom sold it at a yard sale," says *Antiques Roadshow* pop-culture expert Gary Sohmers, "in twenty years, you'll want it back."

Humble but homey glass: Federal's refrigerator jar is typical of collectible kitchenwares.

TIPS
for
collectors

Antiques Roadshow appraiser Eric Alberta offers a few words of advice regarding collecting and investing:

◆ *Collectible* is perhaps the most misunderstood and overused word in the English language. Two of its definitions are frequently used interchangeably. Collectible, "such as may be gathered," is an accurate definition of practically any object new or old. People often confuse this with another definition, "exchangeable for cash or value." Just because an item is described as "collectible" doesn't mean that you can exchange it for more than, or even as much as, you paid for it.

◆ Dedicated collectors usually say that they collect for fun, and if the prices of their items increase, it's a bonus. If the value of their collecting area goes down, they can then afford to add more items to their collection.

◆ In reality, however, most collectors rationalize and justify their passion with the thought that their collection is a good investment. As we all know, collecting is not necessarily rational. People who invest in memorabilia run the risks of fluctuating markets. What goes up can come down. A savvy collector recognizes rationalizations and assesses his tolerance for risk. The up side of collecting is that—monetary value be hanged!—whether your collection increases in value or not, you'll always have the pleasure of the objects themselves.

HOW DO YOU DECIDE WHAT TO COLLECT?

Actually, collectibles probably choose you. If you are thinking about starting a collection, however, and the choices seem almost limitless, the criteria you apply should be yours and yours alone. Whether you concentrate on excellence of manufacture or cuteness, your choice and collectible yardstick should reflect only your own preferences. Don't be influenced by what others collect or by what they have told you is a good thing to collect. And never, never—say *Antiques Roadshow* appraisers in unison—collect purely as an investment. If the objects you can't help but love turn out to be unexpectedly valuable, that's a plus. Even if at first you're the only one around who is interested in Corgi toy garages, it's not altogether impossible that in years to come many people will want Corgi toy garages, a development that, naturally, will make you look smart while it makes your own collection that

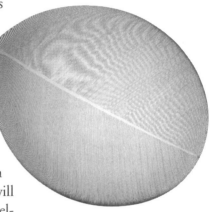

Virtuosic glass: An Iittala bowl, designed in 1958 by Tapio Wirkkala, as viewed from beneath.

much more valuable. But if no one else ever shares your passion, it will still offer you the enormous satisfaction of both discovery and ownership. The real joy of collecting is a lifetime of pleasure and becoming more knowledgeable—not richer.

COLLECTING STYLES

You may, nevertheless, be happy to have some help making your initial choice. So be aware, first, that there are different collecting styles. Some people like to collect items that are inherently useful, like eggcups or handbags. Others collect for shape or color or beauty, although none of these attributes is mutually exclusive. It will help to begin by noticing if the same sorts of things seem always to attract you. Maybe you're drawn to little round vases or certain shades of blue or electric trains? When you're wondering what to collect, keep notes of what attracts you, and look for patterns.

Once you've settled on a type of object, however, you should also realize that a collectible as simple as the eggcup, for example, is divisible into numerous collecting categories. There are silver-plate eggcups, treen (turned wood) eggcups, and ceramic eggcups; if you prefer one type of material to the others, then that's one possible way to collect them. There are also chicken-shape eggcups, and those painted with human faces, both of which allow the eggcup collector (or pocillovist) to generalize or specialize within the field. There are also, to further tempt collectors, souvenir eggcups, cups made in Art Deco styles, cups that are "Made in Japan," cups that are all yellow and white, and those that have one large end and one small—that is, doubles. Such a wealth of choice is hardly restricted to this one field. Twentieth-century glass or advertising memorabilia or toys can—happily—be broken down into the same sorts of specialties.

Don't forget the display element, either, when choosing what you want to collect. Functional or not, many collectibles are suited to being "cabinet pieces"—in other words, to being amassed solely for display rather than use. Wristwatches and vintage evening gowns may present a challenge, but shoes, toy soldiers, and Barbie dolls all lend themselves well to display. (Eggcups do, too.) So despite the fact that the item you've chosen to collect actually has a function, it can still be enjoyed as pure display. Catcher's mitts look super on a wall; and Andy Warhol, you can bet, never used those cookie jars.

WHAT MAKES A GOOD COLLECTION?

A good collection, first and foremost, is composed of things you truly love. If it pleases you, if it reflects your own taste and individuality, it will be a satisfying and wonderful collection, whatever it is.

There is, nevertheless, a formal definition of a good collection, one established by the taste and preferences of the general community of your fellow collectors. When a category of object

Lionel's 1936 scale model "Torpedo" locomotive is the very essence of "streamlined."

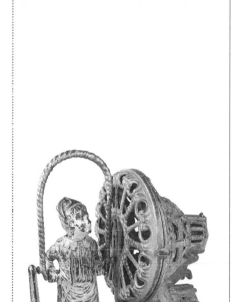

Because "Girl Skipping Rope," an 1890 cast-iron mechanical bank, was difficult to manufacture and correspondingly expensive, it is a particularly rare collectible today.

is of national or international interest, enthusiasts frequently set standards to help them evaluate their subject.

Consequently, when you decide to collect something really popular, like Fiesta ware or dolls, you should make yourself aware of how these things are classified by your fellow enthusiasts—of what makes one piece of Fiesta more desirable than another piece, for instance, or which are the really rare Shirley Temple dolls.

As your collection grows and you seek out and read specialty publications to learn more about your favorites, you may find that like all of us, you've made a few—well—mistakes or that you need to narrow or expand your focus. You may choose to weed out your duplicates or to give away or sell at auction, on eBay, or at a local show those pieces that no longer appeal to you or that no longer fit in with the focus of your collection. Eventually, if you work at it (for the dedicated collector, however, this really isn't work), your collection will someday be refined to the point that it contains only the things you really care about and really want to own. When it reaches this stage, it will probably have become a collection that other collectors admire, not just because it conforms with accepted standards, but because it also contains rarities, pristine examples, or early examples. You should be gratified, then, to know that you've assembled a good—maybe even a great—collection.

From a practical point of view, a good and satisfying collection is usually made up of collectibles that can be easily displayed and enjoyed. You want to be able to touch and handle your favorites, to show them to other collectors, or, at least, to be able to see them easily. It's not a satisfying collection if it has to be packed up and put away in boxes or a vault for safety's sake. What is more, a good collection is never so large that it makes your living room—or any other room—un-navigable.

Consequently, if you're new to collecting, try to pick some specialty that you can live with comfortably, not one that will make you feel anxious. Are you simply all thumbs? Don't decide to collect Italian glass. Do you have seven cats? Textiles may not be for you. Always be guided in your choice by a combination of aesthetics

Small studio pottery, such as this dappled stoneware vessel by Vivika and Otto Heino, can be easily displayed.

In contrast, chairs such as this "Airline" model armchair by Kem Weber, are useful, but large.

and practicality. It never hurts to check out a mate's preferences, either, before putting heart and soul into a collection of breweriana. It's not everyone, after all, who wants to entertain guests in a room full of Budweiser ads.

One way to avoid making embarrassing or costly mistakes is to choose a collectible that hasn't been or isn't currently being reproduced. It's not too hard to determine if this has happened. Visit a reputable dealer or collector in your field (there are reference books at libraries that list clubs and dealers) and mention the word reproduction. Because specialists usually get pretty hot about reproductions (once an item is being copied, it clouds the whole field), they will often be happy to tell you how to recognize impostors. In fact, even the best can be taken in. *Antiques Roadshow* appraiser David Rago comments, "This is an inexact science at best. Part of what makes experts experts is their willingness to learn from new experiences." Reproductions are particularly painful in the area of twentieth-century collectibles because scholarship is often so sparse that frequently collectors feel safer avoiding areas in which there are reproductions.

Antiques, which have been around for a longer period of time, tend to have lengthier histories of reliable scholarship than collectibles, and—theoretically anyhow—it's easier to distinguish the genuine from the reproduction. Once the expert collectors, curators, and dealers sort out all the recognition factors for twentieth-century objects, however, there's no reason that the existence of reproductions should continue to affect collector interest in the genuine article.

Incidentally, don't confuse legitimate reproductions with fakes. Fakes intend to deceive; they won't be addressed here because they require books of their own. You should begin to collect by learning, first, to recognize the genuine. Reproductions, thankfully, are often clearly marked with the name of the reproducer. (The Metropolitan Museum of Art's reproductions of Eva Zeisel's Town and Country dinnerware, for example, are clearly marked as such, as are most museum reproductions—which, by the way, are generally of excellent quality.) These reproductions should be considered (as the Chinese think of all those copies of Ming

Vintage posters such as this one, in which toucan—or two can—enjoy a Guinness stout, are favorites with breweriana collectors.

On the cover of a 1933 Little Orphan Annie game—an Ovaltine premium—that "Leapin' Lizard" comes to life.

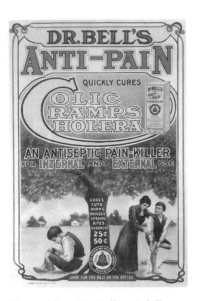

You could pat Dr. Bell's painkiller on a cut or drink it, says this lithographed poster (which neglects to list those active ingredients).

ceramics) as significant tributes to design and the continuing popularity of a classic original.

BECOME A SUCCESSFUL COLLECTOR

How? First of all, learn to focus. Decide once and for all whether you want to own examples of all the Bakelite bracelets in existence, or only the Bakelite bangle bracelets. Decide if you love the color green well enough to restrict yourself to collecting the hundreds of examples of Jade-ite kitchenware that would constitute a complete collection or if you really need a touch of red among the plates and bowls. Decide if you want to own only vases by Weller or if you'll allow yourself that great piece by Hull that's a virtual steal.

Before you go out hunting, get yourself a notebook so you can jot down information on the pieces you discover. Include where you found the piece, price, condition, portability (size and weight), and manufacturer. Also keep track of your plans for your growing collection. Are you willing to have it include some examples that are in mediocre condition? Do you prefer exciting design to excellence of manufacture? Is it important to you to know that you own things that are rarities or unique in the field? The more you know about your own likes and dislikes as they apply to collecting, the better satisfied you will be with your collection.

Work on self-discipline. Try not to purchase a piece that doesn't fit within the parameters of your collection just because it has an attractive price tag. And always be prepared to spend more on occasion than is entirely wise. If you're pricked by guilt as you cart home find after find; if you fret about spending far too much on your "frivolous" passion, try to remember that compared to numerous other compulsions (some of them carved in stone), collecting is a harmless vice. Keep in mind, too, that the pain of paying more than you intended will eventually ease and pass into forgetfulness, but the pain of letting some irreplaceable treasure go will return to haunt you for decades to come—usually at 3 A.M.

Finally, keep in mind that melding rarity, fine condition, great design, and high quality in a single assemblage of objects is possible to achieve, but unbelievably difficult. So, be prepared to give it half a lifetime, for starters.

So sleek and clean it's sculptural, this 1905 Talbot fly reel was retailed by Abercrombie and Fitch.

EVALUATING COLLECTIBLES

It is helpful that, almost across the board, collectors use the same criteria to judge the objects they love. From dolls to furniture to fishing rods, there are standards for valuing collectibles and the same vocabulary can be used almost interchangeably. Whether you're examining a find in your great-aunt's attic or a potential purchase, whatever it is, you can ask yourself the same questions.

OVERALL APPEARANCE

As a preliminary to handling the item, stand back and look at it. Is the object pleasing to look at? If it exhibits a distinctive style (Art Deco or retro, for instance), does it look its age? Is it a good example of its kind?

STYLE

Style is, essentially, a distinctive and characteristic manner of expression, and there is a style, fortunately, to appeal to every taste. Most collectors begin with, or develop, a preference for a particular style. One person likes Art Deco design while another prefers the biomorphism of the 1950s. If you've familiarized yourself with the design characteristics of the style you've chosen for yourself, you will seldom develop eye fatigue at a collectibles show because your selective eye will automatically rule out everything that doesn't conform. Developing an eye for a style will also help you recognize the great mirror in the junk shop that everyone else has ignored or the one Balenciaga gown in a thrift shop otherwise full of secondhand clothes.

FORM

Form refers to the shape of an object as separate from its materials, and is an important component of its style. The ability to discern form is important. If you're starting to collect dinnerware, for example, you'll get to know that frequently the same decorative patterns were applied to different shapes of plates, cups, and bowls. You'll learn to "see through" the decoration to the form of the underlying ceramic. As you become increasingly familiar with your field, you will increasingly be able to recognize the unusual form and to ask yourself if the toy or vase

Style is as important to collectibles as it is to clothes. These minidresses and thigh-high boots are as distinctly 1969 as the hair styles.

Hollywood costume-designer and couturier Adrian designed this "barnyard" dress in the mid-1940s; the print on the bodice is a hen house, while the skirt is covered in roosters.

Beauty, design, and significance combine in this 1888 advertising display incorporating a pictorial array of the cigarette cards portraying nine baseball Hall of Famers.

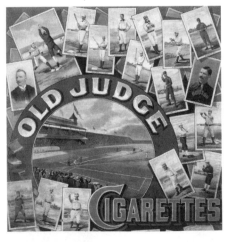

you're considering is a rare form of that particular collectible or simply run-of-the-mill.

MATERIALS

Materials can give you an immediate sense of an object's age. Plastics are postwar. Chrome finishes tend to be from the twenties and thirties. Satin evening gowns are often from the 1930s. Aluminum kitchenware is from the very late 1940s.

The materials of any collectible should be consistent throughout. If four buttons on a Chanel suit are labeled with Chanel's double C's and one is unlabeled, then the unmarked button is likely to be a replacement. That makes a difference to Chanel collectors.

ORNAMENT

The buttons on a dress, the handles on a desk, the engraving on a piece of glass—all are categories of ornament. Ornament is often an indication of the quality of a collectible, so study it carefully. Is the decoration made of exotic materials (ivory, jade, or lacquer, for instance)? Is it painstakingly rendered or incongruously crude? Does it seem to be stamped out by machine, or is it cast? Does it appear to be handmade? Is there a great deal of ornament, and if so, does it suit the style of the piece? Since certain types of ornament—such as inlay, figures, animal forms—are typical of certain designers, they can aid in attribution. The study of ornament brings out the latent Sherlock Holmes in many collectors.

CONDITION

As location is to real estate agents, condition is to every *Antiques Roadshow* appraiser. Indeed, for twentieth-century collectibles, condition is absolutely paramount, because when nearly everything has been mass-produced, the piece that survives in the best condition will necessarily be the most desirable. And when there are some two million of a thing out there, the one that you choose for your collection can even be one of the perfect ones.

In fact, it can be almost more than perfect when it's unused and still in its original, unopened box. "Mint" collectibles like these are infrequently available, and in some categories, they may be extremely rare, so your fellow enthusiasts have agreed to allow certain deviations from perfection—dirt, dings, and slight discolorations, for example. If a thing is suitably rare, however, even scratches, dents, and chips may be acceptable if you keep in mind, always, that some-where, perhaps, an unopened box awaits.

FINISH

Anyone who watches *Antiques Roadshow* knows that original finish is the absolute bottom line—on toys, on tables, on paint-ings or dolls. If someone in your family, with the best of inten-tions, repainted an otherwise rare clockwork toy ship, your ship may still float, but its market value has sunk. Original finish—whether paint, varnish, the set of a doll's hair, an unaltered hem-line on a dress, or an unshellacked baseball—is always preferable to any type of prettying up.

This hasn't always been the case (which explains all those well-meant repairs), and the experts may change their minds again. Until they do, however, don't touch a thing.

Patina—otherwise known as dirt—is always a personal prefer-ence. Some collectors like it, others don't. Patina, however, is most acceptable on furniture and metal wares. You can't call perspiration stains on a dress patina. Nor can you dignify the brown spots on posters with that name. Note and be wary of creases, tears, trimmed edges (on paper memorabilia), old repairs, replaced parts, miss-ing veneers, rust, cracks, and splits in whatever category of collectible attracts your interest. To be safe, and to deter-mine what is dirt for yourself, when you're out hunting, keep a flashlight and a magnifying glass handy at all times.

COLOR

On posters, in tablecloths, on Nancy Ann Storybook dolls, on vintage peanut-butter tins, on every sort of collectible, color is at its most desirable when it is as strong and fresh as the day it was printed, woven, painted, or dyed. Any sort of fading, staining, or discoloration is detrimental to collectibility. One exception to this rule is Bakelite. Clear Bakelite, over the years, has turned the color of apple juice, and collectors have come to love it.

Original bright red paint and gold highlights that are barely worn add to the value of this 1930s Hubley Air Ford cast-iron airplane.

Its feathers are slightly ruffled, but collectors of Jean Harlow memorabilia don't really mind, when it comes to owning a fan that once cooled off the star.

While it may be in like-new condition, this gold-tone metal handbag can barely hold a wallet—let alone a cell phone—and isn't very functional.

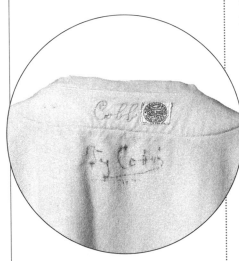

With its 1928 Spalding label and its famous owner's name stitched into the collar, the only known example of a Ty Cobb signed uniform is unquestionably authentic.

Color can also be a useful gauge of the approximate age of a collectible, because certain color combinations typify their eras. Art deco ceramics, for example, are often boldly colored in primary hues, while Italian glass of the fifties is particularly noted for its vivid—some say too vivid—color combinations. (Vaseline yellow and tomato red are typical.) When you recognize that the colors on a piece you're examining are appropriately combined with a characteristic shape of the era, you'll go a long way toward satisfying yourself that it's legitimate.

FUNCTION

Functional items are neither more nor less desirable than nonfunctional items in themselves. Among glass and ceramics collectibles, in fact, it is often the decorative wares (vases, cachepots, figures) rather than the functional tablewares (plates and cups and saucers) that are most highly sought after. Collectors generally prefer their furniture to be functional, however. There's not an active market in unsittable chairs.

If the object does have a function, it should be in working order and retain all its parts. While it may not be working at the time you're thinking about buying it (many old watches, for example, are not), if all the parts are there, it may still be repairable.

ATTRIBUTION

The wonderful thing about twentieth-century collectibles is their frequent and reassuring labeling. Yet labels and makers' marks don't necessarily guarantee quality, and they can also be faked, so look at the entire piece carefully. Attribution to a particular maker is most convincingly made on the basis of a label, but the piece itself should support the attribution. Some experts, in fact, think that the label is the last thing you should look at. When there is no label, scholars and collectors can often make an attribution based on the object's stylistic and material resemblance to known, labeled pieces. Despite the possibility of eventually making an accurate attribution, however, almost every collector prefers to own an item that retains its original label to owning the identical item, unlabeled.

HISTORY OF OWNERSHIP

History of ownership is among the least reliable methods of evaluation for twentieth-century objects, but luckily, it is usually

Different Kinds of Value

As *Antiques Roadshow* appraisers demonstrate on every show, there are many kinds of value, a number of which can operate simultaneously.

SENTIMENTAL VALUE:

Anyone who has watched *Antiques Roadshow* guests carefully unwrap and show their preserved and cherished family artifacts is familiar with sentimental value. Indeed, sometimes sentimental value is the only value an object has.

HISTORICAL VALUE:

Many of the objects brought to *Antiques Roadshow* are significant (sometimes even important) documents of their own time: they're our national heritage. Photographs taken by your GI grandfathers, for instance, of subjects as dissimilar as Polish prison camps or celebrities at USO shows, have real historical value.

AESTHETIC VALUE:

Photographs of GI's in Europe taken by important photographers like Margaret Bourke White, however, have more than simple historical value. They have aesthetic value, that element of artistry, indefinable and indelible beauty that appeals to audiences other than just war historians. The plywood splints once designed by Ray Eames for wounded soldiers are beautiful and rare, and because they are as much biomorphic sculpture as they are splints, they, too, have acquired aesthetic value.

INTRINSIC VALUE:

Items made from costly materials, such as silver, diamonds, and gold, have intrinsic value. A silver wristwatch has some intrinsic value, but a platinum wristwatch is considerably more valuable, because in the precious-metals market, platinum is more expensive than silver.

The soda fountain sign has sentimental value; Mickey Mantle's ring has both intrinsic and celebrity value; and the early (1965) Beatles album is valued internationally.

CELEBRITY VALUE:

Not surprisingly, collectors love those artifacts that once belonged to the famous. There is magic in acquiring John Lennon's piano or a set of presidential golf clubs. It's almost as if the original owner's spirit has somehow infused the object he or she once used.

MARKET VALUE:

The legal definition of market value is the price agreed upon by a willing buyer and a willing seller. It can be stimulated by design trends or diminished as time passes and interest fades. Witness the late twentieth-century fashion for midcentury furnishings, sparked initially by interior designers and vintage dealers simultaneously discovering a neglected, but aesthetically worthy field. As the design world moves on to the next discovery, however, second-tier midcentury furniture (not the top-of-the-line things) becomes correspondingly less desirable. And while badly designed or manufactured objects may be collectible for a moment, in the long run they don't hold up in a volatile marketplace.

An example of a collectible that might have all the bells and whistles, so to speak, would be a platinum Patek Philippe wristwatch worn by your uncle John Fitzgerald Kennedy during his presidential debate with Richard Nixon. Here you have not only sentimental, historical, aesthetic, intrinsic, and market value, but you have celebrity value, too.

Because the same market may have differing values worldwide, our hypothetical wristwatch may not be as desirable in Brazil, for example (because JFK is not as much of an icon there) as it is in the United States. Other collectibles, however, such as certain types of entertainment memorabilia—say, Beatles collectibles—do enjoy worldwide currency, and for these, international interest magnifies market value. (An aging collector base, however, weakens a market, and the Beatles, and their fans, are aging. Imagine.)

The theaters that once displayed this Citizen Kane lobby card may be long gone, but on the walls of film buffs, Orson Welles as Charles Foster Kane lives on.

Not just any old sweater, this one belonged to Marilyn Monroe.

one of the least important ones, as well. Consequently, it appears fairly low on this list.

Twentieth-century objects haven't had time to accumulate much of a history. Despite the wonderful things that have been saved and brought into the *Antiques Roadshow,* a great deal of the past century was more about disposability than about preservation. Many Americans no longer saved their material culture to the extent that their ancestors did. Thus, the history of ownership of many objects is often no more than anecdote, and anecdote is almost always dubious. It is altogether a different horse from the far more rigorous history of ownership known as provenance, which is a very important part of evaluating antiques and works of art. A painting by Monet with a complete, documented history of ownership from the time it left the artist's studio is much less likely to be a fake than one that has mysteriously appeared on the market for the first time. An eighteenth-century desk from Newport is more likely to be authentic if it has been passed down in one Rhode Island family for the last two hundred years.

For most collectibles, on the other hand, unless a piece is known to have belonged to illustrious owners (in which case, most if not all of its value is "celebrity" value—see previous page), provenance is not of much importance. A well-marked Weller vase in excellent condition is unmistakably that, and knowing who all its owners have been since it came out of the factory won't really add much to how the market values it.

But history of ownership is an important aspect of evaluating some collectibles. Certainly, in entertainment memorabilia as well as in sports, there are endless questionable claims. This is why it is particularly important to keep that photograph of the celebrity or sports figure wearing or playing with that item in your collection. If you've ever owned a signed game ball or photograph, for example, you know that it's hard to verify that the star actually signed it himself. He may have had a representative do it for him.

A FINAL WORD

Have faith in yourself and your love of dolls, toys, furniture, glass, ceramics, vintage clothing, textiles, posters, photographs, fishing tackle, entertainment memorabilia, baseball bats, costume jewelry, and watches, etcetera, etcetera, etcetera. If you're not an expert now, you will be.

Chapter One

CERAMICS

Pottery and porcelain, among the most popular of collectibles, offer an almost limitless variety of lovely and gutsy objects in all shapes and colors and at all prices. Collectors can select among dinnerware, vases, art pottery, studio pottery, or some of all four. From Homer Laughlin bowls originally sold in dime stores to investment-level Pablo Picasso plates, there's a ceramic for every passion and wallet. And all offer a real plus: In common with many twentieth-century wares (and in contrast with many antiques), ceramics are generally well marked, enabling even newcomers to the field to research them with relative ease.

Not only are plates and bowls and vases often marked with the country of origin or the factory where they were produced (or both), the more interesting ceramics can also be—and these will be your "finds"—marked or labeled with their designers' names. So there are fewer mysteries here than there are with older ceramics. No imitation Chinese symbols, for instance. No mysterious and frustrating initials. There's very little unmarked vintage china at all, just plenty of straightforward lettering to tell you when, who, and where—everything but how. It's no wonder that ceramics are such a popular collectible, for if it looks like Weller, and says "Weller" on the bottom, it almost certainly *is* Weller. If it says "Made in England," it definitely won't have been made in the United States. And if you find a raised "LR"

Notables from many creative disciplines have tried their hands at ceramics. At top, a streamlined bowl by architect Keith Murray for Wedgwood. Above, Pablo Picasso's Aztec vase.

WHAT'S WHAT

Pottery, stoneware, bone china, and porcelain are all ceramics—most often useful articles made by subjecting clay and related substances to fire. Pottery is probably the most familiar: At its simplest, a "snake" of clay, coiled, baked, and painted or glazed becomes pottery.

Stoneware is baked at a higher temperature than pottery, which makes it stronger. While it can be difficult to tell from porcelain, stoneware is usually thicker in appearance.

Porcelain is created from a mixture of clay, feldspar, and flint, baked in a really hot kiln. The delicate, translucent results are frequently covered with a glaze (a glassy, protective coat). Porcelain is also known as china. Add bone ash to this mix to make bone china.

on the base of a fabulous vase, you may have a prize by noted British ceramicist Lucie Rie (see page 31).

A distinctive teapot that turned up at the *Antiques Roadshow* in Tucson revealed many of the best attributes of ceramics. Designed by Clarice Cliff, a noted Art Deco ceramicist (see page 18), the unusual teapot was from her line of 1950s "Teepee Teapots," and unmistakable in style. Clearly marked with both the name of the artist and the factory in which it was made, it had been picked up in an Arizona thrift store for around $50. The teapot was decorated with maple leaves, and had a "totem pole" handle and a headdress-wearing chief for a spout. Appraiser Nicholas Dawes told the owner that Cliff's Teepee Teapots, made for North American consumption, remain among the most collectible of all novelty teapots.

The renowned English ceramicist Clarice Cliff produced these whimsical "Teepee Teapots" for the North American souvenir trade in the 1950s.

Pointing out the markings on the bottom of the pot, he noted that they indicated it had originally been sold as a souvenir in Canada. Although a small crack in the lid detracted slightly from its value, the teapot was worth $1,000 to $1,500—making this thrift-shop purchase a top-notch find.

A BRIEF HISTORY

After World War I, it was a new world, a world in which the Exposition Internationale des Arts Décoratifs et Industriels Modernes, held in Paris in 1925, could shock a war-weary public with decorative arts—ceramics not least among them—that trumpeted exuberance with sharp, geometric contours and bright, bold hues. These exciting new designs, today called art deco (a name inspired by the exhibition), quickly trickled down from the avant-garde worlds of painting and sculpture, and particularly from the world of architecture, to all the arts. As a result, everything looked like either a bold, sharp-angled skyscraper or wasp-waisted, lyrical naiad—even jewelry, glass, and ceramics.

Production was prolific. Ceramicist Clarice Cliff was a chief proponent of this style, but even the venerable British ceramics manufacturer Wedgwood tried its hand at Jazz Age riff, producing a line of highly stylized figures of tigers, monkeys, and some characteristically Art Deco deer.

World War I moved mechanization forward and, at its close, established American firms like Rookwood (see page 25) were able to mass-produce a consistently perfect product. Moreover, there was scarcely a decorative technique that commercial manufacturers could not employ. In the twenties and thirties, ceramics factories used underglazing, hand coloring, stenciling, and even hand painting—the most expensive and time-consuming technique—with heretofore-unparalleled success.

Technology reached new heights in the twenties, and it seemed, then, that the good times would roll on forever. When the bubble burst in 1929, stylish Art Deco design slipped reluctantly but docilely into the quiet brown housedress of practicality. The Depression years were particularly hard on many of the old line manufacturers that had sold luxury wares for so long, and those that intended to hang on realized it was time to pay attention to things the public could actually use: refrigerator containers, inexpensive and increasingly informal tableware, restaurant china, and even bathroom fixtures, anything to keep the factories running. While some Works Progress Administration (WPA) ceramic sculptures were created during the 1930s, and local handcrafts continued, as always, this was truly the moment for industrial design—design that everyone could afford. Out of a mixture of necessity and philosophy came classics like the brightly colored, inexpensive Fiesta ware (see pages 4, 15) and Russel Wright's wonderfully casual but forward-looking American Modern (see page 15) tableware.

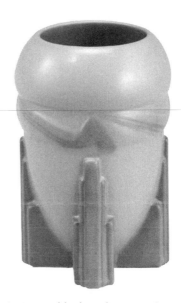

An inverted beehive-shape vase from Roseville's Futura line of Art Deco–inspired pottery, introduced in 1928.

Deer were a popular decorative motif of the Art Deco era. Here, a tenderly rendered example produced by the venerable English firm of Wedgwood around 1930.

FIESTA WARE

A cheerful set of Fiesta ware dishes was inherited by a guest to the Hartford *Antiques Roadshow* from an aunt. She has been using them as her everyday dishes ever since. When appraiser David Lackey saw the set it brought back memories of the dishes his grandmother used at her Texas farmhouse when he was young.

Fiesta ware was introduced by the Homer Laughlin China Company in 1936. The original line consisted of five colors, which increased to eleven, and the rarity of the color of a piece is one of the determining factors in valuing Fiesta. Common colors, such as yellow and turquoise, are worth less than hard-to-find colors like gray, dark green, and chartreuse.

There were a total of 107 pieces in this visitor's set, which Lackey valued at $2,500 to $3,500. While he encouraged the owner to continue using and enjoying the dishes, he also reminded her to be careful with the small bowls and the large serving dish, which would be quite difficult to replace.

POSTWAR POTTERY

It was the conclusion of World War II that both revolutionized and reinvigorated the industry. Studio ceramics, made by hand by artists in a studio or art school, were the happy result of the artistic ferment of the postwar era. Americans, Italians, and especially Scandinavians remembered how to "get their hands in the clay." This truly idiosyncratic output was so refreshing—and so successful—that firms like Royal Copenhagen and Arabia began to factory-produce studio-type ceramics. That is, they had "name" ceramic artists design pieces intended for mass-manufacture. In contrast to this particularly Scandinavian program of artist support, very few American ceramicists, according to leading midcentury ceramics expert Mark McDonald, earned a living making pottery, although the potteries of Gertrud and Otto Natzler (see page 30) and Vivika and Otto Heino (see page 30) are two notable exceptions. Most ceramicists lived by teaching, even the most famous among them. This difficult and financially unrewarding road is followed by studio artists to the present day, and many lovers of ceramics—*Antiques Roadshow* appraisers among them—have befriended such potters and collected their works.

Some late-twentieth-century studio pottery—like this large stoneware bowl by Vivika and Otto Heino— is already highly collectible.

EVALUATING CERAMICS

A s you'd expect, experts always examine carefully the ceramics they intend to buy. They pay particular attention to four components:

◆ Is the piece the *age* that its design says it ought to be or is it a reproduction of some sort? Even some quite recent ceramics, such as Fiesta ware, have been reproduced.

♦ Is the piece a *rare example* of its kind or is it a dime a dozen? (You will have to have seen a lot and read a lot to know the difference.)

♦ Is the piece in collectible *condition*? This needn't always mean perfect, but at the same time, if it's wearing a "perfect" price tag, it ought to withstand close scrutiny.

♦ Can the piece be *attributed* to a particular factory, factory designer, or studio ceramicist?

Here are some tips to help you evaluate like an expert.

AGE

Probably the best indication of age is style. Elements of style can be found in both the shape of a piece and in its decoration, and if you've read and looked carefully, you can spot style at a distance, on a shelf or in a case. If a rimless, somewhat ovate plate is decorated with poodles or sheaves of wheat on an avocado green background, that's its "style," and in this instance, there's a good chance that it was made in the 1950s. If a vase is shaped like a stepped-back skyscraper, it's likely to be Art Deco. If a cream pitcher is smooth, monochromatic, and distinctly organic looking, it's probably 1930s.

Crazing is another sign of age. Crazing is an age-related crackling of the glaze that looks rather like a severely cracked automobile windshield. Chinese potters crazed their wares intentionally, but twentieth-century ceramics are generally crazed only if they're from the early part of the century or if their makers have an imperfect grasp of glaze techniques. There are a couple of exceptions. Pottery glazes have an inherent tendency to craze, as do glazes on chintz ware (see page 22), and pottery and chintz ware collectors accept this as a characteristic of the medium. It doesn't affect the value of these collectibles, although *Antiques Roadshow* appraiser David Rago adds that "on some ceramics, crazing decreases value dramatically."

Wear and staining of the foot ring (the ring beneath your cup or plate) indicate age, as does the serendipitous presence of an occasional actual date on the bottom. (Don't get too excited about a date, however, because it

GLAZE

For many ceramic lovers, the distinction between a pot's decoration and its glaze remains muddy at best, says *Antiques Roadshow* appraiser Riley Humler, a Rookwood pottery expert.

"The two appear to be the same thing, but they're very different. Potters first apply decorations— flowers or maidens or geometric patterns. Then the glaze, a layer of silicate glass that (usually) coats the entire piece, is applied on top of the decorations."

With utilitarian ceramics, such as vases or pitchers, that glaze seals the clay and waterproofs the object. In much of American art pottery, however, the glaze is integral to bringing out the colors and depth of the decoration it coats, giving it a shiny finish. Humler explains: "Like a layer of varnish on a painting, it gives a rich look to the piece."

A Weller vase from the Etna line. A decorator working at the factory painted the vase with pink roses on a shaded gray ground before it was glazed and fired.

An authentic piece of limited-edition "Picasso" pottery has the artist's distinctive signature on the bottom.

Because fewer were purchased, serving pieces are generally harder to find than cups or plates. This Russel Wright American Modern collection includes oblong serving dishes, a sugar and creamer, covered casserole, pitcher, salt and pepper shakers, celery tray, and oval platter.

may actually be the date of the company's founding or of the pattern's introduction!) In fact, *Antiques Roadshow* expert David Lackey warns collectors that if they see any number that looks like a year, they shouldn't assume that it is the date of manufacture—unless a book of ceramics marks indicates otherwise.

It helps to know that most factories changed their labeling with the passage of time. Numerous books exist on ceramics marks, listing the original marks, plus accruals and alterations for almost every manufacturer, with dates for each change (see the Reading List on page 543). If what you see on the bottom isn't a name, some of these texts allow you to look up a mark by its shape (a shield, a human figure, a flower, perhaps) or by the name of the pattern (Virginia Rose, by Homer Laughlin, for instance). If the piece in question was hand painted, the painter's marks, monograms, or signatures were often added by the (usually female) artists who did such handwork at the ceramics factory. Most of these women remain forever anonymous, but at several modern factories—Rookwood being among the most reliable—numerous artists can be identified by name. The works of some, naturally, are more highly prized than the works of others. "Designer" ceramics—like mass-produced tablewares created by Russel Wright—will have their designer's name on the bottom.

And now, the $64,000 question: You see a piece that looks convincingly vintage, has the right name on the bottom, and seems to be an outstanding example of its kind (there is that full-page picture in the pottery book the shopkeeper showed you). How can you tell it is not a fake?

Until the late seventies or early eighties, there was such a small market for twentieth-century ceramics (except for studio ceramics, which collectors often bought directly from the artist or from his or her gallery) that they just weren't worth faking: forgers, for the most part, don't bother to counterfeit things that are not remarkably valuable. Nevertheless, check the specialty books on the ceramics that especially interest you, for counterfeiters have been at work quite recently. (One notorious example is the Little Red Riding Hood cookie jar marked "McCoy"; all are fakes.) Such books will often tell you how to distinguish the genuine article (see the Reading List on page 543).

RARITY

Unlike furniture and metals, ceramics—when they break—break more or less irreparably. A smashed vase is devastating to its owner, but a smashed vase also means that all such vases remaining are now a little bit rarer. Rarity, naturally, can be achieved less dramatically. There are times, for instance, when what was once an ugly duckling becomes a swan. If a piece was offered for sale that didn't sell well because it was an undesirable color or shape, or because it was just plain homely, and if the collecting community has rediscovered its fashion or style, that unloved and unsalable cygnet can metamorphose into a collectible, desirable "swan."

Studio pottery tends to be rare almost by definition, because a single pair of hands can only produce so many pieces in a lifetime (although studio potter Bernard Leach—see page 30—claimed to have personally made over 100,000). Mass-produced Fiesta ware, on the other hand, isn't rare in itself, but certain pieces and colors of Fiesta are rare. Production Rookwood isn't rare, either, but the work of several of its more interesting decorators fits into that category.

CONDITION

Here is the bottom line on commercially mass-produced twentieth-century ceramics: there probably shouldn't be one. Because unless you intend to study a special type of ceramic, are collecting on a tight budget, or simply can't live without a particular vase, bowl, or candlestick, cracks—even hairline cracks—are generally unacceptable. In common with all sorts of modern,

Danish ceramicist Axel Salto built his ceramics like sculptures; they weren't thrown on a wheel. His originals were used to make production molds for limited runs at Royal Copenhagen.

TIPS *from the* experts

In magic and ceramics, the wise viewer never relies on his eyes alone. "If you use your ears, and your sense of touch, along with your eyes, you can catch ninety-nine percent of ceramic defects," says *Antiques Roadshow* appraiser and ceramics expert David Lackey. "All you have to do is be careful and thorough."

Lackey realizes, however, that imperfections are frequently unavoidable in older pieces. "Some of my favorite pieces have some damage," he admits. "As long as an imperfect piece is valued accordingly, feel free to buy it."

Uncracked porcelain "tings" when tapped, while cracked examples sound dull. "And if it sounds dull, you'll want to look a lot closer," Lackey says, for close visual inspection can reveal hidden cracks. Carefully feel the curves and corners of a piece, as well.

"If the chip is on the back of a plate, it's not nearly as important as one on the front," Lackey notes. But don't let your own inspection of a piece replace the direct question to a seller about its condition. "I always ask," Lackey says. "If you ask someone point-blank, they usually tell you the truth."

interchangeable objects, ceramics that have been mass-produced have a really good chance of being in top-notch condition. On the other hand, for ceramics that are exceptionally fragile or rare, minor nicks, chips, dings, and flaking paint are all right, even on top-of-the-line Rookwood. "Minor damage," says *Antiques Roadshow* expert Riley Humler, "will be tolerated on very important pieces."

On more ordinary ceramics, however, keep an eye out for the hairline crack that has been made to "disappear" with Clorox (just sniff). Bleach might hide a crack temporarily, but over the long run, it will cause additional damage. Don't just look and sniff, however. Pick up that bowl or vase and feel it. Run your fingers over it. Not only should you be able to feel chips on handles, spouts, and cup and plate rims—the most fragile areas— you can also often detect the ever-so-slightly roughened surface that indicates someone has touched up the paint.

Tap it, too, and listen. An intact piece will sound like a bell. A fateful, dead "clunk" indicates a crack. You won't want to buy a piece that has a hole in the bottom, either, unless you're just in love and have to have it. That hole marks the spot where the vase (usually) was drilled to be a lamp, and ex-lamps seldom appeal to collectors. Fortunately for fans of mass-produced ceramics (though not necessarily for studio-ceramics aficionados), a perfect example is probably out there. Wait for it.

ATTRIBUTION (LABELING)

On "designer" or commercial ceramics, the best thing to see is the paper label or factory name on the bottom of the plate or cup. Unused pieces may have paper labels; if the pieces have been used, however, they are likely to have been washed off, so the most durable (and convincing) label is always the mark impressed directly into the wet clay. It can't be imitated and can only be reproduced from—literally—scratch. The majority of American dinnerware factory identification marks, nevertheless, are simply printed or painted on the bottom of the ceramic. Sometimes, all or part of these marks

The Franciscan mark includes the information that this plate was made in California and hand decorated, along with a series or product number.

has been dishwashered off or rubbed away, although any little remnant can sometimes lead you to the maker. If, for some reason, you find yourself trying to research a piece that looks very much like a certain type of Hall, Blue Ridge, or Metlox (American dinnerware) but is entirely unmarked, original catalogs and vintage magazine advertisements can help you identify it. For studio ceramics, the puzzling or illegible mark on a vessel that looks like the mate to one pictured in a studio-ceramics book can direct you to the author of the book or even, for more recent works, to the artist himself, who may still be working. There is surely no higher authority.

Italian potter Guido Gambone's fanciful bowl in the shape of a dove, wittily punctuated by an applied orange beak.

COLLECTING CERAMICS

Perhaps one of the nicest things about collecting ceramics is that, as with glass, you can use your collection. Ceramics are as attractive, inventive, and colorful as glass, but tougher. So, if tableware or dinnerware attracts you, collect it and *use* it.

You will find you don't often come across complete sets of collectible dinnerware, so be prepared to start your collection with individual pieces—two plates, one cup, a cereal bowl—that you love. One of the pleasures of collecting is the eternal search for one more plate, that saucer for that cup, or even for the rare-as-hen's-teeth teapot. Eventually, you may succeed in assembling your service for twelve, or you might change your mind altogether and switch over from tableware to unmarked, really eccentric studio ceramics. In either case, if you're just starting out, you should restrict your purchases to ceramics that were fashionable when they were new, because these usually bespeak the aesthetic of their era.

SHAPES AND PATTERNS

A Shelley Dainty Blue plate.

Collecting tableware may be confusing at first, since in some cases names have been assigned to both the shapes of the pieces and the patterns. Thus, the shape that the Shelley company named Dainty could be bought in innumerable patterns, as well as in pure white. Homer Laughlin Eggshell is another shape that recurred in several patterns.

On the other hand, shape doesn't always define one particular type of dinnerware. Blue Ridge from Southern Potteries actually came in many different shapes and many different patterns, yet it is all called Blue Ridge.

To add to the confusion, popular patterns were often applied to more than one shape, and sometimes several manufacturers used the same pattern. Some collectors accumulate shapes they like in an assortment of different patterns; others collect one pattern in a variety of shapes. And some collect it all. The important thing is to enjoy the sport.

TIPS *from the experts*

Antiques Roadshow appraiser David Rago offers some good advice for beginning collectors of ceramics. Before you spend a nickel:

♦ **Buy from a reputable dealer**. Of course, you may not know who the reputable dealers are, so request a written description of the piece you have just bought listing its age, condition, factory, and the artist's name (where applicable). Pay by check, and the moment you get home, wipe the entire piece with acetone. (It will not hurt the original finish, but it will dissolve paint touch-ups and instantly reveal every repair and touch-up.)

♦ **Buy the best piece you can afford.** The six unimportant pieces you buy with the money you might have spent on one fine piece will, over the years, provide you with less enjoyment and less value, should you ever want to sell them, than that best piece.

♦ **Unload from the bottom**. After you have been collecting for five or six years, get rid of the bottom 10 percent of your collection, either by putting it into auction or by selling it online. The next year, do the same. Ultimately, you will have a small, but superior, collection. (Most collections, Rago adds, would be 50 percent better if they were 30 percent smaller.)

(Moreover, you may not be sufficiently familiar with the output of any one factory to know which are the ugly ducklings and which are the swans.) *Antiques Roadshow* appraiser Eric Silver recommends that new collectors look for "quirky, funky things; pieces that were the new designs in their time," not retreads of long-dead fashions. Eric discovered that (even without his advice) his mother instinctively seems to have known this. She still owns a set of dinnerware designed by noted American industrial designer Walter Dorwin Teague. Proof, perhaps, that a good "eye" is genetic.

Here is a selection of the twentieth-century American dinnerware manufacturers most popular with collectors, together with their European counterparts. These are followed by factory-produced art pottery and studio pottery.

AMERICAN DINNERWARE AND TABLEWARE

A number of American ceramics manufacturers concentrated on making dinnerware; some produced art pottery as well. Many of these companies were located in the Midwest—particularly in Ohio—although West Virginia and California also had their share.

BLUE RIDGE

Beginning in 1917, Blue Ridge dinnerware, made by Southern Potteries in Ervin, Tennessee, was decorated mainly with decals applied by hand. In 1938, the firm started adding hand-painted accents to the decals, and by the early forties all Blue Ridge patterns were being designed and hand painted at the factory by

The Blue Ridge hand-painted Crab Apple pattern, from Southern Potteries.

local women artisans. The 1940s and 1950s are known as "The Golden Age of Blue Ridge," for the china was sold in showrooms and department stores, and thousands of pieces were offered as premiums at movie theaters. These wares, which came in thirteen different shapes decorated in many different patterns, are strongly rural, yet manage not to be "cute." Their hand-painted decoration is part of their appeal, and although the names of the individual artists aren't considered to be important, some collectors of Blue Ridge ceramics look particularly for artist-signed wares.

An advertisement for the Blue Ridge Night Flower pattern touts the fact that the dinnerware is hand painted under the glaze.

CASTLETON

Castleton China, which specialized in contemporary shapes and decorations, was a joint venture of the American Shenango Pottery Company in New Castle, Pennsylvania, and the German manufacturer Rosenthal.

After the Museum of Modern Art's "Organic Design in Home Furnishings" exhibition in 1942, Castleton asked the museum to help it select a ceramicist to create a definitive pattern for modern china. The museum chose noted designer Eva Zeisel, whose early work was influenced by the Bauhaus and by sculptor Jean Arp. Born in Budapest, Zeisel emigrated to the United States in 1938 and became an important freelance ceramics designer and teacher at Pratt Institute in New York. (She also designed Red Wing's Town and Country dinnerware; see page 14.) The Museum ware Zeisel designed for Castleton was sponsored by the museum and was issued in 1946. Every piece of this creamy, curving, and elegant ceramic, popular in both Europe and the United States, had to be approved by the museum before it was produced.

Eva Zeisel's Museum porcelain line— sponsored by the Museum of Modern Art—seems as fresh today as it did in the 1940s.

Franciscan proudly advertised its best-selling pattern, Desert Rose, in 1950s magazines, above. Above right, the company's hand-painted Ivy dinner plate.

FRANCISCAN

Produced from the mid-thirties by Gladding, McBean & Co., Los Angeles, California, Franciscan ware was immensely popular, especially with three embossed, hand-painted top-selling patterns: Desert Rose, Ivy, and Apple. Desert Rose, introduced in 1941, was among the most popular dinnerware patterns ever manufactured in the United States. Like other dinnerware collectors, many Franciscan collectors—and there are thousands—are "filling in" missing pieces in sets they have inherited. Certain serving pieces (of which, usually, fewer were sold) are highly coveted. Currently, Franciscan collectors are expanding their collections to include more modern, decal-decorated patterns, among them Starburst and Oasis.

HALL

Although Ohio's Hall China company produced several standard lines of dinnerware that are now enthusiastically collected—Autumn Leaf (once a premium for the Jewel Tea Company), Red Poppy, and Cameo Rose, among others—collectors of Hall are always on the lookout for certain 1920s and 1930s patterns of figural teapots (the Aladdin's Lamp is a choice one) and for refrigerator storage wares. Refrigerator containers, which Hall also made for appliance manufacturers such as Westinghouse and Sears, were wonderfully streamlined ceramic "sculptures" that also happened to be nicely functional. They are popular with collectors today.

Now a collectible, Hall's Autumn Leaf china was originally given away with the purchase of tea.

IROQUOIS CHINA COMPANY

The American midcentury designer Ben Seibel worked for several ceramics firms. For the Iroquois China Company of Syracuse, New York, for instance, he designed a number of lines of "Flameproof for Cooking" stoneware with names that began with the letter "I," such as Informal, Impromptu, Intaglio, and Inheritance. A 45-piece set retailed for $69.95. The Informal line, which proudly advertised itself as a dinnerware that "not only fries, but bakes, broils, roasts and serves with gourmet distinction," was thought to be so well made and so durable that *Good Housekeeping* magazine gave its seal of approval.

EDWIN M. KNOWLES

The Edwin M. Knowles China Company of Chester and Newell, West Virginia, produced a number of lines of dinnerware from the 1930s to the 1960s. Among styles popular today with collectors are Deanna, Yorktown, Utility Ware, and Esquire, which was designed by Russel Wright. All were available in a variety of colors or patterns.

HOMER LAUGHLIN

Best known for its immensely successful Fiesta ware (see box on page 15), the Homer Laughlin China Company of Newall, West Virginia, also made many other lines of dinnerware, some of great interest to collectors. Fiesta designer Frederick Hurton Rhead created Century, Newell, Wells, Kitchen Kraft, and Trellis. Don Schreckengost, the brother of Viktor (see page 27) was chief designer for Laughlin from 1945 to 1960; collectible patterns by Schreckengost include Epicure, Rhythm, and Jubilee.

MCCOY

The subject of McCoy pottery can be confusing, because the McCoy family had interests in several different companies with "McCoy" in their names. However, interest today is in the gently colored (celadon green, soft white, yellow) twenties and thirties stonewares of the Nelson McCoy Sanitary and Stoneware Company of Roseville, Ohio. Early in its history, McCoy produced kitchenware, but by 1926, it was marketing more ambitious products like

This 1950s Levittown housewife practically swoons over her Russel Wright–designed Iroquois Casual china. Many collectors today feel the same way.

Hungry little cowboys and Indians once raided teepee-shaped McCoy cookie jars. Today, they more likely cause showdowns at collector corrals.

jardinieres, umbrella stands, vases, and other decorative items. McCoy is known for floral industry ware (vases, flowerpots, and so forth); cookware, such as bean pots and casseroles; some dinnerware, like sugar and creamers and mugs; and kitchenware, like mixing bowls and pitchers. Cookie jars are particularly popular today, but novice buyers should beware of reproductions.

A colorful crowing rooster struts across assorted pieces of Metlox's California Provincial dinnerware.

METLOX

The name of this California company is actually a contraction of "metal oxide," which was used in ceramic glazes to create colors. Metlox's initial products were outdoor ceramic signs. The firm's 1930s to 1980s ceramic dinnerware, however, and its lines of miniatures, figural pottery, and later, cookie jars (especially a Little Red Riding Hood model) are the pieces collectors prefer. Among several favorite Metlox tableware lines are Antique Grape (made from 1964 to 1988), Colonial Homestead (1940s), Homestead Provincial, California Provincial, and Red Rooster (1950s). Metlox ceased production in the 1970s.

RED WING

Red Wing Pottery had its origins in the mid-nineteenth century, when the residents of Red Wing, Minnesota, started several potteries to take advantage of the rich clay deposits near the Mississippi River. Initially, the potteries manufactured utilitarian items, such as stoneware pickle jars, crocks, and churns for local farmers. By the 1890s, many of these factories had merged. When the demand for their usual products declined in the 1930s, the company began to make dinnerware, and changed its name to Red Wing Potteries in 1936.

In the mid-1940s, Red Wing requested the highly successful émigré industrial designer Eva Zeisel (see page 11) to create something "Greenwich Villagey" for the firm (i.e. "hip" and bohemian), and the artist responded with the novel, biomorphic

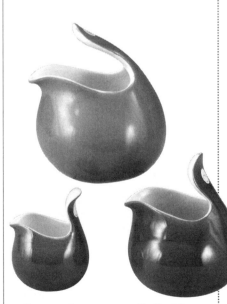

Creamers from Eva Zeisel's playful Town and Country dinnerware, produced by Red Wing Pottery.

dinnerware Town and Country. The salt and pepper shakers looked like cartoonist Al Capp's shmoos (endearing amoebic characters from the *L'il Abner* strip), while the creamer and teapot had curly "noses" or "ears," and the plates and bowls were decidedly and playfully off-kilter. When all were grouped together, Town and Country resembled less a set of tableware than a strangely lovable ceramic family. This pattern is actively collected today. Pieces have been reissued—some by the Metropolitan Museum of Art. The reissues are all marked; the original Red Wing pieces, however, have no marks whatsoever.

STEUBENVILLE POTTERY

American Modern dinnerware by designer Russel Wright, introduced to stave off bankruptcy by Ohio's Steubenville Pottery Company in 1939, became a huge success. In contrast to the weight and simplicity of the popular glazed earthenware Fiesta,

Luckily, the sinuous curves of Russel Wright's American Modern dinnerware struck a chord with the modern American housewife. It saved the Steubenville Pottery from bankruptcy.

PERFECT TIMING

There are auctions, today, of nothing but Fiesta ware. There are encyclopedias of Fiesta and dedicated, scholarly clubs that meet to discuss the minutiae of Fiesta. But who would have dreamed it in 1936, when Frederick Hurton Rhead designed this Art Deco–inspired pattern for the Homer Laughlin China Company? After all, there's nothing to Fiesta but simple color and a few concentric bands of rings. Yet it is, undoubtedly, as Laughlin claims, "among the most collected china products in the world" (a category that includes, mind you, Meissen, Royal Worcester, and Sevres).

Rhead, a studio potter, intended Fiesta to look handcrafted. To that end, he made it heavy and straightforward. Fifty-four items were introduced in five colors, to begin with: a matte-finished light green, yellow, ivory, dark blue, and red. (Turquoise was added in 1937.) The red hue was actually derived from uranium, and was (harmlessly) radioactive. When uranium became a priority for the builders of the atomic bomb during World War II, the Fiesta red was temporarily discontinued. Because of a 1977 scare about the safety of color-glazed dinnerware, the current reissue of Fiesta is being offered as "Lead-Free China for the New Millennium," although the old wares are perfectly safe.

Simply irresistible: Legions of collectors are drawn to Fiesta—plates, pitchers, and vases.

A 1939 advertisement sings the praises of two renowned artists and the dinnerware they decorated for Vernon Kilns. Below, from the Our America series, Rockwell Kent's bird's-eye view of Manhattan.

American Modern offers sinuous curves—especially in the serving pieces—and is seemingly made to be held, while exaggerated spouts and comfortable handles facilitate pouring.

American Modern was produced, initially, in five subdued colors—chartreuse curry, bean brown, granite grey, sea foam blue, and white—all of which could be combined and recombined as the purchaser chose. Its versatility and easy shapes made Wright's innovative design a cornerstone of the growing informality of the American dinner table. American Modern dinnerware is always marked.

VERNON KILNS

Originally named Vernon Potteries, in the 1930s and 1940s this California manufacturer produced many patterns of brightly colored earthenware dinnerware, including examples designed by such noted American artists as Rockwell Kent (see below) and Don Blanding (Hawaiian Flowers, Coral Reef). Many Vernon Kilns patterns were hand painted, and the firm also produced specialty items, such as historical and commemorative wares picturing historic sites like Mount Rushmore, cities (for example, St. Louis, Missouri, and Winston-Salem, North Carolina), and colleges and universities, along with notable human subjects like General Douglas MacArthur.

In 1939, well-known painter and illustrator Rockwell Kent designed a line of tableware for Vernon Kilns called Our America. Its simple forms were decorated with transfers of wood engravings of American scenes—from shipping, to bridge building, to maps of the United States, to plate-filling palm trees. They were printed in red, blue, or brown on a white ground, and each of the pieces was rimmed with stars on a dark ground. Probably no commercial ceramic has ever more thoroughly combined American innocence, bravado, and patriotism.

Also in 1939, Vernon Kilns issued dinnerware based on Kent's illustrations for *Salamina,* a book about his stay in Greenland. This set was not successful and was produced for only one year, making it rare and collectible now. In the 1940s, Kent designed a more successful set of dinnerware based on his illustrations for a Random House edition of *Moby Dick*. All pieces are marked "Moby Dick, designed by Rockwell Kent, Vernon Kilns, Made in USA."

WALLACE

The Wallace China Company of California made four restaurant china patterns depicting the down-home, ride-'em-cowboy motifs that were once a staple of restaurants throughout the West. These patterns—Rodeo, Pioneer Trails, Longhorn, and Boots and Saddles—were all intro-duced in the 1940s and designed by Till Goodan. Their introduction coin-cided with the country's increased interest in an idealized American West, in Western films, and in movie stars like Roy Rogers, Gene Autry, and John Wayne. In fact, Autry and Rogers both owned Wallace's Rodeo pattern. Wallace Western-ware patterns were also conveniently sturdy and useful, and well suited to that new American pastime—the cookout.

Wallace's come-'n-get-it Rodeo pattern features a buckaroo, a bronco, and a border of cattle brands.

EUROPEAN DINNERWARE AND TABLEWARE

Twentieth-century European dinnerware has much in common with its American counterparts. Europe's factories, old and new, were eager for modernity, and to that end, they cut back on the manufacture of expensive and dressy pre–World War I wares in favor of making practical wares, simple in shape and pattern, and eminently affordable.

Hundreds of people visiting the *Antiques Roadshow* want to know more about their heirloom china. Appraiser David Lackey says the way to begin identifying a pattern is to look for the manufacturer's label, the pattern name, and the pattern number on the bottom of the piece. If a plate, cup, or bowl lacks this information, Lackey recommends that you send a color photograph, drawing, or photocopy of the pattern to a china-matching service.

China-matching companies can usually tell when the pattern was made, provide a brief history about the manufacturer, and refer you to specialist books. They provide this service at no charge.

One way to locate china-matching services is to look in antiques, interior design, or women's magazines. Also check telephone listings under "china" or call the china department at your local department store.

If you're hoping to sell, take note: "For a desirable pattern," Lackey says, "services will pay up to one-half their selling price." And unlike that replaced leg on your grandmother's table, if you've added pieces to an old set, that doesn't diminish its value. "It's not like you're buying a newly manu-factured piece that may be different," Lackey says. "It's usually the same vintage and you can rarely tell the difference."

Mix 'n match: The simplicity of Arabia's Kilta line, designed by Kaj Franck, made it possible to combine different colors and still have a harmonious table.

ARABIA

Arabia was Finland's most important pottery manufacturer, with a stable of ceramic artists creating handsome and commercially successful dinnerware throughout the 1920s and 1930s. Nothing of international merit, however, came from this factory until the postwar era, when Kaj Franck became its chief designer. Typical of that period was the very "modern," enormously simple Kilta line of tableware, produced in a variety of colors. Franck designed the Kilta line so that the consumer could mix and match pieces and colors, avoiding an investment in large, uniform dinner services. The Kilta customer could buy only what he needed and replace pieces easily. A later version of the Kilta line was called Teema.

The sunny yellow Buttercup breakfast set from Carlton made any morning brighter. The toast rack is particularly rare.

CARLTON WARE

Carlton Ware was manufactured at the Carlton Works in Stoke-on-Trent, England, beginning in 1890. Among its most collectible lines is a readily available molded earthenware salad service embossed in relief—usually with vivid red tomatoes or lobsters. Another popular collectible is the Fruit Basket line. The floral embossed line is, however, the most popular of all Carlton Ware, especially the teapots. Combining bright colors with embossed shapes of flowers and plants, it can be had in Foxglove, Primula, Wild Rose, and Apple Blossom. Carlton lusterware pieces are all exuberance and sparkle. Their red, orange, pink, and blue fireworks of Art Deco florets and fans perfectly embody the 1920s, although this desirable characteristic has resulted in a highly competitive market and high prices.

CLARICE CLIFF

English ceramicist Clarice Cliff is renowned for hand-painted and bold geometric Art Deco designs. A decorator at Newport Pottery in 1928, Cliff began to refinish unsold pieces in vibrant colors. Called Bizarre, the experiment was an instant success, and Cliff designed new shapes and patterns for the line. Her shop within the company quickly grew. In tribute to her success,

Cliff was named art director of Newport, and the entire company was devoted to producing only her designs.

Cliff's tea things are of particular interest to collectors, although all of the factory's work is highly desirable and commands a high price, even the common patterns like Crocus.

SUSIE COOPER

It has been reported that the influential English ceramics designer Susie Cooper "wanted to do nice things for people who had taste but didn't have the money to satisfy it." In the course of a long career, she succeeded well beyond her modest dreams, designing numerous pleasant dinnerware patterns that were affordable and well suited to current tastes. Cooper opened her own business in 1929. Her designs were hand painted or lithographed on earthenware until about 1950, when the firm's acquisition of a bone-china manufacturer allowed it to produce china as well. In 1966, the Cooper works became part of Wedgwood, and although Wedgwood closed down the Susie Cooper lines in 1979, Cooper continued to work on a freelance basis until 1985.

Currently, the Susie Cooper geometric and lusterware designs—the coffeepots, plates, and even cups and saucers from the Art Deco era—are enthusiastically collected. If the bold, stylized patterns of the late 1920s are especially desirable, however, it is the midcentury patterns that are readily available (many more Susie Cooper ceramics can be found in England, naturally, than in the United States).

A coffee pot, cups, and creamer in Susie Cooper's Raised Spot pattern. Her various sugar bowl and dinnerware patterns include floral and geometric designs, incised decoration, and transfer prints.

SCANDINAVIAN CERAMICS

Between the 1930s and 1950s, Scandinavian ceramics factories returned to an old tradition of hiring the best native artists and giving them free rein to design as they liked. In contrast to American ceramicists, who were isolated and likely to be making their pots in garages, Scandinavian innovators first designed the wares and then assisted in their day-to-day production in the factories.

Both Royal Copenhagen of Denmark and Rörstrand of Sweden produced artist-designed studio-type vases, bowls, and platters after World War II. For collectors of these ceramics, pieces with artist's signatures command a premium.

Perhaps the most important artist to work for Royal Copenhagen during this period was Danish potter Axel Salto (see page 7), who was also a printmaker and designer. In the interwar and postwar years, Salto designed for Royal Copenhagen utterly singular stoneware in fruitlike shapes, sometimes encrusted with bizarre protuberances, creating pots and vases that effectively blended earthen shades (browns, greens, bronzes) with geometric patterns.

The Swedish ceramics manufacturer Rörstrand, once noted for Art Nouveau pottery, produced droll works by Gunnar Nylund and others.

Three plates from Fornasetti's Themes and Variations series, featuring women's faces and architectural elements, black transfer decoration on simple white blanks.

FORNASETTI

In the late 1940s and the 1950s, Italian artist Piero Fornasetti attracted international attention with decorated porcelains printed in surreal and arresting patterns. Neoclassical in concept, his products were often variations on the arresting face of the early-twentieth-century Italian opera singer Lina Cavalieri (he had seen her picture in a vintage magazine), as well as radiant suns, architectural themes, and playing cards. All were produced by Fornasetti's carefully guarded, secret printing process. The artist opted to manufacture his own products and also to market them, and while his wares were commercially well received, some authorities suggest that Fornasetti may have sacrificed even greater success. Had he been willing to let experts handle his business, they contend, it might have been far more efficient and profitable.

Although Fornasetti did manufacture teapots, he preferred working with plates and cups. These were always printed on ordinary, white, commercial blanks (undecorated pieces of china). His skill as a draftsman—all the drawings are his own—is particularly well suited to the several series of plates.

Gifted industrial designer Raymond Loewy, father of the Studebaker Avanti and many other twentieth-century icons, created the Form 2000 set for Rosenthal.

ROSENTHAL

During the Art Deco era, the venerable German firm of Rosenthal became enthusiastically avant-garde, hiring sculptor Gerhard Schliepstein to create highly exaggerated figurines and painter Tono Zoelch to create figurines from porcelain.

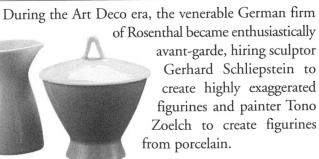

In the 1940s, in the hope of restoring its flagging post–World War II fortunes, Rosenthal decided to collaborate with the American firm of industrial designer Raymond Loewy to create modern dinner services with basic shapes that would be available in twenty different patterns. Raymond Loewy Associates designed for Rosenthal its Form 2000 dinner set (also referred to as Model 2000 and Shape 2000), which is angular and evocative of the Bauhaus in style. Its sleek stylishness perfectly sums up the internationalism of the postwar period.

In the 1950s, Rosenthal hired the cream of the international design field to create porcelain for the firm, employing a group of formidable artists, architects, and sculptors, among them Finnish Renaissance man Tapio Wirkkala, Walter Gropius, Bjorn Winblad, Timo Sarpaneva, Henry Moore, and Salvador Dalí—a veritable Who's Who of Modernism. Collectors, unsurprisingly, look particularly for work by these major artists.

SHELLEY

Staffordshire's Shelley China Ltd. (Staffordshire was long the center of English ceramics manufacture) was renowned for its fine bone china, but the firm also produced earthenware in a wide array of forms: from jelly molds to table lamps, nursery ware, and figurines. Shelley china, like that of all successful manufacturers, came in many shapes and styles.

Frederick Rhead, the English ceramics designer who is best known in the United States for designing Fiesta ware, also designed several patterns for Shelley.

Among the most popular Shelley shapes today are Queen Anne (the cups are octagonal) and Vogue (a futuristic design with square plates and cone-shaped cups with triangular handles); the Queen Anne shape comes in more than 160 different patterns and Vogue, in more than fifty. Dainty is a popular shape, and the pattern Dainty White is especially collectible.

Shelley is a quintessentially British ceramics firm, and since gardens are also quintessentially British, it's only

CHINTZ

By the 1920s, transfer-printed china with allover patterns of tightly placed, small flowers, called chintz ware, was being produced in abundance at the English firms Crown Ducal (A. G. Richardson & Co.), James Kent Ltd., Lord Nelson Ware (Elijah Cotton), Royal Winton (Grimwades Ltd.), and Shelley.

Chintz patterns on ceramics were based on the printed floral cotton fabrics, originally imported from India, called chintz. These floral-patterned ceramics were so successful that by the twentieth century, chintz ware was not only mass-produced, but individual patterns were refreshed or reimagined every year. (Frequently, only the background color would be changed and a new name assigned.) In the 1950s, chintz ware fell from favor, but the numerous chintz patterns exported to North America during that thirty-year period are being avidly collected today. Some collectors concentrate on a favorite manufacturer or shape, while others are happy with any piece at all. Chintz ware was inexpensive when new, but it is not uncommon today for a single plate—depending on the desirability of the pattern—to be valued at more than $100. (Royal Winton's Summertime, introduced in 1932, is thought to be the most popular chintz pattern.) As with all collectible tableware, the more unusual forms, such as butter dishes or toast racks, command a premium.

natural that Shelley would be one of the leading manufacturers of bone china chintz ware (see box this page), that most floral of dinnerware.

WEDGWOOD

The venerable English firm of Josiah Wedgwood and Sons in Staffordshire has enjoyed acclaim for its tableware and other ceramics since the eighteenth century. Today, many people associate Wedgwood with the blue-and-white Jasperware that the firm has manufactured continuously for some two hundred years, giving rise to the distinctive blue known as "Wedgwood blue." But the company has always produced a variety of wares, and the work of two of Wedgwood's twentieth-century designers is particularly collectible today.

In the 1930s, architect and designer Keith Murray created Modernist shapes in monochromes (single colors) for Wedgwood. Decoration, if there was any, was sparse and incised, the embodiment of the streamlined style that was so typical of the era. (Some of Murray's dinnerware, however, was more conventionally decorated.) The artist designed vases, bowls, cigarette boxes, ashtrays, beakers, mugs, and some tableware shapes and patterns, and while his work may not be particularly well known in America, in Great Britain, the market for Murray is quite large—and currently, extremely volatile.

Keith Murray's elegant Wedgwood vase from about 1940 is squat but bold, and has a banded shoulder.

During this same period, Wedgwood also employed artist and expert wood engraver Eric Ravilious, who created light-hearted and traditional wares. Decorative and charming commemorative mugs and a "Travel" dinner service, depicting trains, buses, sailboats, hot-air balloons, and other forms of transportation, depended less on shape than on sprightly decoration. Ravilious was killed during World War II, and many of his designs were, in fact, not issued until the postwar era. His drawing of celebratory fountains of fireworks was adapted for the 1953 Coronation mug.

ART POTTERY

A rt pottery had its heyday in the United States in the late nineteenth and early twentieth centuries, although it maintained residual popularity even after World War I. Art pottery vases, jardinieres, plates, and other decorative objects were still designed and decorated by professional artists and designers, but these were usually created, now, in a factory. Most entries in this category, consequently, are manufacturers (both American and European), although a few individuals merit inclusion.

RENÉ BUTHAUD

Monumental glazed stoneware shapes and highly stylized Art Deco patterns typify the work of French ceramicist René Buthaud. Having designed simple stoneware forms for fabrication by local potters, he coated them with crackled glazes. Buthaud's decorations were generally drawn from life and are frequently stylized, sturdy flowers rendered in colorful glazes. Buthaud's female figures—often, sensuous nudes—were traced directly on the pot.

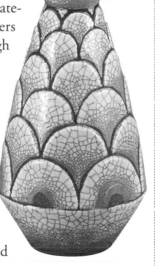

Crackle glazing—as seen in this Raku vase—is a hallmark of René Buthaud's work.

GUIDO GAMBONE

Guido Gambone was an imaginative and versatile Italian potter who produced everything from world-class pottery for major exhibitions to commercial lamp bases. His work is usually classical in shape and decorated in exceptionally vivid colors with bubbly glazes. Gambone also created figural pieces, of which animals like anteaters are typical. (Potential collectors should be

MEISSEN AND ROYAL COPENHAGEN

B oth the fine and old German firm Meissen and the noted Danish manufacturer Royal Copenhagen produced costly, formal ceramic dinnerware between 1920 and 1950. Meissen manufactured figures, as well, just as it had in the eighteenth century; these were the usual maidens and putti (cherubs), but all were stylized and updated. Royal Copenhagen's traditional Flora Danica line, a luxurious tour de force of botanical-patterned china, was, and still is, coveted worldwide. Royal Copenhagen also produced highly successful lines of Christmas plates and figures that have attracted thousands of collectors. The twentieth-century wares of both firms usually command a premium, as much for their glorious old names as for their quality.

Finely rendered, with gilded rims, Royal Copenhagen's hand-painted Flora Danica is popular worldwide.

Italian ceramicist Guido Gambone fabricated a veritable Noah's ark of faience figurines, among them this mild-mannered lion.

An example of Hull's art ware, this urn-shape vase is delicately colored in the pinks and yellows of the Ohio pottery's distinctive pastel palette.

aware that the artist's son is making ceramics today and signing himself "Gambone." *Antiques Roadshow* appraiser David Rago believes that the pieces designed by Gambone senior include a signature plus a stylized image of a donkey.)

GUSTAVSBERG

In the 1920s and 1930s, under the direction of designer Wilhelm Kåge, the Gustavsberg factory, located near Stockholm, acquired an international reputation for Argenta stoneware. Argenta may be unique among purely ornamental Art Deco ceramics in combining an imitation verdigris surface (a turquoise green that resembles patinated bronze) with chased silver. This highly collectible Gustavsberg innovation is a successful blend of Asian, ancient European, and modern styles. Other collectible Gustavsberg ceramics include the spare, classsical works of Berndt Friberg.

Classically shaped and subtly glazed—a Gustavsberg vase from Swedish ceramicist Berndt Friberg, from 1946.

HULL

In its Ohio factory between 1905 and 1985, Hull produced both commercial pottery and "art" wares. It is best known, currently, for baskets, jardinieres, and ewers. These are particularly desirable to collectors in the Woodland, Poppy, and Iris patterns. Cookie jars were another Hull specialty, especially the Little Red Riding Hood open-basket model. Items made with a matte finish, produced prior to a 1950 fire at the pottery factory, are more highly valued than the glossy pieces made after the factory was rebuilt.

MOORCROFT

The successful Arts and Crafts potter William Moorcroft, with the financial support of the famous London retailer Liberty, opened his own factory in 1912, and manufactured art-pottery jugs, vases, and plates. In the 1920s, Walter Moorcroft, his son, produced elegant, hand-painted floral designs on dark-blue backgrounds using a technique that seems to owe a debt to simple finger painting. Walter decorated his later work—reflecting, perhaps, the austerity of the Depression years—in muted earth tones and salt glazes. Rare miniature pieces by Moorcroft are highly desirable.

PABLO PICASSO

Although the limited-edition glazed earthenware objects produced at the Madoura pottery in Vallauris, France, were intended to be commercial products, not museum pieces, from the very outset they *were* museum pieces. Picasso first visited the Madoura pottery in Vallauris in the South of France in 1946, and returned every year thereafter to work at the pottery, where he made more than 3,500 vases, plates, pitchers, and other forms. From this large body of work, hundreds of designs were turned into limited-edition Picasso ceramics that were made in multiples of from twenty-five to five hundred. The technique was as follows: The artist himself painted the decoration on the prototypes of the plates, vases, and chargers; subsequent pieces were copies, each hand painted by a competent ceramic artist. These Picasso plates or vases, while technically not "original Picassos," do manage to capture the spontaneous quality of the artist's work. As the pieces began to be of interest to collectors, prices increased, and today even the smallest Picasso limited-edition ceramics command a premium.

ROOKWOOD

Rookwood Pottery, founded by Maria Longworth Nichols in 1880 as an amateur pottery club, became a successful business in 1883 after William Watts Taylor was hired as general manager. Taylor instituted market surveys to find out what people wanted, standardized the product line, and marketed the pottery through fashionable stores. Under his stewardship, the company developed its characteristic and unique matte glazes.

In the post–World War I era, Rookwood hired artists attuned to contemporary movements in international art. Jens Jenson, for instance, at Rookwood from the late twenties through the forties, seems to have thought of himself as "the American Picasso," says *Antiques Roadshow* expert Riley Humler. When Jensen first introduced ceramics decorated with nude, Deco-esque figures, he caused a scandal on the quiet banks of the Ohio River that was, indeed, worthy of Picasso.

At the height of his fame, Pablo Picasso brought his inimitable genius to the decoration of limited-edition ceramics.

Quirky twisted handles and a blue-green matte glaze are the distinctive features of this bottle-shaped Rookwood vase from 1921.

Fabulous or faux? Forgers are busily knocking off highly collectible Roseville ceramics. The left-hand vase is a fake; a genuine piece is at right.

DISTINGUISHING ROSEVILLE

Success often results in both praise and envy. For Roseville Pottery of Zanesville, Ohio, it produced a slew of less-than-honorable copy-cats. At the Salt Lake City *Antiques Roadshow,* a woman from Duchesne, Utah, brought in what she believed were two Roseville vases. "One of these is fake," appraiser David Rago informed her immediately. "And it's important to know why people would bother faking this, who is faking it, and how you can recognize the real."

Looking at the two vases before him, Rago continued, "the one with the snowberry pattern is authentic. It's not the best thing Roseville ever produced, but it is still very popular,

with pretty colors. You can tell it's authentic because of the sharpness of the colors." The water lily–pattern vase, on the other hand, is one of numerous copies of the Roseville original that have appeared in the last decade, he added. "There's a muddiness to the background. It has a kind of murky airbrushed look to

it, which I'm sure is how they made it." The authentic vase is marked "Roseville USA," while the fake is made of a heavier clay and is marked merely "Roseville."

"This was made in China," Rago said of the fake. "They're making them by the tens of thousands, and a lot of people have been taken in."

Another Rookwood artist, William Ernst Hentschel, painted his vases with figures, until that time an unaccustomed subject for Rookwood.

Sara Sax, according to Humler, was Rookwood's great Art Deco technician. Her assured and elegant works combine repetitious pattern with various types of glaze. As with all pottery of this period, colors at Rookwood were more vivid than they had ever been; moreover, the palette was lighter, and the glazes, due to the aforementioned advances in technology, were less crazed than previously.

ROSEVILLE

The Roseville Pottery Company, located in Ohio until the 1950s, produced enormous quantities of pottery decorated with relief-molded flowers or fruits and competed with Weller for the mid-level market. In 1928, Roseville introduced an interesting, stylized, multi-planar line called Futura, which—because of its distinctly Deco style—is of great interest to collectors today. Other lines from this era, Baneda for example, shared glazes with the standard Roseville product, and both attract Art Deco and Roseville collectors. Other exceptionally popular Roseville patterns are Blackberry and Pinecone, from 1931. All were the work of Frank Ferrell, who designed some ninety-six lines for Roseville between 1918 and 1953.

SAXBO

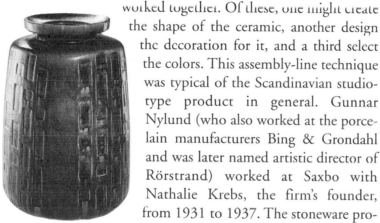

The Danish Saxbo factory employed several designers who worked together. Of these, one might create the shape of the ceramic, another design the decoration for it, and a third select the colors. This assembly-line technique was typical of the Scandinavian studio-type product in general. Gunnar Nylund (who also worked at the porcelain manufacturers Bing & Grondahl and was later named artistic director of Rörstrand) worked at Saxbo with Nathalie Krebs, the firm's founder, from 1931 to 1937. The stoneware produced by this team, in conjunction with Edith Sonne-Bruun and Eva Staehr-Nielsen, combines Asian overtones with classic shapes and glazes.

Too many cooks did not spoil the lovely, team-designed Danish Saxbo art pottery.

VIKTOR SCHRECKENGOST

Working in the Art Deco idiom, and influenced by the art of the Futurists and Cubists, Viktor Schreckengost, the son of a commercial potter in Sebring, Ohio, created vases, bowls, and plates at the Cowan Pottery Studio in Cleveland in the 1930s and went on to a long career as an industrial designer. (He designed, among other things, bicycles, trucks, lawn mowers, exhaust fans, lawn furniture, children's pedal cars, and printing presses.) His "Jazz" bowl, a punch bowl commissioned by

"No chips, no cracks, and a perfectly uniform glaze," describes the condition of the most collectible Rookwood pottery, such as this bulbous vase from 1942, embossed with stylized flowers and a basketweave design.

The "Jazz Bowl," commissioned by Eleanor Roosevelt in 1931, was called "New Year's Eve in New York City" by its creator, Victor Schreckengost.

Eleanor Roosevelt for the New York State governor's mansion in 1931, is vividly colored, graphic, and stylish and a ceramic icon of the era. Schreckengost's later designs include one of the first Modernist dinner services mass-produced in the United States, the Manhattan dinner service for American Limoges in Sebring, Ohio, and Free Forms for the Salem China Company in Salem, Ohio. Salem issued Free Forms in several patterns that Schreckengost designed, including one called Primitive, inspired by prehistoric cave paintings and aimed at the male customer. Free Forms included an innovative dripless teacup, the first patented teacup improvement in one hundred years.

WELLER

Weller, one of the many Ohio potteries, was also one of the largest pottery works in the world prior to World War II. During the twenties and thirties, the company produced innumerable baskets, bowls, ashtrays, figures, jardinieres, pitchers, vases, and umbrella stands. It made hundreds of patterns, as well, among them Dickensware, with designs inspired by the writer's work; Sicardo, which rather resembled iridescent art glass; and Woodcraft, a pattern that imitated wood. There were also hand-decorated lines, among them Hudson. Weller artists painted scenes and portraits and even attempted to copy Rookwood's successful vellum glazes.

STUDIO POTTERY

S tudio pottery is exactly what it sounds like—one-of-a-kind ceramics created by individual artists (and sometimes pairs of artists) working in their studios.

HARDING BLACK

A pioneer in the field of studio ceramics, and a serious student of the technology of glazes—especially ancient Chinese glazes—San Antonio potter and autodidact Harding Black taught ceramics to children and produced wheel-thrown earthenware pots during the thirties. When, in the forties and fifties, Black

This Weller umbrella stand (front) and Dickensware vase attest to the variety of the firm's tremendous output.

was able to move to a better-equipped studio—one with kilns capable of reaching the higher temperatures necessary for stoneware and porcelains—his choices of materials broadened. Over a long career, Black created vessels, including jars, bowls, compotes, vases, pitchers, even birdfeeders. Authorities in the field of ceramics confess to being awestruck by Black's special facility for difficult glazing techniques such as oxblood, black oil-spot, and flambé.

HANS COPER

A German refugee who worked with famed ceramicist Lucie Rie (see page 31) in London after World War II, Hans Coper experimented with a series of single shapes until he felt he had exhausted each one's potential. Although Coper's work can be seen as sculpture, the artist insisted that because everything he produced was a form of container, it had to be considered utilitarian. Typical Coper pots have a distinctly Modernist look—although many also recall ancient and primitive objects—and have little or no color. Sometimes, oxides have been rubbed into their unglazed, stonelike surfaces. What glazes are used are often heavy and textural. Like his colleague Lucie Rie's work, Coper's pots also seem to be architectonic and brooding.

The startling lines of Hans Coper's work were inspired by both Modernist and primitive sources.

MAIJA GROTELL

Finnish émigré Maija Grotell taught ceramics in New York in the mid-1920s while researching and improving her glazing techniques and developing an idiosyncratic series of strict and sleek Art Deco patterns. Grotell made a major mark on the design and ceramics worlds in 1938, however, when she became head of the ceramics department at Cranbrook Academy of Art in Michigan. There, she was inspired by working with members of a faculty that included architect Eliel Saarinen, sculptor Carl Milles, weaver Marianne Strengell, and eventually, designer Charles Eames. It was while teaching at Cranbrook that Grotell did her finest work.

Grotell spent decades resolving esoteric glazing problems. Both her difficulties and her resolutions are most apparent, perhaps, to other ceramicists. Rather, it is the restraint and sophistication that speak volumes to the general community of discriminating ceramics collectors.

The virtuosity of Maija Grotell's pottery is revered by fellow ceramicists and prized by serious collectors.

CURTAIN OF THE NIGHT

The owner of this vase inherited it from her aunt, a business-woman in Dallas, and brought the

vase to the Charleston, South Carolina, *Antiques Roadshow.*

Appraiser David Lackey noted that the vase was signed by Frank Klepper, a Dallas-based artist who occasionally worked in ceramics.

This unusual piece has a metal rim, and it is inscribed on the bottom "Curtain of the Night"—a rare detail for a pottery vase. According to additional markings, it was made in 1932 and sold for $50, quite a bit of money at the time. Lackey told the owner that it was a great example and for collectors interested in regional Texas art, it would be quite valuable. He valued the vase at $5,000 to $8,000.

VIVIKA AND OTTO HEINO

The husband-and-wife team Otto and Vivika Heino were studio potters who produced midcentury ceramics, predominantly vessels (vases, bowls, jars), which were neither flashy nor groundbreaking, but subtle, earthy, and more Japanese-inspired than the work of most of their contemporaries. Heino joint creations are sturdy and accessible. Almost uniquely among American potters, their works were commercially successful, even when new.

A Heino chalice demonstrates the powerful subtlety of the couple's work.

BERNARD LEACH

As a young man living in Japan, Bernard Leach became a serious student of the potter's craft. He spent his lifetime working in clay and is today recognized as one of the great ceramicists of the twentieth century. Leach moved to England in the 1920s and there he produced glazed stoneware pots that, not surprisingly, look distinctly Japonesque. Vessel walls are thick, usually exhibiting simple but elegant brushwork decoration, with stylized representations of carp being among his favorite motifs. In contrast to the restricted output of teacher-potters who must combine their passion with lecturing, Leach estimated that in his lifetime he created more than 100,000 pieces (although many are minor variations of others exactly like them). He was particularly influential in the postwar period, and his manifesto, *A Potter's Book,* is a standard text for ceramicists.

East meets West in the Japanese-inflected pottery that Bernard Leach produced in England.

GERTRUD AND OTTO NATZLER

The Natzlers, Austrian émigrés to the United States, were a husband-and-wife team of ceramicists. Gertrud was the potter, crafting shapely, elegant vessels of all sorts, while Otto, using his own formulas, fired and glazed her work. Otto's glazes, rich lavalike layerings of hue, imitation bronze patinas, and jewel-like colorations often incorporating iridescent crystals, complemented Gertrud's pristine shapes. The Natzlers' early work is more utilitarian in form than their later output. Working together for more than three decades, they perfected innovative glazes and refined forms within a body of work that comprises some 25,000 pieces. After Gertrud's death in 1971, Otto continued working on ceramic constructions of geometric forms with metallic glazes.

POLIA AND WILLIAM PILLIN

Polia Pillin, an aspiring painter born in Poland, and her husband, poet and Russian émigré William Pillin, set up a pottery studio in Los Angeles in 1948. Working together, William shaped and glazed the pots and Polia hand painted their decoration. Polia's designs frequently included dancers, fantastic animals, particularly birds, fish, deer, and horses, and women of mysterious allure. Some experts, among them Mark McDonald, consider the Pillins' ceramics to be more interesting for the painting than for their ceramic body. In fact, like Picasso, whose work Polia admired, the vessels and plates created for her by William may have simply been vehicles for her paintings. William also experimented with glazes in solid colors and with unusual textures, and also produced ceramics without Polia's paintings.

All Pillin pieces are marked with a stylized signature. Appraiser David Lackey notes that the Pillins produced thousands of pieces. Because there is relatively little written about their work, and the signature can be hard to read, there may still be many undiscovered pieces.

LUCIE RIE

Destined to become one of the most noted and respected ceramicists in the world, Lucie Rie began her career in design in Vienna as a student of Josef Hoffmann, the architect and designer who was a major figure in the Austrian Art Nouveau movement and a founder of the Vienna Secession, a group of revolutionary

Partners in work as in life, Gertrud and Otto Natzler together created unusual pottery like this pear-shaped vessel.

William Pillin fashioned what were essentially ceramic canvases for his wife, Polia, to decorate with her fanciful paintings.

ART AND THE ARTIST

At the Louisville, Kentucky, *Antiques Roadshow,* two pieces of Newcomb College pottery—along with the woman who made them—found their way to appraiser David Lackey's table.

From 1927 to 1929, Lackey's visitor had attended Sophie Newcomb College in New Orleans, famous for the art pottery created by its students. She brought with her two of her own pots and coasters.

"I have long been a fan of Newcomb pottery," said Lackey, "But I've never had the pleasure of meeting one of the artists."

Lackey told her that Newcomb coasters usually sell for $500 to $700 each, and small, simple vases such as hers usually sell for $1,000 to $1,200. With their incontestable provenance, however, these might sell for appreciably more.

Lucie Rie distilled a number of influences to create a thoroughly personal and distinctive style.

artists and architects. Rie also studied under the noted Viennese potter Michael Powolny and was deeply influenced both by the Bauhaus and the Scandinavian Modernists.

Rie moved to London in 1938, and to support herself during the war years, she made glass buttons for dressmakers. During the 1950s and 1960s, she produced tableware, until financial stability ultimately allowed her to concentrate on one-of-a-kind functional objects—bottles, vases, and bowls—that are clearly handmade and, generally, of elegant form. Her most distinctive glaze is a thick, chalky, pitted white, although she also worked in bright mustard yellows and cerulean blues.

PETER VOULKOS

In the late 1940s, California was the center of innovative pottery making in the United States, and Peter Voulkos, a major, nationally acclaimed, and revolutionary figure in postwar American ceramics, was teaching there. By the 1950s, his groundbreaking work was inspiring the generation of potters who would succeed him. Voulkos's work is dynamic—some have called him the Jackson Pollock of clay. Glazes are dripped directly on the surface of the pot, surfaces are slashed, and forms have an exhilarating brutality.

Peter Voulkos's powerful creations—like this stoneware charger—confound traditional expectations.

Chapter Two

ADVERTISING

dvertising, that most American of enterprises, may also be the ideal mirror of our popular culture. All our fantasies, values, and desires are ultimately reflected in our advertising. It tracks, too, advances in media, technology, and medicine, and it chronicles subtle changes in our language and daily life. In the United States, advertising is so intertwined with popular culture and language that it's hard to say which came first, the need for a product or that product's promotion. Everywhere you look there is something to buy and a more-or-less-convincing inducement to buy it.

To the noncollector, advertising may seem to be simply television commercials, color glossies in magazines, or highway billboards. To the knowledgeable and passionate collector, however, it is a colorful archive of ownable images, products, objects, and promotional items; it is signs, serving trays, packaging, point-of-purchase displays, secret decoder rings, dolls, toys, and giveaways—all waiting for a home. What an amazing trove for collectors.

A perfect example of the appeal of vintage advertising can be seen in the group of fourteen early-twentieth-century lithographed tin signs that were brought to the Tulsa *Antiques Roadshow.*

Top: A solemn "expert" on a lithographed sign exhorts you to "Drink Moxie." Above: A rosy-cheeked girl entices customers to buy Sunbeam Bread in a die-cut "standee" sign from the 1940s.

A visitor to the Tulsa Antiques Roadshow *shows appraiser Noel Barrett her collection of signs advertising the Chiclets Zoo—a series of promotional rag-doll animals—which Barrett thinks might be the only complete set in existence.*

To school well fed on
Grape-Nuts
"There's a Reason"

This self-framed lithographed, embossed tin sign once advertised Grape-Nuts cereal—although children who eat this for breakfast today are rarely taken to school by a Saint Bernard.

They were signs advertising Chiclets gum that had originally been displayed in a grocery store opened by the visitor's husband's family in 1879. Appraiser Noel Barrett immediately identified the signs as advertisements for the "Chiclets Zoo," a collection of animal-character rag dolls created by Chiclets to promote its gum. Twelve animal characters existed in all, and consumers could buy rag dolls based on each of the different characters. The visitor told Barrett that the signs had survived because her mother-in-law never threw anything away, and consequently the set was remarkably complete, with a separate sign for each animal as well as two larger signs advertising the entire zoo.

Barrett was thrilled with the collection because he had never seen all twelve animal signs, and he told the delighted owner that while the animal signs alone could easily bring $8,500 at auction, together with the two larger Chiclet signs, the whole set might fetch between $10,000 and $12,000. Barrett conjectured that this might be the only complete set in existence—unless, of course, somewhere, there is another lucky owner whose husband's family owned a grocery store in the first decades of the twentieth century and whose mother-in-law never threw anything away.

A BRIEF HISTORY

America has always been the land of the best next thing, from the time Columbus set out to seek a more lucrative trade route to the Indies to the Gold Rush prospectors to immigrants hoping for a new start and a better way of life. With the coming of industrialization and new technologies in the nineteenth century, the race for bigger, better, faster, and stronger was definitely on. Burgeoning industry and trade inevitably meant greater prosperity, more leisure time, and stronger competition for new markets.

From the late nineteenth century until today, America has offered a particularly fertile soil for advertising, a specialty that arose to fulfill (and often create) the need for commercial products and services. It did this by unrelentingly persuading Mr. and Mrs. Householder that this soap, or that cereal, gasoline, scouring powder, brand of children's shoes, or headache remedy was essential to their happiness and well-being.

Advertising became an inextricable part of the American scene largely because about one hundred years ago, a few little-known firms like Kellogg's, H. J. Heinz, and Coca-Cola decided that they would need to invest unheard of sums of money to promote their brand-new, untried products. Kellogg's claims for its cereals may have been modest, initially, but they were persistent. The Heinz Company discovered that giving away countless thousands of little green pickle pins encouraged sales of both pickles and other condiments. Coke put its logo on a multitude of soft-drink related objects, like glasses and trays.

GO FOR THE GIMMICK

Even Burma Shave, a small company making a brushless shaving cream, came up with an innovative "hook." When the fledgling firm was first struggling to market its product in 1925, the owner's son had the brilliant idea of using consecutive road signs to send the message. Five or six yard-long signs spaced about twenty yards apart began to appear on America's highways, each one bearing a single line of Burma Shave's advertising verse (cars moved at a more leisurely pace, then). Travelers looked forward to seeing the signs as they traveled down lonely roads, and laughing at jokes like: "Henry the Eighth/Sure had trouble/Short-term wives/Long term stubble/Burma Shave." Or: "Ben met Anna/Made a Hit/Neglected Beard/Ben–Anna split/Burma Shave." The signs were a sensation, and the effectiveness of the campaign was borne out by one self-referential verse: "If you don't know/Whose signs these are/You can't have driven/Very far/Burma Shave." The little company flourished until the sixties, when it was sold. The signs were discontinued, but shortly thereafter, the highway Beautification Act of 1965 put an end to all roadside signs,

AN AMERICAN TRADITION

Advertising has a long history in America. Within only twenty-five years of the Declaration of Independence, the first illustrated advertisement, offering paper products for sale, was distributed in Massachusetts. (Before that time, all advertising was simply text.) By the mid-1870s, the United States had both color lithography and its first full-service advertising agency, N. W. Ayer & Son (still in existence), making more scientific and elaborate advertising possible.

The last sign of the five- or six-sign series that carried the Burma Shave Company's signature roadside rhymes was a simple board with only the name of the company.

METAL TRAYS

Metal trays, offered as inducements to soda-fountain and bar owners to handle a manufacturer's product, are among the most attractive and noteworthy of vintage giveaways. Most often made of tin (although they could also be of celluloid, glass, or plastic) and lithographed in eye-catching, brilliant colors, the trays were available, generally, in two sizes: small oval tip trays, and large round drinks trays. Naturally, the beverage industries—marketers of soft drinks and beer—made most use of tray advertising, often hiring exceptionally well-known artists, like Norman Rockwell for Coca-Cola, to provide attractive images. When placed edge to edge along the rear shelf of a soda fountain, tin trays made particularly attractive, albeit commercial, decorations, and became, in fact, a widespread style of fountain decor. Eye-catching pictures of smiling beauties were often the centerpieces on these trays, and the commercial message itself was fairly unobtrusive.

The lithographer's name generally appeared somewhere on the tray, often along one edge. Because the working dates of most lithography firms are known and fairly accessible, such information can sometimes help in dating.

anyway. While Burma Shave signs may no longer be found on the sides of the nation's highways, they can be seen on the walls of numerous advertising collectors.

THE ADVERTISING CENTURY

As the twentieth century unfolded, advertising followed many roads to mass merchandising. Cartoon characters were born, sports celebrities turned into product spokespeople, and matinee idols lured millions to movie theaters and cigarette brands. Dozens of automobile manufacturers raced to produce and sell better cars, and oil companies clamored to fuel them. The late twenties brought radios into every living room (to be replaced by television sets in the 1950s) and America willingly embraced every convenience and appliance that promised more free time. Then, the job shortages during the Depression and the labor shortages created by World War II forced women, increasingly, to work outside the home. Through all of this, advertising tracked every current and drift, incorporating or co-opting trends and, frequently, redefining the national taste.

A Donald Duck Chocolate Syrup can appeals to collectors of both general store memorabilia and Disneyana.

Ultimately, as large, wealthy chains began to replace small, independent stores, consumers were forced to become ever more dependent on manufacturers' claims. In the absence of a recommendation from the grocery-store clerk, the picture on a box and the text on a sign were the means for a product to persuade the public of its effectiveness or tastiness. Familiar advertising images and company logos that changed only infrequently and almost invisibly reassured consumers that despite a changing world, some household staples, comfortingly, would stay the same. To some extent, this may be why certain manufacturers' labeling (Heinz, Campbell's, Proctor & Gamble, Hershey) has changed surprisingly little in more than one hundred years, although containers and packaging have changed considerably—not to mention shrinkage in the amount of the product supplied.

As the United States flourished, it began to appear that there was almost no technological marvel that couldn't, somehow, be put into service as advertising: film, radio, television (most recently the Internet); cars, trucks, buses, blimps, airplanes, even space ships (remember Tang?). There was also no shortage of testimonials from newly venerated celebrities and stars. Every advance in media brought fresh, new talent willing to promote a host of products.

Entertainers aren't new to endorsing products and some of the best-known stars show up in surprising places. This packaging for Valley Farm's Bing Crosby Ice Cream (in an appropriate vanilla flavor, and carrying Bing's reassuring "Pledge of Quality") might whet the appetites of both general store memorabilia collectors and entertainment memorabilia collectors.

EVALUATING ADVERTISING

Advertising memorabilia embraces so many materials and objects that the individually listed criteria and standards for evaluating all of them would require a whole book. Condition, nevertheless, weighs heavily in determining value, as it does with all collectibles. Pieces in excellent condition command higher prices than items that have suffered careless or extensive use. And poor condition can devastate pieces because collectors of advertising memorabilia seek predominantly image and color. If a metal sign or tray is rusty or its colors have faded, the value diminishes rapidly. This is particularly true if the central image, rather than just an edge or rim, has been compromised. Paper items are especially vulnerable, and those that are brown and tattered lose significant desirability and value.

COLLECTING ADVERTISING

The reasons people collect advertising art and memorabilia vary, but the most obvious reason seems to be nostalgia. Even years after their original appearance, certain combinations of advertising color, image, and slogan still have the power to seduce. Advertising's wonderful graphic component, naturally, adds to our pleasure in the individual object. These are things that were always designed to draw the eye and

This porcelain enamel flange sign advertising Texaco Motor Oil hangs from the side and thus can be seen from both front and back.

Buster Brown and his dog, Tige, seen here in a cardboard store sign, were popular comic strip characters who went on to sell a variety of goods, including puzzles, toothbrushes, bread, whiskey, cigars, and—of course—shoes.

scream, "Pick me! Pick me!" So it's no surprise that we pick them. Whether it's a gasoline sign, beer tray, or tobacco tin, collectors by the thousands yield to advertising's siren song.

Advertising is indeed nostalgic. It evokes fondly remembered moments of each generation's youth—filling up the Harley at the Esso station, going for a drive in the Studebaker, sipping a Coke at the soda fountain.

Beyond both design and nostalgia is advertising's uncanny ability to capture the language of its era. Assembling a collection of items that document society's change appeals to the archaeological urges of many collectors. Others seem fascinated by the content: the drolly exaggerated claims of patent medicine cure-alls, for instance, or those white-coated "doctors" selling cigarettes. Taken out of the context of their time and place, much advertising makes us cringe, laugh, or both. Would you buy Chocolate Worm Cakes? The purveyors of this English product

An Appraiser's Collection

Many *Antiques Roadshow* viewers are curious as to what the show's appraisers collect. Well, memorabilia from the 1904 St. Louis World's Fair was an early passion of George Glastris, a regular appraiser on the *Roadshow*. Glastris collects glasses, sheet music, silverware, and other items from that world's fair because, as he explains, "I grew up in St. Louis." The fair was a huge success for that city.

Over the decades, World's Fair promoters everywhere did everything they could think of to draw visitors, tourists, and even businesses to their city. Alexandre-Gustave Eiffel was commissioned to build his eponymous tower for the International Universal Exposition in Paris in 1889. The first Ferris wheel, which still ranks as the largest ever made, was

unveiled at the World's Columbian Exposition in Chicago in 1893 (where visitors were also introduced to Cracker Jack).

Miniature versions of all these wonders were for sale as souvenirs, but today they have little monetary value, nearly always selling for less than $50. Glastris says that's because the markets for these items are regional; most buyers live in the city or state in which the fair was held. Secondly, most World's Fair souvenirs were produced quickly and inexpensively, so the quality is low. Online auctions have increased availability of World's Fair memorabilia, deflating prices further. Glastris says, "Today there are 170 different items for sale on eBay from the St. Louis World's Fair alone. Many of these items don't even get bid on."

A cardboard sign from the late 1940s shows a post-war American beauty enjoying the all-American drink.

were not intending to offer a snack crawling with fish bait, only a remedy for curing parasites.

Because advertising memorabilia comes in so many guises and encompasses an endless number of themes, it is also the ideal crossover collectible. Salt- and pepper-shaker collectors may covet a set in the form of RCA's trademark dog, Nipper, but so will collectors of Victrolas. Disneyana enthusiasts can compete with general store collectors for a Donald Duck Bread sign, while collectors of toy vehicles might be as happy to find Metalcraft's Goodrich Tire truck as a collector of Metalcraft toys would.

With so much to choose from, advertising collectors are frequently most comfortable focusing on a specialty or subspecialty. Many are drawn to collecting by vendor, such as country store, soda fountain, or gas station, and buy only items associated with those places. Others concentrate on a particular industry, like tobacco or beer, or on brand-specific items, like Coca-Cola or Planters Peanuts. Some enthusiasts specialize in premiums and giveaways; others prefer specific objects, such as signs or tins. Character advertising always warrants a section of its own because so many collectors

RCA's trademark dog, Nipper, eagerly listening to his master's voice, has a rabid following among advertising collectors in whatever form he appears.

Antiques Roadshow appraiser Tim Luke believes that collections are not meant to be packed away. "I just hate it when collectors have gone crazy buying what they love and then put it all in the attic," he says. "It's almost as if they're afraid to enjoy their collections. People should display what they own."

Luke says "almost every inch" of his house is covered with advertising signs, posters, and vintage food containers from the turn of the twentieth century, most of which feature an edible treat, such as chocolate, fruit, or bread. His favorites depict the world of children. Among them is a cardboard sign advertising Butternut Bread, a company that promoted its loaves by featuring wholesome boys and girls at play. On another die-cut cardboard sign in Luke's collection, a tired Sleepy Bear, nightcap on head and suitcase in hand, eagerly awaits a Travel Lodge bed. It's not the text on the advertisement that draws Luke to the images he takes home. "It's the whimsy attention-getting of it all," he says. Luke's pursuit of this kind of advertising memorabilia includes a search he routinely conducts on eBay. "Sometimes I'll just type in 'bear' and 'cardboard' to see what comes up."

Persuasive Packaging

As any collector of advertising eventually realizes, certain images on twentieth-century packaging recur regularly. Images of women are particularly effective in helping all sorts of things sell. For example, the makers of fruit-crate labels realized that their product needed to be attractive to the wholesale fruit merchant—usually male—not to the ultimate purchaser, so labels on their boxes began to include illustrations of increasingly seductive-looking women. Conversely, when a product hopes to convince female consumers to use it, the image will be of a clearly competent woman. Mothers and adorable babies are used to good effect, too.

The intent of packaging is to inspire trust in the quality of the product. Vintage beer cans display medals won at fairs, and heraldic emblems decorate the labels of such everyday products as soap. Occasionally, the white-coated doctor or some solemn male figure appears on a label, or a manly race-car driver pitches batteries.

Housewives have always looked for a guarantee of purity and security in products. So Nabisco crackers were "triple wrapped for freshness," and claimed so on the box. Alka-Seltzer was sold in airtight, handsome, blue

glass tubes, and tooth powder came in sealed, shaker-top cans, like talcum.

As the century progressed, packaging became more complicated, but typography and shapes grew simpler. From the fussy, elaborate typography of the pre–World War I era, to the bold, stylized lettering of Art Deco, to the somewhat austere and practical sans-serif graphics of the thirties and the years of World War II, packaging reflects the aesthetic of its time.

By the end of the 1950s, the growth of the supermarket and the resulting demise of the old-fashioned grocery store caused a lasting change in packaging that continues to this day. Instant recognition is the name of this game, and an immediately identifiable logo or image is a commercial grail. The black-hatted Quaker of Quaker Oats, Mr. Peanut, the Pillsbury Doughboy, Mr. Clean, and the Jolly Green Giant all inspire trust and consumer loyalty.

Far left: Kirkman Cleanser uses a comic image of the Swiss Alps to convey its effectiveness. Center: A woman with flowing tresses and an hourglass figure lends her glamorous image to Newbro's Herpicide, an otherwise unappealing product. Right: A girl and Reliance Baking Powder are both helping Mother in the kitchen on baking day; an actual can of the product is incorporated into the porcelain enamel sign.

pursue specific characters. Finally, there are advertising displays, which enhance any number of collecting specialties, as well as being an area of specialization unto themselves.

Part of the fun and excitement of collecting advertising is the possibility of coming across some previously unknown object in your own special field. It is this very unexpectedness, combined with the thrill of the chase—and the pleasure of going to advertising shows around the country or local flea markets—that keeps collectors enthralled.

This chapter includes some material from the end of the nineteenth century and the beginning of the twentieth, in addition to that from the period between World War I and 1975, because, on the whole, advertising memorabilia is considered to be "collectible" rather than "antique"—even if it is more than one hundred years old.

The Lone Ranger and Silver help to sell Merita Bread (It's Enriched!), one of the show's regular sponsors, in this poster from the 1950s.

COLLECTING BY VENDOR

The following are a few general vendor categories and examples of the types of memorabilia they include. These categories illustrate only one way of organizing material that can be collected in an almost infinite number of ways. Part of the fun of collecting, of course, is in choosing and pursuing the area that you most enjoy.

GENERAL STORE

Before the post–World War II advent of the large grocery- and hardware-store chains, shoppers, particularly those in small towns and rural areas, went to the general store for all their needs—coffee, tea, spices, flour, candy, tobacco—even yard goods and farm equipment. This, of course, was why it was called a general store. General-store collecting, a field crammed with products, furnishings, signs, and containers, is often broken down into numerous, more manageable subspecialties.

General-store advertising memorabilia includes product displays like J. & P. Coats Thread Company spool cabinets, Diamond Dyes cabinets, or counter display tins for Sure Shot

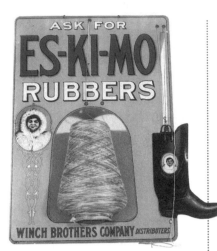

Before the invention of shopping bags, when purchased goods had to be wrapped in brown-paper packages, string cutters were standard fixtures in general stores. The cutters frequently carried advertisements, like this one for Es-ki-mo Rubbers.

Tobacco, which show an American Indian taking aim with a bow and arrow.

The diversity of store advertising signs is amazing. Many early examples are still around—though many of the products they promoted aren't. There's an Ivory Soap cardboard sign featuring a little girl washing doll clothes; a colorful paper sign advertising Dixon's Stove Polish that depicts a woman at the seashore (presumably she's there as a result of Dixon's labor-saving attributes); and a self-framed Austin's Dog Bread tin sign picturing a dog-owner opening a box of "dog bread" as her well-behaved pack watches in happy anticipation. A Heinz "Pure Foods" hanging sign with a cutout pickle suspended from it would be appetizing not just to general store collectors, but to Heinz and sign collectors, as well.

In addition to display and storage cabinets and counter scales, general-store memorabilia embraces string cutters, once an essential tool in the packaging process. String cutters can be plain and utilitarian or as handsome and idiosyncratic as a much-sought-after example put out by Dutch Boy Atlantic

A Treasury of Tins

Tins are among the most widely collected advertising memorabilia. Before the age of plastic, tins were produced in a diverse and gratifying array of shapes, colors, and sizes to contain countless products. The following are some of the different types of tins and the terms that collectors use to describe them.

BISCUIT TINS: A collecting field unto itself because of the number and diversity produced and, also, because of an old bias concerning where they were made. Most biscuit (cookie) tins were of European origin, with the majority being from England. In the early days of advertising collecting, many Americans focused solely on American tins, leaving the field to be dominated by English and European collectors. But the biscuit-tin category includes some of the most imaginative and beautiful containers ever produced. Among the best are the clever figurals; designed to look like stacks of plates, faux books, and simulated crocodile skin handbags, they are shaped and lithographed to fool the eye. Some of the most popular with both American and European collectors today are those in the form of buses, cars, trucks, and ships. The pride of many biscuit-tin collections, these vehicles are also avidly sought by transportation toy collectors and can command thousands of dollars apiece.

FLAT POCKET: Small tins in varying sizes with either lift-off or hinged lids, made to fit in pockets.

LUNCH PAILS: Any of several types of containers that resemble the lunch pails of the late nineteenth and early twentieth century—so much so that they were often recycled to carry lunch to school or work.

White Lead Paint. The die-cut tin sign features the firm's name-sake trademark child striding along with his trademark paint bucket, but in this case, it's a real bucket housing the string. Another desirable store counter item is one of the numerous versions of glass jars that held Planters Peanuts in bulk. General-store collectors take note: The originals have become so sought after that several versions have been reproduced.

The largest category of general-store advertising memorabilia is the box, tin, or crate the original product was sold in. (Tins are a huge area of specialization on their own; see "A Treasury of Tins" box below.) Many collectors fill their kitchen shelves with the hundreds of decorative empty tins that once held coffee, tea, or other foodstuffs, and even collectors of kitchen implements often include advertising items in their collection. Tins like the ones for King Cole Coffee, depicting the nursery-rhyme character, or for Monarch Cocoa, featuring a brightly lithographed Lion, or Gorton's coconut, with its elegant lithography, have tremendous visual appeal, as does an Elephant Brand Salted Peanuts container featuring a profile portrait of a proud pachy-

Decorative tins like this one, which once held Savarin Orange Pekoe Tea, are popular with many advertising memorabilia collectors; some even store other small collections in such tins.

One common form is a round container with lift-off lid, fitted with a bail handle for carrying. Another style is a rectangular form with two fold-down handles and a hinged or lift-off top.

SAMPLE: Miniature versions used as an inducement for the consumer to try a new product. Sample tins were just like the small trial-size bottles of mouthwash and shampoo that we know today.

STORE BIN: A tin used for storage and as a point-of-purchase display in a commercial establishment. The store bin held either a quantity of loose product, like tea or tobacco, or smaller, consumer-size containers of the product. Designed to catch the eye, store bins are often large and colorful and make striking display pieces. Many fewer were made than individual tins, of course, and even fewer survived—and they are particularly prized by today's collectors.

STORY TINS: Tins with storybook or nursery-rhyme characters that incorporate rhymes or other accompanying text.

UPRIGHT POCKET: Usually refers to tins with a hinged or lift-off cover that is at the top of the tin as opposed to flat-pocket tins.

Far left: A Planters Peanut peanut butter lunch pail tin, decorated with a circus made up entirely of Mr. Peanuts. Center: This decorative store bin once held Blanke's Coffee—Always Uniform, Always the Best. At left: A Peter Rabbit story tin appealed to young consumers, who might urge their mothers to buy the brand.

The decorative logo for Cascarets, a precursor of Ex-Lax, presumably and tastefully depicts the product at work.

Right: A flower-filled chromolithographed metal sign advertises two patent medicines—Boschee's German Syrup and Green's August Flower—remedies for, respectively, cough and depression.

A clock advertising Ever-Ready Safety Razors superimposes the dial over a picture of a man—fully lathered— using their new and improved product.

derm. Large tins, of course, can also provide storage space for smaller collections.

Some of the most serious collectors have employed a particularly dramatic means for displaying their collections: They have recreated an actual old-fashioned general store, from countertop to shelves, and stocked it with vintage tins and products.

DRUGSTORE

Collections of apothecary advertising memorabilia include the bottles, tins, and signs for patent remedies, salves, balms, and pills. Not so long ago, successful panaceas for a host of physical complaints had nearly irresistible names—Dr. Kilmer's Swamp Root Kidney, Liver & Bladder Remedy, Kondon's Catarrhal Jelly—along with lavish promises. A sign advertising Dr. Bell's Anti-Pain medicine describes this marvelous product as "An antiseptic painkiller for internal and external use," and claims to "quickly cure colic, cramps, and Cholera." But wait, there's more! It also "cures cuts, burns, bruises, sprains, bites, and headache." Ah, where is Dr. Bell's today?

Some items fit into several vendor categories. Candy, for example, was sold in general stores, service stations, soda fountains, and drugstores. (In fact, soda fountains, with their marble-topped counters and soda pumps, originated in drugstores.) Examples of these multi-venue collectibles include Lifesaver countertop display racks and a three-tier rack for Curtis candies. (The first two of the three sections advertise the familiar Baby Ruth and Butterfinger candy bars; the third is for the now-forgotten Easy Aces.) The illustration of NuGrape Soda on a blotter may have tempted early twentieth-century fountain-pen users, but some advertising copy leaves us mystified today: "Chew Carnation Gum and taste the smell" (unwrapping the package must have been an interesting olfactory experience).

More recent drugstore memorabilia, like a sign for Alka-Seltzer advising "Be wise, Alkalize," or a 1950s Speedy Alka-Seltzer die-cut easel display sign featuring the trademark

"Speedy" character, are especially familiar and desirable. Many readers will remember Speedy, with his Alka-Seltzer–tablet body and hat. Speedy appeared in newspapers and in a series of television spots between 1954 and 1964 and, along the way, became a vinyl bank and a vinyl doll that is a favorite with postwar figural advertising collectors. A giant Speedy advertising figure, in fact, made a memorable visit to *Antiques Roadshow* in Milwaukee (see sidebar, Great Big Speedy, page 60).

GAS STATION AND AUTOMOBILE

The automobile changed the American landscape in a variety of startling ways, not least by promoting the growth of thousands of service stations and car dealerships. Automobilia ranges from Bakelite ashtrays featuring the seated Bibendum (Michelin's trademark tire man) to objects that rival full-size cars and trucks in scale—complete early gas pumps, for example. Collectors with limited space content themselves with just the glass globes, the pumps' decorative tops. Usually, they are decorated with the company's name or logo and set into a metal frame. Among more interesting examples are those that once advertised Mutual Gasoline, incorporating a rabbit motif, and the three-dimensional glass crown of Crown Gasoline. Although automotive signs and memorabilia constitute a specific collecting area, there is a great deal of crossover collecting by owners of vintage automobiles.

Automobilia advertising signs are made of paper, tin, wood, glass, plastic, and a variety of inexpensive metals.

A World War I–era ad from the Saturday Evening Post *explains the delays in filling orders for Indian Motocycles because of their time-consuming, high-quality construction.*

Sign Language

Most of us think of signs when we think of advertising memorabilia, and signs do indeed comprise the largest category in the field. Here is a brief list of some of the terms collectors use in describing them:

A 1950s-vintage tin menu board from a diner or coffee shop none-too-subtly suggests what the establishment wants you to drink.

COUNTER DISPLAY: Just as the name implies, a sign that sits atop a counter—often near the actual product—and acts as a point-of-purchase advertisement.

DIE CUT: A shaped sign that is other than a standard rectangle, circle, or square. Die-cut signs can be stamped or cut out rather than solid. They are also referred to as cutouts.

FESTOON: A cardboard or paper cutout that typically is hung above the bar back of, usually, a soda fountain.

FLANGE SIGN: Named for the flange at the side or the top that allows a sign to be affixed to a wall or side of a building. The flange allows a sign to be viewed from both sides.

MENU BOARD: A sign with space for both product advertisement and notes. Menu boards generally have the product logo on the top and space below for messages. One popular style is the blackboard used by waitresses and short-order cooks to list daily specials. Since most customers read the specials, the menu board is ideal for an ad.

NEON: A sign composed of electric lamp tubing through which the inert gas neon flows. Neon signs advertise products and services and indicate the whereabouts of motels, restaurants, and Las Vegas casinos. Figural neon signs set collectors aglow, although the size of large, elaborate examples can be intimidating. Small neon signs do exist, however. Advertising clocks, for instance, often feature a ring of blue or pink neon tubing that illuminates the face.

This counter display from the late 1950s has a die-cut top and held Tarzan 3-D Trading Cards from Topps Gum, better known for its baseball cards.

PORCELAIN ENAMEL: A sign that takes its name from the finish bonded to the underlying base metal, a finish that creates a glassy surface and a virtually weatherproof gloss. Collectors desire these signs because so many still retain their original brightness and sheen. Although quite durable, porcelain signs can chip and age, which diminishes both their beauty and their value.

PUSH PLATE: A small sign, usually of metal, that functions as a means to push or pull a door open or closed. Mounted at eye level on the outer stiles of doors, push plates make simple but effective sales tools. Placed on exit doors, they can be last-minute reminders of forgotten purchases.

REVERSE GLASS: A sign in which the image is painted on the back of a piece of glass. The resulting ad—most frequently, it hangs—gives the illusion of a glass-covered painting. The best are treasured for their beauty and depth of image.

SELF-FRAMED: Any type of sign that has an integral frame. Late-nineteenth- and early-twentieth-century metal advertising signs often incorporated brown or printed wood-grain "frames." The inclusion of such a frame was a decorative and distinctive touch. Some later examples of self-framed signs were made of cardboard.

STANDEE: A sign fitted with a means of support, such as a foldout brace (also known as an easel back) that allows it to stand. Many examples, like the Philip Morris bellboy (see page 59), are figural.

TROLLEY CARD: A reminder of a time when trolleys plied the streets of major U.S. cities, these are cardboard signs designed to fit into brackets mounted above the windows in these streetcars. The standard size for a sign is 11 × 20½ inches. Today's equivalents are subway and bus ads.

Favorites among collectors are the enamel or porcelain enamel signs that provided the ideal, more or less impervious, canvas for advertising, for example, Goodyear tires, Pontiac automobiles, and General Motors Company Trucks. Other desirable signs range from the 1950s cardboard Texaco countertop example, urging a service checkup (justified by the statement "Expert care means longer wear"), to the red figural sign of the winged horse Pegasus, which all motorists of a certain age instantly recognize as the symbol of the Mobil Oil Company. Many handsome and collectible automobile-dealership signs represent cars no longer in production, such as the Studebaker, the Whippet, and the Hudson Terraplane.

Of course, there are more than cars on the road. Motorcycle memorabilia keeps many fans in hot pursuit. "Motorcycle memorabilia has been big for the past five years," says *Antiques Roadshow* appraiser Leila Dunbar. "The most desirable, of course, is Harley-Davidson." One porcelain-and-neon Harley dealership sign, for example, recently changed hands for $15,000. Although Indian Motorcycles closed its doors in 1953, posters and signs advertising this extinct bike are widely sought after, too. A 1920s Indian poster featuring a chief or Indian scout in full color, for instance, can fetch several thousand dollars.

In the prosperous years following World War II, gas stations actively competed for customer loyalty by giving away or selling items that either advertised their products or bore their logo. An Esso ("Put a tiger in your tank") pitcher and glass set featured that trademark tiger. Sinclair offered individual boxes of soap in the emblematic form of its familiar green dinosaur. Numerous firms emblazoned their names along the sides of toy tanker trucks and other vehicles. For young firefighters, there was a hard plastic Texaco fireman's helmet with its white star ("You can trust your car to the man who wears the star"), and thrifty dog lovers could obtain a Flying "A" Gas plastic savings bank in the form of Axelrod, a worried basset hound. Maps, once a service-station freebie, are sought by collectors, too. Frequently,

A porcelain enamel sign for Beacon Penn Motor Oil—its name is the result of a merger between the two companies—retains all of its original color and sheen.

Studebaker's porcelain enamel sign incorporates the streamlined design that distinguished the car. Memorabilia for many automobiles that are no longer in production are still highly collectible.

Opaline Motor Oil, a product of the Sinclair Refining Company, featured an illustration of an early roadster on its metal gas can.

A trio of sturdy Eskimos supports the Eskimo Pie "Magic Jar," which kept bars of "real ice cream enrobed in chocolate" cold if a soda fountain had no freezer.

they depict the rambling blue lines that mark the routes of the old, languidly traveled highways that preceded the interstates. Usually, these display the company logo (see Tips from the experts, page 45).

SODA FOUNTAIN

Soda fountains, like their close cousins ice-cream parlors and soda shops, bespeak the innocence and joy of the (guiltless) consumption of hot-fudge sundaes, milk shakes, malteds, and root-beer floats. Soda-fountain memorabilia often include items that are not advertising pieces—such as ice-cream scoops, straw dispensers, wrought-iron "sweetheart" chairs, and marble-top tables—but for many, it's the advertising that is most evocative. Collectibles range from porcelain syrup dispensers splashed with the product's name (Cherry Smash or Orange Crush, for example) to calendars, thermometers, clocks, and signs. A sign might be an elaborate cardboard festoon used to decorate a wall, or it might incorporate a menu board. It can even be a push plate for a door.

Serving or tip trays (see Metal Trays, page 36) were manufactured by soft-drink, candy, and ice-cream makers, and displayed advertisements for well-known firms, such as Coca-Cola and Pepsi-Cola, as well as for obscure or regional products, like Klondike Bars, once sold only at Isaly Stores in Ohio and Pennsylvania. A tray picturing a woman in Asian attire seated in a rickshaw proclaims, "Ging Seng, the Beverage of purity," while an unusually narrow tray for Cherry Blossoms beverage proclaims it to be "a blooming good drink."

Pocket mirrors are small but popular advertising collectibles, and soft-drink manufacturers produced a great variety of them. Usually made of tin or celluloid, they range from a 1909 Pepsi-Cola mirror featuring a pretty woman in a feathered hat and flowing gown holding a glass of Pepsi to a whimsical Chero-Cola example picturing a man's face. Held one way, this fellow's expression seems downcast and glum and is captioned "Don't worry." Held the other way, our Chero-Cola drinker looks chipper and pleased, and the caption now reads "Drink Chero-Cola and smile."

Working women were encouraged to take a 7-Up, rather than a coffee break, in this cardboard sign from the late 1940s. The women and the clock are depicted in black and white, while the soft drink bottles are in color.

Crowning the Bottle

There's a beauty to crown bottle caps—those crimped-edged toppers that require a bottle opener for removal—that attracts thousands of collectors to search out pristine examples. The designs and messages on these mini ads for sodas, beer, and juice are meant to be as lively and inviting as that first refreshing sip—and often they're even better. Collectors may start out in a fairly general way—buying caps from all beverages and any country—but many eventually focus on specific beverages (beer, not surprisingly, is popular) or on the beverages of a particular country. Placed in wooden frames fitted with ridges to hold them, crown caps make colorful and eye-catching displays.

DINER AND DRIVE-IN

Diner and drive-in memorabilia, predominantly from the 1950s and 1960s, seem to be attracting nostalgic baby-boomer collectors. Many examples—signs, clocks, and calendars—are versions of the kind of material once made for the soda fountains of a generation or two earlier. Yet, what serious fifties collector, for instance, wouldn't love to have a "playroom" fitted out with a vintage jukebox spinning golden oldies while, nearby, on a formica-top counter a Squirt display is highlighted by the cheery Squirt boy proffering a bottle of the grapefruit-flavored soda? An alternative might be the sign for Dad's Old-Fashioned Root Beer, depicting a

Left: The pompadour on this hard-plastic figure of Bob's Big Boy (a West Coast drive-in) indicates that the chain originated in the late 1950s.

FAST·FOOD COLLECTIBLES

The successor to the soda fountain and the diner is the fast-food chain. Although White Castle and similar burger palaces had been around for years, the era of the fifties and sixties saw the expansion and ascendancy of McDonald's, Burger King, Kentucky Fried Chicken, Pizza Hut, and, later, Wendy's and others.

The rise of fast food coincided with the growth of the American television audience, and the big chains soon peppered viewers with memorable jingles, sayings, and advertising characters. Early fast-food memorabilia are likely to be based on a company's advertising character or spokesperson, like the nodding (bobble) head Colonel Sanders figure of Kentucky Fried Chicken, the 1970s stuffed cloth Burger King Doll, or the circa 1969 Pizza Hut Pete plastic bank.

Ronald McDonald appeared in 1963 (off-air and out of costume, he was known as Willard Scott). He was eventually reincarnated as a cloth doll and as the pivotal point on a watch dial, and as a decal on the sides of drinking glasses. Ronald today is recognized around the world.

Above: Early collectible fast-food memorabilia includes this stuffed-cloth doll from the 1970s of the Burger King himself.

black cow eyeing a slogan that enjoins the thirsty consumer to "enjoy a Dad's black cow—it's delicious with Dad's Root Beer." (A black cow, by the way, is a drink made with root beer, chocolate syrup, and scoops of vanilla ice cream.) Hanging on the wall, a yellow-and-white Borden's Ice Cream clock featuring fifties star Elsie the Cow lends additional bovine charm. Some collectors seek to fulfill their childhood dream of having an unlimited supply of soft drinks by installing a vintage Coke or Pepsi machine that dispenses sodas for a dime.

COLLECTING BY INDUSTRY

Some advertising enthusiasts concentrate on a particular industry, rather than on one sort of vendor. The following are a few of the major categories pursued by such collectors.

BREWERIANA

According to rock star Frank Zappa, "You can't have a real country unless you have beer and an airline." America may not have had an airline until the 1920s, but its first known brewery opened in Manhattan in 1612. As our nation grew, so did its brewing industry. By 1873 there were a record 4,131 breweries in the United States, not substantially fewer than the 5,608 votes received by Prohibitionist candidate James Black in the 1872 presidential election. Despite Black's defeat, the following decades actually saw the number of breweries decline, as beer makers merged and smaller firms were absorbed or eliminated. However, thousands of breweries remained, all eager to slake America's growing thirst, and competition was fierce. The survivors, eager to maintain and increase their market share, turned to advertising.

Late-nineteenth- and early-twentieth-century breweriana—including beer trays, signs, taps, coasters, and other items produced before the Eighteenth Amendment to the Constitution was ratified in 1919—is often referred to as pre-Pro (pre-Prohibition). One popular and attractive motif of late-nineteenth-century brewery advertising was the rendering of the actual brewery on beautifully lithographed signs and trays. Beer companies, displaying their modernity, wealth, size, and success to nineteenth-century consumers—many of whom were immigrants and inclined to admire this evidence of American commerce and industry—attracted loyal devotees.

A tray advertising the Fred Bauernschmidt American Brewery in Baltimore, for instance, sums up the sentiment of the day. It pictures this mighty brewery with numbers of horse-drawn carriages bustling to and fro, while on its rim patriotic stars-and-stripes decorations are framed by sprays of barley and hops. A Central Brewing Company tray illustrates a handsome building that once stood by the East River in New York City. Inset with a picture of a horse's head (an appeal to the racing crowd, perhaps?), it also depicts a flotilla of sailing ships and a steam tugboat.

An immense amount of history can be captured on a vintage sign, and history is always intriguing to collectors. Any sign that portrays the rare likeness of an architecturally interesting but long-demolished building, of a vanished vehicle or antiquated mode of transportation, will find a home. For example, a large and elaborate paper sign depicting a sprawling Pabst Brewing Company brewery amid billowing smoke is replete with both the allegorical figure of Columbia (representing the United States) and glimpses of the most modern ships and trains. It may not say much about the taste of Pabst beer, or anything about how the brew was made, but it does offer a

This desirable beer tray from the 1890s depicts the I. Leisy Brewing Co. plant in Cleveland, Ohio, including details of the factory and street life at the turn of the twentieth century.

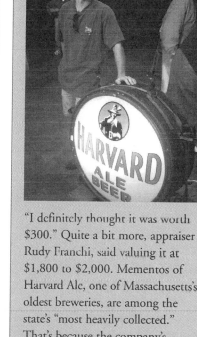

HARVARD ALE SIGN

A novice breweriana collector who found a mint-condition Harvard Ale sign at a yard sale a few years ago brought it to the Boston *Antiques Roadshow.*

"I definitely thought it was worth $300." Quite a bit more, appraiser Rudy Franchi, said valuing it at $1,800 to $2,000. Mementos of Harvard Ale, one of Massachusetts's oldest breweries, are among the state's "most heavily collected." That's because the company's memorabilia are still available, but not too abundant, the perfect situation that Franchi says savvy collectors prefer. "There's no point collecting something where there's just one," he explained. "You buy it and you're done."

BOTTOM'S UP

"So tell me what you know about this wonderful giant Gambrinus beer mug?" asked appraiser Noel Barrett at the Chicago *Antiques Roadshow* of an elderly visitor. He replied that all he knew was that his grandmother stored string in it. "Well," said Barrett, examining the mug, "There's an original maker's label on the inside, which tells us that the piece was made in New York City by W. T. Murphy & Company." The mug, which advertises Gambrinus Lager Beer, dates from around 1880. "This is a wonderful piece of breweriana."

Bottles—liquor bottles in particular—are a more common form of this kind of advertising memorabilia; the glassware was meant to be displayed behind a bar.

The mug's maker used a reverse-glass label, a fairly complicated process that produces a crisp, colorful image. Such expensive labels were more often used to advertise hard liquor, generally a more lucrative product than beer. That's what makes this Gambrinus beer mug so rare and worth $2,000 to $4,000.

Beer-coaster collecting is not as widespread as beer-can collecting, but it is gaining in popularity. Many enthusiasts collect by brewery, by state, by region, by country, or by time period—pre-Pro (pre-Prohibition), for example, or only during World War II.

Collectors look for minor variations in coasters from a specific brewery, such as the presence or absence of a union label (or printer's bug), different color schemes, and changing brewery locations and numbers of years in existence.

nostalgic, historic image the likes of which will never be seen again.

Other, more droll pre-Pro images include ethereal and scantily clad sirens—luring ships to their doom to advertise, naturally, Lorelei Beer; or a perfectly appointed table heaped with lobsters that—somehow—proclaims the thirst-quenching properties of Saltzberger's Beer. A simple but elegant sign in reverse glass depicts the Anheuser-Busch "A" and eagle, and a paper sign featuring a group of early motorists being served a glass of beer—even the female driver is imbibing—captures that time when automobiles were novelties and the designated driver had not yet been assigned.

Prohibition forced many breweries out of business, but others cleverly switched to producing nonalcoholic "near beer." A tin sign manufactured around the end of World War I pictures a soldier, a bottle in one hand and raised glass in the other, offering a toast to Famo, a Schlitz near beer.

By the time Prohibition was repealed in 1933, a revolution in beer drinking—and in future breweriana collecting—was only two years away. Long used to brew in bottles or kegs, beer drinkers were introduced to canned beer in 1935 by the Kruger brewery.

Label collecting is an international collecting area, with many collectors focusing on the beers of one region or one country.

A porcelain enamel sign for the Boston Beer Company's Reliance Ale, dating from before the passage of the Volstead Act, is a treasure for pre-Prohibition collectors.

Beer-bottle labels are excellent collectibles for those without enough room to collect beer cans, trays, signs, point-of-purchase displays, and other room-filling objects.

The Kruger can had a flat top; the Schlitz brewery, however, opted for a cone-top shape with a crimped "crown" cap. Aluminum cans first appeared in the 1950s and the tab top in 1962.

Beer-can collecting is a relatively new enthusiasm, and to have any value, cans must be free of dings and rust. More problematic is the fact that they should also have been opened from the bottom, so the tab is intact. Some collectors put a protective coating of polish or wax on their cans, but others find such a corruption of the original finish offensive and won't purchase waxed cans. Prices of cans, as is the case with other collectibles, can be affected by new discoveries; the rare can that commands a premium price today becomes more common if a cache of other examples is found.

Beer signs, trays, and cans are merely the surface of the breweriana sought by enthusiasts. Collectors want not only original beer bottles but they are also keen to acquire bottle labels and caps and decorative tap handles. In addition, they buy great numbers of point-of-purchase display pieces (see page 62), many of which typically feature a metal or composition figure on a base. The Blatz Beer beer men, their bodies formed by a keg, bottle, or can of Blatz beer; the Falstaff man standing next

Beer-can collectors search out early cans with cone-shaped tops, like this Old Tap Select Stock Ale, which once was sealed with a crown cap.

to a bottle of the beer; and the Bert and Harry Piels images flanking a can of Piels—all helped sell mugs and mugs of beer.

Breweries owned many early sports teams and consequently the tie between sports and beer advertising was (and still is) very strong. Old campaigns fade, but new ones arise, and the best leave collectible reminders. Although Spuds McKenzie, the Budweiser spokesdog, has retired, a host of Spuds-related products—among them, a large plastic lamp in his image—still pay homage to this memorable breweriana character.

A 1944 advertisement for Valliant and Sons Vineyards sings the praises of California Ruby Port and promotes the patriotic benefits of American wines during wartime.

LIQUOR AND WINE

For fans of advertising who prefer more costly potables, liquor and wine offer an alternative. Liquor memorabilia, like beer, is a mainstay of many bar or saloon collections, and some of the most beautiful advertising signs ever produced were for liquor. A Gilt Edge Whiskey sign is a splendid example: a superb, brightly lithographed image on paper features a beautiful woman on a chaise reclining by a bottle of "the treat that can't be beat," Gilt Edge Whiskey. Produced for a San Francisco distillery, this sign is also a fine example of Western advertising art. *Antiques Roadshow* appraiser Brian Witherell says "Western advertising signs are a hot area right now," one that sees prices in excess of $50,000 for the rarest items in mint condition.

Not all advertisers choose to use images of beautiful women, however, no matter how eye-catching. A paper sign for Old Capitol Pure Rye depicts a bearded gentleman sniffing an open bottle with the caption "That's the stuff!"

There seems to have been less wine advertising than beer and whiskey advertising, reflecting the fact that there were fewer wine drinkers in the United States. A paper sign for the Diamond Wine Co., circa 1905, depicts three women in Edwardian finery enjoying a glass of champagne, an elegant image from an elegant age.

A calendar produced by a California winery for a Goldfield, Nevada, retailer is a crossover collectible appealing to wine advertising buffs along with calendar collectors.

Your wartime meal ends on a happy note when you serve THIS BRILLIANT RUBY PORT

Expect great things from Valliant Ruby Port . . . delightful bouquet . . . full flavor . . . pleasant sweetness. Served with dessert or coffee, it transforms wartime meals into a refreshing occasion.

The choice wines of Valliant & Sons include appetizer wines, table wines and dessert wines. All are bottled at the winery in California and are the product of infinite care . . . reasons why Valliant Wines are distinguished by that well-finished flavor and aroma that are so delightful to lovers of fine wine. Sole Distributors for U.S.A., W. A. Taylor & Company, New York City.

VALLIANT CALIFORNIA WINES
Appetizer wines
Table wines
Dessert wines

Interestingly, while such items are rare and coveted by enthusiasts, prices for wine memorabilia are not as high as those for liquor and beer.

TOBACCO

Pipe tobacco, chewing tobacco, cigars, snuff, and, of course, cigarettes have been responsible for a wealth of containers, signs, and accessories, all appealing to advertising collectors.

Cigar signs alone make diverse and interesting collections. A late-nineteenth-century tin sign for Admiration Cigars featuring a smiling moon face contentedly smoking a cigar bears the legend "Mild and mellow to the last inch," while a circa 1905 Colonial Club Cigar cardboard sign is illustrated with the picture of a woman in a jauntily crimped sunbonnet, sans cigar—although what this has to do with smoking is a mystery! An amusing Cyclone Twister sign from around 1920 captions a flattened landscape and twisted cigar with "Looks crooked but smokes straight."

Cigar bands—those paper rings encircling individual cigars—have long been collected for the intricacy and beauty of their design. They can be decorated with a simple logo or portrait of a dark-eyed beauty or a U.S. president, elaborately embellished in gold.

You don't have to love cigars to appreciate the boxes they come in. Much thought went into the image displayed on the inner

Not all tobacciana is advertising memorabilia. Collectors also search for remarkable objects like this submarine-shaped lighter.

Cigar-box labels resemble miniature posters from the turn of the twentieth century, and many display the same high-quality lithography. This brand, celebrating the famous Victorian genre painter Sir Lawrence Alma-Tadema, was produced by Arguelles, Lopez & Brother Cigars in Tampa, Florida.

It may seem surprising that a child's comic strip character was used to sell cigars, but Buster Brown and Tige appeared regularly on the cans that today are eagerly sought after by both tobacco memorabilia collectors and Buster Brown collectors.

lid, often a larger version of the cigar band's decoration. A speeding train in a landscape (S. S. Pierce's "Overland") or a señorita in a richly embroidered shawl ("La Palina") are picturesque possibilities. Cigar boxes have been collected for years, but most have only modest value, even the older examples. In recent years, however, prices have begun to increase, particularly for rare, special-theme boxes. At one auction of legendary sports memorabilia, several baseball-theme cigar boxes, box lids, and labels sold for major-league prices, ranging from $345 for a 1930s Al Simmons Cigar box to $17,250 for a lot comprising an apparently unused Hans (Honus) Wagner lid label and matching cigar band.

Implements for opening cigar boxes, such as the metal hammer-shaped tool produced for and inscribed "Muriel Cigars," attract collectors, as do advertising ashtrays, pocket cutters, and larger figural counter cutters, employed by stores both as a practical convenience for customers and as advertising. Many of these are sculpturally appealing and have an amusing action. "Smoke Morey's Fat Hog Cigars" is the slogan on a cutter in the form of a copper-colored, electroplated metal pig. When you place a cigar in the pig's mouth and pull its tail, the end is nipped off the cigar. "Artie, the best cigar of the year" is the caption on a cutter with a particularly clever action featuring a man, cigar in hand, sitting atop a column. When its ingenious

CIGAR BANDS

Gorgeous? Yes. Valuable? No. Introduced in Cuba in the 1830s as an easy means of identifying superior brands of cigars, cigar bands were once a favorite collectible—especially of children—who were drawn to their colorful images of famous personalities, tropical birds, and scenic views. There's little fan activity nowadays, but a well-preserved collection is still quite striking.

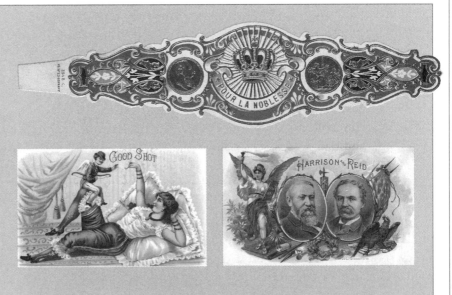

A label for Tiger Brand Cut Plug Tobacco exhibits the beautiful graphics found in many early advertisements—a large part of their appeal to collectors today.

mechanism is wound and a cigar is inserted in a hole in the base, the cigar is cut while Artic lowers his cigar and sticks out his tongue—as if spitting out the tip.

Chewing- and smoking-tobacco memorabilia include signs like that for Velvet Smoking Tobacco, depicting an upright pocket tin of the product and an ashtray with a pipe from which wafts a wisp of smoke spelling "Velvet" in billowy letters. Another, for Pinch Hit chewing tobacco, is made of tin and features a happy fan with outstretched arms exclaiming, "Wow, it's a homer." This is a baseball crossover piece with a twist; it is a testimonial by a baseball fan rather than by an athlete.

Tobacco-tin collectors find scores of superb examples in every color and size. A large Genuine Sweet Cuba Fine Cut store bin was (and is) an impressive display piece. More manageable are the flat pocket tins; although they are small, they often have superb graphics.

The tins of some products came in several sizes. Enthusiasts of Tiger Brand Cut Plug Tobacco tins can collect the large red tin store canister, a large cardboard-and-tin store container, a smaller rectangular container lithographed to simulate a picnic basket in red or blue, or a small pocket tin. Prices vary, based not

JOE CAMEL SURVIVES

Controversy or the withdrawal of a product often attracts, rather than deters, collectors. After the tobacco industry was forbidden to broadcast advertising, it found innovative ways to get its message across. It sponsored races, tennis, and other sporting events for instance. Joe Camel, the animated pitchman of Camel Cigarettes, was one of the most successful— and controversial—characters in advertising. Under pressure that this engaging, cool character was targeting the youth market, encouraging children to smoke, RJR Nabisco retired him in the late 1990s. A virtual caravan of Joe Camel advertising material is now showing up at flea markets and in online auctions.

Among the most popular collectible tobacco tins are the "roly-polys," represented by this Singing Waiter, from the last decade of the nineteenth century.

Not all tobacco advertising relied on the beauty of its graphics; R & B Cigars ads chose to be cute with a bare-bottomed little girl reaching for a cigar for her Daddy.

only on condition but also on the availability and desirability of a particular size or style.

"Roly-poly" tobacco tins are among the more unusual groups of collectible tins. Six different characters were produced for several brands of tobacco—the Satisfied Customer, the Storekeeper, the Man from Scotland Yard (The Inspector), the Mammy, the Singing Waiter, and the Dutchman. Each had a rotund body with lift-off head, and each was clothed in a decorative lithographed costume. Part of the fun for roly-poly collectors is acquiring all the variations. Beware, however: These tins are so appealing that they, like so many collectible favorites, have been reproduced.

Cigarette manufacturers have always been particularly adept marketers, selling the glamour of smoking along with the product itself. Sports heroes, cartoon characters, Hollywood idols, and radio and television personalities have all sold smokes. Although cigarette advertising has been banished from the airwaves since 1971, its images and jingles live on. From the Marlboro Man's rugged depiction of the American West to Virginia Slims' appeal to the women's movement, "You've come a long way, baby," decades of saturation marketing have produced a wealth of collectible material. Early in the marketing of cigarettes, exotic images were emphasized, like the pyramid and camel on the pack of Camels or the mysterious veiled beauty on Fatima Turkish Blend Cigarettes. Sweet Caporal featured a young woman dressed in dark red wearing a fez.

Often, advertisements remind us of just how much attitudes have changed. We aren't too surprised today to come across old ads featuring Ronald Reagan touting Chesterfield cigarettes or Spencer Tracy hawking Lucky Strikes, but what about the Walt Disney Company, now an international entertainment empire that protects its wholesome image as fastidiously as it maintains its theme parks, using Mickey Mouse and Walt himself to advertise Willis's Cigarettes? Now, that's worth a double take. Produced in England around 1931 as a cigarette card, the Willis ad was part of one of the

Willie the Penguin, a plastic advertising figure, looks debonair in his dinner jacket. Willie touted Kool cigarettes from the mid-1940s until he was retired in the late 1950s.

many series or sets of tobacco cards featuring Hollywood luminaries. Non-sport cigarette cards do have a following, but they are not as popular or as pricey as many baseball cards (see the Sports chapter, page 111).

Still, not all corporate pitchmen started out as stars; some were so identified with one product that they became celebrities. Johnny Roventini, for example, a four-foot-tall bellhop at the New Yorker Hotel, was known as "The Smallest Bellboy in the World." Johnny had a big voice, nevertheless, which he used to advantage on radio shows hosted by Philip Morris, where he announced or commanded (the line was equivocal), "Call for Philip Morris." His manner of delivering the line was memorable, and his red-uniformed image in its pillbox hat became synonymous with the company.

Another popular cigarette character, Willie the Penguin, was employed to promote Kool Cigarettes. Willie appeared in print, on radio, and later on television, before retiring in the late fifties. He decorated such items as the handheld fans that advertised Tommy Dorsey's band, which Kool sponsored on the radio. As Dr. Kool, Willie was adorable as a plaster statue, and as himself, he collaborated on a pair of plastic salt and pepper shakers with his wife, Millie.

Two of the rarest and most expensive areas of tobacco memorabilia actually transcend the field of advertising collectibles. Cigar-store Indians are seldom grouped with the collectible tobacco tins, signs, and cigar cutters. Rather, they have been recognized by museums and collectors as enduring pieces of Americana and folk art.

The fact that early baseball cards (put out by cigarette companies) and baseball players tobacco silks (lithographed silk rectangles and squares inserted into early paper cigarette packs and intended to appeal to the new female smokers) are advertising items is quite secondary, today, to their crossover appeal to sports collectors. Nonetheless, enthusiasts of tobacco advertising have a vast selection to choose from.

A "standee," or die-cut easel-backed sign of Johnny Roventini, the famous bellhop at the New Yorker Hotel, has a "call for Philip Morris," as Roventini had weekly on the radio programs sponsored by the tobacco company.

This tobacco tin, made so it could be recycled as a lunch pail, advertised Brotherhood Tobacco long after the tobacco had been smoked.

GREAT BIG SPEEDY

"I was working at a bakery in Los Angeles in 1969," said a man visiting the Milwaukee *Antiques*

Roadshow who had brought with him a huge fiberglass statue. "My supervisor told me to throw out all the junk in the attic, and I did, with the exception of Speedy. I thought he was kind of cute and took him home." Speedy was created by Alka-Seltzer in the mid-1950s to sell antacid tablets. *Antiques Roadshow* appraiser Noel Barrett was very pleased to see it. "What you have here is absolutely wonderful," he told Speedy's savior. "I've never seen a Speedy figure this size before," Barrett said, noting that Alka-Seltzer figurines that are only eight inches tall routinely sell for $300 to $500. "I would expect that a collector would pay $4,000 to $5,000 for this."

CHARACTER-RELATED ADVERTISING

Character collectibles are advertising products appropriated from cartoons, comic books, movies, radio, television, or corporations. Character advertising and merchandising began with the success of the comic strip *Yellow Kid*, drawn by Richard Fenton Outcault in the 1890s. The likeness of the rough-and-tumble but beloved "Kid" began to appear on everything from toys and dolls to cigarettes and cigars. Among *Yellow Kid* items to be found today is a bucket picturing the Kid carrying a pail of Ginger Wafers, his trademark yellow gown providing the space for this tortured verse, delivered in true *Yellow Kid* lingo: "Say dis is de greatest snap I ever struck, de're fine, take a pail to Liz. Dat Brinckerhoffer & Co. knows dere biz." Another desirable *Yellow Kid* piece is the Pulver Gum machine. Gum buyers saw, behind a pane of glass housing the gum, a miniature figure of the smiling Yellow Kid.

In 1902, Outcault introduced another character, one that would become one of the longest-running character trademarks ever created: Buster Brown, a mischievous little boy with a Dutch-boy haircut and saucer hat, and his dog, Tige. This feisty duo was enormously popular in the first part of the twentieth century, and their image was

Jackie Coogan, the first child star, on a highly collectible tin pail that once held peanut butter.

Howdy Doody, the popular puppet television star, was put to work convincing kids that it was time for Royal Instant Pudding.

licensed by Outcault to an astonishing number of manufacturers, including those that made puzzles, toothbrushes, shoes, and perhaps most peculiarly, whiskey and cigars. A tin Golden Sheaf Bakery sign for Buster Brown Bread seems more in character than a cigar tin sporting his name, as does the immortal ad for Buster Brown shoes. ("I'm Buster Brown/I live in a shoe/That's my dog Tige/he lives there, too.") The Brown Shoe company (named for George Warren Brown) purchased the rights to the name Buster Brown from Outcault for its line of juvenile shoes (still in existence today) introduced at the St. Louis World's Fair in 1904. Over the years, Buster Brown shoes were responsible for millions of giveaways—whistles, ink blotters, buttons, and small bisque dolls among them. There were also good-sized figural displays, like the wooden pair featuring Buster and Tige separately and the neon sign outlining a smiling Buster and Tige, heads together. The longevity of both the brand and the image has made Buster and Tige shoe memorabilia attractive to more than one generation of collectors.

The Brownies—drawn by Palmer Cox for magazines, a series of books, and eventually a comic strip—were a short-lived but wildly popular phenomenon and another marketing marvel of the late nineteenth and early twentieth century. The Brownies endorsed a host of products, including Kodak's Brownie Camera, the first simple camera designed for amateurs and marketed especially to children. But the Brownies weren't just camera buffs. They were ubiquitous. In what may have been a play on their

A plastic advertising figure of Colonel Sanders, in his trademark white suit, looks too dignified to eat his own "finger-licking good" chicken.

R. F. Outcault's Yellow Kid helps sell gum by appearing in the window of a Pulver Chewing gum machine.

Popeye, a cartoon favorite, is a natural to sell spinach.

Dennis the Menace seems an unlikely match with cocktail napkins, but that match was made in the 1960s.

An animated window display made by Baranger Studios and used by a succession of jewelers proclaims, "She is a happy bride with one of our beautiful diamonds," even though the groom and the father of the bride struggle to fix a flat tire on the honeymoon car.

A 1940s standee promotes, cheesecake style, Sparkling Life, a long-forgotten soft drink.

creator's name, a 1920s cardboard sign depicts a group of elfin, grinning Brownies hoisting a gelatin mold sculpture made from Cox's gelatin.

As the twentieth century progressed, screen stars—human and animated—were increasingly co-opted for the promotion of commercial products. A Felix the Cat Toffee tin features a winking Felix on the front, while the side panel offers this cross-promotional plug: "If you like my toffee, see my films." There are several variants, too, of a tin pail that initially held "Jackie Coogan" Peanut Butter. Naturally, it bore a likeness of Charlie Chaplin's "Kid," the first child star.

Mickey Mouse has been a staggeringly successful merchandising tool. Mickey and his many comic friends have made untold thousands of promotional appearances as toys, dolls, watches, and games. Collectors of Disneyana particularly covet the advertising items that tie in with their collections. A sign featuring a marching Mickey advertising National Biscuit Company's Mickey Mouse cookies would be a sweet addition to collections in a few fields: Disney, Mickey, grocery store, and Nabisco, for starters. A cardboard flashlight display features a large Mickey at the entrance to the Mousekeeters Clubhouse, flanked by the actual flashlights being sold, with their 1950s price of 69 cents.

DISPLAYS

Figural cigar cutters (see page 56) and Blatz beer men (see page 53) are point-of-purchase displays, and fans of tobacco and beer memorabilia often include such items in their collections. The same is true of a wide range of interesting counter and floor displays, such as the cutout of Johnny Roventini (see page 59).

A second fascinating area of display advertising is the animated display. The best examples of these moving displays combine strong, bold design with an interesting action often made possible by electricity. The Mechanical Man Company was one of the premier producers of such displays. A particularly good example of this firm's work was the circa-1947 Dobbs Hat display, featuring a fisherman dressed in waders and a hat. When the mechanism is activated, the fisherman pulls back his fishing rod and extends his net for his catch. An illuminated sign "explains" the key to the angler's success: "It's the Dobbs." For collectors who aren't fond of hat tricks or who opt for truth in advertising, however, there's a 1950s Slinky display that features a wholesome-looking young man cradling his Slinky. The concealed electric motor lifts one hand, then the other, making the Slinky "walk." It made a hugely effective display.

Another firm, Baranger Studios, produced a wide range of eye-catching electric-powered window displays for jewelry stores and opticians. Subscribers received their new display as they shipped their last one back to Baranger to be cleaned, reconditioned, and sent on to another client. Between 1925 and 1959, Baranger created 167 different displays, with themes ranging from a stagecoach captioned "Hold your horses—don't forget that diamond" to the famed Little Old Woman Who Lived in a Shoe: "Her Diamond was bought here, too."

PROMOTIONAL ITEMS

Promotional items—giveaways and premiums—were used to advertise products as different from each other as soft drinks and prescription drugs. Giveaways, like calendars and pens, and premiums, like secret decoder rings and wrist radios, are collecting categories in themselves, although as with so many other advertising collectibles, they also attract other specialized collectors.

GIVEAWAYS

A giveaway was the original "something for nothing," and the giveaways that pleased sponsors and consumers best were pens, calendars, or cigarette lighters, all fairly inexpensive and all capable of carrying advertising. Pens sporting the names of patent medicines, dairies, or soap manufacturers reminded the users of a product—sometimes years after the original acquisition.

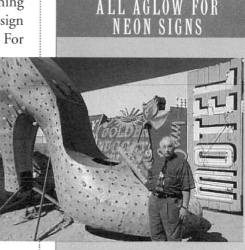

ALL AGLOW FOR NEON SIGNS

When appraiser Rudy Franchi traveled with the *Antiques Roadshow* to Las Vegas, he visited the Neon Museum. "We are in what's called a bone yard," Franchi told viewers, standing in front of a neon shoe the size of a garbage truck. "It's a graveyard for neon and other signs."

Neon may be considered an American roadside standard, but it was the French who created the first neon sign, for the Paris Opera House in 1920. "As soon as neon hit the United States, it took off like wildfire," Franchi says. In the 1940s, Las Vegas discovered its lure at about the time the rest of the country lost its taste for it. "Neon was thought to be a little garish and was relegated to movie theaters and motels," Franchi said. "There were actually zoning laws that forbade neon in certain neighborhoods." Yet neon has become fashionable with collectors, and even a Joe Six-Pack beer sign from a bar window can sell for $300 to $400.

SALESMAN'S SAMPLES, NOT TOYS

Over the last fifteen years, *Antiques Roadshow* appraiser Noel Barrett has augmented his personal collection of toys with late-nineteenth- and early-twentieth-century salesman's samples, miniaturized versions of products carried by traveling salesmen. Barrett's interest in them grew out of his interest in toys. "Because of their size, they seem toylike," he explains. "But samples are rarer because they were never mass-produced.

They were designed to inspire a purchase, so they have lavish detail," Barrett says. "They were made to look exactly like the full-sized object."

Two salesman's samples as seen on Antiques Roadshow *when it visited Austin.*

Barrett notes that many *Antiques Roadshow* visitors mistake small toys for the more valuable salesman's samples. "Just because it's a miniature doesn't make it a salesman's sample," he says. "Take a miniature violin, for example. A salesman could easily show a standard-sized violin. He didn't need a miniature."

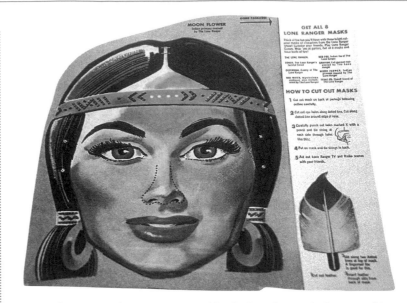

Moon Flower, an Indian princess rescued by the Lone Ranger, is shown on this premium face mask, one of nine Lone Ranger masks featured on the back of Cheerios cereal boxes in the 1950s.

Not surprisingly, the giveaways that collectors come across most often are those that were most widely circulated when new, like calendars. One Massachusetts soft-drink company, for instance, actually gave away six to seven million calendars a year. Other paper giveaways were matches, postcards, blotters, and trade cards, and each has a dedicated following.

Some types of giveaway are purely regional. No need to explain why cardboard, straw, and celluloid hand fans, for example, turn up more frequently in the South than they do in the North. Southern funeral homes, particularly, liked to advertise on hand fans, although the makers of buttermilk and chewing gum were partial to fans as well.

PREMIUMS

Premiums might be considered a step up from giveaways, in that the consumer had to "do" something to get his or her gift—usually send a proof of purchase to the company.

In the 1930s and 1940s, heroes and heroines such as the Lone Ranger, Little Orphan Annie, and Captain Midnight kept American kids glued to their radios day and night. The shows' canny sponsors quickly realized that these fictional stars were the perfect sales force for selling their products, so they

employed them to encourage young listeners to join a club or society and receive the free pins, badges, rings, membership certificates, club identification cards, and a host of other promotional items. In an all-out bid to build brand loyalty and sell goods by getting the kids to ask Mom to buy a specific product, they had hit upon a sales tool that worked exceptionally well.

Radio was more than a technical marvel. It was a magic carpet for listeners of all ages eager to escape the realities of the Depression. What better way to be transported to the twenty-fifth century than on superhero Buck Rogers's spaceship? Buck's radio show aired from 1932 to 1939, during which time its sponsors included Kellogg's, Cream of Wheat, and Cocomalt, and many premiums from this era remain as superb examples of the field, including paper masks of the characters, a ring that glowed in the dark, a shoulder patch, and a futuristic cardboard popgun. The Cocomalt Map of the Solar System is particularly desirable. This was a large, gorgeously lithographed paper sign illuminated with an Art Deco–style futuristic spacecraft and interplanetary creatures.

The Lone Ranger also had several sponsors, starting with Silvercup Bread in 1933, and going on to include Merita Bread, Kix, Wheaties, and Cheerios cereals. Although radio broadcasts of new Lone Ranger shows ended in 1955, Cheerios-sponsored rebroadcasts lasted until 1956. That famous "Hi-Yo Silver," however, was heard on television between 1949 and 1957, and for decades thereafter it echoed on in syndication. Lone Ranger premium memorabilia includes rings, buttons, and pins, and all these were produced almost continuously over the Masked Man's long, multimedia run. Naturally there were several types of premium badges, including the Silvercup Safety Scout membership badge and the Safety Sentinel badge in brass for Miami Maid Bread. A 1942 Kix Blackout Kit reflects wartime concerns, as does a Cheerios or Kix Victory Corps membership kit from the same year. Trademark silver bullets and masks were also offered, and an inducement to buy Cheerios included a black paper mask on the back of the box.

In the mid-thirties, comic-strip darling Little Orphan Annie was a princess of the airwaves. The show's sponsor, Ovaltine,

Captain Midnight pitched hot Ovaltine "the heart of a hearty breakfast," on a promotional mug.

A premium tin-tab button for Buck Rogers Rocket Rangers Satellite Pioneers is remarkable in that its tab is still unused.

Little Orphan Annie—with her dog, Sandy—also pitched the charms of Ovaltine, but as a cold drink in summer.

The value of premiums like this 1946 Captain Midnight Secret Squadron Decoder is greatly increased if they are accompanied by the original pamphlets, instructions—even the mailers they came in.

The Quaker Oats Company introduced a propeller-headed pink alien to promote Quisp cereal in 1965, and Quisp premiums are highly collectible today.

offered listeners a lucky coin with a radio-program decoder along with Radio Orphan Annie's Secret Society pamphlet. The pamphlet was filled with secret handshakes and signs as well as codes for encrypted radio messages, and Ovaltine produced several decoder badges, as well, for deciphering Annie's secret radio messages. There was, however, a rigorous procedure for receiving the coin "absolutely free": It required drinking Ovaltine three times a day for fifteen days and recording each draught on a chart. Then the chart had to be signed by the child and one parent and mailed to the company.

One item that may have presaged the phenomenal popularity of the television western was the Sky King Electronic Television Picture Ring. It featured a movie-camera–style box, an instruction sheet, and a filmstrip that, when fed through the ring, displayed images of Jim, Penny, Clipper, and Martha from the television version of the original radio program. *Sergeant Preston of the Yukon,* set in the gold-rush days of the 1890s, broadcast the adventures of a Royal Canadian Mountie and his trusty dog, Yukon King. It was another example of a radio show that made the successful switch to television, and it offered some of the most imaginative premiums. A Klondike Land Pouch, featuring a likeness of "our hero," contained dirt reputedly from the Klondike. The pouch is worth considerably more today if it still contains the original dirt, and like all premiums, the mailer that the prize was sent in. If a bag of dirt wasn't enough, Quaker enclosed a miniature deed in every box of cereal that allowed young television fans to "own" one square inch of Yukon Territory. Twenty million such deeds were distributed.

COLLECTING BY BRAND

Many advertising collectors choose to concentrate on ads for specific brands, and many of the brands collected today are still in business—which is one reason why they are widely collected. Such longevity keeps them firmly in the public eye, reminding modern consumers of their past while simultaneously creating memories for future collecting generations.

:

0

It is a truism of collecting that when there is no one around to remember a product, its nostalgia value is often diminished—what is familiar from our youth speaks loudest to our hearts. It's also true that the arcane and whimsical charm of some long-defunct brands, such as patent medicines, continues to attract new collectors.

COCA-COLA

Introduced in 1886, Coca-Cola is one of the first, and best, examples of an American branded food product that has come to symbolize American culture to the worldwide consumer. Even in the most remote regions of countries far, far from American shores, Coke *means* America. Here, in the United States, a collection of old Coke trays arranged chronologically can seem rather like watching the flow and progress of our country's changing tastes.

Initially, Coca Cola was developed as a headache and stomach remedy. When this humble potion was inadvertently mixed with carbonated water, however, it was suddenly, magically, and wildly successfully metamorphosed into a soft drink. Pre-1900 Coca-Cola advertising material is "to die for," says *Antiques Roadshow* expert Leila Dunbar, but particularly to-die-for is large paper material. The very first poster advertising Coca-Cola, circa 1886, is perhaps the Holy Grail for Coke collectors.

Metal Coca-Cola trays with elegant images from the early part of the twentieth century are perennially popular collectibles.

There is a profusion of twentieth-century Coca-Cola material on the market—calendars, signs, trays, bottles, carriers, syrup dispensers, pocketknives, toys, glasses, mugs, coolers, pocket mirrors, openers, menus, bookmarks, blotters, playing cards, clocks, thermometers, and more.

The popularity of Coca-Cola memorabilia has inspired numerous reproductions of earlier pieces as well as "fantasy"

COCA-COLA AT WAR

"The Second World War was a major marketing opportunity for American consumer corporations," stated *Antiques Roadshow* appraiser Rudy Franchi as he examined a box packed with Coca-Cola–labeled board games made for World War II soldiers. Decks of cards, score pads, cribbage boards, checkers, and more were all marked with a Coca-Cola stamp. The box was brought to the Austin, Texas, *Antiques Roadshow* by a man who also had one containing a table tennis setup in pristine condition with Coca-Cola imprinted on the handle of each paddle. "In my thirty-one years in collectibles, I've handled everything in this box at one time or another, but I don't think I've

ever seen them all together," Franchi said. "Before the war," Franchi explained. "Coke was very popular, but it wasn't dominant. This was how it got its huge market share." A conservative estimate for this game set is $1,000 to $1,200.

BUY ME SOME PEANUTS AND CRACKER JACK

The popular song "Take Me Out to the Ballgame" has forever paired baseball and Cracker Jack in America's mind, but there are other reasons to associate the two. Among the earliest prizes inserted in boxes of the snack were hand-tinted lithographed baseball cards.

A woman who came to the Milwaukee *Antiques Roadshow* had found her great-grandfather's boyhood collection of Cracker Jack baseball cards, including a rare one of Hall of Famer Honus Wagner, in some old cigar boxes that had belonged to him. "They're hand-tinted lithographs on very thin paper," *Antiques Roadshow* appraiser Kathleen Guzman said, "with numbers and biographies on the backs."

The visitor's great-grandfather had collected 95 of the 144 cards in the series. In the 1970s, however, the family had glued the cards to a backing and framed them, and the glue had caused some discoloration.

If the great-grandfather had the complete set and if the family hadn't glued them down, the collection would be worth about $65,000. As is, its value is $2,000 to $3,000.

items, pieces that resemble earlier Coca-Cola memorabilia—like pub mirrors depicting late-nineteenth- and early-twentieth-century images. But these were never produced during the period they seem to represent. They are often offered as vintage, but their value is nominal compared with true period pieces. Several were produced in the 1970s and 1980s.

A selection of Cracker Jack prizes: More than seventeen billion have been given away since 1912, when the company began including these small tokens in every box.

CRACKER JACK

The success of Cracker Jack owes a lot to the fact that almost everyone finds the combination of molasses-slathered popcorn and peanuts irresistible. It also owes much to the company's canny advertising and promotion. Cracker Jack's secret formula, based on a snack introduced at the World's Columbian Exposition in Chicago in 1893, kept the coated popcorn from becoming hard and sticky. After sampling the innovative, as-yet-unnamed product, a contemporary salesperson proclaimed it "crackerjack" (a turn-of-the-century expression for "great!"). In 1912, the company began to insert prizes in every box, and since that date more than seventeen billion prizes have been given away. The trademark, Sailor Jack and his dog, Bingo, first appeared in advertisements for this snack in 1916 and on the box itself in 1918. Cracker Jack collectors certainly enjoy the usual signs and other advertising memorabilia, but it's the prizes they prize. Over the years, thousands of different examples have delighted Cracker Jack buyers—paper toys and games, flip booklets, tinplate whistles, plastic charms, and tops. Some of the most valuable prizes are an early series of baseball cards (see page 118). The first series, consisting of 144 cards, was introduced in 1914. A second series of 177 cards was issued the following year. These cards are so coveted by baseball-card collectors that they have inspired fakes and reproductions, so beware.

"Cracker Jack prize" is a term that is often misattributed. There are other gumball-machine trinkets and giveaway tokens that may be small and appealing but have never nestled amid the peanuts and popcorn. These are, therefore, of no interest to Cracker Jack collectors, who tend to know just what was in every box in every year.

A circular porcelain enamel sign advertising Dr Pepper. Sometime during the 1950s, the period after "Dr" was dropped, making it easy to date this sign to post–mid-century.

DR. PEPPER

Dr. Pepper, today a national brand but once just a regional soft drink, has been known for its clever advertising since its founding in Waco, Texas, in 1885. Today there are many devoted Dr. Pepper collectors looking for cellophane pencil clips, wall thermometers, clocks, signs, bottles, and tin trays. The brand's longevity gives collectors a lot to choose from, although early material can be scarce and often costly. Recently, a rare circa-1910 Dr. Pepper beverage tray changed hands for close to $9,000. Prices for other material, particularly for later pieces, are more modest. In a recent auction, a large, round metal sign finished in bold red and white and adorned with "10," "2," and "4" (the hours at which consumers were supposed to reach for the soda) and the slogan "Drink Dr Pepper" sold for $270.

MOXIE

The soft drink Moxie was originally developed in 1876 by Dr. Augustin Thompson, an itinerant pharmacist, and sold over the counter in Lowell, Massachusetts, as a patent medicine to be taken for "nerves." Just as with Coca-Cola, the addition of carbonated water (sometime between 1900 and 1920) turned Moxie into one of the most popular soft drinks in the United States. (The saying "You've got a lot of moxie," meaning pluck, is occasionally heard even today.) Moxie collectibles include store signs, hand fans, and signs depicting the usual pretty girls, but also, in one instance, a young, white-coated physician or druggist pointing authoritatively at the viewer and suggesting the purchase of Moxie, "the sensible drink."

Moxie is still being produced today, although its appeal is predominantly regional.

Moxie is more popular with collectors than with consumers today; only a small regional market for the beverage remains. An example of its vintage advertising (above) featured a bizarre image of an early automobile driven by a man astride a horse.

ANTIQUES
DISCOVERY
ROADSHOW

A FAMILY TRADITION

Unfortunately, the value of a collectible can evaporate when its condition is altered. A rather painful example is a jigsaw puzzle made from a turn-of-the-twentieth-century Coca-Cola advertisement that appeared at the Hartford *Antiques Roadshow*. In the 1910s and 1920s, the owner's great-great-uncle used to collect colorful advertisements from his brother's drugstore. He would glue these ads to poster board and cut them up with a jigsaw to make puzzles. He signed the puzzles, dated them, boxed them, and shared them with his extended family, thereby beginning a family tradition. "We still make them today," the owner noted. Appraiser Gary Sohmers told the owner that although there are lots of people who collect jigsaw puzzles, their value is small compared to the value of mint-condition vintage Coca-Cola ads. "I would have to estimate this puzzle in the $50 to $150 range," Sohmers said. "But if it wasn't cut up, it could be worth $10,000 to $15,000."

Mr. Peanut, the advertising figure for Planters Peanuts, looks dapper even as a soft, stuffed doll.

PEPSI-COLA

Druggist Caleb Bradham's customers wanted him to call his soda recipe "Brad's Drink," but Pepsi-Cola—its actual name since 1898—seemed, somehow, catchier. Through world wars and bankruptcies, Pepsi's fortunes waxed and waned, but by 1938 the soft-drink company was second in sales only to the giant Coca-Cola. In its early years, Pepsi apparently produced fewer calendars, trays, and other memorabilia than did its archrival, so Pepsi memorabilia are rarer and can be quite costly. Despite the scarcity of early pieces, there are wide varieties of Pepsi advertising available. These include, among other items, metal outdoor thermometers, banks, bottle carriers, and tie clips. Collectors look for items featuring Pepsi and Pete, the Pepsi-Cola cops, who were created by the famed Rube Goldberg and introduced in a 1939 newspaper cartoon strip.

PLANTERS PEANUTS

The Planters Nut and Chocolate Company was founded in 1906 by the young Italian immigrant Amedeo Obici, but it wasn't until 1916 that a thirteen-year-old student responding to a Planters contest came up with the idea for its spokesnut, dapper "Mr. Peanut," a large unshelled peanut with anthropomorphic arms and casually crossed legs. A company artist later made him even more sophisticated by adding a top hat and monocle. Mr. Peanut turned out to be the ideal representative of Planters and was soon being made into cloth and wooden dolls. Toward the end of the 1920s, his image began to appear frequently in children's stories and coloring books. Planters Peanuts serving dishes, nut spoons, and jars are usually adorned with his natty figure, and a pair of plastic Mr. Peanut figural salt and pepper shakers make a perfect crossover collectible.

GLASS

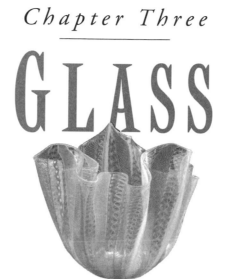

The range of collectible twentieth-century glass is so vast and varied, it's no wonder it's one of America's most popular hobbies. Collectors scoop up kitchen glass and tableware, and blown glass and decorative ornaments, that have no purpose other than to look absolutely beautiful. The hunt for these lustrous treasures encompasses not only the one-of-a-kind studio creations of innovative glass artists, but also the mass-production of companies as diverse as Steuben and Fenton.

A collection of glass can begin innocently. You just want to track down the missing pieces of the 1930s dinnerware pattern your grandmother got as a giveaway at the movies. Or, at an auction gallery, you spot an irresistible bowl created by a major figure of twentieth-century design and think, "Just this once." A collection of glass can even begin with a rediscovery, as a visitor to the Tucson *Antiques Roadshow* learned when he brought in a vase belonging to his father, who had inherited it from his father, who in turn had inherited it from his mother. Appraiser Nicholas Dawes was utterly delighted to see this never-before-appraised Escargot (Snail) vase, a tour de force from the factories of the great glass designer René Lalique. "This particular vase was designed in 1919 and continuously made throughout the twenties and into the early thirties," said Dawes. "It happens to be one of my favorite glass pieces."

Top: Venini fazzoletto handkerchief vase by Fulvio Bianconi. Above: Imperial's popular Cape Cod-pattern plate.

This elegant Lalique Escargot vase saw the light of day (and the cameras) at the Tucson Antiques Roadshow *after having spent over forty years in the owner's closet.*

Dawes pointed out that the condition of this example was exceptional, "pretty much like the day it was made. . . . You can see by looking into the neck that it's yellow on the outside and kind of opalescent, milky on the inside. This is 'casing,' where two layers of glass are fused into one piece. Casing gives the whole vase a kind of luminescence." The brownish staining on the outside (which might easily be mistaken for grime) is actually a sepia patina original to the glass, he noted. The vase has the engraved signature "Lalique" on the bottom, which Dawes said is authentic. "This is a great, rare example of a colored Art Deco Lalique vase," Dawes added.

"Well, it's been in a closet for at least forty years," the visitor said, "and my dad thinks it might be worth anywhere from $500 to $5,000." Dawes enjoyed telling this guest that his Escargot is worth far more than that—at least $15,000, and maybe more. "I won't drop it," the visitor laughed.

Like so many twentieth-century objects, most glass was mass-manufactured and, in its simplest form, was made of the least costly ingredients: silica, potash, and lime. A good deal of glass was produced by pouring molten glass into basic molds, allowing that to cool, removing the newly made solid form, and then repeating the process. A variety of inexpensive decorating techniques were employed to turn this simplest glass into something special. Intricate patterns were incised on molds to produce pieces very similar to those that had been expensively cut or engraved by hand. Some items were engraved on a copper or stone wheel, while others were needle- or acid-etched.

A more time-consuming and labor-intensive process was blowing the glass into molds. This produced multiple copies of a design, but not boxcar loads of it. More elaborate multipiece molds, such as those used by Lalique, formed the glass into intricate, ingenious patterns. Throughout the century, however, in creative defiance of commercial manufacture, some glass continued to be blown free-form, in the traditional way, by studio glass artists as well as in the glasshouses of Europe, particularly Venice.

In the following chapter, you'll find information on the most interesting developments in twentieth-century glass, and learn a good deal about being a smart collector.

Still modern after all these years: iridescent Dugan Venetian vases, made in 1906.

A BRIEF HISTORY

Although the public bought and enjoyed Art Nouveau art glass at the turn of the twentieth century, colored glass did not become ubiquitous in homes until the years following World War I. At that time an invigorated glass industry launched tempting barrages of decorative wares and dinnerware in rainbows of pinks, gentle greens, warm ambers, yellows, and chic blacks into a newly happy and peaceful economy. Mass production at last allowed the ordinary housewife to enjoy a pantryful of dainty colored glass, but mass production was far from the whole story. It was an impressive artistic moment, too, one led by a small group of talented men and women who were committed to crafting singular, innovative, beautiful glass objects.

Since the nineteenth century, international exhibits have been held to show off the work of major decorative artists and their art. The Exposition Internationale des Arts Décoratifs et Industriels Modernes was one of these. Held in Paris in 1925, it rocked the international design community with displays of furniture, silver, and glass in a startlingly modern style—a style that ultimately took its name from the exhibition itself: Art Deco. The best French glassmakers were right on top of this bold new trend, creating many of the finest examples of Art Deco glass. Other glassmakers followed suit, abandoning suddenly outdated Art Nouveau designs and creating truly modern wonders in fluent glass.

Five graceful water nymphs swirl across the surface of this opalescent Calypso plate by the French master Lalique.

LATE TIFFANY?

American glass giant Louis Comfort Tiffany is closely associated with Art Nouveau, the late nineteenth- and early twentieth-century decorative arts movement. That is why appraiser Arlie Sulka was so surprised to see a Tiffany vase at the New Orleans *Antiques Roadshow* that was *not* Art Nouveau. The owner's aunt had given it to her with the warning "not to sell it at a yard sale." The piece was made in 1921, during the waning days of Tiffany Studios.

"Tiffany glass was falling out of favor," Sulka explained. "So their designers asked, 'How can we continue to attract buyers for our glass?'" The answer was to design pieces in more fashionable, abstract styles rather than in Tiffany's early naturalistic idiom.

This piece also reveals how the firm was casting about for new color combinations. "I've seen yellows before in Tiffany, I've seen green leaves, but I don't remember ever seeing this orange," said Sulka, noting that the color was popular in Europe. Its value: about $7,500, in Sulka's estimation.

Sensuous bleeding hearts and their foliage wind their way around this Art Nouveau cameo vase, signed Gallé.

The Art Deco era might even be thought of as the Age of Glass. Indeed, glass was the ideal material for the Jazz Age—slick, brittle, and probably a bit too sharp for its own longevity. It was these very properties that stimulated the imaginations of artists and commercial manufacturers alike. René Lalique, for instance, trained as a jeweler but found his true calling in glass. And while Lalique created and exhibited actual, usable (but needless to say, fragile) glass furniture for that 1925 exhibition, he didn't neglect more conventional wares. Relief-molded, rather than individually blown, these wares could be mass-produced in factories and thereby assure the commercial longevity of Lalique's designs. (The major kinks of mass production had been ironed out during World War I.)

As if to prove the value of mass production, many of the pre-war luxury firms that made handcrafted products went quietly out of business after the stock market crash of 1929. Tiffany glass had already ceased production by 1928. Argy-Rousseau closed in 1931, and Gallé ceased making glass in 1936. Had Steuben not developed its 10M lead crystal, a brilliant glass of dazzling clarity, it too might have failed.

Handle With Care

At the glass table at each *Antiques Roadshow,* appraisers grasp and lift and turn whatever piece of glass presents itself. "It's a touchy-feely process," explains appraiser Louise Luther, who also notes that one of the places that glass lovers can actually get their hands on glass is at glass auctions, where customers are permitted to handle the fragile merchandise. Held to the light, glass reveals its clarity, color, swirl patterns, imperfections, minor fractures, air bubbles, and perhaps, a maker's mark. Lifting, too, gives a good idea as to heft. "I expect certain thin-walled and fragile glass to be light," Luther says. "If it's heavy, I suspect that the piece is a replica." When Luther and other glass appraisers aren't lifting, they're rubbing. If the glass feels "greasy," as they call it in the trade, Luther suspects lower-quality glass or a reproduction. Also, fingertips can find a roughness where a signature should have been. If there's a chance that a less-valuable piece might be confused with one that will bring a good price, a giveaway signature may have been ground off. Touch can also help distinguish between a Gallé cameo-glass vessel that was acid etched or one that is wheel carved (the latter is sharper, usually, and definitely more valuable).

GLASS FOR THE MASSES

The 1930s, then, became a time for finding ways to offer American consumers who were financially shaken by the Great Depression the absolute most for the absolute least—a feat that glass manufacturers accomplished both by increasing product standardization and by providing glass that was simultaneously attractive and utilitarian. Streamlining—of design, of function, and particularly, of cost—was the order of the day. Consequently, good-looking, useful glass tableware for dining rooms and kitchens came pouring by the ton from the patterned molds of every factory that hoped to weather the economic storm. Mass-produced molded glass was ideal for giveaways, since it was discovered that women could be induced to buy a particular brand of cereal or soap if, at the same time, they could fill their Hoosier cabinets with the attractively colored Depression glass tucked inside that box of laundry detergent or sack of flour. Homemakers were thrilled, too, by the delightful new colors of mundane glass kitchenware—rolling pins, citrus reamers, homely refrigerator boxes—and, eventually, when the repeal of Prohibition made it possible, by cheery bar accessories like shakers, stirrers, and martini glasses.

During the Depression, glass refrigerator jars, like this one from Federal, were an inexpensive and attractive way to keep foods fresh.

With the coming of World War II, however, America's rose-colored glasses—along with most of those in blue, green, and amber—disappeared. Mineral coloring agents, it seemed, were somehow crucial to the war effort, and everyday glass turned perfectly clear, ornamented now with bright, primary-color paints. Those pineapples, cherries, and Latin dancers cavorting on juice and highball glasses lent much-needed cheer to an era of ration stamps and war bonds.

In Europe, however, glass production had almost ceased, except in neutral Scandinavian countries. Scandinavian glassmakers like Orrefors and Kosta continued to produce the distinctly modern, high-quality mass-produced glass they had been making since the 1920s. These firms achieved international prominence after the war, when the world was ready to embrace their fresh, minimalist style.

In postwar America, an influx of inexpensive imports from Japan and Taiwan dealt a deathblow to several of the old-line American glass manufacturers, including Heisey and Cambridge. Others, like Steuben, flourished. Internationally, Lalique and Kosta (as Kosta Boda) stayed afloat, as well, and continue in business today.

This unusual pitcher is from Consolidated's "Elegant" Catalonian line (first produced in 1927) which mimicked the bubbles and raised rings of glass found in Catalonia in Spain—hence the name.

RECYCLING BIN SURPRISE

At the Charleston, South Carolina, *Antiques Roadshow*, appraiser Louise Luther examined an interesting bowl from Italy. She described it to its owner as a centerpiece, probably made in the 1930s in Murano, near Venice.

"This is the sort of thing that Dale Chihuly and other contemporary artists have borrowed from Italian designs," said Luther. "As a good piece of collectible Italian glass, its value is about $1,500. And it will increase."

Luther asked the owner what she used it for. "Well," she said, "it's on a chest by the back door. I put cans and things in it before I take them outside." Luther, realizing that this handsome object was being used as a recycling bin, responded with a laugh, "Well, it's certainly a shape that lends itself to being useful!"

Continental Europe's glass industry as a whole, however, was vastly changed by the war. Czechoslovakia, for instance, which had once been a preeminent exporter of fine-quality glass, became Communist and had to submit all its factories and decorating workshops to the supervision of a single central administrative corporation. Surprisingly, and quite contrary to expectations, it was a development that created truly innovative Czech glass. This could happen because, while most Czech art was carefully monitored, the Communist government felt glass was not a medium with the potential to be "subversive." Glassmaking flourished, therefore, attracting Czech artists from other media.

GLASS AS ART

After the war, Italy, too, developed into a major force in artist-designed glass, particularly in Murano (a group of five islands off Venice). There, a tight-knit fraternity of glassblowers long reputed to make the finest of all Continental glass, invented (or reinvented) challenging glassmaking techniques like *filigrana, latticino,* and *fazzoletto*—all of which they used for novel, superb, and distinctively modern glass. Major glass exhibitions held in the 1950s in Milan and Venice invited both Italian and foreign designers to display their products, most of which were whimsical, ebullient, and technically dazzling.

European glass of the forties and fifties—Venetian, Scandinavian, and Czech—was individualistic. Designers often blew or shaped their glass designs themselves. When factory production involved elaborate techniques or hand-detailed elements, this was done under the artist's supervision. It was an antidote to years of mass production, and it helped, too, that after the war people could actually afford to buy this sort of glass again, and that there were no materials shortages. After decades of made-by-machine, the best and most imaginative glass began once more to come, not from

A dimpled, tear-shape Murano bottle in latimo, brown, and clear glass.

the world of commerce, but from the furnaces and blowpipes of artisan glassmakers.

Most of the current advances in technique and design in the United States in the last half of the twentieth century came from the studios of glass artists. The American studio-glass movement that began with Harvey Littleton in the 1960s inspired, among others, Dale Chihuly, a contemporary force in glass. Today there are a number of talented glassmakers creating fine and innovative glass that is both an art form and a marvel.

EVALUATING GLASS

Mezza filigrana is the technique that produces the delicate filigreed swirls in this Murano vase.

Basically, there are two kinds of twentieth-century glass: art glass (handblown, or one-of-a-kind, as *Antiques Roadshow* expert Reyne Haines defines it) and mass-produced glass. Much collectible glass falls neatly into one category or the other, but some glass falls (softly) between. René Lalique, for example, created art glass in factories using techniques of mass production. Other manufacturers employed artists to design reproducible pieces that were then handcrafted in fairly limited numbers by teams of glassmakers in a workshop or a factory. Many glassmakers, too, combined mass-manufacturing techniques with details applied by hand.

Consequently, *Antiques Roadshow* glass expert Louise Luther urges collectors, new or experienced, to "Lay your hands on the glass" (see Handle With Care, page 74).

Luther also agrees with her fellow appraisers in fields as distant from her own as sports memorabilia, textiles, and toys in suggesting that "You should *always* buy the best you can afford." Her advice applies equally to Depression tableware and to the fine and rare engraved glass that Edward Hald designed for Orrefors (see page 102). In theory, this seems easy. In practice, it means developing the self-discipline to walk away from a well-priced piece of glass that you somewhat like if its design or execution doesn't fit into your collection. It may mean, too, putting a deposit on something you're desperate to own but can't afford, and paying it off slowly. In the 1960s, a young glass collector, a university librarian living on a tiny income, longed for a Tiffany Wisteria

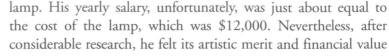

The Hazel Atlas Glass Company mass-produced these cobalt Royal Lace glasses during the Depression. Originally inexpensive, they are now coveted by collectors.

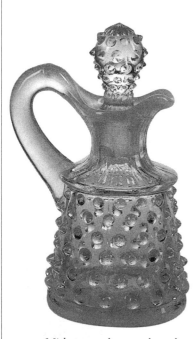

Mid-century hostesses brought out their "Elegant" glassware when company came for dinner. Here, a Fenton hobnail cruet.

lamp. His yearly salary, unfortunately, was just about equal to the cost of the lamp, which was $12,000. Nevertheless, after considerable research, he felt its artistic merit and financial value were worth the risk. It took him several years to buy that lamp—but what courage, what connoisseurship! According to *Antiques Roadshow* glass appraiser Arlie Sulka, his Wisteria lamp, among the most sought-after of Tiffany designs, would today be valued at somewhere between $250,000 and $400,000.

AGE

Because the glass that was made in the collectible era—from 1920 to about 1970—is not antique, the collector shouldn't feel obliged to learn the chronology of manufacturing techniques, for it isn't nearly as useful here as it is for glass made earlier. In addition, manufacturing and ornamental techniques that had been in use for centuries were employed throughout this era, so identifying a technique won't necessarily help you date a piece. Nevertheless, the very newness of twentieth-century glass provides a number of really efficient and satisfactory ways to determine its age.

Mass-produced glass is frequently labeled (see page 80), for example, and the companies that made it generally changed their labeling over the years. Old Lalique (pre-1925), for instance, will have a pattern number and the inscribed signature "R. Lalique France," or the engraved "R. Lalique." From the mid-1920s until 1939, the "R. Lalique" was molded or acid etched. After Lalique's death in 1945, the "R" was dropped. Such neat and well-documented factory labeling means that the collector can be fairly confident in the attribution and age of certain kinds of mass-produced glass.

Not every manufacturer labeled its work all the time, so the origins of some pieces will forever remain a source of speculation. Remember, too, that a forged signature added to a genuine piece will compromise its value. Fortunately, numerous specialty

Glass Techniques

Some glassmaking techniques were invented by twentieth-century glassmakers and became, like the Graal technique developed by Orrefors, a signature style. But others were traditional techniques that continued to be used, and a number of modern glassmaking techniques were shared among different manufacturers and countries. Here is a look at some of the most common methods of creating and decorating glass.

CREATING GLASS PIECES

Most glass objects are made by either blowing or molding.

BLOWN GLASS: To make a blown-glass vessel, the molten glass (called the gather) is placed at the end of a metal tube and inflated by the glassmaker blowing air through the tube. The glass is then free-blown and shaped by the glassmaker using other simple tools, or blown into a mold, so that it takes on particular dimensions and designs each time.

MOLDED GLASS: Mold-pressed glass is created when molten glass (the gather) is dropped (not blown) into a metal mold and then pressed with a metal plunger.

MOLD-ETCHED GLASS: For this process, the mold itself is incised with a design that, impressed on the finished piece of glass, leaves a busy, shallow tracery that imitates—albeit poorly—the expensive look of acid etched glass (see below). It is less expensive for commercial glass factories to produce a design by mold etching because it is less labor-intensive. Depression-era glass, which had to be affordable, was commonly mold-etched. If such cost-cutting techniques in manufacture were lamentable, they were more than compensated for by the varied and delicate colors of Depression-era glassware.

BLOWN-AND-MOLDED GLASS: Sometimes both blowing and molding are used to create a piece, the mold shaping either the inside or the outside of the partially blown glass.

DECORATING GLASS

The following are some of the most widely used techniques for decorating a cooled, finished piece of glass.

HAND-ENGRAVED GLASS: Glass is most often engraved using a rotating copper wheel that has an abrasive applied to its edge, although stone wheels are also used. A less common method involves scratching the design onto the surface with a diamond or other hard material. Because engraving requires considerable time and, often, delicate handwork, it is generally reserved for more expensive pieces.

ACID-ETCHED GLASS: Acid-etched glass is first coated with wax or resin. Then either the design is scratched through the coating with a sharp tool

This 1935 Venus vase from Steuben has an engraved pattern on its bowl.

A Lalique vase is partially acid-etched.

or a stencil or etching plate is affixed to the glass. Next the piece is either exposed to the fumes of hydrofluoric acid or dipped into the acid. The fumes or the acid eat away the exposed areas on the surface of the glass, and the finished etched design is revealed only when the coating is removed.

CAMEO GLASS: To make cameo glass, the original piece is encased with a layer of glass in a contrasting color. Once cooled, the outer layer of glass is cut, carved, engraved, or etched away to reveal that image or design in the color of the underlying layer.

The letter "R" in the signature on the bottom of this Lalique piece suggests that it was created prior to the designer's death in 1945.

In the 1920s, when avocados were a delicacy, Indiana Glass changed the name of their Pear pattern to Avocado. This salad bowl is very hard to find today.

books include both modern and fake labels and tell how to distinguish one from the other (see the Reading List on page 543). There is also the problem of modern reproductions. Factories often reissue their own best-selling older products, which clouds the issue of age.

Manufacturers' original trade catalogs are another aid to identifying what you have. If you're interested in the work of Fenton Glass Company, for example, you can date any of its countless patterns from the actual Fenton catalogs, several of which have been reprinted by national societies and collectors' clubs. Moreover, photographs of exhibition installations, magazine articles, and advertisements are an excellent source for dating objects. And if the company you're interested in is still in business, it may respond to a written request for information.

Glass made in 1920 or 1930 is not necessarily more valuable than glass made in 1965. (Indeed, because, as previously mentioned, many manufacturers continued to make the same styles for years, it may be virtually impossible to tell the older example from a more recent one.) Also, any piece of glass that shows poor workmanship and clumsy or impractical design will be no more valuable now than it was when new. There are, nevertheless, examples of glass that sold for pennies once but are amazingly costly today, like the oh-so-rare Horseshoe butter dish and cover that the Indiana Glass Company made in the early 1930s. As a corollary, if a piece of glass was exceptionally expensive when it was made—whenever that was—it should be even more costly today. So if you come across one that for some reason is not, you may have a "find"—or a fake. Read before you spend.

ATTRIBUTION (LABELING)

"You can never say 'always,'" warns *Antiques Roadshow* appraiser Louise Luther. "Public opinion to the contrary, glass is not always signed. So the signature should be the last thing you look at, since it's easy to fake. If you buy only by signatures, you're going to make mistakes."

Signatures are not always "signatures" either, for that term has come to refer to any and all kinds of factory labeling rather than handwritten names. These include actual incised signatures, paper labels, and marks molded into the glass. Yet, correct attribution is as important to glass as is to all twentieth-century collecting. Attribution can be determined by style, pattern, color, texture, and other characteristics of the glass. A signature is an added plus only if these other criteria check out. Once all these are in place, look at the bottom of the piece, not just for an incised or molded name or mark or logo, but also for a label. Paper labels were commonly placed on new mass-produced glass at the factory, though all too frequently they washed off. (Depression glass, in particular, often bears no type of mark or identification, in which case you can fall back on shape, design, and color.) Original paper labels on art glass and studio glass always add value because a surprising amount of this glass is not reliably signed and, also, because few genuine paper labels survive. Keep in mind, too, that incised (inscribed with a sharp tool) factory or artist names can always be added (or erased) "after the fact," so labels molded into the glass are, all in all, "the best kind," says Luther. "They can't be washed off or applied later on."

RARITY

It's a given that every piece of collectible glass becomes more rare when another like it breaks. Fortunately, there are several less damaging determinants of rarity and many that don't depend on your wishing bad luck on your fellow collectors.

The first of these is the technical difficulty of making a particular piece. While mass-produced glassware is primarily designed

AMERICAN STUDIO GLASS

In the early 1960s, Harvey Littleton, founder of the American studio-glass movement, led a rebellion against factory-produced glass.

After teaching himself the fundamentals of blowing glass using a crudely made furnace and a blowpipe, Littleton began teaching other interested artists how to do it, including his prize pupil, Dale Chihuly.

Dale Chihuly was introduced to glass when he was an interior design student at the University of Washington. His interest led him in 1966 to the University of Wisconsin, where he enrolled in the glass program and studied with Harvey Littleton. He continued his studies at Rhode Island School of Design and later at the Venini firm in Murano (see page 107). Chihuly creates art using glass, including many series of glass sculptures (names familiar to collectors are Seaforms, Persians, Ikebana, and Putti), as well as a number of decorated cylinders, glass "baskets," and glass chandeliers. He has also overseen glass architectural projects and founded Pilchuck Glass School in Seattle. His work is exhibited worldwide.

Collectors now call them "pineapple" vases; Anchor Hocking named them for their colors—like Royal Ruby— rather than their shape.

Ruba Rombic, introduced in 1928, was modern for its time and wasn't a huge seller. Its planar form was difficult to manufacture, and due to the Great Depression, it was only produced for four years. Its rarity makes it especially desirable today.

Once called the "poor man's Tiffany," carnival glass, such as this Raspberry Water Set from Northwood, is easier to find than Ruba Rombic, but complete sets are hard to assemble.

to be efficiently mass-produced, art-glass designers enjoy a challenge, and the very nature of their medium almost demands it: Glass is so "plastic," so malleable, that it begs to be played with. Consequently, craftsmen in glass try to outdo each other, to invent un-reproducible techniques (or methods that are too costly for the competition to reproduce easily). Thus, when Swedish designers developed Ariel glass in 1936, a complex technique in which shapely air bubbles are trapped within the crystal, it was not only difficult to execute to begin with, but was even more difficult to copy. For both reasons, Ariel glass is rare today.

Sometimes, a type of glass is rare simply because its manufacturer produced very little of it. This happened when a particular style wasn't popular and didn't sell well, or even at all. Problems with molds and other production difficulties also resulted in limited production. In either circumstance, those few pieces that have managed to find their way into collections or museums are rarities. And naturally, these are the pieces that everyone wants. Take the example of the Fostoria rooster (also called a chanticleer), made in three colors: white milk glass, clear glass, and black glass. Due to a flaw in the mold, many of the roosters made of the experimental milk glass fractured, while the other colors emerged from the mold whole. Today's collectors of Fostoria poultry find flocks of clear and black roosters, but the milk-glass model? That is a very rare bird.

CONDITION

Cracked glass has no place in any serious collection, except on a high shelf as a study piece or as an example of a style (a "cabinet piece"). Perhaps with the exception of everyday Depression glass tableware (see page 88), glass, of all decorative objects, needs to be absolutely mint to have monetary value. Mint means "just as it came from the factory" (if it did come from a factory). No wear. No chips. No gold or enameled decoration missing

These festive striped tumblers, introduced in the 1950s, were intended to accompany the hugely popular Fiesta dinnerware.

or worn away. The older a piece is, of course, the more likely it will be to have scratches, stains, worn decoration, and chips. So collectors should always be alert to the possibility of repairs or restorations.

For example, glass that has been nicked or chipped on the rim or foot is frequently ground down (placed against an abrasive wheel and polished until the edges are smooth again). How does one recognize ground-down glass? If there has been significant repair, the proportions of the entire piece might seem a little "off." Top-heavy, perhaps. Or, if it is the foot that has been ground down, a little off-round. If it is the rim, the lip may be missing a bit of pattern. Reground rims can feel sharper than the original, too. Because fine condition is so vital in glass collecting, you will need good lighting in order to do a proper examination. And along with a good lighting source, touch is the most important method of examining glass.

It is not unheard of to find a collectible still in its original packaging. Although most consumers who bought new stemware or bottles of perfume simply threw the packaging away, some—maybe a never used house gift—is still as pristine as the day it was purchased. For commercially produced glassware like sets of ice tea glasses or barware, the original packaging can make the set significantly more desirable than it would have been without. Perfume bottle collectors, in fact, are particularly keen to have those original boxes; they were integral to the presentation of the scent. Bottle and box, with their complementary designs, showed best for side-by-side display. The Art Deco packaging of Lalique is collectible itself, actually, even without its original glass contents!

CURING SICK GLASS

Appraiser Reyne Haines says, "Besides cracks and chips, the number one turnoff in glass is cloudiness."

A symptom of "sick" glass, cloudiness most often afflicts vases, bowls, and drinking glasses, because these are generally filled with water, which often leaves minerals, especially calcium, behind. Although collectors usually shun sick glass, Haines says that the ailment is not always terminal. She recommends a mix of water and vinegar to clean up a light calcium deposit. Toothpaste or a denture whitener also takes calcium off glass (as well as tar deposits left from cigarette smoke). Tub and tile cleaners, along with cleaners designed to remove calcium deposits from glass shower doors, can sometimes cure sick glass.

"These remedies work best on crystal," Haines says. "Oftentimes it's impossible to remove thick calcium buildup from iridescent glass." Whatever cleansing agent you use, Haines suggests rinsing it off immediately with mild soap and lukewarm water (extreme temperatures crack glass). Easier than any cure, however, is prevention. "Don't let water stand too long in glass," Haines suggests. And do not let wet glass air-dry, Reyne says; use a dish towel and a little elbow grease to keep your glass healthy.

"Two Kids"—a young boy and a young goat—in a Cambridge Glass flower frog.

Lotus-blossom candlesticks by Westmoreland dressed up Depression-era tables.

Before concentrate, Americans began their day with fresh-squeezed juice from a Federal Glass reamer.

COLLECTING GLASS

Collectible twentieth-century glass can be clear or colored. Even the most modest juice glass of the 1930s could, using inexpensive mineral oxides, be colored to rival precious rubies, emeralds, and sapphires. For countless owners, it is glorious color that attracts them to glass in the first place.

Happily for the collector, much of the twentieth-century glass that we collect today was mass-produced, and much of that is affordable. American mass-produced glass includes the familiar objects so many of us grew up with: salad plates, tumblers, citrus reamers, and fruit bowls. It has no pretensions to being fine art, but often, because of its airy colors or inventive shapes, it is truly beautiful as well as being fun to collect.

Art glass, in particular glass from manufacturers in the Scandinavian countries and Italy, was designed by artists working on the cutting edge (so to speak) of technical possibility. Although made in quantity, it is generally more expensive than other mass-produced glass.

Studio glass, by contrast, is designed by individual artists who very seldom make tableware, although every now and then you will find a gorgeous—and eminently breakable—goblet. Most often, studio glass is a decorative vessel—some form of bowl, vase, or footed compote.

Between mass-produced tableware and Venetian tours de force, there is much to enjoy and much to collect. When it comes to what collectors long to own, table glass—goblets,

A Grape and Cable pattern Northwood centerpiece bowl.

plates, finger bowls—is generally in as much demand as decorative glass like vases, fruit bowls, and candlesticks.

As in every field of twentieth-century collectibles, there are trends in collecting, and the "hot" new market, whatever that may be, is always rather volatile. Once collectors figure out approximately how many of a particularly desirable vase or bowl are out there, the market settles down, with the rarities at the top and the rest falling into place. The new collector, consequently, might feel more comfortable starting in one of the traditional fields, where she or he won't be ambushed by unpleasant surprises.

Another helpful hint for beginning collectors is that some types of glass were heavily distributed only in certain regions of the country. There are some Depression glass patterns, for example, that were marketed primarily in the Northeast while others were localized in the Midwest. (For example, Federal Glass Company shipped boxcars full of iridescent Normandie to New England, and very little made it to the South.) So if you're having difficulty locating your dream piece close to home, try shopping away from your own backyard. The Internet, too, has opened regional markets to the world—and the savvy collector knows how to take advantage of it.

Generally speaking, the value of a piece of glass is not rigidly based on labeling but on the quality of design and workmanship. That is why, if an unmarked piece speaks to you, listen to your heart and buy *that,* rather than some piece of late—and perhaps mediocre-quality—Lalique.

It is important, too, for you as a beginning glass collector to establish your position on condition. If you're buying vintage tableware with the intention of using it, for instance, you need not be *too* concerned with the condition of the piece. After all, you're probably going to add a scratch or three yourself. However, if the glass you collect is going to be your children's inheritance, then every piece—from the very first one you buy to the most recent— should be carefully checked to make sure it is

McKee's Depression-era Laurel pattern cheese dish protected cheese from spoilage and pests.

A star was born when the Federal Glass Company introduced its Star pattern in the 1950s.

THE LATENT COLLECTOR (AND HOW TO BECOME ONE)

Because she thought it was pretty, *Antiques Roadshow* appraiser and glass expert Reyne Haines had been buying Depression glass for years—and using it, too. When a dinner guest remarked to her that she "didn't know you collected glass," Haines replied, "I don't," because she had never thought of herself as a collector. She had only bought what she liked. Yet when her guest returned with the gift of a book on glass, Haines found herself instantly absorbed. "Until I read that first book," she says today, "I thought it was all just 'stuff.'" Now, years, books, and thousands of pieces of glass later, she knows better.

Yet there is more to collecting glass than buying a lot of something pretty that you like. There is the romance of owning the old and learning the history of the glass you've chosen to collect. There is also the pleasure of using your glass, as Haines still does. Along with that, there is the satisfaction of acquiring and owning useful things that, ideally, retain their value.

perfect before you buy it, and then kept far from guests, children, cats, and stainless steel sinks.

The glass manufactured in the United States and Europe between 1920 and 1970 is possibly the most abundant (and varied) glass ever produced. Enthusiasts search for particular plates, saucers, platters, serving pieces, dishes, pitchers, stemware, glasses, mugs, teacups, bowls, vases, boxes, ashtrays, figures, candlesticks, stoppered bottles, and perfume bottles. Even collectors on a modest budget can own truly beautiful examples of twentieth-century glass. Mass-produced Depression may have been less time- and labor-intensive than the "Elegant" glass made during the same period, but it is as beautiful in its own way as the rarest of Lalique perfume bottles.

There are so many possibilities in twentieth-century glass collecting that there is a niche to suit the taste and budget of every collector. Perhaps you have a favorite shape (swans, elephants, roosters) or technique (etched glass, opalescent glass) or function (salt and pepper shakers, ashtrays, vases, shot glasses). Perhaps you like a certain color (green, ruby, or blue), era (Scandinavian glass of the fifties), or brand (Fire-King ovenware). If ever a collectible was "eye candy," it is glass.

AMERICAN GLASS

Collectible American glass ranges from machine-produced Depression glass to singular works of art by Steuben. Mass-produced glass can most easily be discussed by broad categories (carnival glass, Depression glass). More ambitious glass—from "Elegant" to art glass—is treated here by manufacturer (some of whom, interestingly, made Depression glass, as well).

CARNIVAL GLASS

Carnival glass is among the most popular of glass collectibles, and it's no wonder: It comes in a variety of highly attractive shapes, colors, and patterns, and the more common examples are generally affordable.

Known at one time as the "poor man's Tiffany" (from its inception in 1907, it imitated expensive Tiffany art glass), carnival glass has an iridescent finish achieved by spraying or selectively daubing inexpensive metallic salts on pressed colored glass. Many of the factories that manufactured carnival glass were American: Northwood, Imperial, Fenton, Dugan (later Diamond), and Millersburg. Each called its iridescent glassware by some proprietary name, such as Rainbow Lustre, Iridill, or Venetian Art. All produced innumerable patterns, and American exports of carnival glass eventually made this glass so popular abroad that by 1920, Germany and England (where manufacturers were happy to be able to reuse their old Victorian molds) began to produce a carnival glass of their own. By this time, it was already out of fashion in the United States, but overseas its popularity continued until the 1930s, and ultimately, it was manufactured as far away as Australia, South America, and India. During the late 1950s, glass collectors discovered carnival glass, and some companies began to manufacture it again.

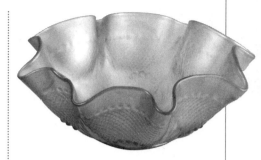

Although there are many ruffled carnival glass bowls, each is one of a kind, because the ruffles were formed by hand as the glass was cooling.

Dugan created what must be the ultimate "brand name" glass by incorporating cattle brand marks into its Round Up pattern.

Carnival glass is valued for pattern, iridescence, color, and shape. The patterns, as various and distinctive as the companies that manufactured them, are frequently naturalistic subjects, such as grapes, roses, and acorns; butterflies, peacocks, and other birds; and even entire summer landscapes. Collectors can choose to collect by pattern, color, or maker, and sometimes, all three.

The rims of Fenton's Open Edge Basket Weave bowls were shaped by hand, making each piece unique.

It can occasionally be difficult to tell the true color of carnival glass due to its very iridescence. In order to determine color, hold the piece up to a strong light—the base color you see is the true color. Certain shades, like the too abundant marigold, are less desirable, while the reds and pastels, which are rarer, are avidly collected.

Covered compotes, plates, and the more unusual large pieces can be quite costly, as can any size piece in a particularly rare pattern or color. Collectors usually

POOR MAN'S TIFFANY

At the *Antiques Roadshow* in New York City, a guest unpacked a carnival glass pitcher and five tumblers in the Grape and Cable pattern made by the West Virginia glass manufacturer Northwood that she had inherited from her grandfather. The set, made around 1908, had an iridescent finish—like that of soap bubbles.

"Northwood is one of the most desirable of carnival glass manufacturers," explained appraiser Reyne Haines. "They made anything and everything."

"I would love to own a Tiffany piece," the visitor noted. Instead, she has found about thirty additional pieces of carnival glass to add to her collection. "There are so many varieties and shapes and colors, you can always find something you like."

Although it is hard to assign value to a collection without knowing what pieces are included, if any make up a complete set, that set will add to a collection's worth.

examine the color and iridescence of a piece and consider the rarity of the pattern. Because there are reproductions (made using re-created molds) and restrikes (new pieces using the original molds) on the market, new collectors may find it difficult to differentiate between "old carnival" (1907 to 1920) and "late carnival" (made after its revival in the 1950s). As with all collectibles, visiting shows and examining pieces, talking with reputable dealers and knowledgeable collectors, and of course, reading as much material as you can find, is the best way to gain confidence.

STRETCH GLASS

Stretch glass was manufactured in the United States from 1916 to about 1930. Although its iridescence is reminiscent of carnival glass, stretch glass is another animal altogether—or vegetable, if you prefer, as it's often called "onion skin" because of the texture of the fin-

A well-proportioned Fenton compote, of blue stretch glass.

ish. Where carnival glass usually has a strong molded pattern, stretch glass is typically plain. Carnival glass was also worked (shaped) before the iridescence was applied, while stretch glass was iridized before it was shaped. The glass was pressed or blown into the mold, and while it was still hot, metallic salts were sprayed onto the surface to produce the iridescence. The piece was then shaped by hand—flared, crimped, cupped or pulled—causing the iridescence to "pull" on the surface and creating the characteristic "stretched" or "onion skin" finish. Depending on how much the piece was worked, the "stretch marks" may be obvious or very fine.

DEPRESSION GLASS

The inexpensive glass tableware manufactured by American firms from 1925 to 1940 has come to be called Depression glass. In just the four years between 1930 and 1934, the major

Evoking New York's Art Deco architecture, Hocking's Manhattan pattern appeals to both glass and Deco collectors.

manufacturers—Anchor Hocking, Indiana, Federal, Jeannette, MacBeth-Evans, and Hazel Atlas—introduced some forty patterns, not to mention those of Westmoreland, McKee, U.S. Glass, and Lancaster.

Depression glass was as diverse as it was inexpensive. Some designs were based on old patterns like the Indiana Glass Company's Indiana Sandwich, which was a reinterpretation of the nineteenth-century glass made in Sandwich, Massachusetts. Many others were influenced by Art Deco designs. The shapes and colors of this very commercial but attractive glassware were often inspired by earlier glass designs, the work of Tiffany, Gallé, and Loetz, for instance. Unlike its predecessors, however, Depression glass was neither blown nor hand detailed. It was pressed by machine into molds, and with the exception of "Elegant" glass (see page 91), it was treated to little or no hand finishing. Such cost-efficient manufacturing techniques left much Depression glass with sharp mold lines and, often, with extraneous clumps of extra glass adhering to handles and feet (filing them off would have added to labor costs). Sometimes there were flaws in the mold itself, and some pieces bear a "straw mark," a line on the surface of the glass that is the result of manufacture, not a crack (it won't widen). Some pieces lean or wobble a bit, and the same pattern may come in differing shades of the same color. For collectors, this is all part of the charm of Depression glass and doesn't affect the way they value individual items.

Depression glass is widely collected. In its gentle pinks and greens and ambers—colors the public loved and still loves—it

Sherbet was served in pleasing footed bowls like these in the Mayfair pattern produced by Hocking in the 1930s.

Jeannette Glass produced the Iris and Herringbone vase from 1928 to 1932. It was brought back by popular demand in the fifties.

Federal's cheerful Normandie berry bowls brightened oil cloth–covered thirties kitchen tables.

has its own charm. The use of color, in addition to the incised decorations on the glass mold, helped to conceal any defects or flaws in the glass. Huge and affordable services of colored dinner and kitchenwares could serve the Depression-era consumer everything from soup to nuts. Pieces of this popular colored glass were frequently given away as premiums in movie theaters or in boxes of laundry powder. In the 1930s, the Jeannette glass company's Sunflower cake plates were placed in bags of flour, and samples of Fire-King's Jane Ray pattern came "Free" with a fill-up at the gas station. Only the smaller pieces—the saucers, plates, small cups—could be packaged in soap and cereal boxes. Thus, there are many more of these smaller items for today's collectors than there are large pieces—pitchers and serving bowls, for example. Glass that still retains its original lid (many did not survive) is always desirable, too: butter dishes, sugar bowls, and candy dishes. Not surprisingly, even the lids by themselves are collectible!

There are dozens and dozens of Depression glass patterns, if not from A to Z, then at least from Adam to Windsor. New collectors often build their collection around pieces they already own or around patterns that are traditional or of visibly rising value. (If you'd like to use your collection as tableware, note that not all patterns include a full range of pieces, and choose your pattern accordingly.) Among the most popular patterns are: American Sweetheart and Dogwood by Macbeth-Evans; Cherry Blossom by Jeannette; Princess, Mayfair, Open Rose, Cameo, and Old Colony by Anchor Hocking; and Sharon by Federal. Some collectors assemble sets by color alone, choosing among royal ruby, forest green, Moroccan amethyst, and cobalt blue (especially popular in Royal Lace by Hazel Atlas). Jade-Ite, a translucent light green, has many fans, mainly in the numerous Fire-King items made by Anchor Hocking, although McKee's rival pattern, Laurel, is an almost identical green and has its own following. The most desirable colors can vary from pattern to pattern.

While most Depression glass was manufactured in brilliant colors and graceful pastels, there were still some popular patterns made of clear glass, including Iris by Jeannette and Manhattan by Anchor Hocking.

"ELEGANT" GLASS

"Elegant" is the term professionals apply to the glass stemware and dinnerware that brides from the twenties to the fifties received as wedding presents or purchased for their holiday tables. Thin, finely polished, decorative (it might be gilded, etched, cut, or plain), and sometimes colored, the "Elegant" Depression glass category includes large pieces as well as tableware: rose bowls, cruet sets, candelabrum, and compotes. It also includes the more expensive lines manufactured by many of the same companies that produced "everyday" Depression-era glassware: Heisey, Cambridge, Fostoria, Imperial, Tiffin, Duncan and Miller, Paden City, Morgantown, and others. This was the sort of glass that was saved for "company," and you can distinguish it from ordinary Depression glass by its somewhat more costly to manufacture hand detailing—fire-polishing to remove mold lines; applied feet or handles (added separately after the glass was taken from the mold), sometimes in contrasting colors; and by the generally high level of factory finishing. Collectors often try to assemble complete sets of patterns, Rose Point by Cambridge, for example, or Heisey's popular Orchid pattern (see page 94). In general, blue and red tints are more avidly sought after than yellow and amber.

IMPORTANT AMERICAN GLASS MANUFACTURERS

The following companies produced much of the American glass that attracts collectors.

CAMBRIDGE

The Cambridge Glass Company in Ohio first produced glass in 1901. The initial heavily pressed patterns imitated more labor-intensive and costly etched glass, and were marked "Near Cut." The 1920s saw the introduction of the Cambridge logo, a "C" within a triangle, which appeared on many (though not all) of the subsequent pieces. There was also a line of opaque colored glass, which included Crown Tuscan, an opaque pink color dating from 1932, and a black glass often encrusted with gold. Cambridge also produced popular figural pieces, called the "Statuesque" line.

Named for the opulent French Royal palace, Fostoria's Versailles pattern stood out among more prosaic Depression glass designs.

Cocktail party goers would have had a happy hour indeed pouring libations from Cambridge's "tipsy" amber decanter into matching shot glasses.

Two for tea: a multifaceted Ruba Rombic sugar and creamer (below), inspired by Cubist painting. At right, Consolidated's sensuous 1927 Catalonian vase.

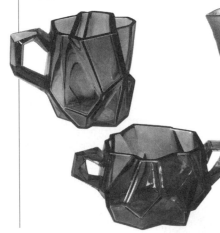

The 1930s saw the production, too, of ornate dinnerware, such as Caprice, Chantilly, and Rose Point. Despite choosing to make relatively expensive glass, the company survived the Depression and continued through the 1940s. In the early 1950s, an influx of cheap imported glass hastened Cambridge's demise. Imperial (see page 94) acquired some of the Cambridge molds in 1960 and reproduced a number of their pieces.

CONSOLIDATED

Consolidated is known today particularly for Ruba Rombic, perhaps its most collectible line. Produced by its art glassware division in Coraopolis, Pennsylvania, from 1928 to 1931, Ruba Rombic is quintessentially Art Deco in its Cubist appearance. About three thousand pieces of this geometric, angular colored glass, designed by Reuben Haley, are known to exist today. Because it exemplifies the most strongly Art Deco design of all commercial American Depression glass, Ruba Rombic is hotly pursued by collectors. Appraiser Reyne Haines comments, "One can hardly believe it was made by Consolidated, whose usual glass was always so much more derivative." The line included thirty-seven pieces, including dinnerware, vases, perfume bottles, and decanters, and appeared in sophisticated hues like jungle green, smoky topaz, and lilac.

Two other Consolidated lines are of note. One is the hand-wrought glass called Martele, also designed by Reuben Haley, which imitated Lalique's sculptured art glass so thoroughly that some pieces were, in fact, copies. Catalonian, the other well-known line, was produced using a technique whereby air bubbles were purposely introduced into the glass as part of the design. First produced in 1927, its rustic appearance lived up to its advertisement as "a replica of seventeenth-century glass made in the province of Catalonia, Spain."

FENTON

A pioneer in the making of carnival glass, Fenton Art Glass Company, based in West Virginia, created kaleidoscopic wares in the manner of the popular Tiffany Favrile glass. Fenton's Iridill or "Rainbow Lustre" glass was a huge success, and from 1907 through the 1920s, the company produced vast quantities of carnival glass in a variety of patterns. Fenton was innovative in developing new techniques as well as colors. One of the best was used to produce a glass that was patterned differently inside and out. This was achieved by carving both the mold and the plunger that pressed the glass into the mold, and the patterns didn't compete because carnival glass is opaque.

During the mid-1920s, Fenton briefly made a relatively costly line of decorative iridescent glass in brilliant shades of turquoise and the always difficult-to-manufacture red. With the onset of Depression-era economies, however, the firm adapted, as did so many of its competitors, by manufacturing kitchenware (citrus reamers and mixing bowls for electric mixers, among other items) and industrial glass. Toward the end of the 1930s, Fenton found great success with the Victorian-inspired Hobnail pattern. (Hobnail glass is covered with a regular pattern of raised knobs, rather like the hobnail studs on the soles of boots.) Hobnail perfume bottles made for Wrisley fragrances helped save the company from bankruptcy in 1937, and hobnail milk glass was successful again in the 1950s.

Sweet and low: Fenton's squat Hobnail pattern covered candy dish dates from the early 1950s.

FOSTORIA

Fostoria was one of the premier manufacturers of "Elegant" glass in the United States, competing with Heisey and Cambridge. (Such close competitors were these three, in fact, that their designs often closely resembled one another.) Fostoria Glass Company was established in 1887 in Fostoria, Ohio, but relocated, ultimately, to West Virginia, where it produced more than 1,150 glass patterns in its century of operation, many designed by George Sakier. Like other manufacturers of "Elegant" glass, its output was greatest from the late 1920s through the 1940s, when lines like Kashmir, June, Versailles, Trojan, and American were particularly successful—and they continue to attract today's collectors.

An unusual combination console bowl with attached candlesticks was designed by George Sakier for the Fostoria Glass Company.

The "Impromptu" pattern from Heisey features widely spaced circular bosses like those on this water pitcher from 1953.

The Heisey Glass Company's plain-Jane Yeoman line was the basis for many, more elaborate etched patterns. Here— an item rarely found on modern tables—the lemon dish.

HEISEY

Along with standard molded glass, the Heisey Company, founded in 1896 by a former glass salesman, produced quantities of blown glass in its Ohio factories. Heisey was originally known for making such good-quality pressed glass in such intricate patterns that it rivaled cut glass. In the 1920s, the company began producing "elegant" tableware in a number of brilliant colors. Its trademark, an "H" in a diamond (see page 80), was molded into the glass or attached as a paper label. Heisey Orchid etched glass—the line included everything from cocktail shakers to cigarette boxes—is perhaps its most highly sought after line.

IMPERIAL

Bring out the best—with Imperial's stylish beaded-glass Candlewick mayonnaise dish.

Because great quantities of energy and water are necessary to the manufacture of glass, the Ohio Valley, near rich coal deposits and rivers, has long been a crucible of American glass manufacture. The Imperial Glass Company, located in Bellaire, Ohio, was known particularly for its skillful mold cutting, and its expertise gave its products a distinct advantage over those of its competitors, since its well carved molds allowed Imperial to imitate expensive cut glass, especially in such lines as the pressed-glass Nucut. Imperial's Nuart line of iridescent glass, which, like so many others, imitated Tiffany, is also highly popular with glass collectors, as is its carnival glass. Produced in colors like blue, purple, green, and the always rare red, Imperial carnival glass typically incorporates elaborate patterns combining floral and geometric motifs. The company also produced several lines of Stretch glass (see page 88).

A ready to party Libbey late 1960s punch bowl with matching cups came all decked out with celebratory balloons.

Imperial introduced Freehand iridescent glass (unusual multicolored pieces made—as the name implies—without the use of molds or presses), which was a critical success but an economic failure, and further lines of iridescent glass such as Lead Lustre were unsuccessful as well. In 1931, the Quaker Oats company decided to use Imperial's new Cape Cod pattern as premiums in its products. It was this that enabled Imperial to last through the Depression and into more prosperous times, when Candlewick, a tableware pattern, became a huge seller. In 1973, Imperial became a subsidiary of Lenox, and changed hands a few more times before eventually declaring bankruptcy.

Imperial's beaded-glass Candlewick butter dish matches the mayonnaise dish on the facing page.

LIBBEY

Prior to World War I, the Libbey Glass Company of Toledo, Ohio, had enormous success with icily brilliant cut glass, a product that helped make it the largest glass manufacturer in the world. After the war, however, cut glass was deemed passé, and in order to survive, Libbey was forced to produce, among other things, garden-variety, machine-made drinking glasses. In 1933, the firm tried to resurrect its former glory by hiring prominent designers, including Walter Dorwin Teague and A. Douglas Nash, who had formerly worked with Louis Comfort Tiffany in New York. Nash created lines of expensive luxury ware for Libbey, glass that was sometimes cut, engraved, or hand etched. Some of the pieces were embellished with "tears" of contrasting colored glass—red on clear, for example. Libbey-Nash, as the work of Nash at Libbey is called, also produced a currently collectible stemware, including patterns such as American Prestige,

Due to Millersburg's brief life, everything made by the company is now highly collectible. Here, the Hanging Cherries pattern butter dish.

New Martinsville's Moondrops cordial and wine glasses, accompanied by a matching decanter.

Syncopation (very rare today), Silhouette (which featured a different animal on the stem of each type of wine glass), and Skyscraper. Nash's designs, however, were too expensive for the Depression era, and the line failed in 1935.

During World War II, Libbey was reduced once more to making restaurant wares and even vacuum tubes for radios. Although it produced some decent-quality glass lines in later decades, Libbey eventually turned away from luxury glass entirely. It is still in business today, manufacturing affordable tableware for restaurants and the home.

MILLERSBURG

John Fenton, who had started Fenton Glass in 1905 with his brother Frank, broke away in 1909 to establish his own glass-making business, hoping to match Fenton's success in manufacturing carnival glass. His Millersburg Glass Company in Millersburg, Ohio, produced glass for only three years before financial difficulties forced it to close, although it was briefly reorganized as Radium Glass Company in its final months. During that brief time, Millersburg made some of today's most collectible carnival glass. Sold as "Radium" glass, Millersburg's popular patterns include Morning Glory, Cherries, Courthouse Bowl, and various Peacock patterns. Due to its beauty and quality—as well as its rarity—Radium glass is highly sought after by collectors of carnival glass. While the firm is best known as a manufacturer of carnival glass, Millersburg also produced attractive crystal and satin glass.

NEW MARTINSVILLE

New Martinsville Glass Company was founded in 1900 in New Martinsville, West Virginia, and first distinguished itself by producing a type of Murano-style glass known as New Martinsville Peachblow. It manufactured a wide variety of "elegant" glass items during the Depression years, including tableware, tumblers, vanity sets (highly sought after by today's collectors), and lamps, in patterns such as Moondrops and Radiant. Strong, modern shapes in black glass are of particular interest to collectors. The company also manufactured a number of crystal animals, from squirrels to swans. In 1943, the company was purchased and renamed Viking Glass Company.

STEUBEN

Frederick Carder, an English glass designer, was long the resident genius of Steuben Glass Works, which he and a partner, Thomas G. Hawkes, founded in 1903 in Corning (Steuben County), New York. Initially, the firm produced iridescent art glass, competing particularly with Tiffany. In fact, some glass historians believe that Steuben's techniques for producing such glass actually predated Tiffany.

Steuben's line of "Aurene" glass, produced from the early part of the century until 1930, was one of Carder's greatest successes. Pieces today command steep prices. An advocate of brightly colored glass, Carder developed more than a hundred new glass colors during his tenure at Steuben, as well as thousands of shapes and styles of etched, cut, and cameo glass (see page 79).

Although Corning Glass Works acquired Steuben in 1918, Carder remained in charge. By the early 1930s, however, his aesthetic was going out of style, and in 1932, Carder stepped aside, although he continued to design art glass for the remainder of his life.

Industrial designer Walter Dorwin Teague was brought in for one year to refocus Steuben. He suggested that the company phase out its colored glass in favor of the clear, lead crystal Corning had recently created (10M). Thoroughly rejuvenated by the success of its new product, Steuben hired sculptor Sidney Waugh as chief designer. Waugh designed and executed, among other works, the noted copper-wheel-engraved Zodiac and Gazelle glass bowls of the 1930s.

Post-1932 Steuben glass can be easily recognized by its clarity and brilliance. Decorative vessels generally have thick walls and stand on some type of plinth or pedestal. Most Steuben glass is marked with the company trademark, a fleur-de-lis, which may have the name "Steuben" on a banner across it. Some Steuben glass is simply marked "Steuben," and the pre-1932 colored pieces by Frederick Carder are sometimes signed "F. Carder" or marked with the name of the glass—"Aurene," for example. Carder-era Steuben is also identifiable by its bright colors and elegant, romanticized forms.

A sinuously shaped Aurene vase, designed by Steuben's co-founder Frederick Carder in the early twentieth century.

The lively Gazelle bowl—one of sculptor Sidney Waugh's triumphs for Steuben Glass Works in the 1930s.

MEET IRENE GLASS

When the owner of this urn-shape vase brought it to the Tucson *Antiques Roadshow,* she explained that she had received it from her mother-in-law, who had owned it for about fifty years. The family always referred to the piece as Irene glass, though the guest

was not sure if that was the proper name.

Appraiser Reyne Haines was able to clear up the mystery for her. Although the piece was unsigned, Haines identified it as a piece of Aurene glass from Steuben. Usually found in simple blue or gold designs, this unusual example was decorated with a beautiful grapevine trailing around the shoulder of the vase.

The owner was delighted to hear it valued at $3,500 to $4,000.

EUROPEAN GLASS

While twentieth-century European glass varies widely from country to country and, to some degree, from glassmaker to glassmaker, there are a few qualities that all European glass shares. Centuries of tradition support its glassmakers, but the most successful of the twentieth-century craftsmen did not simply rest on old laurels or rely on decades-old patterns or styles. They enlivened and enriched their traditional techniques to suit the contemporary eye, and they all experimented, inventing scores of new processes. New materials and more sophisticated tools, many developed after World War II, challenged Europe's glassmakers to create amazing new styles. Because traditionally, European glass was often identified by the process used to make it, modern techniques, such as Ariel (Sweden), *battuto* (Italy), or *pâte de verre* (France), identify glass today.

The glass covered in the section that follows falls mainly into the category of art glass, although even when mass-manufactured, it was of the highest quality and design. There is little tableware here; the pieces that most interest collectors tend to be vessels: vases, bottles, and bowls.

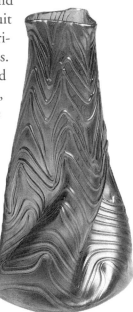

Loetz straight up with a twist! An unusual cylindrical vase of iridescent green pulled glass.

CZECHOSLOVAKIAN GLASS

Czech, or Bohemian, glass has a reputation for being either very good or very ordinary; indeed, the history of Czech glass is filled with highs and lows. Two companies that represent the "highs" are Moser and Loetz, both of which have roots in the Austro-Hungarian empire.

The Moser company was founded by Ludwig Moser in

1857. After Edward VII of England ordered a set of Moser crystal in 1907, the company came to be known as makers of "The Glass of Kings" and was commissioned to produce luxury glassware for other royalty and heads of state. Much of this crystal was elaborate and could combine cutting and etching with embossed gold and, of course, crests. The Germans took over Moser during World War II, but the company was reorganized in 1945 by the Communist party and ultimately was granted the right to operate independently. Moser is still in existence today, producing glassware based on designs created before the mid-1930s.

At the beginning of the twentieth century, Loetz's Art Nouveau and iridescent art glass, including Papillon (also called "oil spot") and Phenomenon (featuring colors applied to the pieces in a manner that looks almost free-form), acquired international renown. While it had some financial difficulties, Loetz continued to produce equally imaginative pieces through the Art Deco period.

After World War II, when Czechoslovakia was cut off from the West, the relative artistic freedom granted to glassmakers there resulted in a resurgence in the making of an idiosyncratic art glass. Cut and engraved pieces by artists like Jaroslav Horejc, and pieces in the Harrtil style—blown and inlaid internally with ribbonlike colored glass (much like Italian glass)—are only two examples of the imaginative styles of Czech glass of the postwar era.

The market for Czech glass, *Antiques Roadshow* appraiser Reyne Haines observes, is driven primarily by Loetz collectors. Although much Czech glass is vivid red or bright orange, the examples that collectors seem to prefer are the "Tango" pastels—pale blues, pinks, and white. (Tango glass vessels usually incorporate two different colors of glass, generally brightly colored, so the pastels are rare.) They are "driven wild," says Haines, by glass with unusual vertical stripes and ball feet. Other Czech glassmakers of note include Kralik and Rindskopf.

Moser's rectilinear yellow perfume bottles and powder box would have been right at home on the vanity table of a 1930s silver-screen star.

Czech mates: Two elaborately etched and gilded faceted glass vases by Moser.

SCANDINAVIAN GLASS

Throughout much of Scandinavia's glassmaking history, production consisted of inexpensive tableware, bottles, and glasses that imitated other styles, but in the twentieth century, an explosion of innovative glassmaking occurred almost simultaneously in Norway, Sweden, Denmark, and Finland. While each country has its own major manufacturers and designers, they share a similar aesthetic and vision.

When, in 1917, the Swedish government began to encourage its industrial manufacturers, including its glassmakers, to hire artists as designers, brilliance combined with innovation created remarkable glass. Between the 1920s and 1930s, acclaim for Swedish glass grew, with Orrefors and Kosta leading the way.

Taking advantage of Scandinavia's political stability and neutrality between the two world wars (a luxury enjoyed by few other European glassmaking countries), Sweden's neighbors followed suit. Norway's Hadelands glassmakers gained prominence; in Denmark, Kastrup and Holmegaards were the leading glassworks (the two companies merged in 1954); and from Finland came Nuutajärvi and the great Karhula and Iittala. Highly successful, all these factories followed Sweden's lead in hiring talented designers, and by the late 1940s and 1950s, Scandinavian art glass as a whole had achieved international prominence. Quintessentially "modern," Scandinavian glass was innovative, sleek, and minimalist.

Collectors of Scandinavian glass today search out pieces by favorite designers rather than manufacturers, because each had a distinct vision. In fact, some designers created designs for more than one company. None were studio artists, however. They were designers whose pieces were produced and marked by the individual manufacturers, the most important of which—with their most significant designers—follow.

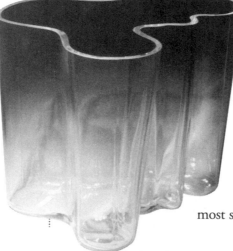

Iittala popularized elegant, avant-garde design with pieces like this 1950s mold-blown glass bowl by Tapio Wirkkala.

Designed by Alvar Aalto, the timeless Savoy vase has been in production for more than 70 years.

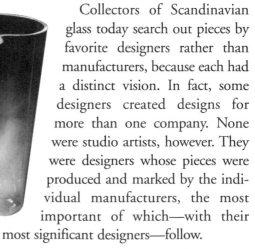

IITTALA

Founded in 1881, the Finnish company Iittala employed many important designers over the years, but perhaps the most prominent was Alvar Aalto. A virtuoso, Aalto designed buildings and furniture in the 1920s but did not work in glass until 1932. The enormously successful 1936 Aalto vases (also known as Savoy vases, after the restaurant in Helsinki in which they were used), with their undulant walls, reflect and echo Aalto's genius in furniture and architecture. They are still being produced successfully by Iittala today.

Tapio Wirkkala was a dazzlingly versatile Finnish designer who, like Aalto, worked in glass as easily and successfully as he worked in wood and metal. After World War II, Wirkkala designed for Iittala a series of abstractly organic vases that were inspired by the shapes of mushrooms. These were so unusual and seemingly so difficult to make that the company's workmen despaired of being able to reproduce his prototype successfully. Their fears proved groundless, and the Kantarelli (Chanterelle) line became enormously popular with the public, another triumph for avant-garde Finnish design.

A third important designer, Timo Sarpaneva, is known for his textiles and cast-iron cookware as well as his glass. Like his compatriot Tapio Wirkkala, he produced designs for Iittala in the 1950s, one of which, the Orchid vase, won *House Beautiful* magazine's award as "The Most Beautiful Object of the Year" in 1954. The Orchid vase remained in production at Iittala for nineteen years; a limited number of reproductions are now produced every year, with the date of manufacture clearly marked on each one. Wirkkala's Lancet vase, like the Orchid vase, features uniquely located or shaped interior cavities.

Working directly with the glassblowers on the factory floor, Sarpaneva experimented with many novel and unusual techniques, including a steam-blowing method that resulted in sculptural pieces called Kajakki. Later works, like his "i" decanters in blue, green, gray, and lilac, are cool and restrained, representing all that was satisfyingly minimalist and contemporary in Scandinavian glass design.

KOSTA

The glass created by Kosta's artists after World War I was clear and simple, and often wheel-engraved (cut with rotating abrasive

The internal bubble in Timo Sarpaneva's Orchid vase—today a classic of Iittala's output—will never pop.

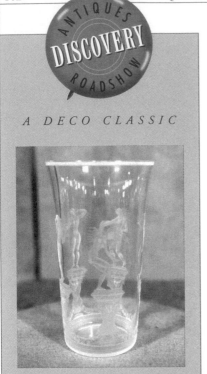

A DECO CLASSIC

This etched, clear-glass vase was a gift to the owner's father in the 1970s, given to him by a friend who had moved to California from the east in the mid-1900s. When appraiser Arlie Sulka spotted it at the San Diego *Antiques Roadshow* she pointed out that two artists were responsible for it: Simon Gate, a glass designer with a preference for the classical, and Gustaf Abels, the engraver who brought Gate's designs to life by etching them onto clear glass vases.

When she located a nearly invisible signature, Sulka was able to determine that this piece was produced by Gate and Abels for Orrefors in 1922, and she valued it at $2,500 to $3,500.

disks), like that of its archrival, Orrefors. Over time, Kosta's work became more sculptural, but by the late thirties, the glass was once again being engraved or deeply cut in stylized natural motifs.

In 1950, the talented Vicke Lindstrand joined Kosta. Refining the production of both its table glass and art glass, Lindstrand made Kosta the top name in Swedish glassware. While there, he worked in a number of techniques, designing engraved pieces, pieces that incorporated color, and vessels featuring controlled bubbles. Kosta is known today for welcoming guest artists to its factory, and the firm continues to produce noteworthy commercial glass, too, under the name Kosta Boda.

NUUTAJÄRVI

Although Nuutajärvi is an old and venerable Finnish company, it is primarily known for the work it produced after World War II, under the aegis of designer Gunnel Nyman, who created noteworthy household and art glass. Her pieces were often formed of thick glass walls encasing controlled patterns of air bubbles or spirals of opaque colored glass. In the 1950s, Kaj Franck took over design at the firm, creating streamlined, understated colored objects.

ORREFORS

Orrefors, perhaps the best known of the Swedish glass manufacturers, first achieved international prominence in the 1920s, when its two top designers, Simon Gate and Edward Hald, engraved the firm's distinctive crystal-clear product with witty stylized figures and animals. Working with master glassblower Knut Bergkvist, this team developed the complex and highly successful Graal technique, in which layers of colored glass are placed over clear glass, then cut through to create the pattern. Designer Sven Palmquist developed several techniques as well, among them Ravenna glass, wherein color is revealed through patterned openings in thick glass.

Orrefors' innovative techniques made possible remarkable patterns, as on the Ariel vase.

At Orrefors in the 1930s was Vicke Lindstrand, the star of Swedish post–World War I glass. He and his colleague Edvin Ohrström created Ariel glass, layering a coating of clear molded glass that entrapped shapely air bubbles over an opaque core. (Orrefors laid off Lindstrand during World War II, but the talented designer had no trouble finding employment with his former employer's chief competitor, Kosta.)

After World War II, Orrefors glass became heavier, and the firm's creative drive, as well as its considerable commercial success, was lost to competitors. Most Orrefors decorative objects found today in the United States are heavy, clear glass pieces with conventional designs. Although attractive, they are not as collectible as the firm's early, more imaginative work.

FRENCH GLASS

During the years when the Art Nouveau style was the rage, French glassmakers introduced several important new techniques, among them *pâte de verre,* cameo, and acid-etched glass. The Ecole de Nancy, an artistic association founded in 1904 by designer and glassmaker Emile Gallé and located in the town of Nancy, included among its members some of France's most important glass designers. When the fashion for French glass reached its height in the 1920s, French glass manufacturers like Lalique and Daum created the best of Art Deco glass. Listed below are the most important French glass designers of the twentieth century.

ARGY-ROUSSEAU

Argy-Rousseau is best known for *pâte de verre* glass. In mixing finely crushed glass with a binding agent, then molding it into the desired form and fusing it together at a high temperature, Gabriel Argy-Rousseau created a translucent, multicolored material. During the Art Nouveau period, Argy-Rousseau vases and bowls were appropriately delicate and floral, but after World War I, the firm was in the forefront of those incorporating Art Deco motifs, such as Egyptian details, gazelles, and stylized female forms into their products. Argy-Rousseau also produced a series of enameled glass perfume atomizers decorated with flowers, birds, and butterflies. The glassworks closed in 1931.

Two Argy-Rousseau pâte de verre *glass vases: top, "Lizard," with an ancient dancer, circa 1930, and "The Garden of the Hesperides," a place where golden apples granting immortality grew on golden trees, circa 1927.*

The beauty of Jean Daum's creations (like this cameo and enamel vase) indicate that this former French lawyer had found his true metier.

DAUM NANCY

In 1878, the French lawyer Jean Daum reluctantly took over a glassworks near Nancy in partial payment of a debt. With his son Auguste, he manufactured everyday glass such as watch faces and commercial drinking glasses advertised as "very heavy, for use in self-defense."

In 1889, after seeing the art glass of Emile Gallé at the Paris International Exhibition, Daum began producing Art Nouveau glass. Unlike some of its French contemporaries, Daum Nancy, as the company was called, was able to change with the times. While other glassmakers struggled after the end of the Art Nouveau movement, Daum went on after World War I to make interesting Art Deco wares, producing thick bowls and vases, typically monochromatic, with geometric patterns deeply etched in the glass. The finest Daum dates from before 1935.

Somewhat less in demand is the Daum lead crystal glass created in the 1940s and 1950s, known as Crystal Daum, as well as a thick-walled art glass infused with thousands of tiny bubbles.

GALLÉ

Those who know only the pre–World War I Art Nouveau work of Emile Gallé (the factory closed in 1914) may be surprised to learn that Gallé's son-in-law reopened the works after World War I to manufacture Art Deco glass. He produced predominantly lamps and vases but also created pale-colored cameo-glass pieces—most with landscape and floral designs, some with animal motifs—that compare favorably with the best decorative glass of the 1920s. Gallé finally ceased production in 1936.

LALIQUE

"Lalique was the best glass designer of the twentieth century," says *Antiques Roadshow* appraiser and Lalique expert Nick Dawes. Yet French designer René Lalique didn't begin his career in glass. He achieved his first success with idiosyncratic, naturalistic jewelry designs. When he did turn to glass, his designs for perfume bottles were so well received that he ceased making jewelry altogether. It was Lalique's intention to popularize his glass without cheapening it in any way. To that end, and with great success, he himself designed everything his glassworks

René Lalique's satiny frosted glass is instantly identifiable even to non-collectors. Here, a stately vase enlivened with decorative birds.

mass-produced—picture frames, chandeliers, even car hood ornaments—employing assembly-line techniques, with nothing made by hand. Standards of production were unusually high at the factory, as well, and the molded glass created there was so crisp as to seem almost carved.

Mass-produced, but impeccably designed, Lalique's hobnail Mossi vase.

Strong Art Deco design was Lalique's forte, and the company's popularity and commercial success engendered innumerable imitations. Before 1930, Lalique glass is clear with a partially frosted finish. After that date, it is almost all frosted, whether clear or colored. Lalique glass is always marked. Signatures are molded, engraved, stenciled, or wheel cut. Although there are exceptions, generally glass made before Lalique's death in 1945 is marked "R. Lalique." Glass made after his death is marked "Lalique."

Although it is stylish and easily recognizable, much of the mass-produced Lalique glass is of limited collectibility, because so much of it was made. The good news is that there are plenty of less-expensive pieces available. This means that genuine pieces can be quite reasonably priced and unquestionably authentic, as well.

MARINOT

French Art Deco glassmaker Maurice Marinot began his artistic life as a painter. (He was one of the original artists, in fact, to be involved in the Fauve movement, led by Henri Matisse.) When he began to blow glass in 1919, he developed textural vessels that combined "accidental" flights of air bubbles with visible handwork. Later, he blew metallic oxides between layers of glass to add colors. Typically, Marinot bottles (usually stoppered) and vases are small in scale. A true "studio" artist, Marinot worked each of his heavy pieces of glass himself, employing no assistants, thus Marinot glass is always one of a kind. He created over two thousand pieces before bad health forced him to stop glassmaking in 1937; he spent his remaining days painting and drawing.

RARE BERRIES

The visitor to the Miami *Antiques Roadshow* who brought with him this interesting perfume bottle had purchased it more than twenty

years before, paying $110 for it. After he brought it home, he noticed that the bottle was signed "R. Lalique," and that the bottle and stopper were each marked with the same number.

Appraiser Louise Luther explained that the design of this Lalique piece was named Blackberry, after the beautiful blue color used on the "tiara" stopper. The matching numbers ensure that the stopper is fitted to the bottle it was made for.

The Blackberry design is extremely rare, and the bottle's value is between $20,000 and $25,000.

One of a kind: As with all his creations, this diminutive stoppered bottle was fashioned solely by Maurice Marinot.

The bold modern designs of the venerable Venetian firm of Barovier & Toso are shown to advantage in this teardrop-shaped vase.

SCHNEIDER

Charles and Ernest Schneider began their careers working at the French glass firm Daum Nancy (see page 104), but left to open their own glass factory outside Paris in 1913. Closed during World War I, the company reopened afterward, becoming a noted producer of chic Art Deco styles.

Several lines were sold simultaneously, of which two are especially collectible. One—luxury glass—simply carried the Schneider signature on the bottom; the other, less costly, was Le Verre Français (and was signed "Charder," *Char* for Charles, *der* for Schneider). Brilliant orange and lemon colors, splashed, mottled, and swirled, are typical of the Schneider line, along with applied handles and feet in contrasting colors. Early on, the Le Verre Français line (made from 1918 to 1933) was primarily inexpensive molded glass, frequently decorated with enameled floral designs. Later, the line was expanded into better-quality cameo-glass lamps and vases.

ITALIAN GLASS

Since the thirteenth century, the center of the Italian glassmaking community has been on the Venetian islands of Murano. From there, Italy led the entire glassmaking world in complex techniques like *millefiori* (which really does resemble "a thousand flowers") and *lattimo,* opaque milk glass. Proprietary techniques were passed down from father to son, and foreigners were unwelcome.

In the nineteenth century, Italy's supremacy was challenged by glassmakers from Bohemia (now the Czech Republic), England, and France, and Venetian glassmakers found themselves struggling to catch up to the rest of the world. While many glassmakers never broke away from the old ways, several of Murano's best, in the early decades of the twentieth century, proved that they could combine centuries of tradition with modern processes to create brilliant, innovative, distinctive glass.

BAROVIER & TOSO

Both Barovier and Toso are Venetian families with centuries-old glassmaking traditions. Ercole Barovier, who became a managing director of his family's company in 1920, was a noted designer of Art Deco glass, but he also oversaw the merger of the Barovier and Toso glassmaking interests in 1936. (The company went through several name changes, finally becoming Barovier & Toso.)

The combined firm of Barovier & Toso continued to create traditional pieces like the high-quality *murrine* glass that both families had long been known for, but together they developed new techniques, including, in the 1930s, *crepuscolo*, in which steel or copper wool was used to create patterns between layers of glass, and *primavera*, a milky white glass in a cobweb pattern that Barovier is said to have invented by accident. Barovier & Toso glassmaking reached its peak in the 1950s with glass in bold designs and bright colors, some incorporating touches of gold or rough, matte finishes. The firm is still in business today.

There were two other Murano glassmaking companies started by (and named for) different branches of the Toso family, neither associated with Barovier & Toso. One, a Murano glass company called Fratelli Toso, originated in 1854. Much of its output, therefore, is before the era of collectibles, though it did produce high-quality art glass in the early part of the twentieth century. The other company, named for its founder, Aureliano Toso, opened for business in 1937. Designer Dino Martens produced brilliant modern art glass for Aureliano Toso from 1939 to 1959. One of Martens's characteristic techniques was *zanfirico*, in which glass threads are embedded in blown glass to create a pattern. Martens's work for Aureliano Toso is highly collectible today.

VENINI

The Murano firm of Venini, founded in 1921, dominated Italian glass from the moment it was awarded a Grand Prize at the Art Deco exhibition in Paris in 1925. Famous for both witty glass animals and large architectural pieces—even chandeliers and stained glass windows—Venini glass combined fine, improvisational design with masterful craftsmanship. In its first years, Venini's art director was sculptor Napoleone Martinuzzi, who in the late 1920s produced plants and animals and vases using techniques like *vetro pulegoso*, in which hundreds of tiny bubbles make the glass virtually opaque.

A masterfully wrought Barovier & Toso free-blown bottle with black corroso surface, colored by metallic powders and gold insertions.

A member of Venini's noted glass menagerie, this bird is the work of Tyra Lundgren.

UNAPPRECIATED

At the *Antiques Roadshow* in Baltimore, Vivian Highberg was asked to appraise an unusual vase—shaped like a female

nude with an hourglass figure. The vase had been purchased by the father of the owner for $50, and he had named it Evelyn after his wife—who did not appreciate the gesture. Somewhat less controversially, this vase also can be seen as a cat with two eyes and two ears.

Highberg explained that the piece was designed and signed by Italian glass designer Fulvio Bianconi and manufactured by Venini (see page 107) in Murano, Italy, between 1929 and 1956. Perhaps Evelyn would appreciate her namesake more today—the rare vase is currently worth $8,000 to $10,000.

The architect Carlo Scarpa, design director of the firm from 1933 to 1947, employed traditional Venetian processes to create innovative glass, but under his stewardship, Venini successfully modernized its *filigrano* (glass having an internal ornament of preformed filigree glass rods creating weblike designs) and *murrine* (glass incorporating slices of glass canes—*millefiori*—to create a mosaic effect). Scarpa invented new techniques, too, among them, *tessuto* (woven), where freely applied threads of color were incorporated into the glass, and several new wheel-grinding techniques. *Velato* (veiled) gives the surface a matte finish, *inciso* (incised) scores it with spiraling lines, and *battuto* (beaten) does the same with small cuts that resemble fish scales in appearance.

Venini closed down during the war but resumed production afterward with a number of talented and versatile designers. Fulvio Bianconi created flamboyant figures from the commedia dell'arte, invented the *pezzato* designs that resemble multicolored patchwork, and the famous *fazzoletto* (handkerchief) vase, resembling a billowy kerchief frozen in glass. Other great postwar designers include Gio Ponti, Riccardo Liccata, Massimo Vignelli, and Tobia Scarpa (the son of Carlo).

In an unprecedented move, Venini eventually opened its glassworks at Murano to foreign glass artists, among them Finland's Tapio Wirkkala (see page 101) and America's Dale Chihuly (see page 81), finally sharing the secrets of Murano's glassmakers with the rest of world.

VETRERIA ARCHIMEDE SEGUSO

Descended from a long line of famous Murano glassmakers, Archimede Seguso is acclaimed for lacy *merletto* vases and other *filigrano* (filigree) pieces that his company made and exhibited at several Venice Biennales during the 1950s. His gold leaf–dusted human figures, birds, and fish are popular with collectors. Seguso's glass pays homage to the traditional shapes of antique Venetian wares while employing variations on the old techniques. (The *filigrano* technique dates

A rare filigreed gourd-shaped bottle by Murano master Seguso.

to the thirteenth century, but Seguso is credited with reinvigorating it.) His work is also distinct and modern in its simplicity of volume and shape.

DUTCH AND GERMAN GLASS

While neither the Netherlands nor Germany enjoys the reputation for masterful glassmaking that some of its European neighbors do, both countries produced notable twentieth-century glass that is enthusiastically collected today, Holland's Leerdam and Germany's WMF, particularly.

LEERDAM

Leerdam, outside of Rotterdam in the Netherlands, has been a glassmaking center since 1765, but it wasn't until 1878 that standard tableware, decanters, and containers began to be produced there. At the beginning of the twentieth century, Leerdam rejected the flowery excesses of Art Nouveau in favor of a Modern aesthetic intended to reflect modern life. It was influenced by Holland's De Stijl movement (led by painter Piet Mondrian), which advocated simple, logical design with an emphasis on function. In 1912, under the direction of P. M. Cochius, Leerdam commissioned talented architects and designers to create well-designed glass for everyday use. In the twenties, architect Hendrik Pieter Berlage and his colleague Piet Zwart created stylized, modern, and somewhat impractical tableware for the firm: a tableware in which cup handles, for instance, lacked the usual, usable loop and were, instead, pads of solid glass. Potter Chris Lanooy soon joined the company to design colorful glass, including the "Orange Apple" vase created for the eighteenth birthday of Princess Julia in 1927.

Pieces from Leerdam's strongly sculptural, free-blown Unica series, designed by its foremost designer, Andries D. Copier, received a silver medal at the Paris Art Deco exposition. Copier's Serica, a less expensive line, followed in the 1930s. Its thick-walled pieces contain combinations of controlled bubble patterns and cracked glass effects. Both are highly sought after by today's collectors. Copier also produced his own Orange Apple vase for the birth of Princess Beatrix in 1938, although perhaps his most famous design is the Gilde wine glass. First

A masked bird ready for Carnivale in Venice is by Fulvio Bianconi for Seguso.

Dutch treat: A perfectly proportioned crystal bottle and stopper from the Netherlands, by Andries Copier.

Aerodynamic freeform bowl (circa 1950) with spiraled ribbons of color, by Floris Meydam for the historic Dutch firm of Leerdam.

WMF Ikora-Kristall bowl with an elaborate pattern of air bubbles and an abstract, multi-color design in the center.

produced in 1930, it is considered a modern icon and is still being made today.

After World War II, Floris Meydam created glass designs for the Unica and Serica lines that were in keeping with the tastes of the fifties and sixties. His crystal objects feature geometric shapes like cylinders, circles, and teardrops. At one point, Frank Lloyd Wright designed glass for Leerdam, but the forms proved to be too technically difficult to manufacture, and most of his designs remained in the production stage; only one of Wright's vases was ever made.

WMF

WMF, or Württembergische Metallwarenfabrik, in Stuttgart, Germany, was primarily a metalworks, but glass was also made there. After the original glassworks was destroyed during World War I, a more modern facility was opened in 1922, and new glass designers were employed. Noted in the mid-1920s for Myra-Kristall, a glass with an iridescent surface, this German firm also manufactured Ikora-Kristall, a line of glassware incorporating colored inlays and patterns of bubbles in forms like free-blown wide and shallow bowls, touched with iridescent powders and sometimes enameled in colors. WMF's best glass was produced between 1926 and 1936.

Chapter Four

SPORTS COLLECTIBLES

A century ago, an Italian immigrant to America discovered a new passion in a new home. "He came here at the turn of the century and fell in love with baseball," his daughter told appraiser Kathleen Guzman at the Hartford *Antiques Roadshow*. "The game was the American dream to him." Following that dream, her father had befriended legendary baseball personalities and collected everything associated with them: Autographed baseballs, signed photographs, and some fifty fascinating letters.

The most valuable piece in the collection turned out to be a personal letter he had received when he was ill, from New York Yankees great Lou Gehrig, then in the fourteenth year of his Hall of Fame career. Guzman told the visitor, "This letter is so wonderful because it is a personal letter from Lou Gehrig on Lou Gehrig stationery saying he's sorry about your father's illness." She then noted, "And 1936 was probably not long before Gehrig began to realize that he was seriously ill himself." Three

Top: A panoramic photograph of the 1952 New York Yankees, signed by twenty-four of the players. Above: The cover of the 1887 Allen & Ginter Champions Album which inside pictured all fifty cards from the N28 set—including ten baseball players.

A 1950s advertising sign for Yoo-Hoo Chocolate Beverage (The Drink of Champions) shows Yankee greats Yogi Berra and Mickey Mantle enjoying a cool drink while the game goes on in the background. The value of this sign is greatly enhanced by having signatures of both players.

years later, the "Iron Horse" would walk away from the Yankees lineup after playing in a record 2,130 consecutive games. Two years after that he was dead of amyotrophic lateral sclerosis (ALS), which would come to be known as "Lou Gehrig's Disease." Gehrig, a New York Yankee and a Hall of Famer, was a beloved figure whose fame transcended sports, all of which makes anything associated with him extremely collectible. Letters from Gehrig are quite rare, as the surprised visitor learned when she was told that her father's treasured letter was worth $6,000 to $8,000.

This *Antiques Roadshow* vignette illustrates two important points about sports memorabilia collecting. The first is that it is no longer a male domain. In the past, it seemed as if a woman's only interest was to toss out all of her son's baseball cards the moment his back was turned, and with the advent of tag sales, clean out the attic and sell her (otherwise occupied) husband's old gloves, footballs, hockey sticks, autographed bats and balls, basketballs, and Kentucky Derby and Daytona 500 programs for a total of $1.75. These days, the sports collecting business is so ubiquitous that women who don't know the Jets from the Mets do know that cards and artifacts can be treasures. Moreover, many women are becoming sports memorabilia collectors themselves.

The second point to be gleaned from this *Roadshow* discovery is that sports fans have long collected memorabilia to "connect" with their heroes. They hope to capture forever, in a tangible way, a part, even just a moment, of the famous athlete's life, and share in a bit of sports history. They keep this alive for years by displaying their keepsakes and telling their stories. Not coincidentally, collecting sports cards, autographs, and artifacts always has been a way to preserve Americana. The collecting of sports memorabilia, particularly of baseball's treasures, has saved a distinct, romantic piece of the past.

A pair of Rawlings size 8 Mickey Mantle baseball shoes from the 1950s, with their original box, featuring a picture of Mantle on the label.

With the twentieth-century boom in sports memorabilia, nearly every sport (and the Olympics as well) acquired thousands of devotees trying to build interesting collections of personal and, at least potentially, financial value. Autographs, trading cards, equipment, clothes, posters, prints, media guides, flags, commemorative coins, cereal boxes, programs, medals, pins, board games, figurines, bobble-head dolls (nodders), plates, miniature stadiums, photographs, pennants, magazine covers, books, recordings, signs, stadium items, tickets, beer cans, bottles, mugs, caps, and innumerable sports-related items are coveted by fans of everything from baseball, basketball, football, and hockey, to boxing, horse racing, golf, and tennis, to the increasingly popular motor sports and wrestling. Indeed, the sports collecting field is so vast and diverse that it seems the better part of valor to limit this chapter to three time-honored, very different sports, each with a strong collecting base. While enthusiasts of baseball, golf, and fishing items may never rub shoulders, what they do share with one another and with collectors in other sports as well, is a methodology of collecting, and extensive knowledge of and passion for their sports.

The collecting of sports memorabilia is largely concerned with the athletes we've come to love and hate with the passions that the ancient Greeks reserved for their gods. Not all sports, however, have gods. There are sports for introverts—thoughtful and quiet—such as fishing, a solitary communion with nature and only incidentally with strength and ego. And there is golf, a sport that has heroic aspects and introspective ones. People who collect golf memorabilia are collecting its stars, Ben Hogan, Arnold Palmer, and Tiger Woods, to be sure; but they are also collecting an experience: the scent of mown grass, the passage of sun and clouds on hot summer days.

Even grand old baseball is not solely about heroes (though baseball memorabilia collecting is undeniably star driven). It's also about sunshine and grass and equipment.

A bulger made by Robert Forgan circa 1890. This type of driver, shorter and broader than a long-nose golf club and with a bulging face, was introduced by Henry Lamb in 1888.

R. FORGAN

OHIO STATE HOMECOMING BANDANA

Most sports memorabilia was not made for posterity, but merely for the day of the game. A football bandana, to be waved by Buckeyes' fans attending an Ohio State homecoming game, appeared at the Columbus, Ohio, *Antiques Roadshow.* Appraiser Daniel Buck Soules noted that the runner depicted on the bandana, his arm extended to ward off tacklers, is carrying a football that is longer and leaner than the earliest ones. This more aerodynamic football, introduced in the early 1900s, could be thrown more accurately, and added an exciting passing element to what had previously been a solely ground game. The bandana's owner paid $40 for it. Soules told him, "It's got the history. It's got the right sport. It's got a great litho on it. It's just an incredible piece and we feel that it's worth somewhere between $1,000 and $1,500." That is, providing that the sale be made in Ohio. Outside Ohio, and away from the Buckeyes' ferocious fan base, the bandana loses some of its value. Referring to regional football rivalries, Soules noted: "If I tried to sell that bandana in Michigan, someone might hang me."

OLYMPIC MEMORABILIA

A collection of Olympic memorabilia brought to the Sacramento *Antiques Roadshow* for appraisal included a 1924 gold medal and a bronze one.

Appraiser David Lackey (eventually) confirmed that in 1924, rugby was an Olympic event, and valued the gold medal at $2,000 to $3,000, the bronze at $500. Lackey explained that had the medals been acquired in an individual rather than a team sport, they would have slightly higher values.

The real gem of the collection, however, was a commemorative vase made by the premier French porcelain company, Sèvres. The pate-sur-pate design on the vase depicts athletes surrounded by a laurel leaf pattern, and is marked on the bottom with the names of both the designer and the sculptor. A real *pièce de résistance,* this vase would have been desirable even at the time it was made. It alone has a value of $5,000 to $7,000. As a collection, these items from the 1924 Olympics might bring $8,000 to $12,000 at auction.

It's a still continuing saga of immigration and integration; a story of photography, of advertising, of technology, and of big business, as well. At its best, baseball will always be America at its best. At its worst? Well, even that's collectible.

BASEBALL

Baseball memorabilia is a rich amalgam made up of the history of a 150-year-old game ("town ball" was played in the 1830s; soldiers played "base ball" during the Civil War; and the first professional league was formed in 1871), hero worship, nostalgia, and—in recent years—financial speculation. Look up baseball collectibles on the Internet and you will find an astonishing number of sites leading you to collectors, dealers, historians, clubs, publications, auctions, price lists, and innumerable areas of specialization. There is perhaps no better indicator of the size of the current baseball market, and no better caveat for the new collector.

Frequently, when a field undergoes such great expansion, the fallout is mixed. Increased popularity, for instance, brings increased understanding of historical significance and of the need for preservation. It also results in a profusion of convincingly marketed "collectible" merchandise—and enough collectors gullible enough to buy it—with a significant amount of misrepresented or out-and-out fake material being sold. As a result, it is a challenge for collectors of baseball memorabilia to determine authenticity and value before making a deal.

When starting a collection, the temptation is to buy a little bit of everything, and that's not a bad idea while you're familiarizing yourself with the field. But once you learn how much is available and come to realize that it is impossible to buy even one one-thousandth of everything that tempts you—there are more than 10,000 sets of baseball cards alone!—you'll begin to focus on what really appeals to you and what you can afford. If you want to collect things that are more likely to retain their value or increase in value in addition to being personally satisfying, make sure they are also things that a substantial number

The 1912 New York Giants World Series Press Pin. The medal lion features an image in relief of a batter and catcher and reads "New York Giants vs. Boston Red Sox" in relief.

of collectors want. Hold on to those things you absolutely love, but remember that in selling off what you don't really need, with the proceeds you can buy items that improve your collection.

Collectors believe this is part of the learning curve of collecting. A new collector, however, can shorten or soften that curve by concentrating on a player, a team, or a particular type of collectible, and ultimately, become an expert in a neatly circumscribed field. As an expert on certain cards, or bats and balls, or autographs, or All Star–game memorabilia, for example, you will know where to look for essential items; how to find the dealers who will give you the best prices; be able to identify and determine the age and condition of examples of your specialty; and develop a knowledge of and keen eye for what is authentic and what is fake.

With the escalation of prices has come a proliferation of forgeries and misrepresentations. Many dealers of memorabilia offer letters of authenticity. If legitimate, these can be a valuable source of information and provide documentation of an item's history and provenance. Bogus letters of authenticity, however, can be used by the unscrupulous to create spurious provenance

A photograph of George Herman (Babe) Ruth signing baseballs in the Yankee dugout, circa 1927. The Babe elevated baseball signing to an art.

A BASEBALL OF HER OWN

Not all sports memorabilia is masculine. Kathleen Guzman appraised an unusual artifact from women's baseball at the Chicago *Antiques Roadshow.* "I went to a house sale, and found this baseball from a 'girls' league," explained the *Roadshow* guest. "So I bought it's for, I think, a quarter." Years later, when the movie *A League of Their Own* came out in 1992, she took it out of the drawer and, sure enough, it was from the All-American Girls Professional Baseball League.

"Ninety percent of the sports memorabilia market is baseball," Guzman told her. "Mostly Babe Ruth and Lou Gehrig, and mostly it's men." This 1950 team ball, however, crammed with signatures of female players, included pitching star Beverly Hatzell.

The visitor had taken the ball to several sports memorabilia shows, but none of the male experts there could give her any idea of the ball's value. Guzman said she had seen only one other signed ball from the AAGPBL. Despite its having been shellacked, which compromised its condition, that ball still sold for $4,200. Of her 25 cent purchase, the stunned visitor said, "This is going to the vault!"

A card from Allen & Ginter's 1888 set of baseball cards, showing pitcher John Clarkson of the Boston Beaneaters, a predecessor of the Braves.

An early baseball card featuring Boston Beaneaters pitcher John Clarkson in a wooden pose is from a series put out by Old Judge Cigarettes.

and establish a false value, and such ploys are often used to soothe a consumer's qualms. Letters of authenticity and guarantees are only as good as the people that provide them. Because fluctuating market trends and authenticity issues are compounded by the unusually high prices being paid for superstar material these days, sound practice means dealing only with people who have a proven track record and who stand behind their claims. Collecting involves both heart and mind, and enthusiasm should be tempered by knowledge and caution.

BASEBALL CARDS

To many, baseball-memorabilia collecting means card collecting. Certainly every true baseball fan—including many who aren't memorabilia collectors—has spent pocket change on cards, and almost everyone who does collect memorabilia has at least a few cards.

A BRIEF HISTORY

Although the very first baseball card has yet to be identified, it is known that baseball cards were in circulation in the later part of the nineteenth century. Many credit their origin to the trade, or advertising cards first issued in the late 1860s by Peck & Snyder, a distributor of baseball equipment. These cards, with their photographs of prominent teams of the day pasted to a cardboard mount, are rare, and today a Peck & Snyder Trade Card of the 1869 Cincinnati Red Stockings, the hard-drinking, heavy-gambling first professional team—subsequently the dominant team of the first pro league, the National Association (1871 to 1876)—is worth around $20,000.

It's pretty well accepted that the first legitimate, nationally distributed baseball cards were package (or box) inserts with Old Judge, Gypsy Queen, and other Goodwin & Co. cigarettes. Sold between 1886 and 1890, they featured such National League stars as Cap Anson and King Kelly, and at 1½ by 2½ inches, they were smaller than the cards of today. Allen & Ginter, D. Buchner & Co., Lone Jack Cigarette Co., and P. H. Mayo & Brother issued other early tobacco cards. A few companies also made larger examples called "cabinet cards" or "cabinets." In 1891, several tobacco companies, Allen & Ginter among them, consolidated into the American Tobacco Company, a behemoth that so dominated the competition that the company saw no need to continue to insert cards into its products in order to attract customers. That is, until Turkish tobacco products came to the United States, sometime prior to 1910.

Card collecting was a national craze from 1909 until 1915, as caramel candy companies joined American and Turkish cigarette companies in offering beautifully colored cards depicting America's ballpark heroes. (Twentieth-century tobacco cards are designated with the letter "T"; early candy company cards are marked with the letter "E.") Today's high-end collectors seek premium-condition cards from such sets as the T3 Turkey Reds, the most popular cabinet cards ever produced; the T202 Hassan triple folders; and the E145 Cracker Jacks, the only major set to feature players from the short-lived Federal League. However, the most important set of the era was the T206 cards issued by the American Tobacco Company in 1909. It includes the most valuable item in the entire sports collecting field—the Honus Wagner tobacco card. Because the eight-time National League batting champion didn't want children to think he advocated smoking, he insisted that his image be removed after only a few cards had been issued. (There are those, however, who claim the real reason was that he wanted more money for the use of his image.) Of this small number of Wagner cards, only a few have survived in near-mint condition, and these are the trade's Holy Grail. At an auction in 2000, one went for $1,265,000! An Eddie Plank card, limited because of a broken printing press plate, and the Sherry Magee cards on which his name was misspelled are two of the other rare cards from this set that are coveted by most dedicated collectors.

After World War I and until the early thirties, caramel candy companies—and to a lesser extent, ice cream companies—supplanted tobacco companies as the major producers of trading cards. Most of these cards were in black and white, however, and lacked graphic interest, and as a result collectors have never been especially enthusiastic about this era. The development of chewing gum, nevertheless, spurred a new boom in cards, and by 1933 and 1934, four Boston-based companies had issued

WAGNER, World's Champions

An early Honus Wagner card, but not the Honus Wagner card. This example is from a regional set issued in 1910 by a Pittsburgh bakery, Tip Top Bread.

A page from a Cracker Jack album with eight baseball cards, including Pittsburgh great Honus Wagner. These albums were available by mail and used for saving the baseball cards included as prizes in boxes of Cracker Jack. The cards are very desirable, but minor caramel staining is a common conditional problem.

inaugural sets: Goudey, George C. Miller Co., Delong, and National Chicle. These cards were 2½ inches square and were the first to feature expanded statistics on the reverse. Goudey's "Big League Gum Cards," with their impressive designs and full-color drawings on thick stock, were far more beautiful than those produced by its predecessors or competitors and are the priciest set of the era. Near-mint 1933 Goudey cards of Babe Ruth and fellow Hall of Famer Nap Lajoie (whose 1933 card was distributed with the 1934 set) have been auctioned in recent years for more than $100,000.

Depression-era paper shortages curtailed the production of baseball cards in the mid-thirties. Oddly, it was during this time that serious baseball card collecting developed, thanks to the efforts of Jefferson Burdick of Syracuse, New York. The "father of baseball card collecting" became interested in old cards not because he liked baseball (he didn't) but because he loved paper products. After corresponding with baseball card collectors, he realized their need for solid information. In 1937, a year, ironically, when no major company produced a major, nationally issued set, Burdick published the groundbreaking first checklist, *The American Card Catalog.* In 1947 he donated his own card collection, dating back to the 1880s, to New York's Metropolitan Museum of Art.

The burgeoning interest in card collecting caused Goudey to come back with a 1938 set; and a new company, Gum, Inc., of Philadelphia, issued its own Play Ball cards between 1939 and

LEROY "Satchell" PAIGE

Ted Williams

JIMMY FOXX, Red Sox

1941. The Goudey, Play Ball, and Double Play prewar cards are very popular with today's high-end collectors. In fact, a mint condition Joe DiMaggio 1941 Play Ball card was purchased at auction in 1999 for $109,000. Collectors who are more interested in history than investment value can find less-than-mint-condition cards from these, and other old sets, at reasonable prices.

World War II shut down card production, but in 1948, a new era in card collecting began when Bowman (formerly Gum, Inc.) and another chewing gum company, Leaf, issued card sets. The single 1948–49, 98-card set manufactured by Leaf—with its higher-priced cards of Satchel Paige, Joe DiMaggio, Babe Ruth, Bob Feller, and Jackie Robinson—now sells in mint condition for $20,000 to $30,000, almost ten times more than the going rate for the easier-to-find 48-card Bowman set.

In 1951, baseball card collecting was changed forever when Topps Chewing Gum Company of Brooklyn, New York, entered the market to challenge Bowman. Although its first set of blue- and red-back cards weren't as attractive as Bowman's, they were successful. The following year it produced a 407-card set that would set the standard for card size (2½ by 3½ inches) and come to be regarded as the most desirable of all sets produced after World War II. Mint cards of ordinary players sell for $60 to $100; scarce cards of Willie Mays, Eddie Mathews, Roy Campanella, Jackie Robinson, and Andy Pafko (the first card in the set) go for four-figure sums. The prize is the fabled Mickey Mantle card, which has changed hands privately for an astounding $275,000.

Three classic baseball cards from three different years, in three different formats. From the left: The 1949 Bowman rookie card of Cleveland Indian Leroy "Satchell" [sic] Paige (they should have spelled it "Satchel"); the very rare 1954 Bowman number 66 Ted Williams card, pulled by Bowman because of a contractual problem relating to Williams's endorsement of their competitor, Topps Gum (subsequently, the 1954 number 66 pictured his teammate Jimmy Piersall); and Boston Red Sox batting star Jimmy Foxx from the 1938 Goudey "Heads-Up" set, comprised of 48 cards showing each of the twenty-four players twice (the photographs of the player's heads are superimposed on cartoon bodies). Foxx won the league's Most Valuable Player award that year.

The 1952 Topps 407-card set is the most desirable post-World War II set of baseball cards. This 1952 Topps Mickey Mantle card has changed hands privately for six figures, and it isn't even his rookie card.

Ironically, the Mantle card was produced in the same quantity as all other cards in the set and is just his first Topps-issue card, *not* his rookie card. Yet it is worth far more than his 1951 Bowman rookie card because dealers and avid collectors have hoarded it, driving up prices. In fact, Mantle cards from all years are worth more than nonrookie cards of comparable players—including Willie Mays, Hank Aaron, Stan Musial, and Ted Williams—because dealers have always promoted the one-time Yankee idol as the post–World War II poster boy of baseball card collecting.

Topps was so successful with its first cards that it was able to buy out Bowman after 1955, and would, without a serious challenge (Fleer Gum produced four smaller sets beginning in 1959; Kellogg's and Hostess Cakes issued limited sets to promote their products), monopolize the industry until the 1980s. A court decision allowed Fleer and Donruss to enter the market with full card sets of their own beginning in 1981, although the new companies had to discontinue putting bubble gum in their packs after the first year. This marks the beginning of today's collecting era; cards from 1981 to the present are, in general, the cards today's budget-conscious collectors sell, trade, and buy. Now Topps, Fleer, Donruss-Playoff, and Upper Deck compete by issuing annual standard sets and specialty sets using gimmicks to attract buyers. More than eighty sets are produced each year at varying prices (including a $100 pack), meaning that all serious collectors must carefully select which cards to buy.

COLLECTING BASEBALL CARDS

Rookie cards are an important subspecialty of the field, and naturally, superstars rule. With few exceptions, each player's rookie and first-issue cards will be the most valuable of their cards, but remember that buying a current rookie's card in quantity as an investment can be risky (unless the cost is very low) because he may not pan out. If a player is on his way to the Hall of Fame, on the other hand, you might want to pick up his rookie card (and other cards as well) before he makes it to Cooperstown and the price escalates dramatically. Some collectors also believe that sound investments include unopened factory sets, boxes, and wax packs (the typical packs you buy in stores). Even if they disappoint by not going up dramatically in price over the years, there is virtually no chance they will depreciate in value. Of course, it's not fun to buy things you can't open, so if you have some extra money, buy two of everything, one to open and one to store away. Opening packs of cards and discovering who is inside is a thrill, however, even if the newest Barry Bonds is worth only fifty cents and the rest of the players are worth only a dime a piece.

Be sure to consult annual price guides, because every dealer and collector refers to "book price" when making a card deal. It's very important to remember that the price in a guide is the price for which a dealer will sell the card to you. If you hope to sell the same card to a dealer, expect only 50 to 60 percent of the book price. Some dealers might want your card but claim it is not in good condition. That's why savvy collectors should have cards evaluated by reputable grading companies (a new phenomenon in the field) or, even better, learn how to grade the cards themselves.

CONDITION

Baseball cards, like watches and posters, are rated according to a scale that weighs how close they are to perfection, because value is dependent on condition. There are several grading systems, and collectors and dealers often use differing methods. It is important, therefore, to understand the criteria and the accuracy of your grader. Make sure that the grader provides detailed definitions of his grades; one person's "excellent" may be another person's "good." There are several firms that provide grading services, including Professional Sports Authentication (PSA) and Sports Grading Corporation (SGC). Collectors and dealers often use these firms' scales and terms in describing a card.

Because this is a complex subject, a few words from expert Leila Dunbar are in order here (see box, page 122).

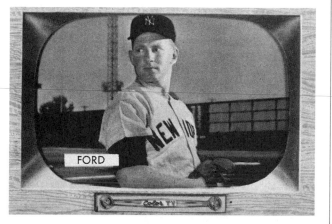

Whitey Ford, from the unusual 1955 Bowman set of 320 cards that places the photographs of players within brown TV-set borders. These brown borders chip easily, so many 1955 Bowman cards have conditional problems.

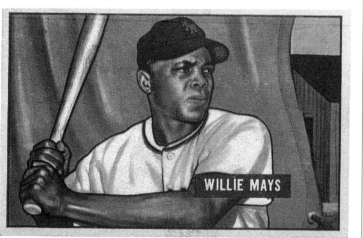

A horizontal New York Giants Willie Mays rookie card from the 1951 Bowman set of 324, which included rookie cards for both Mays and Mantle, as well as Whitey Ford.

Baseball Card Grading 101

Leila Dunbar, a veteran *Antiques Roadshow* appraiser, is senior vice president and director of the collectibles department at Sotheby's. Dunbar handles sports memorabilia at Sotheby's, in addition to being a lifelong sports fan herself. Here's how she grades baseball cards. "I think that people find a lot of grading systems confusing because they often use the same words in different combinations. At Sotheby's, we use a simple grading system, ranging in descending order, from Mint to Good. I have added numerical equivalents for those who prefer to grade by numbers."

All four of these Babe Ruth cards are from the Goudey "Big League Chewing Gum" series of 1933, the first year that company issued baseball cards.

When grading, I start with a first-look inspection of the front and back of a card, to get an overview and see what stands out—the good, the bad, and occasionally the ugly or the sublime. Because first impressions can be deceiving, I then do a step-by-step analysis, starting with the corners. Corners should be perfect right angles. I note any rounding or wear. I then examine the borders to make sure they were machine cut and not trimmed to improve the card. I also check for tears and edge wear and assess the whiteness of the borders. I move on to the image, starting with the most obvious—looking for any creases, stains, staple holes, or soiling. I also check for factory flaws, such as lines or spots from the printing process, and out-of-register or poorly focused images.

Next, I determine if there is any fading or discoloration and evaluate the card's gloss or luster, how close it is to having its original shiny finish. I also make sure there are no other alterations, such as touching up or filling in of color or bleaching, a process for cleaning dirt and stains. Then I return to the borders and look at the centering. Centering is really a comparison of the borders' measurements from left to right and from top to bottom, expressed as the percentage of difference at the most off-center part of the card. The most recognizable problems here are miscut cards, which have part of the border of another card, and diamond-cut cards, which have tapering borders that resemble a diamond.

Finally, I turn the card over and repeat the relevant steps of the procedure on the back. Although the back is not as crucial as the front, any flaws and stains on it still affect its grading and therefore its value. Unless extremely rare, I avoid cards below a rating of "good."

(M) MINT (10)

Also known in other grading systems as Gem-Mint or Pristine. The mint card is the standard against which all others are judged, the best of the best. Pack fresh, it is as crisp and clean as can be, so clean that it might have just come out of the pack. It has never seen a smudge, tear, or crease; there is no residue or stain from the gum it was packaged with or the wax used to seal the pack. All four corners are sharp and crisp, with no hint of wear. The borders are super white and are machine cut, with no trimming. The image is well focused and has no printing faults, the colors are bright and strong, and the card retains all of its original gloss. Centering of the image on the front should be 50/50.

(NM) NEAR MINT (9)

A card that, at first glance, appears to be mint. Closer inspection reveals that it may have one minor flaw, such as borders that are slightly off-white, a minor printing imperfection, a very slight wax stain on the back, a tiny nick on one corner, or a minor surface scratch. Centering must be better than or equal to approximately 60/40 to 55/45.

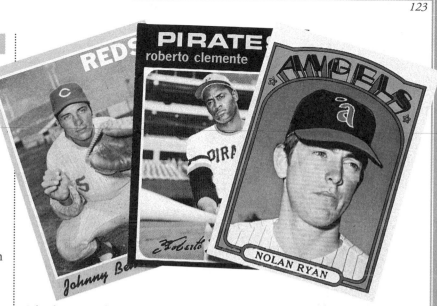

The three Topps baseball cards of Hall of Fame players from the early 1970s show Cincinnati Reds catcher Johnny Bench, Pittsburgh Pirates batting champion Roberto Clemente, and California Angels pitcher Nolan Ryan.

(EX) EXCELLENT (7-8)

Under close inspection, a card that exhibits one or more of the following: slight surface wear, minor rounding or wear on some corners, slightly out-of-register picture focus, with a minor printing blemish or slight wax stain on the back. Centering must be better than or equal to approximately 70/30 to 65/35.

(VG) VERY GOOD (5-6)

A card that has noticeable surface wear or minor printing defects and may exhibit one or more of the following: corner rounding or wear, slight chipping on the edges, off-white borders, light scratches, or one very light surface crease on one side. Centering must be equal to or better than approximately 85/15 to 80/20.

(G) GOOD (3-4)

A card that shows obvious surface wear, which may include slight to moderate rounding of corners, yellowing of border, edge wear, light scratches, staining, discoloration, or printing faults—including focus or color imperfections—and loss of gloss, ranging from substantial to most. There may be a light to moderate crease to one or both sides. Centering must be equal to or better than approximately 90/10 to 85/15.

ADVICE FOR AUTOGRAPH COLLECTORS

When your hero signs a bat or a ball instead of a piece of paper, index card, or program, that's a step or two up in collectibility. Choose a ballpoint pen with blue ink for baseballs, and offer your favorite superstar a new, official American or National league ball. These will be far more desirable down the road than some scuffed old ball you've tossed around at home. Have him use a blue or black Sharpie on a bat, or a silver or gold paint pen on dark items like shoes, because the legibility and the longevity of his signature will have a great deal to do with how your collectible eventually fares n the marketplace. And by the way, don't ask him to dedicate the autograph to you. Personalized signatures are not as valuable as plain signatures, unless they are written to another well-known person.

SIGNED BASEBALLS

After the trading card, the most ubiquitous baseball collectible has to be the autographed ball. At most *Antiques Roadshows,* Leila Dunbar will appraise twenty to thirty balls; at a *Roadshow* in Tampa, Florida, she appraised forty. Balls of course, are easy to take to games and to have autographed during batting practice. Once signed, they become treasured keepsakes of one memorable day when a fan met a hero.

COLLECTING BASEBALLS

For maximum value, a ball should be signed on the "sweet spot," the narrowest area of the "dumbbell" formed by the stitching on the ball. This was the traditional spot for the team manager to sign, but because it was the place of honor, eventually it became reserved for the heroes of the game. Many balls have multiple signatures, having been signed by a mixed bag of players, while others ("team balls") are signed by members of one team. It's an irony, comments Dunbar, that the ball with a single star player's signature is usually more highly valued than the ball that has several.

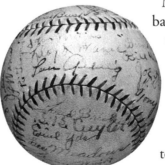

An official National League baseball from the 1927 World Series has the signatures of forty-two members of the New York Yankees and Pittsburgh Pirates teams. The Yankees swept the Pirates in four games.

Many collectors create "theme balls"; balls that require more than one signature. These may have the autographs of Hall of Fame pitchers, Hall of Fame position players, Negro League players, players who all reached similar milestones, players linked by a famous game or event, teammates, and so on. But serious collectors want only one signature on one ball. Certainly, the price of a ball with signatures of, say, future Hall of Famers Barry Bonds and Sammy Sosa will appreciate in ten years, but its value after ten years' time will definitely not equal the

Three signed portrait baseballs from a set of thirty-seven— Yankee Reggie Jackson, Giant Willie Mays, and Indian Bob Feller— painted by Judy Everets on official American or National League balls, as appropriate.

total value of individual balls, each signed by Bonds and Sosa. Online, you can find dealers selling single-signature balls at reasonable prices. For instance, among Hall of Famers you can find Ralph Kiner for $49; Joe Moran for $69; Juan Marichal for $59; Harmon Killebrew for $79; and Nolan Ryan for $135. Among the deceased Hall of Famers, a Richie Ashburn brings $99 and Mickey Mantle, $350. A future Hall of Famer, Greg Maddux, is offered currently for $119. Bring a ball to a card show or business promotion featuring ballplayers, and you may get it autographed for the price of admission, or maybe for $20 more. Have your ball autographed inside or outside the ballpark, perhaps at spring training, and it's no charge. If you don't have a ball, you can probably buy one at the park. But avoid buying signed balls at the park. Souvenir balls with stamped signatures have been sold at ballparks for years and have little value.

The history of a ball may be wholly unknown, or its history may be full of inaccuracies. Team balls provide a great opportunity for detective work. Deciphering signatures and determining teams and years is the key to balls. One team ball—that of the champion 1927 New York Yankees—breaks the rule about single-signature balls being the most valuable. The fabled '27 Yankees are considered by many experts to be the greatest baseball team ever assembled. Its "Murderers Row" lineup included Babe Ruth, who smashed 60 home runs (a record that would last 34 years), Lou Gehrig (who drove in 175 runs), and future Hall of Famers Tony Lazzeri and Earle Combs. Star pitchers Waite Hoyt and Herb Pennock also would be selected for Cooperstown. Yankee team balls from 1926 or 1928, and even from the 1961 team featuring Mickey Mantle and Roger Maris (when he hit 61 homers to surpass Ruth) are also highly sought after, but a ball signed by

A NEAR-PERFECT BALL

A visitor to the Richmond, Virginia, *Antiques Roadshow* brought not one, but four baseballs from the same game. He told appraiser Leila Dunbar, "In the 1956 World Series between the Brooklyn Dodgers and the New York Yankees, a major event took place: Don Larsen pitched a perfect game. I was nine years old. Hank Soar, an American League first base umpire at the game, was a very good friend of my father's, and after that game, Hank showed up at our house with four baseballs that he gave to me: the ball that Don Larsen pitched to the Dodgers' twenty-sixth batter, the next-to-last out; a ball that six umpires had autographed; a ball autographed by the Dodgers; and another ball autographed by the Yankees. One day my Dad came home from work and took me aside and said, 'Don't lose those balls.' A few days later he died. For 42 years I've kept them. . . ." The visitor noted that he had recently met Larsen in Richmond at a card show, and showed him his "perfect game" balls. "So that's where they went!" Larsen laughed.

all of the 1927 Yankees would always bring a premium. (A team ball of the 1920 Chicago White Sox, bearing the autographs of players who were banned from baseball for fixing the 1919 World Series, is also worth a fortune, mainly because it includes a rare signature of "Shoeless" Joe Jackson, who couldn't read and usually signed his name with an "X.")

NEGRO LEAGUE COLLECTIBLES

When Jackie Roosevelt Robinson joined the Brooklyn Dodgers in 1947, he became the first black player in the major leagues, and broke a racial barrier that had existed since blacks were ousted from professional baseball in the late 1800s. Denied the chance to play with white players, blacks eventually formed their own professional leagues, starting the Negro National League in 1920. Although that league folded in 1931, a second Negro National League was formed soon after, and other leagues featuring outstanding black players sprang up in succeeding years, as well.

Most of the leagues had six or fewer teams and played between fifty and eighty games a year,

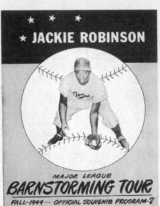

Top: A 1949 program for a Jackie Robinson Barnstorming Tour.
Right: This Jackie Robinson doll, dressed in a Dodgers uniform, came with its original box.

not including their exhibition games against major leaguers (in which they fared very well). Losing Robinson, a former Negro League player, and the many Negro League stars (including Larry Doby, Roy Campanella, Satchel Paige, Willie Mays, Monte Irvin, Hank Aaron, and Ernie Banks) who followed him into the majors caused the Negro Leagues to struggle with attendance and die out by 1960. They left behind, however, a remarkable legacy of great players, and a legendary history. Today sports fans may wonder wistfully what the game would have been like before 1947 had Negro League players, in their prime, been able to compete in the same arena as their major league counterparts.

Leila Dunbar notes that "memorabilia from early black players, particularly Negro League players, is now appreciating quickly. They are valued both because they are rare and because they are an important part of American history." The two players whose artifacts are most in demand were the Negro Leagues' greatest pitcher, Satchel Paige, and its greatest hitter, Josh Gibson.

The tricky part of team balls is differentiating the teams from one year and another. The lack of a few signatures or the presence of a few others are the only means of determining the year of the ball and ultimately its value. Collectors are more likely to seek team balls from championship seasons. There are many reference books that can help you ascertain the values of signed balls (see the Reading List and Bibliography, page 543.)

CONDITION

Signed baseballs should never be shellacked. They should be white as clouds on a perfect summer day. Signatures should be completely legible. (Legibility, of course, is relative. Like doctors, ballplayers aren't noted for their penmanship, although Babe Ruth, Lou Gehrig, and Christy Mathewson all had beautiful signatures.) You want to see a clean signature, not one that is smudged or faded, and clear enough to recognize a few letters in the name. (Unfortunately, if our hero hurriedly squashes the letters together or writes only his initials or someone else's for all you can tell, you can't ask him to do it over.) If your ball has only a single signature, you want it tucked right into the sweet spot (see photo, left). Baseballs are the one item that should be autographed with a ballpoint pen rather than a sharpie or paint pen.

A perfect, desirable, and legible signature in the perfect spot on a clean ball.

AUTOGRAPHED EPHEMERA

In addition to baseballs, autographs appear on multitudes of other items—in autograph books, on contracts, menus, programs, photographs—or on blank index cards and postcards, which are what savvy autograph collectors mail (with stamped, self-addressed envelopes) to a player's team or directly to his home.

THE GOOD DIE YOUNG

Top-notch baseball signatures need not come from Hall of Famers. In New Orleans, a guest handed appraiser Simeon Lipman a decades-old ball signed by famous Boston Red Sox players, among them Ted Williams. Although the owner believed the ball was from the 1948 Red Sox, Lipman explained it was actually from the 1954 or 1955 season. The clue was the autograph of a player named Harry Agganis, a local kid who was known by loyal New England fans as the "Golden Greek," and it was that signature that gave the ball its value. Agganis joined Boston in 1954 and in June, 1955, was starting at first base and hitting .313 when he died unexpectedly at the age of twenty-six. He is still remembered throughout New England, "and his signature makes this ball rare," noted Lipman, who valued the ball between $1,500 and $2,000.

KNOW YOUR AUTOGRAPHS!

Not all autographed items, even those passed down with convincing stories, have authentic signatures. There are skillful forgeries, and even more often, people other than the athlete—trainers, batboys, or secretaries—may have signed that ball. Perhaps the greatest hitter of the "deadball era," the Chicago White Sox's illiterate Shoeless Joe Jackson (made infamous by the "Black Sox" scandal), usually had his wife sign for him. Advanced collectors ascertain the provenance of each piece and check signatures against known, authentic examples. If you aren't sure about a signature, consult a professional.

Another common mistake made when evaluating signatures on photographs and paper is the confusion of real autographs with facsimiles of autographs or stamped signatures. Facsimile annotations and signatures were made right on one photograph, and then duplicated in subsequent prints. These may appear real to the naked eye, but if you take a closer look, the real autograph has usually left an impression or added texture to the surface, while the facsimile autograph seems to be part of the image. Collectors should do side-by-side comparisons to train their eyes to such differences. Facsimile signatures have little if any value, but they may be on a photograph or other item that has value independent of the signature.

Left: The endorsed side of Mickey Mantle's first professional check, for $1,150, dated July 11, 1949. It was a bonus for signing a minor-league contract with the Independence Yankees in Kansas. At right: A one-page letter of encouragement and advice written on Babe Ruth's personal stationery and signed by him, addressed to Christy Walsh Jr., the son of Ruth's agent, when he enrolled in military school in 1935, signed "Babe Ruth."

COLLECTING AUTOGRAPHS

Collectors place the greatest value on autographs that have historical significance, such as the Babe Ruth signature on his 1920 contract with the New York Yankees, a document that finalized his sale from the Boston Red Sox to the Yankees. Collectors also pursue handwritten letters, particularly superstar letters including "good content" about the game. One way to get a letter is to send one (with a stamped, self-addressed envelope enclosed) to a player asking about his career and how he pitched, fielded, or batted. If the player is kind enough to answer (and isn't a whiz at

A 1949 Sports Illustrated *cover featuring Joe DiMaggio and signed by him in blue sharpie, is part of a collection of eighteen signed magazine covers all featuring DiMaggio, and dating from 1936 to 1993.*

the computer), chances are you'll receive a handwritten response.

A huge star in New York City, Babe Ruth signed autographs by the dozen for the kids who followed their idol through the streets, and started the tradition of players signing autographs for fans. Because there were few signed balls before the twenties, there is a premium on autographs of early stars such as Cap Anson, Cy Young, and Christy Mathewson, no matter what they are written on. Also in demand are autographs of deceased Hall of Famers who played the game before baseball-card shows hired ballplayers to spend the day signing anything the public handed them. Collectors also covet the autographs of stars from special teams, among them the sensational 1907 and 1908 Chicago Cubs, the last Cubs teams to win the World Series, and the infamous 1919 Chicago White Sox, who threw the Series to the Reds. Rarity, age, and condition are key.

A famous publicity photograph of Babe Ruth and Lou Gehrig distributed to children during a 1927 cross-country tour. In addition to the facsimile signatures, this photo has the authentic signatures of both players, greatly enhancing its value.

Collectors treasure rare photographs of sports heroes and events. In 1911, for example, panoramic photographs were taken of an all-star game played to benefit the widow of pitching great Addie Joss, who died in the prime of his Hall of Fame career. These photographs commanded a premium when they appeared recently at auction. While they were expected to sell for $10,000 to $15,000, they actually brought $32,200.

For collectors, autographs give photographs added appeal and authenticity. A promotional photo of Lou Gehrig and Babe Ruth, for instance, sold recently at auction. In this photograph, both men are leaning on their bats and smiling; Babe has his arm around Lou's shoulders. Babe's shirt reads "Bustin Babe's" and Lou's shirt reads "Larrupin Lou's." This famous image, with only *facsimile* signatures, was distributed on a 1927 cross-country

JACKIE ROBINSON SIGNATURE

A visitor to the Boston, Massachusetts, *Antiques Roadshow* recalled sitting in the stands with her brother at Brooklyn Dodgers games, watching Jackie Robinson during the year he broke into the majors. "We used to go to Brooklyn's Ebbets Field to see him play," the visitor recounted. "Since I am an African American, it was big for me. I used to go down on Sundays. I saw pitchers throw brushbacks at Jackie's head. I also saw him steal a lot of bases to get back at them. It was really exciting."

After moving to New Orleans, the visitor attended a Negro League all-star game that Robinson, who had once played in the Negro Leagues, also attended. She handed her ticket stub to the history-making player and he autographed it in pencil. "I knew it was something, even then." Appraiser Philip J. Merrill told the thrilled visitor that her signed stub is worth approximately $1,500 today.

RICH AS A GEORGIA PEACH

Sports autographs are usually written on sports paraphernalia, such as Louisville Slugger bats or pigskin footballs. But there are other kinds of sports stars' signatures that are also collectible. For example, the two deeds signed by Detroit Tigers great Ty Cobb that were brought to the *Antiques Roadshow* in Austin, Texas. The first was from 1933—the twilight of Cobb's baseball career—when he sold some property in his home state of Georgia. "With signed legal documents, you always know the signature's real," commented Simeon Lipman. "You know they're not going to have their sister or the batboy sign it."

The visitor also brought a second deed, signed by Cobb in 1909, when he was a young player. "This is what I would call a vintage signature," Lipman said. Cobb signed thousands of autographs after he played, but this signature is from his playing days, when he set the all-time record for career batting average, .367. Lipman told the visitor that the two signed deeds together are worth $4,000 to $6,000 today.

tour. The photograph that sold at a recent auction, however, was one with Ruth's and Gehrig's handwritten signatures in *ink*, in addition to the facsimiles. The value of this rare image was greatly enhanced by the stars' actual signatures, and it sold for $22,000.

A common practice today is to mat and frame a "cut autograph," a signature that has been cut out from a letter or document, with a photograph of the star. These may make attractive display pieces, but collectors do not value them as highly as signed photographs for the simple reason that the player did not hold the photograph in his hand and sign it directly. It doesn't have a legimate history. At card shows and promotions, you can ask players to sign "flat items," like index cards and photographs, usually for less than they charge for bats and balls.

CONDITION

Photographs and autographed ephemera follow the same conditional guidelines as all paper collectibles. Creases, discolorations, tears, and mends affect their desirability. Autograph hounds, take note: Signatures should have a whole page of the autograph book to themselves. If several autographs are crowded on one page it may make a fine display item, but every additional autograph has less value than if it were alone on a page. Unfortunate, but true.

GAME-USED EQUIPMENT

Declares *Antiques Roadshow* appraiser, Leila Dunbar, "gloves, bats, and uniforms are the weapons of the gladiators." And that's why they're so popular. It's all too true that those items that bear a player's sweat are the most valuable— the bats, balls, gloves and mitts, shoes, hats, jerseys, and even catcher Yogi Berra's jockstrap from Don Larsen's perfect game in the 1956 World Series (which Berra gave to a Yankee teammate). It's

A game-used Brooklyn Dodgers cap that belonged to Jackie Robinson in the early 1950s was lent to a farm-team player by a trainer during a workout and never returned.

great to bring home press pins, programs, yearbooks, ticket stubs, and so forth, but there's something really special about items touched by players on the field. For example, Mickey Mantle's game-used glove sold at auction for an astonishing $239,000. That makes the $2,195 list price for a Barry Bonds' game-worn Giants uniform from 1998 seem like a bargain.

BATS

Major League teams pay manufacturers about $30 per bat, and today they are made predominantly by two companies: Louisville Slugger (known from 1884 to 1979 as Hillerich & Bradsby) and Adirondack. Most players opt for one or the other, although Mickey Mantle liked both. How does the collector match the player to his bat? Factory stock numbers are stamped on the butts of the bat handles, and, conveniently, these can be used to identify the player to whose specifications the bat was made. Sometimes the player's name is also stamped on the business end of the bat. Today, who ordered what is a matter of record, which makes identification a lot easier. However, if you come across a bat that is imprinted with a player's signature, don't assume it was made for that player. Bats marketed to the public in sports stores or sports departments, with imprinted players' "signatures" on them, are not collectible. The star didn't order them, use them, or ever set eyes on them. They are ersatz, and

A very rare, uncracked Jackie Robinson game-used Louisville Slugger bat, model number S100, circa 1950-1954, is traceable through factory records. Robinson, the only player in baseball to have his number retired by every team in both leagues, ordered this model bat in 1951 and 1952, with a final order in 1954.

At left: This circa 1932 H&B bat with the engraved signature of Lou Gehrig shows heavy game use but is uncracked.

Middle: A bat, showing no evidence of game use, but signed by twenty-seven members of the 1938 New York Giants.

Right: A 1961 World Series game-used bat made especially for Roger Maris for the series—the Yankees defeated the Reds in four games—has an engraved facsimile signature. 1961 was the year Maris broke Babe Ruth's record by hitting sixty-one home runs.

A Mickey Mantle game-worn glove—a model made exclusively for Mantle by Rawlings, with a deep well pocket design—from around 1960. The original stitching has frayed and broken in two places and the back of the pocket has been signed "Mickey Mantle" in black. The glove shows heavy game use, considered excellent condition in an equipment collectible.

An all-black Rawlings glove, used in the 1986 playoffs (vs. Houston) and World Series (vs. Boston) by New York Mets outfielder Darryl Strawberry, has Strawberry's authentification on an accompanying index card.

unlike such replicas, bats ordered for major league players' use will always have distinguishing marks.

Game-used bats are collectible bats of choice. But how to know if yours is a game-used bat? A nice selection of dings and smudges and a soupçon of dirt can indicate game use. A really good crack in a bat is considered a badge of authenticity, since it usually means the player took a good cut at the ball. And what about prices? A cracked early nineties game-used bat signed by Harold Baines, a star but not a future Hall of Famer, is $80. An uncracked and unsigned early seventies Adirondack used by Hank Aaron sells for $2,300.

If Joe DiMaggio was photographed presenting his bat to a batboy, and if that bat, handed down in the batboy's family, eventually appeared for sale, it would then have a solid provenance: a verifiable history of ownership, a pedigree. This type of authentification is important to collectors, and should always be demanded of the seller of any important material. Just being told that "DiMaggio used this bat" isn't any more reliable than seeing a sign at an old inn claiming "George Washington Slept Here." Intelligent baseball collectors require solid proof, and Major League Baseball has initiated an Authentication Program in conjunction with players and dealers (who have become licensees) to assure collectors that the autographs on bats, balls, and the other items they are purchasing are genuine.

GLOVES

The value of gloves depends on the maker and style of the glove, its age, condition, and the player's name that is embossed on it. Collectors usually divide gloves into pre– and post–World War II, which they distinguish by their laces: Gloves with laceless fingers are prewar models, those with laced fingers are postwar models (though, to confuse matters, various companies produced both types prior to and after the war).

At the Major League level, gloves, like bats, are custom made for specific players. The Spalding Company was one of the early producers of professional gloves. The most notable of the thousands of gloves manufactured was the first-baseman's mitt used by Lou Gehrig on April 30, 1939, the last game he played. Rather than order a new glove, he had sent his old one back to the manufacturer to be completely refaced and relined. In 1999, this overhauled glove was sold at auction for a record price: $387,500.

As with game-used bats, collectors want proof that the star in question actually used the glove. For autographs on gloves, collectors like to see the signature in the player's own hand in a heavy ink.

JERSEYS

Ty Cobb, "one of the fastest and meanest stars of all time," says Leila Dunbar, simply gave away his 1928 Philadelphia Athletics home jersey. (Recently, it turned up at auction and sold for more than $350,000.) These days, however, with jerseys and bats valued as if they were spun gold, players are keeping closer tabs on their old equipment. Game-worn jerseys are still fairly common, because Major League teams clean out their clubhouses on a pretty regular basis and sell their "old clothes" to waiting fans. But all kinds of jerseys are in demand; from individual players' home or road jerseys to team jerseys. Jerseys from bygone eras are particularly popular, including those from teams that no longer exist. Authentic jerseys of well-known players are extremely popular with collectors, especially when signed, but signed replica jerseys shouldn't be overlooked because they, too, can sell for several hundred dollars, and more if a player is deceased.

To find out if a jersey is authentic, you'll look at the inside rather than the outside. Begin by turning it inside out, and first make sure the label is the correct label for that team's shirt. For example, since the Rawlings Company made uniforms for the Pittsburgh Pirates, you should expect to find a Rawlings label on a Pirates jersey. It's worth knowing that well into the middle of the twentieth century, ballplayers wore wool flannel uniforms with the players' names stitched into the fabric. Check to see if there are stitch marks that shouldn't be there, or more moth holes than absolutely necessary. Once again, legitimate letters of authenticity from the player or a team will greatly enhance a jersey's value, so before paying a fortune, check out the seller's reputation thoroughly.

A 1966 gray-flannel road jersey signed by Sandy Koufax, the star Los Angeles Dodgers pitcher who famously refused to pitch the first game of the 1965 World Series against the Minnesota Twins because it fell on Yom Kippur.

A signed gray-flannel Detroit Tigers road jersey from 1945 that once belonged to Hank Greenberg, baseball's first Jewish superstar and one of only three players to be named Most Valuable Player in two positions.

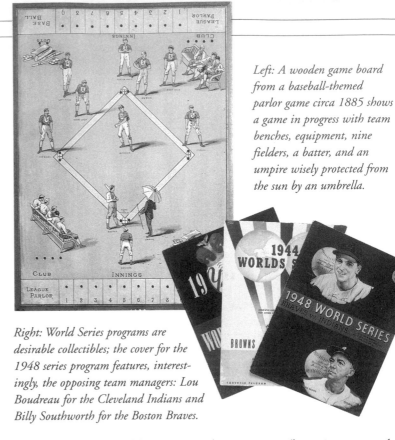

Left: A wooden game board from a baseball-themed parlor game circa 1885 shows a game in progress with team benches, equipment, nine fielders, a batter, and an umpire wisely protected from the sun by an umbrella.

SOME HEAVY HITTERS

In Tampa, Florida, a woman brought to the *Antiques Roadshow* a few pieces collected by her husband, a former pitcher with a Los Angeles Dodgers farm team from the mid-1960s through the early 1970s. Her first treasure was a piece of hotel stationery her husband found in the pocket of a pitching jacket he was handed as part of his uniform in 1966. It was a crib sheet prepared by Dodgers Hall of Fame pitcher Don Drysdale for the first game of the 1965 World Series, with notes on how to pitch the Minnesota Twins lineup. Because the sheet helped the Dodgers win the World Series, appraiser Leila Dunbar estimated its worth at somewhere from $1,000 to $1,500.

The real treasure was a baseball from a game between the Washington Senators and the New York Yankees. Babe Ruth signed it and then pressured Lefty Grove, a Hall of Fame Yankees pitcher who usually avoided signing autographs, to sign, too. Maybe a Ruth autograph alone would have made the ball even more valuable, but finding a ball with a rare Grove signature is a real coup. The ball's value? Between $2,500 and $3,500, said Dunbar.

Right: World Series programs are desirable collectibles; the cover for the 1948 series program features, interestingly, the opposing team managers: Lou Boudreau for the Cleveland Indians and Billy Southworth for the Boston Braves.

Any list of desirable game-used equipment (bats, jerseys, and gloves) would have to include equipment used by the following Hall of Famers: The holy trinity, of course—Ty Cobb, Lou Gehrig, and Babe Ruth—plus Christy Mathewson, Honus Wagner, Cap Anson, Walter Johnson, Hank Greenberg, Grover Cleveland Alexander, Tris Speaker, Cy Young, Eddie Collins, Jimmie Foxx, Rogers Hornsby, John McGraw, Joe DiMaggio, Jackie Robinson, Hank Aaron, Ernie Banks, Carl Hubbell, Duke Snider, Johnny Bench, Joe Morgan, Roy Campanella, Mickey Mantle, Willie Mays, Stan Musial, Bob Feller, Roberto Clemente, Reggie Jackson, Ted Williams, Eddie Mathews, Casey Stengel, Nolan Ryan, Tom Seaver, and numerous others.

ASSORTED MEMORABILIA

There is a seemingly endless list of baseball memorabilia that attract enthusiastic collectors. Board games, souvenir pennants, bobble-head dolls ("Nodders are really

Top: A pennant celebrating the 1912 Boston Red Sox championship, features a Red Sox pitcher winding up. The Red Sox have won four World Series, the last in 1918.

Right: A set of bobble-head Yankee dolls of teammates, friends, and rivals Roger Maris and Mickey Mantle, from 1962.

hot now," Dunbar notes), programs, ticket stubs, and advertising posters and signs are avidly sought. Two particularly popular areas of collecting are press pins, given out to the media at various games, and stadium buttons, such as those picturing the 1953 New York Yankees—the entire team on one button. Seats and turnstiles from stadiums that no longer stand, statues of ballplayers, paintings or drawings by prominent artists depicting the game or its players, cartoons—and even pitcher Don Drysdale's crib sheet, written to remind him of how he wanted to pitch the Minnesota Twins players in the first game of the 1965 World Series (see sidebar, opposite page)—warm the hearts of devoted collectors. Condition issues vary, so examine objects closely, get accurate condition reports from experts, and, like Don Drysdale, do your homework.

Firmly rooted in the American psyche, baseball and its collecting community it has spawned continue to delight and dismay us. There is a constant supply of new memorabilia from today's stars and possibly tomorrow's legends. Only time will tell if this material is as avidly sought in the future as nineteenth- and twentieth-century material is pursued today.

ORVIE OVERALL

A collection of baseball memorabilia including a cartoon and photographs once belonging to Orval Overall, a star pitcher for the Chicago Cubs from 1906 to 1910, was brought to the Portland, Oregon, *Antiques Roadshow* by Overall's grandniece. "Orvie" pitched splendidly in the 1907 and 1908 World Series, helping the Cubs beat Ty Cobb's Detroit Tigers. (Unfortunately for today's Cubs fans, that marked the team's last World Series victory to date.) A sketch by the noted cartoonist Clare Briggs, drawn while working at the *Chicago Tribune*, depicts Orval's former manager from the Cincinnati Reds, Ned Hanlon (who had traded Overall to the Cubs), enviously watching his World Series pitching performance. Among the photographs are pictures of two future Hall of Famers, pitcher Mordecai "Three Finger" Brown and Cubs manager Frank Chance. Chance was also the team's first baseman, immortalized by the famous "Tinkers to Evers to Chance" double-play combination. "It's a beautiful collection," said appraiser Simeon Lipman. "I'd estimate the whole thing at around $1,500 to $2,000 dollars."

GOLF

British passions combined eccentrically: a circa 1900 golf-themed picnic tea kettle stand, its copper tea kettle and spirit burner supported by three wood-shafted golf clubs—a driver, a mashie, and a putter, with brass golf ball feet.

Tiger Woods didn't initiate the collecting of golf memorabilia, but he is undoubtedly responsible for increasing its popularity. So great is his impact that new golf collectors are snatching up not only anything associated with perhaps the sports world's most famous figure, but also the autographs and memorabilia of his chief competitors—Sergio Garcia, David Duval, and John Daly, to name a few—along with legends on the Seniors Tour, and keepsakes from PGA and LPGA tournaments and the Ryder Cup. While golf memorabilia has, like all other collecting fields, been tainted by the influx of needless "instant collectibles" in the marketplace, most new collectors begin to collect because of a budding passion rather than for financial considerations. For now, their focus is on current and recent players, trading cards, and other contemporary collectibles, but because many new enthusiasts have a refreshing curiosity about the history of the sport, it's likely that they will eventually seek out the vintage artifacts that have long been the province of the experienced golf collector.

A BRIEF HISTORY

When did golf begin? A clue may very well be in the Great East window of England's Gloucester Cathedral, installed around 1340. There, a stained-glass roundel depicts a small figure in a tunic, tights, and soft, pointy shoes, swinging what appears to be a golf club. Although this rendering in glass predates any Scottish written records of the game by about sixty years (and although it has been argued that the game being played is actually cambuca, which was popular at the time), it is more likely that most people viewing that window today envision that medieval sportsman somewhere

British passions combined: This Sylvac pottery Scottie who has (unfortunately) retrieved a golf ball, advertised the North British Rubber Company.

on the first fairway with his three buddies. After all, it isn't cambuca that gets millions of us up and out early on weekend mornings all year long.

It appears that the word "golf" comes from the Dutch, who played a game with a ball or disk and curved sticks that they called *"kolven"* or *"kolf."* Yet Scotland (from which many mercenaries traveled temporarily to Holland), is considered modern golf's homeland. In fact, by the middle of the fifteenth century, golf had become so popular there that it was interfering with military training. So, in 1457, Scotland's King James II banned the game, encouraging his men to practice archery instead. Evidently the ban didn't work, and James IV took it up himself a few years into the sixteenth century. In an early example of "if you can't beat 'em, join 'em," he bought "golf clubs and balls and wagered at golf with the Earl of Bothwell."

By the end of the sixteenth century, golf had been embraced in Great Britain by the rich and powerful. Mary, Queen of Scots, is the first woman known to have played the game, and her son, James VI, is said to have taken his clubs with him when, as James I, he ascended the English throne in 1603. (The word "caddy," signifying the carrier of the golfer's equipment around the course, came from the term by which a student in a French military school was known—cadet.)

Golf arrived in America early. A 1729 inventory of the estate of the royal governor of New York and New Jersey included nine woods and one iron, plus seven dozen balls. However, the unusual expense of the equipment limited the game's appeal to the wealthy well into the nineteenth century. Balls, in particular, were expensive to produce, and their effectiveness was relatively short-lived. But, by the late 1880s, mass-produced equipment and—at long last—the invention of a well-made, affordable ball made the game more accessible to the middle-class duffer (though it would long be burdened with an elitist tag).

Pre-1850 golf equipment rarely turns up. It is easier to find equipment made between 1850 and 1914, because about 700-odd golf-related patents were taken out during that period. Items fabricated after World War I, including those that were mass-produced, are, with exceptions, even easier to come by. Consequently, and happily for the collector, there is a wealth of

For the golf enthusiast who has everything: an English toast rack, perfect for serving pre-round breakfasts.

This square-toe iron from around 1700, with its original alder shaft, is similar in design to clubs from the late 1600s.

THE GREAT ONE'S CLUBS

One visitor who came to the Charleston *Antiques Roadshow* brought with him a special set of golf clubs, which came to him by way of his son-in-law, a doctor and friend to the television personality Jackie Gleason. Gleason, best known to an entire generation of television fans as Ralph Kramden of *The Honeymooners,* was an avid golfer. Not only did he do a special episode of *The Honeymooners* entitled "The Golf Classic," he participated every year in a Pro-Am tournament started by Bing Crosby in 1937 at Pebble Beach.

The monogrammed clubs are marked "J.G. The Great One." Included are two special golf balls—one marked "The Great Gleason," and one featuring a picture of a crown.

Appraiser Leila Dunbar postulated that these clubs were most likely given to Gleason as a gift, since the actor actually had a line of custom-made golf clubs of his own called The Millionaires Club, all of which were marked with Jackie Gleason's signature.

The clubs themselves have no inherent value in the world of sports memorabilia, but because they belonged to a celebrity, they are of great interest to collectors. At auction they could easily bring $3,000 to $4,000.

A money clip presented to British golf champion Max Faulkner in 1957, when he was a member of the winning Ryder Cup team for the second time.

remarkable material in existence. Balls, clubs, autographs of famous players (even from the 1800s), scorecards, paintings, ceramic and glass objects featuring golf, trophies, medals, trading cards, golf bags, pins, passes, flags, and—yes—tees all interest collectors. (Pick up a price guide for tees, tee boxes, and tee bags, and you'll be surprised at the going rates.)

The field is so large that collecting golf memorabilia necessitates making thoughtful choices. Collecting a little bit of everything is the surest way to assemble a formless collection that is neither particularly satisfying nor valuable. It's preferable, by far, to specialize, and by focusing on one or two types of collectible, you won't be overwhelmed by the abundance of golf-related material in the market. You will also have a chance to become an expert on the items that appeal to you. With the help of a good library of books on the subject (see the Reading List and Bibliography, page 543) try to learn all you can about your favorites including their age, historical significance, availability, and rarity, along with what is coveted by other collectors and dealers and what doesn't interest them (among which are scorecards, golf markers, golf-bag tags, and pencils). Of course, items that haven't much value on their own will stir interest if they have an illustrious provenance, such as having been used by a Ben Hogan or an Arnold Palmer. What is most interesting, however, is that while baseball collectors casually ignore most old items not autographed by famous players, golf memorabilia collectors seek out those clubs and balls used by amateur or unknown players, because they document the development of the game. They are sports purists who believe that the game is more important than the players. Tiger Woods might agree.

A circa 1935 advertising figure promoting Dunlop golf balls depicts a bag-carrying caddie with a golf ball–shaped head.

GOLF CLUBS

To the uninitiated, a golf club might not seem to impart much information, but collectors read in it the development of the game and the history of industrialization. Early wooden golf clubs, beginning in the mid-eighteenth century, were made by woodworkers, carpenters, bow makers, coopers, and others with wood-working skills. Hugh Philp in St. Andrews, Scotland, Robert Forgan, James Wilson, Alexander Patrick, J. Jackson, Alexander Munro, and the Peter McEwan family were among the skilled craftsmen who made golf clubs. As the nineteenth century unfolded, more professionals specializing in golf equipment emerged. In addition to playing matches, during a time when amateurs were more respected than professionals, such men cared for golf courses, perhaps caddied, and produced clubs and balls. It was a group that included Old Tom Morris, Willie Park (Sr. and Jr.), and Willie and Jamie Dunn. The dominant golfer of the 1860s (despite losing at least two highly publicized matches to Willie Park, Sr.)—and probably the first golfer to recognize the value of autographed items—Old Tom Morris set up his shop in St. Andrews in 1864, across the street from the eighteenth tee of the world's most famous golf course. (Like his father, the even more talented and storied Young Tom Morris would win four British Opens before dying at the age of 24 in 1875.)

EARLY CLUBS

WOODS

Clubs prior to 1800 were seldom marked, but by the nineteenth century, club makers were stamping their names on wooden club heads. Unfortunately for today's collector, most of those markings have worn away, and because identification can be difficult, those clubs that do come with evidence of their ownership and approximate dates of use command a premium.

As balls became less fragile (see page 145), wood clubs (or woods) became a bit more robust; a thicker neck could stand up

WOULDN'T YOU RATHER OWN A MASHIE?

Golf club nomenclature has evolved and changed over the years. Before matched sets became popular in the 1920s, and the numbering system was adopted by manufacturers in the 1940s, a late-nineteenth-century golf bag would have contained clubs with names that had a distinct Scottish burr. There might be several woods: a play club, used for teeing off a mound of dirt (called a 1 wood or driver today), a brassie (2 wood), and a spoon (3 wood); as well as several irons: a cleek (2 iron), a mashie (5 iron), and a niblick (8 or 9 iron, although there were wooden niblicks, too). The names gave great character to the clubs; it's almost a shame they're seldom used today.

This circa 1880 play club (driver) made by Old Tom Morris is the oldest known club using steel in its shaft. The shaft is constructed of twelve pieces of cane—six inner and six outer—around a tubular steel core.

A CHARLES HUNTER BRASSIE

A vintage golf club, known as a "brassie" because of the brass plate on the bottom of the club (the modern equivalent of the #2 wood), was brought to the Toronto *Antiques Roadshow* by a woman who had received it from her father in England. It had been made circa 1880 for Charles Hunter—a head professional at the venerable course at Prestwick, Scotland, beginning in the 1860s.

Appraiser Christopher Mitchell pointed out features to look for in an old golf club. A piece of horn, for example, had been inlaid on the front side of the club to protect the wood and make it last longer. On the back, a channel had been cut and inlaid with lead to give the club weight and help elevate the ball.

This club was in very good condition. The inlaid horn was still intact—rare in clubs this old. Also rare was that Charles Hunter's name engraved on top of the club's head was still legible. Most important, the club hadn't been refinished or altered in any way. Considering its excellent condition and that clubs from the 1880s are very scarce, Mitchell valued it between $3,000 and $4,000. The visitor's comment? "Thank you, Dad."

From left: On June 19, 1876, the first patent ever issued for a golf club was given to Thomas Johnston of Edinburgh, the maker of this spoon (for short-range shots). Middle: An early presentation putter engraved with the Celtic cross, made by Hugh Philp, whose putters are particularly sought after by collectors. Right: A left-handed play club once owned by Willie Dunn, from the 1840s.

to the harder new ball. Around 1860, American hickory started replacing ash, lemonwood, redheart, hazelwood, lancewood, and other woods as the material of choice for shafts. Woods made around 1880 are known as long-nosed woods, a term that accurately describes their shape. The clubhead was spliced to the shaft, glued, and wrapped in twine known as whipping. Long-nosed woods were suited to their job, which was to send balls airborne from sheep-mown fairways. As the 1880s progressed, the manufacturers began to shorten the heads of wooden clubs from heel to toe. Collectors refer to these clubs as semi long-nose. A more convex club with a protruberant clubface, known as "the bulger," also developed during this transitional era for golf equipment.

In the 1890s, persimmon, a native American wood, became the material of choice for producing the clubhead for woods, and would remain so for decades. Another major change was that spliced necks were being phased out by socket heads, although they would continue to be produced as late as the early 1920s. For these new socket-head clubs, the neck was drilled out to create a hole into which the shaft was fitted and secured.

IRONS

Early irons, made by armor makers, toolmakers, and blacksmiths, were necessary for playing out of difficult lies: balls that landed in cart ruts, sand, or the dreaded rough, for instance. Prior to 1850, irons were not used often, perhaps due to the fragility of the balls, so irons that *were* made in the first half of the nineteenth century are rare and highly desirable. In the late nineteenth century, however, blacksmiths and other iron producers increased their iron production to include the long-faced "cleek" iron (which produced little loft), the small-headed "rut" iron (for bad surfaces), and the "sand" iron. They did so by using first, steam- and then electric-powered hammers and, eventually dies. Called cleek makers, they used methods that allowed them to bridge the transition from hand-forged, blacksmith-produced irons to drop-forged, mass-produced factory irons. Proud cleek makers stamped their products with their names and with symbols (such as stars) known as cleek marks. The pursuit of cleek marks has become a passion of many collectors and, therefore, a large part of club collecting. According to experts, there are more than 150 known marks. (Note that because professionals and retailers often purchased club heads for assembly, clubs might also bear a seller's mark.)

Iron-head golf clubs produced by blacksmiths prior to about 1880 were seldom marked. The absence of a mark, however, does not necessarily mean that the iron was made by a blacksmith, because the markings may have been removed. Once again, provenance is important to determining value.

Left: A circa 1880 cleek (1-iron) made by F. & A. Carrick of Musselburgh, Scotland, who took over their father's blacksmith and tool manufacturing business in the 1850s. For the Carricks, forging clubheads was a sideline to their main business: making hand tools.

THE 1890S THROUGH THE 1940S

An increase in the game's popularity and rapid advances in technology led to a golf boom in the United States that started in the 1890s, increased dramatically after World War I with the emergence of star American golfers Walter Hagen, Bobby Jones, and Gene Sarazen, and lasted into the 1930s. This was a time of innovation and experimentation, with patents being applied for and granted on the dizzying array of clubs that provide today's collectors with a wealth of unusual material to choose from. You can find, fairly readily, patent clubs that have an unconventional shape, are made of unusual materials, or are embellished with striking motifs. Individual patent clubs may exhibit bold redesigns of traditional features. For example, Brown's patented perforated irons (which resemble rakes) were so popular in the early twentieth century that they were offered in at least nine styles.

The majority of irons made before 1900 had no identifying markings on their faces, and for some collectors, this obscurity adds

Osmund's Patent Automation Caddy, manufactured—probably in the 1920s—by John Jaques & Sons, a venerable British sporting goods manufacturer founded in 1765. This device allowed a person playing without a caddy to keep his clubs off the ground. Variations are still used today.

to the clubs' appeal and value. Players, however (with little concern for future collectors), discovered that patterns scratched onto the faces of irons increased backspin on the ball, leading to greater control of the shot. So, from the 1890s on, manufacturers put design dots on the faces of irons, and within a few years these patterns included, among others, hyphens, dot punches, deep grooves, crisscrosses, and scored lines, some of which are still being used today. A few of the designs on what were often called "fancy-face irons" were controversial, however. For instance, a deep-groove pattern introduced in 1914 was widely criticized for making the game less challenging. After Jock Hutchinson won the 1921 U.S. Open using the deep-groove clubs, there was such a backlash that the pattern was discontinued. But golf collectors love it.

Some collectors hunt for old clubs with unusual neck designs, such as A. H. Scott's patented fork splice, or clubs that resulted from early experiments with compressed wood, marketed under such "futuristic" names as Forganite and Kroydonite (delete the

THE 1890S THROUGH 1940

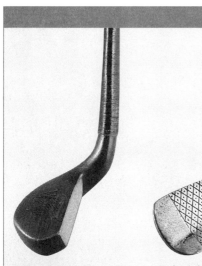

This one-of-a-kind offset putter crafted by Charles Brand of Carnoustie, Scotland, circa 1895, is the only known wooden long-nose club made with a wry-neck (the lower neck curves back to offset the blade).

A dual-face mashie (5-iron), designed and patented by Thomas Sharpe in 1906. This club provided increased backspin, negotiated stymies (shots taken when an opponent's ball is in the way), and hit short, elevated shots.

The A. G. Spalding & Sons Cash-In Putter, produced from the 1930s to the 1980s, was one of its most popular putters and used by many PGA Tour Pros. The Cash-In was designed by Robert Cash, who received a patent for the club on June 10, 1930. This is one of his original models.

A patent club designed in 1935 by Edmond Glover of Tenafly, New Jersey, allowed a player to change the position of the iron's blade to respond to a ball's lie.

"ite" and you have the manufacturer's name). Others pursue the Farlie, Smith, and other clubs featuring patented designs that were not only pleasing to the eye, but also by guaranteeing that the ball was struck squarely with the clubface, promised to prevent the dreaded shank shot. Although such innovative clubs were produced in large numbers, they are justifiably popular with collectors.

Even at the end of the nineteenth century, golfers were clamoring for better putters. In 1894, Scotsman Willie Park came up with his famous Park Patent Bent Neck Putter. Park bent the hosel, which connects the shaft to the clubhead, giving players a better view of the blade (the bottom edge of the clubhead). By the first decades of the twentieth century, European and American companies, such as Standard, James Anderson, MacGregor, the Newark-based The (William) Burke Golf Co. (which also made hickory buggy whips), and A. G. Spalding were producing mallet-head putters in a variety of materials, including brass and aluminum. French golf professional Jean Gassiat produced a putter around 1910 that had a large rectangular head that resembled a grand piano. Called "the Gassiat," this distinctive wood putter in top condition fetches over $1,200 today.

Some of the most sought-after clubs of the 1920s and 1930s are those fancy-face woods. Featuring inserts with appealing, often humorous, designs directly on the clubfaces, they have a lot of character. Steel, brass, or other hard materials strengthen their hitting surfaces, and while the majority of these clubs have hickory shafts, steel-shafted clubs were produced as well.

Even after steel shafts became legal for tournament play (1926 in America and 1930 in Great Britain), hickory-shaft clubs continued to be manufactured by manufacturers such as MacGregor, Spalding, and Gibson. By the mid-1930s, millions of wood-shaft golf clubs had been produced by American factories and today, they exist in such quantities and are so common that collectors ignore them. Golf clubs with wooden shafts, therefore, aren't necessarily valuable.

When the steel-shaft club, after many years of experimentation, supplanted the hickory-shaft club in the mid-1930s, that ended what today's collectors refer to as the "antique golf club era." Of the many steel-shaft clubs that were produced then, perhaps the most coveted today is the bullet-shaped MacGregor "Streamliner," an unusual wood bearing an evocative name.

"The Gassiat," originally called the Chantilly putter, was named for Jean Gassiat, a professional at the Chantilly golf course, who won the French Open in 1912.

Manufactured in 1937, MacGregor Streamliner drivers were aerodynamically designed to concentrate all their weight directly behind the ball. Great in theory, they did not perform—nor were they legal for play. They are, however, highly collectible.

A Ben Hogan Saber 4 Iron from his second design, produced from 1955 to 1957. Hogan destroyed the entire first production run in 1954 because he was dissatisfied with the quality.

A Tommy Armour Silver Scot Tourney 3852S putter, manufactured by MacGregor in the late 1930s or early 1940s and modeled after the Spalding HB putter first offered in 1919. All Tommy Armour putters were very popular. They featured shallow blades and remained in use for high-level play long after they were discontinued.

The Wilson "Designed by Arnold Palmer" putter was produced in 1962 and 1963. In 1963 and 1964, Wilson produced an identical putter without Palmer's name, marked "The Wilson 8802." Both versions have a devoted following and have been used by major players— among them Lee Trevino and Ben Crenshaw.

THE 1940S THROUGH THE 1960S

"Classic" clubs are those clubs that were manufactured throughout the forties, fifties, and sixties, after the "antique" golf club era. Not all clubs of this period, however, qualify as classics. A classic is determined by age, maker, fame, and quality— with an emphasis on quality. Classic woods were fashioned of the finest oil-hardened persimmon and crafted by skilled woodworkers. Classic irons, wedges, and putters were fashioned from high-quality castings, expertly hand-ground. Many classic clubs were so player friendly that, even until the late 1980s, they were sought by amateur and professional alike for play as well as for collections— often twenty or thirty years after they were produced. A prime example is the Bristol George Low Sportsman Wizard 600 putter. Years after the last club was produced in 1962, it was used by Jack Nicklaus to win major championships. A Low Sportsman 600 could easily bring more than $10,000 today.

MacGregor is credited with most of the collectible classic clubs of the forties and fifties. The chief designers and innovators of this period, Tommy Armour and Toney Penna, worked with some of the greatest male and female players of the game: Ben Hogan, Byron Nelson, Jimmy Demaret, Louise Suggs, and Jack Nicklaus, to create superb clubs that today sell for well over $1,000 in top condition. In recent years, Fred Couples and Nick Faldo won major tournaments using vintage MacGregor drivers. Other classic club makers favored by collectors are Wilson (which produced better collectible clubs than MacGregor in the sixties) for irons, putters, and wedges; H & B for its PowerBilt woods; Ben Hogan for irons; and Spalding for irons and putters.

No one can predict whether classic clubs from this era, or any other era, will increase in value, so it pays to look first for quality, no matter what club you collect. Keep in mind that some clubs that appear to be old and fabulous are modern and valueless reproductions of valuable antiques. Also remember that the dating of golf clubs is not an exact science, and that it's always possible that a manufacturer might produce a favorite style of club many years after it was first in fashion. This doesn't mean it isn't necessarily collectible or valuable. It just might not be exactly the club you thought you were purchasing—and it should be.

EVALUATING GOLF CLUBS

As with all collectibles, condition is important for ascertaining value, and naturally, clubs in poor condition are not as desirable or valuable as those in mint condition, excellent condition, or even fair condition. Never try to restore your own club collection, however, because refinishing, reshafting, rechroming, and even regripping will lessen the value of a club even more. If you must restore, go to a professional!

When considering a purchase, you'll want a club that hasn't been used much. The closer it is to mint condition, the better. With woods, check to see if there are cracks in the head or if the club face has been filed or sanded. Any epoxy repairs or wood grafts in the toe and heel areas reduce desirability. Lettering and identification stamps should be clear and deep.

With irons, look for wear on the chrome if the club is chrome plated (1930 or later). Stamps should be clear. For steel-shafted clubs, check the entire shaft for dings and dents, pitting, and rust. Make sure the shaft is straight and check the condition of the shaft band.

For older clubs with wooden shafts, make sure there is no splitting, cracking, or warping. (If the shaft has warped, a professional restorer can repair this without a loss in value.) Many wooden shafts were stamped just below the grip; check to see if there is a stamp. Check the length of the club, too, to see if it has been shortened for use by a child.

GOLF BALLS

The balls that Renaissance-era royalty played with were most likely made of boxwood, but by the seventeenth century, a far more successful ball was developed, known as the "feathery." This was a leather ball, soaked in alum and stuffed with a top-hat-ful of boiled feathers, which dried to nearly the hardness of wood. It provided the player with more give than boxwood and a much better flight. A good drive with a feathery might be 150 to 180 yards. When the hide covering got wet, however, the ball tended to drop like a stone and come apart. The manufacture of the feathery was so difficult, more-

IS IT REALLY A GOLF BALL?

Identifying early golf equipment can be difficult. Unusual clubs may be rare finds, but they may also be reproductions or period clubs from games other than golf. Balls can pose problems, as well. Feathery balls have been reproduced, and old leather-covered balls from other games can be misidentified as rare featheries. Savvy collectors know that any ball that has stitching on the outside can be eliminated, because the stitches on a true feathery are concealed within.

It may take considerable detective work to tell the difference between a solid gutty ball and a rubber-core ball without destroying either. This is particularly a difficulty with balls of gutta-percha mesh (or bramble) covers, because this was used on both types of balls. One way to get it right is to ask an expert; another is to try to match the ball to known examples in books.

THE ELUSIVE FEATHERY

The most sought-after of the collectible golf balls is the feathery, and the rarest of these have commanded five-figure prices. Smooth gutta-percha balls from the mid-nineteenth century and balls that have been hand-hammered or line-marked with a chisel also command a premium. A Henry's rifled ball from 1903, its cover pattern spiraled like the rifling of a gun barrel, recently changed hands for $40,000!

over, that it took cobblers a full day to craft just three or four balls—and because they were so fragile, a player needed six or more to complete one round of golf. Featheries, consequently, were more expensive than clubs.

It wasn't until the development of the gutta-percha (or "gutty") ball, around 1850, that golf became widely affordable. Gutta-percha is a tough, plasticlike substance made from the latex of various Malaysian trees. The gutta-percha was shaped into golf balls

A rare and expensive feathery made and labeled by William Gourlay circa 1840, about a decade before the development of gutta-percha revolutionized the making of golf balls and, consequently, the sport.

with a smooth finish, but they didn't fly very well, so golfers began to mark their surfaces to make them fly truer and farther, 200 yards or more. One method was to use the claw end of a hammer to dent the surface. Today, collectors refer to these balls as "hand hammered." Robert Forgan, a ball and club maker at St. Andrews, is credited with selling the first balls with surface patterns.

By the 1880s, markings on the balls were cast in molds. The 1890s saw dozens of pattern designs, and the "bramble" (a hobnail or bumpy finish) emerged as the favorite. In 1898, American Coburn Haskell introduced rubber-core balls, made by winding thin elastic rubber-band-like threads around a small rubber core and coating the whole with gutta-percha. This wrapping was initially performed by hand, until a machine was invented to accomplish the task and increase production. The original Haskell ball had a mesh cover, but it was replaced with a superior bramble cover. The improved Haskell ball was so successful and so high-flying that golf courses had to be redesigned around it. It ended the gutty ball era.

In 1909, Spalding began to produce the dimple pattern ball that would become the standard. Manufacturers continued, however, to experiment with cover designs through the teens and into the twenties, until Spalding's American patent expired. By the 1920s, the gutta-percha cover was giving way to the softer balata cover that is still in use today.

Another golf ball improvement was the liquid-core ball, based on patents obtained by Eleazer Kempshall in 1902. The liquid core was the ball

An unpainted, solid gutta-percha ball from 1902, with a rifled pattern, made and labeled by Henry.

A hand-hammered "gutty," circa 1860 (right), with a pattern said to have been designed by early clubmaker Robert Forgan, the nephew of Hugh Philp. Its patterns were hammered into the ball's surface to improve its flight.

of choice until the 1960s, when the one-piece rubber ball was introduced.

Signature balls, imprinted by the manufacturer with a professional's name or signature, are a popular and—for the most part—accessible category of golf ball collecting. These balls should not be confused with autographed balls signed by a pro with a pen. Technically, the signature ball began in the feathery era, when players and makers stamped their own names on balls, but turn-of-the-twentieth-century British golfing great Harry Vardon was the first professional player to "be paid for the use of his name on a golf ball: the Vardon Flyer, a gutty manufactured by A. G. Spalding & Bros. In the 1920s, sporting-goods companies, including Wilson and Worthington, started to imprint balls with the names of the stars who used them, among them Walter Hagan, Tommy Armour, and Jock Hutchison. By the mid-thirties, major golf-ball producers were promoting Sold-Only-in-Golf-Stores lines of professional-quality balls, leaving lesser signature balls to sporting goods and department stores. Although the dimple cover standardized the look of most balls produced after World War II, there were so many signature balls that collectors today have a lot to choose from. For instance, a collector might track down all the variations of MacGregor's Jack Nicklaus ball—there are approximately 140 variations. Note one interesting subgenre in this specialty: signature balls with the names of celebrities and politicians rather than golfers.

If you find an empty vintage golf ball box, don't throw it out. Collectors crave those as well.

With Coburn Haskell's introduction of rubber-core golf balls in 1898, gutta-percha balls quickly became outmoded. This example of a Haskell ball is from 1899.

SIZE COUNTS

Standardization of the size and weight of golf balls in the United States was finally hammered out in 1932, when the United States Golf Association established the weight at a maximum of 1.62 ounces, and the diameter as not less than 1.68 inches. In the United Kingdom, the Royal & Ancient Golf Association standards were slightly different: The weight was the same, but the diameter could be as small as 1.62 inches. This big ball–little ball rift lasted until 1983, when the U.S. standard was adapted in Great Britain; it has now become nearly universal.

WORKS OF ART

One of the primary attractions of golf paintings, prints, and sculptures is that they capture the personal and private pleasures of the pastime of golf: The sky, the grass, the trees, the weather. What they don't usually depict are the game's frustrations.

Signature balls, such as this mid-1960s one from Arnold Palmer, make good golf collectibles for the fan just starting out.

A photogravure of Old Tom Morris (1821–1908) after a portrait by Jermyn Brooks. Morris was a golf champion, course designer, club maker, and pioneering professional at St. Andrews in Scotland.

A somewhat primitive painting signed "Wood Club" and entitled "Holing Out" is probably from the early twentieth century. It depicts players and their caddies on the green.

There are a number of early prints and paintings depicting golflike games, many of which come from seventeenth-century Holland. (One Rembrandt etching is often referred to as "The Golf (or Kolf) Player," when in fact it depicts an early Dutch game called beugelen.) A portrait of William St. Clair of Roslin—club in hand, addressing the ball—painted by Sir George Chalmers in 1771, is perhaps the first professionally painted portrait of a known golfer. A painting of the Old Course at St. Andrews, dating to around 1820, is believed to be the earliest depiction of golf in Scotland.

Some golf images have proven to be so popular that they have been reproduced over and over. One fine example is the *Blackheath Golfer* print depicting William Innes, the captain of the Society of Golfers at Blackheath. Originally painted by Lemuel Francis Abbot, it was published as a print in 1790. The print was issued in numerous editions from 1790 to 1926, and it is important to find an expert to distinguish between them because that affects their value. (The earliest versions are the most desirable.) Most of these prints are marked "Engraving by V. Green Mezzotint," whether they are originals or not; later printing simply copied the original engraver's name.

Many of the portraits of golfers dating from the early nineteenth century are life-size, and some of these were reproduced as smaller mezzotints. Works of art picturing golf and golfers in this earlier period were much like the game itself, a luxury of the wealthy. As the game spread—and as improved equipment such as the gutty ball and then the solid-core ball expanded golf's reach—artists responded. With the golf boom of the 1890s came more prints and paintings, along with illustrations in magazines and books. The first print to depict a *professional* golfer was a photogravure by H. J. Brooks of Old Tom Morris. A four-time British Open champion, a renowned ball and club maker, and the greens keeper and professional at St. Andrews, Morris the elder was the subject of various paintings and prints throughout the late nineteenth and early twentieth centuries. (He was known to sign limited-edition prints long before the collecting of such autographed sports items came into vogue.)

When the English magazine *Vanity Fair* published eight caricatures of golfers in a "Men of Their Day"

A 1906 calendar distributed by a Scottish life insurance company features the British Open champions of 1905 gathered together at St. Andrews, where the tournament was played that year. Four-time winner Old Tom Morris is recognizable at center.

A postcard with Howard Chandler Christy's "The Golf Girl" from a series of six drawings entitled Types of the American Girl *from 1900. At least a few women were getting on the course.*

feature, these became almost instant collectibles. Sir Leslie Ward, known as "Spy," created seven of the eight caricatures; the last was the work of Liberio Prosperi, who signed his work "Lib." Copies of the lithographs could be obtained separately from the publisher, and many enthusiasts still pursue the individual images in the hope of assembling a complete set. Well-known American illustrators, such as Howard Chandler Christy, Charles Dana Gibson, and Harrison Fisher, drew images of golfers that were used to create prints, cartoons, and postcards. The Perrier water company commissioned a series of humorous golf cartoons entitled "The Rules of the Game," comprising twenty-four illustrations by Charles Crombie (for more on Crombie, see the Ceramics chapter, page 1). The illustrations were so popular that they were often removed from the book and framed, making the complete book that much more difficult for collectors to find.

Practically any work of art that depicts golf courses or golfers has become collectible: cartoons, posters advertisements, photographs, and paintings—including very bad paintings of famous golfers, and very good paintings of unknown golfers.

Sculptors have also explored the subject of golf. Works range from elegant bronzes depicting such greats of the game as Harry Vardon (who battled fellow Britons J. H. Taylor and James Braid for golf supremacy early in the twentieth

From the early twentieth century, a silver-gilt six-inch figurine of golfing great Harry Vardon (1870–1937) after the original by Hal Ludlow. Number 1 of a limited edition of 60.

A Royal Doulton plate with one of Charles Crombie's Classic Rules of Golf illustrations. The legend reads "Every Dog Has His Day and Every Man has his Hour."

This Weller Dickensware vase, decorated with a lady golfer, would be a sought-after collectible by both Weller and golf memorabilia enthusiasts.

century), to the amusing papier-mâché golf ball–head golfer used to advertise Silver King golf balls. With golf art, the collector can enjoy his favorite sport even as he sits by the fire in winter, dreaming of spring.

DECORATIVE ARTS

The game of golf turns up on decorative works in a variety of materials, particularly glass and ceramics. Countless representations of golfers tee off on tobacco jars, beer steins, ashtrays, jardinières, and vases, as well as on Copeland Spode stoneware ewers. England's Royal Doulton porcelain factory has made a specialty of golf-related ceramics, producing scores of commemorative plates and a series of golf ware that collectors crave. And for decades, ashtrays and humidors with golf themes have been the gift of choice for the golfer who has everything.

For the young golfer, there is a 1930s children's breakfast set with a "Bunnykins" teeing off in perfect form, or a true crossover collectible—a Brownies cup and saucer set adorned with Palmer Cox's Brownie characters playing golf.

There is also an interesting selection of golf-themed glass items, many of which reflect the social aspect of reviewing the game over cocktails and regaling guests with stories of great moments on the green. Barstool golf memorabilia includes cocktail shaker sets along with decanters, bottles, ice buckets, and pitchers, all adorned with golf scenes. It bears remembering, however, that smart golfers always designate their driver.

Antiques shows are excellent venues for winkling out the golf motif cocktail shakers and glasses that awaited at the nineteenth hole. Or the 1920s Carltonware humidor that was the

A tyg—a large ceramic drinking vessel with handles—from Lenox sports a sterling silver rim and hand-painted scene of a male and a female golfer.

family's gift to Dad on Father's Day (for more on Carltonware, see page 18). The pursuit of such golf memorabilia may put you in competition with collectors outside the field, so don't be surprised if the cocktail shaker you covet is also on the list of a determined cocktail-shaker collector.

GOLF TROPHIES AND MEDALS

Once upon a time in the collectibles world, golf trophies were among the things that dealers simply couldn't get rid of. Particularly below the radar were silver trophies, which were frequently sold for scrap and melted down. But today, handsome golf trophies find good homes, and that formerly despised silver tray, *if* won by a famous golfer or *if* commemorating an important match, is now a sought-after collectible.

The custom of awarding some kind of prize, such as a trophy or medal, is well established in the United States and abroad. Generally speaking, experts say, trophies are more commonly American than British, while medals are more commonly British than American. In addition to the good old-fashioned loving cup, all sorts of objects have been made into golf trophies: Ashtrays, statues, cigarette boxes, mugs, trays, crystal decanters, clocks, and watches. Although the British Open championship belt is no longer awarded, the winner of that Grand Slam event is always given a silver replica of the original ceramic claret jug. And each year in Georgia, the Masters champion is awarded a replica of the original trophy depicting the Augusta clubhouse. A medal also goes to the low-scoring amateur at the Masters Championship and to the winners of various amateur tournaments.

Golf medals can be made of brass, silver, bronze, pewter, gold, or combinations of these. Medals are undeniably handsome, satisfyingly weighty in the hand, and easy to display, and they can be miniature works of art. Golf medals, say

SILVER SPOONS . . . AND MORE

Along with trophies and medals, there is considerable collectible golf memorabilia in silver and gold. Sterling silver souvenir spoons, for instance, were sold at the famous old courses for tourists to take home. Silver golf-motif whisky flasks, hat pins, match safes, and nut trays, as well as gold cuff links, brooches, and cigarette cases, were all offered at jewelry stores and were made by the best American manufacturers: Whiting, Gorham, Unger Brothers, and Tiffany, among them. These can be exciting yard sale and eBay finds.

One large and one small golf gold medal from the Professional Golfers Association of Great Britain. The large one is from the 1951 British Open, which was won by Max Faulkner.

Examples from a collection of 49 demitasse spoons of various dates from golf courses around the world, among them Walton Heath, Little Aston, Singapore, New Delhi, and many others. Silver spoons made tidy souvenirs for traveling golfers.

A Mecca Golf card featuring George Low, a Scottish golf professional who came to the United States in 1899. For many years, he was the professional at the Baltusrol Golf Club in New Jersey.

medal enthusiasts, are especially pleasant to collect because there's a little romance, a little story, behind each one.

Naturally, medals from important championships are more attractive to collectors than medals from the local public course. Gold medals are more highly valued and, of course, more valuable intrinsically than bronze medals. Still, if that gold medal or sterling trophy was won by the vice president of the local Kiwanis club, it's not likely to be as collectible as even nonprecious prizes won by, say, Sam Snead or Jack Nicklaus. Celebrity players' awards are always most desirable, as are those from major tournaments. One example, the 1897 U.S. Open Gold Medal sold for $50,000.

TRADING CARDS

The first golf cards appeared in England around 1900, and they depicted not famous players but golf strokes and views of well-known courses. Around 1910, the American Tobacco Company published a series of cards of champion athletes, and in that series were the images of six golfers. This Mecca Cigarette Set included cards picturing American golfers Gil Nicholls, Finley Douglas, Fred Herreshoff, Jack Hobens, Alex Smith, and George Low.

Around the same time, a set of photographic cards was produced in England for Ogden's Guinea Gold Cigarettes that pictured Old Tom Morris, Harry Vardon, and James Braid. This set also included golf match cards, among them one depicting Vardon vs. Braid. In the 1920s, W. A. and A. C. Churchman produced a set of 50 famous golfers. Other tobacco cards followed, to be joined by cards for chocolates, newspapers, and a variety of other products. Simultaneously, complete golfer card sets were produced in the United States. Collectors of American golf cards look for Bobby Jones and his competitors Walter Hagen and Gene Sarazen (whose claim to fame was winning the 1932 U.S. and British Opens with his new invention—the sand wedge). But collectors should be aware that some early cards have been reproduced in recent years.

Left: The front and reverse of a W A & A. C. Churchman cigarette card, from its series of fifty famous golfers, issued in the 1920s. This card features the U. S. phenomenon, Bobby Jones. Right: A tobacco card issued by J. Millhoffer & Co. Ltd. pictures Miss Doris Chambers, a British golf champion who won the Ladies Open in 1923.

Among the more whimsical prizes for golf card collectors is the National Exchange Bank of Providence, Rhode Island's "The Seven Ages of Golf." This seven-card set from 1902 features various golf vignettes, from a baby teething on a club to a gentleman so elderly that his caddy has to tee up his ball. The very last card, and the seventh of the Seven Ages, depicts a bearded old man seated on the terrace at the eighteenth hole, longingly watching as the players come in.

Although there are dedicated collectors, the market for golf cards has never reached the fever pitch of the baseball card market and therefore prices, for the most part, are much more reasonable. That may be changing, however, as an increasing number of card sets have come on the market since the arrival of Tiger Woods. Not surprisingly, the most valuable cards picture Woods, among them a 2001 SP Authentic that currently brings well over $1,000. Other golfers on pricey cards include Sergio Garcia, Matt Kuchar, John Daly, Jack Nicklaus, David Duval, and Woods's female counterpart, Annika Sorenstam.

A useful first step in exploring golf memorabilia is assembling a strong library; the books in the Reading List and Bibliography (page 543) are a good place to start.

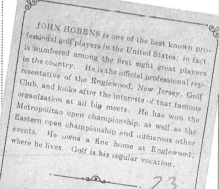

In the early 1900s, Mecca Cigarettes, an American Tobacco Company brand, issued a series of cards featuring champion golfers, Jack Hobens among them. Hobens was the professional at the Englewood, New Jersey, golf club and founding member of the U.S. PGA.

FISHING TACKLE

Kentucky watchmaker George Snyder revolutionized the fishing reel in about 1820 by adding gears, making them more efficient and simpler to use. "Kentucky" reels, especially those made by Snyder, such as this example from the 1830s, are highly collectible.

This 1950s Doc's Menhaden Minnow Motion Lure, here with its original graphic-covered box, was made by the Sanford Metal Bait Company in Florida and undoubtedly would lure collectors.

A dramatic, three-dimensional celluloid die-cut counter display from about 1920 for fishing tackle from Shakespeare, a company that originated in Kalamazoo, Michigan, in 1897 and is still a leading fishing-tackle manufacturer today.

Sports enthusiasts have long considered fishermen a breed apart. In the nineteenth century, Grover Cleveland, a fine fisherman and perhaps the sport's most vocal proponent among United States presidents, griped whimsically about "the narrow and ill-conditioned people who snarlingly count all fishermen as belonging to a lazy and good-for-nothing class, and who take satisfaction in describing an angler's outfit as a contrivance with a hook at one end and a fool at the other." Cleveland, who spent many a day fly-fishing on the Potomac, took pride in being part of a "separate class or sub-race among the inhabitants of the earth."

Certainly fishermen comprise a separate class among collectors of sports memorabilia. Members of the National Fishing Lure Collectors Club take special pleasure in referring to themselves as that imaginary genus and species, *Hoardplugens enmassus,* their own tongue-in-cheek term for plug collectors. With the same unfailing determination, joy, and canniness they use to reel in the most elusive fish in the lakes, ponds, streams, rivers, seas, and oceans of our planet, fishing tackle collectors set out to acquire those aged and rare rods, reels, lures, and flies, some splendid fishing ephemera (including catalogs and posters), and miscellaneous old tackle.

The knowledgable and avid collector will gaze at a lineup of old lures on a shaky table, or at rods leaning on a garage wall, and be touched by their beauty, impressed by their history, and stimulated by their value. He will know, as well, which items to keep and which to throw back.

A BRIEF HISTORY

Two Famous Fishermen

A true crossover collectible for enthusiasts of all three sports featured in this chapter: A baseball card of Red Sox hitter Ted Williams, showing him fishing with golf legend Sam Snead.

Euuropean settlers brought "angling, with a rod and a line and hook" to the New World, where the native people, of course, had been fishing for centuries. Few colonists had time to indulge in fishing for sport, but by the late eighteenth and early nineteenth centuries, American fishermen were casting flies for trout and salmon and lures for bass and pike, using tackle imported from old-line English purveyors such as John Cheek, John Haywood of Birmingham, and the Ustonson and Chevalier families of London. In 1810, the English-made Phantom Minnow became the first artificial lure to appear in the United States. This fabled creature had a distinctly triangular metal head, metal fins, and a silk body, and seems to have been superb at its job, for by the end of the nineteenth century, the little lure was being offered in twelve different lengths and touted in advertisements as the "Celebrated phantom minnow, very fine for black bass and pickerel."

American craftsmen set to work improving fishing tackle, however, and they came up with a number of innovations. Kentucky jeweler, silversmith, and watchmaker George Snyder introduced the world's first precision, free-running bait casting reel around 1820, which improved on the multiplier reels made by the British. Snyder's brilliant stroke was to incorporate watchmaking technology   that is, gears—into his reels. Reels with gears quickly became the standard. Soon, Kentucky had a fine community of reelsmiths and today's collectors covet the vintage Kentucky Reels for their history and craftsmanship. In 1997, a brass bass-fishing bait casting reel designed by Snyder changed hands for $31,350, the highest price ever paid for a piece of American fishing tackle sold at auction.

The Boke of Hawkynge and Huntynge and Fysshynge, *which includes the* Treatise on Fishing with an Angle, *circa 1486 to 1503, is the first known English-language book on fishing. It is attributed to Dame Juliana Berners, although the attribution is tenuous.*

FLEXIBLE RODS

The fishing rod developed rather more slowly than the reel. Until the mid-nineteenth century, rods were made of stiff, solid wood—most often, fine-grained American green-heart and West Indian lancewood. Then a certain Sam Philippi of Easton, Pennsylvania, discovered the secret to creating a flexible fly rod. He simply glued together four long strips of bamboo. Until the 1880s, bait casting rods were an unwieldy 10 to 12 feet long. Then, James Henshall, another Kentuckian, developed a shorter, lighter 8-foot-3-inch version. This "Henshall Rod" would be the prototype for today's bait casting rods, although it was improved upon several years later when James Clark created a rod out of split bamboo. Called the "Chicago Rod," it combined with the Kentucky Reel and the newly introduced artificial plug to increase interest in sport fishing substantially.

Bamboo would remain the choice material for rods of both bait casters and fly fishermen until after World War II; and collectors today who acquire vintage split-bamboo trout and salmon fly-fishing rods and bamboo casting rods often use them as well as display them.

EVALUATING FISHING TACKLE

The rods, reels, lures, and creels (the containers carried by anglers to hold the day's catch) that flooded the market prior to 1900 are extremely desirable to collectors today. Most were put to use when they were originally purchased, and the many that still exist are in poor condition—which is why those in particularly good shape are extremely popular with serious collectors. Unfortunately, lures from this period (their mass production is credited to James Heddon, see box, page 164) have almost entirely disappeared.

After World War II, there was greater prosperity, more leisure time,

A seven-piece bamboo fly rod made by H. L. Leonard, circa 1875, can be assembled as an 8½-foot rod or as a 10-foot-3-inch rod. The butt cap is stamped with the name of John Krider, a Philadelphia tackle dealer.

The seams of this seventeenth-century English leather creel are covered with tar to make them watertight.

Far left: The Florida Shinner was made by F.L.B. Flood for, unsurprisingly, the Florida Shinner Bait Co. in Frostproof, Florida. Lures made by F.L.B. Flood—with their metal fins and carved tails—resemble folk art and are very popular among collectors today.

Left: James Heddon & Sons Tackle Co., of Dowagiac, Michigan, produced this "genuine" Heddon giant Musky Vamp Minnow Lure, circa 1925. The box features a diving bass.

and new materials such as fiberglass and boron. To date, rods constructed from these materials are not considered collectible, but because boron rods were manufactured for little more than a decade, there are far fewer of them in existence than fiberglass rods, and, thus, they may have a better chance of becoming collectible in the future. Today, high-tech rods are made of fiberglass, of the lighter and more powerful graphite, or of a combination of the two. Intriguingly, despite the technological breakthroughs of the second half of the twentieth century, there has been little change in the basic rod and reel.

Dull and cheap plastic lures have found their way into the fisherman's kit, certainly, but fishermen tend to be conservative by nature, and the collector of fishing memorabilia is, at heart, nostalgic and a purist. His collection therefore, usually evokes something of the beauty of his sport, the simplicity and virtue of the man, the water, the rod, and the fish. Plastic may catch a lot of fish, but, currently at least, not the eye and heart of the dedicated collector.

COLLECTING FISHING TACKLE

There are motherlodes of vintage fishing equipment lurking in old tackle boxes, at the backs of garages, and in basements and attics. But collectors don't want *any* old tackle and certainly not rusty lures, reels with tangled lines, cracked rods, or weatherbeaten creels when there is tackle in good condition, perhaps with a pedigree, available. So look for and buy only pieces that improve your collection—or that can

An H. L. Leonard three-piece (with two tips), 11-foot Calcutta bamboo fly rod from 1873 has the usual brown dappling left by the flames commonly used to straighten crooked Indian bamboo.

IDENTIFYING EARLY RODS

Early, handmade fishing rods may be marked, either on the butt cap or on the reel seat itself, while later factory-made rods are usually labeled on the shaft. Because the animal glues that held vintage bamboo fly rods together were prone to fail, the rods had to be bound every few inches with silk thread to hold the strips together. When better glues were developed early in the twentieth century, such safeguards were required only at the ends of the rod sections. The collector should know that early rods will always have intermediate windings, unless they've been refinished—and even then the ghosts of the missing windings will be visible. The presence of intermediate windings, therefore, is usually indicative of age and a good reason to add the rod to a collection.

Minnow buckets such as this one made by Old Pal would have been standard equipment for every weekend fisherman in the late 1950s.

be swiftly sold or traded to someone who needs that item for his own collection. If fly-fishing is your thing, seek out fly-fishing tackle and leave the bait casting tackle to those who collect it. And if you love lures, leave those flies for the fly fisherman.

Because prices have been rising, vintage rods, reels, and lures are now starting to turn up in general antiques and collectibles shops. There are also shops specializing in sporting collectibles that carry fishing items, particularly in parts of the country where fishing is a major pastime. Auctions provide a good way to add to your collection, but if you feel you aren't well enough informed to bid, catalogs of past sales can provide a wealth of information about values. Because many people naively assume the contents of their old tackle boxes and the rods standing in the corner are worthless, tag sales can still hold happy surprises for intrepid and discerning collectors.

Of course, you will find everything imaginable at tackle shows, but interestingly, you might find a better deal at a gun show. Dealers who are experts on rifles and pistols often bring along some vintage fishing tackle and know relatively little about its history and value. If you are the only person attending a gun show seeking fishing tackle, you might just land a big one.

Many collectors and dealers are trawling the Internet as well, hoping to find a rare reel, rod, or lure. Several fishing collectibles Web sites listed in the bibliography offer valuable information (see page 543), but perhaps the greatest source will be other collectors. They know the value of what they have, so you may not find bargains, but they'll supply information, trades, and friendships. They can often steer you in the right direction—to fellow collectors, reputable dealers, or useful links on the Web.

FISHING RODS

Fishing rods are "poles" (considered slang by fishermen) with a handle, a seat for a reel, and guides for a line. The two most commonly collected rods are fly rods, which are long and flexible and are used with a simple reel (mounted on the underside of the rod) that winds a tapered line; and bait casting rods, which are shorter, less flexible, and are often used with a lighter line and a more complex reel (mounted on top).

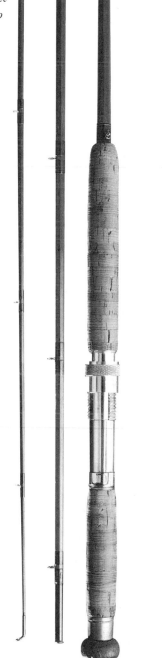

Above: A four-strip bamboo fly rod, made in 1938 by W. E. Edwards. The first bamboo rods were made of four strips, but Hiram Leonard increased the number to six, making the rods both stronger and lighter. Because the glues weren't reliable, the rods were tied at intervals with silk thread.

At right: A ten-foot, three-piece bamboo salmon rod, with two tips and a butt extension, made circa 1930 by Jim Payne.

Although it is collectible, the split-bamboo bait casting rod will usually sell for less than $100, while the best examples of split-bamboo fly rods might bring in the neighborhood of $4,000. Steel, beryllium copper, and modern types of bait casting rods have little, if any, value to collectors.

The fly rods preferred by enthusiasts are the split-bamboo trout and salmon rods that were made from the 1860s until shortly after World War II. Constructed in sections so they could be taken apart for transport, these rods frequently came with two tip sections, because this was the most fragile part of the rod and the most easily broken, and a spare was a good thing to have. Prior to the turn of the twentieth century, fly rods that were used to catch trout and other small fish tended to be 10 to 12 feet in length. More recent fiberglass and graphite rods, however, are generally between 6 and 10 feet long. For larger streams and salt water, longer rods and heavier lines are used.

Salmon rods are substantially longer than trout rods. Two-handed salmon rods made in the United States prior to the 1940s were 14 to 18 feet in length; in Britain, they could be up to 20 feet in length. Both types are sought by collectors. Also collectible are the one-handed bamboo salmon rods that were built from the 1920s into the 1970s. These are generally 16 feet in length and never shorter than 13 feet.

Collectors look for early split-bamboo rods in good condition, and cherish unused examples. Unused rods built by Leonard, Thomas, Edwards, and especially Jim Payne have the highest value—$1,200 to $4,000. Because split-bamboo rods have always been so popular with collectors, some recent brand-new examples produced by Thomas & Thomas, Lyle Dickerson,

Many early fishing rods were equipped with guides made of German silver (also known as nickel silver), an alloy of copper, nickel, and zinc. When German silver corrodes, it turns a dull gray-green. According to A. J. Campbell, a fly-fishing expert, gray-green fittings can be the "kiss of death" to a vintage fishing rod. He adds, "If German silver fittings are dull gray-green, the rod probably has little or no value, so don't bother cleaning it. The energy expended usually reveals pitting from corrosion; and the corrosion itself indicates that moisture has destroyed the rod's integrity, that the glue is no longer sound, and the wraps might be rotten. Also, nickel-plated brass guides often turn gray-green, and those poor-quality fittings are only found on cheap rods."

A very early brass salmon or saltwater reel probably made in New York City is engraved with the name of the owner, G. C. Furman, and the date, 1826; the maker is unknown.

Sam Carlson, and others can command prices equal to the older fly rods—but these are primarily bought by fishermen needing equipment, not by collectors.

OTHER FISHING RODS

Spinning rods, developed in the forties, are popular with fishermen on boats and beaches, and are used on lakes and ponds. These differ from bait casting rods in that the reel mounts under the handle rather than on top, and the guides, therefore, are mounted under the axis of the rod. This arrangement, like that on a fly-fishing rod, facilitates casting. Spinning rods have larger guides than bait casting rods do, to accommodate larger amounts of line when casting. Spinning rods, even bamboo examples, are not yet collectible.

Big-game rods are built to the highest standards because of the stress and weights they must endure to pull in tuna, swordfish, and marlin. They are also known as offshore rods, billfish rods, tuna rods, and deep-sea rods. Big-game fishing, which was made feasible by the motorized boat, was pioneered in California in the late 1890s. It spread to the Atlantic and was given a tremendous boost by Julius vom Hofe of Brooklyn, who in 1913 invented a reel with internal drag. Offshore rods were introduced in the late 1920s. Big-game rods are typically very thick in diameter but just 6½ or 7 feet in length. Boat rods, which can be as short as 5 feet, are best at 6 and 6½ feet. Downrigger rods can be as long as 8 feet. These rods are collected, especially the early ones, but their value depends on their being in very good condition and marked with a high-quality maker's or retailer's name, such as Tycoon, Edward vom Hofe, Hiram L. Leonard, and Thomas Rod Co.

REELS

The use of spoollike fishing reels has been traced to around A.D. 1200 in China. The French may have used wooden reels in the 1500s; the first iron and brass reels probably came from the foundries of Birmingham, England, circa 1650. In 1651, in the earliest known printed reference to a reel, a "wind," installed within two feet of the lower end of a rod is mentioned.

High-quality reels go back to the 1700s, although very few are extant. American reels from the 1800s to the 1870s are referred to as "smith age" reels because much of the finish work was done by hand. (The side plates, however, usually were formed by a drop hammer at a foundry.) Smith Age reels are extremely rare and can command prices from $500 to $3,000.

Very few of Kentuckian George Snyder's improved reels (see page 154) from the 1820s to 1840s were produced and fewer survive today. Collectors of "Kentucky Reels" look for the works of his contemporaries, Meek, Milam, Gayle, Hardman, Conroy, Shipley, and Sage. They also may seek out the "New York Reel" (usually a ball-handled multiplier made of brass or nickel silver), reel makers from Edward and Julius vom Hofe, Conroy, Krider, and Crook.

During the last quarter of the nineteenth century, drag and line levelers were developed, turning the simple fishing reel into an object of mechanical beauty. The reels made during this period, the so-called "Golden Age of the Reel," fuel the collecting market. Because most late nineteenth century reels are unmarked, however, identification can be tricky. Comparing them to illustrations in old advertisements or to any marked reels you may have is the best way to confirm their lineage.

Among reel connoisseurs, Meek has been a name to conjure with since 1835, when B. F. Meek, a Louisville watchmaker, began making reels with his brother J. F. He later worked with fellow reel-maker B. C. Millam before opening his own shop in 1882. His son Sylvanus joined the firm, which was known as B. F. Meek & Sons until 1916 when it was sold to Horton Manufacturing in Connecticut. This No. 3 jeweled free-spool reel was made there, circa 1920.

FLY REELS

A fly reel stores line, provides smooth, uninterrupted tension (drag) when a fish makes a long run; and counterbalances the weight of the rod when casting. It consists of a foot that secures the reel to the rod, a handle, an outside frame, a spool that turns around a pillar that is attached to the frame, and if appropriate, a drag system that puts tension on the revolving spool. The drag system prevents spool overrun and line entanglement and tires the hooked fish by exerting tension on the line. A trout fly reel doesn't need a drag system because of the smallish size of the fish. Salmon reels are larger than trout fly reels and usually have some form of drag mechanism, similar to, but not as heavy as, a saltwater drag. Rachet-and-pawl drag systems are the simplest and most common.

Fly reels have three types of retrieve systems: single-action, which is the most popular because it's light and simple (one turn

A Peerless trout fly reel, made circa 1890 by Edward Vom Hofe, with a nickel-silver frame, aluminum spool, and hard rubber side plates.

Top left: This Pflueger Medalist trout fly reel from 1930, once belonged to noted fly-fishing writer Alfred W. Miller (who wrote under the nom de plume Sparse Grey Hackle). Top right: Orvis is credited with designing the first trout fishing reel. It used a narrow spool to increase the retrieval rate. The perforated sides and spool reduce the reel's weight and also make it easier for the line to dry. This example of an Orvis First Model, circa 1875, has been modified by its owner.

A Pflueger Supreme No. 1573 level-wind, anti-backlash bait casting reel, circa 1920, with its original box. Its level wind feature spreads the line evenly on the spool as the fisherman reels it in.

of the handle completes one turn of the spool); multiplying (which retrieves faster); and the heavier automatic, which incorporates a large coiled spring around the inside of the reel spool.

Collectors particularly seek fly reels from the 1880s to the 1930s, built by Meisselbach, South Bend, Malloch, Julius or Edward vom Hofe, Hardy Bros., Heddon, Shakespeare, Pflueger, and all the other major firms of the "Golden" and "Expansion" ages. Vom Hofe reels, including large salt-water reels, made at the turn of the century with the alloy German silver (also known as nickel silver) and hard rubber, or just German silver, are especially desirable, when they are in good condition. Because they exhibit such fine detailing and craftsmanship, collectors pay a premium for these reels. Recently, a 1902 German silver reel with hard rubber plates, a wood handle, a universal drag system, harness holders on the reel, and a click lever and free spool lever was offered at $1,400.

BAIT CASTING REELS

Bait casting, despite its name, isn't a method of fishing employing live bait; in fact, it uses artificial bait and employs small revolving spool reels that, typically, are equipped with "level wind" mechanisms. (It's also called "plug casting.") Based on the British fly reel, the American bait casting reel was invented at the beginning of the nineteenth century—a time when flies and natural bait were the sport fisherman's only choices. George Snyder's reel (see page 154) was fitted with a spool that would pay out line during the cast. It also featured a multiplying mechanism; turning the handle caused the spool to revolve a greater number of times than the handle was turned. This became known as the multiplying reel or multiplier. The addition of a mechanism to distribute the line on the spool evenly, referred to as a line leveler, was developed in the late nineteenth century, and tangled lines became far less common.

Bait casting reels should correspond to the size of the rods, which are usually 5½ or 6 feet for one-handed rods and from 4½ to 7 feet for two-handed ones. Unlike fly reels, bait casting reels are mounted on top of the rod, to make it easier to

A James Heddon & Sons Model 3–35 bait casting reel from the 1920s. Heddon, who is credited with making the first plug in the 1890s, later founded a tackle company, which became one of the largest in the country.

control fighting fish and retrieve lures. Bait casting reels made before 1900 are extremely collectible and, for the most part, are much higher priced than later, mass-produced reels.

SPINNING REELS

This reel became popular after World War II with anglers who wanted easy-to-use, multitask equipment. The spinning reel—at one time called the open-faced spinning reel—uses a stationary spool around which the line is wound. The size of the reel can vary according to the weight of the line, which ranges from ultralight to heavy. Although spinning reels are nearly all in use rather than on display, enthusiasts should look only for older spinning reels in pristine condition in their original cardboard boxes. By far the most collectible are those made by Illingsworth, as well as the Malloch Side Caster.

SALTWATER REELS

Saltwater reels are extremely well crafted and feature drag mechanisms superior to those on conventional reels. They are built for performance. When freshwater reels started to be used for catching larger saltwater fish, improvements—such as an interior drag mechanism—were added. The star drag applied pressure to the spool so that the hooked, running fish had to work harder for the line. (Drag systems eventually became a standard feature on all bait casting reels.) Collectors are interested only in saltwater reels from the 1920s.

The Seagate reel, manufactured by the Penn Fishing Tackle Manufacturing Company in Philadelphia, was used for deep-sea fishing, primarily for stripers and other sea bass.

IS THIS REEL COLLECTIBLE?

To be considered collectible, a reel should have all its original parts, its screws and nuts, and most important, be in working order. The more common a reel, the more important it is that it be in top condition. Although top condition will always command top dollar, the collecting community is more accepting of imperfections when it comes to rare reels. What collectors want are sharp edges, crisp markings, still-polished hard rubber (and perhaps silver), and intact plating. What they don't want is heavy corrosion, chips and scratches, cracked rubber plates, damaged screws, and missing parts.

Reels are often marked with the name or logo of the retailer (rather than the producer) and the store address. Two examples: Andrew Clerk and Company of New York (succeeded by Abbey & Imbrie); and Bradford & Anthony of Boston (succeeded by Dame, Stoddard, & Kendall). Congress Tackle and Abercrombie & Fitch are twentieth-century retailers that stamped reels with their names. Today's collectors avidly seek reels sold by all these establishments.

A Doddsi dry fly, tied by Preston Jennings, author of A Book of Trout Flies *(1935) and the first American to take a scientific approach to tying flies that simulated the mayflies and other insects that trout actually fed on.*

FLIES AND LURES

Originally known as artificial lures, the fishing lure can be defined, in the broadest sense, as an organic or inorganic object that is meant to deceive its prey—bass, trout, bluefish, pike, or sailfish—into making an unfortunate miscalculation. This is not, however, an angler's definition. In proper tackle talk, real worms, fish, eels, and chunks of meat are bait, and any nonnatural substance with a hook (and a means of being attached to a line) that attracts and snares fish is a lure. Except— and there's always an exception—sometimes bass fisherman in the United States use the word "bait" to describe artificial lures.

Flies were once called artificial flies to distinguish them from the real insects that were commonly used as bait. In the most general interpretation, a fly is a lightweight lure, but don't say that to a fly-fisherman. Lures, which are designed to look—sort of—like small fish and other food that might interest larger fish, are usually about 3 to 9 inches in size. Flies are usually smaller, ⅜ to 1½ inches, corresponding in size to mayflies, grasshoppers, and other insects that fish customarily dine on.

FLIES

The hand-tied fly is a beautiful thing, even to the uninitiated. That is why even nonfishermen collect them. The fly consists of a hook disguised by an attractive arrangement of feathers, string, and sometimes fur. Some flies are designed to float lightly on the water's surface (the dry fly); others are made to sink (the wet fly). Salmon flies, dry or wet, are usually larger, more elaborate, and more colorful than those created for trout, although both trout and salmon flies are made in different sizes to be used in different weather and stream conditions.

The original flies from the 1860s, today termed "classics," were made from feathers. Some of the feathers used in classic salmon flies are from species of birds, such as egrets and eagles, that are now protected, so other types of feathers are dyed today to resemble those that are unavailable; fur or manmade substitutes are also used.

Every fly-fishing region is home to fly-tying experts. Some have been so good at fooling fish with their realistic, tempting handwork that they have achieved national and international status. The following are among the better known fly-tiers: Joseph Bates, Ray Bergman, Megan Boyd, Elsie and Harry Darbee, Winnie and Walt Dette, Charles DeFeo, Syd Glasso, Theodore Gordon, George Grant, Edward Hewitt, James Leisenring, Frances Stearns, Roy Steenrod, and Lee Wulff.

Some of the more famous and collectible fly tiers, such as Carrie Stevens of Maine, "signed" their work. The Stevens signature, for instance, is a tiny red stripe on the head of the fly. (Stevens's striking patterns from sixty and seventy years ago are still being used on contemporary flies, and the originals are extremely valuable.) If a fly lacks a signature, a collector can only identify the maker by having the good fortune to find the fly either in its original wrapper or in its envelope or paper backing, or to locate an old illustration in an advertisement. Try to be sure of your source, because flies with fake signatures or incorrect attributions exist.

Until World War I, most salmon tiers came from England, Scotland, and Ireland, and worked for firms such as Hardy Bros., Samuel Allcock, John Forrest, and Martin Kelly. However, the most sought after and valuable flies are those tied by George M. Kelson, the illustrious author of the classic *The Salmon Fly*, first published in 1895. Some well-known modern-day salmon fly tiers are Charles Defeo, Bill Hunter, Poul Jorgenson, Alex Rogan, and Paul Schmookler.

Three trout flies tied by Catskill tier Walt Dette, from the top, clockwise: Blue Dun, Hare's Ear, and Leadwing Coachman.

A Beauly Snowfly, a nineteenth-century salmon fly that originated on the River Beauly in Scotland, tied by George M. Kelson, author of The Salmon Fly *(1895), whose flies may be the most collectible of all.*

LURES

There is no question that even those who have never used a rod and reel can get caught up in the lure of lures—if for no other reason than their names. Who wouldn't be curious, after all, about lures named Dunk's Double Header, Flange Wobbler, or Wauckazoo Surface Spinner? What about a Dummy Double, a Glutton Dibbler, the Croaker, the Baby Pikie Kazoo, and Goo-

These three Iris Sedge variation salmon flies were tied by Preston Jennings.

MALLOCH FLIES

A visitor to the Boston *Antiques Roadshow* brought in a japanned box filled with fishing flies that had belonged to his grandfather. Appraiser Christopher Mitchell told the visitor that the box was made in Scotland circa 1875 by Peter Duncan Malloch, a famous fisherman who designed the first spinning reel.

Inside the box were more than 200 flies, all in impeccable condition, and all gut snelled (instead of having a metal eye through

which to attach the fly to the line), indicating that they were early examples.

The sheer number of flies in the box, and the fact that they were in perfect condition added to their value. Mitchell told the visitor that the salmon flies were worth $40 to $60 apiece, while the trout flies were worth $10 to $15. Because of the family history, he estimated the box and its contents collection at $4,000 to $6,000.

Eger Baits, in Bartow, Florida, "The World's Greatest Proven Fish Getters," produced this Frogskin Nature Frog Lure circa 1940. Perhaps its most novel lure design, it utilized real frog skin, which was slipped over the lure's wood body and allowed to shrink and cure.

Goo Eyes? And for good measure, how about Husky Musky, the Surface Dingbat, Killer, and the Snagless River Runt?

Lures more than live up to their names. Both new and veteran collectors are attracted to their shape, color, character design, and quasi-realistic form. There are glow-in-the-dark lures for night fishing, luminous painted lures, water sonic plugs, battery-illuminated plugs, and even a small rubber mouse, covered with genuine mouse skin.

Because of the abundance of lures, most collectors wisely narrow the field by focusing on a particular type. Some opt for an all-wood collection; others enjoy collections based on color variations. Some limit their interest to lures that are still in their original boxes, or the lures of a single producer, perhaps Heddon, J. T. Buel, Creek Chubb, Paw Paw Bait Company, Pflueger, Shakespeare, or South Bend.

An original box can greatly increase a lure's value, and empty boxes—particularly for rare lures—can have substantial value on their own. Collectors should also seek old advertisements and catalogs listing sizes and color options. Careful attention should be paid to hardware (the hooks and the rings with which the

Heddon, the company formed by the man who may have invented the wooden fishing lure, manufactured many lures during its long history, including this circa 1920 "Playfair" wooden minnow, with its original wooden box.

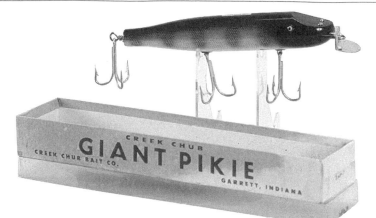

A "Giant Pikie," circa 1960, made by the Creek Chub Bait Co. of Garrett, Indiana, as a muskie lure, with its original box. Creek Chub lures, manufactured from 1916 to 1978, are highly collectible today.

hooks are attached to the lures). Different styles and finishes can help identify the lure's age and maker, which can be crucial in establishing accurate value. Older lures made by famous manufacturers are the most desirable.

Lures should be as close to original condition as possible. Missing parts, refinishing, repainting, replacement parts, and rust are flaws seldom tolerated by dedicated collectors. Reproductions are shunned outright.

When collectors talk about lures, they usually mean plugs. Plugs developed toward the end of the nineteenth century, amid the rising popularity and technological advances in bait-fishing rods and reels. The first plug, reputedly, was made from a plug (a piece) of wood to emulate a fish. Almost all its descendants have a built-in swimming action, so that, unlike the earlier metal lures, plugs didn't always sink, but usually stayed at the depth the fisherman desired. As the first buoyant or semibuoyant lures that did not require fly-casting tackle, they filled an important niche in the fishing world and became one of the most popular types of lures.

Surface, floating, and diving plugs can be made from wood, plastic, or a variety of other materials. They can be used for salt-water fishing, but freshwater lures are far more numerous.

Collectors also look for shiny spoons and spinners (artificial lures that are used primarily in fresh water). Each type comes in various colors and sizes. Spoons are often painted only on one side—usually in silver rather than gold—and they are most often treble-hook for casting and single-hook for trolling. A typical spinner has a single or double spinner that revolves above a dressed hook in a V-wire configuration that looks much like an open safety pin. Standard spoons and spinners do not command high prices,

From the Blue Spring Bait Manufacturing Company, a Croft's slant-headed, jointed lure from the 1950s. Croft, a fisherman and woodworker, formed the company with John Barefield in 1949 but only a small number of lures were ever produced and very few exist.

THE PHANTOM MINNOW

Since the early nineteenth century, when the "Phantom Minnow" first appeared in America, lure makers have attempted to create faux minnows that appeal to fish. One of the most interesting attempts was made in 1916 by the Detroit Glass Minnow Tube Company. A real minnow was pressed into service for a lure consisting of a transparent glass tube filled with water and a live minnow, while the outside was fitted with four sets of treble (three) hooks. One model was made with glass that magnified the minnow, offering a larger, and presumably tastier, temptation.

One of the first lures produced by Pflueger—when it was still called Enterprise Manufacturing Company— was the glass-bodied Crystal Minnow spinner, a lure that is now a highly sought-after collectible.

but there are exceptions, such as the early, patented Buels, Manns, and the famous Riley Haskel Minnow that was patented in 1859. A copper-bodied version in the Phantom style (see left), a Riley Haskel Minnow can sell for $8,000; when the first one came on the market in 1988, it brought a then-record price of $22,000!

MISCELLANEOUS FISHING COLLECTIBLES

Collectors of fishing memorabilia are also in search of paper ephemera relating to fishing and fishing images. So in addition to valuable catalogs (a few years ago a 1911 Heddon catalog sold for $1,650), enthusiasts look for calendars, paintings, and prints depicting their favorite sport, or for letters on company stationery signed by famous personages, or for ephemera with significant content about a manufacturer or the history of his products.

Some collectors seek equipment other than rods and reels, such as fly vises, fishing knives, gaff hooks, and landing nets. Creels are a welcome addition to a fishing tackle collection because they make highly sculptural displays, especially when combined with period lures, rods, and reels. Prices for creels can range from $10 to $2,000. Rare and desirable creels range from handmade examples woven by the Pima Indians to solid copper British creels made in the seventeenth century. At the other end of the scale are the standard—but handsome—wicker creels, selling in the $30 range.

In order to fish, you need a license, and this collectible porcelain enamel sign from the early 1930s announced where you could buy one.

This high-quality Tillamook-style creel made of split willow in a French weave pattern has hand-tooled leather reinforcements, strap, handle, and pouch, and was made by the George Lawrence Company of Portland, Oregon, in the 1920s.

Chapter Five

TOYS

Toys, like advertising art, can capture the essence of the era in which they were produced, existing as three-dimensional models of comic-strip heroes, every type of transportation, passing fads, and cultural obsessions of all kinds. The appeal of toy collecting, however, is too often dismissed as nostalgia, an attempt to regain the treasured possessions of childhood. That is only part of its allure. Indeed, toy collectors customarily pursue all kinds of items that were created well before they themselves were born, and their motivations for collecting can be as varied as the subject itself. Toys have been avidly collected for decades, and what ultimately makes a toy enduringly popular is good design, sculptural appeal, brilliant color, and historical relevance.

What's more, toys are fun. And just when the toy enthusiast thinks he or she has seen them all, there's some new, diverting surprise.

Such was the case with a toy Ferris wheel brought to the Baltimore *Antiques Roadshow*. The visitor told appraiser Noel Barrett that he'd bought it from a coworker who'd had to clean house after his wife and mother-in-law died. "I'm a train collector

Top: boy's toys— Lehmann's Daredevil Zebra Cart, circa 1924, features a cowboy and an unlikely steed. Above: from the mid-fifties, Linemar's rare, battery-operated Smoking Robot.

An exceedingly rare, steam-powered Ferris wheel made in Germany by Doll & Cie is complete with flags and composition riders.

A wooden Pete the Pup toy, based on the silent-era cartoon character drawn by Woody Woodpecker's creator, Walter Lantz.

and I'd offered to purchase one of his trains," the guest explained. "But then he told me there was more stuff up in the attic, we went up and there this was, just sitting there, wrapped in a 1933 newspaper. Of course, my wife fell in love with it right away."

Barrett was equally impressed by the still-operable Ferris wheel. "When I saw it, I said, 'Oh, boy,' because it is a marvelous thing and I had never seen one in such remarkable condition." He told the visitor that it had been made by Doll & Cie, a German manufacturer of toys powered by steam engines that also made wonderful cars, gas stations, and merry-go-rounds. This Ferris wheel was in completely original condition, including having all its composition figures and original flags. Having nothing to compare the Ferris wheel to, Barrett consulted with a few of his *Antiques Roadshow* colleagues—a common procedure before appraisers face the cameras. The conclusion? At auction, the likely price for this very special toy would be between $8,000 and $12,000. When the visitor said he paid only $200 for it, Barrett exclaimed, "Holy mackerel!"

Such responses are common in the growing field of toy collecting, because the difference between the prices originally paid (or what a lucky collector might pay at a tag sale) and the prices these vintage toys fetch in today's market is astonishing. It's important to point out, however, that there would be far less toy collecting if the fun was only about escalating prices. The fact is that although vintage toys were designed with children in mind, it is grown-ups, of course, who are the most passionate collectors.

A BRIEF HISTORY

When it came to toys and games, Americans predominately "bought American" until the early twentieth century, when imports rose in popularity. By 1914, they made up half of the market, but World War I and the accompanying disruption of international trade helped to save the American toy industry. In 1917, the newly formed trade association Toy Manufacturers of America successfully lobbied for stiff tariffs on imports as well. With fewer imported toys on the market, American companies did exceptional business.

Ferdinand Strauss, Louis Marx, and J. Chein were three companies that mass-produced colorfully lithographed tinplate novelty and transportation toys. Manufacturers like Arcade, Dent, Kenton, Kilgore, and Hubley made the heavier cast-iron toys, including all kinds of trucks (with realistic parts), cap guns, and soldiers. In 1913, A. C. Gilbert of Connecticut had a major success marketing Erector Sets, the first American construction toys with moving parts and motors; Charles Pajeau, of Evanston, Illinois, introduced Tinkertoys around 1915; and in 1916 John Lloyd Wright, son of architect Frank Lloyd Wright, started the Lincoln Logs toy company in Chicago, creating one more phenomenon. The growing automobile industry prompted pressed steel toys from firms like John C. Turner, Girard Model Works, Keystone, and Buddy L (called Moline Pressed Steel until 1930). In addition, Parker Brothers and Milton Bradley competed head-on in the field of board games and puzzles.

In the late twenties and thirties, many toy companies went out of business or merged with other firms to adapt to the realities of the Depression. Surprisingly, however, a few new companies, among them Fisher-Price (specializing in wooden pull toys), were founded. In 1933, Frank Hornby of Liverpool, England, who earlier in the century had created Meccano Ltd., introduced a popular line of diecast vehicles known as Dinky Toys. Also, in 1935, Parker Brothers struck gold with Monopoly.

Giant American companies like Marx and Lionel, and German firms like Märklin, Lehmann, and Schuco Toy, survived World War II, but the innovative Japanese became the stars of the postwar market. Among the most popular Japanese toys of

Wind up this German-made mechanical toy (circa 1912) and the dapper billiards player takes his shot. The ball is returned automatically.

HANDMADE MONOPOLY

A mid-1930s handmade copy of a Monopoly set was brought to the Des Moines, Iowa, *Antiques Roadshow*. "It was made by my grandmother's uncle while he was in a sanitarium in Detroit," explained the owner of the unusual piece. It's maker had transformed the original properties, based on Atlantic City, New Jersey, into their Detroit equivalents. "I love the little Fox Theatre, which is still in existence in Detroit," observed *Antiques Roadshow* appraiser Wayne Pratt. "This is one the funniest and most interesting games I've seen in a long time."

The maker printed his own cards and even went so far as to put a Michigan license plate on the car piece. While hard to appraise, Pratt noted that "a normal old Monopoly game will bring a couple hundred dollars." For this one, a Monopoly collector—especially a collector from Detroit—might pay as much as $1,500 to $2,000.

A unusual Depression-era cast-iron baby carriage, manufactured by Kilgore, stands a mere 5 inches tall but weighs nearly 2 pounds.

the fifties and sixties were tinplate, keywind, or battery-operated space toys and robots. The Japanese toys, nonetheless, faced fierce competition from American companies—many of which used the less-expensive plastic. For instance, in the fifties, Hassenfeld Brothers (later known as Hasbro Industries and Hasbro Inc.) introduced Mr. Potato Head (the first toy advertised on television), following it, a decade later, with a cultural icon, G.I. Joe (see the Dolls chapter, page 263, for more about Joe). Among newer companies entering the fray were the English-based Lesney (Matchbox) and Corgi Toys (which specialized in diecast vehicles) and the American firms Tonka, Smith-Miller Toy, and Doepke.

EVALUATING TOYS

Toy desirability and price are determined by condition, and each specialized area has its own rules and criteria—not surprisingly, for there are numerous differences between a ninety-year-old Märklin boat and a fifty-year-old robot. Yet they have one thing in common: Top-condition pieces are in a league of their own. And the newer the toy, the less forgiving collectors are of its faults.

Scale also comes into play, because a small spot of rust on the bumper of a large Buddy L truck is a lot less damning than the same-size spot on a small penny toy. Experienced collectors master their specialty and learn where problems are likely to occur, so they know what to look for when examining a toy. They also develop a sense of how a piece compares with others they have seen.

Collectors hail Arcade's 1927 model Yellow Cab Taxi Limousine. It comes equipped with spare tire, separate license plate, nickel-plated cowl lamps, and a cabbie.

Rarity plays an important part in value, too. A slight flaw or two in a rare toy may be acceptable, whereas it won't be tolerated in a readily available or quite new toy. Completeness is another issue: A cast-iron auto missing a tire that can be replaced is not as seriously compromised as a space van missing a molded plastic radar shield that can't be. Familiarizing yourself

Children like a (little) scare, which this tin litho keywind chomping alligator— probably made by Lindstrom—provided.

with what was included in a toy's original equipment is always a good idea. Sometimes this information is listed on the box, but if the toy you're interested in has no box, books on the subject can be helpful.

If a collectible toy comes complete with its box, that can more than double its value. Collectors thoroughly examine both the original packaging and the toys, or they ask for accurate condition reports if they are buying online or sight unseen. Tears and creases in the packaging devalue the overall worth of a boxed toy, particularly if they deface an attractive graphic.

Restoration is really a matter of personal taste, with many collectors believing in careful cleaning but also in leaving the piece in as original condition as possible. Others demand that toys look like new and have them completely repainted. A commonsense approach is to think about the long-term integrity of the toy; if the paint is worn and faded, that may well be more appealing over time than the toy that looks newer than it should. Refitting a toy with appropriate replacement parts—for example, putting new slot-and-tab arms on an incomplete keywind walker—can enhance a toy's appeal. Do not, however, attempt repairs or restorations on your own, unless they can be achieved without altering or harming the toy. Amateur repairs, soldering, and repainting have damaged or ruined countless toys. At the very least, consult a professional for his or her opinion.

Mechanisms are another tricky area. While the working toy is always preferable to a nonworking example in the same physical condition, much depends on the characteristics of the toy. For the toy that in perfect condition has little action,

W O O D S Y - W E E
C I R C U S

A visitor to the Milwaukee *Antiques Roadshow* told appraiser Leila Dunbar that he had come across an old boxed toy called Woodsy-Wee Circus. "It was in good condition, so I bought it." Dunbar, impressed with the buy, inside found a giraffe, a camel,

and an elephant. This toy, she explained, was one of the first sixteen produced by Fisher-Price, founded in 1930, "a horrible time to start a toy business." Today the Woodsy-Wee Circus is among those most-prized by Fisher-Price collectors, and this one looked like it had "never been played with." It did have some mold damage and a crease on the box but the owner's return on his $60 impulse purchase was $1,000 to $1,500.

any loss of movement may not be nearly as devastating to its value as that loss would be in a toy that bases its appeal on terrific action.

COLLECTING TOYS

Although some people collect a little of everything, most focus on a specialty or two that best represents their preferences: American tin, German automotive, character toys, mechanical banks, still banks, paper-on-wood, cast-iron automotive, aeronautical, pressed steel, keywinds, diecasts (toys made from metal cast under pressure in a mold), trains, Japanese automotive, guns, celluloid, rubber, plastic (starting small in the thirties but usurping the market from the fifties on), horse-drawn toys, and robots and space toys. They also hunt for toys—and games—made by specific manufacturers, among them Buddy L, Lehmann, Marx, Schoenhut, and Schuco.

As with any collectible, you will do best to buy with your head as well as your heart. To become expert, read as much as you can in your area of interest, attend shows and ask questions of others with similar interests, and develop good working relationships with reputable dealers and auction houses. Examine as many pieces as you can, and learn to recognize those in top-quality condition that have not been restored. Learn how to tell originals from reproductions. Most of all, have fun. These are, after all, toys.

Buddy L is the best-known and probably most collectible American toy-truck maker. This 25-inch 1921 dump truck rolls out on Firestone rubber tires and has a hinged tailgate and chain-operated bed.

Fill 'er up: Toy cars could be serviced at this tinplated steel Marx Roadside Rest Service Station. The 1935 toy includes pumps topped by glass bulbs and even an ailing aluminum roadster.

This chapter gives you an overview of a few of the most popular collecting areas and of some of the companies that produced the toys collectors love. Because *Antiques Roadshow Primer* covered the magnificent toys produced in the nineteenth century, these are only touched on here. The major focus is on collectible toys of the twentieth century.

Meier's 5-inch tin touring car, circa 1914, proved that good things come in small, long packages.

PENNY TOYS

Penny toys are the perfect small-apartment collectible. They take up little space, yet pack a lot into a diminutive package. These toys, popular between the late 1890s and the mid-1930s, were sold for one penny on city streets and in stores, offered in boxed sets—often as Christmas decorations—or sold to other manufacturers to be used as parts of boxed toys and games. Penny toys were made of many different materials, including tinplate, wood, paper, celluloid, or diecast metal.

Although there are collectors for all categories of penny toys, the ones that are currently propelling the penny-toy market are made of tinplate. German firms produced penny toys in several materials, and a few of the more prominent tinplate toy producers were Johann Distler, Issmayer, Georg Levy, Georg G. Kellermann (often marked "CKO"), Johann Phillip Meir, and J. L. Hess. Parker Brothers and other American game companies usually obtained the penny toys they used for their board games from German manufacturers. The French produced penny toys as well. The Charles Rossignol (CR) company created spirit-painted and, later, lithographed tinplate toys; firms such as Simon & Rivollet (SR) manufactured diecast vehicles. The Japanese produced tons of penny toys, especially in wood,

TINPLATE TOYS

Noel Barrett, an *Antiques Roadshow* appraiser, theorizes that the term "tinplate toys," often used to describe tin toys made during the late nineteenth and early twentieth centuries, was first used *after* these toys were originally made. "It's a dealer's term. It's similar to calling 'windup' toys 'clockwork' toys." Tinplate is actually the more accurate term, as the toys are made from thin sheets of steel plated with tin. They were lighter and less expensive to ship than cast-iron toys, their major competition. These had to be transported in wooden crates. The earliest tin toys were often soldered and handpainted, lending them a folk-art look. Around 1900, offset lithography replaced hand painting and the true mass-produced tinplate toys began to come off assembly lines faster, in brighter colors, and with far more detail. "Once offset lithography was used, tin became almost synonymous with cheap," Barrett says. Their demise was hastened by the ascent of plastic in the post–World War II era. "Plastic was even cheaper than tin," Barrett says. "And you had the safety issue with all those sharp edges on tin toys." Today, fewer and fewer tinplate toys are turning up. "American tin toys from the late nineteenth century are quite scarce," says Barrett. "The attics where all these toys would be found have all been cleared out by now."

paper, and plaster. Most of their toys, even the lithographed tinplate examples, are unmarked or bear the marks of unknown manufacturers.

Earlier toys may have handsome translucent spirit finishes, but collectors lust after the most brilliantly lithographed pieces loaded with detail. Tinplate transportation penny toys constitute a large and desirable segment of the penny-toy field, and there is a rich assortment of horse-drawn carriages, early horseless carriages, racers, sedans, coupes, limousines, and buses to choose from. For collectors who prefer a nautical theme, there are speedboats, paddle wheelers, gunboats, ocean liners with smoke billowing from their stacks, and even one elaborately lithographed sailboat that rocks back and forth on a "choppy sea" wheeled base. Train collectors can choose from trolleys and locomotives as well as from sets featuring locomotives and cars. A double-decker bus by Meier was one of the best toys a penny could buy. Attractively lithographed in red with yellow piping, it features lithographed passengers at all three windows and an assortment of passengers on the open upper deck. Its astounding detail lures collectors to pay over 120,000 times its original price. (You can do the math.) Other transportation penny toys sought by aeronautica collectors include airplanes, zeppelins, and hot-air balloons.

Many toy collectors love action, and a large number of the better penny toys provided it, despite their original one-cent price tag. The easiest way to achieve action is with wheels, but there is large variety in the penny toys that are not simply miniature platform toys—vehicles, or animals, or people attached atop a wheeled base—that roll back and forth. A great many also incorporate other actions. For instance, an elephant penny toy by Georg Fischer moves its trunk up and down as the platform rolls forward. The action is provided by a small piece of metal that runs from the front wheel to the pachyderm's trunk, which is suspended by two tabs to allow movement.

Penny toys are so popular that several firms are creating new ones today, often patterned on or copied from old designs. Novice collectors should familiarize themselves with these newer products so as not to pay vintage prices for them.

Pennies from heaven—a Meier Wright Brothers penny-toy biplane (circa 1907) is brass-plated with a pilot—and is just 3¼ inches long.

Officers and gentlemen—two American dime-store lead soldiers from the 1930s. The striding figure at left is by Barclay; the sailor on the right is by Gray Iron.

TOY SOLDIERS

Toy soldiers are enjoyed as much on the shelves of collectors today as they were decades ago when they were first deployed by young commanders on nursery floors. Their poses are varied and often action packed, with figures firing guns in any of a number of positions, drawing bows, or challenging an enemy with swords or lances. It is not battle alone that attracts most collectors to toy soldiers, but the pomp and ceremony of the miniature fighting forces and military bands. Toy soldiers bring history to life.

Lead-soldier collecting as we know it today originated some two hundred years ago. The French firm Lucotte began producing three-dimensional soldiers in the late eighteenth century (and their successor Mignot still produces them). Following Bismarck's triumph in the Franco-Prussian War, the Dresden-based firm of George Heyde became the preeminent German manufacturer. Heyde not only produced sets of figures celebrating German military might, but also such diverse figures as American Indians, the Chinese soldiers of the Boxer Rebellion, the opposing forces in the Greco-Turkish War, Arab caravans, and the gallant explorers battling the elements on polar expeditions—themes appealing to adventure-seeking children everywhere.

The most famous name in toy soldiers is Britains Ltd. of England. Near the end of the nineteenth century, the already prestigious firm introduced the first hollow-cast lead soldiers, cheaper to produce and thus cheaper to purchase. From its first slightly crude sets—#1, the Life Guards (the Queen's household cavalry), and #2, the Royal Horse Guards—Britains built a force of soldiers far larger than the Queen's, one that would outlive numerous monarchs and survive two world wars.

Britains cleverly packaged its 54-mm figures in attractive boxes. At first it used simple labels listing the set's contents, but

A British army general and field marshal—manufactured by Britains Ltd. in the late 1850s—on the lookout for Russian soldiers during the Crimean War.

Made by Britains Ltd. during the Civil War, a mounted Union Army bugler rallies the troops.

Four World War I Belgian infantry-men by Britains Ltd. take their positions against advancing enemy troops.

eventually the boxes became more ornate, often featuring a drawing of one soldier representative of the set. Of particular interest are sets in boxes designed by artist Fred Whistock.

American companies produced metal soldiers in the first two decades of the twentieth century, but when Americans think homegrown, what comes to mind are the distinctly rugged figures sold in five-and-dime stores from the 1920s to the 1950s. These hollow-cast lead, rubber, and cast-iron figures were larger than their European counterparts, usually around 3½ inches tall. Although their uniforms were not painted as accurately as those produced by the Britains firm, they were cast in a variety of exciting action poses. Three of the largest producers of these small-scale "dime-store soldiers" and accessories were Barclay Manufacturing, Manoil Manufacturing, and Grey Iron.

Composition soldiers (as well as dolls, figures, and parts for some toy vehicles) were made from a mixture of white china clay, sawdust, and glue. Two extensive and well-known lines of German composition soldiers dominated that area of the market from early in the twentieth century until the late fifties. These figures, made by O. & M. Hausser, were marked "Elastolin," the name the company used for its composition material, and ultimately the name by which its soldiers have come to be called. The other sort, "Lineol," were made by Osker Wiederholz.

In the world of toy soldiers, there are also "connoisseur" figures crafted to appeal to adults interested in military history. These finely sculpted, meticulously painted miniatures do not detour to a toy box en route to a collector's shelf—they go there directly. As with toy soldiers, specific regiments are what many collectors look for. Early in the twentieth century, English toy maker Richard Courtenay crafted some of the handsomest metal soldiers ever produced. Intended for the connoisseur market, they even included the knights of Agincourt and Crecy, on foot and mounted, in a variety of appropiate poses. These miniature masterpieces celebrate the pomp and splendor of chivalry and include, in minute detail, heraldic devices on shields, armor, and weapons. They are among the treasures sought by serious collectors of toy soldiers.

AUTOMOTIVE TOYS

Automotive toys, a huge collecting area, can range from the meticulously hand-painted toys of the German manufacturers to the diecast toys that crowd the shelves of Tootsietoy and Matchbox collectors. Over the last one hundred years many materials have been employed in their production, including wood, pressed steel, die-cast metal, tinplate, celluloid, rubber, and, eventually, plastic.

Just as the real newfangled contraptions captivated turn-of-the-century adults, toy versions of automobiles, some with highly unusual designs, enraptured the Edwardian sandbox set. The vis-à-vis was one particularly memorable style, because of its unconventional seating arrangement. Fitted with two seats across from each other, the driver faced his other passengers!

By 1906, larger, more elaborate toy cars were created, some based on very specific models and some on generic designs, a formula that would continue throughout the twentieth century. As each new actual car came on the market, toy manufacturers would replicate it in miniature. This is still true at the beginning of the twenty-first century, and toy versions of the latest models continue to increase the collecting pool.

Toy-car collectors vary greatly in their approach. Some are eclectic, while others focus on era, material, company, or even type of car. Some enthusiastically collect German and Japanese automotive toys, while others buy strictly American.

Typically, cast-iron toys, such as this 1912 Fischer taxicab, were not fitted with propulsion mechanisms. They relied on child power to make them go.

GERMAN AUTOMOTIVE TOYS

German toy manufacturers brought a fine eye for detail to their early automobiles. The first roadsters, with their simple designs, gave way to more elaborate limousines and pre–World War I luxury cars, both hand painted and lithographed. These were more likely to resemble actual, finely crafted machines than their American counterparts.

In 1911, George Carette, one of the most prolific producers of pre–World War I toy automobiles, offered a limousine that came in three lengths: 8½ inches, 12½ inches, and 15½ inches, with a choice of option packages. For instance, the deluxe version of the 12½-inch model was hand painted, had headlamps, molded front seats, rubber tires, a reverse mechanism, a composition driver, and nut-and-bolt (rather than tab) construction on the front seat and roof. The firm closed in 1917, when Carette, a French citizen, was deported from Germany.

After World War I, newer companies such as Tipp joined old competitors such as Märklin, Bing, S.G. Günthermann, and Karl Bub. Styles had changed and the labor-intensive hand-painted finishes available before the war were, for the most part, no longer produced. Lithography was now the finish of choice. Although not as deep and rich as the fine, enameled finish, lithography allowed toy-car makers to accessorize their products inexpensively, adding piping around windows and doors, faux vents on hood panels, and simulated canvas roofs for convertibles. Details that were too time-consuming to paint by hand—even necessary details such as drivers and passengers—could be incorporated into the design to add color and interest to the toy. This worked well for such cars as Bub's taxi from the early twenties, presumably made for the American market. It was lithographed in yellow and black, had a checkerboard motif below the windows, and sported fancy lithographed spoked wheels.

Bing, a German manufacturer of stuffed animals that walked, tumbled, and growled, also built tinplate cars, among them this lovingly detailed 1915 model.

The sides of delivery vans and buses allowed the really creative manufacturer to reproduce the actual advertisements seen on vehicles plying the streets of the day. Bing produced lavishly lithographed examples, including a circa-1920 bus for the English market fitted with an accurate destination board and with the sides of its upper deck emblazoned with advertisements for Wright's Coal Tar Soap. A circa-1928 version by the same firm for the American market features an advertisement for Heinz Spaghetti, complete with the proper "57 Varieties" logo.

By the 1920s, fewer toy cars employed clockwork mechanisms and more were powered by the lighter and less-expensive key-wind motor. (The terms *clockwork, windup,* and *keywind* are generally synonymous in the language of toys. Some collectors, however, distinguish between the heavy-duty clockwork mechanisms of early German and American manufacturers and the lighter, less-expensive mechanisms that were popularized by novelty toy makers and eventually were embraced by the wider industry.)

In this massive 21-inch tin "bus," made by Bing in 1915 and featuring "real Dunlop balloon tyres," a uniformed chauffeur commands the playroom floor.

Checking under the hood of most tinplate automobiles does not reveal much, but there are exceptions. A Moko (named for the firm's founder, *Moses Kohnstam*) limousine features a hinged hood panel that when open reveals a lithographed engine fitted with tiny pistons that pump up and down when the key is wound. Also innovative were the electric lights that manufacturers were placing in some vehicles, among them a Karl Bub limousine. Bub, which was founded in the 1850s, was one of the largest producers of toy automobiles during the twenties and thirties. It even made battery-powered cars.

Collectors of fire-fighting toys are especially attracted to the many different brightly lithographed Tipp fire trucks. However, Tipp's most beautiful automotive toy may have been one based on one of the sexiest cars of the 1930s, the Mercedes Autobahn-Kurier. This vehicle is Art Deco on wheels—low slung, with an elongated hood leading to a rounded roof, terminating in a sloping rear end enhanced by a V-shaped trunk. The car is lithographed, too, with the curvilinear design connoting modernism, movement, and speed to that era—and to us!

Propelled by a toy locomotive, this 1920s cast-iron Märklin snowplow could easily clear toy trucks of pretend blizzards.

World War II brought an end to Germany's long reign as premier producer of tinplate automotive toys. In the postwar period, many firms regrouped, including Tipp, which continued to make automobiles, motorcycles, and other toys until it closed in 1971. Märklin and Lehmann survive to this day, producing trains and other toys; Märklin has even issued high-quality copies of some of its classics. However, even these superior and innovative postwar tinplate toys were overshadowed by the impressive products of Japan.

JAPANESE AUTOMOTIVE TOYS

Japan, which has a long toy-making tradition, began exporting toys, paper toys mainly, to the West in the nineteenth century. Although some tinplate automobiles were produced in Japan before World War I, very few are known to still exist. Japanese firms increased toy auto production in the 1920s and 1930s, often modeling their toys—not too subtly—on toys produced in Germany. These are scarce as well. (Rumors of pre–World War II Japanese tinplate automobiles are often heard in the collecting field, but very few ever come on the market.)

The golden age of the Japanese toy in the United States was from 1950 to 1970, when Japan inundated five-and-dimes with literally tons of inexpensive toys and novelties. Thousands of these items sold for cents rather than dollars and they were not designed to last. Today's collectors, however, realize that many of these inexpensive Japanese toys were better designed than was first thought. Moreover, the ascendancy of the Japanese toy coincided with what many believe to

At the height of America's obsession with exaggerated tailfins, the Japanese firm Bandai produced this classic 1959 Cadillac.

be the zenith of American auto design, so it was Japan, ironically, that produced the most desirable toy versions of the best American cars.

Which firms made these toy cars? Well, no one knows exactly. True, some toy companies that flourished after World War II, such as Bandai and Masudaya (MT, or Modern Toys, is their trade name), are still in existence, and several trademarks have been deciphered and makers identified. However, there is still a woeful lack of information about Japanese toy companies and a great deal of confusion as to whether the names that appear on the toys and boxes actually referred to the wholesalers or the manufacturers. That lack of information, however, does not deter collectors.

Although the Japanese did make keywind vehicles, their more impressive toy automobiles ran on a simple friction mechanism or were battery operated. At the top of the Japanese toy automobile line is the 1962 Chrysler Imperial, powered by friction. The car really doesn't do much more than roll forward, yet it causes much excitement when it appears at auction and has sold—in its original box—for over $20,000. Its surprising value is determined by its beauty and its extreme scarcity—either few were produced or few survived playroom highways. On the other hand, a common late-1950s battery-operated Ford, featuring a remote control allowing the driver to go both forward and backward and also to slide the convertible top back into the trunk, often brings merely $500 or less. Bells and whistles do not always mean higher prices.

Remote control may be a nifty idea, but it can also deflate the value of Japanese automotive tinplate. Remote controls usually mean wire connections, and these cause awkward display problems and clutter collector's shelves. Wrapping the wire around the battery box is no solution because that can damage both wire and box. It's such a vexing problem that in the early days of automotive toy collecting, enthusiasts often cut the wires off and threw away the remotes. This made the vehicles easier to display but reduced their value. In today's market, of course, serious collectors demand that toys be complete and in original condition.

Although toy automobiles were made in several sizes, including an impressive 24-inch Mercedes, the most collectible seem to be those in the 11-to-13-inch range, often referred to by collectors as "12-inch." The 8½-inch models follow these in popularity. Although there are some very pricey cars in the 14-to-16-inch range, most collectors agree that anything above 18 inches simply takes up too much shelf space.

La dolce vita for toy car enthusiasts comes in the form of a sophisticated Ferrari 2+2 by Bandai.

Intact boxes enhance the value of collectible toys. Here, from Bandai's "Automobiles of the World" series, a 1964 Cadillac sedan.

AMERICAN AUTOMOTIVE TOYS

The first American-made toy cars and trucks were, for the most part, more primitive than their European counterparts, but the materials American manufacturers worked with were far more diverse. Whereas Europeans concentrated on tinplate, the American firm Converse, for example, produced toy automobiles incorporating wood, light pressed steel, and cast iron as early as 1896. Although these lack the meticulous detail of German toy automobiles of the period, collectors admire their simple charm.

Most American firms that specialized in automotive toys continued to use cast iron and light pressed steel along with tinplate until World War II.

CAST-IRON AUTOMOTIVE TOYS

By the late nineteenth century, after the discovery of huge deposits of iron ore in the United States increased that metal's availability, there was an influx of cast-iron products, and even toys, such as mechanical banks, horse-drawn carriages, trolleys, and trains, were cunningly molded in cast iron. With the exception of mechanical banks, most of these toys were not fitted with intricate mechanisms but were powered by their young human owners pushing them across Victorian parlor floors or, heaven forbid, richly polished dining room tables.

Automobiles were a natural continuation for manufacturers of cast-iron playthings. Ives, Kenton, and Jones & Bixler produced several cast-iron toy automobiles before World War I. A circa-1905 creation by Kenton was an open-air bus called a charabanc (French for benched carriage), patterned after a vehicle introduced at the World's Columbian Exposition in Chicago in 1893. By the turn of the century, charabancs were plying the streets of Chicago, New York and other large American cities. Kenton's souvenir version came with a driver and four passengers. A particularly desirable set—referred to as the "comic-character" version (because of its use of familiar strip characters)—employs the Sailor as driver, Happy Hooligan, his brother Gloomy Gus, Mama Katzenjammer, and the Professor.

Although actual construction slowed down during the Depression, thirties children continued to build with toys like this Jaeger concrete mixer by Kenton.

The nickel-plated revolving drum of Kenton's rare 1932 Jaeger cast-iron cement-mixer truck was turned by a large chain driven by the rear axle.

The Roaring Twenties were as hot a time for the American toy industry as they were for American jazz. Cast-iron toy makers such as Arcade, Dent, Hubley, Kenton, Kilgore, Vindex Toys and Novelties, and A.C. Williams turned out veritable fleets of heavy cast-iron beauties with glistening paint. Practically every kind of road vehicle was produced in a variety of sizes: coupes, sedans, luxury limos, dump trucks, moving vans, motorcycles, and buses. Manufacturers emulated real vehicles so that Johnny or Jimmy could own a miniature version of the family car or the moving van delivering the new neighbors' furniture or even the Harley-Davidson with which that the hellion at the end of the block was terrorizing the town.

Determined to give youngsters more of what they wanted, Arcade Manufacturing Company of Freeport, Illinois, began to produce a series of Ford Model T's and A's. In 1921, it entered into an agreement with Yellow Cab Company to make toy taxis. This wildly popular taxi line was extensive and inventive and included models with a coin slot in the roof and a trap under the car that allowed young motorists to save their change while they played—these are sought by both cast-iron car collectors and collectors of toy banks.

At the height of the Depression, Greyhound Coach Line's commissioning of the General Motors Company trailer bus may have saved Arcade from bankruptcy. Arcade produced a toy blue cab pulling a bus-style trailer patterned after the "people movers" that were used at the 1933 World's Fair. It came in five sizes, and on its roof were three lines of print: "A Century of Progress," "Chicago 1933," and "Greyhound Lines." At the World's Fair, not surprisingly, it sold by the thousands. Arcade also sold an

Dent was among several companies that produced toy versions of practically every type of vehicle, including this 1950 milk truck.

extensive line of trucks, including tankers, stake-side trucks, and dump trucks. Collectors particularly like the early Mack C-Cab dump trucks, as well as several White trucks. In 1943, Arcade ceased production, but during the last twenty years of its existence, it produced hundreds of different automotive and other cast-iron toys truly worthy of its slogan, "They Look Real."

Founded in 1894, the Dent Hardware Company of Fullerton, Pennsylvania, began life as a producer of refrigeration hardware, but it soon expanded to a line of well-crafted toys, producing beautiful horse-drawn toys—including some fantastic fire pieces—as well as boats, planes, trains, and automotive road toys—sedans, coupes, taxis, buses, and trucks. Dent's handsomest automotive products were its large Mack dump trucks. Several firms produced toy versions of the Mack, but those made by Dent are possibly the most desirable. Perhaps its proximity to the Mack factory in Allentown, Pennsylvania, gave Dent an edge over its competitors. Its truck series comprises a realistic tanker, dump truck, flatbed truck with removable stake and chain sides, and a Junior Supply Company van marked "New York" and "Philadelphia." The van is the standout among these special items; its back is fitted with working doors cast with difficult-to-make matching open grillwork.

Kenton Hardware Company, founded as Kenton Lock Manufacturing Company in Kenton, Ohio, in 1890, issued its first line of cast-iron toys, including banks and horse-drawn vehicles, a few years later. In the 1920s and 1930s, Kenton rolled out an automotive fleet that included sedans, coupes, fire trucks, tankers, dump trucks, and fleets and fleets of buses. In addition to

Hubley's "Midget Series" included this 1930s 3¼-inch Art Deco–style dump truck with chubby rubber tires and a nickel-plated dump bed.

Wyandotte produced an elaborate 16-inch long-nose dump truck in 1937 with chrome grille and bumper and black rubber tires on wooden hubs.

several versions of spiral staircase double-deckers, it also made five versions of an odd-looking bus with an enclosed upper deck called the Pickwick Coach, patterned after a bus used mainly in the late 1920s and early 1930s on the California coast. Curiously, the upper deck of this bus was fitted with sleeping compartments. Kenton's Jaeger Drum-Type Concrete Mixer Truck, initially produced from 1932 to 1941, is fitted with the revolving nickel drum seen on real trucks (the revolving drum prevented the concrete from drying). Kenton ceased production in 1952.

A single-seat "cigar" racer by Hubley (circa 1940), made from aluminum and cast iron.

The Hubley Manufacturing Company, founded in Lancaster, Pennsylvania, in 1894, was a major producer of cast-iron toys, including buses, a fine line of motorcycles, several race cars, fire engines, automobiles, and construction equipment. However, if it had produced only one car—the 1927 Packard Straight Eight—its place in toy history would be assured. Based on one of the most beautiful and luxurious vehicles of its day, this splendid toy features a hinged louvered hood that open to reveal a realistically cast model of the car's famous engine, side doors that open and a spare tire at the rear. It was an expensive toy when it was released just prior to the stock market crash of 1929, and it was dropped from the line immediately afterward, adding rarity to desirability. Despite the fact that cast iron is considered a durable material, this car is fragile, and most examples, when they do appear on the market, have replaced hoods or doors; damage or repairs to the back end is also common. Regardless, five-digit prices are usual.

During the Depression, Arcade stayed afloat on the back of the hugely popular Chicago World's Fair souvenir edition of GMC's trailer bus, made for Greyhound.

A GIFT FROM SANTA

At the Louisville, Kentucky, *Antiques Roadshow,* appraiser Noel Barrett was pleasantly surprised to see a man and his granddaughter bring in a 1922 toy truck that looked like it had never been driven off the lot. "Well, I hope you play with it as carefully as your grandfather played with it," Barrett said to the granddaughter, "because he took very, very good care of this truck." Made by Keystone from pressed steel, the truck was a Packard, "as you can see by the original decal," noted Barrett. Pointing out that the toy was an old police patrol truck, he commented that "most kids would prefer a dump truck that has some action. They want something that they can put some sand into and then dump. A truck that hauls malefactors to jail is an odd thing for a child to play with." Barrett asked how much the grandfather's Dad had paid for it back in 1922. "Santa Claus brought it," explained the old man. Replied Noel: "Well, Santa Claus probably paid $5 or $6 dollars, which was a lot of money in those days." At auction today, the truck might sell for $2,000 to $2,500. Grandpa's response? "Thank you, Santa!"

Buddy L dubbed this 1936 stylized version of the Chrysler Airflow "the Scarab" for its beetlelike shape.

Hubley was licensed by many companies and had much success making realistic cast-iron toys modeled on Bell Telephone trucks, Borden's milk trucks, and Harley-Davidson and Indian motorcycles (with rubber tires and spoke wheels). After World War II, it produced a few fire engines in cast iron, but switched eventually to the more affordable diecast metal and plastic. Hubley changed its name to Gabriel Industries in 1955 and continued making toys until 1978.

In the 1930s, several cast-iron toy producers, Hubley among them, began to make smaller, less expensive cars and trucks. These became dime store staples and are referred to as NDQs, which is short for the nickels, dimes, and quarters they originally sold for. The New Jersey–based J. Chein, however, took a different approach. Long known for lightweight, inexpensive tinplate cars and trucks, Chein produced a series of Mack trucks, such as the Dan-Dee Skid truck, that in the late 1920s and early 1930s sold for just 19 cents. The Dan-Dee was good-size, just over 9 inches long, and brightly lithographed in orange with black piping, green running boards, and whitewall tires with bold red hubs, all for less than a quarter!

PRESSED STEEL AUTOMOTIVE TOYS

In the late 1800s, steel had been used primarily for toy parts, but in the new century, some manufacturers began to make entire toys of steel, and it would continue to be utilized in the toy industry well into the post–World War II era. Automotive pressed steel toys were produced in a wide range of gauges and thicknesses by such firms as Turner, Wyandotte Toys, Keystone Manufacturing (whose toys included the Packard truck), Metalcraft, Smith-Miller Toy, Steelcraft, and Toledo Metal Wheel. However, it was Moline Pressed Steel, later renamed Buddy L Manufacturing, that produced the best-known and best-loved steel toys. The

Tonka's to-scale farm truck replicated Ford's 1950s stake pomel truck, down to its rubber mud flaps and chrome grille.

mammoth, finely designed, well crafted line of Buddy L pressed steel dump trucks, tankers, lumber trucks, fire engines, moving vans, and railroads were rugged, outdoor toys capable not only of ruling the sandbox but of entirely rebuilding it. The company was dissolved in 1939 but was reborn during World War II, when, with metal unavailable, Henry Katz and his partner Milton Klein produced a line of wooden Buddy L automotive toys in Glens Falls, New York. Buddy L returned to making metal toys after the war, using lighter weight steel, but eventually it moved, as had so many of its competitors, to cost-saving plastic.

Pre–World War II Buddy L toys are what collectors with large shelves and a love of construction vehicles look for. Because they were meant to be played with outdoors, many Buddy L toys were left outside, where rain and time combined to corrode even these most durable of playthings. So devoted are Buddy L collectors, however, that scores of the toys have been repainted and refurbished—some amateurishly, others professionally—and parts have been replaced. In recent years, new toys based on the originals have also been produced in small quantities, and the craftsmanship on many of these rivals that of the originals. Although collectible, restored and reproduction Buddy L toys bring far less than clean, original examples.

Although metal was still scarce in the post–World War II era, America's love of large, heavy toys continued, and Tonka, Smith-Miller, and Charles William Doepke Manufacturing joined Buddy L in trying to satisfy young customers. Although rather svelte in comparison with prewar fleets of Buddy L's, Tonka's trucks gave youngsters plenty of toy to play with. The company originated as Mound Metalcraft in Mound,

MY BUDDY

The "Buddy L Manufacturing Company probably made some of the finest pressed steel toys ever," appraiser Noel Barrett told a visitor at the Richmond, Virginia, *Antiques Roadshow.* His guest owned Buddy L Model T cars from the "flivver" series, made in 1919 and 1920. "These were given to me by friends of the family in about 1938," he said. "Their boys were too old to play with them and I've had them ever since." Replied Barrett, "Well somebody took good care of these toys." The owner explained, "I

only played with them in the house. I don't think I ever took them outside, because I was always told that they were special." That was good advice, because the two cars are today worth about $2,600. The owner's plans for the toys? "I'm going to pass them on to my grandson."

This 15-inch pressed steel GMC dump truck, made by Buddy L in 1957, came equipped with rugged rubber tires and a manual dump bed.

Minnesota, and produced hoes, rakes, and shovels as well as racks for ties, shoes, and hats. Toys were a sideline. The first two offerings, which were produced in 1947, were a steam shovel with a red cab and a crane and clam with a yellow cab.

In the 1950s, the firm's line grew to include a suburban pumper fire truck with a working fire hydrant, ladder trucks, tractor trailers (such as livestock vans, a grain hauler, and moving vans), utility trucks, wreckers, pickup trucks, and dump trucks, among them a state highway department dump truck with a plow for snow removal (they were made in Minnesota, after all). Tonka still produces toy vehicles, but those early pressed steel automotive lines from the 1940s to the early 1960s are being avidly collected by enthusiasts who owned them as children.

Smith-Miller began making large aluminum vehicles in 1945, producing an impressive line of Ford, Chevrolet, GMC, Cabovers, and Mack trucks. One of the firm's handsomest vehicles is the 1952 "L" Mack Blue Diamond dump truck, which was finished in white with blue accents.

Doepke or Model Toys began operation in 1946 and is regarded by some experts as one of the finest postwar manufacturers American of toys for its superior quality and exact replication of actual vehicles. Although Doepke produced two fire trucks and a searchlight truck, it is best known for its line of construction equipment. This includes a bulldozer, concrete mixer, crane, Euclid truck, and a giant road grader measuring 26 inches and weighing 14 pounds. Both Smith-Miller and Doepke had short life spans, closing in 1955 and 1959, respectively. Among collectors, they each have avid followings.

DIECAST AUTOMOTIVE TOYS

A ⅟₄₃-scale, two-tone 1927 Oldsmobile rumbleseat roadster from Tootsietoy's GM series.

Starting in the 1930s, for safety reasons, a new alloy replaced the lead in diecast metal, mostly in the production of "penny toys." This new material, adopted by Tootsietoys and eventually by Dinky, was a zinc, aluminum, and copper alloy with traces of magnesium. Called mazac, (as well as mazak, zamac, and zamak), it is still used today. In automotive toys, five manufacturers led the way with diecast toys.

Tootsietoys were the product of Dowst Brothers Company of Chicago—which took the "Tootsie" portion of its name from one of the brother's grand-daughters—whose first toy vehicle, made in 1910, was patterned after the French Bleriot plane and was produced in three amazingly successful versions. A rather generic limousine followed in 1911, and in 1914 came a flivver, a ¹⁄₄₈-scale model of a Model T Ford.

Although the company produced only five different models in its first decade as a toy-vehicle manufacturer, the twenties and thirties saw it expand the line to include a series of delivery vans. These inexpensive vehicles were well suited to the Depression-era pocketbook and sold at five-and-dime stores, either individually or in boxed sets with attractive, brightly labeled boxes. In the thirties, Tootsietoys produced several of the toys that today's collectors love, including a series of Funnies cars featuring cartoon-character drivers. These were sold individually or in boxed sets of six. The boxed sets had more elaborate paint, and the figures bobbed up and down, thanks to eccentric cams on the axles.

Another star series, the "Grahams," was introduced in 1933. Subsidized by the makers of the Graham Blue Streak, these were ¹⁄₄₃-scale models of that vehicle. Elegant and beautifully crafted, the Grahams were Tootsietoys' first three part vehicles. Instead of being cast as one piece, the Grahams were constructed from three separately cast units: the radiator and headlight unit; the chassis, which included the running boards; and the body. This technique provided greater detail with higher quality.

Tootsietoys continued to produce vehicles after World War II, making its last all-metal car in 1969. There are fans for its postwar vehicles, but it is the prewar vehicles that automotive collectors admire and desire.

Dinky was a line of diecast toys produced by the famed English firm

Calling all cars: Dinky's patrol car's crime-fighting tools included a roof-mounted siren and a police-radio antenna.

A finely detailed Esso panel truck from the Dinky division of the English toy company Meccano, made in the days before plastic windows.

From the identical die, but this time doing duty as a delivery vehicle for the terribly British Chivers ("Always turn out well") Jellies.

TIPS
from the
experts

You know how it goes: The original book is almost always superior to the blockbuster movie, which is almost always better than the subsequent remakes and sequels. In terms of value, the same is true for the spin-off toys and action figures that some blockbuster movies spawn by the tens of thousands. Those collectors who snapped up merchandise from the *Harry Potter* and *Lord of the Rings* movies because they assumed they were good investments should probably listen to the wise counsel of *Antiques Roadshow* appraiser Tim Luke. "With *Star Wars,* only the stuff from the original 1977 movie has much value," he says. "And while the *Star Trek* and *Batman* movies have made a lot of money, it's only the pieces associated with the original sixties television shows that have appreciated much at all. You're lucky to get half the original retail value," says Luke, noting that sales prices are inevitably inflated during the hype days surrounding a picture's original release. Value in the secondary market, Luke explains, is determined by the three criteria that apply to all collectibles: desirability, condition, and rarity.

Although licensed products show up in the market boxed and in mint condition, these are so extensively mass-produced that, at least for now, few collectors want them. (For more collectibles based on popular characters, see page 210.)

Tootsietoy's 1924 lilliputian laundry van, from the Federal delivery truck series, was cast in a single piece and featured gold-tone wheels.

Meccano, founded in 1901 by Frank Hornby. Noting the success of America's Tootsietoys, in 1933 Hornby introduced a set of six diecast cars. The name Dinky Toys was not applied to the vehicles until the following year, and mazac didn't replace lead until 1937.

After World War II, Dinky swung back into production and in 1946 it introduced its first new postwar toy, a Jeep, followed by commercial, racing, sports, and additional military vehicles. In 1947, a new, larger line of Dinkys was introduced, called Supertoys. These toys were well built and quite successful; the name was dropped in 1950 but was reintroduced in 1955. In response to its competitor Corgi Toys, Dinky began installing clear plastic windows in its vehicles in 1958. Then, in the 1960s, Dinky responded to the market and improved its products again by adding windows, doors, and trunks that opened. In 1964, the firm was taken over by Lines Brothers but survived the restructuring. Today, Dinky has a huge following in England and a large number of collectors in the United States, as well.

Matchbox's parent company, Lesney, was founded in England in 1947 by two unrelated Smiths, *Les*lie and Rod*ney,* school chums who later served together in the British Royal Navy. In 1952, the company scored a huge success with the 15½-inch-long coach produced in anticipation of Elizabeth's coronation in 1953. In the same year that Elizabeth became Queen, it introduced toys considerably smaller than the original product line. These new toys ranged roughly from 1½ to 3 inches in length and were packaged in a container that resembled a matchbox—hence the name Matchbox. These are referred to as 1–75 (for the scale), and Matchbox produced several lines over the years, including the slightly larger Yesteryear models.

A 1960s three-axle Matchbox farm truck looks as weathered as its working prototype.

The most surprising feature of 1–75-scale Matchbox toys is their action. Here, a cab-over dump truck with functioning dump bed.

Antique and collectible stores are filled with scratched, rusty, and worn-out Matchbox toys, but collectors should avoid buying examples in poor condition unless they are extremely rare models, and because there are different versions of the same models, identification can be tricky.

Corgi diecast vehicles were introduced in 1956 by the South Wales-based Playcraft Toys. In designing its line of toy vehicles, Corgi targeted Dinky as its main competition and aimed to produce a superior product. The first Corgis were made in two styles: one without a motor, the other with a flywheel motor, (phased out in 1959). Corgi toys were fitted with plastic windows for a more realistic look. In fact, the company's proud slogan was "The Ones with Windows." Corgi became known, too, for high quality and innovation, introducing, for example, spring suspension in 1959. Hundreds of different Corgi models have been produced, including Air Force vehicles, cars, boats, planes, and farm equipment. Some of the most popular with collectors are a series of 1960s character vehicles from popular television shows and movies, including several James Bond Aston Martins, a Batbike, Batboats, Batmobiles, and a Beatles Yellow Submarine.

Hot Wheels has the most descriptive name in the world of antique and collectible toys. And these diecast cars live up to their showy moniker. Hot Wheels tore up the retail road when Mattel introduced them in 1968, forcing competitors to redesign their products or get out of the way. Hot Wheels were built for speed and could easily lap their competitors. That first year,

Mini muscle car—an early example of Mattel's aptly named Hot Wheels, with jacked-up suspension, oversized tires, and quad exhaust pipes.

For Hot Wheels fans seeking Grand Prix thrills, Mattel produced this Ferrari racer, complete with rearing horse hood decal.

Sean Connery drove the original of this Corgi in the James Bond film Goldfinger. *The tiny Aston Martin was outfitted with many 007 gadgets.*

sixteen diecast cars were produced to capture the spirit of the California hot rods that youngsters, and oldsters, yearned for. One, the Beatnik Bandit, was based on a show car designed by Ed "Big Daddy" Roth. Customized versions of muscle cars such as the Firebird, the Custom Barracuda, the Corvette, and the Camaro were designed with the same slick lines and promise of speed as their full-size counterparts, besides being fitted with mag wheels and red-line tires. Mattel called its metallic finishes Spectraflame, and they were hot indeed.

Those original sixteen models were produced in as many as fourteen different finishes. The cars were packaged on blister-pack cards with a matching collector's button, and its new vehicles were such a huge success that it seemed Mattel could not produce enough of them. That changed in 1973, when in an attempt to cut costs Mattel changed the Spectraflame finishes to less costly and less exciting enamels. Demand dropped, and production was cut—the 1973 line was carried for only one year, making those cars some of the rarest models produced.

Perhaps the most famous Hot Wheels vehicle is the 1969 VW Beach Bomb, a van with plastic surfboards hanging out the back. There are conflicting stories about surviving examples, but it is believed they are prepro-duction, or prototypes of a model that was never mass-produced. Whatever the real story is, these little vehicles, based on the VW microbus, are dream cars for Hot Wheel collec-tors. In recent years there have been reports of this car changing hands for astronomical sums, even tens of thousands of dollars. But don't confuse this model with the similar, but much less valuable, VW Beach Bomb Hot Wheels produced between 1969 and 1971. The major difference is in the posi-tion of the surfboards; on the more com-mon model they slide into side-mounted panels.

Hot Wheels still are being produced and some of the flashier classics of years past have been reissued. Since Hot Wheels were often offered in several different colors, collectors have an added element to look for and argue about; rare color variations can command a premium. Collectors are particlarly condition-conscious, right down to the blister pack containers. There are piles of damaged Hot Wheels and other diecast cars in antique stores and at flea markets, so clever collectors should not buy any in poor condition, unless the toy is quite rare.

TRAINS

Trains were a natural for toy makers, and, naturally, they were produced in great numbers both in Europe and the United States. Early American tin toy makers created floor locomotives that didn't run on tracks and were based more on imagination and whimsy than on scale-model accuracy. Much more accurate miniatures of real trains were created in cast iron by American firms such as Pratt & Letchworth, Wilkins Toy, Welker & Crosby, and Ives. Paper-on-wood trains made by R. Bliss Manufacturing and Milton Bradley were inexpensive to produce yet colorful, thanks to their lithographed paper finishes.

In the early 1890s, the German company Märklin introduced trains in three different gauges (defined as the distance between the rails)—#1, #2, and #3—and today's collectors distinguish toy trains by their gauges, as well as by wheel configuration (the number of wheels in the front, middle and rear of the locomotive). Märklin also introduced the toy train switch point and the crossover that made figure-eight track layouts possible. Märklin is credited by many experts with creating the train set that could be added to and reconfigured.

Ives is one of the most important names in nineteenth-century American toy production. Its line included clockwork

A wonderfully detailed 1920s tin windup train—engine, coal tender, and coach with opening doors—from Märklin.

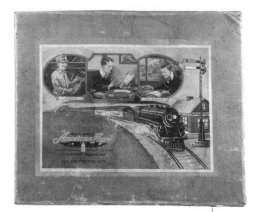

A wish-fulfilling illustration of boys doing man-sized jobs enlivens the box for American Flyer's 1926 train set. Inside was a cast-iron clockwork locomotive and tin-litho tender, baggage, and passenger cars.

toys, cast-iron floor trains, even clockwork cast-iron locomotives. In 1910, it added locomotives with electric motors. Ives is credited with establishing the O gauge as a popular gauge.

Baltimore-based Voltamp served the high end of the train market. Its founder, Manes Fuld, first produced an electric train for his son in 1879; by 1903, his company was marketing a line of toy trains that rivaled in quality the elaborate imports of the German firms. Carlisle & Finch, however, is credited with being the first American firm to manufacture electric-powered trains. Of course, the most famous electric trains *ever* produced were made by Lionel.

At the turn of the twentieth century, inventor Joshua Lionel Cowen of New York City was creating store window displays incorporating trains and trolley car themes. He began to produce small electrical motors to power these vehicles, and while there is some controversy as to what his first product actually was, it is believed that sometime around 1901 he began to sell an electric trolley car and an electric express train. By 1903 he was manufacturing a 2⅞-inch gauge trolley that was being advertised in the Montgomery Ward catalog. Catalogs of this period show that "train" was not used to describe a Lionel product until 1906. In that year, the Lionel Manufacturing Company produced an oddball gauge measuring 2⅛ inches between the outside rails. Cowen called the new gauge "standard." And this, in effect, made all other gauges being used by other firms appear to be non-standard, and therefore inferior.

Claiming that his company produced the best product, Cowen used the slogan "The Standard of the World" in his advertising. Until around 1913, Lionel would produce only standard-gauge models, but later it had great success with a smaller O-gauge train as well. Although the company continued to produce trains patterned after steam engines, Lionel recognized early that the railroad world was hurtling toward electricity. Unlike many of its competitors, Lionel went full throttle with electric toy trains that replicated actual electric trains. Lionel always seemed to be one step ahead of its competition.

A classic, superbly detailed "standard gauge" electric locomotive from the innovative Lionel Manufacturing Company.

World War I had a profound effect on the toy train industry, as it did on the toy industry as a whole. Afterward, with high tariffs greatly reducing toy imports, American toy-train producers flourished, while their German competitors struggled with a weak economy and a greatly diminished export market. Lionel's standard gauge became the product to which others were compared. (Yes, it became the *standard*.) In fact, Ives was forced to abandon #1 gauge and produce the new "standard" size, calling it "wide gauge." Voltamp's line also switched to standard gauge after the firm was taken over by Boucher.

Louis Marx & Co., a major American toy manufacturer, produced a large number of inexpensive train sets, such as this keywind tin-litho Streamlined Train from the 1930s.

In 1910, William Hafner, founder of the then-struggling toy auto manufacturer W. F. Hafner Company, entered into a partnership with William Coleman, a Chicago hardware-store owner. Coleman and Hafner focused on the production of clockwork trains, renaming their company American Flyer. (Hafner would eventually leave American Flyer to form a competing train company, Overland Flyer.) Although American Flyer would for a time manufacture a successful line of mechanical airplanes, it was best-known for its exceptional trains, and became Lionel's only serious competitor in the American train market—particularly after A. C. Gilbert bought it in 1937 and redesigned the line. American Flyer's main innovation was its conversion from the standard gauge three-rail system to the two-rail S gauge of only ⅞-inch. (German and American manufacturers would ultimately produce even smaller gauges, such as OO and HO.) It was the product itself, however, that made the trains so popular. American Flyer produced splendid locomotives, passenger cars, freight cars, and cabooses well into the fifties.

Latecomers to the train business were Milton and Julius Forcheimer, founders of Dorfan in Newark, New Jersey. The brothers' German family in Nuremberg were the originators of Fandor trains, and the name Dorfan, of course, reverses the

STEAM ON, STEAM ENGINE

A friendship brought an impressive handcrafted locomotive into the family of a guest at the Hartford, Connecticut, *Antiques Roadshow*. "This is a handmade replica of the camelback locomotive that the New Jersey Central used," explained the train's owner to appraiser Nancy Druckman. "It was given to my grandfather by a man who was in prison." It seems the grandfather, a railroad foreman, visited a prisoner as part of his work with the Knights of Columbus, and when he got news of a job transfer, his prisoner friend gave him a good-bye gift: a locomotive ingeniously cobbled together from a cigar box and a length of birch branch

(the boiler). Druckman said the memento is part of a tradition of prisoner-made handcrafts, and noted the locomotive could sell for $6,000 to $8,000. She concluded, "If you run into a couple of railroad fans, it could go for significantly more."

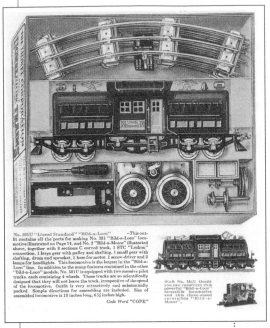

No. 381U "Lionel Standard" "Bild-a-Loco" —This outfit contains all the parts for making No. 331 "Bild-a-Loco" locomotive illustrated on Page 14, and No. 2 "Bild-a-Motor" illustrated above, together with 8 sections C curved track, 1 STC "Lockon" connection, 1 large gear with pulley and shafting, 1 small gear with shafting, drum and sprocket, 1 base for motor, 1 screw-driver and 2 lamps for headlights. This locomotive is the largest in the "Bild-a-Loco" line. In addition to the many features contained in the other "Bild-a-Loco" models, No. 381U is equipped with two massive pilot trucks, each containing 4 wheels. These trucks are so scientifically designed that they will not leave the track, irrespective of the speed of the locomotive. Outfit is very attractively and substantially packed. Simple directions for assembling are included. Size of assembled locomotive is 18 inches long, 6½ inches high.
Code Word "COPE"

With No. 381U Outfit you can construct this powerful "Bild-a-Loco" reversible locomotive and this three-speed reversible "Bild-a-Motor".

Lionel sold kits as well as finished trains. Here, the Bild-a-Loco, containing all the parts and tools necessary to construct a standard-gauge locomotive 18 inches long and 6½ inches tall.

This O-gauge model train from American Flyer is based on the Burlington's famous diesel electric-powered Zephyr, a streamlined stainless steel train that took twelve hours off the travel time between Denver and Chicago in 1934.

syllables. The company first made its mark in 1924 with take-apart motors and electric reversing units. Unfortunately, while the Dorfan train was tough, durable, and striking looking when new, its diecast metal had impurities, making the trains susceptible to disintegration. Because most Dorfan trains and accessories, including impressive cranes, have crumbled into piles of dust, those that survive are coveted by collectors.

In England, Frank Hornby's Meccano Company (discussed earlier in this chapter) launched a separate line of Hornby trains in 1920. Its tin railroad line grew and Hornby introduced a large assortment of lithographed tinplate accessories.

In Germany, Märklin rebuilt, cutting its pre–World War I line to concentrate on #1- and O-gauge trains, and became the dominant German manufacturer once again. The train business continued to grow in the early 1930s before Märklin turned to less expensive 00-gauge trains in a smaller scale (3.5-mm-to-the-foot scale, on 165-mm track; half the size of O this combination became known as HO). Its longtime competitor Bing made some highly collectible clockwork trains with passenger cars, Pullman cars, U.S. mail cars, and observation cars for the American market in the twenties, but business declined when the stock market crashed and Bing ceased toy production in 1932. Karl Bub eventually took over the Bing train production (while Fleischmann took over the company's toy boat inventory).

American Louis Marx, producer of a vast assortment of toys, weathered the Depression quite well. Aided by the acquisition of one of its former subcontractors, Girard, Marx produced inexpensive locomotive and train sets. Other American firms like Ives and American Flyer struggled in the Depression. Even Lionel nearly went bankrupt and, as mentioned elsewhere, was saved in part because of a deal with Disney to produce a Mickey

and Minnie Mouse handcar, which became a sensation. Lionel also introduced the "City of Portland," based on an actual streamlined train, further exploiting the public's thirst for sleek, new designs. A successful line of O-gauge Streamliners followed, and helped in the firm's escape from financial ruin. After World War II, Lionel was up and running quickly and adapted easily to the realities of plastic and the Cold War. In the late 1950s and early 1960s it produced a series of fairly martial flatbed cars fitted with helicopters, rockets, and missiles.

BOATS

Toy boats of all kinds have long held an exalted position in the toy world; often, they are auction stars and the seaworthy apples of collectors' eyes. Paper-on-wood toy collectors admire brightly lithographed ships by makers such as R. Bliss Manufacturing and W. S. Reed Toy. American tin collectors yearn for late-nineteenth-century paddle wheelers by James Fallows & Sons and others. Even cast-iron transportation collectors have some heavy metal boats to choose from, among them the Hubley *Penn Yan* and Dent battleships.

In most instances, however, when collectors talk boats in hushed, reverential tones, it is the late-nineteenth-century and early-twentieth-century products of German makers, such as Märklin, Bing, Fleischmann, Arnold, J. Falk, and Carette that they are discussing. At the top of the list are the early Märklin boats, both the battleships and pleasure or commercial craft. In 1997, a rare Märklin paddle-wheel steamer wowed the crowd and sold at auction for $108,000. It encapsulated many of the features that have convinced collectors that Märklin boats are some of the most beautiful toys ever produced. Meticulously painted, the steamer is fitted with two slanting funnels, a three-tier captain's walk with stairs, and a passenger observatory building above a hand-painted first-class deck featuring tassel-draped windows painted to give the illusion of depth.

The King Edward, *a 1912 battleship made by the German toy manufacturer Bing, was perhaps all too ready for action in the North Atlantic.*

Tin boats—some hand painted, some lithographed—were fitted with clockwork mechanisms or friction motors. Two of the more interesting manufacturers are the French company Radiguet and the American manufacturer Orkin. Radiguet boats are usually painted black with copper trim and are fitted with gleaming brass live-steam boilers. Orkin boats lack such sophisticated effects but make up for that in scale and charm. Large models include battleships and speedboats, often fitted with wooden deck details.

Japan was an active toy-boat builder after World War II, producing large battery-operated lithographed tinplate toys in several styles, many of which still sell for under $300 in their original boxes.

A note to new collectors: Because backyard admirals often floated early toy boats, condition can be problematic. Restoration in various forms, particularly repainting, is common, as is rust. If a boat has a mechanism, check to be certain it is shipshape.

A hand-painted zinc-hulled single-screw pleasure craft with a working rudder, circa 1888, manufacturer unknown. The propeller is powered by the centrally located brass alcohol burner.

Bon voyage. This intricately detailed 1930s twin-funnel ocean liner by Fleischmann is a masterpiece in tin.

AIRPLANES AND ZEPPELINS

This dragonfly-sized 1930 Hubley Giroplane is made of cast iron, with white rubber tires and a nickel-plated motor and propellers.

Mankind's restless nature kept man (and woman) from being satisfied with conquering only land and sea. The sky beckoned, and anywhere adventurers went, toys soon followed. Early aeronautical toys, however, were often incorporated within other toys—a tower fitted with a balance arm might suspend a weight from one end and a dirigible with a man in a gondola from the other, for example. Wind the toy and the dirigible "flies."

As air travel became more prevalent, so too did the toy airplane. Produced in lithographed tin, pressed steel, and diecast metal, toy planes came in sizes ranging from the tiny Tootsietoy to the much larger pedal plane.

After the daring exploits of World War I flying aces, toy plane production flourished. The 1920s saw Chein, Strauss, and other toy companies producing inexpensive, colorfully lithographed handheld planes. Keystone produced large pressed steel aircraft, including a 1932 Ride 'Em Air Mail Airplane. Measuring 25 inches, with a 24-inch wingspan, it was fitted with a seat and made a clicking sound when pulled along but, alas, never got off the ground.

In 1927, Charles Lindbergh became a Jazz Age superstar when he piloted his plane, the *Spirit of St. Louis,* from New York to Paris. That airplane was a natural, if there ever was one, for toy companies. So the St. Louis–based company Metalcraft offered a *Spirit of St. Louis* construction kit that allowed fledgling aviators (and their dads) to assemble the toy from the ground up. Strauss produced a tinplate *Spirit of America,* the wing lithographed with a plane soaring over the Atlantic Ocean, bounded by North America and the Statue of Liberty on one wing, Europe and the Eiffel Tower on the other.

Although their products are far from being lighter than air, cast-iron toy manufacturers produced planes ranging from the 3½-inch Kilgore T-5 monoplane to a Hubley Tri-motor with a 17-inch wingspan. Hubley also produced several Lindy airplanes, even an early open-cockpit "Lindy Glider."

For wing walkers, a whimsical Tippo three-propeller tin-litho biplane from the 1930s.

Marx's plastic circa-1953 "Sparkling" fighter jet, with a friction motor and a Stars-and-Stripes decal on the wing.

Rosko's remote-controlled battery-operated Rocket Man in Space Armor walked and fired rockets on command.

In the 1930s, Tipp offered numerous planes and several keywind silver zeppelins. The French firm JEP (Jouets en Paris) produced a tinplate seaplane, brightly lithographed in red with oversize pontoons. In the late 1930s, Märklin manufactured a constructor plane based on the JU-52 Junkers, a plane so popular that it was reissued several decades later. In the postwar era, German firms like Tipp continued to produce toy airplanes, and the Japanese turned out a diverse line of planes, including several commercial airliners. Many postwar Japanese planes depict now-defunct airlines such as Pan Am. Toy planes have now been produced for nearly one hundred years, offering toy collectors more choices than most of today's frequent flyers.

ROBOTS AND SPACE TOYS

The concept of the automated figure is centuries old, but it wasn't until 1921 that Czechoslovakian playwright Karel Capek first used the term *robot* in his play *R.U.R (Rossum's Universal Robots)*. It was coined by his brother Josef, who derived it from the Czech word *robata,* meaning "forced labor." By that time, there had been numerous films about mechanical, electric, and synthetic men and women and animated dolls, and soon there would be even more robotic creations, including the evil Maria in Fritz Lang's 1927 German film classic *Metropolis* and the silly-looking robot in the 1935 Gene Autry western-sci-fi serial *The Phantom Empire*. Soon after, space travel went weekly in the wildly popular Saturday afternoon serials *Flash Gordon* and *Buck Rogers*.

Despite the popularity of science fiction in the 1920s and 1930s, it was not until after World War II that the toy industry began to create an array of robots, astronauts, flying saucers, and interplanetary explorers. There were several reasons for this sudden boom. The 1950s were fraught with cold-war anxieties, and there was paranoia about "aliens"; moreover, there was a wave of UFO sightings beginning in 1947. Then too, the United States and the Soviet Union were involved in a space race; the computer industry was being born; Isaac Asimov's seminal *I, Robot* was published; and there were scores of science fiction movies about space travel and alien invasions. Two of the better films, the cult classics *The Day the Earth Stood Still* (1951) and *Forbidden Planet* (1956), featured memorable robots. And further fueling this increasing fascination and paranoia regarding the future, American and German toy companies began to make some very fine robots and space toys. It was the Japanese, however, who introduced Americans to truly impressive space vehicles, ray guns, and robots. For the most part, these were painted and lithographed tinplate toys, and some had simple friction or keywind mechanisms. But the ones with mind-boggling action were battery operated.

ROBOTS

Because Robby the Robot from *Forbidden Planet* became famous soon after the film's release, Nomura Toys created a Robby look-alike called Mechanized Robot. A slew of robots followed, made by various firms and bearing a strong resemblance to the film star—they are now called Robby or Robby-style robots.

Masudaya Toys produced a series of five large robots that has been dubbed by collectors "The Gang of Five." Each is approximately 15 inches tall and has arms that swing back and forth as it walks.

Radicon Robot adds 5 inches to its height with an antenna, which receives signals from a wireless remote control. Produced in a fifties high-tech gray-blue wrinkle-textured finish, Radicon has really gratifying action: His head glows, his ears spin, a bulb in his chest lights up, and he rolls forward unless stopped or redirected by command of the remote-control box. One of the first wireless remote toys, Radicon was featured on the cover of a 1958 issue of *Popular Mechanics*. In mint condition, with its box, it can bring over $10,000.

WHAT'S IN A NAME?

Identifying robots and space toys poses a challenge to collectors. That's because various Japanese firms produced the same style of robot, often with very similar lithography and only slightly different features. The easiest type of identification, naturally, would be by the name on the original box. Unfortunately, the exact same names were used for both look-alikes and completely different toys. Photographs and a good memory consequently are requirements.

A fearsome Japanese Giant Sonic—also known as Train Robot—in multi-colored tin-litho, with flashing lights, locomotive whistle, swinging arms, and "bump-and-go" action (circa 1955).

The awe-inspiring Japanese GEAG superhero robot, manufactured in the 1960s, is tin-litho with a painted plastic head.

A remote-controlled Nomura Piston-Action Robot from the late 1950s. As it walks, its three lighted, cranial pistons move up and down.

Non-Stop Robot features bump-and-go action; that is, when the robot meets an obstacle, he changes direction. Collectors usually refer to this toy as Lavender Robot, for his unusual color. Giant Sonic Robot (also known as Train Robot) is bright red with a black head fitted with one red eye and one green eye and yellow ears that, when in action, flash on and off like a railroad semaphore. He is also known for the ear-piercing locomotive-style whistle he emits in action. Target Robot may have the most terrifying action of any robot. Finished in violet blue with yellow-and-red accents, he is packaged with a dart gun for the owner and has a bright red target disk centered on his chest. When in action, he rolls forward, attacking, and when the owner's dart hits the robot's target, he stops and turns as if in retreat; but then he turns again to renew his assault, his eyes and ears flash, his mouthpiece illuminates, and he emits a roar. Ah, the stuff of collector's dreams, built on the stuff of childhood nightmares!

Finished predominantly in red, like Giant Sonic Robot, Machine Man is the fifth in the Gang of Five. His name is lithographed prominently on his chest (don't confuse him with Ideal's plastic Mr. Machine). He is the rarest Gang of Five member, and in 1997 sold at auction for $74,000.

Other desirable robots include two keywind examples: Lilliput, an early Japanese robot from the 1940s, is believed to be among the first mass-produced toy robots. Finished in orange with a boxy black head, 6 inches tall. Diamond Planet Robot, introduced by Yonezawa Toys in the early fifties, is unconventional. It is 10 inches high, with its wide head attached directly to the body, giving it the neckless solidity of a professional weightlifter; the body is fitted to a rounded platform rather than legs, and it originally came with a massive winding key, for its keywind mechanism provides enough power to enable it to perform actions equal to most battery-powered toys. The arms raise and lower, the chest meter sweeps back and forth, and sparks bubble through a red gel in the base.

By the early 1970s, almost all robots were being made in plastic in Japan, the United States, and elsewhere. Although plastic in the robot world usually means both "made later" and "less desirable," there are some exceptions. There is growing interest in plastic robots from those put off by the high prices of tinplate and from advanced collectors as well, who are always restless for something new.

Interestingly, some of the earliest American robots were plastic. Ideal produced Robert the Robot, which had a hand-crank remote-control and speech mechanism—Robert talks! Louis Marx created a huge, statuesque robot named Big Loo, which was 38 inches of maroon, gold, and green plastic. His size could be intimidating were it not for his big, cheesy grin. More in scale with other robots are the 10½-inch Ranger Robot and the 14-inch Dux Astroman. Ranger Robot by Daiya is constructed of ribbed, clear plastic with a smooth, clear chest panel that reveals his tinplate gears. When in action, he walks forward, stops, raises his arms, and bellows smoke while an illuminated color wheel spins. At a recent auction, a boxed Ranger Robot sold for $8,400, while a Dux Astroman brought $1,560. Made in Germany, the Dux Astroman looks more like an alien astronaut than a robot. He has a red antenna on a clear, Plexiglas-domed helmet, a dark green body, and hands fitted with foam. When activated by the multibutton remote control, a bulb illuminates his transparent green chest, displaying the working mechanism. He moves forward, lifts his arms, and bends at the waist as his hands pick up and clasp an object.

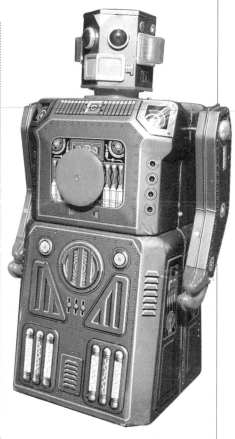

Matsudaya's circa 1955 Target Robot, one of the scarcer members of the so-called Gang of Five, emits a terrifying roar when he's hit by a dart on his chestplate.

A robot's best friend—the battery-powered Magic Space Dog (circa 1955), by Yoshiya, has multiple moving parts, including a flying saucer on a tether encircling its head.

SPACE TOYS

Numerous keywind and battery-operated astronauts were also produced by the Japanese in the post–World War II era. Although not technically robots, robot collectors make little distinction between the two. Astronauts come in a variety of styles and sizes. Some examples, such as Interplanetary Explorer Spaceman and Porthole Robot Spaceman, look more like deep-sea divers than astronauts. A spaceman by Yonezawa features a

It's a bird. It's a fish. It's a baby squid. It's Buck Rogers Rocket Police Patrol. The 1935 action hero takes aim with his ray gun in this fanciful Marx toy.

boxy robot body with a domed helmet encasing a smiling astronaut's head. Although finished in blue, it is virtually the same as the Cragstan Toys red-finished Astronaut (imported from Japan by the U.S.-based firm). Both are configured in the "skirted style": A flaring legless lower body conceals the wheels it moves on.

Wouldn't space travel be unbearably lonely without "man's best friend"? Several versions of Space Dogs have been produced and even reproduced, and illustrate the fact that manufacturers like to increase product lines by adding features, using a different type of mechanism, or simply changing the lithography. Because robot- and space-toy collectors love rarity and obscurity, some variations of particular toys are more desirable and worth substantially more than other models. A popular keywind silver-gray Space Dog pads forward, opens and closes his mouth, and flaps his ears as sparks illuminate the red gel on his back and his bubble eyes roll. A much rarer female version, the Magic Space Dog, is battery operated, finished in orange, features a bow on her head, and is fitted with a tether suspending a tiny flying saucer. In addition to having the same action as the silver-gray canine, she has a flying saucer that revolves around her head. At a recent auction, Space Dog brought a respectable $840, but his rare sister variation took best in show at $10,200. For those wishing to expand their space-age menagerie, Space Whales and Space Elephants are also out there somewhere.

Forbidding price—Nomura's Robby, inspired by the robot in the 1956 movie Forbidden Planet, *brings top dollar at toy auctions.*

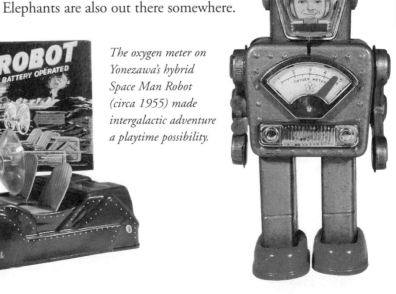

The oxygen meter on Yonezawa's hybrid Space Man Robot (circa 1955) made intergalactic adventure a playtime possibility.

Rockets, space cars, capsules, saucers, satellites, space stations, and other deep-space toys are highly sought after by collectors, with many selling for thousands of dollars. A special few have reached the stratosphere. An extremely rare friction-powered Space Patrol Car, with a robot driver in its original box, for example, sold at auction for $39,850. The presence of a robot, figural or lithographed, almost always adds to the value of a toy.

One series of space stations by Horikawa Toys was made in several versions. Resembling a tin-plate doughnut, the early version was offered in blue or red and can sell for around $2,000, while the New Space Station, which features an updated radar shield and a plastic bottom, sells for about $1,000 less. Like robots, many whirl, beep, and light up and are packed with intriguing "mystery action"—a term that appears on the boxes of many space toys and is usually synonymous with bump-and-go.

The innovative Masudaya produced a Sonicon Rocket in the early sixties that bears a closer resemblance to a hybrid airplane-cum–flying saucer than a rocket. The toy included a large whistle that could be used to activate the battery-operated mechanism.

Flying saucers have been made for decades but seldom on the scale of Masudaya's aptly named Space Giant. This was 12 inches in diameter, and its size was enhanced by a large domed astronaut-housing cockpit that tapered back, was topped by one fin, and flanked by two others. Moon

Long before Star Trek, Star Wars, and E.T., kids were moving at warp speed to alien spacecraft like this 1950s Japanese tin flying saucer.

Rosko and other toy companies were light years ahead of NASA with battery-operated astronauts (left) well-equipped for walks on the moon.

Although not exactly a space toy, Yonezawa's Atom Jet racer (circa 1958), which featured three tail jets and large dorsal fins, appeals to space toy collectors today.

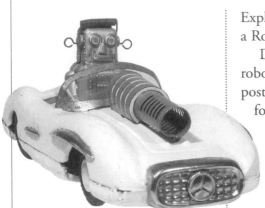

Cragstan's Mercedes Space Patrol sports car (circa 1959) combined the best of two worlds in which even tin robots could keep up with the Joneses.

Linemar toys were made in Japan by various manufacturers for Marx. This 1956 Mark II Lincoln Continental Coupe has a prominent hood ornament, antenna, and front and rear directional lights.

Explorers, Robot-driven Bulldozers, a Satellite Interceptor, and a Robot Torpedo were among other vehicles produced.

Despite astronomical prices for stellar pieces, the world of robots and space toys still offers hundreds of great toys from the post–World War II era for under $1,000, and a super selection for less than $500. Keep in mind that condition is all-important. So if you purchase one of these toys, don't throw out the boxes or even the cardboard inserts that secure that robot or saucer. They may be a nuisance to keep, but collectors believe they enhance the toy.

Collectors should note that many classic robots and space toys have been reproduced and sell for a fraction of the original, so don't pay top dollar for a replica.

BATTERY-OPERATED TOYS

Battery operated is often shortened to *battery op* by collectors and the term refers, in its broadest sense, to any robot, space toy, automobile, or other toy that is powered by a battery. Since many of these toys warrant their own categories, collectors use the term most often to refer to the Japanese-made post–World War II lithographed tinplate clowns, bartenders, bears, cats, dogs, elephants, monkeys, monsters, and the long list of other creatures that cleverly iron clothes, serve drinks, draw pictures, blow balloons, smoke cigars, style hair, play musical instruments, and amuse their owners. These toys combine the charm of the smaller key-wind Japanese toys with the size and action of robots and space toys. An example of one you can find fairly readily is the Bartender, a snappily dressed gentleman with martini glass in one hand and cocktail shaker in

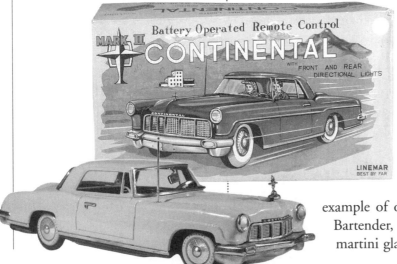

the other. He stands behind a small lithographed tinplate bar. When activated, he vigorously mixes and shakes the drink, pours it in the glass, raises the glass to his lips, and drinks. The results are immediate: He sways slightly, his vinyl face turns red, and smoke pours from his ears. This amusing toy with its sensational action can be bought for under $100 because it is so plentiful.

One of the more bizarre battery ops is a plush bear on a lithographed tinplate base marked "Cine Bear." He holds a camera, from which he shoots tiny plastic snakes or worms. Equally strange is the rare Japanese Pleasant Kappa, also known as Funny River Creature. Nobody has really figured out what Kappa is. Made of green-finished tinplate, Kappa is dressed in a spiffy plaid jacket and has a birdlike beak and a circle of straw hair around a bald spot. Perhaps even funnier than its appearance are the directions on its box. "If you pull string, Kappa will laugh, shake his head, and his eyes will shine and then you will have a clear head of thought."

Frankenstein, the Hootin Hollow Haunted House, and Spooky Kooky Tree are an elite trio of toys from Marx (which had a Japanese subsidiary, Linemar) that collectors adore. They are also marvelous additions to a Halloween collection. Frankenstein has a green plastic face and wears a lithographed tinplate mortuary tux. A push of his remote control and he walks forward, bends at the waist, raises and lowers his arms, and brings his ghoulish green hands together.

Hootin Hollow Haunted House is a lithographed tinplate tour de force depicting a spooky, decrepit old house packed with scary images. It has multiple actions controlled by eight side-mounted buttons. The buttons can be employed to illuminate the shadow of a ghost at a window, open a door to reveal a Dracula-like figure, or cause a skeleton to rise from the chimney.

The bark-pattern lithographed Kooky Spooky Tree is reminiscent of the crabby, talking apple tree in the classic film *The Wizard of Oz*. It rolls forward with mystery action and raises and lowers its branch-form arms; its eyes roll up and down as it emits a shiver-inspiring whistling sound.

This battery-operated, flocked Dentist Bear (circa 1953) by Suzuki & Edwards actually boasted that it came complete with a "crying baby bear" patient!

CHARACTER TOYS

Hundreds of popular characters from newspaper comic strips, comic books, movies (including animation), radio, and television have been the subjects of toys, action figures, and dolls, from the cast-iron Yellow Kid goat cart to the Howdy Doody hand puppet to the lithographed Peanuts tin drum to a key-wind lithographed tinplate George Jetson hopper. But who are the two most consistent performers, both pre– and post–World War II? A mouse and a rough-and-tumble sailor.

Mickey Mouse burst on the scene with the release of the Walt Disney cartoon *Steamboat Willie* in 1928, and soon after, Mickey Mouse merchandise took the marketplace by storm. Mickey Mouse collectors particularly love the memorabilia of the early 1930s. A lot of these early toys feature a Mickey with a sharp, long nose and a toothy grin, making him much more rodentlike than the rounded Mickey we know and love today.

Not all prewar Mickey toys are rare or stratospherically expensive, not even the 1934 Mickey Mouse Handcar that helped save Lionel from bankruptcy. Made in electrical and key-wind versions, the toy handcar retailed for $1 and Lionel received orders for over 350,000, putting the company to work around the clock in the midst of the Depression. An example of this Mickey toy in excellent condition can usually be had for $1,000 or less (not cheap exactly, but remember, some rare, desirable toys go for tens of thousands of dollars). The rarer box for the toy can double that figure.

Mickey Mouse was the subject of some delightful post–World War II toys. For instance, a Linemar battery-operated Mickey Magician can make even a skeptic believe in magic. Featuring a large and impeccably dressed Mickey standing on a stage with a top hat on a podium, he lifts his hat to reveal a tiny metal chick, then lowers; Mickey waves his wand, and lifts the hat again. *Voila,* the chick is gone! The illusion is created by

An indefatigable Mickey and Minnie Mouse worked overtime on Lionel's Handcar toy, riding the tracks while saving the company from bankruptcy.

means of an electromagnet concealed in the hat.

Today, Mickey Mouse is over seventy-five years old and still going strong. (For more on Mickey Mouse memorabilia, see page 374.)

In 1919, comic-strip artist E. C. Segar began to draw the "Thimble Theatre," a strip revolving around the Oyl family: the patriarch Cole Oyl; his wife, Nana; their children, Castor and Olive; and Olive's first boyfriend, Ham Gravy. In 1929, the family bought a boat, and Castor Oyl and Ham Gravy went down to the docks, looking for someone with seagoing experience. Spotting a scrubby-looking fellow with an anchor tattoo and a squinty eye, Ham queried, "Hey there! Are you a sailor?" The feisty response was "Ja' think I'm a Cowboy?" Popeye was hired and soon supplanted Ham Gravy as Olive's beau. He also was embraced by a Depression-era America in need of simple, honest, and big-hearted, if slightly rough-and-ready, heroes. This spinach-eating, mumbling muscleman would be the inspiration for some of the finest character toys ever made.

Years before Superman came on the scene, toy producer J. Chein touted Popeye's super strength. The company created, for instance, Popeye the Heavy Hitter, a toy that has Popeye, a hammer in his hands, standing on a comic-strip lithographed

At the height of his popularity, the beloved Popeye popped up everywhere. Tin versions of E. C. Segar's scruffy seaman pummel a punching bag (left), blow bubbles (center), and wind up for a walk with his parrot (right).

THE MOUSE ON THE FLYING TRAPEZE

"I've seen Mickey Mouse on planes, trains, and automobiles, and now on a trapeze," said *Antiques Roadshow* appraiser Leila Dunbar. "He's got to be the most talented mouse ever." The visitor who brought the swinging mouse to the Nashville *Antiques Roadshow* said her father received it in the 1930s when he was recovering from surgery. She had brought it in "because we have the original box, and we heard that toys in their box were worth something." Dunbar told her that the toy itself was made between 1931 and 1934 and imported from Japan. "See how light this is?" she asked. "It has almost the feel of a Ping-Pong ball. It's very delicate and fragile." Then pointing to Mickey's crushed nose, Dunbar noted, "It's obvious he's been played with often." Turning her attention to the box, which was actually much rarer than the toy itself, she continued. "In those days, the lithography was just spectacular," Dunbar said. "If you look here on the side, you see Minnie and Mickey playing the piano. They're having a great time. This is one mouse you definitely want to keep in the house!" She valued the toy at $500 to $700 and the box at $800 to $1,200.

base fitted with an amusement park–style strength-tester complete with a numerical meter and bell. When the toy is wound, our hero raises the hammer, strikes, and maybe rings the bell. Popeye's scrappy reputation of not looking for a fight, but never avoiding one, resulted in several "pugilist" toys, including two in which our hero works out on celluloid punching bags. These are known as the Upright and the Overhead punching bags by Popeye collectors. The box for the Popeye Overhead Puncher is one of the most amusing in toy collecting. One side features a heated Popeye in midstride, as if on his way to meet an opponent, muttering, "Blow me down—He's my meat! I'll lay 'im among the cactussus." Not English exactly, but Popeye's fans need no translation. This 1932 toy is rare and valuable and has sold for $4,000 on several occasions—even without the box.

Another Popeye boxing toy is Popeye the Champ, also known as Big Fight. It's a Louis Marx gem that combines a popular character with stunning lithography and great action. It consists of a tinplate four-post boxing ring, its sides adorned with Thimble Theatre characters and the celluloid figures of Popeye and his nemesis, Bluto, mounted on a disk. When wound and activated, the disk rotates and the combatants slug it out. When a bell rings, either Popeye or Bluto is knocked out—the action is random and unpredictable. The box is also a beauty, decorated as it is with a close-up of the ring showing Popeye connecting with a right to Bluto's chin.

Considering Popeye's occupation, the boats would seem to be the natural Popeye toy, but surprisingly only a few were made. A prewar rowboat by Hoge Manufacturing, finished in bright red,

A rare, turn-of-the-twentieth-century cast-iron Buster Brown toy made by Hubley features an oversized Tige pulling his young master in a tin cart.

is fitted with a lithographed Popeye manning the oars. His rowing action is provided by a powerful clockwork mechanism. In 1998, this toy sold at auction for $9,900. The rarer version, also by Hogue, features Popeye in a speedboat, and it was purchased for $18,150. A battery-op Popeye in a rowboat with a remote control and the original box brought $9,200 at another recent auction.

Popeye remained a popular character well after his creator's untimely death in 1937, going on to become the star of animated cartoons that are still run on television, and of a float in the Macy's Thanksgiving Day Parade. After World War II, several Popeye toys were produced in Japan for Linemar, Marx's subsidiary. A keywind favorite has Popeye balancing Olive in a chair. A popular battery-op Popeye sits on a can of spinach and blows smoke from his pipe.

In the 1950s, there was much toy merchandising connected with television shows that were geared to children. *The Mickey Mouse Club, Howdy Doody, The Roy Rogers Show, Gene Autry, Hopalong Cassidy, The Lone Ranger, Davy Crockett* episodes on Walt Disney's *Disneyland Show, Zorro, The Adventures of Superman, Captain Video and His Video Rangers,* and cartoon shows were among the programs for which there were toys, games, and other merchandise, all bearing the likenesses of popular television characters. (Children would even send away for some toys promoted by the stars in commercials.) Cap pistols and rifles based on those toted by TV cowpokes alone constitute a specialized area of collecting. In the 1960s, the animated *Flintstones* and the *Jetsons* inspired Stone Age and Space Age toys. *Batman* and *Bullwinkle* also spawned mass-produced toys.

Today, in the rush to find the character toys of their youths, many collectors pass up those of earlier times. Some earlier character toys, such as the Toonerville Trolley and Marx's keywind Joe "Wanna buy a duck?" Penner, may actually sell for less today than they did ten or twelve years ago. The Toonerville Trolley has great action, and the Joe

Criminals couldn't get far with Dick Tracy in hot pursuit in this 1949 Marx squad car with its friction motor and a battery-operated flashing red light.

A 1966 Batmobile by Ichimura provided curious multiple views of the superhero and Robin in their three-wheeled, elaborately decorated tin-litho vehicle.

A 1920s German-made tin-litho Toonerville Trolley—based on the cartoon created by Fontaine Fox—sold in the United States by the noted toy distributor Geo. Borgfeldt & Co.

The goat-skin bellows tucked beneath Lehmann's (circa 1903) Tut Tut car (German for "toot-toot") let the dapper Sunday driver clear the road with his little horn.

Penner is one of the most elaborately lithographed keywind walkers ever made. They would be fine additions to novelty or keywind toy collections.

THE MANUFACTURERS

S everal toy companies played especially important roles in the history of twentieth-century toys, while others are particular favorites of collectors. Here are a few described briefly.

LEHMANN TOYS

A manufacturer of novelty toys founded in Germany in 1881, the Ernst Paul Lehmann Company was adept at packing action and whimsical charm into small packages. It was known for lithographed tinplate people and for novelty vehicles.

Lehmann created toys based on current events around the globe. When colonists in South Africa began to raise ostriches for their plumage and the public became fascinated by these exotic birds, Lehmann created a two-wheeled "Africa" mail cart with a black driver being pulled by an ostrich.

Local news was also inspirational. In 1906, cobbler William Voigt, an ex-convict, dressed up as a Prussian captain and stole money from the treasury of Köpenick, a suburb of Berlin, right under the noses of the military who controlled it. He was soon caught and sentenced to prison, but he had become such a folk hero that Kaiser Wilhelm pardoned him. Lehmann redressed its old toy sailor figure in a military uniform and within a couple of months had a new toy, the Captain of Köpenick, to sell.

Lehmann produced many of the same toys for years, even decades. Tom the Monkey, who climbed up a string when it was pulled, was so popular that Lehmann produced it from 1895 to 1945, and other manufacturers copied it as well.

During its long and still ongoing history, Lehmann has produced collectible dancing figures, bands, motorcycles, cars, cabs, trucks, buses, and a delicate airplane named Ikarus. Its toys are easy to identify because they are almost always marked with the firm's name and bell-shaped spindle-press logo. Most toys are also marked with their own names, which are quite often a prominent part of their design.

SCHOENHUT TOYS

Albert Schoenhut, a German immigrant who settled in Philadelphia, began producing toy pianos in 1872, although he didn't begin to make other toys until the beginning of the twentieth century. For the next thirty years, his company produced clowns, roly-polys, horse-drawn wagons, wooden boats, guns, dolls, and other toys. What the Schoenhut Company of Philadelphia may be best remembered for, however, is the Humpty-Dumpty Circus, introduced in 1903. Original sets contained only a few carved wood pieces, but as the circus grew in popularity, Schoenhut added dozens of animals and circus performers as individual pieces or in boxed sets. Accessories, such as cages, circus wagons, trapezes, and tents, were also produced.

One of the most desirable circus accessories for collectors today is an elaborately embellished band-wagon with six removable, poseable musicians playing various instruments, and a driver, with four horses that are fitted onto two separate, wheeled platforms. Also sought after is the circus tent introduced in 1928—a wooden frame supporting a red-and-white-striped "canvas" roof with the words "Humpty-Dumpty Circus" lithographed on it. Printed on the interior of the tent are a clown, an elephant, and a ringmaster entering the ring. These are flanked by grandstands with a band and full house of spectators. The *pièces de résistance,* however, are the rare side banners depicting sideshow attractions such as the Beautiful

Before his great fall, Humpty Dumpty had a career in the circus. The finely detailed wooden Schoenhut play set is complete with ringmaster, clown, acrobats, and a bevy of performing animals.

Snake Charmer, the Smallest Man on Earth, the Bearded Lady, the Siamese Twins, the Living Skeleton, and the Wildman of Borneo.

Another Schoenhut classic, Teddy's Adventures in Africa, came in a box with a lavishly lithographed interior depicting an African savanna. Also included were a bespectacled Teddy Roosevelt (a convincing likeness) and a photographer patterned after the former president's son Kermit.

Some assembly required—the Schuco Studio 1050 Racer kit (circa 1952), with working steering wheel and leather seat, was sold in parts and assembled by the buyer.

SCHUCO TOYS

Founded in Germany in 1912, the Schuco Toy Company first made mechanical novelties but became famous for its windup toys. The company produced plush teddy bears, walking felt figures, automotive toys, character toys, and a line of small keywind walkers that featured metal bodies covered in cloth. Although most are only around 4½ inches tall, their tiny mechanisms still allow them to raise a stein of beer, shuffle forward, or beat a drum.

Schuco thrived after World War I, under the direction of Adolph Kahn. In the mid-1920s, it produced perhaps its most famous creation, the Tricky Yes-No Bear, with a tail lever that enabled the toy to nod "yes" or "no." Because the bear was popular with all ages, Schuco marketed it to adults as well as children, a practice it would continue until it ceased production in 1970.

After World War II, the company made many handsome vehicles with ingenious action, some of which have been reproduced in recent years.

FERDINAND STRAUSS TOYS

When Ferdinand Strauss emigrated from Germany to New York at the turn of the twentieth century, his initial interest in toys was as a "creative" distributor rather than a toy maker: Purchasing toys from European and American makers, he marketed them under his own name. Emboldened by his success and aware that the importing of toys to the United States would be curtailed by war in Europe, he eventually opened his own toy factory in East Rutherford, New Jersey, following that, in 1914, with the first of several toy stores stocked with his own products.

His first toys were pretty much copies of a Lehmann's dancing toy and the Climbing Monkey, but they are also the first American mass-produced tinplate toys. By the late 1910s, Strauss was known as the "Founder of the Mechanical Toy Industry in America."

Although Strauss continued to produce mechanical toys, including tinplate transportation vehicles like the Yell-O-Taxi and Scout Flyer airplanes, sometime in the late 1920s or early 1930s he ceased production to concentrate on his stores. Direct attribution of his toys is sometimes difficult, because although many are marked with his name, subcontractors may have produced them. It is believed that Strauss stopped all toy-making activities in the mid-1930s, but as late as 1944, the company was still listed in trade directories as a manufacturer of gliders, mechanical toys, and popguns.

LOUIS MARX TOYS

In 1912, Ferdinand Strauss hired sixteen-year-old Louis Marx as an errand boy. Career-minded, Marx moved up quickly in the ranks to salesman, and by 1917, the twenty-one-year-old was running the Strauss factory. When Marx couldn't convince Strauss to sell his retail stores and concentrate on toy production, however, he left, eventually opening an office at the Toy Center in New York City with his brother David. Through the 1920s, Marx redesigned toys, often subcontracting them to other manufacturers in order to fill all his orders from chain stores. Like Strauss, he ordered in such quantities that manufacturers were willing to place the Marx name on their toys.

A millionaire at twenty-six, Marx was a master at finding ways to produce toys at lower costs while improving them. Toward the end of the decade, he sold more than 100,000 toys based on an

Above: Pretend bus drivers could double their fun with the Strauss 10-inch tin-litho mechanical double-decker Inter-State Bus (circa 1927). Below: More affluent toy passengers could make their way about town in the company's 8½-inch Yell-O-Taxi (1919), driven by a uniformed cabbie.

obscure Philippine string toy that would eventually be known as the "Yo-Yo."

Marx deftly kept his product line fresh by adapting toys from existing dies, so that without the expense of retooling, a key-wind B. O. Plenty Walker became a Mortimer Snerd Walker and a Miniature Drugstore became a miniature Fire House or Movie Theatre—a technique he applied throughout his career.

At one time, Louis Marx & Company was the largest producer of toys in the world. In the 1930s, Marx began buying factories and other companies, including Girard Model Works and C. E. Carter in the early 1940s. With the acquisition of Girard, Marx protected its source of inexpensive train sets, a large part of the business. By 1950, Marx was producing more than 12 percent of the toys made in the United States. At the Erie facility, the company churned out tanks, cars, and tractors at the rate of over one million each per year. Marx's first foreign factory was in England, and by 1955, it had factories or production agreements with companies in Mexico, Australia, South Africa, France, and Japan.

Collectors have long valued the keywind and battery-operated toys marked Linemar, made by various manufacturers in Japan for Marx. Some of the best Linemar toys, including Roller Skating Mickey Mouse and Unicyclist Popeye, were produced by TPS (Tokyo Playthings, Ltd.) for Marx.

For six decades Marx anticipated changes in the toy market, providing it with what was wanted. Easily adapting to the reality of plastics, Marx produced such favorites as the Rock 'em Sock 'em Robots and a line of play sets (the Western Ranch and scores of others) that featured lithographed settings for plastic figures. In 1972, Marx sold his company, claiming that the making of toys was a young man's business.

Because even toy figures need to learn how to operate their vehicles safely, Marx produced the keywind Driver Training Car (circa 1950).

In classic rags-to-riches fashion, Louis Marx became one of the leading manufacturers in the world, making toys like this relatively streamlined Gravel Mixer Truck (circa 1934).

Chapter Six

FASHION AND TEXTILES

Wearable, touchable, and best of all, usable, clothing and textiles of the twentieth century attract hordes of passionate collectors who, just a few years ago, would have walked right by those feed-sack quilts and beaded bags. Soft goods of all types—from handkerchiefs and aprons to blankets and ball gowns—are attracting unprecedented interest, as vintage textile dealers set up booths at specialty shows in major American cities, and thousands—among them famous designers and superchic celebrities—attend.

Here's why. Unlike most of its fragile, nineteenth-century predecessors, vintage twentieth-century clothing—much of it mass-produced—is gratifyingly durable and (if you're not going to leave it to a museum) can be unconcernedly and casually worn. The development of synthetics has something to do with this, but even more to the point is our growing expertise in textile preservation and the technology of climate control. Veiled cocktail hats and felt circle skirts aren't for everyone, of course, not even museum curators. Yet the courage it takes to dress in

Top: A long, lean handbag from the 1950s. Above: An elegant 1950s evening gown by Mainbocher with a fitted bodice and an asymmetrical peplum.

SHOES FOR BOUND FEET

Most of us are familiar with the sad and long-standing Chinese practice of binding little girls' feet to keep them small and delicate "like a lotus blossom." Appraiser Caroline Ashleigh examined an unusual pair of these lotus shoes at the Cleveland *Antiques Roadshow.*

Beginning in the tenth century, young Chinese girls of the upper classes were subjected to the painful process of having cloth strips tightly wound around their feet, the toes bent under, to inhibit natural growth. This resulted in deformed but tiny feet, most no more than four inches long. Not only did bound feet indicate that a girl came from a wealthy family, but small feet were viewed as being sexually attractive. Foot binding was only abandoned in 1911, with the founding of the Chinese Republic.

The pair of lotus shoes examined by Ashleigh was made of silk, the traditional material, and embroidered in cotton. Because the shoes are smaller than the usual four inches, Ashleigh believed they were made for a child, which adds to their rarity and value. She estimated their value at between $450 and $650.

such apparel brings real sartorial distinction to the wearer, since—a little like a lettered T-shirt—it sends a message as to who you are, who you think you are, or who you'd like to be.

So, at many large antiques shows today—where dealers who are experts in white linens, hats and bags, men's clothes, and couture are frequently found—collectors are buying vintage. They search for vintage clothing on the Internet. At garage sales and in thrift shops, canny enthusiasts unearth 1930s handbags to carry on their twenty-first-century arms. They snap up hats, shoes, dresses, and uniforms: for everything old, unsurprisingly, is new again. If it feels good in the hand or good in the heart, then it will look good in your closet, or on you.

Often, to complement this personal style, collectors accent their homes with vintage soft goods as well, using twentieth-century quilts and blankets, tablecloths, tea towels, and bedspreads to create a "look." This chapter covers both areas, but focuses primarily on fashion.

FASHION

To some people, old clothes are just old clothes: Worn fur coats from the 1940s, outmoded 1950s evening gowns, little 1930s day dresses that look like they've spent much too much time hanging out on the clothes line or stretched on an ironing board. To a new generation of sophisticated, party-going women, women who want to stand out from their tank-topped, blue-jeaned peers, these clothes—plus the shoes, bags, and gloves that go with them—are the surest means of making, in an suitably dated phrase, a "fashion statement." (Another sort of fashion statement altogether is being made by the scores of men who attend the annual polyester leisure-suit convention, dressed, for better or worse, in their crease-free synthetic best.) Fashion models and Hollywood stars turn up increasingly at grand events in grand vintage turnouts, so that once again, dresses by those masters of couture Charles James, Coco Chanel, and Christian Dior are seen at all the top premieres. There is a definite retro movement afoot, one that prefers the outfit that you won't see yourself coming and going in. In other words, there's a fashion for, well, old clothes.

Vintage garments aren't just any old clothes, however. They are stylish clothes above all; and "stylish" seems to come in two categories: the wearable and the unwearable. Wearable vintage, not surprisingly, is often less expensive than unwearable vintage because it is frequently newer and thus, more durable, or it is less "important." Unwearable vintage clothes—because of their fragility, rarity, or association with a noted celebrity (like Marilyn Monroe's glittering JFK "birthday" dress, for instance, see page 356)—are generally purchased for display. Often, it is their very costliness that makes them unwearable. No one wants to be responsible for dribbling caviar down the front of a rare Fortuny gown, which is why so few real collectors of unique clothing actually wear their vintage couture. (*Couture,* by the way, along with being custom-made for the wearer and frequently one-of-a-kind, is legally defined by the French government as being limited to garments that have required at least thirty hours of handwork.) Currently, not only the coats, dresses, and gowns, but even the mannequins on which such clothes were draped and exhibited are collectible. Representatives of well-known American designers (Ralph Lauren comes to mind) are continuously scouting flea markets and thrift shops for inspiration. Moreover, while many museums have been steadily acquiring vintage garments for years—couture, most often—they are also on the hunt for even the most humble of

Four LBDs—little black dresses—of the fifties and sixties, from left: a strapless silk cocktail dress by French designer Jean Dessès; a silk cocktail dress with three-quarter length raglan sleeves and a deep decolletage with rose by Traina-Norell; a sequined cocktail dress with see-through sleeves by Galanos; and a pleated chiffon cocktail dress (unhappily, much altered) by Chanel.

HOW HIGH IS HIGH?

If the original cost of a garment was high, it will also be high today. And high can mean stratospheric. The American designer Mainbocher's clothes could be twice as expensive as Parisian couture. His garments were so expensive, in fact, that it was not unknown for his wealthy clientele to hand their husbands only half the bill, paying the rest from their own—necessarily ample—pockets.

This bronzy evening gown from Christian Dior's fall 1954 collection, seen at the Sacramento Antiques Roadshow, *has a full skirt and a scratchy horsehair crinoline slip.*

everyday men's and women's wear. The Lower East Side Tenement Museum in New York City, for instance, has a curator busily acquiring workday clothes made by and for New York's early Russian immigrants.

Intriguingly, plain old work clothes and housedresses can sometimes be harder to find than luxurious, costly gowns. This is because overalls and housedresses were worn, for the most part, by people of modest means, and so were worn until the clothes wore out. Costly gowns and couture, however, were the privilege of the well to do, according to Keni Valenti, a New York expert on vintage fashion. They were frequently considered almost "too good to put on," an attitude that accounts for the wonderful condition in which so many high-priced and fragile garments are found today. Women who could afford expensive clothing felt obliged to take care of it, too—or had maids who did that for them—stuffing sleeves with tissue paper and putting everything away in fabric garment bags, the perfect textile storage: safe, dark, and dry. On the other hand, while some garments were, indeed, too good to put on, others weren't too good to put out with the trash. One wonders if it was a mistake or an angry spouse who draped a $3,000 Chanel gown over a garbage can on a Manhattan street for a very lucky collector to find.

A vintage Christian Dior evening gown from the fifties—not found on the street, but given to the collector by a friend— showed up at the Sacramento *Antiques Roadshow*, and appraiser Linda Donahue explained how the dress fit into the history of post–World War II fashion.

After those far-too-Spartan war years, Dior at last had the freedom to create fanciful, luxurious dresses in collections that were presented twice each year—spring and fall—from 1947 until his death in 1957. The dress the visitor brought in, with its full skirt underpinned by a horsehair crinoline slip, was from the designer's Bronze-Green Collection of fall 1954. And its all-important Dior label was still attached to indicate that it was custom-made for a client. This particular design, published in the French fashion magazine *Silhouette* in 1954, was an important dress in that it was characteristic of its era.

Fortunately for its current owner, this dress had received proper care and was in "untouched" condition, meaning that it had no alterations or damages. Donohue told him, "If it had been hemmed or taken in or changed, the whole idea of the dress and the integrity of the original design would have been altered." She also congratulated the owner on the care he takes of his collection, which he keeps wrapped in acid-free paper and stored on hangers encased in cloth bags. (Many people think vintage clothes should be kept in plastic bags, but these are simply dust attracters.) Donohue counseled him to continue to keep this dress in a dark place and to dry-clean it seldom, if at all. The optimal way to store it would be flat in a trunk or drawer. She estimated its value to be between $1,500 and $2,000.

A man's khaki wool "Eisenhower jacket" from 1951 has its original applied Eighth Army patches, certain to be of interest to collectors of Korean War–era uniforms.

Men's clothes are not in equivalent demand, despite the fact that they can be as well made as couture. The beautifully tailored suits and jackets of the 1920s, for instance—influenced as they were by a singularly natty Prince of Wales and by starry swashbucklers like Douglas Fairbanks and Rudolf Valentino—are unquestionably elegant and dashing. Yet, collectors and museum people are far more interested in women's garments, perhaps because these are less conservative and tend to reflect the spirit of almost any era more completely and colorfully than men's clothes do. Nevertheless, menswear has its dedicated collectors, among them designer Helmut Lang, who specializes in collecting military uniforms. One American museum has been scouting recently for a 1940s zoot suit. (For inveterate attic rummagers, a zoot suit can be recognized by its double-breasted jacket with oversize lapels, its high-waisted, wide-legged trousers nipped in at the cuff, and the inevitable, looping-to-knee-level key chain dangling from one pocket.) On the whole, however, "A suit is a suit is a suit," says Keni Valenti. Unless it's a zoot.

BOY SCOUT UNIFORMS

Many people explain their collecting habit by citing a formative childhood passion. In Louisville, Kentucky, one *Antiques Roadshow* visitor's youthful enthusiasm was for the Boy Scouts, and was an Eagle Scout himself (a feat matched by his *Antiques Roadshow* appraiser, Tim Luke). He now collects—naturally—scouting memorabilia, and brought in one of his prizes for Luke to look at: A scout uniform from 1915. "I wanted a world-class uniform," he explained. "And I saw this in a mail auction. I didn't know what condition it would be in. When it arrived I was flabbergasted," for the uniform was in fine condition and came, unexpectedly with membership cards and washing instructions. His purchase was enhanced by a Boy Scouts of America pin, the original owner's troop number, and a patch with the Boy Scout motto, "Be Prepared."

"This is very collectible," noted Luke. The value of the $300 auction purchase? About $2,000.

A French beaded evening dress from the 1920s, with the characteristic dropped waist and "tubular" form.

A BRIEF HISTORY

"The language of fashion shapes and reflects the spirit of the times and offers telling insights into who we were at the beginning of the last century and how we had changed by its end," says *Antiques Roadshow* appraiser Caroline Ashleigh. The real history of twentieth-century fashion begins during World War I, when the about-to-be "liberated" woman developed both a desire and a fondness for more comfortable, less restrictive clothes. When the war ended, all the "modern" girls cut their hair, rolled their stockings down, and overnight became "flappers," a term stemming from a phrase in Robert Graves and Alan Hodge's book *The Long Weekend,* which described the 1920s woman as "a comradely, sporting, active young woman who would ride on the 'flapper bracket' of a motor cycle." This "active young woman" took full advantage of every sort of postwar technical advance, elastic and plastic among them (both of which were welcome replacements for the unyielding whalebone of Edwardian corsets), as well as the "invention" of the brassiere, which initially consisted of two handkerchiefs, attached to lengths of ribbon. The flapper's head-hugging cloche hat, waistless dress, and carefree, sporty look were all intended to evoke and emulate the look of such plucky modern heroines as aviator Amelia Earhart and tennis star Helen Wills Moody.

During the flapper era, silk, jersey, cotton, and wool dresses were tubular in shape, easy, unstructured, and often, seductively revealing of bare arms and back. The racy illusion of bare legs was furthered by beige and buttercream stockings, as hemlines, rising throughout the decade, revealed more and more of them. Contemporary author Aldous Huxley noted that the ideal twenties woman was "angular and tubular like a section of a boa constrictor dressed in clothes that emphasized this serpentine slimness."

The detailing of these sinuous clothes, hats, jewels, shoes, and bags was equally exotic. Many twenties garments and accessories made some stylized reference to King Tut's tomb, just discovered in 1922, and sported those new-all-over-again Egyptian motifs of scarabs, locusts, and gazelles. Dresses, hats, and bags also came in for their share of Art Deco's stylized representations of greyhounds, baskets of flowers, and lithe young women—usually nude and usually gamboling. The large, stylized flora, asymmetry, and striking colors of the period were features that could be seen to wonderful advantage on soft and flattering clothing styles that somehow also managed to incorporate the bold, architectonic geometry advocated by the 1925 Exposition Internationale des Arts Décoratifs et Industriels Modernes in Paris.

THE 1930s

Novice collectors often confuse clothes from the twenties, characterized by low hip belts and asymmetrical details, with the clothes of the thirties, because early in the twenties, hemlines were long, like the skirts typical of the thirties. They rose above the knees only toward the end of the decade.

Throughout the Depression years, however, hemlines plunged along with the stock market and stayed long. (Hemline length, potential collectors should know, was once a major fashion issue. Only recently, with the advent of the American do-your-own-thing attitude—and the popularity of trousers—has the subject been treated with indifference.) Fashion in the thirties was cool and dignified. Bias cutting allowed crepes, satins, and jerseys to flow languorously, following the natural line of the body, and waistlines, which had disappeared in the twenties' rush to comfort and androgyny, returned to their accustomed spot. In the thirties, too, the ladies' suit became as popular as the dress, while both appeared in alluringly feminine styles—frequently with capelet sleeves or incorporating cape effects—on smart and increasingly self-possessed young women.

In 1935, nylon, the first synthetic fiber, was

A short-sleeved crepe evening dress from 1938, with gold feather decorations accenting the waistline. At left: A wool jersey evening dress from 1934, cut on the bias, with a halter neck and a long, graceful scarf providing a capelike effect.

In the United States, a signature 1940s silhouette was Joan Crawford's broad-shouldered profile, created by designer Adrian. His sometime rival Edith Head called it "Hollywood's single most important influence on American fashion."

invented at the DuPont Experimental Station in Delaware. DuPont began to produce nylon yarn in 1939. Named by its creator for the two cities in which it was hoped the new material would have its greatest success—New York and London—it was successful beyond DuPont's wildest imaginings, particularly for the stockings that superseded the traditional hose in expensive, relatively hard-to-launder silk.

THE 1940s

That nylon stocking, however, became as rare as sugar and French perfume during World War II, as did all kinds of textiles. The manufacture of uniforms took precedence over fashion. Consequently, the coats, suits, and dresses of the war years were economically designed; specifically, they used far less fabric than they had in earlier decades, becoming plain, short, slim, and tailored. While such austerity may have been prompted by wartime shortages, it also managed to become fashionable in itself, for fashion and style are nothing if not adaptable. Then, in 1947, as the rest of the world settled gratefully into peacetime, a young French couturier named Christian Dior shook the very foundations of the fashion world with his "New Look," a Gallic reappraisal of aesthetic and form. Dior's new dresses employed yards and yards of fabric for skirts, and in their billowy extravagance, they emphasized both tight-fitting bodices and tiny waists. It was a style immediately embraced by millions of women who had been yearning to leave behind the overalls and economies of the war years: to be feminine once more. Silks, woolens, and taffetas were back in stores after a long absence, and taffetas, especially, lent themselves to the New Look. (In order to achieve the look, corsets—also called girdles—returned with a boned and zippered vengeance.) Accompanied by pert veiled hats and pristine white gloves, Dior's New Look was a perfect minimalist's take on Victorian style. If it occasionally pinched or kept one from breathing deeply, it was always flattering.

Not everything fashionable came from France. Walk-in closets full of fine clothing were made in Hollywood for movie stars. Oscar-winning costume designer Edith Head developed her own ready-to-wear line, for which she "knocked off" the original dresses and suits she had designed for Joan Crawford. Hollywood designer Adrian did the same.

THE LATE 1940S AND EARLY 1950S

Sophisticated vintage clothing collectors consider the late forties and early fifties to be the high point of twentieth-century couture. "The look" was still dictated by Paris, although American designer Charles James was at the height of his fabric-sculpting powers in the fifties, and fellow designers like Pauline Trigère were dressing the confident Manhattan sophisticate. While most of the clothes that turn up in vintage shops are a long way from couture, the 1950s were also a high point for accessories, and there is an abundance of these.

Hats, bags, gloves, and shoes in matched sets—all four, if possible—were very much de rigueur, since there were formulas for dressing in the fifties, an era of rules. One didn't wear white after Labor Day, for instance, or wear a cocktail dress to dinner. A cocktail dress was "dressy"—most appropriate for nonblack-tie parties—and its suitability for cocktail parties was usually a matter of neckline and fabric. The cocktail dress was always short: It inevitably had some serious décolletage or bared shoulders, and was dark—preferably black—with velvet or silken trim, perhaps. The dinner dress, worn for dinner parties or at restaurants, was less formal. It had a higher neckline, exposed little flesh, and was frequently topped by a matching small jacket. Satin and brocade fabrics usually stayed home until after 6 P.M. Elegant cardigan sweaters, often of cashmere—silk lined and appliquéd with beads, sequins, embroidery, lace, and rhinestones—were typically thrown over the shoulders of a dressy dress on chilly evenings or were worn "at home."

THE 1950S

Despite unprecedented American optimism in the 1950s, a truly "American decade," French and Italian designers took the lead when it came to fashion. The clothes of the fifties were svelte, luxurious, and sophisticated. They were generally well made,

Pauline Trigère, who designed this silk lace evening gown in 1953, was one of the first American couturiers whose clothes could compare to those from Europe.

If Joan Crawford typified the look of the forties, then Audrey Hepburn defined the fifties. More natural, Hepburn's gamine look called for pixie-cut hair, bateau-necked jerseys, and Capri pants.

DUNGAREES, BLUE JEANS, DENIMS

Long before James Dean wore jeans, without the saddle shoes, in *Rebel Without a Cause*—in 1873, actually—Levi Strauss and Jacob Davis received a patent for a denim work pant with an innovative riveted pocket and made the first blue jeans. (The word *jeans* come from "jeans fustian," a type of cotton fabric. The *jean* part comes from *Jannes,* the French word for "Genoa," while *fustian* comes from the Latin for cotton cloth.) Made of a wonderfully durable denim called "501," the jeans of Levi Strauss & Co. were enormously successful, particularly because they were the only manufacturers allowed to make riveted clothing until the patent ran out around 1891. After it expired, other companies, like Lee (and somewhat later, Calvin Klein), began to stitch up their own variations.

Collectors throughout the world today, particularly the Japanese, want jeans, especially Levis jeans, and particularly if they were man-ufactured before 1950. There is also a market for Levis jeans made before 1971, easily identifiable by the use of all capital letters on the red tab label. (A lower case "e," incidentally, means it was made *after* that date.)

whatever their country of origin. As cou-ture had done in the past (and continues to do today), the work of the best design-ers influenced ready-to-wear.

In those hallowed realms of fifties French couture, the great Christian Dior still reigned more or less supreme, but his supremacy was ultimately challenged by a Spaniard, Cristobal Balenciaga, and more especially by fellow Frenchman Hubert de Givenchy, who achieved fame by designing for film star Audrey Hepburn. Givenchy designed structured, coolly ladylike clothes. Even more widely copied than Givenchy couture, however, was Hepburn's gamine look, especially her pixie-cut hair, casual bateau-neck cropped jerseys, and Capri pants. These same tapered slacks, however, when worn skintight and particu-

The small waist and long, grace-ful skirt are typical of Christian Dior. Here, a black wool dress with matching jacket trimmed in velvet, from 1956.

larly when combined with high heels, became a "vulgar," unabashedly tarty fifties look. It wasn't so much tarty as sexy on Marilyn Monroe, however, that model of strapless, backless, see-through, off-the-shoulder, fur stole, and evening wrap glamour. Monroe's snug sweaters, low-cut necklines, and too-tight-to-sit-in skirts even went to high school, the original stomping ground of yet another fifties look: Peter Pan collars, penny loafers, and pink felt poodle skirts. There, it rubbed elbows with snug-bodiced strapless prom dresses of tulle, chiffon, satin, and lace net, with bows, beads, and sequins, creating a schizophrenic fifties style that was innocently provocative. Today's collectors like it all, mixing tart and pixie with rolled jeans and prom.

THE 1960s

The fashions of the 1960s are an eye-popping potpourri from which the miniskirt emerged triumphant. Girlish and saucy—its brevity virtually demanding the invention of tights to replace those suddenly visible stocking tops—the miniskirt, all by itself,

Designers of the 1960s, 1970s, 1980s, 1990s . . .

Although the market has not yet shaken out for the following designers, they may still be the ones to watch in the future:

GIORGIO ARMANI Armani brought men's suiting to women's fashion. The unstructured jacket and loosened suit provided easy elegance.

STEPHEN BURROWS Known for his draping technique, lettuce edges (soft, loose ruffles), and creative use of knits, leather, and suede.

OSSIE CLARK One of the designers who made London the center of fashion in the 1960s, Clark popularized the motorcycle jacket and hot pants. He often used fabrics designed by his wife, Celia Birtwell.

COURRÈGES Made his name with a futuristic, space-age style: Short skirts and pants with trapezoidal lines and white midcalf boots (known as go-go boots).

JAMES GALANOS Known for ready-to-wear clothes with silk linings, embroidery, and beadwork that approximated couture.

RUDI GERNREICH Notorious for inventing the topless bathing suit, Gernreich was also known for his radical color and pattern combinations—pairing stripes with checks, for example.

GUCCI The firm's touch-me velvet hipster pants, body-skimming tops, and white jersey dresses with strategically positioned see-through cutouts are rock-and-roll glamorous in a casual, sexy way.

HALSTON America's first minimalist designer was the jet set's favorite during the 1970s. Halston designed the pillbox hat made famous by Jacqueline Kennedy.

JEAN MUIR Known for precision cut clothes. Her motto: "When you find something that suits you and never lets you down, why not stick with it."

EMILIO PUCCI Pucci, known as the "Prince of Prints," caused a revolution in textile design with his op-art patterns and colors on slinky fabrics. Worn by the likes of Elizabeth Taylor in the 1960s, and thirty years later by Madonna.

MARY QUANT The queen of the sixties British "mod" looks, Quant popularized the micro mini skirt, tights, and the poorboy sweater. "By raising the younger generation's hemline, she raised the older generation's hackles," quips appraiser Caroline Ashleigh.

ZANDRA RHODES Designer of eccentric and glamorous clothes who helped put London at the forefront of the international fashion scene in the 1970s.

Ossie Clark

Zandra Rhodes

Rudi Gernreich

SIGNS OF THEIR TIMES

Period newspapers, mail-order catalogs, advertisements, and even old postcards (depicting beach scenes, for instance) can be an aid in dating vintage garments. These last are a particularly effective way of attributing dates to such specialty items as bathing costumes. Here are a few other tips to help you identify designers or eras:

◆ Small, allover patterns were typical on dresses of the thirties and forties.

◆ Beaded sweaters were popular during the 1950s. (They were first shown by American designer Mainbocher.) These are often decorated with flowers, scrollwork, or appliquéd, beaded animals.

◆ Chanel buttons frequently have a lion's head motif and are stamped "Chanel" on the reverse.

◆ Characteristic of 1950s detailing are appliqués of "sophisticated" symbols, such as telephones and Eiffel towers, and stitched-on mottoes. Other popular motifs are masks, harlequins, playing cards, and images of Venice and Hawaii.

◆ Dog breeds, too, offer keys to decades, appearing on (and as) handbags, hats, and skirts. The dog of the twenties was the Borzoi and the dog of the forties was the Scottie. The dog of the fifties was—no surprise—the poodle.

Two sixties icons in one—the "Souper dress," a paper dress covered with images of Andy Warhol's Campbell's Tomato Soup cans—from 1966–67.

might have provoked the all-too-true observation that, in the fifties, children wanted to dress as adults. In the sixties, it was the other way 'round. Among the many fantasy styles of the sixties were the space-age look (exemplified by the Pucci- and Halston-designed uniform for Braniff airlines, with that "bubble" hat, and by the little white dresses and white go-go boots of Courrèges); the mod look (Carnaby Street, London); and the tie-dyed beginnings of the hippie look.

Emilio Pucci, whose brightly patterned garments hide a tiny script "Emilio" within the print, rose to prominence in the sixties, and was also a favorite of the fashionable well to do. But there were also Rudi Gernreich's truly shocking topless bathing suits, Paco Rabanne's plastic disk chain-mail dresses (which, surprisingly, could be flattering to the right wearer) and paper dresses sold in cans and imprinted with op-art patterns. Even pop-art icon Andy Warhol designed paper clothing, imprinting it with images of Campbell's soup cans, Brillo boxes, and S&H green stamps. Because these are now considered a part of Warhol's "artistic output," they have soared to a current value well beyond that of conventional vintage clothes.

There was a more conservative side to the sixties, however, one that was epitomized by the regal Jackie Kennedy, whose minimally adorned sleeveless sheaths set the style for all those women who couldn't envision themselves in miniskirts. The "Jackie look," as practiced by such designers as Valentino and Pierre Cardin, was traditional and safe, and it seemed to carry with it subtly, a presidential imprimatur.

For now, the end of the sixties marks the end of the collectible fashion era, although that will change as a fondness for the seventies look starts to make its way into the collectors' closets. And it will. For who would have dreamed that poodle skirts would fly out of thrift stores?

EVALUATING VINTAGE CLOTHING

Learning to shop for collectible clothes might seem redundant, initially, since shopping for clothes is nothing new—we've done it most of our lives. Yet, as with all collectibles, you need to shop with a special intelligence and focus, since there are particular things that clothing collectors look for, and other things they avoid. A few tips should help you to collect wisely and to separate the silk purse from the (possibly polyester) sow's ear.

The three most important criteria for selecting a collectible vintage garment are: Establishing that it is by a known designer and who that is; determining its condition; and finally, establishing rarity. The last criterion really requires either extensive shopping or extensive reading—especially books on specialist subjects (see page 543) and auction catalogs, the majority of which include mainly those vintage clothes that are considered to be the most desirable (and costly) examples.

First Lady Jacqueline Kennedy started the sixties fashion for sleeveless sheaths and pillbox hats, setting a more conservative style for the lady who didn't want to wear miniskirts.

Trendy young women of the sixties took their fashion cues from swinging London and adopted "mod" caps, vests, dark tights, and skirts well above the knee.

A sumptuous stenciled velvet cape from the 1930s—with a quilted red border, silver and gold stenciling, and red lining and edging—by Maria Monaci Gallenga, a Florentine designer who developed a method of stenciling metallic paint on velvet so the design appeared to "float" on the fabric.

In addition to these important criteria, there is also an unusual and quite specific hierarchy of desirability for vintage clothing, even apart from such considerations as designer or date. In general, this hierarchy corresponds to the function—basically, to the dressiness—of the clothes. For instance, evening gowns are generally considered to be most valuable, followed by cocktail dresses, dinner dresses, suits and coats, day dresses, and separates. Fundamentally, this also has to do with price, since things that were originally costly are also costly and desirable now. Here are a few guidelines.

DESIGNER

The designer is possibly the easiest of these categories for the new collector to recognize and deal with, because, happily, most designer clothes are labeled—although their exceptionally fine detailing and hand stitching make them stand out from the run of the mill in any case. (In clothing, hand stitching is always a good indication of either dressmaker or couturier manufacture, although it's also found on homemade things.) Labels are often sewn into one of the side seams of couture garments, and French garments sometimes bear a date. On a dress marked *"Carven, printemps 1938,"* for example, Carven is the name of the French couturier and the date tells us that the piece is from his 1938 spring collection. Not all top-quality apparel is labeled, however. In the 1920s, dressmaker gowns were still a luxurious necessity for many fashionable women, and scores of anonymous, talented dressmaker-designers—many of whom did fittings in their clients' homes—never thought to label their creations.

Since the usual way to find out if a vintage dress is labeled is to unzip, unbutton, unsnap, or unhook the closure and check the inner seams, experienced dealers in vintage designer clothes can walk into a thrift shop and immediately know if their competitors have been there before them. "Unzipped," say the disappointed bargain hunters, turning to leave.

However, for those of us who need a little more time and effort to separate the fine from the ordinary and the zipped from the unzipped, materials are as good a guide to quality as any. Materials are perhaps key for those garments that have no labels at all. (Surprising as it may seem today, many of the original owners of fine clothes intentionally cut them out, as they were considered vulgar!) So just as the connoisseur of paintings needs a good "eye," the clothing collector needs a good "hand." If you have first determined that the fabric of a garment has a high-quality feel or "hand" (this takes practice and perhaps a session with a helpful salesperson at a good fabric store), then look for hand stitching and such dressmaker details as expensive buttons and unusually rich linings. Items made of cashmere, for example, or of expensively embroidered silks or brocade, are always worth a second look, even when unlabeled.

CONDITION

Alterations on vintage clothes are seriously frowned upon. If you inherit a sequined twenties dress with a too-long-to-wear pleated skirt, don't, whatever you do, shorten it. Such high-handed treatment of original fabric, original cut, and the original intent of the designer simply destroys the resale value of what would otherwise be a collectible dress. Don't cut anything away, either—trim, cuffs, or collars. (Fraying ends or loose threads, however, can be neatly repaired without harming the integrity of a garment.) Buttons should be original and the fabric itself—whatever that may be—ought to be unstained and unfaded. Colors should also be as bright or, if not inherently bright, at least as intense as when the garment was new. Cleaning vintage clothing is often costly, and sometimes risky, so it is preferable to try to buy things that won't require cleaning, although improvements in solvents and cleaning techniques have enabled conservators to remove and lighten food stains better than they were able to do in the past. If sequins or metallic trim have discolored, however, these will be virtually untreatable, so keep this in mind when you are shopping. Specialist textile conservators, often affiliated with museums, can sometimes salvage especially important pieces for you, although this type of work can be very expensive. Tears, rips, and holes can be repaired, but if any

Left: A strapless short evening gown in aubergine silk faille with flat bows at the shoulders, designed by Christian Dior in 1953 or 1954, came with a matching coat (above) with huge, ruffled sleeves and a coordinating stole. Imagine the closet space and suitcases—or rather, trunks—needed to hold or travel with such a wardrobe!

When not designing costumes for Joan Crawford and Greta Garbo, Gilbert Adrian designed a line of "Adrian Originals," including this monkey-print silk dress in an Asian-inspired design from the 1940s.

part of the original piece is missing—cuffs, trims, belts, or numbers of handsome buttons—the garment has been irreparably devalued.

RARITY

The aforementioned work clothes or housedresses made by Russian immigrants may be hard to find and the object of a museum search, but that doesn't make them valuable. Value resides in the market's being keen to own a particular piece of clothing. Consequently, rarity in vintage garments frequently boils down to finding something that was originally one of a kind and expensive to boot. Finding, for example, something of Yves Saint Laurent's from the two years during which he designed for Dior. Or discovering, rolled up in an attic trunk, one of Fortuny's amazing pleated gowns. Or happening on a ball gown by Charles James, who labored so long over each of his sculptural extravaganzas, and charged so much for them, that they are silken hen's teeth, now.

While plenty of rich women could afford expensive clothes, they didn't all have wonderful taste by any means, and unattractive clothing doesn't have the value of the beautiful or exquisite. Some specialists, among them Keni Valenti, believe that only sexy apparel is really desirable, and the sexier the better. And *Antiques Roadshow* appraiser Caroline Ashleigh reminds us that the more "star power" and provenance a dress has, the more allure and value it has as well. Think of the dress that Princess Diana wore when she danced with John Travolta at the White House.

COLLECTING VINTAGE CLOTHING

Fortunately for the collector, there are thousands of vintage garments to look through and thousands of places in which to find them. Church sales, thrift shops, tag sales, and yard sales are good beginnings and fun, even if one doesn't find Dior. (At tag sales, incidentally, don't forget to ask the seller if there's still a wedding dress in the closet. For if that is your passion, it may not have been offered for sale because it's assumed no one will buy it.) Internet auctions (such as eBay) can be an interesting source for vintage clothes if you have a good idea of what you're looking for and know what questions to ask. Keep in mind, however, that in fashion, the market can be volatile. Also, don't buy things just to pack them away. They've been in the dark long enough.

THE MAJOR DESIGNERS

Although, realistically speaking, designer or couture clothing is actually rather rare and seldom to be found at local garage sales, it *can* still be discovered at thrift and consignment shops, especially those that are in or near big cities. Throughout the country, too, when the larger auction houses conduct vintage clothing sales, they focus primarily on designer clothing, since this is the only type of vintage apparel that is sufficiently costly to be worth the effort of cataloguing. Auctions, then, are a good place to find designer apparel. But even if you are never going to stumble across a Charles James ball gown at a flea market, it's important to know something about the creators of fashion and the clothes they designed, since variants on and dilutions of their particular visions eventually became the clothes that everyone wore.

BALENCIAGA

From the late thirties on, Spaniard Cristobal Balenciaga, considered to be among the great couturiers of the twentieth century, designed in his Paris atelier perfectly cut and perfectly tailored dresses, simple in form and without much ornamentation. Balenciaga creations made during the 1940s and 1950s may be labeled with his mother's name, "Eisa," which was the name of his couture house in Spain. (Some knowledgeable buyers preferred to shop there, in fact, since it was considerably less

A 1950 beige wool coat with dolman sleeves by Cristobal Balenciaga, a designer known for incomparable tailoring.

A regal Balenciaga evening gown from the 1960s with an ivory satin skirt, a cocoa-colored chiffon bodice, and a matching tulle bolero jacket covered with hand-cut gold and olive-green sequins in a variety of square and round shapes.

expensive than the Paris establishment.) Balenciaga's "sack" dress (the chemise) of the late 1950s was the antithesis of the New Look of the previous decade (see Dior, below) and was controversial in its time because, although it was unaccustomedly comfortable, it camouflaged the shape of the body completely.

CALLOT SOEURS

The three Callot sisters dominated Paris couture of the 1920s, offering their well-to-do clientele richly embroidered, seed pearl–embellished chemise dresses styled, quite often, in an opulent, Asian-inspired aesthetic. Callot Soeurs offered fashion as theater, beginning in the 1890s through the late 1930s.

CHANEL

The inventor of modern dressing—no corsets, no flounces, no beading, no fuss—the French designer Gabrielle "Coco" Chanel found instant success after World War I with exquisitely well-made casual styles in humble fabrics. Sporty, braid-trimmed cardigan jackets and easy skirts in which a woman could step out, suited a newly relaxed, postwar mood. Chanel's wool jerseys and red and neutral corduroys appealed not only to chic women of the twenties, but also to thousands of smart women for decades thereafter. Her easy, boyish look was the antithesis of Christian Dior's, whose corseted waists Chanel termed "boned horrors." There is much vintage Chanel ready-to-wear available—suits, dresses, and blouses—and such garments are collectible, although aficionados keep a sharp eye out for Chanel couture.

CHRISTIAN DIOR

Famed creator of the post–World War II "New Look," the brilliant French designer Christian Dior transformed, overnight, the way midcentury women dressed. Subtly influenced by bouffant, Victorian dress styles, he designed clothing that overemphasized the body's natural shape—clothing that virtually required a corseted waist. Because French couturiers had ceased to suffer from wartime fabric restrictions, Dior was also free to create skirts that were wonderfully full and flattering to "wasp" waists. Experts disagree on the exact number, but Dior's skirts seem to have required anywhere from twenty-five to fifty yards of fabric.

The designer's talent was wide-ranging and versatile. In

For many stylish women, a Chanel suit is the epitome of sophisticated daywear. This example, in wool tweed, with jacket, skirt, and coordinating blouse, is from the fall 1959 collection.

1956, several years after creating the New Look, he designed a trendsetting A-line dress. He also pioneered in the licensing of his own name, ultimately allowing exclusive rights to the name "Dior" to be used by various manufacturers of sleepwear or leather goods, for instance, as well as by department stores. For a short while after Dior's death in 1957, Yves Saint Laurent took over the firm as head of design, and the clothes he created during that brief period are in great demand.

Christian Dior, surrounded by his models at a fashion show in 1950. His clothes brought back the corseted waist, and some of his skirts reputedly used fifty yards of fabric.

FORTUNY

Throughout the 1920s and 1930s, Mariano Fortuny's dresses were favorites of the young, of women who were modern and forward-looking. He was renowned for the patented, fine accordion-pleated silk dresses that became his signature. These dresses were also capable of being twisted and knotted for travel and storage, and yet magically and mysteriously (to this day), they retained

MARIANO FORTUNY TEXTILES

A dramatic wall hanging made of cotton fabric stenciled in an exotic pattern turned up at the Hartford *Antiques Roadshow*. The visitor explained to appraiser Titi Halle that the red-and-black textile had been purchased by her grandfather.

The fabric, Halle said, was a circa-1920 creation of renowned

designer Mariano Fortuny, known for his knife-pleat gowns (see photograph, this page) and for stenciled cottons such as this one, which the company still makes. Halle conservatively estimated its value at $2,500.

their pleats. Fortuny was also a master of rich stenciled velvets.

The lines of Fortuny's dignified gowns combined the deluxe detailing of Renaissance Italy with the spare simplicity of classical Greece. Perhaps his most famous creation was the Delphos gown, a silken column of rippling pleats. But many of Fortuny's pleated dresses were sprinkled or spangled with Venetian glass beads, and indeed, his work is thoroughly associated with Venice, where he lived and worked.

In addition to clothing, Fortuny's workshops produced deluxe upholstery materials, which are still being made.

CHARLES JAMES

A highly original English-born American designer of the 1940s and early 1950s whose gowns are rare and remarkably valuable today, James saw himself as a sculptor of clothing. A perfectionist, he often spent years on a single dress and liked to combine two or more of the rich fabrics he preferred (satins and velvets, for example) into gowns with interesting and unique variations of color, sheen, and texture. James gowns are noted for their asymmetrical cut and distinctive arc seaming. Perhaps to subsidize this very costly "art," James also occasionally contracted with manufacturers and stores to create ready-to-wear Charles James clothes. His ready-to-wear, however, is generally not the focus of James collectors. They yearn to own the gowns.

CLAIRE McCARDELL

Although she never designed "grand" dresses, American designer Claire McCardell is collected because she shaped what is internationally considered to be the all-American look. Sportswear, that signature American style, was Claire McCardell's

Fortuny's most famous design was the Delphos gown; he made the first in 1907 and continued making variations until the 1940s.

almost single-handed invention. While her label was quite successful before the start of World War II (her 1938 tent dress could be belted to metamorphose into a comfortable shirtwaist), McCardell's easy style was, in fact, forged by a combination of wartime frugality and her own belief that clothing should be functional. Her fabrics were simple—seersuckers, cottons, wool jerseys, and denims—but unfortunately the cottons used in some of McCardell's garments have not held up well.

YVES SAINT LAURENT

After briefly working as chief designer for the house of Dior, the very young Algerian-born Yves Saint Laurent opened his own atelier in Paris in 1962 and quickly became fashion's darling. His heterogeneous collections were influenced by the gridlike art of Piet Mondrian, by pop art, by the casual street wear of the Left Bank, and by menswear tuxedos and trousers. All of Saint Laurent's original creations, especially those from the early years of the 1960s, are collectible today, as are his A-line dresses. The firm's ready-to-wear line, Rive Gauche, is of good quality but shouldn't be confused with the couture garments.

SCHIAPARELLI

An Italian and a lover of Surrealism, Elsa Schiaparelli found some success retailing handmade sweaters in Paris in the 1930s but quickly graduated to creating couture tours de force—like Kelly-green velvet gloves that would magically blossom into dress sleeves and jackets embroidered with

Claire McCardell's stylishly informal "Monastic" dress of circa 1949 is made of windowpane-checked wool with a black chiffon waist wrap.

Yves Saint Laurent, circa 1966, designed this jaunty sequined and striped nautically inspired minidress.

Schiaparelli began her career making sweaters in the 1930s and was still making sweaters like this example in black rhinestone-trimmed orlon twenty years later.

A salmon pink matte silk "Grecian" evening gown, with puffed sleeves and a high waist, designed in the early 1920s by Madeleine Vionnet. Gold beads, gold lamé ribbon, metal tassels, and a classical cameo provide the decoration.

droll optical illusions. In an era when clothing was dominated by neutral colors, Schiaparelli marketed her new, super-vibrant "shocking pink" and even enlisted surrealist painter Salvador Dalí to help her design quirky handbags, hats, and costume jewelry. Her motto was "Never fit a dress to the body, but train the body to fit the dress." With embroideries of fountains, mosaics of mirrors surrounded by silvery scrollwork, and great flaming sunbursts on shocking pink capes, "she took willful illusion," says one commentator, "and pounded it into wearable apparel."

MADELEINE VIONNET

Often referred to by her peers as "the Euclid of dressmaking," couturier Madeleine Vionnet created solemn, fluid gowns that were based on precise, mathematical principles and her own eye for the sculpturally beautiful. Cut on the bias, her almost minimalist 1920s dresses successfully combined the two most important criteria of dressmaking: They hung gracefully, and they allowed their wearer unrestricted movement.

OTHER DESIGNERS OF INTEREST

ADRIAN

American designer Gilbert Adrian was discovered in Paris by Irving Berlin and brought to New York to design costumes for Broadway, eventually moving to Hollywood. Considering himself a costume, not a fashion, designer, Adrian believed that film costumes should enhance the character while maintaining a high level of glamour. In 1941, he opened his own couture house, dressing Joan Crawford, Greta Garbo, Judy Garland, and Jean Harlow. Adrian is perhaps best known for creating Joan Crawford's broad-shouldered profile, a look that became popular nationwide.

BALMAIN

French designer Pierre Balmain was well known for design classics that often incorporated long silhouettes and full jackets.

Balmain's "New French Style," as it was dubbed by his friend Gertrude Stein, featured richly embroidered gowns and ensembles for luxury-starved clients. During the postwar forties, Balmain apprenticed alongside Christian Dior at the atelier of Lucien Lelong, and during the sixties his uncluttered designs became truly sculptural. In the course of Balmain's career, he created personal wardrobes for such dissimilar celebrities as Brigitte Bardot, Marlene Dietrich, and Katharine Hepburn.

GEOFFREY BEENE

Known for clean-cut clothes and a fluid use of materials—which he referred to as "liquid geometry"—American Geoffrey Beene's designs celebrated the female body while allowing complete freedom of movement. Beene's well-known sequined football jersey evening gown is only one droll example of his knack for melding masterful construction techniques with whimsical patterns. He was active from the 1960s through 1999.

BILL BLASS

Known for flawless tailoring, Blass became famous for the innovative use of menswear fabrics for women's clothes. The typical Blass client was a well-dressed upper-middle-class woman of the sixties through the nineties who was "not obsessed with fashion."

PIERRE CARDIN

An Italian-born designer of elegantly cut women's clothing and a pioneer in the field of men's fashion, Cardin was once Dior's assistant. Cardin's "Bar" suit, a fitted jacket with long black skirt in silk shantung, is notable, and his style is epitomized by clothes with bias cut, soft semifitted lines, and a lavish use of color. He was the first couturier to create a ready-to-wear collection for both men and women. He launched the space-age look of the late 1960s with stark, short tunics, the use of vinyl, and helmets and goggles.

This organdy Balmain evening gown from 1969 features double rows of appliquéd rings—a very slight "mod" touch on an otherwise conservative dress.

Thoroughly "mod," in contrast, is Pierre Cardin's space-age "Egg Carton" dress of 1968, made of dynel permanently molded in a three-dimensional diamond pattern.

Jacques Fath designed the very feminine strapless circa 1952 evening gown, at right, near the end of his career. Although sober in design, its colors are flamboyant—aqua silk georgette with a midnight blue and mauve satin sash.

A 1950s wool jersey afternoon dress with elaborate side pleats by Madame Grès reveals her training as a sculptor.

JACQUES FATH

A Parisian dress designer with a family tradition in fashion design (his great-grandmother designed dresses for Empress Eugénie, consort of Napoleon III), Fath is credited with creating the fluttery short skirts worn by the thousands of bicycle-riding French women who were victims of wartime gasoline rationing. Following World War II, Fath's ultramodern designs and modern publicity seeking made him, along with Dior and Balmain, one of "the big three," and a force in the French haute couture. His early death in 1954 has left him less well known today, perhaps, than his colleagues.

MADAME GRÈS

Trained as a sculptor, Alix Grès created extravagant asymmetrically draped gowns inspired by the styles of ancient Greece, but with updated details, like dramatic butterfly-like pleated sleeves fanning out from the back. Grès's designs, known for their purity and simplicity, were created with the traditional technique of hand pinning the fabric. Among her clients during a career that spanned the thirties to the nineties were Princess Grace of Monaco and Marie-Hélène de Rothschild.

LANVIN

Founder of one of the premier Paris couture houses, in the 1910s and 1920s Jeanne Lanvin found fame with a fresh and modern approach to fashion. Continuing to produce the romantic styles of those decades even after the prevailing fashion called for a sportier aesthetic, she thus supplied a welcome alternative for women who preferred a feminine silhouette. Lanvin's designs were influenced by Indian saris, Coptic embroideries, and Persian silks—all of which she had seen in her extensive travels. These clothes meshed nicely with the public's renewed interest in the exotic.

MAINBOCHER

Main Rousseau Bocher was the first American designer to be successful in Paris, where he was especially well known for creating elegant evening wear. He became an international star after designing the Duchess of Windsor's tailored satin wedding dress and was the first couturier to show strapless evening gowns and gowns ranging from long, high-waisted styles to those that were lacy and transparent. Another Mainbocher "look" was the dressy cardigan sweater, often made with jeweled buttons. Mainbocher also designed for the stage and for the war effort, creating uniforms for WAVES and SPARS in the 1940s that continued to be worn, virtually unchanged, until the 1970s.

EDWARD MOLYNEUX

The English-born Molyneux served in the army during World War I and, after a Parisian apprenticeship, opened his own couture houses in London and Paris in 1919. Molyneux is known for master-tailored bias-cut garments, frequently displaying oriental styling. Actresses Gertrude Lawrence and Lynn Fontanne were Molyneux clients during the 1930s.

NORMAN NORELL

The tailored, careful work of this American designer succeeded in convincing the fashion world that Paris was not the only place to buy elegant clothes. Norell originally worked for Hattie Carnegie. Then, in 1941, he joined dress manufacturer Anthony Traina and launched Traina-Norell, a label known for its feminine, colorful clothing. Following Traina's death in 1960, Norell worked alone, always spurning superfluous detail and specializing in perfect tailoring and bright, cheerful hues, while not neglecting simple black and white. The excellent workmanship of Norell garments is particularly admirable in that they were ready-to-wear, not couture.

From her summer 1929 collection, a Lanvin chemise dress covered with tiny silver bugle beads. The asymmetric hem, beads, and dropped waist summarize that era.

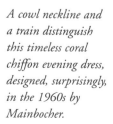

A cowl neckline and a train distinguish this timeless coral chiffon evening dress, designed, surprisingly, in the 1960s by Mainbocher.

NONDESIGNER VINTAGE CLOTHING

This circa 1923 silk velvet evening dress with rhinestone beading came from Henri Bendel in New York City. Many top-quality American clothes of this era carry only the store label, not that of the designer.

The majority of apparel seen in dealers' booths at vintage textile shows and flea markets and at tag sales and thrift shops is good-quality clothing made between the 1920s and the 1960s. It is the decades of the forties and fifties, however, that seem to attract most collectors today, although there is growing interest in clothing from the sixties. Cheek by jowl on crowded colorful racks—and vying with each other to become part of your collection—are sunsuits, housedresses, beach attire (including the dreaded wool bathing suit), skiwear, and all the styles of wearable day dresses, skirts, sweaters, men's suits and coats, and furs that you've loved in hundreds of Hollywood films. There is plenty of specialty sportswear for skating and tennis enthusiasts, as well; and for the collector of uniforms, there are thousands of military and domestic items, including maids' and nurses' uniforms.

New collectors will find that, compared with the massproduced clothing available today, even the most pedestrian midcentury garment is better constructed, of better-quality fabric, and generally more richly embellished (if it is embellished at all) with unique and currently unreproduceable "dressmaker" details such as lace insets, ruching, appliqués, or handworked embroidery. Fabrics, for the most part, will be all natural—wools, cottons, and silks—although the occasional bit of rayon creeps in. For the price, many of these garments are goodlooking bargains. Strapless tulle gowns and body-hugging sheath dresses are stylish again and easy to wear. Ballerina skirts are flattering. Velvet lounging wraps with ermine collars can be had for less than the cost of some polyester bathrobes, and nearly every dress or gown has belt buckles, buttons, or details that—by today's standards—are marvels of design and quality. With so much to choose from, however, it is easy to forget that as with designer clothes, label and condition are important.

Curiously, there are few collectors for vintage coats, which are just as well made and attractive in their way as chiffon gowns or silk lounging pajamas. (Centenarian socialite Brooke Astor, who has lived long enough to know, once advised that one should never get rid of a coat, because it will always come back in style.) Warm and fashionable coats, then, might be an interesting niche for the new collector, who should also keep in mind that coats (and dresses, too) bearing the label of well-known and high-quality regional stores will generally command a premium. Hand-sewn detailing will also add to the price, and needless to say, freedom from moth holes and perspiration stains will be reflected in that price tag.

The collector of a particular period of midcentury apparel can find much useful information about styles and original relative costs in both vintage newspapers and mail-order catalogs, since American, English, and European department stores published seasonal catalogs of clothing appropriate for everything from christenings to weddings to funerals. Such ephemera can sometimes be picked up at flea markets. (Another useful tip, especially for those who have difficulty distinguishing between some twenties and thirties garments, is that the zipper was not widely used until the 1930s.)

To find good-quality, stylish, and pristine clothing, dedicated collectors should haunt shops run by hospital or institutional auxiliaries and keep abreast of when and where good benefit clothing sales are being held. Wonderful finds from the best stores and even some important designer things have been discovered on the racks of used clothing at charity resale shops, not to mention at old standbys like Goodwill and the Salvation Army. Nevertheless, as the competition for vintage garments heats up, it is becoming increasingly hard to get there before the superenthusiast who has taken the time to learn just what day that new merchandise comes in. The early bird most definitely gets the Bergdorf Goodman gown.

It is very likely that you will take better care of your vintage apparel than the original owners did, since you don't think of these well-made, stylish clothes as disposables. However, don't

TIPS *for* **collectors**

♦ If you're looking in the Yellow Pages to find used-clothing stores, be sure to check under all the following headings: Clothing Bought and Sold; Secondhand Clothing; Used Clothing; Thrift Stores; Resale Shops; Consignment Shops; and Vintage Shops.

♦ Bring cash, a large, light plastic bag (for carrying home your purchases), and a measuring tape. Avoid bringing a purse or wallet that you have to keep your eye on—if there are no dressing rooms, you may be trying on clothes (right over what you are wearing) in the aisles, in the middle of a field, or even in the street.

♦ If you find a piece with a label, take a look at it. If the label is woven, not printed, and sewn down on all four corners, that's a sign of good quality. If it is made of fabric other than nylon or it is yellowed, that is a sign of age—which is good. If it is sewn on with thread that looks different than the thread used elsewhere in the garment, it may not be authentic.

Another 1920s dress, this one in deep pink silk with metallic bead trim, is typically sleeveless and collarless.

CHARLIE CHAPLIN VINTAGE MESH BAG

When *Antiques Roadshow* visited Cleveland, appraiser Caroline Ashleigh was surprised and delighted to see a "Charlie Chaplin" mesh bag made by Whiting & Davis—an example of this firm's "Hollywood Star" series. A mere twenty-five years old, the Charlie Chaplin bag was the only black-and-white portrait bag to be included in a rare set of four portrait handbags—the other three depicting color likenesses of Renée Adorée, Marion Davies, and Clark Gable. The bags had extra-long carry chains with a rounded spider-mesh link. They were originally sold for $10 each.

Experts disagree about why the series was discontinued. It was once assumed that it was due to lack of demand, but it is rumored that the bags may have been recalled and destroyed as a result of lawsuit threats made by the stars' heirs. Ashleigh believed the retail value of this bag to be between $1,200 and $1,400.

expose them to too much sunlight or make major tailoring changes, because both are anathema to value. These are not simply clothes, remember, they're collectibles.

HANDBAGS AND OTHER ACCESSORIES

The story of vintage accessories is, for the most part, the story of handbags. Scarves and aprons have their fans, as do fans, and certainly there are scores of collectors longing for dashing hats and luxurious kid gloves. Because most of these things have fallen out of fashion, the collector base for scarves, aprons, fans, hats, and gloves is significantly smaller than that for dresses, suits or handbags. Shoes, of course, are an interesting and attractive field, but shoes frequently have serious conditional problems. You can wear a pair of shoes out, but you'll rarely wear out a Lucite or alligator handbag. Also, shoes come in sizes, a restriction not shared by handbags. You might prefer a small handbag to a large one, but it doesn't have to fit.

HANDBAGS

Handbags are almost more popular than vintage clothes, perhaps because they can be arranged to make interesting, almost architectural displays, and because they don't take up anywhere near the space that organza evening gowns or even fifties circle skirts do. Consequently, the collector can show off a handbag collection in her living room, if she likes, or keep it in glass cabinets, or store it in the closet.

Because the various handbag materials are inherently tougher than the textiles of vintage clothes, handbags can pretty much be used with impunity. The following selection represents only a sampling of the more popular possibilities, because almost everything—from feathers to silk flowers, to aluminum, to cardboard, to solid gold—has at some time or another been pressed into duty to carry our lipsticks, combs, glasses, handkerchiefs, gum, aspirins, credit cards, cell phones, keys, personal digital assistants, and, every now and then, wallets.

EXOTIC-SKIN BAGS

Handbags are fashioned from leather, cloth, silk, straw fibers, plastic, and metal—from any material, in fact, that's ever been deemed light enough to be portable. For most collectors, however, exotic skins are the hands-down—or forearm-up—favorite. Bags can be made of reptile skins, like lizard and snake; of fish skins, such as shark (otherwise known as shagreen); even of birds, like ostrich; but alligator and crocodile skins (almost indistinguishable from each other) top most bag collectors' charts. (Legal restrictions, by the way, have been relaxed because they no longer are endangered species.)

Crocodile bags were expensive when they were new, and like most collectibles, things that were costly when new, are costly today. Crocodile bags are available in many colors, but in vintage bags, the neutral blacks and browns have always been most common. The reason is simple. A new crocodile bag can cost thousands of dollars and most women who are able to spend that amount of money on a handbag want it to "go with" as many outfits as possible. This is why colored vintage crocodile bags—the reds, maroons, or greens, usually—are harder to find and more costly than brown or black. Despite the collectibility of alligator and crocodile, it is an interesting sidelight that handbags

A red crocodile Hermès Birkin bag, named for Jane Birkin, an actress who shocked audiences with a nearly nude appearance in the 1966 movie Blow-Up. *This bag was a classic when first offered and it still is today.*

BATA SHOE MUSEUM

The Bata Shoe Museum in Toronto is not just the only shoe museum in North America, it also has the world's largest collection of footwear, housing more than ten thousand pairs of shoes. According to *Antiques Roadshow* appraiser Titi Halle, if you lined up all these shoes heel to toe, they would stretch for three miles.

The museum's holdings reveal how shoes evoke not only time, place, and culture, but also indicated social status. In seventeenth-century Italy, for example, the higher the heel, the more socially

elevated the wearer; while in France, the longer the toe point, the greater your income. (In 2002, shoe designer Manolo Blahnik managed both at once.) The museum also has an unrivaled collection of work shoes, among them a

A pair of opera boots from the 1890s, made by François Pinot, part of the collection of the Bata Shoe Museum.

pair with long iron spikes attached to its soles, which were used in nineteenth-century France for crushing chestnuts. There are shoes made specifically for logging, and twisted hemp shoes worn by sailors in the 1800s.

The Bata Museum collects today's shoes, too. On view are the footwear of Marilyn Monroe, Elton John, Ginger Spice, and that most notorious of shoe collectors, Imelda Marcos.

Recognizing the Fine Handbag

A Tiffany evening bag with a flower basket over a chocolate brown ground in fine petit point, with a coral slide clasp.

Any object that is expensive and desirable is coveted and ultimately copied. In the periods in which they were especially fashionable, therefore, needlework handbags were as susceptible to imitation as Impressionist paintings. Fortunately, genuine handsewn needlework can be distinguished from machine-made needlework: Viewed through a magnifying glass, every stitch of the handmade object will appear to be slightly raised, while the reproduction—simply printed on the background—will look flat.

Keep in mind, too, that the best-made beaded bags feel surprisingly heavy. Also remember that coarsely applied beads are not much in demand.

In both needlework and beaded bags, examples depicting people and landscapes are usually more highly valued than those with only floral motifs.

One interesting detail about evening bags is the very real possibility that the bag frame itself might be valuable. Look carefully on the inside to see if the frame is stamped "14K," "sterling," or "800" (a European silver mark). Gold does not tarnish, and an unusually clean surface can be a clue. Clasps can be set with precious or semiprecious stones. Even

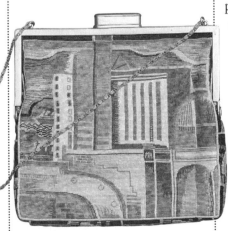

A beaded Art Deco bag decorated with skyscrapers, from the 1920s.

diamonds and sapphires were mounted in clasps. Art Deco clasps are often of bold and angular enamel and a few bags of that era were made by jewelers Mauboissin, Lacloche, and Chaumet. One collector tells of purchasing in a consignment shop (for an almost embarrassingly small sum) a stone-studded evening bag, its gilt metal frame marked "VCA." The stones turned out to be amethysts, rubies, and emeralds, and the "VCA," the stamp of the jewelers Van Cleef and Arpels.

Not all handbags are "jewelry," or are meant to look like jewelry. Tasseled vanity cases of Bakelite, celluloid, and tortoiseshell mark the post–World War I period, when the growing acceptability of cosmetics for women made it fashionable to carry them. Saucy vanity case–handbags were carried during the twenties and thirties and often resembled highly extravagant lamp pulls more than pocketbooks.

Look for forties beaded bags marked "Charlet" or "Fre-Mor," as well. These command a premium.

This early twentieth-century jeweled mesh Whiting & Davis bag is painted in a black and white diamond pattern and set with large, dark red glass stones.

incorporating taxidermy—that is, those that are ornamented with stuffed croc heads, arms, and tails—are deemed far less desirable than those made simply of reptile skins. In evaluating any vintage alligator or crocodile accessories, look for a glossy finish (skins can dry out) and solid, well-made fittings.

Hermès bags (retailed by the French equestrian outfitter Hermès), and particularly the trapezoidal "Kelly" bag, named for film star Grace Kelly, were made in exotic skins, as well as in calf, and the Kelly bag represents the pinnacle of bag collecting for many enthusiasts. The Hermès rectangular "Birkin" bag, named for singer and actress Jane Birkin, is also desirable. Simple bags with the characteristic Hermès "H" closure seem not to be as interesting to collectors.

BEADED AND NEEDLEWORK BAGS

Various types of beaded and needlework bags have been popular since the eighteenth century. In the twentieth century, however, they were customarily saved for evening wear. To an extent, this is because they are fragile and really don't hold up well to everyday use. It is also because beading and needlework are labor-intensive techniques and, at their best, incorporate a great of deal of handwork, which makes them expensive. If an expensive bag is fragile, it will usually be saved for grand-ish occasions.

Many of the fine vintage needlepoint and petit-point bags that enthusiasts value today were manufactured between 1920 and 1960 in Austria, although Walborg, a Belgian maker, is one of the most collectible. Conveniently for needlework enthusiasts, a label denoting the country of origin and often the name of the bag's maker is frequently stitched into the lining.

MESH BAGS

Collectors of mesh bags, made of links of interwoven metal, tend to prefer those made by two firms: Mandalian and Whiting & Davis. The American-made mesh bags manufactured by Turkish

TIPS *for bag collectors*

♦ Monograms diminish value.

♦ Colorful telephone-wire bags—yes, made from coiled handset wire—were a forties frivolity that were certainly the ideal accessory for that era's broad-shouldered Joan Crawford suits and upswept hair.

♦ Box bags and figural bags in all materials have become particularly collectible. A bag in the shape of a beaded poodle recently brought several thousand dollars at auction, and bags in shapes such as telephones and ice buckets are equally desirable. Let's leave the last word in purses to designer Elsa Schiaparelli, however, who created a particularly droll and famous bag in collaboration with Surrealist painter Salvador Dalí. Made in the shape of a telephone with a lobster "receiver," it has become an icon.

A 1960s op-art pattern beaded bag, hand-made in Japan for Walborg of Belgium.

BAKELITE PURSES

Around the turn of the twentieth century, Belgian-born scientist Dr. Leo Baekeland stumbled upon a revolutionary, non-flammable plastic known today as Bakelite.

Bakelite jewelry made a splash during the Depression, because of its cheerful, vibrant colors and its affordability.

Another use of Bakelite was to make distinctive Art Deco purses, such as the three examples that were brought to the Denver *Antiques Roadshow* from the visitor's large collection. According to appraiser Kathleen Guzman, all Bakelite has become very collectible. Two of the purses were marked, one "Llewellyn" and one "Rialto," two of the premier manufacturers of Bakelite purses. About the third, Guzman told the visitor, "Sometimes they're marked. Sometimes they're not. Sometimes they're just great style, like this one." These purses could bring from $500 to $1,500 apiece at auction.

An American hard plastic "tortoiseshell" handbag, probably from the 1930s, with a chain handle.

immigrant Shatiel Mandalia were particularly popular in the twenties and thirties, and their geometric, essentially Eastern motifs make them easily recognizable. Original bags will be labeled "Mandalian Mfg. Co." (although imitations do exist), and as often happens when a style achieves widespread popularity, other mesh bags combining any of a certain type of bold Art Deco coloration (reds and yellows, for example) with distinctly geometric designs have come to be termed "Mandalian," whether they are or not.

The best metal mesh is so finely woven that it feels like fabric. The Massachusetts firm of Whiting & Davis developed a technique for manufacturing silver- and gold-colored mesh that was so much finer than that of their competitors that, for decades, theirs was the leading name in the field. Founded toward the end of the nineteenth century, Whiting & Davis made several popular styles, among the most fashionable of which was "Dresden Mesh," with its gentle patterning, and "Bead-lite," billed as being chip resistant (it wasn't). In the thirties, the firm commissioned, among others, the couture house of Schiaparelli to create designs for mesh bags. These eventually became staples of the line.

After World War II, gold and silver fish-scale mesh bags were increasingly in vogue, and slinky Whiting & Davis mesh bags spent much frivolous time at the Stork Club and at coming-out parties. Incidentally, the linings in mesh bags can make damage to the metal mesh hard to see, so look carefully before you buy, and make sure that the chain handles are original.

PLASTIC BAGS

Lucite handbags from the 1940s and 1950s (in uncracked condition, of course) are a popular collecting niche. A man who is one of the great editors of the twentieth century has assembled a major collection. Plastic box bags can be made of Bakelite, as well, and in the field of plastic bags, figural examples, such as animals, are most highly sought after. Experts advise that you sniff the inside of Lucite. If there is a strong chemical odor, the material is probably on the verge of self-destructing and may not be a candidate for your collection. Top names in the plastics category are Willardy, Llewellyn, and Gilli.

HATS

Although hats are not generally a widely sought-after collectible, there is one American hat manufacturer—Bes-Ben—whose witty work commands an astonishing premium. Other hats of interest to collectors, but far less costly than the Bes-Ben creations, are labeled examples by Lilly Daché, Hattie Carnegie, and Mr. John.

BES-BEN

Bes-Ben was founded in Chicago in 1920 by the brother and sister team of Bessie and Ben Green-Field (he was known as "The Mad Hatter of Chicago"). Until 1941, their firm produced conventional hats. After that date, perhaps to protest the somber mood that settled on the country with the coming of World War II, the company began to create fanciful, tongue-in-cheek hats incorporating such design elements as American flags, tiny frogs, flying insects, cigarette packs, butterflies, records, and genuine jade. Profoundly eccentric, Bes-Ben hats were frequently

This Bes-Ben confection consists of a round ivy-covered crown decorated—and why not?—with embroidered owls and netting.

custom-made for Hollywood celebrities like Lucille Ball and Elizabeth Taylor, as well as for the society ladies who lunched—and liked to be noticed. Although the hats sold new for anywhere from $37.50 to $1,000, depending upon the quality, quantity, and frivolity of their trimmings, once a year, at a midnight sale, Bes-Ben hats would be offered for as little as $5. Then, at 2 A.M.—in typically waggish style—all the unsold hats would be thrown out the door for waiting bargain hunters to scramble for!

HATTIE CARNEGIE

A retail phenomenon who started with a hat and dress shop, Hattie Carnegie was a Vienna-born American who took her name from Andrew Carnegie, "the richest man in the world."

The inventive brother and sister team at Bes-Ben took inspiration from all sources. This Kelly green hat is trimmed with skunks made of pipe cleaners.

Bes-Ben created this "Clasping Hands" hat from padded ivory velvet. The hands have applied red plastic fingernails, set off by a large pearl and gilded metal pinky ring and matching bracelets.

A shallow-crowned brown velveteen modified pork-pie hat, designed by Lilly Daché in the 1930s. Daché was primarily a milliner, but also designed clothing and accessories from gowns to gloves. For a short period, she also created costume jewelry.

Starting as a hatter in 1909, she eventually designed everything from clothing to handbags to cosmetics. Her look was somewhat Victorian.

LILLY DACHÉ

Parisian-born and -trained milliner Lilly Daché, with hat shops in New York, Florida, and Chicago, specialized in turbans draped directly on the head and, most dazzlingly, on the heads of such celebrities as Betty Grable, Carole Lombard, and Marlene Dietrich. Her work also included close-fitting brimmed cloche hats, snoods, and caps.

MR. JOHN

This American hatmaker, born in Germany, gave himself the name John P. John when, in 1948, he opened the salon in New York City, where he created sophisticated and stylish hats. He was known for his forward-tilted "doll" hats, scarf-attached hats, skullcaps held by tight face veils, and fur toques, among other styles. His talents were also called upon by Hollywood, which hired him to design the period bonnets for *Gone with the Wind* (remember the hat Scarlett wore with her green velvet "curtain dress?") and other films.

SHAWLS

Eighteenth- and nineteenth-century Kashmir and paisley shawls have always had a following, but currently there is a growing and discriminating market for Canton shawls, also known as Spanish shawls (although they were not made there, they were exceptionally popular in Spain). These "Spanish" shawls are also called piano shawls after the instrument over which they were often decoratively draped. In fact, from early in the nineteenth century until at least the 1930s, these luxurious and feminine wraps, marvelously embroidered on silk crepe de chine (Chinese silk) and bordered with long, hand-tied silk fringes, were made most commonly not in China or Spain, but in Manila. Ranging in size from four- to six-feet square, the shawls are generally black or ivory, embellished with colorful

A "Spanish" or "piano" shawl with a characteristic long knotted fringe.

embroidery. The most popular shawls, currently, are those in white with black embroidery, black with white embroidery, or white on white. During the 1920s and 1930s, many machine-made imitations were produced.

LINGERIE

For the collector of vintage lingerie, the corset has become a popular—if unconventional—choice. There is a school of thought that assumes that because corsets often turn up unworn in their original boxes, their original owners didn't like to wear them. The truth is, most women loved what they did for the figure. Corsets went in and out of fashion during the twentieth century, but when they were in fashion, they were worth the discomfort for the final effect: A tiny waist and a smooth, flat profile. Young women today may prefer to be free and unfettered, but they sometimes collect these boned constructs. They also enjoy wearing vintage hammered silk slips as gowns. In fact, black full slips are the waitresses' uniforms at one chic New York restaurant.

Silk hosiery in neutral tones can lend authenticity to any vintage turnout, although to hold those stockings up, the dedicated collector of lingerie might also have to collect—and wear garters, girdles, or garter belts. Synthetic, easy-to-launder nylon stockings appeared just before World War II. (During the war, when nylon was rationed, young women faked the look by applying liquid, flesh-toned makeup to their legs, then drawing a "seam" up the back with eyebrow pencil.)

Nightgowns, housecoats, and bed jackets appeal to some collectors, for

This silk, satin, and metallic gold brocade shawl from the mid-1920s—with its repeated stylized flower design and a long, full silk fringe—is a good example of an Art Deco–era fabric design.

Two silk negligees, trimmed with lace (left and far left) and a pair of lace-trimmed silk tap pants (above), all from the late 1930s or the early 1940s—luxurious garments made before World War II textile shortages.

An *Antiques Roadshow* visitor in Boston brought in some rare and unusual World War II memorabilia: souvenir pillow shams from various military divisions and bases. *Antiques Roadshow* appraiser Elyse Luray Marx told the guest that the shams were "a way of say-

ing, 'We're alive, everything is okay, and we miss you.'" Marx explained that few of these shams have survived in such fine condition because they were generally made of fragile silk.

Marx believes the twelve shams are worth between $50 and $100 apiece. "I'm thinking about framing some of them," the visitor said, "and giving some to family members."

the handwork on such garments is often astonishing. The finest examples of handwork were often seen in trousseau lingerie, frequently ordered from Belgian, Irish, and French convents. The quality of such lace and embroideries—created for private viewing only—can be breathtakingly beautiful.

At another extreme, as fifties vintage clothing becomes ever more fashionable, horsehair and starched nylon crinoline petticoats have become desirable. These were not only for the most part unbeautiful, they were also scratchy and uncomfortable to wear.

TEXTILES

Handmade rosepoint lace or nineteenth-century beadwork may appeal to the connoisseur of craftsmanship, but the materials that attract collectors today are not masterpieces of handwork but, rather, homey, nostalgic, and decidedly domestic soft goods. Workaday tablecloths, blankets, bedspreads, and quilts engage the passions of modern enthusiasts for mainly one reason: They are wonderfully textural. The feel of those soft or fuzzy or well-washed textures, added to their gentle colors and a large nostalgia quotient (the lovely sensation of cuddling under a nubbly chenille bedspread), goes a long way toward explaining the popularity of vintage textiles. Familiarly known as "domestics," they are exceptionally handsome on a bed or a table, and happily, vintage blankets or sets of napkins are often less expensive than the new.

EVALUATING TEXTILES

All textiles—clothing, blankets, and tablecloths—share virtually identical criteria. Consequently, the careful collector—no matter what sort of textile he or she collects—learns to look for tears, raveling edges, faded colors, and worn spots, all of which diminish value. The collector also checks thoroughly for stains, which are not always removable, and for erosion and insect damage. (To do this, hold the garment or textile up to a light source and look for holes.) On most textile, however, poor workmanship is usually a sign of poor quality, even for mass-manufactured products. It's surprising how many supposedly quality-controlled factory-made items can exhibit misalignment of color printing, unintentional color variations from one part of the textile to another, or skipped weaves. Keep in mind, however, that if you are good with a needle, that ravel or tear can mean a bargain.

COLLECTING TEXTILES

A turn-of-the-twentieth-century quilt from the southern United States in the "target" or "pine burr" pattern. The top panel is three-dimensional because it is made up of folded pieces sewn together.

While textiles seem homey collectibles, they are not necessarily inexpensive collectibles. Enthusiasts feather their nests with several types of comforting blankets and quilts, and competition can be keen, driving up prices.

QUILTS

Quilting is a particularly satisfying type of handwork, one that perfectly reflects its makers' artistic and nurturing inclinations. Although quilting originated in Europe, it has come to be considered something of an American art form. Quilting in America, in fact, dates to our own colonial times, although it may seem to us today that quilts must have covered beds nationwide during the nineteenth century. In many cases a form of worthy and useful thrift, quilting used up remnants and scraps of fabric and transformed them into both a necessity and a work of art.

Patchwork quilts were fashioned by cutting bits of leftover textiles into pieces and sewing them into square blocks with interesting patterns, then sewing those blocks together. A layer of cotton batting was sandwiched between the patchwork panel and a plain panel of fabric, and the three layers were basted together. This "sandwich" was then stretched on a frame, and the

This fluffy chenille bedspread is unusual in its colors—strong greens, reds, and yellows—because most are in pastels. The bold peacock design makes it very collectible.

actual "quilting" process began. A design—geometric, freeform, or pictorial—was stitched through this three-part coverlet in attractive patterns. Appliquéd quilts were made in a similar fashion, except that the pieces of fabric were sewn, or appliquéd, onto the top panel of the quilt, which was then quilted as usual.

KIT QUILTS

At the end of the nineteenth century, quilting was a less universal pastime than it had once been. It actually came around again in the 1920s and 1930s, when this traditional domestic art experienced a revival because, among other things, there was a renewed interest in America's colonial arts. The majority of the quilting done in the twenties and thirties, however, was a relatively easy-to-do variant of the slower-going original, and was called kit quilting. It was a pastime that found its moment when, in 1916, *Home Needlework* (one of several new, influential needlework magazines) advertised the first quilt kit, called "Kittens." This marked the first time, too, that the accomplished, but possibly not very imaginative, needlewoman could "quilt by number," since the kit provided her with everything she might conceivably need: A design, instructions, illustrations, and stamped, colorful cloth to cut out and stitch onto a (usually) white cloth that came prestamped with the quilt's pattern. Some kits also provided the thread, floss, and binding.

The precut pieces would be appliquéd directly on the accompanying cloth in a variety of "modern" designs—designs that quite often had few traditional antecedents and reflected the technologically advanced twentieth century. So, ironically, planes, skyscrapers, and automobiles—the most streamlined of motifs—deployed on comfy, homey quilts. The profile of sweet, old-fashioned "Sun Bonnet Sue," however, saved the day for the twenties and thirties. The Sue pattern was omnipresent then, as was the ultrasweet and pastel "Ice Cream Cone." In the nursery, the room for which many kit quilts were destined, "Mother Goose" was almost as popular as "Sun Bonnet Sue." This is not to say that no one made old favorites. Traditional patterns like "Lone Star," "Double Wedding Ring," and "Grandmother's

An appliqué kit quilt in a circus pattern, probably designed by Marion Cheever Whiteside Newton, a watercolorist turned children's book illustrator turned quilt-kit designer. Between 1940 and 1965, her studio—Storybook Quilts—sold presewn appliquéd squares as well as quilt patterns for people to make themselves. Her studio also made custom quilts.

Fan" turned up, but mostly on the appliquéd models.

Kit quilts of this era, especially those of the twenties and thirties, can often be recognized by their characteristic minty greens, lemon yellows, and powder-puff pinks. Some, however, were composed of bright primary colors.

FEED-SACK QUILTS

After the development of the sewing machine, and as inexpensive cloth from New England's textile mills became increasingly available, staples like sugar, rice, flour, and seed were frequently sold in cloth sacks. Such cotton or burlap feed and flour sacks were a commonplace for the thrifty and practical farmwife, and the empty sacks were eminently reusable textiles.

During the Depression years, manufacturers—in the hope, perhaps, of encouraging brand loyalty in housewives—made feed and flour bags in pretty printed and solid cottons, many with paper labels that could be easily soaked off. Scores of these sprightly prints and colorful solids wound up in what we call today feed-sack quilts. One of the largest makers of the cloth bags was the Bemis Brothers Bag Company of Minneapolis. These days, paradoxically, part of the charm of feed-sack quilts for collectors is the whole or partial appearance of the bag manufacturer's name on the finished product.

CONTEST QUILTS

Throughout the United States during the nineteenth and early twentieth centuries, quilt contests were a traditional and popular feature of country fairs. Quilts created especially for competitions were expected to be made of as many pieces of fabric as possible; to include up to tens of thousands of pieces of patchwork. The winners of blue ribbons in such contests were those needlewomen (or men and boys—Dwight Eisenhower used to help his mother make quilts) who put the patches together or cut the patterns to be appliquéd and stitched them in the most imaginative and beautiful ways. Quite naturally, collectors consider such quilts to be exceptionally desirable works of art.

A "Flower Basket" pattern kit quilt from the 1930s features thirty-two different baskets, each with a different flower—among them carnations, daffodils, lilies, pansies, and sweet peas.

This feed-sack quilt in a pattern of string-pieced six-pointed stars was made in the American Midwest in the 1930s.

TIPS
from the
experts

♦ Never wash wool blankets, not even by hand. Use only a reputable dry cleaner that has experience with old textiles.

♦ You can wash cotton blankets safely in a washing machine, unless they are fringed, there are holes, or the binding is very loose. Use cold water and the delicate or gentle cycle and dry in a dryer using low heat.

♦ Store clean blankets only. Store them flat, with as few folds as possible, in a place where there is some air movement—not in sealed plastic bags. Remove them from storage periodically to air them. If the blanket has been folded, change the position of the folds when you refold it.

In addition to the quilts mentioned above, there are collectors for specialty quilts, such as those made for fundraising, for occasions like weddings and anniversaries, and for those that display patriotic themes.

BLANKETS AND BEDSPREADS

Two types of vintage American-manufactured blanket are particularly popular with textile collectors: Pendleton blankets, produced by Pendleton Woolen Mills, the first U. S. manufacturer to make blankets for trade with the Indians; and Beacon blankets, also known as camp blankets. There is also collector interest in the English-made Hudson's Bay blankets, traded by the Hudson's Bay Company in Canada for Indian furs beginning in the eighteenth century. Bates bedspreads, especially those with furry chenille tufts, may not be blankets, exactly, but they attracted many textile enthusiasts, too.

PENDLETON BLANKETS

Oregon's Pendleton Woolen Mills, still in business today, has produced machine-woven woolen trade blankets since 1909. From the eighteenth through the nineteenth century, American colonists had been trading the Indians useful and warm wool blankets in return for more valuable commodities—to the colonists, at least—such as furs. By the turn of the twentieth century, however, the "trade" blankets themselves had found a far wider audience than the Indians. Adorned with representative Indian motifs, Pendleton blankets were popular with homeowners, who warmed to their suggestion of long-lost Western romance and woodsy Adirondack camps. Until the 1950s, in fact, Pendleton blankets were such common and popular household staples that the firm could successfully market some two hundred designs, dividing the product into three distinct lines: Beaver State, Pendleton, and Cayuse.

The earliest Pendleton blankets are most valuable today. Enthusiasts make distinctions in desirability between the round-corner blankets that were made before 1910 and the later squared-corner examples. Growing collector interest has created markets for every type of colorful old blanket, and the vintage Pendleton blankets that were once spread on driveways to display

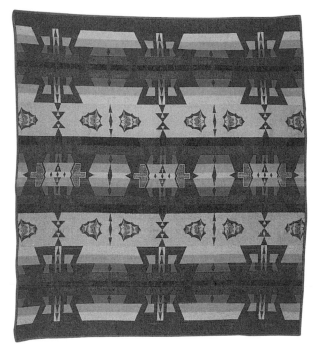

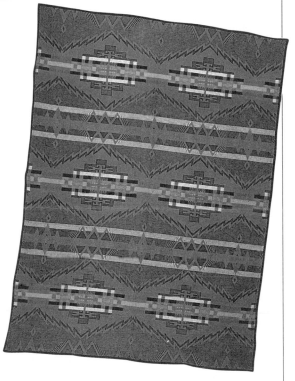

tag sale merchandise might command more than $1,000 today, their value depending on the condition of the blanket and the relative rarity of the pattern.

Other collectible trade-blanket manufacturers include Jacobs/Oregon City, of Oregon City, Oregon; J. Capps & Son, of Jacksonville, Illinois; Buell, of St. Joseph, Missouri; and Racine, of Racine, Wisconsin.

HUDSON'S BAY BLANKETS

The "point" blankets from Canada's Hudson's Bay Company were first made in 1780. Point blankets were so highly prized by American Indians that they eventually became important elements of the fur trade. The handwoven wool of the point blanket was beaten with mallets to prevent shrinkage, and the points—those short, narrow black or indigo stripes on the edge of the blankets—indicated the weight and size of the blanket, which in turn determined the price. One point meant that the blanket would cost one beaver pelt, and the larger the size and weight of the blanket, the more points it would accrue.

Until 1900, many of these high-quality, highly desirable blankets continued to be handwoven, but by the mid-twentieth century, the typical Hudson's Bay Company blanket was

Left: Although not the only North American company to make blankets to trade with the Indians, Pendleton Woolen Mills was the only one founded specifically for that purpose. Their first blanket designs incorporated simple stripes, blocks, rectangles, and crosses, but in 1901 the introduction of the Jacquard loom enabled Pendleton to create more intricate zigzag designs.

Right: A square-corner post-1910 wool Pendleton trade blanket in a green, orange, and black pattern based on Indian designs. Eager to please their customers, some woolen mills sent designers to live among the Indians in the United States and Canada to learn what designs and colors would appeal to different tribes.

manufactured and supplied by any of several English manufacturers. Collectors look for vividness of color, size, and weight (just as the original Indians did), and, of course, freedom from moth holes.

BEACON OR CAMP BLANKETS

Beacon blankets were cotton rather than wool and seem to have been a warm and fuzzy staple of many an American childhood. Manufactured since 1904 by the Beacon Manufacturing Company (which ultimately became the largest manufacturer of blankets in the United States), early camp-blanket patterns were derived from patterns on trade blankets and from Navajo weavings. Between the thirties and fifties, Western images were particularly popular: Indian children, totem poles, tepees, and the familiar if currently impolitic "cowboys and Indians." Retailed through giant merchandisers, such as J. C. Penney; Sears, Roebuck and Co.; and Montgomery Ward, these literally picturesque bed coverings were fixtures in thousands of mid-twentieth-century American children's rooms. While they were all initially made of pure cotton, most, as time went on, became blends of cotton with rayon and other synthetics until (and perhaps contributing to their diminishing popularity) they came to be made entirely of synthetics.

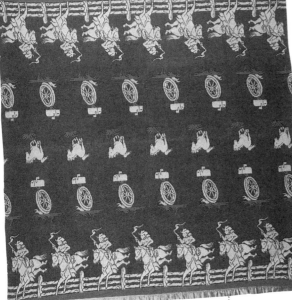

A cotton and synthetic Beacon camp blanket from the 1940s with a fanciful pattern of cowboys, wagon wheels, mail boxes, and ponies—perfect for a boy's room.

Collectors of Beacon blankets prefer the more attractive and innovative patterns made before 1945, the presynthetic era. They also prize rarity of design, good condition, and unfaded and pleasing color combinations. Those that have particularly strong colors—the reds, blues, and greens with the usual touch of black—are preferred, as are those with Indian motifs. Among non-Indian subjects, blankets decorated with Art Deco or floral motifs are most desirable.

Several firms other than Beacon made camp blankets. Among them are the American Woolen Company, Well-Bilt, and Esmond Mills.

BATES BEDSPREADS

Vintage bedspreads from Bates in Lewiston, Maine, are especially popular today for the "period" accent they lend to vintage-style

rooms. Bates pictorial spreads were almost indispensable in boys' bedrooms of the mid-twentieth century, where their cheerful Disney or baseball designs enlivened the private sanctums of future Bates collectors. The firm's cowboy images are currently in great demand, as are images of space travel and especially nautical themes, with bedspreads awash in ropes, sailboats, and compasses. Many white Bates bedspreads were twentieth-century interpretations of the three-dimensional all-white quilting designs of the nineteenth century known as whitework.

TABLECLOTHS

The practical, enamel-topped kitchen table, so prevalent in American homes of the twenties and thirties, was not for every housewife. Good wood tables remained common in many kitchens and dining rooms, and pretty tablecloths were required to protect these wood tabletops, while simultaneously beautifying and enlivening the actual table setting.

Of course, there were gorgeous lace and damask cloths during this period, too, but particularly throughout the 1930s and 1940s, every local five-and-ten-cent store carried substantial selections of brilliantly patterned cloths (often, but not always, with sets of four, eight, or twelve matching napkins). These printed rounds, squares, and rectangles offered durable, inexpensive, and particularly cheerful table coverage at a time when the country as a whole found itself sobered, first by the Depression, then by World War II. Strong geometric patterns and angular, stylized forms mirrored Art Deco in the 1920s, for example. (Tablecloths from this period are somewhat rare and are frequently made of linen, which is unusual in later decades.)

In the thirties, cotton cloths—imprinted with bountiful fruits and flowers in the most dazzling (and durable) of naturalistic colors—abounded. Some examples include as many as twelve colors in a single cloth. By the forties, strong border designs were showing up, and while forties motifs are similar to those of the previous decade, the fruits, vegetables, and flowers

The pattern of this nautically themed Bates bedspread features an assortment of well-known American ships— naval, merchant, and private vessels: the U. S. S. Constitution, *the* U. S. S. Chesapeake, *the* Challenge, *and the* Sea Cloud.

Printed tablecloths with "south of the border" designs were particularly popular in the early 1940s. This one depicts Mexican themes in a colorful pattern printed in red, yellow, brown, and black on a white background.

Fruits and flowers are among the most popular motifs with vintage printed tablecloth collectors today—many of whom search for the tablecloths they remember from their grandmother's kitchens.

Souvenir tablecloths, such as this one from Wisconsin, were a popular vacation purchase in the post–World War II United States, and they are avidly collected today—especially ones from the midwestern states, which were visited by fewer post-War tourists and therefore produced fewer souvenirs for them.

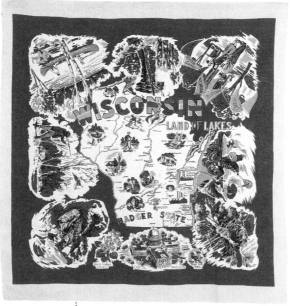

of this era can be distinguished from their predecessors by their being relatively close-packed and combined, often, with thick stripes. Cuban and South American images, reflecting the influence of film stars like Carmen Miranda, and anything "South of the Border" were also characteristic of the early forties, as were combinations of gray and pink. After World War II, with the return of gasoline and servicemen, formerly homebound Americans could travel freely and indulge themselves in that new and uniquely useful souvenir: the tablecloth imprinted with the map of one's vacation spot or a famous sight-seeing destination. (For the many avid collectors of these tourist cloths, Midwest themes are particularly in demand).

By the early 1950s, before the "everyday" tablecloth went the way of the buggy whip, cloths were printed in fewer colors and incorporated simpler abstract floral or fruit patterns, often outlined in the favorite colors of the time: chartreuse, orange and yellow, avocado green, and turquoise. The tablecloth industry virtually disappeared once plastic tabletops took over.

Enthusiasts look for collectible cloths in mint condition: This means unused and preferably bearing the original label. The intensity of the colors in the cloth reflects both the quality of the cotton and the excellence of the printing process. For collectors who collect by subject —Mexico, vegetable prints, or African-American images, for instance—the unusual motif will often take precedence over condition.

Chapter Seven

DOLLS AND DOLL ACCESSORIES

At the Chicago *Antiques Roadshow,* a guest arrived with a complete set of Dionne quintuplet baby dolls, a set she'd owned since she was a girl. Created by noted doll manufacturer Madame Alexander, the tiny quints were tidily dressed in their original matching rompers and sunbonnets, and were lying side by side (by side by side by side) on a pillow in their original wicker basket. Beneath that pillow were their pink organdy party dresses, complete with petticoats, in excellent condition. Not only was their original clothing in fine condition, observed appraiser Dana Hawkes, "every one of the five dolls has its original name tag, which is extremely rare."

No doubt, millions of "grown-up" little girls looked on in envy as the dolls' owner related that they'd been a gift in about 1940 (Madame Alexander began to produce the dolls in 1935, when the actual quints were a year old) from a fond aunt and uncle. And, yes, as fine as their condition was, she had actually played with them. She must have been a very meticulous child, Hawkes commented. But the quints' owner believed that their

Top: a Schoenhut dollhouse. Right: the rare Deanna Durban celebrity doll.

Perfect in every detail, from pleated organdy dress to ringlets to pink ribbons on her wrists, every aspect of the Shirley Temple doll was overseen by the movie star's mother. The tag on Shirley's dress proclaims her "The World's Darling."

Vogue's Black Ginny doll, here wearing a straw hat, is very rare. She was produced only in 1953 and 1954.

remarkable condition was more a factor of her being an *only* child. "I didn't have to share," she laughed. As several young *Roadshow* visitors tried to peer into the wicker basket, Hawkes told the astonished guest that her dolls might bring up to $2,000 at auction.

DOLLS

Nothing summons nostalgia the way our favorite childhood playthings do. What grown woman watching *Antiques Roadshow* that night wasn't wishing that her own treasured doll—a Madame Alexander or a Nancy Ann or a Barbie—had been tucked away somewhere in pristine condition? Maybe, in fact, that quintuplet discovery sparked more than a few attic searches. And if those original dolls didn't turn up, the thrill of that search might even have led her to track down a dealer who had that doll to sell, and just maybe that dealer had other dolls that were so beautiful, adorable, or irresistible that those, too, became must-haves. The doll-owner gene can lay dormant for years, after all, but in the doll-lover, it returns full-force.

Dolls from every era are collectible, but the ones that fall into the collectible, not antique, category, are those made between 1918 and approximately 1975. Dolls made earlier, such as those manufactured by Bru or Jumeau, are termed "antique," even though they may not be 100 years old. "Modern" dolls are those manufactured within the last 25 years, and "contemporary" dolls are those being made today.

Whereas antique doll collectors tend to judge one another's collections by the bisqueness of doll heads or their rosebud mouths being open or closed (closed, interestingly, is often better), twentieth-century doll collections are often built around individual dolls such as Ginnys and Barbies or doll manufacturers such as Madame Alexander or Nancy Ann Storybook.

To the enthusiast, rare attributes (a red-haired Barbie or a black Bye-Lo Baby) matter, but so do age and condition and the outfits the dolls are wearing, since in some instances clothes *do* make the doll. Even the materials used to create the doll add to its collectibility, and surprisingly, formerly despised products like composition (a cousin to papier mâché), celluloid, and plastic have become newly desirable.

A BRIEF HISTORY

Centuries of doll making have left us with some wonderful examples of the beloved playthings of our European and American ancestors. Of wood and leather, wax, papier mâché, and eventually bisque, these antique eighteenth- and nineteenth-century dolls are coveted by thousands of collectors worldwide. Before World War I, Europe (especially France and Germany) was the doll-making capital of the world, and beautifully crafted bisque-head dolls with wooden or cloth bodies, clothed in modish and enviable outfits, came from such companies as Jumeau and Bru (in France) and Kammer & Reinhardt and Simon & Halbig (in Germany).

Just after World War I, American firms began to experiment with new technologies and took the lead from their German and French competitors in the doll market. Improved rubbers and sturdier composition materials, alternatives to beautiful, breakable bisque, produced a wealth of increasingly innovative dolls,

THE TWINS

A pair of Grace Corey Rockwell dolls that appeared on the Charleston *Antiques Roadshow* were given to the owner's mother sometime between 1920 and 1930.

Appraiser Richard Wright noted that Grace Corey Rockwell marketed her dolls through the Century Doll Company of New York, and it's very rare to find a pair of them. Unfortunately, one of the dolls appeared to have been repaired, which greatly decreased its value. The doll in perfect condition is worth $3,000 to $4,000, while the damaged example is valued at only $600 to $800.

Madame Alexander's Sonja Henie Trousseau doll. The young Olympic sensation is shown here dressed in ice skates and a blue taffeta skating dress.

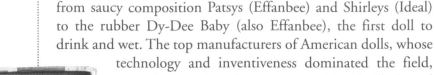

She could drink, wet, blow bubbles, and cry real tears. Lovable Tiny Tears—with "Rock-A-Bye" eyes—delighted children of the 1950s.

from saucy composition Patsys (Effanbee) and Shirleys (Ideal) to the rubber Dy-Dee Baby (also Effanbee), the first doll to drink and wet. The top manufacturers of American dolls, whose technology and inventiveness dominated the field, were the "Big Four"—Horsman, Mattel, Ideal, and Madame Alexander. Their output has become increasingly collectible.

After World War II, plastics swept the industry and spurred another change in U.S. doll manufacture. Hard plastic, more durable than earlier materials, made it possible to create, among other delights, small dolls with better detail. In the fifties, young baby boomers acquired families of dressable 8-inch Ginnys (Vogue); adorable Tiny Tears (American Character), a real "crybaby" that came in a wide range of sizes; and the popular Sweet Sue (also American Character). And the very end of the decade saw the birth of that star of doll stars, Barbie.

The fifties also saw the blossoming of children's television. Favorite characters such as Howdy Doody (a marionette), Lamb Chop (a hand puppet), and Davy Crockett (an historic character and the subject of a television series) offered manufacturers an unforeseen wonderland of marketing opportunities, and these, along with scores of other beloved television characters, were turned into "character" dolls—grandparents of today's Captain Kirks, Chers, and Darth Vaders. We can only hope that more recent creations—not just the aforementioned, but all dolls made today—age as gracefully as their forebears did, and that their place in the American heart remains as fresh as tomorrow's collectors might hope to find each doll's complexion, clothes, and hair.

American Character produced hard plastic dolls of varying heights. Their 14-inch Sweet Sue Formal—still wearing her wrist tag—is at the far right.

EVALUATING DOLLS

While it's fine and desirable to buy only dolls that engage your heart, you aren't going to want to pay a lot for dolls that have been loved to a state of unrecognizability. That's common sense. But just what does a careful and intelligent collector look for when examining a doll? Of highest value to enthusiasts are those dolls that are mint-in-package (MIP) or mint-in-box (MIB). Vintage baby dolls are more likely to be found in good condition than girl, teen, or adult dolls. (They've spent their "working years," after all, cradled in carriages and cribs.)

Take the time to learn what constitutes good condition in a given doll, and to know how to look for flaws. Regardless of the material it's made of, any doll that you are considering for your collection should be submitted to a rigorous physical inspection.

HAIR

The wig should be original to the doll, and in very good condition. It is considered a collectible plus for a wig to retain its original set. Rare hairstyles (for that particular doll) are desirable, as are perfect eyelashes.

EYES

Eyes frequently have condition problems. Hard plastic Shirley Temple dolls, for example, are all too often found with eyes so crazed "they look like 'Children of the Damned,'" says expert Tim Luke. Clear-eyed Shirleys are scarce, and therefore highly desirable.

SKIN

The skin of a composition doll should have an uncrazed finish (although a minimal amount of fine crazing is to be expected, and indeed, has become increasingly acceptable). For white dolls, a finish that is rosy and colorful is a requirement. And while variations in color are not important for black dolls, the paint or finish of the skin should be intact. Realistically modeled features are a rarity and a plus.

Dubbed an "action figure" by Hasbro, G.I. Joe permitted young commandos to act out their battle fantasies without feeling that they were "playing with dolls." This Action Sailor came with a blue denim work shirt, metal dog tag, boots, garrison hat, and a macho scar.

Ideal produced the Cowgirl Shirley Temple doll in 1935 to celebrate the centennial of Texas's independence from Mexico. Her outfit came complete with a tiny six-shooter.

The skin of every doll, in fact, regardless of the material it's made of, should be unblemished and undamaged. Its color should not have darkened or lightened over time, and dirt is definitely unwelcome. A top-quality doll should be as clean and fresh as when it was new.

CLOTHING

Doll outfits should be original and preferably never laundered. Not just dresses, but undergarments, shoes, and socks are most prized when they are in like-new condition. A wrist tag is considered a bonus, as are original jewelry, accessories, and boxes. Says appraiser Richard Wright, "Composition and hard plastic dolls from the thirties and forties particularly, have to be absolutely perfect and wearing their original tags."

A popular doll in a rare outfit, such as that worn by the Cowgirl Shirley Temple, always commands a premium.

SIZE

Dolls—even baby dolls—were frequently manufactured in several different sizes, and those sizes were not standardized, but varied from factory to factory. One firm would make the identical doll in sizes ranging from 10 inches to 28 inches, while another made its character dolls in sizes from 7 inches to 16 inches, but made its child dolls 12 inches to 27 inches tall. Some dolls were offered only in one or two sizes, perhaps because they were only expected to have limited runs. On the whole, the larger example of a particular doll—conditional details being equal—is more desirable.

CATEGORIZING DOLLS

Collectors have traditionally categorized dolls by the material their heads are made of: china, for example, or bisque, a flesh-tinted, matte-finish variant of china, or good old (or new, depending on how old you are) vinyl.

Twentieth-century advances in technology provided doll manufacturers with a hitherto unimagined range of materials for their products. Not surprisingly, some of these materials turned out to be more durable, more lifelike, and, all in all, better suited to making dolls than others. As they experimented, doll makers worked with single materials—say, all hard plastic or vinyl—and combinations—vinyl and cloth, composition and rubber, composition and cloth, and vinyl and hard plastic, for example. In fact, throughout the manufacture of a particular doll, the material from which it was made might change over time. Take Kewpies, for example. These sweet little cupidlike dolls began in bisque; but over their lifetime, they were fashioned of perhaps every material known to dollmaking, including composition, hard plastic, and vinyl.

The materials described below are noted in, more or less, the order in which they came into use during the twentieth century, beginning with a few that had earlier roots.

CLOTH

Cloth is among the easiest and most universally available materials to work with; it is also exceptionally sturdy. Many of the most famous, as well as the favorite, dolls of the twentieth century were fashioned of cloth, sometimes with heads and other parts made of bisque, composition, or other materials: Kewpies, Billikins, googly-eyes, and Cabbage Patch Kids among them. Cloth dolls, made of cotton, stockinette, and even oil cloth, were especially popular in the 1920s.

CHINA AND BISQUE

In the eighteenth and nineteenth centuries, some of the very best dolls were made with bisque and china heads and extremities. Although bisque-head dolls—such as some Bye-Lo Babies and some Nancy Ann Storybook Dolls—were manufactured into the 1930s, the inherent fragility of bisque was the impetus for many of the alternative materials that were being tried. The doll industry required less vulnerable substitutes.

China, the porcelain that is used both for tableware and dolls, is a combination of kaolin (a clay) and petuntse (ground feldspar)

This impish 5-inch bisque Kewpie doll, with heart label, is German-made.

MARKS ON TWENTIETH-CENTURY DOLLS

Most gratifying to doll collectors and potential doll collectors is the knowledge that twentieth-century dolls are generally well marked, either with the name of the manufacturer, with the doll's name, or both. (Half-dolls are exceptions because, along with very few others, they may or may not be marked.) If a doll's mark includes its country of origin—Germany, for instance, or Japan—you can be certain it was made after 1892, when it became a law that all foreign-made imports be identified as such. The country of manufacture can also be an aid in identifying the doll's exact date of manufacture. (Barbie shoes marked "Japan," for example, are older than shoes marked "Taiwan.") And for some dolls, the location on the body where the mark appears (on the back, or under the hair, for instance) can be a great help in dating.

"Patent applied for" dates, however, can be confusing to collectors, because it is all too easy to assume that the date shown is actually the date the doll left the factory, instead of the date on which the company applied to the patent office for its patent, the completion of which process could actually take years. Consequently, a Barbie marked "Pat. applied for 1958," for example, might well have been made in the early sixties.

Effanbee's Dy-Dee baby, a rubber-bodied doll with a hard plastic head, was the first doll with the ability to drink and wet. This lucky doll had a pink dotted Swiss dress and bonnet, undershirts, bibs, washcloths, and her own baby bottle, baby powder, and baby oil.

A rare 21-inch composition Madame Alexander Margaret O'Brien doll, in a starched pinafore and wearing a wrist tag, shows no signs of crazing or the other conditional problems that plague this material.

frequently mixed with bone ash or other additives. It is fired in a kiln, and colored and sealed under a glaze to protect its porous surface. Bisque is simply unglazed porcelain with a matte surface. Both types of ceramic lend themselves particularly well to the realistic rendering of pearly skin and rosy cheeks, and both types, of course, break readily. No parent has ever been happy to give his or her child a plaything that is almost certain to break. Consequently, bisque- and china-head dolls are less common in this age of synthetics.

RUBBER

The process for vulcanizing rubber was patented by Charles Goodyear in 1844 and was widely used for doll manufacture through the rest of the nineteenth century (interestingly, the Goodyear Company itself produced a line of rubber dolls); it remained a popular and inexpensive material for doll making well into the twentieth century. Modern rubber is a longer-lasting substance than its antecedents, and it can also take paint without chipping or flaking. The multiple advantages of modern rubber's softness, washability, and durability, not to mention its capacity to allow dolls to "drink and wet" (and not infrequently, squeak), made rubber dolls commercially appealing.

COMPOSITION

"Composition" is the name doll manufacturers give to a material made from a mixture of sawdust and glue that is heated and poured into molds for doll heads and bodies. Composition has nineteenth-century roots, but only came into its own in the twentieth century, when American toy manufacturers at last figured out how to make composition dolls universally affordable.

Until the Horsman Company wrote down its specifications, however, there were as many formulas for composition as there were doll factories. Consequently, there was little quality control for composition dolls. Horsman used its newly standardized composition recipe to make a highly durable doll, which it aptly and amusingly named "Can't Break 'Em."

Unfortunately, despite dependable formulas, the organic components of composition dolls have made them (like books, which are composed of the same materials) highly susceptible to damage from heat and damp, and particularly, to the doll collector's bugaboo, crazing (a network of very fine cracks).

Composition was produced, mainly, from the teens until after World War II, and dolls made of composition were sold by many well-known manufacturers, although scores were sold unmarked. "There's something nostalgic, almost folksy, about composition dolls," says Tim Luke (whose own dream doll, in fact, would be any of the rare composition Madame Alexanders made in the early years of the company).

CELLULOID

A pair of 17-inch celluloid dolls in traditional costume made by Norwegian doll artist Ronnaug Petterssen.

Dolls made from celluloid, an early plastic composed of nitrocellulose and camphor, were popular playthings in the 1920s and 1930s. These dolls were lightweight and easily molded, but came to be disdained as "second-rate," because their skin was often as fragile as an eggshell, and equally easily cracked. Worse yet, the celluloid was likely to darken in color to a dull, deep yellow or unappetizing brown.

Although most people consider celluloid dolls to be mainly Depression-era dolls, they were actually produced from the last quarter of the nineteenth century until 1950 or so—because celluloid made the lightest-weight doll body before plastics and vinyl came into use. Many of the finest doll manufacturers made all-celluloid dolls or celluloid-head dolls with cloth bodies, among them the famed German maker of lifelike soft dolls, Käthe Kruse (whose celluloid dolls bear the characteristic German turtle mark; see box on page 292). One reason for the demise of this material was the belatedly discovered fact that it was highly flammable and, most disturbingly, that it had an unfortunate tendency to explode when placed near heat.

HARD PLASTIC

Dolls made of hard plastic were a by-product of World War II technology; it was *the* material for a wide range of popular dolls created in the 1950s. From the manufacturers' point of view, the overriding advantage of plastics was that they could be crisply molded and easily

A doll for all seasons: Princess Summerfall-Winterspring, a character from the 1950s show Howdy Doody.

Madame Alexander started making vinyl dolls in the 1960s. This 15-inch vinyl Pollyanna is wearing a jumper trimmed with rickrack and a crisp white blouse.

Two composition dolls from Effanbee, Patsy and Skippy (The Real American Boy), both dressed in their original clothing.

painted and were resistant to chipping, flaking, or crazing. For the young consumer, plastic had the advantage of being very light in weight—ideal for toting around—and it was more or less impervious to frequent baths. (A soft plastic doll material, which turned out to be unstable, was marketed in the United States for a short time in the mid-twentieth century.)

VINYL

Vinyl, for collectors, marks the start of the "modern" doll era. Dolls made of vinyl, a synthetic plastic capable of having a variety of resiliencies, first appeared on the market in the 1950s. They were a definite improvement on hard plastic dolls. Vinyl skin was cheaper to produce than its plastic precursors, and it could be dyed to look exceptionally natural while retaining a remarkably supple, skinlike feel.

COLLECTING DOLLS

Perhaps you've decided you'd like to test the waters of the twentieth-century doll market. But the market is huge, and some ordinary looking dolls come with surprising price tags, making them serious investments as well as pretty, nostalgic collectibles.

Which doll or dolls should you start with? Although there are no hard and fast rules to follow, a quick look at the techniques used by experienced collectors reveals as many approaches to collecting as there are collectors: by specific doll (Kewpies or Barbies or Shirley Temples, for example), by era (dolls of the 1930s or 1940s), by material (only composition dolls or dolls with bisque heads), and by manufacturer (Madame Alexander). And that's just for starters. Whatever your focus, heed the advice of *Antiques Roadshow* expert Tim Luke, and always—and only—buy what you like. The majority of collectors, of course, do this intuitively, purchasing as adults either the doll they loved best as a child or the doll they'd always yearned for. While in search of your childhood favorites, however, it's a good idea to learn as much as you can about them. As with any collectible, make use of books as well as the

Cabbage Patch Kids

The Cabbage Patch doll story is a cautionary tale about a nice, small doll growing large, larger, and very large, and floating off, ultimately, into the clouded realms of doll obscurity.

Cabbage Patch Kids were born in 1977 in the Georgia mountains, where these homey, homely hand-stitched cloth baby dolls—ostensibly discovered under a leaf in a cabbage patch—were offered for "adoption" by their maker, Xavier Roberts, in exchange for a signature and an adoption fee. The dolls captured the imaginations of thousands of children, and thousands of delighted parents

and their small "parents-to-be" lined up for a Cabbage Patch baby and its "birth certificate." Within five years, however, Coleco acquired a license to mass-produce the dolls, and when, at last, 57 million had been manufactured and adopted, the Cabbage Patch fad had run its overblown course. Today, collectors deem the signed examples from the late seventies and very early eighties more desirable than the later models, but the secondary market for the output of that overly cultivated Cabbage Patch is volatile, at best—and sauerkraut, at worst—and might be taken as fair warning to Beanie Babies zealots.

Web. There are plenty of on-line sites to check for information. Search out local doll clubs for upcoming shows and other events. Visit the shows, if possible, and have a look at what's available. Although dealers' prices may seem prohibitive, many also offer dolls in pristine condition, giving you an opportunity to see them at their best. Visit as many dealers as possible and do a little comparison window shopping. Seeing all those dolls in person may seem overwhelming, but you'll get a sense of what's available and of what the going rates are.

Don't be shy about asking dealers questions. The more knowledge you gather, the more intelligent you'll be as a collector—and the more likely it will be that you'll know a "find" when you see it at a flea market or yard sale.

Although condition is important (see page 267), don't pass up less-than-perfect dolls, especially if the price is right. Some

A WORD TO THE WISE

Limited edition dolls, which are offered by the manufacturer only for a short time and in a limited quantity, are a fairly recent marketing ploy. Better to spend your money on proven collectibles. As well, modern and contemporary dolls are considered risky "investments" because they are unproven in the marketplace.

Patti Play Pal, first issued in 1959, is 35 inches tall and could be dressed in real children's clothing. Other members of the Play Pal family include Suzy, Penny, twins Johnny and Bonnie, and Peter.

repairs are not difficult to make and there are many good doll hospitals where a Shirley or Ginny can go for a mend and a rest.

Don't be afraid to take some risks. You're going to come across dolls you'd love to own, but maybe you don't feel knowledgeable enough to know whether or not their clothes or wigs are original. You might not even be sure a doll is really the doll the seller says it is. But, if you set yourself a reasonable budget, you won't lose sleep over a potentially wrong decision.

Experienced collectors know, however, that even if you start small, you'll eventually find that in the pursuit of your passion, you've made a sickening mistake. There's probably not a collector alive who hasn't paid a premium price for a 1930s doll, for example, wearing "original" clothes—only to discover later that its outfit was made in the seventies. Or one who hasn't excitedly brought home what turned out to be an out-and-out reproduction, or a prize purchased for a bargain price, which, on careful examination, turned out to have a replaced leg or arm. Collecting, by its very nature, is a dicey education in an occasionally slippery marketplace. But legitimately earned battle scars simply mark us as veterans, and entitle us to move on: We become knowledgeable and confident enough in our hard-won experience to trade up and refine our collections.

While there are no rules that must be followed when it comes to which doll or dolls to make the focus of your collection, it does make sense for beginners to use the areas established by seasoned collectors as guidelines. So, this chapter is set up in those familiar and easily recognizable groups, and includes doll manufacturers, celebrity dolls, action figures, advertising dolls, and specialty dolls.

MAJOR DOLL MANUFACTURERS

Many collectors build their collections on the dolls of just a few manufacturers, and some among these have produced so many of the dolls that collectors desire that they should be singled out. The following major manufacturers appear in alphabetical order.

CAMEO

The Cameo Doll Company, in business from 1922 to 1970, manufactured two particularly well-known and beloved dolls: Kewpies and Bye-Lo Babies. Kewpies, those impish, tiny-winged cherubs created in 1909 by illustrator Rose O'Neill, were first manufactured in Germany in 1913, but it is with Cameo that the Kewpie is most identified. Cameo made its doll in composition, hard plastic, and vinyl, as well as in several sizes and poses. The company also marketed the Kewpie-like baby Scootles, a baby doll that was designed to be as cute as a Kewpie. Both Kewpies and Scootles come in white-skinned and black-skinned versions. All Cameo Kewpies are marked somewhere on their head or body.

Cameo also became one of several manufacturers licensed to produce the Bye-Lo Baby, the painstakingly realistic newborn look-alike doll that was the work of doll designer Grace Storey Putnam. Bye-Lo Babies could not be termed beautiful, nor even mildly adorable, for they were created in the Winston Churchill-like image of a three-day-old infant. Nonetheless, Bye-Lo Babies were such a huge commercial success (actually, they came to be called Million Dollar Babies) that they went through several incarnations in various materials: bisque, composition, celluloid, and rubber. Bye-Lo bodies could be hard, soft, and even internationally assembled combinations of both. (The 1920 model Bye-Lo, for instance, had a German-made bisque head and celluloid hands attached to an American-made cloth body.)

Cameo also made a segmented Margie doll in the 1920s, designed by Cameo proprietor Joseph Kallus as an affordable alternative to expensive bisque dolls. The Margie doll had a composition head with painted facial features and a segmented wooden body. It could be displayed in a number of different poses because of the segmentation of its limbs.

Some early non-Kewpie Cameo dolls may not be marked at all, or they may wear only a wrist tag.

A cute and highly collectible Kewpie couple from the Cameo Doll Company, complete right down to their socks and shoelaces.

Cameo's realistic newborn Bye-Lo Babies struck a chord with doll buyers everywhere. Their success caused them to be nicknamed Million Dollar Babies.

Wartime materials shortages didn't stop Effanbee from producing Little Lady, shown here with rare yarn hair and a cloth body.

EFFANBEE

Founded in 1910, Effanbee—named for partners Bernard Fleischaker and Hugh Baum, "F and B"—is a firm known for innovation and pioneering manufacturing techniques. Its first dolls had bisque heads (until 1920, many were made by Lenox China), and Effanbee later experimented with all sorts of materials, working with rubber in 1930, and ultimately developing the rubber Dy-Dee baby, the very first doll to drink and wet (a well-placed plug kept the doll from wetting continuously). In 1915, the company became the first to distribute a black doll (a version of their popular Baby Grumpy).

Effanbee's best-known doll is Patsy, introduced in the 1920s. Made of composition, she was the earliest American doll to be created with the realistic proportions of an actual child. A family of Patsys soon followed, including Wee Patsy, Babyette, Patsyette, Patsy Jr., Patsy Ann, Patsy Lou, Patsy Ruth, and so on. Patsy was also the first doll to have a wardrobe and accessories.

In 1926, doll artist Dewees Cochran designed a series of four 21-inch compositions dolls for Effanbee, which she modeled after and called "American Children." Later, other dolls in other sizes were added to the line.

Little Lady, introduced in the 1930s, came dressed in some of dolldom's most desirable clothing, everything from adorable daytime frocks to frilly gowns. Like so many of her peers, Little Lady came in a variety of sizes and was made originally of composition, but during the World War II years, some dolls had to be manufactured with cloth bodies and composition arms and legs.

Also popular with collectors is Effanbee's well-dressed Anne Shirley doll (so marked on the back), that was introduced in 1939 and named for the young Hollywood actress (who named herself after the character she played in her starring role in *Anne of Green Gables*).

In 1949, the company switched over to hard plastics, creating the Honey doll, who

Effanbee's American Children from designer Dewees Cochran came beautifully dressed and were available in a variety of sizes.

Owning a collection of dolls can be a bitter-sweet experience, as it was for the original owner of this large assembly. Her son told Richard Wright during the Denver *Antiques Roadshow* that his mother was never actually allowed to play with any of the dolls she was given, but instead was told to keep them stored in their protective boxes.

Her collection, an eclectic mix of dolls representative of the years just prior to World War II through the beginning of the war, included a Shirley Temple doll made by the Ideal Toy Company and a drum majorette made by Effanbee. There was even a rare Baby Sandy doll, named for a popular child movie star of the 1930s.

Though the majority of the dolls were American, there were a few German-made dolls manufactured by Hertwig & Co. in the 1930s, as well as some German and French celluloid dolls. The entire collection had been carefully preserved over the years, and was valued at $4,000 to $6,000.

could walk—although she seemed to dress for and walk to only those places where girl dolls of that era were expected to walk: in parades, as majorettes, or to the altar.

HORSMAN

Horsman was founded in 1865 by Edward Iseman Horsman, and is notable for having been, circa 1890, the first American company to manufacture durable composition heads. Horsman's innovative composition dolls bore the proud slogan "Can't Break 'Em," and were a genuine boon to parents who had wearied of wiping tears shed over shattered bisque. (Composition dolls are, in fact, "one of the first of the all-American dolls," says

Horsman's Billiken has the fuzzy body of a stuffed animal and the composition head of a doll. The face of this strange-looking doll was supposedly based on a Chinese good luck charm.

Ideal's 13-inch Snow White, faintly resembling the Disney cartoon character, was actually adapted from the Shirley Temple doll mold. The Seven Dwarfs appear on the hem of her gown.

doll expert Tim Luke. "Until quite recently, however, they were the 'red-headed stepchild' of the doll collecting family, yet what those manufacturers could do with a little sawdust and glue is amazing.") Horsman remained a pioneer in the industry, originating Fairy Skin (a soft plastic) and Miracle Hair. The company's products included mama dolls; the odd-looking Billiken, who combined the best of both worlds, the plush body of the teddy bear with the composition head of a doll; and the earliest of the Campbell's Kids (see page 288). Horsman is notable for having always manufactured dependable, high-quality dolls.

IDEAL

The Ideal Novelty and Toy Company has always enjoyed a reputation for innovation. From its "invention" of the Teddy bear in 1902 to the 1930s experiments with hard plastics that culminated in the very first plastic doll, the Ideal company prided itself on being in the technological forefront of toy making. Among its many patents is one for the "mama" voice.

Given the fact that the company was a model of creativity, it's not surprising that Ideal had several highly successful dolls. In the 1930s, it introduced a series of best-selling composition celebrity dolls named for the immensely popular child stars of the Depression era: Shirley Temple (see page 285), Deanna Durbin (see page 286), and Judy Garland (see page 285), plus the inimitable Snow White, based on the Disney cartoon. Later, and true to her aptly chosen name, Ideal's composition and rubber Betsy Wetsy drank from a bottle, then wet. The company's 1949 hard plastic Toni doll, with her nylon hair, could be given limitless sugar-water permanent waves.

One of the company's few missteps was the Sparkle Plenty doll, based on the character from the Dick Tracy comic strip. Her soft plastic "magic skin" truly approximated skin, but also deteriorated rapidly.

In 1959, Ideal began issuing the life-size vinyl and hard plastic Patti Play Pal family—comprising Patti (35 inches), Suzy (21 inches), Penny (32 inches), twins Johnny and Bonnie (24 inches), and Peter (38 inches). Each doll could be dressed in real children's clothing. Other large dolls made by Ideal included Miss Ideal and the preteen 38- and 42-inch Daddy's Girl.

Ideal sold its trademark to Mattel in the 1980s.

MADAME ALEXANDER

Founded in 1923 by Beatrice Alexander Behrman (*the* Madame Alexander) with the help of her sisters, this well-known firm ultimately produced some six thousand personality dolls, including separate lines of "International" and "Americana" dolls. Every Madame Alexander doll was carefully designed and crafted, and all were fashionably dressed.

Dolls could be had in various materials, among them cloth, composition, and vinyl. Collectors particularly prize those made of cloth, manufactured from the 1930s to the 1950s (with a doll or two being made in the sixties). The faces of Madame Alexander cloth dolls are molded from heavy felt suede, with features exceptionally well rendered. From its inception, the company looked to the heroines and heroes of well-known nineteenth-century novels for inspiration, for the firm's philosophy was that dolls should be educational. *Little Women*'s Meg, Jo, and all members of the March family; Alice from *Alice in Wonderland*; Little Lord Fauntleroy; and Dickensian stalwarts like David Copperfield and semi-stalwart Tiny Tim were all turned into Alexander dolls.

Between the mid-1930s and 1948, Madame Alexander produced hundreds of composition dolls (remember those Dionne quintuplets?), and although they carried different names, many, somehow, shared the same face. In fact, one popular style, the Wendy Ann, was named for Madame's granddaughter. Wendy Ann's face not only appeared on a Wendy Ann doll but on a number of other dolls with different names and outfits. (The firm's successful Scarlett O'Hara composition doll had a Wendy Ann face, as did the Ginger Rogers doll and—of all things—the Little Lord Fauntleroy doll.) The same is true of the Maggie face, the Margaret O'Brien face (produced in hard plastic

Madame Alexander's hoop-skirted Scarlett O'Hara commemorates the 1939 release of the film Gone With the Wind.

The four March sisters and Marmee make up a colorful and desirable character set by Madame Alexander.

Shapely Bild Lili, with her signature spit curl, is a 1950s character doll based on a popular comic strip from the German newspaper Das Bild. *Ruth Handler, creator of Barbie, credited the sexy, "grown-up" doll as her inspiration.*

as well as composition) and the Princess (who grew up to be Queen) Elizabeth face. Certain celebrities, with faces too unique, evidently, to be cloned, were recreated with their own distinctive features: Thirties child star Jane Withers was one of these.

In the late forties, Madame Alexander became one of the first companies to switch to hard plastic. Both the Wendy Ann and Margaret O'Brien faces were carried along into the fifties, but new faces were also introduced, including the popular Cissy in 1955. Lissy, her younger sister, showed up in 1956, and Cissette, a smaller version of Cissy (as you might guess from her name), was introduced in 1957.

Then came vinyl. For economy's sake, the vinyl dolls, too, shared just a few faces. Among these were the Little Shaver (based on a drawing by illustrator Elsie Shaver), the Renoir Girl, and the "First Ladies Series"—wives of American presidents. Vinyl bride dolls, the March sisters (the girls of *Little Women* have been a continuing theme for Madame A., as have Alice and Scarlett), storybook dolls, and ballerinas are just a few of the readily available dolls from Madame Alexander's late output.

MATTEL

Mattel became one of the leading doll manufacturers with just a single doll–but what a doll, for Barbie is a doll without peer. She is *the* doll of the twentieth century. The secret behind the doll's phenomenal success can be summed up in the observation, revolutionary at the time, of her creator, Ruth Handler, wife of the cofounder of Mattel: "Little girls want to pretend to be bigger girls." She was struck by this idea during a trip abroad in the late 1950s, when she noticed the popularity of a shapely, lipsticked and mascaraed Bild Lili doll, a "grown-up" doll based on a character in an adult comic strip. When Handler returned to the United States, she convinced others at Mattel, until then a dollhouse furniture manufacturer, to gamble on her insight: Thus, she became the virtual mother of the world's first teenage doll, Barbie, born on March 9, 1959, and appropriately named for her actual daughter, Barbara. The new doll was casually coiffed in a ponytail, had wide doe eyes (accented by black eyeliner and bright blue shadow) and holes in her feet so she could be conveniently affixed to her accompanying stand. She also wore a strapless bathing suit and a good deal more make-up than most fifties mothers approved of. Mattel quickly responded to criticism by changing her face, but Barbie still languished on toy store shelves until, in desperation, the company started to sponsor commercials on the popular TV program *The Mickey Mouse Club.* The rest is history. From that day to this, little girls worldwide—Barbie is one of only a few dolls with an international following—have dressed, walked, danced, and eventually even "talked" with over one billion Barbies. To put that number into perspective, imagine that all these Barbies and her eventual friends, Ken, Skipper, Francie, Midge, Alan, and on and on, are placed pony-tailed head to tiny toe: They would circle the earth more than seven times.

Barbie is not universally beloved, however. There have been any number of objections to the Barbie concept, some more vocal than others. No amount of Barbie bashing, however, keeps two dolls from being sold every second, or undermined Barbie's role as a miniature paradigm of both femininity and twentieth-century popular culture.

As of 1961, Barbie had a lightweight, hollow body, and though she could initially be purchased as a brunette, a redhead, or a blonde, the blonde was far and away the favorite (which makes the other two rarer and, therefore, more desirable as collectibles). Not surprisingly, Barbie collecting has a great deal to do with hair. By 1963, for example, there was a Fashion Queen Barbie, with a trio of different wigs, and a Bubble-cut Barbie. In 1964, that bubble burst, and Barbie returned to her wholesome ponytail—with swirled bangs, however, not curly bangs. The following year, she became Color Magic Barbie, with

Gentlemen may prefer blondes, but Barbie collectors favor brunettes and redheads.

BARBIE MISSPEAKS

For their innovative Teen Talk Barbie, Mattel's marketers taught a few Barbies to say "Math class is tough!" Feminists took umbrage, and while the firm quickly discontinued that model, the impolitic phrase had already created a frenzy among collectors. Eager to purchase a Barbie doll that was certain to be a rarity, they bought boxes of Teen Talk Barbies that held no clue to what the doll would "say." They had to insert the batteries in order to know if they'd bought a worthless Barbie or a collectible Barbie.

ENVIRONMENTALLY FRIENDLY BARBIE

Hard plastic was the doll material of choice over the last half of the twentieth century, but now its days may be numbered. For years, materials scientists and environmental groups, such as Greenpeace, have condemned the making of dolls with vinyl, which consists of soft PVC plastic, because additives in the PVCs—such as cadmium and other toxins—are harmful to the brain, liver, and reproductive system. These additives can be ingested by children, who sometimes suck on the dolls.

Mattel, Barbie's maker, made news in 1999 when it announced it was moving toward plant-based plastics that are "far more environmentally friendly." Greenpeace's Rick Hind responded, "Plant-based plastics could revolutionize the industry. Children born today can realistically look forward to playing with a PVC-free Barbie that is made of bio-based plastic."

In the meantime, as any collector will tell you, it's best to keep yesterday's Barbies, and other soft plastic dolls, out of the hands of infants.

blond or black hair that could be changed to red, and the year 1965 also marked the first time Barbie could bend her knees. By 1968, Barbie had learned to speak Spanish, as well as dance (the Twist and Turn Barbie had a movable waist).

Advanced Barbie collectors look for the mint-in-box Barbie #1 through #4. The original Barbie can be recognized by either her blond or brunette floss hair, and the copper tubing in her legs that exit through holes in the balls of her feet. This tubing allows her to be securely placed on the prongs of her accompanying posing stand. Number one Barbies are marked "Japan" on the arch of the foot. Barbie #2 was made only for three months in 1959–1960, and looked exactly like the Barbie #1, except that she had no holes in her feet and sported little pearl earrings. She was attached to her stand with a wire that ran up to and under her arms. Barbie #3 has no holes in her feet, either, but because Mattel decided that the earlier models looked slightly too Asian, the firm modified her eyebrows and, for the first time, gave her eye color. (Until that time, she'd had black and white eyes, with black eyeliner.) The #3

Ken, introduced in 1961, has been Barbie's one and only boyfriend.

Barbie of 1960 has blue eyes and blue or brown eyeliner, and a vinyl body that is inclined to go a bit greenish around the earring holes. Barbie #4 is exactly like Barbie #3, except that her stand is slightly different.

Barbie may be a teen doll, but with her extensive wardrobe, she is also the ultimate fashion doll. Today, her elaborate outfits can be the creations of top designers, and her lavish gowns could go to the Academy Awards.

NANCY ANN STORYBOOK DOLLS

The Nancy Ann Storybook dolls reclined in fluffy perfection in their perfectly coordinated polka dot boxes. These too-pretty-to-play-with miniature princesses, most based on characters from children's stories and nursery rhymes, were named for their creator, Nancy Ann Abbott, whose first dolls, circa 1936, were fashioned of painted or sprayed bisque, whereas later models were made of hard plastic.

This Little Bo Peep, a Nancy Ann Storybook doll from the 1950s Fairyland series, may have lost her sheep, but she still wears her original outfit and polka-dot box.

Storybook dolls can be found in sizes from 3½ inches to 7 inches, and they are highly sought-after by collectors, although it can be somewhat difficult to tell which model is which. This is because, although their distinctive boxes were generally labeled with the doll's name, the dolls themselves could all too easily wind up being placed in the wrong box by a harried mother, tag sale supervisor, or collectibles dealer. That is, if the original boxes (so important when it comes to the dolls' value) were saved to begin with.

STEIFF

When we think of Steiff toys, we usually think of plush stuffed animals. And from its founding in 1894, the Steiff company was justifiably famous for making the choicest and cheekiest squirrels, elephants, monkeys, giraffes, and teddy bears ever hugged to shreds by adoring children. Less well known, perhaps, are the Steiff dolls they also produced. These, like the stuffed toys, were well crafted of felt, plush, or velvet. Of very high quality and accordingly very rare, these dolls have embroidered or hand-painted faces with glass button eyes and, often, handsewn seams. Some are "jovial lads and buxom maidens" (as the ads for them once proclaimed), while others are children, golliwogs (soft cloth blackface dolls), clowns, or soldiers. Steiff dolls share with the stuffed animals the same identifying Steiff button in the ear. They can also be recognized by the seam running down the center of the doll's face and the unusually large feet that enable them to stand upright.

A Steiff gypsy doll, circa 1910. Since 1894, the company produced dolls along with the better-known Steiff stuffed animals.

Vogue's 1950s wide-eyed Ginny doll (above right) could be bought with stylish accessories, such as (top to bottom) sunglasses, a school bag, and a miniature suitcase.

VOGUE DOLLS

The 8-inch Ginny doll, introduced by Vogue Dolls, Inc., in 1948, was, until the 1960s, one of the most popular of all play dolls. And perhaps because Vogue was founded as a manufacturer of doll clothing and employed hundreds of home seamstresses over the long course of her popularity, the well-dressed Ginny could have arrived at a lucky child's door with elaborate seasonal wardrobes of up to one hundred outfits and matching bonnets. She also came with useful accessories, including eyeglasses, shovels and pails, inflatable pool toys, and a pet dog with a plaid coat (manufactured by Steiff).

CELEBRITY DOLLS

Few of America's legendary personages, whether military hero, sports great, or movie or television star, have escaped being transformed into a plaything. Such was the fate of Charlie Chaplin and General Douglas MacArthur; Jackie Robinson and Cher; Farrah Fawcett and Jackie Kennedy—not to mention Canada's Dionne quints (see page 263). All became celebrity dolls, and perhaps one reason that these dolls are so attractive to today's collectors is that they are wonderfully easy to date. Collectors all know, for example, that a Soupy Sales

(a Knickerbocker doll from 1965) will be marked 1965 Knickerbocker on the back of its head. This definitely keeps it from being confused with a Soupy Sales from 1967, let alone a Soupy Sales from 1942, when the comedian the doll was based on was still in high school.

Shirley Temple, Judy Garland, and Deanna Durbin, three young movie songstresses of the 1930s, are particularly characteristic of the celebrity genre, and have thousands of devoted collectors. The dolls are described below, in order of their popularity.

SHIRLEY TEMPLE

The Ideal Novelty and Toy Company's composition Shirley Temple doll was created under the watchful eye of little Shirley's mother, who allowed the company to put dimples on her bottom along with the requisite dimples in her cheeks. Ideal Shirley dolls, some $6 million worth of them, ultimately, were marketed in conjunction with several of the child star's films, and were dressed in costumes identical to those in which she appeared, from the knife-pleated dress in *Baby Take a Bow* to the Scots-plaid kilt of *Wee Willie Winkie*. Shirley Temple dolls have been eagerly collected since their introduction, and have also been extensively reproduced in the United States, France, Germany, and Japan. An interesting sidelight on such widespread reproduction is the fact that the celluloid pin worn by the original Shirley Temple doll is considered by collectors to be so important that it has actually been faked.

JUDY GARLAND

Judy collectors don't have quite the array of pretty frocks to choose from that Shirley collectors have, but anyone smitten with her performance in the 1939 film classic *The Wizard of Oz*—and there are surely millions—has a slew of Judy dolls to choose from. Probably the most sought-after is Ideal's 1939 all-composition version, featuring Judy in three sizes (13 to 18 inches), and in a perfectly Dorothy-like dress and coif, with the classic blue-and-white pinafore and white blouse with rickrack trim, her hair separated into neat, distinctive "bunches." Other interpretations of Judy as Dorothy have been produced by Effanbee (1984) and Madame Alexander (early 1990s).

THE REAL DR. EVIL

Captain Action, created by Ideal, had masks and costumes that transformed him into Superman, the Lone Ranger, the Phantom, and Captain America. Of course, Captain Action had an arch-enemy, Dr. Evil, billed as "The Sinister Invader of Earth" (not to be confused with Dr. Evil, nemesis of Austin Powers of movie fame).

The Dr. Evil at the Providence *Antiques Roadshow* was found after being missing in action for 30 years. "It has its accessories," marveled appraiser Gary Sohmers. "I mean, how did you manage to keep the original little ray gun and this little medallion?"

The owner replied, "It's been sitting at the bottom of a toy box."

Because Captain Action was reissued a few years ago, the value of the original isn't superhuman. It's a still respectable $600 to $800.

DEANNA DURBIN

Deanna Durbin, an adolescent with the operatic voice of a grown woman, was a remarkably popular movie star in the 1930s and 1940s, inspiring a doll in 1938. Created by Ideal of composition and 21 inches tall, she is a rarity marked "Deanna Durbin/Ideal Doll" on the back of the head. Although the real Deanna's career ended in the late forties, her fan base remains strong, as does the search, by collectors, for her doll.

ACTION FIGURES

Their inspired nomenclature allowing young boys to play unabashedly with dolls, the "action figures" of the mid-twentieth century replaced the toy soldiers and cowboys and Indians that had skirmished for years in every little boy's toy chest.

HASBRO AND G.I. JOE

In the 1960s, the G.I. Joe "action figure" became Hasbro's answer to Mattel's Barbie. Named for the archetypal hero of the film *The Story of G.I. Joe,* the Joe doll, like his female counterpart, was an adult. Like her, he had articulated body parts, and his handsome face was perfectly generic. (He bore a striking resemblance, it has been noted, to the young Al Gore.) Hasbro's Joe also had several friends, including a Frogman, a Green Beret, and the admirable Nurse Jane; but he also had enemies, Japanese Imperial soldiers among them. To combat the latter, he came equipped with assorted vehicles and weapons—almost five hundred auxiliary items altogether. If dolls of the twentieth century are miniature reflections of societal trends, it is worth noting that the first black G.I. Joes were made in the mid-sixties, a time of racial turmoil, whereas the first anatomically correct doll was a few years away. Joe eventually acquired more hair—flocked hair—and in the 1970s (not surprisingly), a beard. He became less militaristic at the same time the country did, retiring from the military and going on to indulge in superfitness and extreme sports, such as mountain climbing and deep-sea diving. It was not peace that finally killed G.I. Joe, however. He was done in by the 1978 increase in the price of petroleum, a crucial component of his vinyl and plastic parts.

Intriguingly, some of the doll's many outfits—the uniforms of air cadets, MPs, and Annapolis midshipmen—are more highly valued by collectors than Joe himself. The earliest G.I. Joes, the 1964 models, are marked on the lower back with the letters "T.M."

IDEAL'S CAPTAIN ACTION AND DR. EVIL

Ideal and other companies retailed heroic action figures that successfully competed with the great G.I. Joe. Captain Action was one star, and was perhaps unique in owning a closet full of clothes—masks and costumes and accoutrements—all of which enabled imaginative, full-of-beans American boys to convert the Captain, with just a change of costume, into other, equally exciting dolls: into Captain America, for instance, or the Phantom. Helpfully, 1960s children trying to cope with the occasional destructive tendency could easily turn to another Ideal action figure, the do-gooder captain's nemesis—the no-good Dr. Evil.

MEGO

The Mego character dolls and superheroes are 8-inch action figures, produced from the early 1970s until 1983, when the firm failed. While Mego thrived, however, it created scores of beautifully outfitted dolls and accessories modeled after comic-book heroes and film and television characters, including those from *The Wizard of Oz* and the mildly wizardly Mr. Spock and his fellow Trekkers; and celebrities, such as a gaudily dressed Cher, Sonny (who sells, today, for more than his mate), Joe Namath, and the all-but-forgotten John Boy Walton. In effect, the Mego dolls were mini-versions of Hasbro's G.I. Joe and Ideal's Captain Action, products of the toy industry's belated but happy realization that a little doll could be sold for the same price as a big one.

Action Pilot G.I. Joe came with an orange jumpsuit and dog tags.

I'm worth more than you, babe: Mego's Sonny today sells for far more than Cher.

CAMPBELL'S KIDS LOOKALIKES

The owner of these dolls appeared on the *Antiques Roadshow* in Madison, Wisconsin, and explained that the pair had been a gift to her mother, though her mother couldn't remember ever having played with them. The owner noted that the side of the box was marked with the date

November 12, 1935, but had no other information.

Appraiser Richard Wright identified the pair as Dolly Dimple and Bobby Bounce, characters that were popular in the 1930s. The dolls are made of painted bisque—and designed by Grace Wiederseim. If they look familiar, it is because Wiederseim, who was also known as Grace Drayton, is also responsible for creating the Campbell's Kids in 1904. Wright appraised this pair in their original box at $3,000 to $4,000.

ADVERTISING DOLLS

A popular and distinct category of collectible dolls, advertising dolls started as commissioned promotional figures. A few, notably Buddy Lee and the Campbell's Kids, had so much child appeal that they were eventually manufactured and sold in the mass market.

BUDDY LEE

Originally, Buddy Lee dolls were made by the Lee Company for a Minneapolis department store to be mini-models for Lee's clothing. Introduced in the early 1920s, these baby-faced Buddys—with their neatly tucked-in shirts, chubby cheeks, impish smiles, and side-glancing eyes—captured the mischievous look little boys get when a tempting mud puddle catches their eye. The dolls charmed the public. Other stores wanted them, and soon it was clear that kids did, too. Lee began selling these 12-inch composition Buddys on their own, and Buddy was so successful, he went to work for other companies, including Coca-Cola (in the uniform of a delivery-truck driver and the standard bottling-plant outfit), as a gas jockey for Shell, Texaco, and Phillips 66, for railroads and John Deere. In 1949, Buddy went from composition to hard plastic and grew to be 13 inches tall. Black Buddy Lees, called Black Magic dolls, are also collectible.

Adorable macho Buddy Lee in his spiffy Lee Rider Cowboy Pants.

THE CAMPBELL'S KIDS

The 1905 brainchild of illustrator Grace Drayton, the illustrated Kids' original "job" was to sell the soup, but they were far too cute and salable to remain two-dimensional soup salesman for long, so Campbell's licensed them to Horsman (see page 277). By 1910 the Campbell's Kids had become the archetypal advertising dolls.

Thereafter, they were also somewhat inadvertent "traveling" salesmen, for while the Horsman firm produced the first Campbell's Kids dolls, competition among doll makers to manufacture these enormously popular toys seems to have been fierce. In 1928, for example, the American Character Doll Company, founded after World War I, won the rights away from Horsman to become their sole manufacturer. Unmarked American Character Doll "Kids" composition dolls dressed in the chef's clothes made famous in the advertisements can be recognized because they are just a trifle pigeon-toed. Some of the dolls made between 1910 to 1925 can be identified by their sateen bodies and horizontally striped sateen legs. When the Ideal Company acquired Horsman in the 1940s, the latter firm produced Campbell's Kids once again, though it sold the rights, ultimately, to a Canadian firm, Dee and Cee. From Horsman to American, to Ideal, to Dee and Cee, everyone loved those Kids.

The Campbell's Kids are the ancestors of food advertising dolls such as Mr. Peanut (the Planter spokesnut) and the Pillsbury Doughboy, who, in his pillowy way, resembles them remarkably (see the Advertising Memorabilia chapter, page 33).

Spokesdolls: The Campbell's Kids were a hit in themselves, and sold countless cans of soup.

SPECIALTY DOLLS

Four idiosyncratic areas of doll collecting are worth mentioning, for they have many fans. These include dolls by doll designer Bernard Ravca, googly-eyed dolls (those close cousins of the Kewpie), half-dolls, and bisque nodders and immobiles.

RAVCA DOLLS

Bernard Ravca, a French doll maker, was visiting the United States, exhibiting his unusual, sculptural dolls, when his homeland fell to the Nazis. In sudden and unexpected exile, he chose to continue crafting his idiosyncratic soft cloth dolls in

Ravca dolls portrayed people of all ages and all walks of life. Here, a smiling old woman peddles her wares.

A TELLTALE SWITCH

Two beautiful painted oilcloth dolls from the Martha Chase doll company were brought to *Antiques Roadshow* when it visited Providence. The girl doll, sold as "Little Nell," was appraised by Richard Wright at $2,000 to $3,000. The second, a boy doll, was worth less than $150, yet both had intriguing stories.

The visitor's mother worked at the Chase factory in Pawtucket, Rhode Island, in its final years. The rare "Little Nell" doll, from a set of Charles Dickens dolls, was given to her by Bob Chase, a descendant of Martha Chase, who founded the company in the 1880s. The boy doll was made especially for the visitor's son by his grandmother, who told him that she switched the left and right foot so that he would know that it was *his* doll.

America. The heads of Ravca dolls (fashioned from cotton, composition, or even dried apples) were covered in silk stockinette; the bodies were stuffed with straw (or sometimes, chemically treated bread crumbs); and the dolls frequently bore aged or thoughtful faces with exceedingly lifelike expressions. Full of eccentric humanity, Ravca's dolls portrayed people from all walks of life, from gnarled peasants to international politicos. Ravca made dolls in several sizes, and they represented characters as different from one another as the doomed Marguerite from Gounod's *Faust,* General Lafayette, and John D. Rockefeller. Their soft bodies are formed on wire armatures, and they are dressed in native or characteristic costume. Unfortunately, because of the delicacy of the silk with which their faces are sheathed, they are easily damaged, especially around protuberant areas, like their noses and chins. Collectors look particularly for the larger dolls.

GOOGLY-EYED DOLLS

"Googly" eyes are flirty eyes, impishly glancing sidewise— possibly at the hordes of collectors who yearn to own the dolls that have them. Kewpie-like in appearance, moderate-to-good quality googly-eyed bisque dolls, or dolls with composition "mask" faces set into cloth bodies, were made primarily between 1912 and 1938 and are rarities. "Roguish" or "goo-goo" eyes were the trademark of cartoon character Barney Google, the inspiration for the popular song, "Barney Google, with the goo-goo-googly eyes." Amusing and impish dolls with this endearing feature were made by many of the good European doll firms, like Gebruder Heubach, Max Handwerk, and Armand Marseille, and are available in several models: a toddler doll, a baby doll, an Uncle Sam doll, and even a bellhop.

An Armand Marseille googly with a particularly sweet expression and perfectly preserved hat, dress, and shoes.

HALF-DOLLS

Known variously as novelty dolls, flapper dolls, bed dolls, and boudoir dolls, these sofa, chaise, and dressing-table ornaments were intended for grown-ups, not children. They were manufactured mainly between 1915 and 1930 (although they continued to be made into the 1950s) in France, Italy, and the United States. They were purely for display, and first came to popularity in the 1920s. Their heads and upper bodies—the best were formed of china or bisque—are those of grown women, whose faces express a post–World War I knowingness mixed with a Roaring Twenties pseudodecadence. Many wore typical, flapper-style bobs and featured heart-shaped, bright red lips from which occasionally dangled a rakish cigarette. Others had decidedly Latin hair and clothes, while still others were fashioned after historic figures, such as Marie Antoinette. Often, the ceramic torsos of both types of half-dolls are attached to powder-puff or pin-cushion "skirts"; those that wear actual skirts, however, reveal beneath them tiny high-heeled shoes on impossibly tiny feet.

To attach the skirt to the upper, doll portion, the bottommost edge of the doll's half-body was pierced around its perimeter with small holes. These allowed the torso to be sewn to the skirt, generally a tour de force of silk or tulle. Boudoir dolls can be made of wax, composition, china, or simple cloth, but they are always dressed flamboyantly (unless, as often happens, they've somehow lost their skirt).

Peculiar to half-dolls is the fact that, although the quality of the material they are made from certainly affects their value, their desirability depends on the positioning of their arms. The doll whose arms extend out completely from her body is most valuable. If the hands touch the body, but the elbows are akimbo, she's worth rather less. Least desirable of all is the doll whose arms are molded to her sides. It might be reasonable to assume that fragility—the likelihood of those extended arms surviving intact—accounts for this distinction, but it may simply be a quirk of doll collectors.

For display, not play: This elegantly attired half-doll was intended for grown-ups.

Arms and hands stand free of the body of this flapper half-doll, making her far more desirable than even her make-up will make her.

SO HUGGABLE

Käthe Kruse dolls are rare visitors to the *Antiques Roadshow,* and when appraiser Tim Luke came across this one in Austin, Texas, he was delighted to see it. Käthe Kruse was a German housewife who hand-crafted her first doll in 1905 as a Christmas present for her daughter. Five years later, the young mother, with the help of a painter and five seamstresses, was creating dolls in her living room. Soon after, she acquired her first big client in America: New York's FAO Schwarz. The famous toy store helped establish her as a doll maker and allowed her to distribute her wares nation-wide. Today, the Käthe Kruse Doll Studio remains the oldest doll manufacturer in operation in Germany.

The owner is a collector who inher-

ited the doll from an aunt she had seen only a few times in her life. A large collection of clothes, which she also brought in, came with the doll, which was still in its original box.

There are several characteristics of

note on a Käthe Kruse doll, beginning with the meticulously hand-painted features of the face. The clothes, too, were made with great attention to detail. Most unusual, however, is the material used to make the body. Käthe Kruse's goal was to make dolls that were huggable and warm, unlike the cold bisque dolls that were popular at the time. To that end, all of her dolls are stuffed with reindeer hair. When you hold her dolls close, they feel real.

This doll also has the original tag, which, in most cases, is thrown away. The tag is marked with reversed Ks, indicating that it was most likely made in the 1920s. The doll itself contains the Käthe Kruse stamp on the bottom of one foot, as well as a serial number.

Taking into account the box, the condition of the doll, and all the wonderful clothes, the doll was valued at $2,000 to $4,000.

A rare breed: Animal nodders (like the sleepy pup above) are harder to find than their human counterparts.

BISQUE IMMOBILES AND NODDERS

Sold originally for mere pennies, and especially popular in the 1920s, bisque immobiles and nodders are exceptionally small dolls, somewhere between 2 and 7 inches tall, made wholly of bisque. Most examples were manufactured in Germany (and are so marked), with their "clothes" molded on their bodies. Immobiles, as the name implies, have no moveable parts. Nodders are immobiles that nod their heads, a variation achieved by attaching head to body with a piece of elastic running up through a hole at the top of the head and knotting it there. Animal nodders dressed in molded clothes are considered by collectors to be more desirable than people nodders. Both immobiles and nodders are often decorated with carelessly applied paint that has not been fired on the bisque. Such "cold paint," as it's termed, wears away easily, making those dolls that retain their original paint in perfect condition more collectible than those that don't.

DOLLHOUSES & ACCESSORIES

Mickey McGuire, an immobile comic figure, stands in a stooping position with his hands on his knees. His frowning mouth has a hole for a cigarette.

Today there is absolutely no doll-related item that avid collectors won't buy—from pocketbooks to shoes to vintage photographs of children just *playing* with dolls. There are scores of enthusiastic collectors for G.I. Joe's every martial outfit, as there were for the bag of Barbie's shoes (marked Japan, not Taiwan) that recently changed hands at auction for $500. Still, along with their camouflage and their slingbacks, dolls need shelter: a place to hang those perfectly-pressed (original) clothes, a place to garage their sleek red Ferraris, a place to put up their tiny heels. That's where the dollhouse comes in.

The forerunners of the modern dollhouse were seventeenth- and eighteenth-century cabinets that opened to reveal beautifully furnished miniature rooms. Some historians speculate that these cabinets were originally made to teach housekeeping skills to little girls, but whatever their initial function, such rooms obviously needed to be furnished with rich, finely crafted miniature furnishings, each piece carefully carved to scale. And they were. Yet this is exactly what distinguishes the "miniature" from dollhouse furniture, which may also be attractive and made to scale, but which is basically an inexpensive (at least when new) toy, specifically made to be played with by children. Collectors of miniatures, which were never meant to be played with, differentiate themselves from dollhouse collectors and tend, particularly, to disdain furnishings that are machine-made. But real dollhouse furniture has a homey appeal—machine-made or not—and a distinct and collectible charm.

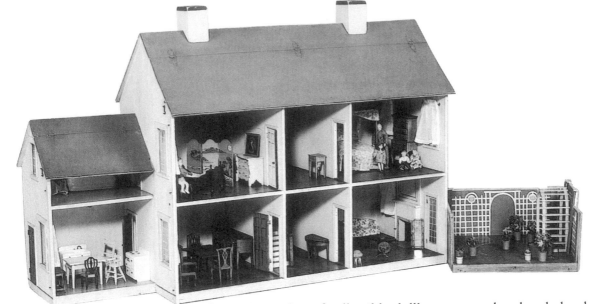

TynieToy's New England Townhouse of the 1920s was a beautifully made and sophisticated miniature copy. This example came with an attached garden and two fireplaces, and was fitted with miniature electric lights.

A number of collectible dollhouses were handmade by doting fathers for Christmas or birthday gifts, which means they are sometimes clumsy or crude, although often they're very finely made, especially when constructed by loving architects for lucky daughters. Commercially made dollhouses, however, are those most sought-after by dollhouse collectors. As with all mass-produced collectibles, examples marked with the maker's name are particularly valued. Toy companies such as TynieToy, R. Bliss Manufacturing Company, McLoughlin Brothers, and A. Schoenhut Company all made popular dollhouses and labeled them, as well.

Since about 1870, most dollhouses have been made on a scale of one inch to one foot, and their furnishings have been made to the same specifications. But the commercial dollhouse itself was never meant to be an architecturally accurate toy. Rather, it was an imaginative recreation of a particular style. Thus, a Tudor-style dollhouse or a bungalow, instead of always imitating the common eight-room dollhouse configuration, might have been manufactured in as many as six different sizes with any number of rooms. Most, however, contained at least four to six rooms, often connected by hinged doors. Although the rumor persists that, like the seventeenth- and eighteenth-century cabinets, such toys were intended to be "instructional" tools, little girls were far more likely to be absorbing the finer points of interior decorating than of cleaning, curtain ironing, or window washing. In fact, it's probable that battalions of today's interior designers first learned their

This two-story Victorian dollhouse opens to reveal four fully furnished and elaborately appointed rooms.

trade on a dollhouse—in all likelihood, a dollhouse made of fiberboard or metal with a beautifully lithographed façade—a façade that reproduced, after a fashion, the popular architecture of its time.

Large, detailed dollhouses with brilliantly lithographed paper exteriors were first made in the United States by R. Bliss, founded in 1832, and these are enthusiastically collected today. Between 1889 and 1914, Bliss created almost fifty types of dollhouse—some quite tiny, some more than two feet tall.

From 1917 to 1925, Schoenhut, the toy manufacturer, marketed a popular one-and-one-half story bungalow of fiberboard, wood, and glass, with stenciled details, embossed "brick" or "stone" elements, and wood corner posts. It also sold "mansions" made of the same materials. (Schoenhut houses were usually labeled on the base, the foundation, or the floor.) Early in the century, McLoughlin Brothers—better known, perhaps, for its gorgeously lithographed games—manufactured a highly successful folding dollhouse.

TynieToy, a small American company that flourished in the 1930s, employed local craftsmen to recreate perfect New England buildings, from farmhouses to townhouses to grandish Nantucket sea captain's houses complete with widow's walks. TynieToy dollhouses were fitted for electricity, and some were even equipped with working fountains. The interiors were furnished with copies of Chippendale, Sheraton, and Hepplewhite furniture, and all were very expensive. In the 1930s, TynieToy charged $145 for a rooming house, an additional $100 for its furniture, and $25 for a garden. If it seems astonishing that a market existed during the

A. Schoenhut Company's large two-room wooden dollhouse.

Dollhouses were often furnished with tiny, to-scale copies of fine antiques, among them these 1920s examples.

Depression era for such a luxury, that is because throughout its brief existence, passionate dollhouse collectors and wealthy, adoring parents were TynieToy's chief clientele. Ultimately, the postwar technology of injection molding and plastics made steel, fiberboard, and even TynieToy's luxury dollhouses obsolete.

DOLLHOUSE FURNISHINGS

The well-appointed dollhouse should be decorated with furnishings appropriate to the architecture of the house. A colonial house, for instance, is definitely at its best when furnished with Chippendale furniture; a Victorian cottage ought to have Victorian furniture—but nothing too dressy, for it is just a cottage. (As with real houses, however, both types should be allowed a few "older" pieces—furnishings inherited from Grandma.) All furniture should be to the scale of the house, and if European dollhouse furniture from the 1930s can be found, a dollhouse of any style can be decorated with some of the most beautifully detailed miniature objects made in the twentieth century: chests, for instance, with dovetailed, moveable drawers, sewing machines with working mechanized parts, and clocks with articulated hands and swinging pendulums. Although plastics have made dollhouse furnishings cheaper and more disposable, collectors still prefer to buy the earlier, well-crafted pieces with the cunning moving parts—the cabinet with doors that open and close, for example, or the more unusual items: the cast-iron ironing boards by Kilgore that currently bring around $20 each, or the 1920 Tootsietoy metal tea cart that recently sold for $25. Paradoxically, a complete ten-piece porcelain miniature tea set can be purchased today for less than $10.

Chapter Eight

WRISTWATCHES

Watch collectors are inclined to believe that vintage watches are inherently superior to watches being made today, that they offer better value. And, they may be right. For starters, consider that old watches offer decades of choice in design, manufacturer, and function. This means that anyone who appreciates old wristwatches can—by carefully picking through the nearly one-hundred-year history of the commercial wristwatch—find one (or more) styles to love.

Like other collectibles, however, vintage watches (and modern watches, as well) are in thrall to the gods of fashion. Clothing styles, home furnishings, and industrial design are capricious and influential. Not so long ago, for example, the rectangular yellow-gold watch was *the* watch that collectors had to have. But, by the first decade of the twenty-first century, with the renewal of interest in mid-twentieth-century styles, the round, white-gold watch had become, unexpectedly, the *new* new thing.

And while one might not think that the traditionally male and basically conservative pursuit of wristwatch collecting would be quite so subject to fashion, the truth is that today's collectors do seem to expect their watches to transmit subliminal messages like: I'm sporty; I'm eccentric; I'm discreet; I'm rich. Not so, however, in the field of women's vintage wristwatches, which are generally smaller and without the muscle of interesting complications (mechanisms that do more than tell

Top: A 1960s Baume & Mercier cushion-shaped wristwatch. Above: A circa 1947 Rolex chronograph with three subsidiary dials, an outer scale for date, an inner scale (calibrated for tachometer), and windows for day and month.

A square antimagnetic Rolex chronograph from the 1930s with two subsidiary dials.

the time of day; see page 308). Until recently, in fact, women's wristwatches have been consigned to the realm of jewelry rather than to the more scholarly realms of serious watch-dom.

Avid watch collectors are predominantly male and mostly interested in collecting men's styles. Some search for the products of only a single manufacturer; a few are passionate about electronic watch technology, buying only electronic watches. Many make their purchases on the basis of beauty (always subjective) or design (less so), always combined with as fine and desirable a movement as they can afford. Still others enjoy owning concept watches like the Tank watch, inspired by a weapon of war—the tank—that metamorphosed into an object of beauty, or watches that have romantic associations: engraved sentiments on the back of the case, for example.

YOU'VE COME A LONG WAY, BABY

Women's watches are often classified as jewelry and, consequently, are only of minor interest to serious watch collectors. Over the years, many women's watches have been scrapped—sold for the value of their precious metals or stones. Recently, however, some of the finest women's watches (Patek Philippe, Cartier, and Rolex among them) have attracted some enthusiasts, as have a select few of the less-expensive watches (Waltham, Bulova, and Hamilton). The watches of these last three manufacturers share stylistic details with their more costly sisters, and can probably still be found in

Women's wristwatches can be jewel-encrusted or sporty. From left, an Art Deco Cartier wristwatch with diamonds; a diamond-enhanced Patek Philippe watch with a cabochon gemstone bracelet; a classic Cartier Tank.

boxes of old watches at flea markets—for flea-market prices.

If you are rooting around in tangles of old wristwatches, keep an eye out for strong design—design that is typical of its era. Of particular interest are Art Deco–era watches—those with highly geometric shapes and calibre-cut stones. These look like stylish mini skyscrapers lying on the wrist. Also of interest are the industrial looking, multicolored gold cocktail watches from the forties and fifties—mainly those with scrollwork cases and convex crystal bubble faces. Some models have related watch bracelets, or have the watch dial itself hidden beneath a hinged cover of gold and stones.

A watch made by Rolex (see page 317), one of the most significant manufacturers in the history of the development of the wristwatch, appeared on the Tulsa *Antiques Roadshow,* and like many family watches, came with its own colorful legend.

The owner's father had been given it at a party thrown by an eccentric Tulsa oilman in the 1940s. His parties were so lavish that *baskets* of Rolex watches were set out as party favors—or so the story goes.

The current owner inherited his father's watch and wore it regularly until he was in a car accident and ended up in the hospital—without the watch. He asked his sister to go to the scene of the accident to see if she could find it. On arrival at the scene, she opened the car door and almost stepped on the watch! Since then, the owner has kept his watch in a vault.

A 1950s Rolex Oyster Perpetual Date model with a lizard strap. Most of these wristwatches have a magnified "cyclops eye" over the date window to make it easier to read.

Antiques Roadshow appraiser Kevin Zavian identified the watch as an Oyster Perpetual bubble-back. Rolex Oysters, introduced in 1926, were the first truly waterproof watches, and perpetual models were self-winding if worn every day. (The mechanism that allowed the watch to be self-winding, a tiny weight on a tiny pendulum, was accommodated in the convex "bubble-back.")

This high-quality watch has twenty-six jewels to reduce friction between the gears—many decent watches have only fifteen—and the serial number indicates that it was manufactured in 1944 (so the story of the oilman's party could be true). It retains its original black dial with radium numerals and hands. While most watches of this period have been retouched or refinished, which greatly decreases their value, this one is exactly as it was the day it was made—which underscores the craftsmanship of its manufacture, because it withstood an accident and time in the street! Its fine condition encouraged Zavian to value this watch at approximately $6,000.

TIME SAVED

A visitor to the New Orleans *Antiques Roadshow* brought in her great-grandmother's "watch necklace," a small watch on a chain.

Appraiser Jonathan Snellenburg dated the necklace to the 1920s. "It's not fine jewelry, like Cartier, but was made to catch the wave of Art Deco," Snellenburg said. "These were a bit like the Swatches of their day." The watch necklace's case is sterling silver and the decorations around the watch include synthetic sapphires and colorful enamels. Commented Snellenburg, "You can wear it to the ball with-

out worrying about losing it."

"I keep it in a safe-deposit box," the visitor said of the necklace, valued at between $1,500 and $2,000. Snellenburg encouraged her to take it out and wear it, at least once in a while. "This was made to be used."

A BRIEF HISTORY

A rectangular 18K gold dress watch with luminescent Arabic numerals and a subsidiary dial for the second hand, manufactured by Patek Philippe & Co. for Tiffany in 1927. Company records show that this watch was sold in 1929.

Portable timekeeping began with Peter Henlein, a young German locksmith who devised the brilliant and justly famed "Nuremberg Egg" in the early 1500s. Henlein's invention was, as its name implies, egg shaped. It kept time badly, and another century and a half had to pass before a portable watch was invented that was mechanically sophisticated enough to accomplish the tricky task of counting the minutes. It was a century and a half after that—1810, in fact—when a watch made specifically to be worn on a wrist was created by the great French firm Breguet, purportedly for the queen of Naples. Interestingly, while women tied pretty watches to their wrists, such frivolities were scarcely considered suitable for men's wear. Men carried sturdy, dependable pocket watches.

The wristwatch we know today evolved from a small pocket watch that late-nineteenth-century French artillery officers, needing to time the flights of gun shells, managed to strap to their wrists. The entrepreneurial Swiss watchmaking community, on learning of this contrivance, began manufacturing wristwatches for European army officers during World War I.

American watchmaker Robert Ingersoll decided that American doughboys had an equal right to be on time. By adding a pair of wire lugs and a strap to his standard ladies'

WRISTWATCH SHAPES

Wristwatches today come in a variety of shapes, but the first were *round,* the shape of a classic pocket watch. The *cushion shape,* a rounded square, developed from the round watch. With the growing popularity of the wristwatch came square and rectangular shapes, and then a multitude of others.

Round Patek Philippe with Breguet-style numerals, from 1948.

watch, he invented the first affordable commercial wristwatch. His support for the war effort didn't end there. Ingersoll concluded that there might also be considerable military advantage to being able to tell time in the dark, so he coated the numbers on his wristwatches with a mixture of radium and paint to make them luminous. (This refinement lasted well into the 1940s, when radium, suddenly discovered to be toxic and dangerous to those who applied it to the watch face, was banned.)

After World War I, that useful round wristwatch shape was joined by all the cushion shapes, squares, and rectangles we have come to know and enjoy, and within fifteen years of the end of the war, the pocket watch pretty much vanished. By 1935, nearly nine tenths of the watches being manufactured throughout the world were wristwatches. Housed in gold, platinum, steel, silver, and gold-filled cases, the modern wristwatch offered an infinite variety of gears and wheels, numbers of jewels, the occasional gem enhancement, and what watch collectors lovingly refer to as "complications" (see page 308). As the century progressed, such refinements became more complex and watches became more dust- and water-resistant as well. Near the end of the century, the wristwatch devolved into the highly accurate, but entirely uninteresting, quartz watch—so easy to maintain and so potentially disposable that an entire watch "wardrobe" was, amazingly, within the price range of the man and woman in the street.

For collectors, three periods in the development of the wristwatch are particularly important.

TIPS
from the experts

Sig Shonholtz, an *Antiques Roadshow* appraiser, learned watchmaking at his father's knee. His experience in taking apart and putting together watches, he believes, gives him special insight into the collecting of vintage watches.

For thirty years, Shonholtz has heard the same question: "What's the best watch?" His response, "The answer depends on the criteria you choose to judge your watch by. The 'best watch' is unquestionably the most dependable, the most durable, the most accurate, and most beautiful watch you can buy for the least amount of money. If the model you prefer meets all these specification, you will have bought the best watch there is. The best watch for formal occasions and the best snorkeling watch have different criteria."

Shonholtz particularly likes three watch companies of the 1930s, 1940s, and 1950s: Hamilton, Longines, and Gruen, whose watches sold for $50 to $250 when new; they sell now in the still reasonable range of $200 to $800. "If properly serviced, they'll last a lifetime," he says. "These companies made some unattractive models, but most of what they did was sophisticated and beautiful. They were wearable for both work and dress, and the average watchmaker can easily service them."

Cushion-shaped Rolex Oyster Army model, from the 1930s.

Square Bulova "Flip," from the 1950s.

Tonneau-shaped 1930s Cartier with curved sides and straight top and bottom.

WRISTWATCH CARE

Wristwatch repair and restoration can be expensive, especially for watches that have complications or complex dials, so it is important to take good care of your collection. If a watch needs to be repaired, never attempt to do it yourself, and be sure the watchmaker you bring it to is expert in handling watches by maker.

Wristwatches should always be protected from sudden changes in temperature and stored in a cool, dry environment that is as dust free as possible. If you are not wearing your watches regularly and must store them, keep in mind that they need to be wound three or four times a year, because the oil that lubricates watch mechanisms can dry out and harden, literally "gumming up the works."

British watchmaker John Harwood patented the first self-winding wristwatch in 1923. His watches—without crowns—cannot be wound manually. Early models were set by turning the back, later ones by turning the bezel.

MILITARY WATCHES OF WORLD WAR I

The first wristwatches were made for military use. During World War I, when much of Europe was contending in the trenches, neutral Switzerland was in a fine position to focus on providing the fighting men with wristwatches. The enormous military contracts awarded during that era enabled many small Swiss houses to make watches for troops while simultaneously consolidating their own reputations. Such military watches were of efficient, not to say minimalist, design, and most had useful subsidiary dials, like day or date indications. For these reasons, certain groups of collectors are very enthusiastic about the prototypical cushion-shaped, steel-cased military watches from World War I, often paying unusually large sums for unrestored, mint examples. In America, naturally, it is American military watches that are popular. In Great Britain, collectors are particularly enthusiastic about Swiss watches made for the U.K. market.

INNOVATIONS OF THE 1920s AND 1930s

Within the decade following World War I, as peace and prosperity returned to America and Europe, an innovative horology developed to capitalize on and exploit this happy return to the good life. Several international firms tumbled over each other in their haste to provide improvements on the wristwatch, the latest toy.

In 1923, the British watchmaker John Harwood created the first self-winding wristwatch. Within three years, the Swiss watch manufacturer Blancpain had developed a worldwide market for its own self-winding watch (based on Harwood's design). Then Rolex, in 1926, produced the famous Oyster watch, the world's first waterproof watch. By 1930, with the Oyster Perpetual, this savvy Swiss firm had discovered a way to manufacture a revolutionary wristwatch that was both waterproof and self-winding.

In 1933, the first shock-protection device, Incabloc, was created, and in the same year, the old Ingersoll company—

still in business today and still an imaginative marketer of popular products—created the first Mickey Mouse character watch, a smashing and perennial success (for more on character watches, see Entertainment Memorabilia, page 351). All this occurred within fifteen years of World War I's end.

POST–WORLD WAR II HIGH-TECH WATCHES

The close of World War II, however, saw the public's delight in such mechanical innovations wind down and virtually stop. The cause was simple enough—the advent of electronic and quartz movements. Even before these developments, however, most American watch companies had discovered that they couldn't compete with the Swiss; in fact, they could produce a less expensive, more dependable watch simply by buying movements in Switzerland and housing them in American cases. It was less costly to import than it was to manufacture. Combined with popular interest in electronic gadgetry, this factor created a public and manufacturing community that was less and less interested in gears, moon phases, and wheels.

This is not to say that fine-quality mechanical watches weren't made during the era, first among them, according to Sig Shonholtz, the 1950 Guillermin Mollet that he himself wears. ("One of the most beautiful watches ever produced.") Nonetheless, such specialty items were easily overshadowed at the time by novelties like Hamilton's 1957 electronic watch, "the first one ever made," according to one authoritative source—or the Bulova Watch Company's 1960 electronic watch, "the first one ever made," claims another source, equally authoritative, offering readers a lesson in the scholarship of so many vintage objects, says Shonholtz, in that both dates are right and both dates are wrong. The Hamilton model was indeed manufactured in 1957, and many thousands were sold, but it was plagued by problems and frequently returned. Consequently, the 1960 Bulova, incorporating a transistorized circuit, actually makes a legitimate claim to being "first," for it was not until the second watch came out that the kinks in the electronic watch were finally eliminated.

A classic Ingersoll Mickey Mouse character watch from 1933, the first year of manufacture. Macy's in New York reported selling 11,000 of these immensely popular watches in one day.

Shown is the visible movement of the 1960s Bulova Accutron Spaceview. Accutron models with invisible dials started as a sales tool for jewelers, but were so popular that Bulova began to produce them for sale.

Geneva-based watchmaker Franck Muller—known as the "master of complications"—makes timepieces today for those who prefer pre-quartz craftsmanship and mechanical elegance.

There is little doubt, however, that in 1960 the Swiss were the first to develop the quartz wristwatch, a revolutionary timepiece with no moving parts. But the Japanese Seiko LCD watch with a digital display was hard on their heels, and it began to seem that quartz flash and dazzle would do little to maintain the health of the old-line European watchmaking firms. As Japanese watch producers thrived throughout the 1970s, many Swiss companies foundered, 80 percent, in fact, having to file for bankruptcy. The crowning blow to the sober, steady craft of traditional watchmaking may have been the Swatch watch—a product of the early 1980s that was destined to make time, frequently wasted and always fleeting, a truly throwaway thing.

It was only reasonable to assume that there would be a reaction to the quartz and digital revolution, and there was. Ingenious contemporary watchmakers like Franck Muller (once the boy genius of Patek Philippe) are once again creating mechanical watches: laboriously handcrafting pinions and fashioning elegant gears for watches that need to be wound and don't enjoy water sports at all. There are also new materials for collectors to lust after; the titanium-vanadium alloys and materials such as those used for the Radio Vision I watch, with its shell of four thousand ground diamonds—industrial grade, one hopes.

In the following pages, you'll become acquainted with the materials wristwatches are made of, how they came to be popular, and the methods collectors use to determine which ones they want to own. You will discover the watches that are currently collectible, learn a little about the manufacturers that produced them, and find out how to distinguish the run-of-the-mill timekeeper from the one that is timeless.

EVALUATING WRISTWATCHES

Basically, there are two types of wristwatches: mechanical watches and battery-driven, or quartz, watches. Manual-wind watches (those the wearer winds by hand) and automatic, or self-winding, watches are both mechanical watches. Battery-driven watches are, of course, powered by

The Vocabulary of Watches

The new collector may be somewhat daunted by the unfamiliar vocabulary of watch collecting, so here are a few key definitions of the parts of a watch.

The movement of a perpetual calendar wristwatch with moon phases and twenty jewels, made by Patek Philippe & Co. in 1944.

MOVEMENT

The timekeeping mechanism, the ticking heart of the watch. It is mechanical, with gears, a balance wheel, and moving parts. (A quartz watch has no movement. Instead it has a module.) To reveal the movement, very carefully open the back of the watch.

JEWELS

The synthetic rubies or sapphires that, because they are more durable than metals, are used in mechanical watches to reduce the friction at junctures where there would otherwise be metal-to-metal contact. Jewels enhance accuracy and dependability in watches, most of which have fifteen or seventeen. Some superior models and those with complications can have as many as twenty-six.

INCABLOC

A factory term for the cloverleaf-shaped mechanism devised to shield the heart of the watch. Basically, this is a shock absorber, used to protect the watch works.

CALIBER

The size of the watch movement.

EBAUCHES

The boilerplates of the watch industry. *Ebauches* are the watch movements at their most basic—blanks, essentially—bought by many watch manufacturers to be embellished with their proprietary complications and refinements.

A 1930s chronograph with a black face, made by Breitling.

FACE (DIAL)

Displays the numbers, minute tracks, and hour markers that indicate the time. It may be made of enamel, metal, paper, or plastic.

NUMBERS

Numbers can be indicated in several ways—as Roman numerals, as Arabic numerals, sticks (batons), or as combinations of these. Some watches have no numbers at all or make use of a single image to mark a number, like the Movado Museum watch (see page 316).

This 1940s Vacheron & Constantine watch has Roman and dot numerals applied to a black face.

HANDS

Indicate the hour, minutes, and seconds. They are usually metal.

WATCHCASE

Offers protective housing for the movement. It may be made of steel, gold, or silver-plated metal, plastic, gold, silver, platinum, aluminum, or titanium alloys.

CROWN

The round button, set on the side of the watch, usually ribbed, with which a watch is set and wound.

CRYSTAL

A protective lens covering the face, made of clear sapphire glass, mineral glass, or plastic.

BEZEL

The metal rim that surrounds the face and holds the crystal.

A Gruen Precision round, gold-filled brass calendar model wristwatch from the 1940s, with windows for day and month and an outer dial for the date.

This Patek Philippe waterproof stainless-steel chronometer from the 1960s has a second hand in a subsidiary dial.

replaceable batteries and don't need to be wound. Both mechanical and battery-driven watches can be found with countless unusual, perhaps intimidating elaborations, among which are repeating mechanisms and chronographs (see page 308).

The collectibility of twentieth-century wristwatches is based, first, on the accuracy and complexity of the movement and, second, on beauty. Factored into this equation are the fine points of intrinsic value (gold, silver, or platinum cases and bands), the maker or retailer (the maker being the most important), the presence of complications, and the age and condition, with occasional adjustments for changing fashions in shapes.

MATERIALS

Watchcases are generally made of metal, which can be as inexpensive as silver plate and chrome or as costly as platinum. These are the major materials from which watchcases are made, from the least to the most expensive:

SILVER PLATE AND CHROME: Both used to coat base-metal watchcases for inexpensive watches and intended to imitate either platinum or white gold.

ALUMINUM: A light, easily worked silvery white metallic element that resists corrosion. It is sometimes used for inexpensive novelty watches.

STAINLESS STEEL: Has the advantage of being rust-free and dependably rugged. An alloy of nickel, chromium, and steel, it is more difficult to work with than other watch materials. Much used for military watches, stainless steel is durable and one of the least costly of watchcase metals.

GOLD-PLATED BRASS OR OTHER NONPRECIOUS METALS: Sometimes termed "gold filled," such watchcases are made of metal with a thin coat of gold applied either by fusion or by electroplating. They are marked "14K G.F." (for gold filled) or "1/20 G.F." Gold-filled cases are among the least-expensive watchcases, and frequently, the gold plating wears away, exposing the base metal underneath.

SILVER: Less expensive than gold watches but also more likely to nick, scratch, and tarnish. Silver is not a common material for wristwatches. A more durable inexpensive "white" watch can be obtained with stainless steel, chrome, or silver plate.

<u>GOLD</u>: Perhaps the most popular wristwatch material. It has durability, beauty, and visual warmth. Gold watches are usually hallmarked (stamped) with the stamp of the country of manufacture. Gold hallmarks indicate carat. The higher the carat, the more gold per 24 parts ("18K," for instance, indicates 18 parts of gold out of a possible 24). And the higher the carat, the softer the gold. Gold doesn't tarnish. (If you are looking through a box of old watches, the solid-gold watches, either 18K or 14K, will usually be bright.)

Gold is manufactured in various colors, among them, pink, rose, white, green, or natural yellow. During the 1940s, there was a fashion for colored gold, created by alloying yellow gold, most often, with copper (for pink) or silver (for white). A gold wristwatch is almost invariably stamped somewhere on the case with its gold content; for example, "14K" if it is American; "750," "18K," and other marks (see below) if it's European.

<u>TITANIUM</u>: A very strong white metallic element that is used in the manufacture of lightweight alloys. Currently, the suitability of such materials for watchcases is being tested. One recent example is a titanium-aluminum-vanadium alloy.

<u>PLATINUM</u>: The most costly of the precious metals used for any kind of jewelry. It is stronger and harder than either silver or gold, and its silvery white color is often enhanced by being set with diamonds, which it shows off well. It was a favorite for pre–World War II wristwatches, as was white gold. A platinum watch will always be more valuable than the same watch in other metals.

Highly elaborate cases, enameled cases, and cases made of gold or gold set with precious gems are more valuable than unadorned cases (unless the movement is by one of the great names, see page 313). Look at the back or inside the back cover of the watch to see what the case is made of. If the case is gold in color, look for the customary stamp that indicates its gold content: "14K" or "18K" (marked in Europe as "585" or "750," respectively). No mark at all often means the watch is not gold. If the watch is stamped "Guaranteed for (*x* number) years," it is not gold, just gold plated or gold filled.

This very early tonneau-shape 14K gold wristwatch — with a gilt face and black Arabic numerals—was manufactured by Patek Philippe in 1917.

A rectangular Patek Philippe platinum dress wristwatch, with graduated hooded lugs and a combination of dot and baton numerals, manufactured in 1947.

Hooded Rolex Oyster Perpetual bubble-back, from the 1940s.

Swiss-made Chronograph, from 1930–1940.

Rolex Oyster Date Precision, from the 1950s.

Complications

While many watches have mechanically sophisticated movements, or complications, the following are among those that are fairly recognizable. Also included in this group are unusual styles, such as bubble-back, reverso, and skeleton watches.

AUTOMATIC WIND:

Because the wristwatch sits on a constantly moving part of the body, it is perfectly suited to the automatic wind, a mechanism incorporating a pendulum. This device allows the owners of such mechanical watches freedom from having to wind them. As long as the wearer isn't immobile, the watch winds itself.

BUBBLE-BACK:

The Oyster Perpetual, known as a bubble-back, was a watch produced by Rolex between 1931 and 1950. With the metal back of the watch made convex (bubble shape), it was able to accommodate the internal oscillating weight that made it self-winding. Over nearly two decades of production, the back of the self-winding Rolex became more "bubbly" as the watch itself got thinner.

CHRONOGRAPH:

A chronograph is a particularly sophisticated type of timekeeper—its second hand functions as a stopwatch.

SPLIT-SECOND CHRONOGRAPH:

A rare and desirable variant on the chronograph, the split-second chronograph, which overlays the chronograph hand with an additional second hand, allows the wearer to clock intermediate times.

DATE INDICATION:

First used circa 1915, the date indication tells the wearer the date, with either a hand on the watch face or a rotating disk displaying the date.

*Rolex Perpetual Day-Date,
from the 1960s.*

*Patek Philippe Perpetual-Calendar
Wristwatch with Moon Phases, 1959.*

*Jaeger-LeCoultre Reverso,
from about 1950.*

DAY INDICATION:
As with the date, the day of
the week can be indicated by
a hand or a disk. Like date
indication, this complication,
too, was introduced in 1915.

**DUO-DIAL, OR
"DOCTOR'S WATCH":**
This watch has two dials on one
face—one for the hours and
minutes, the other for the seconds. It was originally designed
for taking a patient's pulse.

MOON PHASE:
An indication on the face of the
wristwatch of the number of
days since the last new moon,
usually shown through a window on the dial.

REPEATER:
A watch with an integral chime.
Press a button or push a slide,
and the watch can chime the
hour, the quarter hour, and
the minutes. A holdover from
the days before electricity, when
it was difficult to tell time after
dark, the repeater allows its
owner to hear the time.

REVERSO:
A watch with a case that rolls or
flips over to protect the movement. The story is that this
clever refinement protected the
watch crystals of British polo
players in India from inadver-
tantly being smashed by a
mallet.

SKELETON:
This variation allows the viewer
to see the movement through
the face; it is customarily hidden behind the dial.

WATERPROOFING:
With a watertight case and
crystal, a watch can be made
resistant to being dunked in a
bathtub, perspired into, caught
in the rain, or taken diving to
a depth of one meter for thirty
minutes.

Audemars Piguet made this rectangular gold wristwatch in 1925. It has four subsidiary dials—for day, date, month, and constant seconds combined with moon phases.

In the late fifties and early sixties, Hamilton produced this Cross Country wristwatch, which kept local time and that of each U.S. time zone—each zone had its own hand in a separate color. One additional hand kept Greenwich Mean Time.

AGE

The age of a wristwatch can be gauged by weighing several elements. The face, for example, may have a radium dial, suggesting pre-1950s manufacture. The amount of wear on the back of the case can indicate years on a wearer's wrist. Some elements, such as the barrels at the ends of the case that hold the watch pins, may be worn enough to have thinned and become structurally insecure. Wear is only natural, but the less there is, the better.

CONDITION

Watches, like stamps and coins and even toys today, can be sorted into formal categories of conditional excellence. With objects that have been so extensively mass-produced that there are now millions of them on the market, this makes excellent sense. Fine distinctions can be drawn between all these wristwatches to make it easier for collectors to formulate on-the-spot judgments and thus collect wisely. Any watch you consider for your collection should be in good-to-mint condition. A commonly accepted system for the grading of watch condition also makes it easier for people to buy from each other via the Internet or from catalogs, because everyone is, so to speak, starting on the same page. The advantage of such standardized grading systems is that if the rules are adhered to, even the complete novice can feel comfortable judging the external condition of a vintage watch and its relative value.

One important presumption in evaluating watches is that they be working, although because watch oil dries out, a watch may actually be in working condition even if it is not running. All it may really need is a simple cleaning and oiling.

If you are considering purchasing a specific wristwatch, you might want to have the dealer open the back to see if it is dirty or rusty. Wind the watch as well, and check to see if the parts move easily (or at all). And finally, put the watch next to your ear and move it around to different positions. If the beat or pitch of the tick changes, the watch may be too well worn to be worth adding to your collection.

Watchbands are of only moderate importance to collectors; nevertheless, an original leather strap in good condition is always a plus. If you wear the watches in your collection and believe

GRADING A WATCH

The terms for the following grading categories may be somewhat different from wristwatch book to wristwatch book, or dealer to dealer, but the requirements remain the same.

GRADE	QUALITY	WHAT IT MEANS
Grade 10	New Old Stock	A watch that is factory-new, in its original box and wrapping, with all tags and labels intact; in other words, a watch that has never been worn.
Grade 9	Mint	A watch that is still in its original box and appears never to have been worn.
Grade 8	Excellent	A watch that may or may not be in its original box and that exhibits very little use; such a timepiece may have been used briefly and stored. It is original in all its parts and has no faint scratches nor marks of repair on the case.
Grade 7	Very Good	All parts are original; if there are faint marks, they can only be seen through a loupe (a jeweler's magnifying glass); the movement may show evidence of having been cleaned and oiled, and if there *are* repairs, they will have been expertly done.
Grade 6	Good	A watch that has had gentle wear; its crystal may have been replaced, but the hands, dial, movement, and case are original; if there have been repairs, they have been done with original replacement parts; faint, difficult-to-see scratches may be on the case, which has no dents; the dial has no hairline cracks.
Grade 5	Fine	A watch that has its original case, dial, and movement, but may have new hands and crystal; the dial has no chips, though it might reveal hairline cracks; the case will have no large scratches, and if the watch is plated, none of the brass is showing; the parts of the movement show only the most minor of scratches.
Grade 4	Average	The case, dial, and movement will be original; if the movement has any replaced parts, these will be as near to original as possible; gold plating will not be worn away, and the dial will be free of rust and chips, although it may have hairline cracks; insignificant marks on the case and dial can be seen without a loupe.
Grade 3	Fair	A well-used watch; on those that have gold-plated cases, brass can be seen through the worn spots; the case might be dented, and the dial may have small chips and hairline cracks; there will be definite wear to the movement, case, and dial, and the case or the dial may not be original.
Grade 2	Poor	The movement is broken and the watch needs a new dial or a replacement crystal; the case shows excessive wear and has many dents; the watch hands may be missing.
Grade 1	Scrap	If this watch has any value, it is mainly for parts. Its movement doesn't work, the case is damaged, and some parts are not original. There are no hands and no crystal.

THE SWITCH TO SWATCH

From its inception in the spring of 1983 until the fall of 1985, when the fad for Swatch watches peaked, the Swiss firm SMH sold an astounding ten million Swatch watches. Those first Swatches are hotly pursued by Swatch collectors, and Swatch watches are among the very few quartz watches that are currently collectible. (However, collectible models are limited to special editions, like those designed by such artists as Keith Haring and Sam Francis.)

And a word of caution: More than any other wristwatch, a plastic watch like the Swatch needs to be absolutely mint and still in its original packaging to have value in the collectibles market.

An early 1980s geometric design Swatch. To have any collectible value, a Swatch must be mint and in its original packaging.

their bands are too old (for example, the stitching is weak or the watch-pin barrels too worn) to risk wearing, or if they do not fit your wrist, put the original bands away in a safe place and have the original buckles fitted to new bands with new pins.

Metal bands are significant only if they are original to the watch. Precious metal bands are definitely a bonus, although they do not add unusual value to a watch that has an unexciting movement.

COLLECTING WRISTWATCHES

The serious collecting of wristwatches is a rather new hobby, about as old as that Swatch, because wristwatches were considered horologically second rate for much of the twentieth century. It was not until the 1980s that there began to be a significant demand for fine vintage examples. (An exception is the Ingersoll Mickey Mouse watch, which was big in the 1960s, but isn't exactly horologically significant.) The wristwatch market, therefore, certainly can't be said to have jelled, and the values of some of the less expensive watches, especially, have not yet been established.

Watch collectors, like all collectors, should choose to collect only the examples that they are passionate about. Faced with a wealth of choice, however, it helps to focus the passion on, for example, only watches made by one manufacturer, such as Hamilton (which Shonholtz believes to be "mass-produced perfection; easy and inexpensive to service; highly affordable"). Collecting a particular period (such as Art Deco) or country (American made, rather than Swiss made) are other strong focus areas. As with any collectible, reading up on your special area of concentration helps to prevent having to "de-accession" a lot of mistakes before you get your collecting feet under you.

Keep in mind, too, that the maker's name, the materials from which the watch is made, and the condition of the watch are always going to be the main indicators of value. A watch will be more valuable if its dial is clean and unrestored (although there *are* valuable watches with restored dials).

"If you collect wristwatches, wear them," *Antiques Roadshow* expert Sig Shonholtz advises. Unlike some other collectibles, wristwatches are distinctly functional objects that should be used. When they are stopped dead and arrayed in cases, they resemble doleful botanical specimens rather than the vigorous mechanical marvels we know them to be. "If you want to make an investment, go to a stockbroker," Shonholtz adds. "Watches are for pleasure."

MANUFACTURERS

The following are some of the most important wristwatch manufacturers of the twentieth century. But when you are buying, be careful. Imitations of Rolex, Audemars Piguet, Patek Philippe, and Cartier watches are beloved of street vendors but of no value to collectors.

AUDEMARS PIGUET

Watches made by the Swiss manufacturer Audemars Piguet, founded by Jules Audemars and Edward Piguet in 1875, are rather undervalued, despite their being of the highest quality. From the firm's inception, in fact, it was renowned for fashioning watches with many unusual complications, among them, repeating mechanisms and the *heures sautantes* (a refinement in which the watch, instead of being fitted with the customary hour hand, displays the hour through a window in the dial). In 1906, just after the creation of the wristwatch, Audemars Piguet introduced the first wristwatch to incorporate a minute repeater.

BAUME & MERCIER

The Geneva, Switzerland, firm of Baume & Mercier produced relatively affordable wristwatches. The company's classic-design models and its chronographs are of interest to watch collectors.

BREITLING

A Swiss firm known from its inception for chronographs, Breitling has produced several collectible chronograph models, among them the Cosmonaut, the Chronomat, and the Premier. Certain calendar watches, particularly the Unitime, that tell world time, are highly sought after.

A WRISTWATCH AND A BRACELET

A visitor to the Boston *Antiques Roadshow* brought a watch that had been a gift to her grandmother during World War II.

Appraiser Kevin Zavian explained that this watch had been purchased at the famous jewelry store Van Cleef & Arpels, which had branches in both Paris and

New York. The watch, made in the United States by a noted New York goldsmith, is stamped with the French hallmark for import—a small eagle—proving that it was manufactured for sale in the Paris store.

Made of 18K gold in the retro style of the 1940s, the watch is both a bracelet and a timepiece. Its woven snake chain lends drama. Although Zavian had seen unfinished examples of this watch bracelet in the past, this was the first time he had seen a complete one. He estimated its value at $5,000 to $6,000.

A rare asymmetrical 1960s Bulova Accutron, with Roman numerals and a date window. The Accutron, the first electronic watch, uses a tuning fork—rather than wheels and springs—as its prime moving element.

BULOVA

An American watch company, Bulova was founded in the late nineteenth century by Joseph Bulova. From the 1920s to the 1960s, Bulova produced high-quality, dependable, and stylish watches. By the mid 1930s, the company was manufacturing millions of popular and affordable watches. It continued to do so when, in 1960, it marketed the breakthrough Bulova Accutron, the first electronic watch to incorporate a transistorized circuit. Accutrons are difficult to keep running, yet they remained the most accurate of the electronic watches until the end of the decade, when Accutrons were superseded by the quartz watch.

CARTIER

The famous French jeweler Cartier was always an innovator in the field of horology. In 1917, Cartier created what some consider to be the pinnacle of watch design—the Tank watch. This classic shape is said to have been inspired by Louis Cartier's impression of the great juggernauts of World War I. Indeed, actual tanks, when viewed from above, do resemble the firm's most famous design, and the first editions of the watch were, in fact, Cartier's gifts to American tank commanders. Cartier also produced watches with other shapes: the Santos—the first true Cartier wristwatch—a square with beveled corners named for the early-twentieth-century Brazilian aviator Alberto Santos-Dumont and introduced in 1904; the Tonneau, or Barrel; and the Tortue, which—if you close one eye—almost succeeds in looking something like the tortoise it was named for. Many Cartier watches are now collectible; the water-resistant Pasha (commissioned by the Pasha of Marrakech for swimming) and the elegant Vendôme, both of the 1930s, are only two of the more popular models.

A classic rectangular men's 18K gold Cartier Tank watch from about 1955, with eighteen jewels, a white face, and Roman numerals.

GRUEN

Gruen was perhaps the earliest American company to believe that the wristwatch had a future. Like Ingersoll (see page 300), Gruen produced timepieces for the American soldier in World War I. Gruen cases were made of silver, which would not rust. In the 1920s, the company hired many of the Swiss and German watchmakers who were then emigrating to the United States, and in 1935, the firm introduced its most famous model, the Curvex, then the epitome of streamlined industrial design.

Gruen's famous rectangular Curvex wristwatch was a streamlined design introduced in 1935 that neatly echoed the curve of the wrist. This 1940s gold-filled model has a two-tone face and Breguet hands.

HAMILTON

The mechanical Hamilton is considered by some authorities to be the Ford of American watches: inexpensive, durable, attractive, and ubiquitous. The 1957 Hamilton Electric became the world's first battery-powered watch. Although undependable, it ushered in the era of electronic horology, followed in 1972 by the Pulsar, the first digital watch. This "advance," it was (erroneously) thought, would make watch hands obsolete.

INTERNATIONAL WATCH COMPANY (IWC)

Founded by an American in 1868 and taken over later by the Swiss, IWC is located in Schaffhausen, making it the only important watch firm in German-speaking Switzerland. International is known for making watches of particularly high-quality workmanship. Its 1948 model, the Mark XI pilot's wristwatch with its antimagnetic inner case, is popular with collectors. So, too, are the steel Ingénieur model, the first automatic watch the company produced, and the 1958 Mark II, featuring a black dial and crisp white numbers. IWC has supplied watch movements to jewelers throughout the world.

Hamilton named each of its watches. This is a gold Midas, a rectangular wristwatch with hidden lugs, introduced in 1941.

JAEGER-LECOULTRE

Since 1833, LeCoultre has been one of the most important makers of *ébauches* (see page 305) for other luxury watch manufacturers. In 1903, the original Swiss company merged with chronometer-maker Edmond Jaeger, and became known as

Left: A round International Watch Company stainless steel automatic (self-winding) sports wristwatch from the 1940s, with alternating Arabic numerals and dots.

WRISTWATCHES: NOT EASY TO FAKE

Skulduggery in baseball memorabilia can be accomplished with just a pen and an old baseball. Recreating a watch is far more complex. "Watches are hard to fake well," asserts *Antiques Roadshow* appraiser Sig Shonholtz. To fool watch experts, fakers would have to construct their phony watches just like the original. "You need millions of dollars of manufacturing equipment," he explains.

More common is the technique of slapping a fine house name on a nameless dial, watch movement, and its case back. Shonholtz says this technique is a little like adding a Rembrandt signature to a paint-by-number painting. "Right now, a lot of name-brand watches on the Internet are selling for half the value of a real watch by that company," he says. "And I know that company never made the model listed. Remember, if it looks like *too* good a deal, it probably is."

Jaeger-LeCoultre. In 1929, it introduced the Calibre 101: At less than a gram, this is still one of the tiniest watch movements in the world, perhaps *the* smallest. Two years later, Jaeger-LeCoultre came out with one of its best-known models, the Reverso.

LONGINES

Longines is a Swiss watch company that takes its name from its location on a spot called Les Longines, "the long meadows," near Lausanne. The Longines 1932 Lindbergh Hour-Angle watch, a navigating watch designed for pilots that allowed the wearer to determine longitude during flight, was based on Charles Lindbergh's own design. It became one of the firm's greatest successes. Longines chronographs are widely sought after today as well. Longines' "Winged Hourglass" trademark was first used in 1889.

MOVADO

Although this company broke new ground in 1912 with a unique curved movement that followed the curve of the wrist, Movado is perhaps best known for the simple and stylish 1960 "Museum" watch, which is in the collection of the Museum of Modern Art. This model has no numbers or batons on its dial, just one elegant dot.

The Movado watch that is most popular with collectors, however, is not a wristwatch. It is the "Ermeto," a purse watch with an automatic winding mechanism that is activated by opening and closing the cover of the case. The Movado name derives from the Esperanto word for "always moving."

The 1932 Longines Hour-Angle Watch, designed by and for pioneer aviator Charles Lindbergh, has a rotating bezel for the rapid determination of longitude.

The classic Movado Museum watch, introduced in 1947, has a black dial defined by just one dot of gold at the 12:00 position. Designed by Nathan George Horwitt, it was inspired by a sundial.

CERAMICS

Twentieth-century ceramics is an enormous field, one that embraces pitchers, vases, sugar bowls, hand-thrown studio pots, and everything in between. Even vintage tablewares (our everyday creamers and dinner plates) are collectible. Ceramics are graphic, useful, and a delight to the eye. And all are popular with collectors because—unlike glass, a second cousin once removed and something often dropped—they are also durable.

A bright green two-handled vase in Roseville's Futura pattern is characterized by Art Deco lines.

Clarice Cliff's Sliced Circle ceramic vase, circa 1929, is part of her Bizarre ware series and features a brilliant sunburst of Art Deco geometry.

These two pitchers are just a small sample of the variety of hues available in Fiesta ware.

This Weller Sicardo bud vase captures the iridescence that made Tiffany glassware so successful.

This grouping of earthy bowls, vases, and a wall plaque underscores the vivid colors employed by Italian ceramacist Guido Gambone.

A somber Gustavsberg modernist pottery vase has muted flambé decoration.

DINNERWARE & TABLEWARE

AMERICAN

One of the all-time most popular earthenware patterns is Franciscan Ware's creamy Desert Rose, introduced in 1941.

This "Our America" dinner plate was designed by artist Rockwell Kent for Vernon Kilns.

EUROPEAN

A Cheery English chintz ware pattern, above, evokes a lush summer garden in full bloom.

In this Crown Works breakfast set designed by Susie Cooper, the shape of the ceramic is called Kestrel, while the pattern is called Crescents.

Bronze-glazed Eva Zeisel Town and Country tablewares for Redwing: an unusual soup tureen and salt and pepper set.

An unusual covered casserole, in Curry (actually, chartreuse) from Russel Wright's successful American Modern dinnerware.

The branchlike handle on a pitcher in Roseville's popular Pine Cone pattern adds to its woodsy charm.

Despite its mid-century roots, this group of Metlox Potteries Red Rooster kitchenware is engagingly Early American.

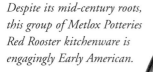

A typical Fornasetti plate, picturing a caged—but happy—harpy.

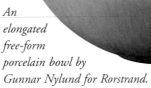

An elongated free-form porcelain bowl by Gunnar Nylund for Rorstrand.

A matte blue glazed Rookwood tapering vase with a Greek key design, circa 1925.

ART & STUDIO POTTERY

A Susie Cooper Cubist coffee pot from 1928. Cooper used a wide variety of decorative motifs on her ceramics, among them floral design, transfer prints, and incised patterns.

Glazed in matte turquoise, a 1968 mysterious closed form by Natzler.

A rustic Weller Ansonia batter jug, with a mottled green and yellow glaze.

With an almost primeval quality, the stoneware studio pots of Hans Coper are monumental and sculptural.

Keith Murray designed this streamlined and formal red stoneware covered jar for Wedgwood around 1940.

The gazelle motif, a favorite of the Art Deco era, is boldly rendered on this small René Buthaud vase.

A ceramic version of the aurora borealis in radiant orange and yellow on a slender William and Polia Pillin bottle.

Picasso's Grand Vaseaux Danseurs, circa 1950.

ADVERTISING

Good advertising usually promises an easier or fuller life. Probably nine out of ten successful advertisements feature a human face to catch the eye, but brilliant color is also important, as are recognizable logos and striking graphics. The best advertising collectibles are pure consumer anthropology.

This ruby glass fountain dispenser for the long-gone Cherry Smash ("A True Fruit Blend") still wears its topper sign.

A smiling diner waitress with a tray of Cokes, in a vintage point-of-purchase sign for Coca-Cola.

A hand-crafted sign for Al Mac's Diner, painted on masonite, is as much folk art as advertising memorabilia.

Sultry Cleopatra, on a mask cut from the back of a Wheaties box, seems an unusual choice for "The Breakfast of Champions."

ONE OF A SERIES OF FAMOUS CARTOON CHARACTERS. LOOK FOR OTHERS IN CRACKER JACK

HERBY

IRON

A hearty washer-woman on a point-of-purchase cardboard sign reminds buyers of the value of Kirkman's wrappers.

KIRKMAN'S BORAX SOAP FOR LAUNDRY WORK

SAVE THE WRAPPERS FOR PREMIUMS

Young and old purchasers alike gobbled their Cracker Jack to find prizes like these three.

CAMEL TURKISH & DOMESTIC BLEND CIGARETTES

Instantly recognizable, the old-fashioned logo of Camel cigarettes on a 1940s tin.

There's much to read (perhaps too much) on these handsomely lithographed cracker boxes from the early twentieth century.

COPYRIGHTED 1896, R. F. OUTCAULT

JOURNAL

N.Y. JOURNAL

SAY IM DE JOURNAL KID IM DE REAL TING CAUSE DE HIGH ADMIRAL HAS ADOPTED ME DEY KNOWS A GOOD TING WHEN DEY SEE IT AN SO DO I

HIGH ADMIRAL

Outcault N.Y. JOURNAL

88

HIGH ADMIRAL CIGARETTES

W. J. SANDS & SONS Biscuits Crackers ERIE, PA. SPECIALTIES

TIDAL WAVE BISCUITS ERIE STEAM BAKERY

HOPE BISCUIT WORKS CRACKERS BISCUITS

ROBINSON BROS BRANCH CRACKERS AND CAKES CLEVELAND O.

ROBINSON BROS CRACKERS AND FINE CAKES

An unlikely ad today: The Yellow Kid sells—and smokes— High Admiral cigarettes in the 1890s.

From the 1890s, this is the only known example of an embossed cardboard die-cut ad for Coca-Cola.

A lithographed box for Mecca Cigarettes, with a romantic view of the "Turkish" skyline.

A porcelain enamel sign for a metal polish seems to promise to do the job quickly as well as thoroughly.

Mickey Mouse turns up in all sorts of advertisements, including this one for Standard Gasoline.

The memorably named (and misspelled) Trop-Artic Auto Oil.

"Let's Make a Date for Tonight"

SAYS VIRGINIA DARE

"So you can enjoy the only wine of its kind in the world!"

As light as sherry, as vigorous as port. Virginia Dare is different than either, more refreshing than either. Its flavor is *hearty* but never *heavy!* Pedigreed grapes are especially cultivated for this only wine of its kind in the world. Virginia Dare is available in red or white wine. You'll probably want *both* when you see how little they cost.

Garrett and Company, Inc., New York

SAY IT AGAIN . . .

VIRGINIA DARE
AMERICAN RED OR WHITE
WINE

Innocently suggestive, Virginia Dare—in a 1940s version of colonial dress—serves her eponymous wine.

The Quaker Oats company employed both the Katzenjammer Kids and a Roy Rogers premium (here, a souvenir cup) to sell its cereal.

In jewelry store windows, Baranger's electrified heart and diamond band display touted diamonds for loving hearts.

With a slot and Kewpie-esque "Thank You," the Calumet tin became a bank.

A swirled, stoppered bottle by Barovier & Toso exemplifies the striato technique.

Typical of American Harvey Littleton's experimental studio glass is this 1964 blown glass sculpture, entitled "Implosion/Explosion."

A Schneider coupe in mottled yellow glass shading to purple.

Perhaps the most familiar of the geometric carnival glass patterns, "Fashion," shown here in a punch bowl, was called 402½ when Imperial Glass first issued it.

VASES

Lalique's clear and frosted blue glass vase from 1919 is called Perruches for the molded parakeets perched on its molded boughs.

Shoulders cloaked in yellow and orange, this intense and glowing red "Jade" vase is quintessential Schneider.

Molten blue Aurene "lava" slides over the shoulders of a rare Frederick Carder Steuben yellow jade vase, its body acid-etched with a "blanket of flowers."

There is speculation that Frederick Carder's iridescent Aurene glass predated that of Louis Comfort Tiffany. This example is marked "Steuben Aurene."

Typical of the 1920s taste for all things Egyptian is Fostoria's Tut vase, designed for the company by George Sakier.

GLASS

Sometimes practical, sometimes cerebral, often magical, and always fragile, the best glassware of the twentieth century may look like liquefied diamonds, rubies, emeralds, opals, and agates, but it is, in fact, the work of ingenious artisans, technicians, and manufacturers. The most collectible examples of vintage glass were always cutting edge (so to speak) and always inspired.

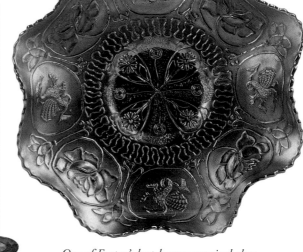

One of Fenton's best-known carnival glass patterns, an undulant and eerily iridescent Dragon and Lotus bowl in blue.

In this 1931 Depression Glass wine goblet, the Cambridge Glass Company's Aurora pattern is characterized by its faceted ball stem.

A pair of candlesticks in Consolidated's Catalonian pattern of 1926, in the rare Spanish Rose color. This glass is characterized by interior bubbles and raised rings on the surface.

From Sweden's Orrefors glassworks, a faintly chartreuse-tinged Apple vase, designed in 1957 by Ingeborg Lundin.

A mere 8 inches high, this Venini vase bears only the factory mark, yet it looks enough like others designed by Fulvio Bianconi to merit its Bianconi attribution.

Austerely elegant, this vivid Sommerso pillow vase was designed by Flavio Poli for Seguso.

Brilliant finger-painting in glass: an unmarked Barovier & Toso pezzato tear-drop form vase.

This early twentieth-century unsigned Loetz vase with iridescent silver pulled designs and applied teardrop decorations emulates Tiffany glass.

SPORTS COLLECTIBLES

T he thrill of victory—and the victor's uniform; the ball that got lost in the sun—and the ball that got lost in the rough (plus the useless club that put it there), not to mention the rod, the reel, and the one that got away. Whatever sports collectors collect, they always win, for they own both the memorabilia and the memory.

Looking more like a war medal than an ID badge, this very rare 1914 Philadelphia Athletics press pin is in near mint condition.

A rare, uncracked Jackie Robinson game-used bat, circa 1950–1954.

A 1950s warm-up jacket signed by short stop and team captain Pee Wee Reese.

A ball signed right on the sweet spot by Lou Gehrig. Single-signed Gehrig balls are hard to come by.

Left: An early game from Parker Brothers, Peg Base Ball, came with a colorful box featuring a batter framed by a base-ball diamond.

Above: The striking graphics on the box cover of this circa 1910 Champion Base Ball game make it ideal for display.

A ticket from the legendary third game of the 1932 World Series at Wrigley Field, when Babe Ruth allegedly pointed to the center field bleachers before hitting a homer right to that spot.

BASEBALL

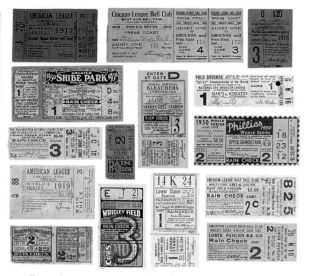

Part of a rare and valuable collection of 256 tickets and stubs that charts the history of World Series baseball from the first World Series (1903) until 1998.

Left: The 1946 Kansas City Royals Winter League road jersey that Jackie Robinson wore while preparing for his Major League debut with the Brooklyn Dodgers in 1947, and right, the jersey

Yankee Mickey Mantle wore on the road in his finest season, 1956, and signed for a fan.

A bit of the original green paint shows through the later "Yankee Blue" on an original seat from Yankee Stadium.

Ted Williams's official team-issue travel bag from the 1940s was signed by "Thumpin' Ted" (or "Toothpick" or "The Kid") himself.

GOLF

Bow-tied Alex Smith's biography is printed on the reverse of this Mecca Cigarettes champion golfers card.

A golf card from the 1980s, signed by PGA great Jack Nicklaus.

RULE·IV·
If a player play when his partner should have done so.....

Whatever works: two circa 1910 patterned balls, the Diamond Chick, right, by North British Rubber Co., and the Tit-Bit, top, maker unknown.

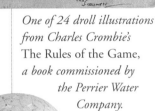

One of 24 droll illustrations from Charles Crombie's The Rules of the Game, a book commissioned by the Perrier Water Company.

This 1920s Round the Clock golf game is frequently mentioned in Agatha Christie novels.

A decorous and sportily dressed lady golfer appears on McCormick's faux golf-bag biscuit tin.

CLUBS

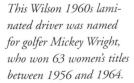

The Penna TP63 6 iron, designed by MacGregor's chief club designer, Toney Penna, in 1963.

Edmond Glover of Tenafly, New Jersey, patented this club with a blade that could be positioned at different angles in 1935.

Devised in 1879 for use in sand, water, or mud, this Roy Water Iron—somehow—hit each ball twice, causing the player to forfeit the hole.

This Wilson 1960s laminated driver was named for golfer Mickey Wright, who won 63 women's titles between 1956 and 1964.

A colorful Ringer putter, with a turquoise non-metallic head.

FISHING

FLIES

Salmon flies created and tied by Charles DeFeo: left, Silver Spate; below left, Miss Mary; below right, Yellow Cains.

Right column: Flies created and tied by Paul Schmookler: top, Corinthian Kate; middle, Davoust; bottom, Le Caford.

Two 1930s Meek No. 55 fly reels made after the company was acquired by the Horton Manufacturing Company of Bristol, Connecticut.

An S-handle Seamaster salmon reel, circa 1960, from H.L. Leonard.

An H.L. Leonard fly-fishing reel from the 1880s. This model was produced until 1917.

Made in 1878, H.L. Leonard's single-action trout reel in nickel silver has marbleized sideplates and knob, and a crank handle.

Two Florida fishing lures with their original boxes: a Beder & Flynn Darter lure, circa 1945, manufactured in Pinellas Park and a Barracuda Lure, circa 1940, from Florida Fishing Tackle in Saint Petersburg.

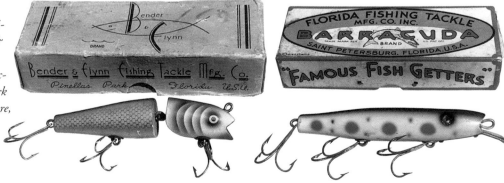

TOYS

From the 1930s, a gravity-driven tin litho Junior Swing made by Buffalo Toy & Tool Works.

When new, the best toys are those that are most ingenious. They roll, float, they make noise, they turn, they crawl, they bleep, and they walk. And they're colorful. Great toys are far less likely to be pastel pink than bright red, yellow, and blue. And the finest vintage toys are all of this, with paint intact, parts in place, and packaging good as new. Like that magical moment when the wrappings come off, they're perfect.

Plume flying, steed prancing, this member of the Queen's Household Cavalry is the soul of British swagger.

A 1936 Wyandotte Circus Truck with a "rooster comb" hood ornament and painted wood spoke wheels has lost its tin animals.

A Scottish battalion, a little the worse for wear, marching toward an engagement with the enemy.

A 1910 Gong pull toy uses opalescent painted cast iron comic strip figures from Little Nemo in Slumberland as bell ringers.

This realistically litho-graphed iridescent German beetle, manufactured by Lehmann in 1903, flutters its wings and crawls.

Linemar's Mechanical Ball-Playing Giraffe, circa 1958, bounces its ball on a wire between its head and front feet.

From Japan's Nomura factory, a 1955 battery-operated Miss Friday the Typist, with six distinctly secretarial actions.

This classic blockhead robot by Yoshiya, left, has flashing lights, swinging arms, a turning head, and makes "coarse electronic noises."

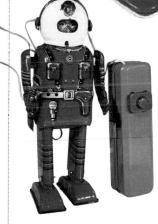

Linemar's Spaceman Robot, circa 1956, shoots his laser rifle while light illuminates his face inside his round helmet.

The Usagiya SP-1 Space Car Robot, from the 1950s, features an unusual friction-drive, dual-exhaust vehicle with a block-head robot driver whose mouth emits sparks.

A mechanically sophisticated Buddy L 1950s crane, below right, with its original wooden log payload, can raise and lower both its boom and hoisting hook.

When the hose nozzle of this battery-operated tin-lithographed Marx filling station is attached to the tank of this toy Studebaker Hawk made by Distler, the gauge in the pump turns as if the tank is being filled.

A diecast Dinky Toy truck, made in England, hauls a typically British load.

A Hauler and Closed Van Trailer from 1955, made by Louis Marx & Co., included an air horn and pull-down tailgate.

Made in England in the 1960s, Lesney's Matchbox trucks include a grit-spreader, an eight-wheel tipper, a container truck tipper, and a stack truck.

Calling all children! A Courtland keywind tin lithographed ice cream truck moves forward while a long rod allows the ice cream man to ring his bell.

Suitcases firmly attached, a mechanical tin lithographed Marx joyrider's jalopy tilts on its rear wheels while his head spins.

Operated by remote control, this post–World War II tin lithographed submarine—here with its original box—was submersible.

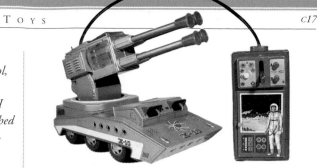

Suzuki & Edwards Atomic Pom-Pom Cannon, a battery-operated tin-litho space-age tank, moves forward and backward, its turret and antenna rotate, and the gun barrels move in succession.

Terrifying suburban aliens. Marx's 1956 plastic Captain Space Solar Scout Atomic Ray Gun, with a rotating tricolor signal light and electric buzzer.

Early aviation toys, such as this 1928 tin lithographed single-wing military aircraft by Chein, are highly prized.

Amos and Andy's taxicab, left, is a crossover toy: of interest both to toy enthusiasts and collectors of black memorabilia.

Extensively and carefully lithographed, this Japanese police motorcyclist was available with or without a sidecar.

FASHION AND TEXTILES

Collectors of vintage fashion and textiles have a curatorial obligation not to wear them out. Even wearing them in—hanging them on walls or spreading them on beds or tabletops—exposes fabrics to the possibilities of spots, tears, and deterioration from damaging sunlight. But the craftsmanship and design of twentieth-century clothing and household textiles make them appealing collectibles.

Top: A 1960s modified cloche hat from Mr. John and, bottom, a witty hat, crawling with pearlized shell- and straw-bodied snails, could only be the work of Chicago hatmaker Bes-Ben.

Around 1949, Charles James employed this bodice design in several dresses, but also made it as a top to be worn with an evening skirt.

Left: Silk velvet trimmed in mink, this Callot Soeurs coat was the last word in 1912 Paris fashion.

Right: Down at the heels, holes in the pocket, and lovingly patched, these 1890s Levis® jeans have a belt in the back (for fit) and buttons for (red) suspenders.

Even the complicated fringe on this 1920s cut steel beaded bag is in mint condition.

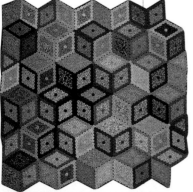

Far left: Scraps of ordinary feed sack bags have been stitched together to make this tumbling blocks pattern quilt from the 1930s.

Left: An African-American quilt from the 1940s, in a strikingly modern abstract design, made from scraps of gabardine fabric.

Yves Saint Laurent's pink peau de soie "Circus" cocktail dress, circa 1967, has a skirt sewn with tiers of ostrich feathers.

Jeanne Lanvin's 1926 black taffeta robe de style has a bodice and skirt front decorated with an Art Deco pattern of silver bugle beads, pearls, and rhinestones.

Witty and surreal at once, Schiaparelli's circa 1938 emerald velvet "sleeve gloves" are completed by a matching snood.

Black-and-white is preferred today by collectors of the embroidered silk shawls so popular early in the twentieth century.

Any wearer would seem goddesslike in this hand-pleated column of liquid silk by Fortuny.

A sleeveless and soigné coral velvet gown attributed to Madeleine Vionnet, circa 1929, trimmed with a beaded tie.

A 1955 "late day" dress from Traina-Norell in rose-covered satin, with a wide, gathered cummerbund trimmed with a rose.

DOLLS AND ACCESSORIES

Accompanied by the Cowardly Lion, Ideal's composition Judy Garland, first issued in 1939, wears Dorothy's gingham pinafore and her hair in "bunches."

B earded or cuddly, chubby or bald, tiny, tall or stuffed, vintage dolls touch childhood's heart. Often, they resemble movie stars (Shirley Temple and Margaret O'Brien), idealized fashion plates (Barbie), or even their young owners. They walk, they talk, they cry and wet, and of course, they need nice homes, so we provide them with furnished dollhouses. Those that have been carefully cared-for grow up to be collectibles.

A trio of German cartoon character nodder dolls—Uncle Walt, Moon Mullins, and Kayo—wearing (mostly) original paint.

This 1950s Ideal Toni comes with her wrist and dress tag, most of her accessories, and her box—which has been repaired, but is still sturdy.

The box that accompanies Hasbro's 1970s G.I. Joe Air Adventurer in his Adventure Team orange coveralls advertises his "Life-like Hair and Beard."

Made of hard plastic, a 1950s Buddy Lee doll in his Phillips 66 uniform is jointed only at the shoulders—the better, perhaps, to pump gas.

Gingerbready and charming, a turn-of-the-twentieth-century wooden Bliss dollhouse exemplifies the beautiful lithography so typical of early toys.

Although the make-up on this 1959 #1 all-original brunette pony tail Barbie (with her #1 booklet) is mint, her bangs could use a little combing.

It's not the rose gold or the painted metal face, but the octagonal shape of this 1930s Patek Philippe that makes it particularly rare.

WRISTWATCHES

Sometimes tiny, sometimes large, sometimes full of "complications," and sometimes simple, sometimes as thin as a wafer or too small to read, wristwatches are attractive—and functional—jewelry. Wristwatch collectors, on the whole, prefer character and mechanical complexity to just another pretty face.

A "retro" Lord Elgin from the 1940s combines bold design elements with a black face.

Vintage wristwatches offer enthusiasts decades of choice in design, manufacturer, and function, which the contents of the modern jewelry store usually do not. Clockwise from top left: A round gold Vacheron Constantine, with stepped bezel, stepped lugs, and stick numerals; a 1948 Universal Tri Compax "square button" (i.e. not waterproof) chronograph; and a Franck Muller contemporary Chrono-Automatique, for those who prefer pre-quartz craftsmanship.

This 1930s two-color gold Rolex Prince doctor's watch has an enlarged second hand that facilitates the taking of a pulse.

Watch bracelets became popular after World War II: This Gruen "Veri-Thin Precision" Curvex—and its movement—conformed to the shape of the wrist.

Made in the late teens or early twenties, an unusual silver Longines of classic tonneau shape has highly legible Breguet numerals.

ENTERTAINMENT

Those faces. Those clothes. Those shoes. Not an iota of celebrity memorabilia is too insignificant or too intimate to engage the collectors of romance and dreams. Film or television props, concert stubs, photographs, recordings: All are preserved for the future by those enthusiastic fans who savor—and save—our collective popular-culture memory.

Sentimental and touching, a poster advertises The Kid, *a film written, directed by, and starring Charlie Chaplin.*

FILM

Marilyn Monroe, "The Talk of Hollywood," on the cover of Life *magazine, April 7, 1952.*

Ushering in the age of science fiction, this lobby card for Fritz Lang's 1926 masterpiece Metropolis *promised high melodrama.*

Showing surprisingly hard wear, these handmade green Munchkin shoes—designed by Gilbert Adrian—were worn in the 1939 classic The Wizard of Oz.

The Munchkins wore green, but Judy Garland as Dorothy donned these ruby slippers.

A 1955 pastel portrait of James Dean by R. Lucas, with a long inscription in Dean's hand to "Kitty."

Over 5 million copies were sold of the photo of Rita Hayworth wearing this nightgown. Now the nightgown has come up for auction.

TELEVISION

Grandpa Munster's tuxedo jacket, with orange satin lapels, was the appropriate formal wear for self-respecting vampires on the popular 1960s television series.

The silvery space suit worn by Leonard Nimoy as Mr. Spock in "The Tholian Web" episode of Star Trek.

From the Eisenhower era, Howdy Doody host Buffalo Bob's cowboy costume and his "campaign" jacket.

On a 1957 one-sheet, the mythic Elvis, his guitar, and his pompadour advertise MGM's movie Jailhouse Rock.

MUSIC

A signed Sekova electric guitar, right, that once belonged to Bill Wyman of the Rolling Stones.

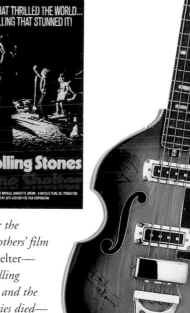

A poster for the Maysles Brothers' film Gimme Shelter—about a Rolling Stones tour and the day the sixties died—touts it as "a mind-blowing trip across young America."

A mid-century serpent-form necklace of enameled "gold" and rhinestones, with matching earrings, by HAR, known for its creative figurals.

Faux rubies surround metal angels and are suspended from a gilt-metal rope on this Joseff of Hollywood medallion necklace.

BRACELETS

Right: In the 1940s, silver jewelry of exceptional creativity and quality was designed, made, and sold in Taxco, Mexico.

Far right: Bakelite came in a variety of colors and could be carved, ground, and polished, threaded, drilled, sanded, and sliced— providing endless design possibilities.

Studio jeweler Art Smith's highly important Positive/ Negative necklace from the 1950s.

PINS & BROOCHES

This stylized peacock pin, with its faux pearl body and colored glass tail, is unmarked, but is thought to be early Chanel.

A Coro enamel and rhinestone tulip pin on which the spring-mounted pink baguette stamens tremble.

A Marvella brooch from 1960 combines gold-tone metal with a dollop of swirly green glass.

Careful detail highlights this enamel and rhinestone figural equestrian pin by Trifari.

This Bakelite bulldog brooch was made for inexpensive fun on a Depression-era budget.

COSTUME JEWELRY

Costume jewelry is like the precious jewelry it imitates, but more fantastic, often bigger, and usually more playful. For much less money, it provides enthusiasts with the glittery pleasures of matching necklaces, pins, bracelets, and pairs of earrings to their clothes, eye color, and wallets. Yet its artistry and inventiveness frequently equals—and sometimes surpasses—the real.

A festive Miriam Haskell necklace of rhinestone circles suspending ruby-colored rhinestone and gilt metal tassels.

Typical of Miriam Haskell's dense style, this pair of earrings combines gilt-metal flowers with clustered rhinestones and pearls.

Twentieth-century glass-making techniques provided clearer and brighter rhinestones than had ever been available. This tiara replicates antique diamond pieces.

Staret jewelry from the 1940s—like this 4½-inch-long torch brooch of enamel and rhinestones—is big, showy, and fanciful.

The diamondlike rhinestones on an Eisenberg "fur clip" from the 1930s are highly convincing.

Hobé collectors value the sterling brooches incorporating glass "stones," such as this one.

A fine rhinestone tremblant flower pin with stones in a variety of sizes.

The odd combination of blue, green, and brown stones in this Schreiner brooch is unlikely to be found in genuine jewelry.

Clear, basic, and graphic, this 1930s Lester Beall poster brilliantly promotes the benefits of radio to America's rural populace.

POSTERS & ILLUSTRATION

Posters and comic books were always throw-aways; the artistic equivalent of fast food. They were made to be viewed or read and discarded. And even when new, the original paintings from which book, magazine, and calendar illustrations were reproduced were also—amazingly—disposable. Fortunately, all these things have always had fans who salvaged them for themselves—and for us.

POSTERS

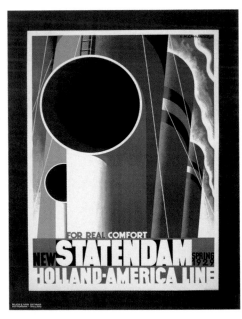

Successful poster artist Cassandre's work was so effective that this Statendam poster, above, brought him five to ten times the customary fee.

Right: Printed in huge numbers for insertion in a Bob Dylan record album, this distinctive Milton Glaser poster encapsulates the 1960s.

A poster for a poster museum: Raymond Savignac created this "museum guard" for the Musée de l'Affiche in 1978.

A convincing World War II photomontage poster by Henrion depicts an efficient telephone operator communicating with various British military personnel.

Bertozzi Parmigiano-Reggiano was good enough to pass a three-judge olfactory test, as graphically presented in this Achille Mauzan poster from 1930.

The unusually busy links at Cruden Bay, pictured here in a 1930 British Rail poster, were a convenient hop from London.

A 1951 poster for BOAC (British Overseas Airways Corporation) by Abram Games suddenly turns the image of airplane steps into an unfurling map of the world.

A 1930s poster for the Hotel l'Arbois, shows it in the vanguard of hotels catering to a new taste for sun bathing on the French Riviera.

James Montgomery Flagg designed more than forty war posters, but this authoritative World War I Uncle Sam remains his best-known image.

Ihap Hulusi, the leading Turkish poster artist, created this exotic image promoting travel to Egypt.

ILLUSTRATION ART

Above: A portrait of Madeline—heroine of a beloved series of children's books by Ludwig Bemelmans—with a large bunch of flowers.

Right: Nostalgia and art winsomely combine in Norman Rockwell's Dr. and Doll, an original 1929 cover for the Saturday Evening Post, considered one of the most popular covers of that magazine.

Cappiello's delectably plump golden goose makes a fitting image for "the queen of fois gras."

Right, Gustav Klutsis's powerful and acclaimed 1931 poster "The USSR is the Avant Garde of the World Proletariat" captures the Revolution's essence.

Illustrator N. C. Wyeth painted this fierce group for endpapers on Scribner's 1911 edition of Robert Louis Stevenson's Treasure Island.

Jessie Willcox Smith's charcoal and watercolor on board illustration for the cover of Helen Hay Whitney's The Bed-Time Book of 1907.

In Haddon H. Sundblom's tender 1940s illustration for a poster, Coke goes with everything, even ball gowns and pajamas.

An illustration from an as yet unidentified book or magazine, circa 1925, of a picnic in a canoe by Andrew Loomis.

FURNITURE

When they were new, these examples of twentieth-century furniture, many designed by architects, seemed startlingly avant garde and modern. The best of them still do. And it is this freshness and strength—this beauty and appropriateness for every decade—that makes them modern classics, and collectible today.

This updated "Marilyn" loveseat is polyurethane covered in red nylon. It is an homage to Salvatore Dali's sofa design based on Mae West's lips, built by Jean-Michel Frank.

Arne Jacobsen's womblike 1957 Egg Chair, in its original blue cloth upholstery, retains the label of its manufacturer, Fritz Hansen.

Although Le Corbusier's groundbreaking chrome and leather lounge chair was first designed in 1928, it has been continually reproduced. (A manufacturer's label helps in accurate dating.)

Eight feet of pillows and tufting on a mahogany frame, this 1950s armless sofa is an Edward Wormley design for Dunbar Furniture.

A 1963 blend of Shaker design and walnut plank, this George Nakashima Conoid bench has its original finish.

Too costly to ship assembled, late models of this popular ESU-400 storage unit by Charles Eames for Herman Miller, below right, were sent in pieces.

Unfortunately, the original pink and black paint on this 1927 Paul Frankl Skyscraper chest has been stripped, but it retains its bakelite, glass, brass, and maple "bells and whistles."

Dappled cowhide, called slunk skin, covers a fifties version of Charles and Ray Eames' LCW (lounge chair wood), first designed in 1946.

Above: The stylized shape and the carving on this 1925 Süe et Mare mahogany armchair epitomize fine French Art Deco design.

Far left: Frenchman Jean Royère's 1937 tribute to the classic Greek stool, as blond and sleek as Jean Harlowe.

Left: Unlike the chest on the previous page, this Paul Frankl Skyscraper bookcase, circa 1928, with cabinets, shelves, and brass pull rings, has its original red and black lacquer.

Although George Nelson's Marshmallow sofa for Herman Miller is here covered in brown vinyl, it is often seen in more colorful fabrics.

OMEGA

The well-known Swiss watch company Omega originated in the nineteenth century and takes its name from the last letter of the Greek alphabet—omega (Ω)—the traditional symbol for "ultimate achievement." In the late 1940s, Omega had a great success with the Constellation, an automatic chronometer. Among Omega collectors, the hand-wound chronometers of Caliber 30 T2 designation are sought after. As the official watch of the National Aeronautic Space Administration (NASA) Apollo Program, Omega had the signal honor of being the first wristwatch to be worn on the moon when Neil Armstrong wore Omega's Speedmaster on his historic moonwalk.

A rectangular gold Art Deco–style Omega wristwatch with cartoonlike, exaggerated numbers and spade hands, from the 1930s.

PATEK PHILIPPE

Patek Philippe, founded in 1833, is considered by many experts to be the premier watch house in the world. It stands first with knowledgeable wristwatch collectors, primarily because of its unsurpassed melding of classic, understated design with exquisite craftsmanship and sophisticated mechanisms. One of the world's most desirable factory-made timepieces is the Patek Calatrava, first produced early in the twentieth century. A round-case watch and an instant classic, it is undoubtedly one of the most popular wristwatches ever manufactured. Sold at auction recently for $1.2 million, a 1932 Calatrava with complications became the highest-priced wristwatch in the world.

ROLEX

Switzerland's Rolex firm—a manufacturer of perennial status symbols of the twentieth, and possibly the twenty-first century—was founded by Hans Wildorf just before World War I. The name, it is said, comes from the French *horlogerie exquise* (maker of beautiful timepieces).

The 1926 Oyster was the first major Rolex wristwatch and the world's first waterproof timepiece, inspired, goes the story,

THE "IT" GIRL'S WATCH

An Ermeto purse watch that had once belonged to the actress Clara Bow, the "It" girl of the silent-film era, was brought to the Los Angeles *Antiques Roadshow*.

The Art Deco–style purse watch, picked up at a tag sale for $26, is inscribed with the silent film star's name on the back and

the original Cartier registration number on the bottom. A close inspection by *Antiques Roadshow* appraiser Sig Shonholtz revealed a tiny note, folded and tucked into the watchcase, reading: "Daniel Freeman to Clara Bow on her 22nd birthday, 29 July 1928 . . ." Freeman stole the watch back, along with an anklet with his and Bow's initials on it, as repayment for his broken heart. Together, the watch and the anklet are valued at $3,000 to $4,000.

A Rolex Prince Doctor's watch (duo-dial) from the 1930s. Rolex designers discovered that they could make a more accurate watch, and one that would run for a longer period of time, if they used a rectangular case rather than a round one. The first Prince, the most accurate watch of its time, was manufactured in 1928.

A Rolex Oyster from the 1920s also carries the name of fashionable London jewelers Mappin & Webb, the store at which it was purchased.

This round gold automatic (self-winding) Universal Genève watch has a two-tone dial, baton numerals, and an Incabloc movement.

by Wildorf's being unable to open a naturally "waterproof" oyster at a party. The Rolex Oyster has a twinlock system that seals the winding mechanism against moisture, and the firm whimsically claims to test each watch in its "Oyster Beds." (Some authorities suggest that collectors ask a Rolex retailer to make such a test before submerging any waterproof watch themselves; others believe it isn't reasonable to expect that a vintage Rolex will remain waterproof.)

Part of the explanation for the continuing investment value of Rolex watches is the company's tight control over the number produced each year, as well as the carefully selected and limited number of Rolex dealers. Such sustained value is also due in large part to the quality of the watches themselves and to the firm's constant pursuit of horological invention. In the thirties, Rolex introduced the self-winding Perpetual; in the fifties, the Date-Just, which displayed the day of the month, and the Submariner and Day-Date models. The Day-Date indicated the day of the month while it spelled out the day of the week.

Genuine Rolex watches are well marked. The most collectible models are the Prince, the Oyster, the Doctor's Watch, and the GMT Master, which has a fourth hand that keeps Greenwich Mean Time.

A luxurious rectangular hand-made platinum and yellow gold Vacheron & Constantin dress watch from the 1930s.

Waltham (see page 320), a noted maker of railroad watches, became equally noted for military watches during World War I. This rare 1918 military watch was an early, experimental waterproof design.

UNIVERSAL GENÈVE

Universal Genève, founded in the last decade of the nineteenth century, began producing the well-known Compax line of watches shortly after 1934. In 1944, it produced the best-selling two-button sports chronograph of the midcentury, the Tri-Compax, which included a complete calendar and moon phases. Considered a masterpiece of Swiss watchmaking, the Tri-Compax is among today's most sought-after chronographs. Among other important Universal Genève watches are the Golden Shadow, with a superthin movement, which was the thinnest automatic watch when it was introduced in 1966, and the Polerouter, developed from the watches worn by SAS pilots on an historic flight over the North Pole in 1957.

VACHERON & CONSTANTIN

Vacheron & Constantin, founded in the eighteenth century, is perhaps the oldest watch company still in operation. The luxury watches produced by this Geneva firm are not very well known, and possibly for that reason they are less highly sought after than those of its more famous competitors. In its own factories, the firm produces watches with several kinds of complications, among them repeaters, chronographs, and calendars.

FAMOUS JEWELERS' OWN BRANDS

Watches having the Tiffany & Co. name on the dial or the case, or both, often contain movements by Patek Philippe, Audemars Piguet, Hamilton, Longines, or International Watch Company. That Tiffany name, however, lends a touch of additional status to anything it touches, and wristwatches are no exception. Tiffany watches—along with others from fashionable jewelry stores like Van Cleef & Arpels or Shreve, Crump & Low—are always popular with collectors.

The Italian jeweler Bulgari introduced a well-known serpent-shaped bracelet watch in the 1940s that is valued more today for its design than for its horological merit.

A GOLD WATCH AND A HANDSHAKE

A vintage Rolex Prince watch that was brought to the Toronto *Antiques Roadshow* originally belonged to the owner's uncle, a driver for the owners of a Canadian department store.

The family gave Rolex presentation watches to their most-valued employees. This watch is inscribed on the back and its unusual face spells out "Quarter Century Club" in place of numbers.

Antiques Roadshow appraiser Kevin Zavian observed that this watch was made fairly early in Rolex history. Although it no longer has the original leather band, the watch is worth between $5,000 and $6,000.

WALTHAM

From the 1930s to the 1950s, the old-line American manufacturer Waltham—in the mill town of Waltham, Massachusetts—maker of thousands of nineteenth-century railroad watches (accurate, inexpensive pocket watches that took their name from those used to keep the railroads running on time), produced sturdy and dependable wristwatches, many for the military. These are among the most affordable watches available to collectors today.

Waltham pioneered the production of watches on an assembly line. The company went out of business in 1957.

WITTNAUER

A Swiss company that ultimately merged with Longines, Wittnauer was the first company to produce a waterproof, shockproof, antimagnetic watch. Wittnauer watches were issued to American soldiers in World War II.

A Wittnauer chronograph with three subsidiary dials and an outer scale (marked for tachometer). The company is known for stylish and dependable watches.

Chapter Nine

PHOTOGRAPHY

Nearly everyone has a family album—or drawersful of photographs of friends, relatives, friends of relatives, and complete unknowns. So most of us already collect photography in its broadest sense. A considerable number of photographs of all kinds have been brought to the *Antiques Roadshow* over the years—daguerreotypes (the earliest photographs), twentieth-century photographs recording important historical events and spectacular natural monuments, and pictures of everyday occasions and ordinary places. Works by masters like Ansel Adams and Edward S. Curtis have appeared along with family scrapbooks assembled during World War II. The range has been enormous, and anyone interested in starting to collect photography seriously has an equally enormous universe of material to choose from. But, like all collectors, photography collectors should collect what they love; a personal—and pleasant—decision.

Collectors of serious photography believe that they are pursuing *the* artistic medium of the twentieth century, and they may very well be right. Photographic images have captured the world in a manner unimaginable before the medium's invention in the mid-nineteenth century. To the collector, however, its chronicling aspect is often secondary to the idea of owning the

Top: A daguerreotype portrait from the 1850s of a little boy and his toy horse. Bottom: Walker Evans's Dockworkers, Havana, 1932. *Some consider Evans to be the finest documentary photographer of the twentieth century.*

beautiful and moving works produced by some of the great artists of our time.

There are all sorts of photography collectors. There are those who seek out only works by the great masters of the medium: Berenice Abbott, Paul Strand, or Ansel Adams, for example. Some are attracted by unusual photographic processes, collecting daguerreotypes, calotypes, or platinum prints. One well-known collector turned to collecting black-and-white photographs, for which silver is used to make the image, only after he had assembled a notable collection of silver and silver-plate decorative objects. Sometimes, a compelling subject inspires a collection. Many collectors choose only landscapes, for example, or only portraits. And even more special interests can come into play. A visitor to the New York *Antiques Roadshow* had been watching his local PBS station in the mid-1970s when a larger-than-life photograph of Albert Einstein appeared as part of the station's fundraising auction. The visitor, an IBM researcher, had long been "an admirer of Einstein," he told appraiser Daile Kaplan. After bidding on the photograph, he went to sleep, and was awakened by a call from the station with the news that he had won the photograph (taken by Philippe Halsman, one of the most famous portrait photographers of the twentieth century) for $125.

Albert Einstein helped photographer Philippe Halsman escape from Nazi Germany. Halsman's 1947 portrait of his benefactor has become the iconic image of the eminent physicist.

There's more, however, to this story. "Einstein had helped Halsman escape Nazi Germany," explained appraiser Kaplan. "Years later, Halsman was honored to be able to meet Einstein, photograph him, and thank him personally." Halsman came away from that meeting with this iconic image. "When I was in college, lots of people had this image as a poster on their dorm walls," Kaplan says. How much is this $125 investment in PBS worth today? Between $7,000 and $10,000, Kaplan estimates.

In order to provide a framework for those interested in this popular collecting area, a brief history of photography and its practitioners in the United States follows, with emphasis on the period from the early decades of the twentieth century to about 1975. Included are summarized profiles of some of the major figures in the field. Many different stylistic labels have been used to describe these photographers—among them, documentary photographer, pictorialist, and photojournalist—but these distinctions are not as important as the fact that they all have enormous talent.

A BRIEF HISTORY

In 1839, French stage designer Louis-Jacques-Mandé Daguerre unveiled the first highly detailed, permanent photographic image, called, with justifiable pride, the daguerreotype. The image was captured on a silver-coated copper plate. Daguerreotypes differed from the photographs we know today not just in their metal surface and silvery appearance, but also in being entirely one-of-a-kind. A daguerreotype could not be reproduced or enlarged, and neither could its successors, the ambrotype and the tintype. No negatives exist for any of these processes.

An elegant rider seated sidesaddle on her well-groomed horse posed for this daguerreotype in the 1850s.

COLLECTING DAGUERREOTYPES

Daguerreotypes were a popular means of preserving family and national history from the moment they were invented. Although they were an expensive way to record a likeness, they were much less expensive than their predecessor, the painted portrait.

Some 30 million daguerreotypes were taken in the United States between 1840 and 1860, when they were superseded by ambrotypes and tintypes. Over the years, most have been lost or damaged, yet many remain.

Daguerreotypes, with their clarity and detail,

A daguerreotype portrait of a man in full masonic regalia from the 1850s.

attract collectors, but those of famous people are particularly sought after, as are those depicting the sitters at their occupation or displaying the tools of their trades, along with outdoor scenes. The slightly macabre genre of posthumous portraits of children taken as remembrances attract some enthusiasts, as do the surprising numbers of daguerreotypes of toys or pets, either with their owners or alone. All are very popular with collectors. Military subjects can command a premium, especially if the images are large and the subject is dressed in full regalia.

FASHION PHOTOGRAPHY

Fashion and photography have a long and intertwined history. In the 1920s, the great Edward Steichen was chief photographer for the fashion magazines *Vogue* and *Vanity Fair.* Irving Penn started at *Vogue* two decades later, and eventually expanded into other areas, including travel and advertising. Another photographer whose fashion work won acclaim is Richard Avedon. His raw and confrontational portraits frequently confound his viewer's expectations of his subjects. Other noted photographers who concentrated on the world of fashion include Baron Adolphe de Meyer (see page 343) and Horst P. Horst (see page 345).

William Henry Fox Talbot's Bridge of Sighs, St. John's College, Cambridge, *circa 1845. With Talbot's calotype process, multiple prints could be made.*

William Henry Fox Talbot, an English polymath and Daguerre's contemporary, took the field one step further when he discovered a way to create a negative from which a positive paper image could be made. Talbot had worked on his process, which he called the calotype, for several years, and although his early efforts predate Daguerre's announcement, he did not patent his process until 1841. Talbot's calotype is the process on which twentieth-century photography was based. (Digital technology seems to be leading photography far away from the negative in the beginning of the twenty-first century.)

The decades that followed the invention of photography saw tremendous technological ferment and innovation. Scientists and darkroom dabblers of all sorts sought to make their photographs reveal increasingly more detail and simultaneously to take less time and be less cumbersome and expensive to develop. Photographers also wanted the resulting photographic images to last longer than the earlier, less stable processes had allowed. What point, after all, was there in a loved one's portrait if it didn't last? Technological changes in photography, consequently, were based on developing more and better printing processes and smaller, more versatile cameras. (See page 326 for a review of a few of the photographic processes.)

Photography quickly became an invaluable tool for documenting historic events and recording likenesses of those both famous and humble. Civil War–era images by Mathew Brady and his colleagues are particularly well known.

By the close of the nineteenth century, groups of serious enthusiasts in Europe, such as the English-based Linked Ring—which broke away from the Royal Photographic Society when the latter steadfastly refused to consider photography an art rather than a science—recognized the medium's potential as an art form. In the United States, however, there were no similar groups, only clubs for amateurs. There were, however, an increasing number of people who thought it was important to distinguish between art photography and the efforts of amateurs.

Gerson Sisters Dressed for Crinoline Ball, New York City, *circa 1906, by pictorialist photographer and Photo-Secessionist Gertrude Käsebier.*

THE PHOTO-SECESSION

The founder of the first serious American art-photography movement was Alfred Stieglitz, an American photographer who had studied in Germany in the 1880s. In 1902, he organized an exhibition entitled *American Pictorial Photography by the Photo-Secession.* Stieglitz's goal was to break away, or secede, from the crowd of amateur photographers and to establish a circle of fine-art photographers on the order of the Linked Ring. (He took the name "photo-secession" from the progressive turn-of-the-twentieth-century German and Austrian artistic movement.) Most Secessionist photographers were pictorialists, creators of romantic, painterly images. In fact, pictorialists often used charcoal and pigments to highlight image areas, making them more closely resemble more traditional forms of art, such as drawings.

That same year, Stieglitz began to publish *Camera Work,* a revolutionary magazine that would become enormously

(continued on page 328)

BUT IS IT ART?

The recognition of photography as an art form worthy of respect has been something of an uphill battle. In its infancy, photography was viewed as a science, and its technical aspect dazzled people—it seemed to be pure magic. As the science of photography rapidly evolved during the nineteenth century, photographers began to explore its artistic potential. Despite the photographic experiments of famous artists like Thomas Eakins and Edgar Degas, the creative aspect of photography was overshadowed in the public's eye by its technical wonders. Crediting the technology of the camera with the resultant image totally ignores the artistry of the person who created it—an attitude akin to attributing the beauty of a Van Gogh landscape to the brush and paint, rather than to the artist himself.

One reason that artistic respectability has been so difficult to achieve stems from the ease with which photographs can be made. Because of technological advances, practically anyone could use a camera, have the film developed, and images duplicated. The first advertising slogan of the Eastman Kodak Company, which developed the first camera designed for amateurs, was "You press the button, we do the rest." Even today, many people fail to understand that photography is a legitimate vehicle of creative expression.

Photographic Processes

The following list of photographic processes, in roughly chronological order, offers brief definitions of what are often highly technical procedures. It is helpful, nonetheless, for collectors to familiarize themselves with the vocabulary. Additional information is available in many specialized books (see reading list, page 543). Some of these seemingly outmoded processes are being resurrected by photographers today.

DAGUERREOTYPE:
Named after its inventor, Louis-Jacques-Mandé Daguerre, who introduced the process in 1839, a daguerreotype is a highly detailed one-of-a-kind photographic image on a silver-coated copper plate.

CALOTYPE:
Invented by William Henry Fox Talbot prior to Daguerre's announcement, the calotype process was not patented until 1841. It created a paper negative, which was then used to create a positive image on paper. Although calotypes lacked the crispness of daguerreotypes, this technique made duplication of images possible.

CYANOTYPE:
Invented by British scientist John Herschel in 1842, the cyanotype is a simple but slow photographic process that does not require a darkroom. The most common method requires that an object be placed on chemically treated paper and exposed to light. Appropriately, the process produces prints with a bluish tint.

COLLODION WET-PLATE PROCESS:
Also known simply as the wet-plate process, it was developed in 1848 and improved upon in 1851 by Frederick Scott Archer. It employed a chemical process on glass plates and was extremely popular between 1855 and 1881, replacing daguerreotypes and calotypes.

CARBON PRINT:
Introduced by Alphonse Louis Poitev in 1855, this process utilizes gelatin and carbon and produces rich, glossy images. It was particularly popular from about 1870 to 1910.

The Three Graces, *photographed by Julia Margaret Cameron, is an albumen print from 1869.*

ALBUMEN PRINT:
A process invented by Louis-Désiré Blanquard-Evrard in 1850, the albumen print was made by coating a piece of paper with various chemicals and egg white (albumen), and exposing a negative on it. Albumen prints have a shiny appearance and rich, golden tones, but they have a tendency to yellow and fade with age. Most photographic prints of the nineteenth century were albumen prints. They were replaced by gelatin silver prints in the 1890s.

AMBROTYPE:
Patented by James Ambrose Cutting in 1854, the ambrotype is a wet-plate process using chemicals for printing on glass, resulting in a grayish image. The plates are mounted on black backgrounds or the backs are painted black to darken the exposed areas and add contrast to clear portions. Ambrotypes had the advantage of being quicker to develop and less expensive than daguerreotypes, for which they are often mistaken. The daguerreotype is generally a brighter image.

TINTYPE:
Introduced by Adolphe Alexandre Martin in 1853, the tintype (also known as a ferrotype) is an image created by the collodion wet-plate process applied to a blackened sheet of iron, a less expensive process than the daguerreotype. Its ease of use and lower cost began to democratize photography, making it affordable even to the less affluent.

PLATINUM PRINT:
A process patented in England by William Willis in 1873, which employed a negative to print on paper coated with iron salts and platinum salts. The process was a favorite among fine-art photographers from the late nineteenth century to World War I, when the rising cost of platinum forced many to use less expensive processes, most notably the

palladium print (see below). The platinum print is experiencing a revival today.

GELATIN SILVER PRINT:

Produced on paper coated with a gelatin emulsion within which light-sensitive silver salts are suspended, an image on a gelatin silver print is not embedded in the paper, but rather is suspended on the surface. The results are long lasting. Introduced at the end of the nineteenth century, the gelatin silver print became the most widely used process for black-and-white photography in the twentieth century.

AUTOCHROME PLATE:

An additive process invented and developed by the Lumière brothers and introduced to the market in 1907. This method produces no negative; each autochrome photograph is a unique image, employing colored potato starches to form a screen, which then acts as a filter. When the resultant black-and-white positive is combined with the color screen, a positive image is produced that creates the illusion of full color. The "plate" refers to the glass plate on which the image appears.

CARBRO:

Dating from around 1919, the carbro process is based on the earlier carbon transfer to a bromide print, and a process patented in 1905 as Ozobrome. It employs gelatin tissues colored with three primary colors—cyan, magenta, and yellow. These are placed on silver bromide prints. When they are transferred onto paper, they combine to produce a three-color print. Carbro prints have the advantage of being long lasting.

Ambrotype of a small town in the Pacific Northwest, taken by Peter Britt in the 1850s.

PALLADIUM PRINT:

This less expensive variant of the platinum print process substitutes palladium for platinum. The print produced by this process is also known as a palladiotype.

CHROMOGENIC COLOR PRINT:

The chromogenic color-print process uses photographic paper incorporating light-sensitized layers of red, green, and blue emulsion. These combine with dye couplers to produce a full-color positive image. The print produced is also known as a "C" print or chromo. The process is not as long lasting as other color processes.

DYE TRANSFER:

A subtractive process also known as dye-imbibition, the dye-transfer process deposits three layers of dyes onto a gelatin-coated sheet of paper. Three separate black-and-white negatives are made from the original transparency, shot through red, green, or blue filters. Each contains information about one of the three colors. From these negatives, molds or matrices capable of releasing and absorbing dyes of the primary colors are made. When

the matrices are precisely aligned or registered, they form a full-color image. Although time-consuming, the results are controllable, producing relatively stable prints.

DYE DIFFUSION:

A modern, technically advanced process, dye diffusion uses three layers sensitized to blue, red, or green. Each layer contains a developing agent, a dye reciprocal to the color, a final backing layer, and a "packet" of additional chemicals. After exposure, the packet releases the chemicals, and the dyes that form the image diffuse through the emulsion layers to form the image on the backing. In earlier processes the negative materials would then be removed from the positive. One example is the unique-image Polaroid process. In later versions, the negative materials remain embedded in the positive. Although not visible, these embedded materials make the newer version less stable than the former.

DYE DESTRUCTION:

Also known as dye-bleach process, dye-destruction makes prints from a negative or transparency created by the use of layers of emulsion, each sensitized to a primary color. Each layer also has a dye corresponding to its color. When the negative is exposed, a silver image is created in each layer, which is then developed and bleached out. When printed, the residual dyes of the three layers create a full-color image by appearing as one. Cibachrome is one brand name for this process. The color in a dye-destruction print is less susceptible to fading than in chromogenic print, but not as stable as in a dye-transfer print.

PHOTOGRAPH OF A TRAGEDY

A visitor from Scituate, Massachusetts, brought an early-twentieth-century photograph of an ice-bound ship, the *Terra*

Nova, to *Antiques Roadshow* in Boston. *Terra Nova* carried the heroic Antarctic expedition led by English explorer Robert Falcon Scott. Appraiser Daile Kaplan told the visitor that the photograph was taken by Herbert G. Ponting, who survived this voyage.

For two months, Scott and four companions dragged heavy sledges across a bleak landscape where temperatures rarely crawled above zero. When they reached their destination, they found that Norwegian explorer Roald Amundsen had arrived there a month before. Scott kept a diary, chronicling the illness, hunger, and blizzards that beset the five men, all of whom died along the way. "Any artifact from this trip is very valuable," Kaplan observed, adding that this photograph's large size and Ponting's signature make it "one of a kind." Its value is $6,000 to $9,000.

important to the development of serious photography. He used the magazine to build the Photo-Secession movement and to establish a group of artists diverse in their work but united in their belief in photography as a separate and legitimate field of fine art. *Camera Work* provided Stieglitz, who edited and published it, with a medium for displaying his own works as well as those of other twentieth-century masters-in-the-making, such as Edward Steichen, Gertrude Käsebier, Alvin Langdon Coburn, and Paul Strand.

In 1905, Stieglitz, encouraged by Steichen, opened a gallery at 291 Fifth Avenue in New York City. He called it the Little Galleries of the Photo-Secession at 291, but it was commonly called simply "291." There he exhibited paintings, sculpture, and drawings of emerging "modern" artists, such as Picasso, Matisse, and Rodin, along with his own and his colleagues' photographs. Stieglitz brought fresh ideas to American audiences, challenging their concept of art. By presenting photography side-by-side with painting and sculpture, he set it on an equal footing with other modernist movements.

Not all American photographers joined Stieglitz, yet many of these also had a lasting impact on serious photography, Edward S. Curtis and Lewis Wickes Hine among them. Curtis, who became a photographer in the waning years of the nineteenth century, is known for romanticized studies of North American Indians. Hine, trained as a sociologist, was a pioneer in investigative photography, and his images brought attention to social issues, particularly child labor.

Chief Joseph (circa 1905) by Edward Curtis, part of the photographer's thirty-year chronicle of the American West.

The final issues of *Camera Work* (from 1916 and 1917) featured the photographs of Paul Strand, a master of bold and simple styles who had turned away from the self-consciously "artistic" techniques of the pictorialists. Strand called his work "straight" photography. He was against using artifice to achieve effects: no scratching on negatives or rubbing oil on lenses; no cropping or manipulating the negative. Such manipulations of photographs, he contended, were "merely the expression of an impotent desire to paint." Strand's photographs, as a result, were crisp, focused, and free of all visual trickery.

The Photo-Secessionists disbanded around 1916, but the artists associated with the movement continued to create important work.

WESTON AND HIS CIRCLE

New York was not the only place in the United States where important photographers were working in the early years of the twentieth century. Edward Weston established his Little Studio in California in 1911. He was already a successful photographer when he met Stieglitz in 1922 and seems not to have been directly influenced by him. Weston's works are crisp, clear studies of light and texture as they relate to organic forms. His most frequently photographed subject was his second wife, Charis Wilson—in images that are famous for their abstraction of the female body. He is equally well-known for his studies of vegetables and expansive landscapes.

In Seattle, Imogen Cunningham, a friend of Weston's, began as a studio-portrait artist. Her early works are influenced by Käsebier and are for the most part romantic studies in the pictoralist style. Later she turned to sharply focused images. She is known for close-up, voluptuous studies of flowers and nudes.

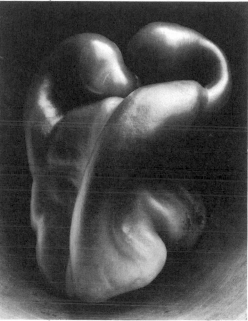

Influential West Coast photographer Edward Weston was known for his abstract studies of "strangely beautiful forms," such as Pepper, 1930.

NEW YORK TO PARIS, PARIS TO NEW YORK

Man Ray, an American who began his career as a painter, became an important photographer in the 1920s. Influenced by Alfred Stieglitz, he began by photographing his paintings to document them and later turned to photography as an art form. After he moved to Paris in 1921, he photographed some of the best-known painters and authors of the period,

In works such as Flatiron Building *(1938), Berenice Abbott meticulously recorded New York's ever-changing cityscape.*

Dust Storm, Cimarron County, Oklahoma *(1936), one of the many stark photographs documenting the plight of the rural poor by Arthur Rothstein.*

including Henri Matisse, Max Ernst, James Joyce, and Ernest Hemingway. He is particularly noted for his photograms, which he called Rayographs—cameraless images made by placing objects on light-sensitive photographic paper, then exposing the paper to light.

Berenice Abbott worked in Man Ray's studio in Paris before starting her own studio there. Abbott specialized in portraits, producing iconic images of such literary luminaries as James Joyce and Jean Cocteau. She discovered and ultimately saved the work of Eugène Atget, a masterly photographer who documented Paris in the early years of the twentieth century, a period when that city was going through intense change. In 1929, Abbott returned to New York and began—in her distinctive style—to do for New York what Atget had done for Paris. Over the next two decades, Abbott recorded New York's fluid cityscape, which culminated in the book *Changing New York*.

THE DEPRESSION AND THE FSA

During the Great Depression of the 1930s, photography explored industrial abstraction (images depicting parts of machinery to symbolize the energy and dynamism of the industrial age), showed an increased interest in the documentary style, and saw the rise of photojournalism. Increasingly, photographers influenced how people received the news and perceived the world around them. New movements arose, too, such as Group f/64, named for a large-format camera's smallest lens aperture, the one used to produce images with the greatest depth of field. Founded in 1932 by Ansel Adams, Edward Weston, Imogen Cunningham, and others, this group embraced clear, crisp, "straight" photography. The Photo League (called the Film and Photo League until 1935), an organization of documentary photographers founded in New York in 1930, influenced scores of photographers, among them Aaron Siskind, to use their cameras for social change—helping to forge better lives for the common person.

In 1935, the Farm Security Administration (FSA), a governmental social agency, employed American photographers to document the effects of the Depression. The resulting studies, detailing the plight of farm workers, were intended to educate the public. Photographers were briefed on their subjects' sociological background, a strategy, it was hoped, that would make their work that much more telling. Dorothea Lange, Walker Evans, Ben Shahn, and Arthur Rothstein were part of the varied group of photographers who employed a documentary style to produce searing, timeless images of the rural poor. Dorothea Lange's unforgettable portrait of a migrant mother—despair and deprivation etched on her face, her weary children leaning into her—is a milestone of the era.

Walker Evans was perhaps the greatest documentary photographer of the twentieth century. Working for the FSA from 1935 to 1938, he produced several books, *American Photographs,* published in 1938, among them. It features his FSA images and some earlier work, including street scenes that resemble carefully crafted snapshots. His best known book, however, is *Let Us Now Praise Famous Men,* published in 1941. Considered a masterwork of American literature, it combines writing by James Agee with Evans's photographs of disenfranchised Alabama sharecroppers, their impoverished living conditions, and their weathered churches. The images are wrenchingly understated, bleak, and serene.

LIFE MAGAZINE AND THE BIRTH OF PHOTOJOURNALISM

In 1936, Henry Luce founded *Life* magazine, an illustrated weekly and the first publication to feature photographic images on a regular basis. *Life's* first cover was shot by Margaret Bourke-White, one of the magazine's original four photographers. Known for hard-edged images glorifying machinery, Bourke-White filled the magazine with these and portraits of the working poor of the Depression era. She also documented the tumultuous times immediately before, during, and after World War II.

American civilians followed the progress of World War II through *Life's* pictures, for they captured the war's devastation. Among unforgettable *Life* images are Margaret Bourke-White's

WORLD WAR II SCRAPBOOKS

A visitor from Arlington, Massachusetts, came to the Boston *Antiques Roadshow* with her grandfather's photograph album. He had served in the U.S.

army during World War II and taken the photographs during the liberation of Germany's Buchenwald concentration camp.

Appraiser Wes Cowan suggested she contact the National Museum of American History, part of the Smithsonian Institution.

"Most people don't have a clue as to what to do with these photographs," curator Margaret Vining said. "They just have an instinct that they are historically important." Collections of photographs from World War I to the present can be sent to The Veterans History Project, part of the American Folk Life Center at the Library of Congress, which is collecting both visual and written war histories.

For information about where to send war photographs or other war memorabilia, contact The Veterans History Project at: vohp@loc.gov.

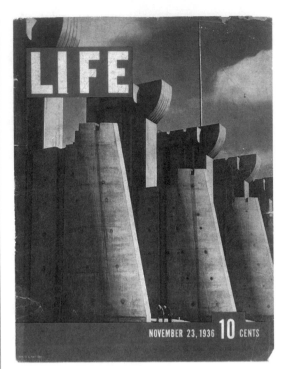

On the cover of the first issue of Life *magazine, November 23, 1936, Margaret Bourke-White's arresting photograph of Montana's Fort Peck Dam.*

photographs of the liberation of the Nazi concentration camps and W. Eugene Smith's wrenching images of the fighting in the Pacific.

Photographers such as Robert Capa carried light and versatile 35mm cameras into battle, revolutionizing the way photographers would cover war. Between 1943 and the end of hostilities, Capa photographed Rommel's retreat from North Africa, the Allied landing and invasion of Italy, the momentous D-Day landing on Omaha Beach, and the liberation of France.

Technological advances in the 1930s allowed photographers to explore old subjects in new ways by giving them new tools to work with. In 1931, for example, photographer and scientist Harold E. Edgerton invented the stroboscope, a flash device using pulses of light to make efficient and effective high-speed photography possible. Stroboscopic, or stop-action, photography allowed photographers to capture images that could not be seen with the naked eye. Edgerton's 1934 photograph of Wesley E. Fesler kicking a football shows in amazing detail the foot connecting with the ball and the indentation in the ball at the moment of impact, an event lasting fractions of a second.

THE 1940S AND 1950S

The forties began with an important step in the history of photography: institutional recognition. Photographs had been exhibited at art museums, but until this time no museum had ever formed a curatorial photography department. In 1940, New York's Museum of Modern Art became the first.

Arthur Fellig (known as Weegee) was a freelance photojournalist specializing in images of New York nightlife. His book *Naked City,* published in 1945, peered into the city's darker, less perfect corners. Weegee was equipped with a police radio and was famous for arriving at a crime scene before the police. Because he was so often the first to arrive, he was nicknamed Ouija, after the board game that "predicted the future."

Although America in the 1950s has been customarily portrayed as innocent and wholesome, the works of at least one photographer contradict such false nostalgia. Swiss-born Robert

Frank employed a documentary approach for his book *The Americans,* shot during a 1955 road trip. Considered a Beat Generation classic today, the book was savaged by critics at the time, who believed Frank's distinctive style, incorporating odd angles and the blurring of images, showed a lack of technical skill. His doleful images of waitresses, mourners, and lonely, open roads exude a nervous desperation and despair that made many viewers uncomfortable.

One of Lee Friedlander's noted self-portraits, in which he appears as a shadow on the back of a woman walking down a New York City street, taken in the 1960s.

In 1955, scores of memorable *Life* magazine images, plus hundreds of other photographs, appeared together for the first time in the Museum of Modern Art's landmark exhibition *The Family of Man.* Organized by Edward Steichen, the exhibition awakened an enormous audience to photography and the catalog became a major bestseller.

ON THE STREET IN THE 1960S

During the sixties, inspired by the work of Walker Evans and Robert Frank, Garry Winogrand shot thousands of frames chronicling New York City street scenes. Winogrand is known for edgy images of urban life, such as the series taken at New York City zoos and published in *The Animals* in 1969.

Winogrand's friend Lee Friedlander described his own 1960s work as documenting the "American social landscape, and its condition." Friedlander is known for self-portraits in which he appears only as a shadow or a reflection, and for a series of images of television sets in motel rooms.

Another photographer of the sixties, Diane Arbus, created images that are deeply personal, empathic explorations of her subjects, many of them "outsiders" to conventional society. Her photographs are not always easy to look at, but they are powerful documents of humanity.

ANSEL ADAMS'S AMERICAN LANDSCAPES

A guest brought a portfolio of signed prints by photographer Ansel Adams to the Hot Springs, Arkansas, *Antiques Roadshow*. The owner told appraiser Daile Kaplan that in 1964, he contacted Adams about mounting an exhibition at a museum where he worked. Adams suggested a selection of sixteen photographs that he had taken in the Yosemite Valley. The visitor purchased the set for $100.

Kaplan explained that Adams photographed Yosemite repeatedly, beginning in 1926. In the 1950s,

he revisited his archival negatives and made the visitor's prints, among others. "These are what we call 'modern prints,' because they are later reinterpretations of the original photographic negatives, rather than 'vintage prints,' which would have been printed closer to the time the negative was made.

"They are also superb examples," she said, appraising the portfolio at $30,000 to $50,000.

A REDISCOVERY IN THE 1970S

As the sixties yielded to the seventies and the antiwar protests evolved to include other issues, environmentalists came to embrace the work of Ansel Adams. Adams, of course, was not a new young talent but a well-respected artist with decades of experience, and his depictions of remote unspoiled and threatened landscapes showed budding conservationists what was being lost. Their beauty inspired Americans to work to save the vanishing wilderness.

COLLECTING PHOTOGRAPHY

Since the invention of photography, the standard method of sharing images and promoting a photographer's work has been through books. There were studios, galleries, and exhibitions, but the marketing of photography as art only gained real momentum in the 1970s, when museums began to mount increasing numbers of retrospectives and dealers began to amass inventory and present it to the public. This gave rise to the creation of flourishing photography departments at the major auction houses, where new price records continue to be set for photographs today.

EVALUATING PHOTOGRAPHS

Photography is still a relatively young and expanding collecting field, and there are vast opportunities for emerging and seasoned collectors alike. As with any other field, the new collector should begin by collecting what he loves—portraits, nudes, dogs, flowers, cats, landscapes, or contemporary work.

Although choice images by top twentieth-century masters routinely sell today for hundreds of thousands of dollars, there are still many great works to be had for far less money. Aside from the

Up Close and Personal

When you look at what may be a valuable photograph, ask yourself the following questions. The answers will help you to evaluate the work like an expert.

1 Is the photograph matted and framed? If so, carefully remove the photograph or have an expert do it for you.

2 Is the photograph printed to the edges of the paper? Does the format of the print conform to preexisting standard sizes, such as 8 x 10 inches or 11 x 14 inches? If not, has the print been trimmed? Does this appear to be the photographer's intention or does it appear to have been done without his or her permission? A trimmed print may indicate that the composition of the photograph has been altered.

3 Is the photograph signed on the front, the back, or on the margin? Is the photograph hand stamped, front or back, with an inkpad stamp, or is it blind stamped (embossed)? Are these signatures or stamps consistent with this photographer's usual type of labeling?

4 What photographic process was used to make the print? (For descriptions, see box, "Photographic Processes" page 326) Is this a process the photographer used?

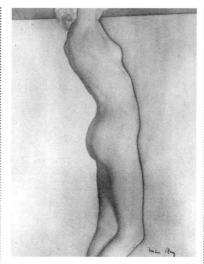

The value of this Man Ray solarized print is enhanced by the signature on the front.

5 Is the print evenly toned or high contrast? When examining a photograph, it is important to pay particular attention to the range of tones to note how different one black-and-white photograph looks next to another. Sometimes the tones sit in gray scale; sometimes the tones are high contrast.

6 Is the paper single weight or double weight? Textured? Shiny? Velvety? This can help determine age, but such subtleties often require advanced knowledge and a qualified professional opinion.

7 What is the age of the photograph? While the process or technique a photographer employs may be helpful in determining the age of a print, vintage prints often have a patina that appeals to some serious collectors. Such prints, which were made near the time the negative was made, are more desirable than later (or modern) prints.

8 Are the size of the image and the sheet size consistent with the photographer's usual output? (The *sheet* is the paper support; the *image* is the picture area.) "Before photography was accepted as a serious art form, twentieth-century photographers tended to work in small sizes," says Daile Kaplan. "André Kértesz, for example, used postcard-size paper in the 1920s; later on in the 1960s and 1970s he revisited his negatives and made larger-format photographs."

9 Finally, what is the condition of the photograph? Are there bends in the paper? Is the photograph clean? Does it have chips, dimples, dings, or tears? Is that appropriate to this photographer's prints? (Weegee's prints are notoriously distressed because newspaper personnel, such as photo editors, handled them.)

work of a few major photographers, it is generally less expensive to collect photography than it is to collect paintings and sculpture. While this chapter only skims the surface of an enormous field, concentrating on American photographers of the twentieth century, there are also important photographs from the nineteenth century available for collectors. Interesting photographers of that era are still being discovered and studied by scholars, as are less-well-known twentieth-century artists. Contemporary photographers and vernacular photography also offer interesting collecting potential. Adventurous collectors can search through local antique shops and outdoor markets for vintage prints, or visit museums and galleries to see the work of contemporary photographers.

VERNACULAR PHOTOGRAPHY

Vernacular photography can encompass such anonymous images as The Archery Club of the Greystone Camp, Asheville, North Carolina, *taken around 1930.*

There is a growing interest in collecting photographs made by anonymous photographers whose intent was more documentary than artistic. In a strange twist, vernacular photography—the work of amateurs—is beginning to be reconsidered, evaluated, and in some cases collected. Interest in such photographs is dictated both by their content and by historical importance.

Museum curators, specialists, and collectors are just beginning to explore and define this genre, which reflects a growing interest in the convergence of photography and popular culture. Vernacular photography can record offhand moments or unusual subjects, capture a particular era, or speak to us with deep historic or cultural associations. African-American family photograph albums, for example, are attracting collectors, as are certain other types of albums, especially those that offer the viewer a casual glimpse into an interesting subject. A good example, appraiser Daile Kaplan says, might be an album depicting life at a women's college in the early years of the twentieth century.

Don't confuse "vernacular photography" with "vernacular style." The latter term is often used to describe photographs depicting everyday objects and scenes, produced by artists like Walker Evans.

RARITY

The big question for collectors is: "How many of these are out there?" The answer is easy to determine when the images are unique: No negatives enabling reproduction were available for daguerreotypes, ambrotypes, and tintypes.

As soon as photographs could be easily reproduced and enlarged, the number of copies a photographer could produce was virtually unlimited. Cognizant of the law of supply and demand, most photographers limit the number of their prints. Too many prints of the same image only undermine value. If an image has developed a following, however, the photographer might choose to revisit it at a later date. For example, there are 1,300 copies extant of Ansel Adams's *Moonrise, Hernandez, New Mexico,* some printed decades apart. Yet, each time a print of *Moonrise* appears at auction, it realizes a strong price and sometimes sets a new record because it is an iconographic image and although all these copies exist, supply still does not meet demand. Don't imagine, however, that every photographer is in Adams's league. Most would certainly not consider glutting the market with twenty-five prints of the same image—let alone 1,300!

Many photographers who have developed a reputation, however, revisit negatives of choice images and sometimes issue limited-edition portfolios of prints. Such limited editions are common among twentieth-century masters. Usually, between four and twenty different images are included in a portfolio, of which, perhaps, twenty-five to one hundred copies will be printed. "The photographs an artist selects for a portfolio generally represent his or her most important images," says Daile Kaplan, an *Antiques Roadshow* specialist. "For the collector, it's a great opportunity to acquire simultaneously a significant body of that artist's work."

THE NEGATIVE AND THE PRINT

The term *vintage print* is often used to describe a photograph, but there is disagreement about what a vintage print is. The controversy is centered on how much time has passed between the creation of the negative and the printing of the

LIMITED EDITIONS

An "edition" is an intentionally limited number of prints made from a single negative. The photographer generally writes that number, with the total number of prints made for that edition, on the print. The inscription "15/20," for example, informs the purchaser that she is buying the fifteenth print out of a total of twenty the artist made. It is to the photographer's advantage to keep the editions of his or her photographs small, because that keeps the demand high.

UNCOVERED ON THE ROADSHOW?

Visitors to *Antiques Roadshow* often arrive with a piece of priceless local history. Such was the case with a woman at the New Orleans show who brought in several photographs taken by E. J. Bellocq, an early-twentieth-century New Orleans photographer.

"Bellocq was a Toulouse-Lautrec-like figure in New Orleans," says appraiser Daile Kaplan. "He took very intimate portraits of prostitutes in bordellos." A cache of Bellocq's glass-plate negatives was discovered after his death by Lee Friedlander (see page 344).

After examining the visitor's prints, Kaplan was uncertain. Were these Friedlander prints from the 1960s or hitherto unknown vintage prints that Bellocq himself had printed? If Friedlander's, Kaplan said the prints might fetch $600 to $900; if Bellocq's, $12,000 to $16,000 could be expected. Only careful chemical-and-paper analysis will reveal the truth.

image. A print is considered vintage if it was produced up to several years after the negative was made.

For clarity's sake, auction houses and galleries are currently cataloging photographs by the year the negative was made, followed by the year the photograph was printed. This is important information to have, because there is often a significant difference in value between a "vintage" print and a "non-vintage" or "modern" print. A vintage print can often bring ten to twenty times as much as a modern print, despite the fact that both depict the same image. The print world supplies the precedent here. Rembrandt etchings, for example, have been endlessly reprinted from the artist's original etched metal plate, and the earlier etchings— those more likely to

This Paul Outerbridge Jr. New York City roofscape was shot and printed in 1923, at the outset of the photographer's career.

have been pulled from the press under the direction of the artist himself—are significantly more valuable. Photographs are valued using the same premise. It is presumed that the oldest print (as determined by paper and technique) is closer to the artist's hand and mindset at the actual time the negative was created.

The photograph market, therefore, is fueled by prices for vintage prints. Photographer Diane Arbus, for instance, made and signed her famous image of identical twins in 1967. A signed image printed by the photographer sold for more than a quarter of a million dollars in 2000; a posthumous print of the very same image, authorized and signed by her daughter, Doon Arbus, brought $25,000.

Naturally, every beginning collector wonders how it is possible to tell the older image from the modern print. Experts suggest that you first look at the paper. Museum curators, faced with the same problem, often use black light to determine if the paper was made before World War II, since prewar photographic paper does not contain brightening agents and, therefore, absorbs black light. Newer paper with brightening agents will reflect the black light, and white areas will have a purplish tint.

If you are uncertain about the age of your photograph, ask an expert, conservator, or appraiser for his or her opinion. Written information anywhere on the photograph or frame can help, as well.

SIGNATURES

As with twentieth-century paintings, signatures are essential to valuing photographs. Not all photographers, however, take pen (or pencil) to paper. Some hand stamp their work; others, like Paul Outerbridge Jr., signed *and* stamped their photographs. A signed print will always be of more interest to collectors than an unsigned one.

Knowing how a photographer endorsed his or her work is important to establishing authenticity and value. If a familiar image isn't signed or stamped, for instance, it may have been printed without the photographer's knowledge. Or the artist may have thought it didn't measure up to his or her usual standards. The photographer wouldn't necessarily destroy these second-rate prints. If they *were* kept, there's always the chance that these unsigned images—prints that the photographer considered mediocre—might come on the market to confuse, puzzle, and tempt collectors. Unsigned or unstamped prints may also be press prints, given out to newspapers for purposes of reproduction. Press prints are printed on lesser-quality paper, and they often have a recognizable shine.

Artists most frequently sign their prints in the lower-right corner, on the mat, or on the back of the print. Should you suspect that there is a signature hidden beneath or behind the frame, and you are buying the photograph from a gallery, ask to see it unframed. "Auction houses," says Leila Buckjune, head of photography at Christie's, "will customarily unframe works for inspection by collectors." If you see an interesting photograph elsewhere, ask to have it (very carefully) removed from its frame so you can check for hidden signatures.

COLOR

For years, black-and-white photography has overshadowed color photography in both the numbers of images produced and collected. Both the film and development for color photography were quite expensive and difficult without extensive equipment. The lack of stability of the various color processes also discouraged some early photographers.

Nevertheless, over the years, photographers have explored various color photography processes. In 1907, Auguste and Louis Lumière invented a process employing Autochrome plates (see page 327). In the 1930s, several photographers, including Man Ray, experimented with color photography. Paul Outerbridge Jr. mastered the complex three-color technique called carbro (see page 327), which turned out to be more stable than several later processes. Eliot Porter (brother of painter Fairfield Porter) began his color photography career around 1939. He used color brilliantly to photograph birds and landscapes.

Thanks to new processes like dye-destruction film (such as Cibachrome), and dye-diffusion film (see page 327), a new generation of artists is exploring color photography, including some of the most sought-after contemporary photographers.

Stone and William Street *by Berenice Abbott, 1936. Inspired by Atget's work in Paris, Abbott photographed changing New York.*

Bagatelle *by Eugène Atget, albumen print, circa 1910.*

The Photographers

The following brief descriptions offer a glimpse into the careers of some of the many artists that have contributed to the field of photography in the twentieth century. They pursued very different kinds of photography—photojournalism, documentary photography, fashion photography, pictorialism, and portraiture among them—each with a special brilliance and idiosyncratic vision.

BERENICE ABBOTT
AMERICAN (1898–1991)
Abbott worked with Man Ray in Paris before opening her own studio. There, Abbott specialized in portraits, especially of literary figures such as James Joyce and Jean Cocteau. In 1929, she returned to New York and began recording street scenes. Over the next two decades she developed a documentary style, recording New York's ever-changing cityscape. In 1935, her project "Changing New York" became part of the Federal Art Project, the New Deal program that aided artists,

and was published as a book of the same title in 1939.

ANSEL ADAMS
AMERICAN (1902–1984)
Ansel Adams was a pioneer, an artist who was concerned not only with capturing "thundering crags and glittering groves," but with the *process* of translating his subjective impressions to the photographic paper. Using exposure and film development to control image area and to achieve the blackest of blacks, the whitest of whites, and the purest variations of the grays in

between, he produced the image he had visualized exactly. Adams is closely identified with a technique called the Zone System, and was also a tireless environmentalist. His stunning images have been embraced by conservationists and photography collectors nationwide.

MANUEL ALVAREZ BRAVO
MEXICAN (1902–2002)
Alvarez Bravo photographed the art and populace of Mexico. Combining the influences of European modernism with those of the thriving artistic environment of postrevolutionary

A New Orleans prostitute photographed by E. J. Bellocq, circa 1911, and printed by Lee Friedlander in the 1970s.

Margaret Bourke-White's haunting image of prisoners at Buchenwald waiting to be liberated by U.S. forces in 1945.

Mexico, he was influenced by the indigenous culture of Mexico throughout his long career, but also remained open to artistic influences from outside his native country. By combining these elements, he created a singular body of work that incorporated the Mexican landscape, cultural and religious artifacts, and the daily life of the people, as well as images influenced by Surrealist aesthetics.

DIANE ARBUS
AMERICAN *(1923–1971)*

Considered one of the greatest documentary photographers of the sixties, Arbus's unsparing, bold, and still controversial portraits of American "outsiders" included transvestites, twins, midgets, and asylum inmates. Arbus confronted her subjects directly with her camera, but they seem to be perfectly amenable to being laid bare by her images.

EUGENE ATGET
FRENCH *(1857–1927)*

Jean-Eugène-Auguste Atget, among the first of photography's social documentarians, is a major figure in the history of photography. His images of Paris may be the most vivid record of the shops and street scenes of a city ever made. In recording the daily appearance of a rapidly changing Paris, Atget made more than ten thousand photographs of this immense subject over a period of thirty years. His work is characterized by a deceptive simplicity.

E. J. BELLOCQ
AMERICAN *(1873–1949)*

Bellocq's chronicling of prostitutes in Storyville, New Orleans' red-light district, became classics when they were published by the Museum of Modern Art in 1970. Discovered in the 1950s by photographer Lee Friedlander, the images often challenge the prevailing perception of prostitutes. Bellocq shot the eighty-nine glass plate negatives in 1912 and reportedly did another series on the opium dens of New Orleans's Chinatown, which has never been recovered.

MARGARET BOURKE-WHITE
AMERICAN *(1904–1971)*

One of the giants of photojournalism and one of the four original photographers to work on *Life* magazine, Bourke-White's early output includes dramatic, hard-edged images of machinery and industrial forms. She documented General Patton's push into Germany, the devastation at Buchenwald, and the establishment of the Indian state and the partition of Pakistan.

Henri Cartier-Bresson, searching for "the decisive moment," found one while peeking through a gap in a fence in Paris.

Alvin Langdon Coburn's Under Dark Arches *was one of 23 plates in Robert Louis Stevenson's book* Edinburgh, Picturesque Notes.

BILL BRANDT
ENGLISH *(1904–1983)*

A student of Man Ray, Brandt is known for photographs of grim mining towns and for dour portraits of miners, as well as for surrealist-influenced portraits of British artists and literary figures.

BRASSAI (GYULA HALASZ)
FRENCH, BORN ROMANIA *(1899–1984)*

Brassaï's most lauded work is a series of Paris night scenes captured in the 1930s. His subjects ranged from artists, writers, and performers to the city's architecture and included the homeless who lived beneath the bridges of the Seine.

HARRY CALLAHAN
AMERICAN *(1912–1999)*

Strongly influenced by Ansel Adams, Callahan photographed landscapes, city streets, pedestrians, and portraits of his wife, Eleanor, often nude. With a characteristic sharpness and a strong sense of design, Callahan transformed prosaic subjects into arresting compositions of simplicity and grace.

ROBERT CAPA (ANDREI FRIEDMANN)
AMERICAN, BORN HUNGARY *(1913–1954)*

Capa first won recognition documenting the Spanish Civil War (1936) and went on to photograph several mid-century conflicts. His photographs of World War II appeared in *Life* magazine, and his images of the Normandy Invasion are among the most recognizable photographs of that historic battle. Capa famously declared, "If your pictures aren't good enough, then you aren't close enough." He died adhering to that principle, the victim of a land-mine in French Indochina.

PAUL CAPONIGRO
AMERICAN *(1932–)*

A master of landscape photography, Caponigro is also noted for his evocative photographs of ancient sites, Stonehenge among them.

HENRI CARTIER-BRESSON
FRENCH *(1908–)*

Cartier-Bresson helped establish photo-

Imogen Cunningham's bold botanical abstraction Amaryllis, *1933.*

A 1920s study of a woman, by pioneering fashion photographer Baron Adolph De Meyer.

journalism as an art form. His style, philosophy, and technique are best documented in his 1952 book, *Images à la sauvette (The Decisive Moment)*. He was among the first to embrace the 35mm camera, which afforded him spontaneity and anonymity.

ALVIN LANGDON COBURN
BRITISH, BORN AMERICA
(1882–1966)

A pictorialist photographer, Coburn—working with Stieglitz—was a founding associate of the Photo-Secession. He took a series of portraits of leading British writers and artists in the 1910s, as well as views of American skyscrapers. Late in the decade, he began to take the first purely abstract photographs, which he called vortographs, although he continued to do portraiture.

IMOGEN CUNNINGHAM
AMERICAN *(1883–1976)*

One of the first women to photograph nudes, Cunningham was her own first model. A friend of Edward Weston, she is best known for her botanical studies.

EDWARD S. CURTIS
AMERICAN *(1868–1952)*

Curtis is a noted chronicler of American Indians. As official photographer of the 1899 Harriman Expedition, he documented both the indigenous population and Alaska's geological features. Curtis's greatest work, however, was his "North American Indian" project, a thirty-year endeavor to document the daily life, ceremonies, and beliefs of the various tribal communities before development and western expansion effected their

cultural assimilation. Curtis visited more than eighty tribes in North America, and although what he photographed was actually his own romanticized view of the Indians, he produced more than forty thousand powerful photographs.

BARON ADOLPHE DE MEYER
AMERICAN, BORN GERMANY
(1868–1949)

In 1914, de Meyer became the first full-time photographer at Condé Nast's *Vogue*. In 1921, he transferred to rival William Randolph Hearst's *Harper's Bazaar,* where he became a trailblazing fashion photographer.

The anonymity of New York City street life, with reflections, by Lee Friedlander, 1963.

ALFRED EISENSTADT
AMERICAN, BORN POLAND
(1898–1995)

One of the four original *Life* magazine photographers, Eisenstädt, using a simple 35mm Leica camera, completed more than 2,500 assignments, resulting in 92 *Life* covers. He is considered one of the fathers of photojournalism.

WALKER EVANS
AMERICAN *(1903–1975)*

Perhaps the greatest documentary photographer of the twentieth century, Evans worked for the Farm Security Administration from 1935 to 1938. An assignment from *Fortune* produced iconic and sensitive work portraying the dignity of poor sharecroppers in Alabama; the photographs were published in *Let Us Now Praise Famous Men,* with text by James Agee.

ROBERT FRANK
AMERICAN, BORN SWITZERLAND
(1924–)

In his book, *The Americans,* Frank took a documentary approach to photographing American culture. He revealed ordinary people without hope or promise and the everyday places where they live and work in a distinctive style that frequently employed odd angles and blurred focus.

LEE FRIEDLANDER
AMERICAN *(1934–)*

One of the "street photographers" of the 1960s, Friedlander is known for working in series: street images, landscapes, nudes, the industrial environment, and self-portraits in which he appears only as a shadow or a reflection. He also photographed obscure American monuments and office workers at computers.

PHILIPPE HALSMAN
AMERICAN, BORN LATVIA
(1906–1979)

From the 1940s to the 1970s, Halsman made his mark with glossy portraits of celebrities, intellectuals, and politicians in magazines such as *Life,* the *Saturday Evening Post,* and *Paris Match.* Halsman also worked with surrealist painter Salvador Dalí to produce collaborations like the "Dalí Atomicus," in which Dalí, his canvas, furniture, cats, and streams of water are all pictured suspended in air. Halsman also captured highly unusual views of many notables, like then Vice President Richard Nixon and the Duke and Duchess of Windsor, leaping in the air, in his famous series of "jumping photographs."

Lewis Wickes Hine's New York Homework, 1910. *This photographer documented the lives of immigrants in early-twentieth-century New York.*

Satiric Dancer, Paris, *1926, is perhaps the best-known photograph taken by André Kertész.*

LEWIS WICKES HINE
AMERICAN (1874–1940)

Working in tandem with the Progressive and Reform movements, Hine was particularly interested in photographing child-labor abuses and was able to use these images to effect social change. From 1904 to 1909, he documented immigrant processing at Ellis Island. He worked, too, as a free-lance photographer for the National Child Labor Committee, chronicling children toiling in factories, mines, and sweatshops in the northeast, southeast, and mid-Atlantic states. He also documented slum conditions in Washington, D.C. In 1930, Hine photographed the construction of the Empire State Building for his book *Men at Work.*

HORST P. HORST
AMERICAN, BORN GERMANY
(1906–1999)

Horst was one of the leading fashion photographers of the mid-twentieth century. One memorable photograph shows a model in an unraveling corset. Horst also photographed such notables as Harry S. Truman, Coco Chanel, Marlene Dietrich, and Jacqueline Kennedy.

YOUSUF KARSH
CANADIAN, BORN TURKEY
(1908–2002)

An Armenian born in Turkey, Karsh fled persecution, arriving in Canada in 1924 and joining his photographer uncle. In 1935, Karsh was appointed official portrait photographer of the Canadian government and became known professionally as Karsh of Ottawa. He first captured international attention with his often reproduced 1941 portrait of Winston Churchill.

GERTRUDE KASEBIER
AMERICAN (1852–1934)

A Photo-Secessionist working in the pictorialist style, Käsebier is best known for portraits and tender images of mothers and daughters in domestic settings.

ANDRE KERTESZ
AMERICAN, BORN HUNGARY
(1894–1985)

While living in Paris, Kértesz contributed to the magazines *Vu* and *Art et Médicine.* In New York, he worked from 1939 to 1949 as a free-lance photographer for the magazines *Look, Vogue,* and *Town & Country.* In 1949, at Condé Nast, he transformed the visual character of *House & Garden* magazine. Returning to artistic endeavors after his retirement in 1962, he focused on bustling cityscapes.

Dorothea Lange's Migrant Mother, *a moving portrait of Dust Bowl desperation, 1936.*

One of ten prints from a Jacques-Henri Lartigue portfolio; the introduction was entitled "Portrait of All the Things I Lovingly Loved."

DOROTHEA LANGE
AMERICAN (1895–1965)

Dorothea Lange is best known for her Farm Security Administration photographs of the Dust Bowl farmers who migrated to California in the 1930s. Between 1935 and 1942, she photographed migrant workers, sharecroppers, tenant farmers, and other victims of the Depression in twenty-two states, primarily in the South and West.

JACQUES-HENRI LARTIGUE
FRENCH (1894–1986)

Lartigue began to take pictures at age seven, focusing on moments of exuberance and spontaneity and chronicling "La Belle Epoque" before the outbreak of World War I. After the war, Lartigue turned to painting, earning a substantial reputation in the field. In 1962, *Life* magazine published a selection of

the photographs he had concealed for years, reviving his dormant career and public awareness of his work.

ARNOLD NEWMAN
AMERICAN (1918–)

Famous for his "environmental portraiture," images of people posed in settings associated with their occupations, Newman captured well-known artists, writers, composers, political and business leaders, and scientists. Among his best-known portraits is a photograph of Igor Stravinsky at the piano. Newman also shot Max Ernst, Alfred Stieglitz and Georgia O'Keeffe, Marilyn Monroe, Alfred Krupp, Pablo Picasso, and Jean Cocteau.

PAUL OUTERBRIDGE JR.
AMERICAN (1896–1958)

Outerbridge's early work was influenced by Paul Strand and it consisted primarily of still-life abstractions composed of ordinary objects: cups, lightbulbs, machine parts, milk bottles, eggs. Later in his career, Outerbridge became a fashion photographer. He also created a series of erotic and fetishistic nudes, few of which he was able to publish or exhibit during his lifetime.

GORDON PARKS
AMERICAN (1912–)

Parks earned his reputation documenting African-American life as a staff photographer for *Life* magazine between 1948 and 1972; he won acclaim for images of ghetto life, the Civil Rights Movement, and black nationalists.

Girl with Leica, *1934, exemplifies Alexander Rodchenko's interesting use of surprising visual angles.*

Eighth Avenue & Forty-Second Street, New York City, *circa 1932–34, by Ben Shahn, a painter and graphic artist as well as a photographer known for his images of ordinary people.*

MAN RAY (EMMANUEL RADNITZKY)
AMERICAN (1890–1976)

In the early years of the twentieth century, Man Ray frequently collaborated with artist Marcel Duchamp in New York. In the 1920s, he established a studio in Paris, and increasingly influenced by the surrealists, became an enthusiastic experimenter with photographic techniques. He may be best known for his "Rayographs"—cameraless photographic images—as well as solarized prints created by exposing a print to light during the developing process, resulting in a partial reversal of light and dark values.

ALEXANDER RODCHENKO
RUSSIAN (1891–1956)

Initially a painter and graphic designer, Rodchenko eventually turned to social commentary using photomontage and photography. He was noted for shooting his subjects from odd angles, usually high above or below, in an effort to shock and disorient the viewer. At the behest of the Communist Party in Moscow, Rodchenko changed his orientation from abstraction to more formal photography in the 1930s, concentrating on images of sport and parades. He organized photography exhibitions for the Soviet government in the 1940s.

ARTHUR ROTHSTEIN
AMERICAN (1915–1985)

One of the photographers hired by Roy Stryker to document the Federal Resettlement Administration (which later became the Farm Security Administration, or FSA) during the Great Depression, Rothstein became famous for images of the Dust Bowl.

BEN SHAHN
AMERICAN, BORN RUSSIA, NOW LITHUANIA (1898–1969)

A painter and graphic artist (see page 450), Shahn produced hundreds of photographs of ordinary people in lower and midtown Manhattan between 1932 and 1935. He also photographed demonstrations for expanded work-relief programs, protest marches against social injustice around Union Square and City Hall, inmates and prison guards at Blackwell's Island Penitentiary and the New York City Reformatory. From 1935 to 1938, working for the Farm Security Administration, he took thousands of photographs of the rural southern and midwestern United States.

A stylized 1930s portrait of actress Anna May Wong, above, by Edward Steichen, one of the masters of the medium.

Marines in Saipan, 1944, left, a vivid image of warfare by W. Eugene Smith for Life *magazine.*

AARON SISKIND
AMERICAN (1903–1991)

Motivated primarily by the desire to instigate social change, Siskind's early photographs focus on the social and political conditions of the poor and otherwise disadvantaged. He photographed regularly in New York's Harlem district during the 1930s and 1940s, although ultimately, Siskind's interest began to shift away from social documentation and toward the more formal, poetic, abstract images of found objects, stone walls, and graffiti, for which he eventually became famous.

W. EUGENE SMITH
AMERICAN (1918–1978)

Smith was a dedicated photojournalist with a deep commitment to practicing his craft ethically. After a brief stint on the staff of *Newsweek,* he published photographs in *Life, Collier's,* and *Harper's Bazaar.* Smith had a long relationship with *Life* magazine, alternating between being a staff member and a freelancer from 1939 into the 1970s. He is noted for the photo-essay, a form that he was instrumental in perfecting. Among these are "Country Doctor" and "Nurse Midwife."

EDWARD STEICHEN
AMERICAN, BORN LUXEMBOURG (1879–1973)

As a photographer and curator, Edward Steichen was one of the most prominent and influential figures of twentieth-century photography. He was a founding Photo-Secessionist, and convinced Stieglitz to open the "291" Galleries. He worked in a variety of styles in black-and-white and in color; his images included portraits, landscapes, fashion and advertising photography, and photographs of dance and sculpture. His early work was in the pictorialist style; but after World War I, he became a proponent of "straight" photography. A curator at New York's Museum of Modern Art for 15 years, Steichen was responsible for many important exhibitions, including the groundbreaking *The Family of Man* in 1955.

ALFRED STIEGLITZ
AMERICAN (1864–1946)

The importance of Alfred Stieglitz—founder of the Photo-Secessionist movement and the "291" Galleries, and founder and editor of *Camera Work*—to twentieth-century photography cannot be overstated. In addition to his extensive efforts to

"Straight" photography advocate Paul Strand's uncompromising yet lyrical portrait, Nancy Thompson, Taos, 1932.

Whatever happened, it's probably not good: A Weegee shot of an accident victim in shock.

establish photography as a fine art are his own memorable images, among others, *The Steerage,* taken aboard an ocean liner en route to Europe from New York in 1907. Later works include a series of portraits of his wife, artist Georgia O'Keeffe.

PAUL STRAND
AMERICAN *(1890–1976)*

The champion of "straight" photography, Strand was introduced to Alfred Stieglitz and the "291" Galleries in 1907 by Lewis Hine. Strand experimented at first with soft-focus lenses in the pictorialist style. Between 1915 and 1917, Strand worked closely with Stieglitz, and at the end of this period, he began to produce a body of sharp-focus work, including quasi-abstract still lifes of kitchen bowls and cityscapes. In 1945, the Museum of

Modern Art in New York devoted its first major retrospective of a contemporary photographer to Strand.

WEEGEE (ARTHUR FELLIG)
AMERICAN, BORN POLAND *(1899–1968)*

A newshound and photographer of New York nightlife, Weegee tuned into police radio bands to be first at the scene whenever a newsworthy accident or crime occurred. Although he photographed the panorama of urban life, on-the-spot coverage of violent crimes, disasters, and their survivors and onlookers are what he is best known for. His seemingly raw and spontaneous work for New York City newspapers and photography syndicates in the 1930s and 1940s brought him international attention.

BRETT WESTON
AMERICAN *(1911–1993)*

The student of his father, Edward Weston, Brett Weston began producing exquisite nature studies and landscapes when he was still in his teens. He became one of the finest photographic printers in the world, constructing abstract and dramatic compositions from such subjects as factories, cars, sand dunes, plants, and rooftops. Toward the end of his life, he reduced his subjects to pure form, producing mostly high-contrast prints of close-ups and abstract details.

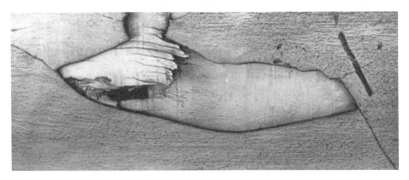

Garry Winogrand's amusing 1963 depiction of a New York pachyderm soliciting a snack, from his series on New York City zoos.

Sequence 15, 1959, by Minor White, a leading abstract photographer of the twentieth century.

EDWARD WESTON

AMERICAN *(1886–1958)*

Weston was among the most influential photographers of the twentieth century. The subtle tones and organic forms of his works set the standard by which much later photography would be judged. Early works include incisive industrial landscapes, although one of his favorite subjects was his wife. Weston is known for his crisp, finely detailed images and abstractions of the female form.

MINOR WHITE

AMERICAN *(1908–1976)*

A leading abstract photographer, White began his career with the Works Progress Administration (WPA). He studied with photographers Edward Weston and Alfred Stieglitz, but his characteristic images are imbued with a feeling of spirituality. White also worked with photographer Ansel Adams, who taught him the Zone System, a method of visualizing the final print before taking the shot.

GARRY WINOGRAND

AMERICAN *(1928–1984)*

Photographs taken in and around New York City won Winogrand praise as an astute chronicler of contemporary life, particularly in the 1960s. In describing his street scenes, Winogrand stated, "I photograph something to see what it will look like as a photograph."

Chapter Ten

ENTERTAINMENT MEMORABILIA

Here's a riddle: *When is a used collectible valued more highly than the same collectible in mint condition?* The answer: *When it's been used by a celebrity.* Film, television, stage, and recording stars inevitably enhance the value of any collectible they sign, wear, handle, or make any kind of (documented) contact with. Moreover, a celebrity instantly turns valueless things into collectible things.

If feisty Judy Garland danced those sparkly little red pumps down the Yellow Brick Road, no one bidding on them at a memorabilia auction cares if they are missing more than a few sequins. Collectors don't ordinarily look twice at men's white shirts with Sulka labels, either—unless they happen to know that a particular one was once worn by Mick Jagger of the Rolling Stones. The closer anything has come to a star, the more desirable it is. Gleaming electric guitars, sweat-soaked stage costumes, blatantly fake pearls, thousands of autographed photographs, programs, and album covers, and a mind-boggling assortment of artifacts touched by celebrities are luring avid and

Top: a Gibson "Lucille,"
signed and dated by blues master B. B.
King. Above: the legendary Garbo on
the cover of a vintage fan magazine.

A collector with an impressive array of early Marilyn Monroe memorabilia at the Baltimore Antiques Roadshow.

A rather sedate pair of Elton John's signature eyewear, along with one of his not-so-sedate costumes.

knowledgeable collectors by the thousands to break open their (perhaps collectible) piggy banks.

Nearly everyone who knows anything about entertainment collectibles would love to purchase even the tiniest lipstick that was part of Marilyn Monroe's life. While most Monroe collectors clamor for things from the peak of her career, one visitor to the Baltimore *Antiques Roadshow* explained to appraiser Gerald Tomlin that he buys the less-expensive memorabilia from Monroe's early years, when she was just Norma Jean Baker. He noted that he had been following the advice of the show's appraisers to avoid sprawling collections, and Tomlin approved, estimating his exciting collection at $18,000 to $20,000. It included, among other things, a German doll in a crocheted dress with porcelain hands, feet, and face, and real hair, that had once belonged to little Norma Jean. "I bought this from Eleanor 'Bebe' Goddard, who was Norma Jean's stepsister," explained the visitor. "Bebe said it was a gift to the little girl from her aunt and that she cherished it throughout her childhood." That such a rarity could still be discovered and purchased by a low-profile collector offers hope to other niche collectors, as well as those of modest means.

The coveting of celebrity memorabilia is not limited to mere mortals. Celebrities themselves purchase objects once owned by the celebrities they idolize—singer George Michael bought John Lennon's piano, for instance—perhaps hoping to find inspiration in the residual aura of greatness left by the previous owners. Gary Busey, who starred in the movie *The Buddy Holly Story,* paid a quarter of a million dollars to acquire a guitar that Holly really played.

Of course, Holly's early Fender Stratocaster guitar and Lennon's Steinway have actual intrinsic value. But, if confirmation is needed that intrinsic value isn't high up on the coveted-by-collectors list, then think about the individual who spent $1.26 million for the notorious sewed-on dress Marilyn Monroe wore when she sang "Happy Birthday" to President John Kennedy. He thought he got a bargain, and perhaps he did. But had anyone else worn that dress, it would be virtually worthless. It's just another reminder that objects touched, drunk from, written on, eaten from, slept on, thrown away, played on, or ridden in by our celebrity idols are saved, venerated—and very collectible.

COLLECTING ENTERTAINMENT MEMORABILIA

Before 1970, the only ways to obtain entertainment memorabilia were through classified ads, fan clubs, photo shops, and personal contacts. Then, in 1970, the financially beleaguered MGM was forced to sell nearly 200,000 props and costumes dating to the time when it was Hollywood's reigning studio. This public auction put into circulation a veritable history of movies and of MGM's greatest stars. The swell of interest it created in movie memorabilia continues to this day.

What the MGM sale did for movie collectibles, a Sotheby's auction held in London in 1981 did for rock and pop music collectibles; thus, this chapter concentrates on those two areas, touching a little on the still-young TV collectibles market.

Entertainment collectibles mostly fall into three distinct categories:

EPHEMERA: Paper and cardboard tickets and stubs, programs, and promotional posters were originally intended to be used once and discarded. While in most cases, they were produced in substantial quantities, any number were taken home as souvenirs and tenderly laid away. Now, many of these are much-in-demand artifacts. Ephemera, therefore, are both accessible and affordable, and a good place for the budding enthusiast to begin his or her collecting.

MERCHANDISE: Outside licensees have traditionally manufactured products to publicize movies, television shows, or "hot" popular singers. These items are as varied as Beatles needlepoint sets, Michael Jackson fan club jackets, Brady Bunch lunch boxes, Zorro hand puppets, Bionic Woman dolls, Pinocchio

AND IT FLOATS

Fans of the movie classic *20,000 Leagues Under the Sea* would have recognized the submarine that was brought to the Los Angeles *Antiques Roadshow* for appraisal. The owner, who picked it up at a swap meet, had always hoped it was from the 1954 film starring James Mason and Kirk Douglas, but he was never able to verify it. Appraiser Michael Schwartz authenticated it for him because not only did he recognize it from the film (which he'd seen a number of times), but he knew it was similar in construction to other props from the same movie that have appeared at auction.

The submarine is made of fiberglass, and a peek inside revealed the many working parts used in the sub's construction that allowed it to light up, rise, and float in the water. Because it is rare to see examples from the film come up for auction, this unusual piece was valued at $6,000 to $8,000.

Modern jazz aficionados would love this vintage poster for an appearance by jazz greats Thelonious Monk and Sonny Rollins at a Harlem night club.

PLEASE SIGN HERE

If you want to get your autographs directly from living stars, you can write studios and production companies, stars' agents, publicists, and fan club members, or send index cards and photographs (with self-addressed stamped envelopes) to the celebrities' homes or offices. There are annual guides that give contact addresses (some are actually correct) for even the biggest celebrities. ("Star Maps" can help you track down certain Beverly Hills residents.) For personal contact with stars, try your luck at celebrity golf tournaments or attend "Hollywood Collectors Shows" (though major stars are rarely, if ever, guests); go where the celebrities go (sporting events or trendy restaurants and clubs); and, if they are performing in your area, wait outside the theater or arena doors for them. Remember: Specialty collecting shows and book and record promotions are venues where the stars come specifically to sign autographs; elsewhere, collectors should be tactful in approaching celebrities, who ought to be allowed their small share of privacy and peace.

cookie jars, and hot-water bottles modeled after the shapely Jayne Mansfield. Merchandise generally has a longer lifespan than ephemera because it is made of durable materials and was intended to be kept. Because it too has been mass-produced, however, it lacks the value of the thing that is unique.

PERSONAL ITEMS AND AUTOGRAPHS: Serious entertainment collectors desire most those rare articles that have come into contact with stars. They follow auctions and private sales for gems such as John Lennon's glasses, Bing Crosby's humidor, W. C. Fields's letters to his mistress, Boris Karloff's signed script from *Frankenstein,* Stan Laurel's original gag and script notes, a copy of Margaret Mitchell's book *Gone with the Wind* signed by the stars of the movie, and so on. Such rarities are always in demand—who wouldn't be interested in one of the four "Rosebud" sleds used in the classic movie *Citizen Kane*?

Some collectors, of course, are content to limit themselves to autographs and signed photographs, and, depending on their budget, to signed letters and documents. They acquire autographs and signed photographs at memorabilia stores, through dealers and other collectors on the Internet, at collectors shows, at auctions, and by making contacts through collectibles magazines.

EVALUATING ENTERTAINMENT MEMORABILIA

How can the collector possibly know if the guitar being offered at the local rock and roll memorabilia show was indeed played by Eric Clapton? There is no "played by Eric Clapton" label on it, after all, and fingerprinting and DNA testing aren't exactly feasible.

With the majority of collectibles, materials, dates of manufacture, and maker's labels can be verified, but substantiating the prior ownership of clothes, props, and musical instruments can be a problem. This can be disquieting for collectors faced with the knowledge that the higher their collecting aspirations, the more desirable and costly things are, the more cautious they need to be.

So if there is a photograph depicting the celebrity wearing, holding, or even smashing the collectible, that's a good beginning. There might even be a signature on the item, or a letter from the celebrity verifying its authenticity. For the thousands of items owned or used by living celebrities, the intrepid collector can try contacting the star and asking if the object in question was really his or hers. Also, she can take her autograph or object to professionals for verification. (Don't send anything in the mail.) Still, for almost all putatively celebrity-related items, *Antiques Roadshow* experts endorse the Missouri state motto: "Show me."

The Givenchy-designed dress Audrey Hepburn wore in her Oscar-winning 1957 Paramount hit Funny Face, *and as seen in the publicity still, below.*

MOVIE MEMORABILIA

The modern "cult of celebrity" began in the twentieth century with the advent of motion pictures. Radio and, later, television added to its explosive growth, but the powder-packed charge of full-blown glamour has always been a Hollywood thing.

THE STARS

Nearly every actor, actress, and film, no matter how obscure or bad, has fans. The entertainment collectibles market, however, is propelled by collectors' passion for a relatively small number of stars and movies. These stars may be famous, but far more significant is their undeniable mystique—the source of their enduring fascination. Box office performance is not nearly as significant for a film as whether it has insinuated itself into our psyche and our shared culture.

Collectors just testing the waters often purchase current movie-personality materials that may have future collectible

potential. From autographed photographs to costumes and props, they concentrate mostly on the stars (and filmmakers) they have repeatedly seen over the last thirty years on magazine covers and talk shows: Gorgeous actresses, highly paid (and usually handsome) leading men, superstar directors and producers. Other collectors hunt down memorabilia dating from the early twentieth century, when the very first movie stars and filmmakers thrilled the public with this new form of storytelling—long before Julia Roberts, Arnold Schwarzenegger, and Steven Spielberg. There are two mid-century stars, however, whose appeal to collectors—and in fact to the general public—seems to know no bounds.

MARILYN AND JIMMY

By far the single most popular entertainer in terms of collectibles is Marilyn Monroe, a star who dominates Hollywood

Marilyn Monroe—in the famous Happy-Birthday-Mr.-President dress—coos to JFK in May of 1962. Years later, the dress itself went for a huge sum at auction.

collectibles. This is hardly surprising, since, as one authority put it, "She crossed so many boundaries and was accepted by so many different types of people" that she has been embraced since her death by new generations. Marilyn memorabilia, in fact, is still being produced, especially dolls and reprints of famous photographs. Collectors particularly want to own Marilyn mementos from between 1953, which was when she appeared in her first three starring roles (it was also the year her famous centerfold appeared in the debut issue of *Playboy*) until her premature death in 1962.

The 1999 auction of Monroe memorabilia, which included the sale of the $1.26 million dress mentioned earlier, totaled an incredible $13 million. Among the items offered were stockings, books, pearls, a plastic cup, blankets, a tissue box cover, a sad slip of paper with the words "he does not love me" written in pencil, and the tags and license for a poodle given to her by Frank Sinatra.

If Marilyn Monroe is the queen of entertainment memorabilia, outselling Lucille Ball, Bette Davis, Marlene Dietrich,

Hollywood Heavy Hitters

From the silent era to the early seventies, what follows is a partial list of movie stars (plus a few filmmakers) who continue to thrill collectors.

They are American, French, German, Italian, British, and Swedish, and represent a century of beauty, and, occasionally, talent.

ABBOTT AND COSTELLO • URSULA ANDRESS (*and later* "*Bond Girls*") • "B" WESTERN HEROES (INCLUDING GENE AUTRY • WILLIAM "HOPALONG CASSIDY" BOYD • AND ROY ROGERS) • THE BEATLES (*also collected by music collectors*) • BRIGITTE BARDOT • JOHN BARRYMORE • JEAN-PAUL BELMONDO • INGRID BERGMAN • HUMPHREY BOGART • CLARA BOW • MARLON BRANDO • LOUISE BROOKS

Clara Bow

• FRANK CAPRA • CHARLES CHAPLIN • LON CHANEY SR. (*and to a lesser degree Lon Chaney Jr.*) • SEAN CONNERY • GARY COOPER • ROGER CORMAN • BUSTER CRABBE • JOAN CRAWFORD • DOROTHY DANDRIDGE • MARION DAVIES • BETTE DAVIS • OLIVIA DE HAVILLAND • THE DEAD END KIDS • JAMES DEAN • CECIL B. DEMILLE • MARLENE DIETRICH • WALT DISNEY

Charles Chaplin

• DOUGLAS FAIRBANKS • FEDERICO FELLINI (*director*) • W. C. FIELDS • ERROL FLYNN • HENRY FONDA • JANE FONDA • JOHN FORD • CLARK GABLE • GRETA GARBO • JUDY GARLAND • CARY GRANT • D. W. GRIFFITH (*director*) • JEAN HARLOW • WILLIAM S. HART • HOWARD HAWKS (*director*) • RITA HAYWORTH • ALFRED HITCHCOCK (*director*) • AUDREY HEPBURN • KATHARINE HEPBURN • JUDY HOLLIDAY • BORIS KARLOFF • BUSTER KEATON • GRACE KELLY • STANLEY KUBRICK (*director*) • LAUREL AND HARDY • BRUCE LEE • VIVIAN LEIGH • HAROLD LLOYD • CAROLE LOMBARD • SOPHIA LOREN • MYRNA LOY • GEORGE

Jayne Mansfield

LUCAS • JAYNE MANSFIELD • DEAN MARTIN AND JERRY LEWIS • THE MARX BROTHERS (*Harpo is even more coveted than Groucho by some collectors*) • HATTIE MCDANIEL • RUSS MEYER (*director-cinematographer*) • OSCAR MICHAUX (*director*) • HAYLEY MILLS • TOM MIX • MARILYN MONROE • MONTY PYTHON • PAUL NEWMAN • LAURENCE OLIVIER • OUR GANG/LITTLE RASCALS (*particularly Carl "Alfalfa" Switzer*) • BETTY PAGE (*queen of fifties fetish shorts*) • MARY PICKFORD • ELVIS PRESLEY (*also collected by music hobbyists*) • ROBERT REDFORD • STEVE REEVES • PAUL ROBESON (*also collected by sports collectors*) • JEAN SEBERG • FRANK SINATRA (*also collected by music collectors*) • BARBARA STANWYCK • BARBARA STEELE • JAMES STEWART • GLORIA SWANSON • SHIRLEY TEMPLE (*as child actress*) • THE THREE STOOGES (*surprisingly, as collectible as the Marx Brothers*) • ELIZABETH TAYLOR • SPENCER TRACY • RUDOLPH VALENTINO • ANDY WARHOL (*director-producer-actor; also collected by art collectors*) • JOHN WAYNE • RAQUEL WELCH • ORSON WELLES (*actor-director*) • JOHNNY WEISSMULLER (*and other Tarzans*) • MAE WEST • PEARL

James Dean

WHITE • ED WOOD (*director*) • *and* NATALIE WOOD.

Clark Gable

THE AWKWARD AGE

"One of the reasons I love seeing collectibles is that I never know what's going to turn up," said appraiser Caroline Ashleigh. The surprise appearance at the Louisville *Antiques Roadshow* was a yearbook picturing photographs of James Dean as a high school junior. We're more familiar with Dean as the epitome of cool, straddling a motorcycle, perhaps, the collar of his leather jacket turned up.

But in this 1948 yearbook, *Roadshow* viewers saw, well, a slightly goofy Dean. A Dean wearing not just glasses for his drama class photo, but unquestionably unbecoming glasses. On another page, there's James Dean in his basketball uniform—showing his definitely uncool knobby knees.

The yearbook's coup de grace, in Ashleigh's opinion, is Dean's signature in the back of the book, actually his nickname, "Rack." Ashleigh estimated that Dean's junior yearbook might be worth between $3,000 and $3,500.

Judy Garland, Jean Harlow, Rita Hayworth, and Elizabeth Taylor, then unquestionably, James Dean is king. And if Marilyn's cross-generational popularity has a lot to do with her being a martyr to the Hollywood system—she was exploited and then crushed for wanting independence—then Dean's enduring popularity has to do with his being *the* symbol of rebellious, self-destructive, misunderstood youth. Their early deaths certainly contribute to the mystique, for the public is particularly in love with stars—film, sports, rock—who died before their time, their youth and glamour thus preserved forever. The reason Dean cultists watch and rewatch *East of Eden, Rebel Without a Cause,* and *Giant* is that these were the handsome, supercool actor's only three starring performances. He died at twenty-four. Naturally, memorabilia from those films is particularly coveted, and the grail would be the red jacket Dean wore in *Rebel Without a Cause* (released soon after his death). Dean merchandise, including dolls, is everywhere. Authentic Dean memorabilia, from original posters and autographed stills to signed letters and documents, is scarce, but still in circulation, fueling an ever-growing cult of collectors.

James Dean memorabilia—the rare and the mass-produced—range from the actor's own script for Rebel Without a Cause *to a 1956 commemorative plate to a modern polymer figurine.*

THE FILMS

The movies of the last thirty years that will appeal to collectors thirty years from now are the blockbusters: films that were star vehicles or that created stars, won Academy Awards, had dazzling special effects, major licensing deals, or any combination of these attributes. In addition to looking for movie-personality autographs and items from these films, new collectors will be acquiring stills, posters, advertising press books, scripts, lobby cards, action figures, costumes, props, ticket stubs, scenic and special-effects designs, models, and other materials.

THE DOMINANT MOVIE

Of all the films ever made, the one that thrills high-end collectors most is *Gone with the Wind,* arguably the most popular movie of all time, surprising even More popular, perhaps, than *The Wizard of Oz* and *Casablanca.* Many fans collect *only* items from the beloved 1939 movie. There are numerous dealers who specialize in "GWTW" merchandise and memorabilia, and there are a few stores and gift shops, among them some in Florida and Georgia, that deal exclusively with "GWTW" items. It's easy to find reissued posters, photographs, mugs, games, key chains, plates, other commemorative collectibles, teddy bears, music boxes, and dolls of Scarlett O'Hara, Rhett Butler, Ashley Wilkes, and Mammy. But for the collector, originals are where the fun is, and these are regularly offered at auction. Gable's script sold for $220,000 (to Steven Spielberg). And at a London auction held in 2002, a petticoat worn by Vivien Leigh went for a tidy sum, as did a sweater worn by Olivia de Havilland. It brought three times its estimate.

George Lucas's *Star Wars* was released in 1977, so it isn't yet of real interest to *vintage* collectors. But *Star Wars* and the sequels and prequels it spawned could, in time, displace "GWTW" as the most popular franchise in the market, because the collecting fervor of *Star Wars* fans increases with each passing year. Available merchandise covers everything imaginable, from action figures to footwear, tinware to toiletries. Carrie Fisher, a.k.a. Princess Leia, caused a stir when she offered several of her private *Star Wars* items for sale, including an

Tomorrow is indeed another day for Gone with the Wind *memorabilia. The wildly popular movie is equally popular with collectors, some of whom concentrate only on "GWTW" memorabilia, such as this vintage poster.*

MARGARET MITCHELL, A.K.A. PEGGY

A visitor to the Birmingham, Alabama, *Antiques Roadshow* presented appraiser Richard Austin with some valuable *Gone with the Wind* mementos.

"What's really interesting is that these things once belonged to a woman who knew Margaret Mitchell," Austin said. The personal inscription from Mitchell in a first edition of the book makes that clear. Personal letters, signed "Peggy" rather than "Margaret," confirm the close connection. In one, Mitchell confides just how distorted her life had become: "For nearly a year everyone I have ever known has brought or tried to bring their friends to meet me, in the firm belief I would give them a day or two. You can't imagine the unbelievable numbers of people that have been on our doorstep. . . ."

Austin figured the collection, which had cost its owner $400, was worth $6,000 to $8,000.

autographed scrapbook, autographed stills, and an original painting of her character. Only time will tell if the *Harry Potter* movie franchise, with its innumerable worldwide licenses, will exercise equally collectible wizardry.

COLLECTING MOVIE MEMORABILIA

Hollywood produces an amazing amount of material of interest to a wide collecting base. Here are some tips to help you focus your interest.

PERSONAL EFFECTS

As you might surmise, the closer any item has been to a star, the more we have to spend to own it. But for the canny collector who can't write a blank check, there are celebrity-owned personal effects that can be had for (relatively) reasonable sums. For example, while you may not be able to acquire Bette Davis's very own baby rattle (which actually came up for sale), you might still be able to buy books bearing her personal bookplates. Similarly, while Jimmy Stewart's own script from *It's a Wonderful Life* is probably out of reach, the dedicated Stewart collector can still hope to own one of the letters he wrote to a fan discussing his work on that movie. Although a dress worn by Elizabeth Taylor at the 1969 Oscars may be too pricey at $167,500, the dedicated star gazer can still buy silver boxes owned by Ethel Barrymore, letters from Joan Crawford, and awards presented over his long life to comedian George Burns. These prizes are out there: Charlie Chaplin's bowler and Orson Welles's

Sling-back rhinestone-encrusted evening shoes, made especially for Marlene Dietrich, are shown with a publicity photo from the 1930s.

The Movie Collecting Cult

When it comes to movies, serious collectors are interested in a wide range of genres (see box, page 362), but "cults" have grown up around a number of specific classics—not just *Rocky Horror Picture Show* and *Eraserhead*. These are the movies that collectors see over and over again, memorize, analyze, and discuss over cups of espresso way into the night. Here are a few must-own favorites.

THE ADVENTURES OF ROBIN HOOD • BREAKFAST AT TIFFANY'S • BREATHLESS • CITIZEN KANE • A CLOCKWORK ORANGE • **Desk Set** DINNER AT EIGHT • EAST OF EDEN • *Bruce Lee movies)* • FANTASIA • FORBIDDEN PLANET • FREAKS • FROM HERE TO ETERNITY • GENTLEMEN PREFER GODFATHER *(and sequels)* • GODZILLA • GONE WITH • A HARD DAY'S NIGHT • HELP! • HIGH NOON IT HAPPENED ONE NIGHT • THE JAZZ SINGER VITA •

ALL ABOUT EVE • BEN-HUR • BLUE VELVET • *(and other films of the French New Wave)* • CASABLANCA • • CLOSE ENCOUNTERS OF THE THIRD KIND • EASY RIDER • 8½ • ENTER THE DRAGON *(and other* **Gentlemen Prefer Blondes** BLONDES • GIANT • THE THE WIND • GRAND HOTEL • HOUSE OF WAX • IT'S A WONDERFUL LIFE • • KING KONG • LA DOLCE LAST TANGO IN PARIS •

LAWRENCE OF ARABIA • THE MALTESE FALCON • MIDNIGHT COWBOY • THE **Mutiny on the Bounty** **The Wizard of Oz** MISFITS • MUTINY ON THE BOUNTY • THE NIGHT OF THE LIVING DEAD *and* DAWN OF THE DEAD • A PLACE IN THE SUN • PLAN 9 FROM OUTER SPACE • THE PRINCESS AND THE SHOWGIRL • PSYCHO • REBEL WITHOUT A CAUSE • THE RED SHOES • SCARFACE • THE SEARCHERS • SHANE • SINGIN' IN THE RAIN • SOME LIKE IT HOT • THE SOUND OF MUSIC • SPARTACUS • STAGE DOOR • A STAR IS BORN • SUNSET BOULEVARD • SUPERMAN *(and sequels)* • THE TEN COMMANDMENTS • **Casablanca** THE TEXAS CHAINSAW MASSACRE • 2001: A SPACE ODYSSEY • VERTIGO • WHAT EVER HAPPENED TO BABY JANE? • THE WILD BUNCH • THE WIZARD OF OZ • THE WOMEN • WUTHERING HEIGHTS • **High Noon** *and* YELLOW SUBMARINE.

MOVIE FAVORITES BY GENRE

The most popular genres, as defined by the market, are:

♦ Academy Award winners
♦ Fred Astaire–Ginger Rogers musicals
♦ "B" westerns
♦ Busby Berkeley–choreographed musicals
♦ the six Marlene Dietrich movies directed by Josef von Sternberg (for example, *The Blue Angel* and *Blonde Venus*)
♦ Disney movies
♦ film noir classics
♦ gangster films from the early thirties
♦ Hammer Studios horror films
♦ Italian westerns starring Clint Eastwood
♦ James Bond films (from 1964 to the present)
♦ musicals from the fifties and sixties
♦ pre-Hollywood-code films
♦ Ray Harryhausen special-effects spectacles
♦ serials
♦ science fiction films from the fifties (some classic, some cheesy)
♦ silent movies
♦ Tarzan movies
♦ Universal Studios horror films from the thirties
♦ war films made during World War II

draft for *Citizen Kane* appeared on the market, and both reside, today, in the homes of satisfied collectors.

In rare circumstances, one can actually purchase a Hollywood legend. In 1995, Charlie McCarthy, the wooden dummy "partner" of ventriloquist Edgar Bergen, was sold at auction in New York. Charlie (with Edgar) was a big radio star, appearing in twelve feature motion pictures. He was actually given an honorary Oscar in 1937. When the winning bidder paid $112,500 for the dapper, monocled Charlie, it set a new record for blockheads.

PUBLICITY SHOTS

During the 1920s alone, two million photographs of film stars were taken at various studios. Moreover, this figure represents only the number of individual exposures; the number of actual copies of 8-by-10-inch glossy prints that were made from the negatives exceeds that quantity by a substantial margin. Imagine, then, the total number of publicity stills that were issued by MGM, Paramount, Warner Bros., Twentieth Century-Fox, Columbia, RKO (for a time), and the smaller Hollywood studios—as well as by studios worldwide—in the thirties, forties, fifties, and into the sixties. There is a treasure trove of collectible, relatively inexpensive photographs (almost all in black-and-white) for every pre-1970s star. Attractive to display and easy to store, publicity shots are the backbone of today's movie-personality collecting.

The epitome of a cool collectible: a personalized, signed early Sinatra publicity shot.

The best publicity stills are the originals, those that were circulated in conjunction with the release of an actor's latest movie or those that were simply meant to be part of a star's portfolio. Of the originals, some of the best are known as "outtake stills" and depict scenes that were ultimately left on the cutting-room floor. Outtake stills frequently provide buffs with

In a publicity still, the aging Bette Davis (as Elizabeth I) jealously eyes the comely Joan Collins in the 1955 costume drama The Virgin Queen.

A Shirley-Temple-as-Heidi autographed publicity shot.

fresh insights into film production. Original stills are recognizable by their being clearly focused, properly exposed, and sharply detailed. By comparison, duplicates seem out of focus or muddy. Collectors look at the back of a still to check its authenticity. It should be printed on durable paper stock and often retain text written (on a strip of taped-on paper) by a studio publicist to identify the star. If it's an action still rather than posed shot, it will have the movie, the star, and possibly identified costars.

Many publicity photos were autographed, but that may not enhance the value. Signed stills were given away by the thousands, and it is well known that the great majority of signatures were forged by studio clerks and others. Prices for signed stills can fluctuate wildly, so it's crucial to verify that signatures are authentic.

FILM PROPS AND COSTUMES

Louis B. Mayer, head of Metro-Goldwyn-Mayer during the many years it was the film industry giant, thought as little of movie props, or properties, as Walt Disney thought of animation cels. Only the actors mattered to him. "This is the only business in the world where the inventory goes home at night,"

BUT CAN HE SING?

One guest at the Austin *Antiques Roadshow* brought in a droll letter addressed to Enrico Caruso and signed by Charlie Chaplin. In it, Chaplin wrote, "I received the picture you sent me and showed it to Bill as requested. Bill gave one look and turned up his nose. He afterwards admitted that you were a very nice-looking dog, but said he could clean up a dozen of you with one paw tied behind his back."

This "Enrico Caruso" it seems, was a dog owned by the visitor's great uncle. *Antiques Roadshow* appraiser Leila Dunbar surmised that "Caruso" had written a letter to Chaplin's dog, Bill—the canine star of Chaplin's *A Dog's Life*—and that Chaplin had responded.

Observed Dunbar, "They were sort of doggie pen pals." Dunbar estimated that Bill's photograph and letter were worth $3,000 to $4,000.

MEMORABLE COSTUMES

A visitor to the San Diego *Antiques Roadshow* appeared with a collection of design albums that had been given to her by her mother, who had worked for costume designer Edith Head from 1938 to 1942. Head was long considered the grande dame of Hollywood costume design, and won more Academy Awards than anyone else in the movie industry. The guest's mother was a "specialist"; it was

her job to hand-paint the fabrics that would be made into costumes.

On the back of each design, a stamp detailed information about the production of the costume. The guest's collection also included a portrait of Edith Head and swatches from all the costumes her mother had worked on.

According to appraiser Rudy Franchi, this was a difficult collection to evaluate, but he assessed it at $8,000 to $10,000.

he said. Nonetheless, years after Mayer's death, MGM held the aforementioned highly successful auction of the 12,000 props and 150,000 costumes it had used in the filming of 2,000 movies since 1925. One wonders if those who run MGM in its current incarnation regret that 1970 fire sale. After all, props from significant movies become more valuable over time. A case in point is the throne of Julius Caesar from *Cleopatra.* Auctioned in 1970, when it reappeared at a Sotheby's sale in 1996, it brought six times the amount it had realized at the MGM auction.

Before you make any decisions about becoming a prop collector, however, you should probably take into account storage considerations. Many props are ungainly, if not huge. Director Cecil B. DeMille, for example, enjoyed making films that were rooted in history (but not necessarily in historical accuracy). Insisting on at least some verisimilitude for his 1956 epic *The Ten Commandments,* he went to the trouble of obtaining red granite from the top of Mount Sinai for the tablets used in the movie. (Another set was made from fiberglass, because even the sinewy Charlton Heston would have had a time hoisting those heavy granite slabs above his head.) Other props don't just weigh a lot but are truly of blockbuster size. Even the actual ship used to film *Mutiny on the Bounty* has been sold.

The surreal chiffon dance costume with a mile-long train that Cyd Charisse wore in the nightclub dream sequence of Singin' in the Rain.

"Orphaned" or "mystery" props are those that were once owned by a studio but are not attributable to any noteworthy movie or scene. These are usually affordable. If you do some detective work (for example, watch films certain items might have come from) and identify the film and scene, then their value can go up dramatically. If you're just starting out, look for those props produced in relatively significant quantities. Usually they come from new movies. Among the examples are the many matchbooks imprinted in bright green for the 1996 picture *The Birdcage.* These can currently be bought for less than $100.

Farther up the collectibles ladder are props from lower-level box-office hits, among them the iron maiden used in 1948's *Abbott and Costello Meet Frankenstein,* or even a "sperm costume" from Woody Allen's early 1972 comedy *Everything You Wanted to Know About Sex (But Were Afraid to Ask).*

At the apogee of prop collecting are the props and costumes that even noncollectors would be happy to own, such as the Munchkin costumes from *The Wizard of Oz.* (Serious collectors look for the dresses, rather than those little green shorts, because the former are not as common.) John Wayne costumes are desirable, even when they have been recycled. A tunic he wore (and probably wished he hadn't) in *The Conqueror* turned up

The white suit in which John Travolta famously discoed in Saturday Night Fever, *below, and a publicity still from the film, above.*

Julie Andrews wore this cream-colored dirndl-style dress in several scenes of the 1965 megahit The Sound of Music.

LET'S NOT FORGET FIDO

A unique trophy appeared at the Los Angeles *Antiques Roadshow*, which appraiser Leila Dunbar declared was not-quite-living proof that California has an award for everything. Unearthed in 1972 when its owner was part of a demolition crew working at an old trophy plant, it remained a mystery for years.

But his discovery, it turned out, is the animal world's Oscar. While everyone is familiar with the Academy Awards, the American Humane Association's award for outstanding achievements in major motion pictures by an animal is unquestionably less well-known. First awarded in 1950, some former honorees are Spike the dog—better known as Old Yeller, from the movie of the same name (1957), Cat, from *Breakfast at Tiffany's* (1961), and the last recipient of the award, Ben the Bear, from *Gentle Giant* (1967).

In attempting to investigate the value of his find, the owner had once been told that his one-of-a-kind trophy (still in its original case) was worth only $15 or $20. Luckily, he brought it to the *Antiques Roadshow*, where Dunbar told him that the trophy could bring $800 to $1,200 at auction.

on television years later in episodes of *The Wild, Wild West* and *Star Trek*. A bigger prize, though, despite its being made in 1978, would be the cape worn by Christopher Reeve in *Superman*.

THE OSCAR

All Oscars are equal, but some are more equal than others. For the Academy of Motion Picture Arts and Sciences, all the awards it bestows upon members of the film industry represent the highest recognition attainable. Among collectors, unsurprisingly, many distinctions are drawn. To begin with, there are the proto-Oscars. In the days before the gilt bronze statuette dominated filmdom, there were several kinds of awards honoring achievement. The first was the *Photoplay* Medal of Honor, bestowed annually for decades from 1920 on. While there *is* a market for such medals, it doesn't compare with Oscar's.

In the category of almost-Oscars, too, fall the slightly bruised plums, like the Academy Award of Merit for Outstanding Achievement. Few collectors would get excited about owning a plaque presented to, say, Farciot Edouart, Hal Corl, and the Paramount Transparency Department signifying the "Academy Scientific or Technical Class II Award For The Engineering And Development Of A Double-Frame, Triple-Head Background Projector"; this medal does, at least, bear Oscar's image, but only in relief.

Slightly more collectible than such plaques are very real Oscars presented to more obscure film talents. Every year, for instance, art directors, sound editors, and costume designers are awarded the gold-tone plated bronze statuette, and should these ever appear in the market, they'll be valued at under $5,000. Worth more than $10,000, usually, are the Oscars awarded to the films or film contributors who may be well known to

The Oscar awarded to Casablanca for Best Picture in 1943.

A publicity still of Humphrey Bogart and Ingrid Bergman in Casablanca, *which won the Oscar for Best Picture in 1943.*

the industry but not to the general public. Into this category would fall Oscars presented to composer Miklos Rozsa for his score of Alfred Hitchcock's *Spellbound* and writer Donald Ogden Stewart for his screenplay for *The Philadelphia Story.*

At the top of the Oscar pyramid, as you might expect, are the statuettes given to major stars and filmmakers. The twelfth Academy Award ceremony was held on February 29, 1940, at the Ambassador Hotel in Los Angeles. Bob Hope was master of ceremonies for the second half of the evening, but he yielded the floor to Spencer Tracy for the presentation of the highly anticipated award for Best Actress. One of the nominees was the star of a film that had been described by *The Hollywood Reporter* as the "Supreme Triumph of Film History." The star was Vivien Leigh, and the movie was *Gone with the Wind.* When the Oscar she won that night appeared at auction in 1993, it brought half a million dollars, at the time a record price. At a recent sale, however, Steven Spielberg purchased the only Best Actor Oscar won by Clark Gable, paying over $600,000 for the award he was given for 1934's *It Happened One Night.* Spielberg unexpectedly and graciously returned the statuette to the Academy, explaining, "The Oscar statuette is the most personal recognition of good work our industry can ever bestow, and it strikes me as a sad sign of our times that this icon could be confused with a commercial treasure."

A 1930s sepia-print publicity photograph of Vivien Leigh in profile carries her very legible signature.

A SIMPLE THANK-YOU

"It is with deep appreciation that I write to thank you for the time you have devoted to the processing of the mail," began a letter presented at the College Park, Maryland, *Antiques Roadshow*. The signature on the letter, in black fountain pen: "Jacqueline Kennedy." The letter's owner explained to appraiser Tim Luke, "I was working at the Pentagon on the mail in November 1963, when the president was killed," referring to the assassination of John F. Kennedy. "All this mail was coming in after the funeral. We set up a mail post at the Pentagon to handle it." In addition to her letter, Mrs. Kennedy also sent a folded photograph of her young family and a color print of the White House's Green Room. When the program first aired in 1997, Luke ventured that "a collector would spend at least $10,000 for this," because the Sotheby's sale of Jacqueline Kennedy Onassis's belongings had just sold for what turned out to be inflated prices; today he values the package at about $1,000.

PRINTED EPHEMERA

The most affordable type of collectible movie material is printed ephemera. In pretelevision Hollywood, movie magazines—Photoplay, Motion Picture Magazine, and Screenland, to name only a few—fed the (usually very) young fans thirsting for images of their favorite stars. Movie magazines featured photos of the stars and page after page of fluff and gossip on particularly alluring subjects, such as "Is Clark Gable Romancing Jean Harlow?" and "How Garbo's Fear of People Started." Cover headlines promised to "tell all," but the studio-controlled content never did. Nonetheless, movie magazines were gobbled up by star-crazy teenage girls, some of whom, fortunately, saved them for decades.

News weeklies weren't above using famous faces to increase sales. Marilyn Monroe appeared on the cover of *Life* magazine no less than nine times, and even winsome Judy Garland struck a "cheesecake" pose for the cover of *Look*. But as much fun as these magazines are to read today, they were mass-market publications, and so widely circulated that it is most unlikely that any of them will ever rise disproportionately in value. (One exception is any magazine containing material pertaining to Orson Welles's controversial 1941 masterpiece *Citizen Kane*.) The same is true of the novels written to coincide with film releases not adapted from

"'Slugger' Raft Pops 'Legs' Dietrich in the Kisser!" Movie Story *and other movie magazines kept fans informed—or at least intrigued—and today are fun, if easily obtainable, collectibles.*

books. Novelizations offered studios a clever method of supplying material to romance-hungry fans. For instance, following the success of the 1936 Gary Cooper movie *The Plainsman*, a novelized adaptation of the film, illustrated with 118 stills, appeared in bookstores—today, this is a great collectible.

Subject-specific publications capitalized on stars as well. In the realm of auto memorabilia, for example, certain early issues of *Auto Racing Digest* feature Paul Newman on the cover. (These are collectible, but their actual monetary value is quite low.) Film and theater trade journals are also desirable, because they often contain images that are no longer available elsewhere and because they were circulated only among the Hollywood cognoscenti.

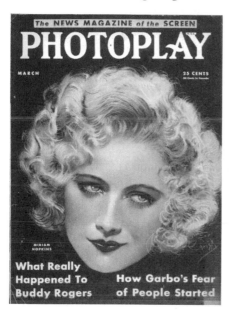

Photoplay, Motion Picture Magazine, *and* Screenland, *among others, featured photographs of the stars and lots of gossip. News weeklies like* Life *also ran famous faces on covers to increase sales.*

Somewhat rarer are the programs given to audience members at various screenings and events. Moviegoers bore them home as treasured mementos. Most desirable to collectors are pre-1920 programs, especially those pertaining to the groundbreaking director D. W. Griffith, maker of *The Birth of a Nation, Intolerance,* and other silent classics. For 25 cents, an audience member could purchase a program replete with photographs and beautiful full-color illustrations. Relatively expensive at the time, they are correspondingly expensive now.

Studios also published press packets just for theater owners, known to insiders as "bally books" because their aim was to generate "ballyhoo" for films. The books contained studio-approved feature stories and ideas for movie ads and promotions. Like trade journals, they were not widely disseminated. And because they also supply us today with a unique perspective on promotion techniques for particular films, they are very collectible.

TIPS *from the experts*

"Avoid movie posters that are signed," *Antiques Roadshow* appraiser Rudy Franchi advises collectors new to the movie poster market. Merchandisers invented the gimmick in the 1980s, Franchi explains, often designing posters long after the movies had come and gone. "They had them for almost every star," says Franchi. However, stars rarely signed the sheets. "The hairdresser in these movies signed some of the posters," Franchi notes. "Always be suspicious of limited-edition movie posters."

Experienced collectors look for the vintage movie posters that were printed by the studios to advertise movies when the movies were new. "The original posters followed the movie from one theater to the next," Franchi says. Most were tattered in their travels, and all were supposed to be returned to the distributors. "But, thank goodness, they weren't," says Franchi, noting that projectionists and ushers habitually ushered movie posters home. But even if the distributors got their posters back and they were discarded, they still weren't safe from movie poster fanatics. Says Franchi, "I had a friend who got jaundice from dumpster diving for posters. That's how some of them survived."

PAPER DOLLS AND COLORING BOOKS

Some of yesteryear's most popular female stars reappeared two-dimensionally in the form of cutout dolls and in coloring books. Marilyn Monroe, Judy Garland, Elizabeth Taylor, and especially, Shirley Temple were all immortalized in paper. If you decide to start collecting in this area, look for uncut, complete books of paper dolls. Similarly, coloring books should be uncolored—although how many children could actually refrain from coloring in Liz's violet eyes or Judy's ruby slippers?

(Hollywood stars often appeared as three-dimensional children's dolls as well; for more information, see page 284.)

LOBBY CARDS

Lobby cards are full color, usually 11-by-14-inch promotional pieces that were, as their name suggests, hung in theater lobbies to advertise upcoming films. Newcomers to collecting, especially those partial to silent movie relics, might find this a fine place to start. Of the relatively small amount of extant material documenting the beginnings of the film industry, lobby cards are among the few still obtainable according to some experts, although opinions differ on this.

Definitely available are lobby cards from every decade of the sound era. The passionate collector, if she works at it, could probably track down attractive lobby cards from fifties and sixties films as diverse as *East of Eden, Singin' in the Rain, Beach Blanket Bingo, Jailhouse Rock,* and *The Creature from the Black Lagoon.* There are interesting needles left in those lobby-card haystacks, too. *King Kong,* for example, was originally released in 1933, then rereleased in 1938, 1942, 1947, 1952, and 1956. Each time, new promotional material accompanied the film. Not surprisingly, the earliest lobby card is the most valued, and the latest is the least desirable.

A lobby card depicting a particularly dramatic scene from To Have and Have Not, *the film that first paired Humphrey Bogart with newcomer Lauren Bacall.*

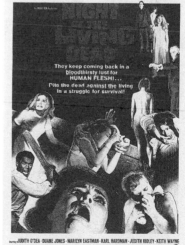

POSTERS

Horror, comedy, action, and more—movie posters in all genres utilized vivid color, eye-popping graphics, and enticing film stills to catch the attention of potential moviegoers.

Prior to the advent of radio advertising, the way to interest an audience in the next must-see movie was via posters. Posters, therefore, had to be eye-catching, and consequently they employed vibrant colors and excitingly overwrought illustrations. They were uncontestably successful at their job. Our grandparents (and great-grandparents) flocked to theaters mainly because of them. These factory-folded posters were printed on standard-size sheets of paper, and are named for their sizes. The one-sheet, which is 27 inches by 41 inches, is the size that was usually displayed, behind glass, in theater lobbies. The larger three-sheet, 41 inches by 80 inches, and the giant six-sheet, 81 inches by 81 inches, are much harder to find, especially in the requisite untorn, unstained condition. More often, they are found in pieces. Less highly valued collectible post–World War II posters, equally lurid, employed photography as commonly as they did illustrations.

Collecting vintage movie posters (from Hollywood and around the world) has been enormously popular since the 1960s, with much of the action, according to *Antiques Roadshow* poster expert Rudy Franchi, taking place in London. Curiously, the majority of surviving pre–World War II U.S.

Posters typically followed films from theater to theater and were often thrown out at the end of the run—which is why it is rare to find one in mint condition.

posters have been found in Europe. In America, the few pre-1939 posters that still exist were discovered years later by theater owners. Most early posters issued by major studios were damaged when in transit between theaters or in being repeatedly put up and taken down. Exhibitors abroad, fortunately, held on to theirs.

For poster collectors, the names Boris Karloff and Elsa Lanchester (who rejected Karloff's lovelorn monster in the 1935 classic *Bride of Frankenstein*) are bigger than Spencer Tracy and Katharine Hepburn. Horror and science fiction posters from the 1950s are particular favorites; among the most popular are *The Thing, The Day the Earth Stood Still, Forbidden Planet, The Invasion of the Body Snatchers, Them, The Incredible Shrinking Man,* and *I Was a Teenage Werewolf.* And don't overlook cult director Ed Wood's hideously and enjoyably bad 1959 *Plan 9 from Outer Space.* Plain old classics, such as *Casablanca* and *The Wizard of Oz,* have plenty of fans too.

There are also collectors who enjoy specializing in the work of a particular artist, and acquire, for instance, all the posters created by one illustrator. Interestingly, well-known artists worked on movie posters—among them Norman Rockwell and Thomas Hart Benton.

(For more information about collecting vintage posters, see *Posters and Illustration Art,* page 423.)

MERCHANDISE

Prior to the 1960s, studios did not engage in licensing to the extent they do today, so most of the early material that has survived was tied to media and theater promotions. Nevertheless, the studios did authorize the marketing of a variety of goods, many of them targeted to younger fans. For example, Roy Rogers pencil cases, shirts, billfolds, felt pennants, cap guns (look for a double set with holsters, in their box), lunch boxes, and toothbrushes were in ready supply. Roy's "safety awards" were presented to schools, and all of this material (except for that pair of cap guns), is affordable today. Take note, however, that for unknown reasons, memorabilia pertaining to those easygoing cowboy stars of yesteryear—Rogers, Gene Autry, Hopalong Cassidy, and others (you might be able to locate a small bottle of Hoppy's "hair trainer")—seems to be gaining in popularity, so prices may rise. Items related to the classic Clint Eastwood "spaghetti westerns" have their following too, though it is highly unlikely that there is much overlap between the two types of collectors.

Of course, there is no scarcity of low-priced merchandise on the market, because new products featuring stars and movies from the vintage era are produced every day. Marilyn Monroe, James Dean, cartoon heroine Betty Boop, and *Gone with the Wind* turn up on countless items, from posters and T-shirts to mugs and plates. Because they are mass-produced collectibles, however, don't expect them to increase in value over the years.

Actually, similar items featuring current stars and movies have a better chance of becoming desirable years from now. How many years, though, is anybody guess. Just keep yours wrapped and boxed, and hope that everyone else unpacks and mangles theirs!

A dancing cardboard puppet of the Little Tramp (circa 1924), with the box it came in, below left.

Below: "FREE! to kids who bring in mom or dad." It was hoped that young fans of Buck Rogers would pull in adult customers with giveaways like this one. Bottom: memorabilia pertaining to the easygoing cowboy stars is always desirable. This Hopalong Cassidy folding chair is an unusual example.

When a Mickey Mouse watch was brought to *Antiques Roadshow* during its first season, appraiser Rudy Franchi told the young guest that thousands of them were sold during the 1930s. In fact, Franchi continued, because the Disney company was still young and looking for its market, dividends from the sale of the watches helped it stay in business until the successful release of *Snow White* toward the end of the decade. This particular watch, however, had a rare add-on—a fob, which attached the watch to a vest. The three little mice on this example and a few other indicators convinced Franchi it was an "M1"—the very first model sold at Marshall Fields department store in Chicago in 1933. While the watch originally sold for $2.95, this young guest had picked it up for $3. Franchi estimates its worth now at $800 to $1,000.

In the 1930s, Disney stars Mickey, Minnie, and Donald were replicated as dolls and set to work on handcars and other toys, as well as having their image appear on children's tea sets.

DISNEYANA

Walt Disney first introduced moviegoers to Mickey Mouse in the 1927 silent film short *Plane Crazy*, but it wasn't until 1928 that Disney and Mickey made history. With *Steamboat Willie*, the first cartoon to feature a synchronized soundtrack, Mickey Mouse became a star!

Two years later Walt Disney began marketing Mickey Mouse toys. Today's children, however, would scarcely recognize that early beloved mouse. In those first cartoons, Mickey was thinner and much rattier-looking, and he had a pie-shaped wedge-cut in each of his round black eyes. (Our more familiar Mickey has wide eyes: expressive white ovals with black pupils.) At first he was barefoot and barehanded, but by his *Steamboat Willie* debut, he had been given shoes and white four-fingered gloves.

Manufacturers realized Mickey's potential immediately, and battled for licensing rights. German companies were among the first to release Mickey Mouse merchandise: pins, books, toys, and figures made of lead, iron, or porcelain. Because early makers based their toys on their own faulty memories of Mickey's facial features, these could change from toy to toy (except for those inimitable ears). Today, Disney lawyers oversee the slightest whisker twitch.

Most Mickey Mouse collectibles are toys. Often he is paired with girlfriend Minnie. One rarity is Tipp & Co.'s circa 1931

Mickey and Minnie on a motorcycle. This toy has changed hands for six-figure sums, and is the current Mickey Mouse record holder. A Mickey the Drummer, manufactured by Nifty, commands a premium, too. You may want to do a bit of mouse hunting in England, since both the motorcycle toy and the highly desirable "Standing Mickey with Moving Eyes and Mouth" were made for the British market.

Together, Minnie and Mickey even saved the day for Lionel trains. In 1934, they teamed up to "power" a clockwork-driven rail handcar made by the then struggling Lionel corporation. According to *The New York Times,* "Mickey and Minnie Mouse, pumping a red-painted hand car around a circular track . . . pulled the Lionel Corporation . . . back into the black."

Goofy, a largeish dog with a dopey, drawly voice, first appeared in 1932 as Dippy Dawg, then he became Dippy the Goof, and finally Goofy. While Goofy's no Mickey, there has always been sufficient interest in him to warrant mass marketing of numerous Goofy toys. A good example of the Goofy market would be found in the Marx Toy Company's 1950 clockwork Goofy the Walking Gardener. The value of this toy (Goofy pushing a wheelbarrow) has never achieved the heights of vintage Mickey toys for three reasons: It was produced relatively late, years after Goofy's creation; like Jiminy Cricket and the Seven Dwarfs, it is a secondary Disney character; and many Goofy the Walking Gardeners are still in existence. Goofys have value only when they're rare and perfect.

The practically unintelligible Donald Duck, who appeared first in a 1934 cartoon, was the last of Disney's major characters. Once Mickey was "prettied up," Donald became, by default, the Disney character with the most bite and irascibility, quite popular in his own right. As with Mickey, the early Donald looked slightly different. In particular, his bill was longer. The most collectible Donald material was made before World War II. Of particular interest are cars (with Donald as the driver); banks; dolls; comic books from the mid-forties to the late sixties supervised by

With tin wind-up toys, children in the 1940s could "animate" their own Disney characters—like Donald Duck and Goofy—at home.

Less cuddly than feisty, an early Mickey Mouse doll from the 1930s has a velvet body and mother-of-pearl buttons.

A SEQUENCE OF CELS

Two albums of Disney animation art that appeared in Los Angeles are a real *Antiques Roadshow* treasure. In 1939, the owner began to work for Walt Disney Studios as an inker and painter. The albums she brought for appraisal contained the drawings she was responsible for.

Each artist was given a sequence to paint and his or her work was timed. Yet despite the pressure of producing 35 to 65 cels per day, the owner declared that it was the most enjoyable work she'd ever done.

Flipping through the album's pages, appraiser Elyse Luray Marx pointed out artwork from Disney classics such as *Pinocchio, Fantasia, Bambi,* and *Sleeping Beauty.*

Though the artwork here has been cut down (trimmed), decreasing the value slightly, she estimated that these albums are still worth $15,000 to $20,000.

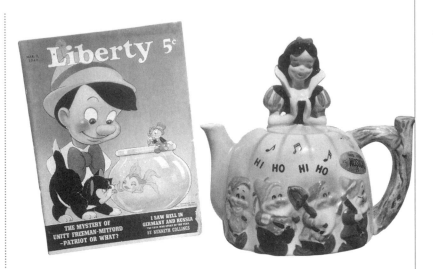

Carl Banks, Donald's illustrator; and figures made of everything from ceramic to wood to lead.

Minnie Mouse, Pluto, and Pinocchio are other Disney characters of special interest to collectors, though none approaches Mickey Mouse's level of popularity and higher-priced items aren't free of risk.

DISNEY CARTOON CELS

Before the days of computer-generated images, the creation of cartoons was a painstaking process; every move required a series of drawings. A cartoon cel was drawn for each individual frame of a cartoon, and when shown in sequence, the cels merged into seamless movement, like a very sophisticated flip book. Considering their current popularity as collectible art—in fact, cartoon cels are among the most coveted artifacts of filmdom— you may be surprised to learn that they were created using, basically, an assembly-line procedure. The first step in producing the Disney Studios cel was the tracing of the image from an artist's final sketch onto sheets of celluloid (hence the term "cel"). Next, the colors were applied by staff artists. Because approximately 1,440 cels were required to net one minute of movie time, you can imagine how many there must have been.

Snow White and the Seven Dwarfs, the first full-length cartoon feature (1937), was a turning point in character animation, and for having created it, Walt Disney was awarded a special Oscar: one large figure towering over seven smaller

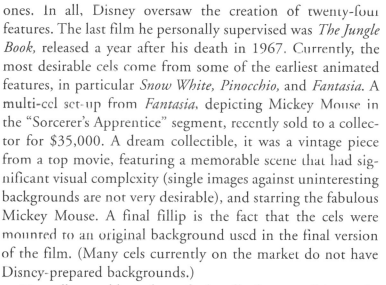

The Disney gang was promoted on virtually everything. From left, a magazine cover, a teapot, and a wooden pull toy.

ones. In all, Disney oversaw the creation of twenty-four features. The last film he personally supervised was *The Jungle Book,* released a year after his death in 1967. Currently, the most desirable cels come from some of the earliest animated features, in particular *Snow White, Pinocchio,* and *Fantasia.* A multi-cel set-up from *Fantasia,* depicting Mickey Mouse in the "Sorcerer's Apprentice" segment, recently sold to a collector for $35,000. A dream collectible, it was a vintage piece from a top movie, featuring a memorable scene that had significant visual complexity (single images against uninteresting backgrounds are not very desirable), and starring the fabulous Mickey Mouse. A final fillip is the fact that the cels were mounted to an original background used in the final version of the film. (Many cels currently on the market do not have Disney-prepared backgrounds.)

Naturally, untold numbers of cels suffer from condition problems. They were never intended to last beyond their immediate usefulness, of course, and their surfaces may not have been properly prepared for the application of color. Years after their creation, therefore, the gouache (opaque watercolor paint) with which they were colored may lift from the celluloid; with areas of paint lost, the value of the cel declines dramatically. Similarly, many cels have been destroyed or damaged over the years, and even those that do survive do not necessarily depict desirable subjects. Collectors always hope to find those rare cels that are in such good condition that they could be shown on the big screen.

Why would any serious collector buy "cels" from classic works of animation? "Because it puts a smile on your face," reasons appraiser Kathleen Guzman.

If the idea of collecting cels appeals to you sense of fun, what deciding factors—besides rarity—go into the value quotient? As with movie stars, the "leads," like the Snow Whites of the world, tend to have more cachet than the "supporting role" Grumpys. "There's a cuteness quotient," adds Guzman. "If the character's eyes are wide open and she's talking, it tends to have more value." But there's no reason for collectors with less deep pockets to despair. They can find cels from newer animated films, such as *The Lion King,* for a few hundred dollars. In the same price range, Guzman suggests buying preliminary sketches done for the cels of classic cartoons, which reveal "the draftsman at work." She notes, "Drawings show how difficult the animation process really is."

LEARNING DISNEYANA

The toys and the commercial tie-ins made in the period between Mickey's creation in 1928 and the onset of World War II are among the most prized of Disney collectibles. It is worth noting that, for the most part, the toys that were made under license generally are considered more desirable than those toys that were not. Fortunately, the dating and origins of many of the earlier Disney character products are fairly easy to determine. Prior to 1938, for instance, those manufactured in America and Germany were marked either "Walt Disney Enterprises" or "Walter E. Disney"; those made in Britain bore the inscription "Walt Disney Mickey Mouse Ltd." In 1939, the name of the firm was changed to "Walt Disney Productions."

Popeye takes on roller skating in this mid-1950s tin toy from Linemar. Popeye's pants are satin and the bowl of his pipe is made of wood.

Walt Disney supposedly once called cels "worthless temporary tracings." He might be surprised, and even gratified, by the fact that today cels have come to be considered works of art in themselves and (heavily laced with nostalgia) are widely collected.

A WORD ABOUT OTHER ANIMATORS

During animation's golden age (the late thirties to the mid-fifties) and concurrent with the work at Disney studios, other studios' cartoonists were dreaming up memorable characters, some of whom would go on to achieve worldwide fame. Walter Lantz's studio created Woody Woodpecker and Andy Panda. Max and Dave Fleischer created Popeye, Olive Oyl, and the most popular female character in animation history, Betty Boop. At Warner Bros., directors Tex Avery, Bob Clampett, Robert McKimson, and Chuck Jones created beloved cartoon characters Bugs Bunny, Daffy Duck, Porky Pig, the Tasmanian Devil, Sylvester and Tweety, the Road Runner and Wile E. Coyote, and Elmer Fudd. For MGM, Avery came up with Droopy Dog and directed Tom & Jerry cartoons. And U.P.A. gave birth to Gerald McBoing-Boing and Mr. Magoo. Despite such variety and lovable eccentricity, none of these characters has the appeal of those created and marketed by what came to be Walt Disney's empire.

ROCK AND ROLL MEMORABILIA

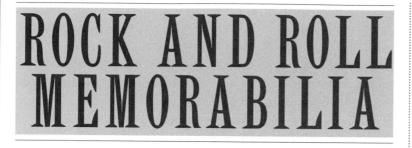

M ick Jagger once sang, "I know, it's only rock and roll, but I like it." Of the countless millions who share that sentiment, there are a growing number of fervent collectors who would rather share the actuality of fellow Rolling Stone Keith Richards's "Crazy Joe" Stratocaster, John Lennon's American-tour sunglasses, or the color slides of the Jimi Hendrix Experience playing at the Cal Expo Show in 1970. Others content themselves with rare recordings and the artifacts of their musical heroes.

Above: a publicity photo of guitar great Eric Clapton in concert. Left: an original Elvis acetate of something entitled "Somthing." Below: Clapton's 1952 maple-neck Fender Telecaster.

The music of rock and roll actually dates to the early and mid-fifties; nevertheless, most major rock memorabilia dates from the 1960s, when rock music became the soul of the youth-dominated counterculture. Folk rock, surf music, the "girl group" sound, Motown, the Mersey beat, soul, psychedelic/acid rock, funk, and even country rock emerged, incorporating folk, protest songs, blues, rhythm and blues, doo-wop, country, rockabilly, and classic rock and roll. Distinct "sounds" came out of Liverpool and London, New York, Boston, Philadelphia, Chicago, Detroit, L.A., San Francisco, Memphis, the Northwest, and the Deep South. Such disparate artists as the Rolling Stones, the Supremes, the Beach Boys, the Shangri-Las, Roger Miller, Petula Clark, the Drifters (one of the rare fifties acts that did not fall victim to the British invasion), Lesley Gore, Simon and Garfunkel, Mary Wells, the Jefferson Airplane, Nancy Sinatra, the Mamas and the Papas, Aretha Franklin, Gerry and the Pacemakers, James Brown, the Lovin' Spoonful, the Four Seasons, and Bob Dylan were all broadcast on Top 40 radio. Popular on alternative and college radio stations were

FIFTIES FAVORITES

Fifties fans collect memorabilia from a full range of individual artists and groups, among them Ruth Brown, the Coasters, Sam Cooke, Bobby Darin, Dion and the Belmonts, Fats Domino, the Drifters (especially with Clyde McPhatter singing lead), the Everly Brothers, Bill Haley and the Comets, Buddy Holly, Jerry Lee Lewis, Little Richard, Roy Orbison, the Orioles (and other early doo-wop groups), Carl Perkins, the Platters, Johnny Ray, the Teddy Bears (with Phil Spector singing), Ritchie Valens, and Jackie Wilson.

A ticket stub to a 1963 London performance of the Beatles, opening for the better-known (at the time) Roy Orbison.

Frank Zappa's Mothers of Invention, the Grateful Dead, and scores of others. Elvis recorded his final hits, Linda Ronstadt (at first with the Stone Poneys) her first, and Janis Joplin (at first with Big Brother and the Holding Company) her only hits. Wonderfully talented solo artists and groups appeared with amazing regularity. And "Louie, Louie," with the Kingsmen garbling the words, achieved immortality.

COLLECTING ROCK MEMORABILIA

For rock and roll material, as for most collectibles, rarity is prime, and serious collectors learn to distinguish between the mundane and the unusual. For example, they know that an autographed Allman Brothers Band album is fairly common and not particularly valuable—*unless* the names on it include the very rare signature of Duane Allman, whose time with the group was curtailed by a fatal 1971 motorcycle accident. Rarity, however, seems subject to continuing "scholarship." Consider the plight of the collector who purchased, for a premium price, an original Yellow Submarine Pop-Out Art Decorations Book only to learn of a subsequent "warehouse find" of quantities of the identical item. Other merchandise from the 1960s has been known to surface in bulk, so collectors can seldom rest easy.

PRINTED EPHEMERA

The majority of printed ephemera available to the novice collector are unsigned promotional items, concert posters, tickets, programs, and handbills; all "ephemeral" things, meant to be thrown away.

Almost anyone who has attended a rock concert has saved a ticket stub as a keepsake. For major concerts by major stars—the Beatles at Shea Stadium, or George Harrison's Concert for Bangladesh—stubs are both fabulous souvenirs and authentic collectibles that can command solid prices. It might seem, then,

It's Not Only About Rock

There are passionate collectors of music besides rock and roll. Some concentrate on Broadway scores, movie soundtracks, or television themes; forties and fifties folk; comedy albums; Dixieland; gospel; and, of course, classical music—if you have $50,000 and can find a seller, you may be able to pick up a signed handwritten letter from Ludwig van Beethoven.

BLUES

BLIND LEMON JEFFERSON • ROBERT JOHNSON • MUDDY WATERS • HOWLIN' WOLF • WILLIE DIXON • BROWNIE MCGEE AND SONNY TERRY • MEMPHIS SLIM • B. B. KING • THE PAUL BUTTERFIELD BLUES BAND • JUNIOR WELLS • BUDDY GUY • LIGHTNIN' HOPKINS • JOHN LEE HOOKER • JIMMY REED • BESSIE SMITH • **B.B. King** *and* LEADBELLY.

JAZZ

SCOTT JOPLIN • JELLY ROLL MORTON • LOUIS ARMSTRONG • BIX BEIDERBECKE • DUKE ELLINGTON • COUNT BASIE • MILES DAVIS • JOHN COLTRANE • CHARLIE PARKER • SONNY ROLLINS • FATS WALLER • ART TATUM • DAVE BRUBECK • GERRY MULLIGAN • THELONIOUS MONK • CHARLIE MINGUS • CANNONBALL ADDERLEY • THE MODERN JAZZ QUARTET • ELLA FITZGERALD • SARAH VAUGHAN **Louis Armstrong** • *and* BILLIE HOLLIDAY.

BIG BAND

• COUNT BASIE • TOMMY DORSEY • JIMMY DORSEY • PAUL WHITEMAN • ARTIE SHAW • GLENN MILLER • GENE KRUPA • BENNY GOODMAN • LES BROWN (*with lead singer Doris Day*) • *and others.* **Glenn Miller Orchestra**

COUNTRY

JIMMIE RODGERS • THE ORIGINAL CARTER FAMILY • UNCLE DAVE MACON • BILL MONROE • HANK SNOW • THE SONS OF THE PIONEERS • BOB WILLS (*especially with lead singer Tommy Duncan*) • LESTER FLATT AND EARL SCRUGGS • MINNIE PEARL • HANK WILLIAMS • ERNEST TUBB • RED FOLEY • KITTY WELLS • LEFTY FRIZELL • JIM REEVES • PATSY CLINE • EDDY ARNOLD • GEORGE JONES • TAMMY WYNETTE • MERLE HAGGARD • DOLLY PARTON • WILLIE NELSON • JOHNNY CASH • LORETTA LYNN • *and* ELVIS PRESLEY.

Elvis Presley

Dolly Parton

A strong market for psychedelic-era concert posters has helped immortalize Janis Joplin and Jim Morrison—hard-living rock stars who died young.

that unused, untorn tickets to such events would be even more collectible. Not so. Not too long ago, a collection of 310 mementos of "missed opportunities" (unused tickets) came up at auction, and failed to find a buyer—possibly because there was speculation that they were fakes.

Rock concert programs are not as rare as tickets, since many fans carried them home. In the programs market, earlier examples seem to be more collectible, with bands such as the Rolling Stones, the Byrds, the Yardbirds, the Grateful Dead, and even the Dave Clark Five attracting the most attention.

Considering how hard it is to get backstage passes, you would expect them to be expensive, and they are. Pass collectors differentiate between "satins" and "laminates," "Before Show," "VIP," "Staff," and a variety of other flavors. Beware of any that come without a secure provenance; these are most likely fakes.

Since the 1960s, thousands of promotional photos have been distributed with press kits. They are also handed out by the band members themselves. (Do you remember Paul's "grandfather" trying to sell Beatles publicity stills in *A Hard Day's Night*?)

In addition, adoring fans take their own snapshots of favorites during, before, and after concerts. Yet even images of famous musicians that are sold with copyrights can be affordable. Photographs depicting, for example, the early British pop star Cliff Richard or the Who (with negatives) have been purchased relatively inexpensively. However, unless you receive formal confirmation that you have been sold the copyright to an image, assume that you do not have the right to publish it or make duplicates to be sold for profit. The artists themselves, or their estates, jealously guard their territory.

Most of the posters that decorate the rooms of today's teenagers are not yet old enough to be collectible. It is the earlier posters from the 1960s (and some from the seventies) that are actively collected. Before that time, strange to say, posters had nothing more than informational text, because budgets were small and the addition of pictures was costly. Collectors don't necessarily care about graphic design. It is the star that makes a poster collectible, not its appearance. Exceptions are the creatively

A counterculture spin on Art Nouveau cabaret posters—a 1969 Rolling Stones tour promotion.

designed psychedelic posters of the sixties and early seventies, including those promoting upcoming concerts at the Fillmore West in San Francisco. These have been exhibited in museums as documents of an era.

Original posters in all sizes featuring the megastars of the sixties and seventies are in demand. At the top of the market are the true rarities—posters advertising concerts by stars before they became stars. These are particularly rare today because they would have been consigned to dustbins. If you had gone to hear Texan Bruce Channel, for instance, at the Tower Ballroom in New Brighton, England, on June 21, 1962, would you have bothered to nab the poster by the entrance wall on the way out? Why would you have wanted a poster of the night's headliner, a minor singer who had only one big hit ("Hey! Baby")? Unless you were prescient, how would you have known that one of the four bands on the bill that night (and on the promotional poster), the Beatles, would achieve success—even if you liked that Liverpool sound.

Beatles posters from their several appearances at the Tower Ballroom are scarce, as are any early posters of the "Fab Four." It's far more likely that you'll find posters for their movies, *A Hard Day's Night, Help!,* the feature-length cartoon *Yellow Submarine,* and the documentary *Let It Be,* or concert posters from the late sixties produced in large numbers by the Dutch firm The Fool.

By the 1970s, the Beatles had disbanded so no new posters were forthcoming, and from that decade, only a few music personalities are actively collected. These include the Rolling Stones (who were touted as the world's greatest touring band), Paul McCartney and Wings, John Lennon, David Bowie (including his seventies "Ziggy Stardust" persona), Blondie, the Eagles, and Led Zeppelin.

ROCK 'N' ROLL POSTERS

On the *Antiques Roadshow* in Austin, Texas, a guest unfurled a collection of rock and roll posters. "You have a history of the music business from the sixties here," said Gary Sohmers. "The value is $15,000, but that's not what's important. It's the history."

History, here, was a 1965 poster of the Rolling Stones, a psychedelic Chocolate Watchband poster, and another announcing a 1972 Austin concert by the Grateful Dead. The guest had purchased most of the posters while living in California in the late 1960s. "Some bookstores

sold posters for a dollar, so I'd pick out the ones I liked," he recalled.

But he also brought along a drumstick that for Deadheads would be a magic wand. "I went to see the Grateful Dead. Bill Kreutzmann let go of one of his sticks and it hit me in the foot."

If you find a great original poster in a shop, at a yard sale, or hidden away in the attic, don't despair if it isn't in the best condition. Professionally executed restorations are acceptable to the collecting community.

SIGNED EPHEMERA

The bread and butter of the serious rock music collector is autographed ephemera. Rock has never been like country music, with annual "fanfests" where the public can meet the friendly, grateful stars. But enough rock stars signed autographs that there are now many thousands in circulation. There is, however, something of a hierarchy among types of signatures.

An autograph buried within an autograph book is not as highly prized as an autograph on a record jacket, for example. Similarly, entire autograph books packed with rock star signatures do not do particularly well on the market.

It goes without saying that the major factor in a signature's value to collectors is the star power of the signatory. For those just beginning to collect autographs, big stars such as AC/DC, Aerosmith, Cheap Trick, Rod Stewart, and Elton John beckon. The secondary members of many of the top acts, however, are the ones that sometimes can be had for a bargain, although when seven items autographed by Bill Wyman of the Rolling Stones, Christmas cards among them, appeared at auction recently, they couldn't find a buyer for even $400. A "Merry Christmas" from Mick Jagger or Keith Richards would have sold for enormous sums.

Keith, Mick, Ronnie, and Charlie—each of the Stones signed this post–Bill Wyman promotional glossy.

Almost always, the signatures of rock idols are more collectible after they are dead, as long as their fame hasn't diminished precipitously once the music stops. Live musicians could, ostensibly, keep signing autographs by the thousands, for years to come. For dead musicians, there is—obviously—a fixed supply.

Handwritten lyrics are understandably at the top of the collector's wish list, but distinctions between types are carefully drawn, for large sums tend to be involved. First drafts are considered more valuable than "rewrites." A rewrite can be identified by the fact that it will, typically, duplicate the definitive version of a song, show no corrections, and be written on plain paper. The collector's prize is always the lyric that the artist first committed to paper, for when the muse strikes, stricken musicians often have only a napkin or a parking receipt on which to pen their verses, making corrections or altering rhymes on the spot. By contrast, the rewrite is most often the handwritten copy of the original that was taken to the studio and handed to an engineer.

It is acceptable, in the collectors' market, for the first drafts of handwritten lyrics to be crumpled or stained. Such features are the ephemeral equivalent of furniture patina, adding a touch of "historical authenticity." A little wear and tear is also forgiven on any particularly rare signed magazines and signed pictures, for these were often taped or stapled on walls.

A signed program from a series of May 1968 Jimi Hendrix concerts at the Teatro Brancaccio in Rome. Hendrix also inscribed "BR Groovy."

AUTOGRAPH VALUES

The autographs of rock musicians are valued quite differently from, say, presidential autographs. One authority ranks them as follows:

RANK	TYPE OF AUTOGRAPH
1	Actual penned lyrics
2	An autograph on a photograph (Check to be sure that the ink on the signature is of irregular consistency; otherwise, the signature may have been printed on the image.)
3	An autograph on a record jacket
4	A handwritten letter (A letter might jump up a couple of notches if its contents are particularly personal or important.)
5	An autograph on a fan-club card
6	An autograph on an official or legal document
7	An autograph on blank paper or in an autograph book

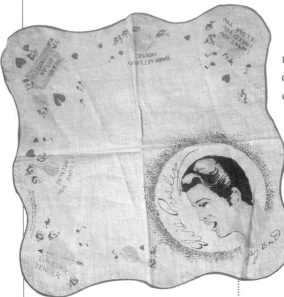

Hit song titles and a likeness of "the King" embellish this 1956 Elvis souvenir handkerchief.

Janis Joplin left this rainbow-colored crocheted hat behind after a Long Island concert. No one dreamed then that it would be a valuable relic of an era.

Signed publicity material, however, should have legible signatures. Letters and contracts should be complete, with no parts of the text missing. Letters should have their original envelopes. And if you expect a high return on your stash of concert programs, they must be in pristine condition. Because fans who picked them up when walking *into* the concerts usually handled, folded, and smudged them for the duration of the performance, perfect examples are rare.

PROMOTIONAL ITEMS

Not long ago, a vast, single collection of 1,400 buttons "representing every aspect of the rock and roll community" became available to collectors. But as big as it was, it merely represented the tip of the iceberg, for along with such buttons, bands have promoted themselves with cardboard stand-ups, decals, backpacks, key chains, paperweights, belt buckles, mini-zeppelins (guess whose?), dog tags, and ashtrays (appropriately chosen by Earth, Wind and Fire). Over time, rock stars became commercially canny and savvy about collectors, so unlike their fifties and sixties predecessors, they made licensing deals for promotional items and put their names on just about everything. As is true of toys, dolls, and probably Pandora's box, unopened promotional items are worth three times more than opened ones.

CLOTHES AND ACCESSORIES

One can literally walk in the shoes of the rich and famous rock stars. Or put on their pants, leather jackets, or racy, lacy bustiers. Such items have been marketable for quite some time, and seem to be increasingly available as time goes on. Why are they so popular? Perhaps because certain rock stars have made such "fashion" integral to their acts. Think of Elvis, the Beatles—from their early collarless suits to their quirkier Sgt. Pepper's Lonely Hearts Club Band uniforms and Magical Mystery Tour costumes—to Prince, Elton John, and, of course, Madonna.

At the top of collectors' wish-lists are those items that once belonged to the biggest stars: Elvis Presley's "Starburst" stage cape, circa 1971; the Buddy Holly crewneck sweater seen in so many

"Take another little piece of my heart now, baby." Janis Joplin at Woodstock.

of his publicity photos; the shawl Janis Joplin wore on the back cover of Big Brother and the Holding Company's *Cheap Thrills* album. Such garments were so closely associated with their owners' images that they became part and parcel of their rock persona. Along with Jim Morrison's stage-worn pants, the aforementioned have macabre connections, since their respective owners met sad and early deaths.

If you want to collect celebrity clothes or accessories, you will need first to satisfy yourself that the items you are considering for purchase can actually be traced back to the star. Forensic testing aside, how can one hope to distinguish between any random soiled, white handkerchief and one used to mop the brow of, say, Tom Jones, James Brown, or Louis Armstrong? Authenticity can be verified to the satisfaction of collectors by:

1. The item's provenance—an unbroken and verifiable chain of ownership leading back to the star

2. The authenticated signature of the star on the item itself

3. A photograph of the star wearing the item

4. A letter from the star attesting to the authenticity of the item

For the most part, top stars' clothing is an area for the experienced collector. The less assured collector or the bargain hunter should consider seeking out atypical items as opposed to iconic ones. For example, three Madonna-related items were recently offered on the Internet: a pair of shoes from the film *Evita*; a pair of gloves worn on tour; and a Dolce & Gabbana bra. The gloves brought twice as much as the shoes, and the bra six times as much.

SUITABLE FOR FRAMING

In 1991, *Rolling Stone* magazine listed the top fifty-four album covers of the seventies—i.e., after *Sgt. Pepper's Lonely Hearts Club Band* and other Beatles albums. The top ten selections by art directors, designers, photographers, and editors were:

1. *Never Mind The Bollocks . . . Here's The Sex Pistols,* The Sex Pistols; **2.** *Sticky Fingers,* The Rolling Stones; **3.** *Exile on Main Street,* The Rolling Stones; **4.** *Hotel California,* The Eagles; **5.** *Hejira,* Joni Mitchell; **6.** *Into the Purple Valley,* Ry Cooder; **7.** *Abraxas,* Santana; **8.** *Candy-O,* The Cars; **9.** *Relayer,* Yes; **10.** *Sailin' Shoes,* Little Feat.

Also notable for intriguing artwork are:

Playing Possum, Carly Simon; *Born to Run,* Bruce Springsteen; *Horses,* Patti Smith (with a photograph of her by Robert Mapplethorpe); *Dark Side of the Moon,* Pink Floyd; *Houses of the Holy,* Led Zeppelin; *American Beauty,* The Grateful Dead; *The Ramones,* The Ramones; *Self-Portrait,* Bob Dylan; *Rumours,* Fleetwood Mac; *Who's Next?,* The Who.

A stage outfit worn by Joan Jett, one of the first female hard rock stars, is valued at less than one-third of the average price of a pair of Madonna's shoes. Despite having big hits in the eighties such as "I Love Rock 'n' Roll", and a teenage past in the pioneer seventies all-girl band (the very collectible Runaways), Jett is still affordable because she is a second-tier star. For fans who prefer her to Madonna, Jett's clothing can be a bargain. But even some superstar clothing isn't rare. A case in point is the wardrobe of Elton John, who has generously donated so many of his belongings to charity that—for the moment, at least—the market is oversaturated.

As the Jett and John examples illustrate, today's market is ideal for new collectors who wish to buy star duds at affordable prices, but only if they intend to keep them for a while. Like other collectibles, they shouldn't come back on the market too soon.

GUITARS AND DRUMS

Not all performers sought to create an image. Some actually earned their celebrity status by being top musicians. One might be hard pressed, for instance, to envision the "quintessential Eric Clapton outfit," since he was never a fashion plate. But all dedicated collectors would be thrilled to own one of his guitars. In fact, one sold recently for a six-figure sum.

Since guitars are so easy to store and display, they are especially popular with rock fans who collect instruments. Even some celebrities collect guitars—movie star Richard Gere, for example, has an extensive collection. At the pinnacle of instrument collecting "wanna-haves" are the guitars used by famous stars such as George Harrison, Keith Richards, Mike Bloomfield, Roger McGuinn, Carlos Santana, Bo Diddley, Jeff Beck, Jimmy Page, blues legend B. B. King, Jerry Garcia, Robbie Robertson, Elvin Bishop, Joe Walsh, Pete Townshend, Johnny Winter, Rick Nelson, Dick Dale, Dave Davies, Lou Reed, Bob Dylan, the influential Les Paul, Chuck Berry, Elvis Presley, and, at the top, Eric Clapton, Buddy Holly, and

Top, guitar great Bo Diddley, one of the progenitors of rock and roll, and above, one of his highly collectible electric guitars.

Even the tiniest object associated with a star is collectible. Here, a guitar capo signed by Bob Dylan.

the man generally considered to be the greatest rock and roll guitarist of all, Jimi Hendrix. In fact, almost anything from the Hendrix legacy is desirable and a Fender Stratocaster that Hendrix played has been valued at more than $350,000.

Curiously, even fragments of Hendrix's guitars are sought-after—making it amusingly clear that the condition of musician-played instruments can often be of low priority. As Hendrix was known for periodically smashing his instruments on stage, bits and pieces have made their way into collectors' hands. The rather droll provenance of a guitar Hendrix smashed at Royal Albert Hall on February 24, 1969, reads, in part: "The second of two nights at the Royal Albert Hall was filmed. . . . The vendor [of this guitar at auction] is captured on the film diving into the melee on stage, as the crowd invaded it during Jimi's climactic guitar-smashing routine, and can be seen rushing past the camera with the fragment concealed under his jacket!" If all of the ostensible fragments of Hendrix guitars currently in circulation were in one room, it would be enlightening to see if any of them actually fit together; or if, when reassembled, they would yield more guitars than his fans have calculated that he smashed.

Drum sets are not popular with collectors because of their size, but single drums, drum heads, or drumsticks often appear

The Prefab Four: a tambourine decorated with portraits of TV's pop music phenomenon, the Monkees.

THE MONKEES

One of show business's most bizarre success stories occurred in 1965, when auditions were held to cast four singer-actors to play a singing group in an ABC comedy called *The Monkees.* Five hundred people tried out, and the four young men selected were Mike Nesmith, Mickey Dolenz, English singer Davy Jones, and Peter Tork. Inspired by the Beatles' hit movie *A Hard Day's Night,* the show was an enjoyable mix of absurd, anarchic humor, silly dialogue, quick editing, and surprisingly engaging performances by the charming foursome.

The Monkees' television show premiered in September 1966 and its popularity was fueled by a run of Top 40 hits that made them one of the most successful acts of the era—amazing because they were a prefabricated group. In fact, the group rose to stardom so quickly that they had little time to rehearse the music together as a live band before going on tour in December 1966. Later, after much arguing, they were allowed to play on their own records.

Along with Ricky Nelson—and to a lesser degree, the Archies and the Partridge Family—the Monkees continue to be the rare performers that have crossover appeal for collectors of both television and rock music memorabilia.

From various sessions recorded during the late 1950s, John Coltrane's lush jazz classic, above. Top: a mid-1960s album cover of a Satchmo concert in Paris.

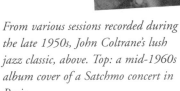

Elvis, during a recording session for RCA.

on the market and are avidly collected by the fans of the relatively few noteworthy rock drummers (Ringo Starr and Keith Moon, for example). Novice collectors should note that drumsticks can be had for quite reasonable amounts.

Because artists often become very attached to their instruments, they are, naturally, loath to give them away. When giving one as a gift, therefore, they tend to sign an unplayed replica of the one they actually use. Among collectors, these are known as "signers," and they are the least interesting of autographed guitars because they've never been played by the musician; a huge difference. To cite one example, when Bob Dylan's 1958 Gibson CF100E guitar appeared at auction with a photograph of Dylan playing it, it brought nearly $10,000; an unplayed guitar he had merely signed brought about one-third as much.

RECORDS

In the mid-eighties, the CD replaced vinyl albums and 45s around the world, but it's never replaced them in the minds and hearts of record lovers. These old records are out of print, but they are still out there, bounty for collectors. There are countless stores that sell old vinyl, and records abound in closets, attics, basements, and garages—even on the shelves of those die-hard record collectors who still have turntables.

So, unless there is major hoarding, there is little danger of records disappearing—and in fact, the most popular, best-selling records are the ones that are out there in most quantity. That's why condition has become the major factor in determining prices for popular old albums. Condition and scarcity both come into play with 45s (and the old 78s) and albums that: weren't produced in large numbers to begin with; were imported; had smaller stereo printings, printings with alternate tracks, or different sleeves (as did the Beatles' *Yesterday and Today*); or just slipped through the cracks. (Usually collectors put a premium on original pressings, promo/demo recordings, and variations that have different tracks or instrumentation.) Scratches, not surprisingly, decrease the value of records. Very Good condition records are worth only half as much as unplayed records in Mint or Near Mint condition; and the warped or scratched Poor-to-Fair condition examples have very little. That said, it should be pointed out that prices vary so much for the same items that there are record collecting books on the market that don't list prices at all.

ELVIS

Former truck driver Elvis Presley is the legitimate King of Rock and Roll. It was Elvis who created the most brilliant mix of rock 'n' roll (of the kind Bill Haley and the Comets were pioneering) with black roots music, earthy rhythm and blues, and gospel; who injected the raw, energetic tradition of Country; and who, by sheer force of personality, made a hybrid music that ignited the world. During his career, Elvis's songs made the Top Forty 107 times, more than twice the number of appearances of the Beatles. And still his fans yearned for more.

Elvis's unprecedented success in the late 1950s prompted a flood of Elvis merchandise, so the King's collectibles exist in great variety, and include everything from key rings to his own Harleys. Among the more unusual pieces are Elvis overnight cases, "Love Me Tender" hair and body products, and the sweat-stained handkerchiefs with which he wiped his forehead during concerts. Today, almost any pre-1970s item is avidly collected, in particular those created by Elvis Presley Enterprises (which produced the majority of Elvis material). Elvis merchandise continues to be produced, however, so collectors should not mistake replicas for originals.

A visitor to the Boston *Antiques Roadshow* was just 14 years old in 1956, when a new record store opened in her hometown of Mayfield Heights, Ohio. A memento from that grand opening was a promotional 45 called "Perfect for Parties," and it contained six songs sung and introduced by the King himself, Elvis Presley. "There were a lot of new singers back then, but he was my favorite," she explained.

Over the years, the visitor said, she occasionally played the record, but put it away while her children were young to avoid a heartbreaking accident. Appraiser Gary Sohmers noted that most 45s from that era are worth less than a dollar. But because few such "premiums" were produced, the value of this particular 45 is considerable. Moreover, its record sleeve is in perfect condition, bringing its value to $150 to $175. What does the show's guest plan to do with her treasure? "Put it back in the box and then give it to my kids in twenty years."

A potpourri of 1950s Elvis Presley promotional items, including fan-club cards and an 8-by-10 glossy.

A CASUAL ENCOUNTER WITH A BEATLE

Imagine this: It's 1967, and you're a young American tourist in England who, above everything, wants an autograph from the soul

of the Beatles, John Lennon. What to do? How about going to his house and introducing yourself? That's what a guest at the Providence *Antiques Roadshow* did when she was 18 years old, as she explained to appraiser Dana Hawkes. "John Lennon's house had a very big fence around it . . . but the gate was open. There were a few other fans there, and we walked in. It was a beautiful day and he was sitting outside painting a picture." The young woman went home with more than her memories; she took some snapshots, each dated August 1967, of her once-in-a-lifetime casual encounter with her hero, and got two autographs. Today, says Hawkes, these authentic early signatures are worth $1,500 to $9,000 apiece.

THE BEATLES

Fab Four collectors give Elvis collectors a run for their money. Even today, traditionally reserved London auction galleries periodically succumb to bouts of Beatlemania, and offer as many as 300 high-quality Beatles collectibles at a time. (A little perspective: If 300 works by one painter, say, were offered at auction on one night, the market would be glutted and the value of every piece would be decreased.) Yet there seems to be an insatiable thirst for Beatles collectibles, no matter how many there are in circulation. Fortunately for collectors, there is plenty, because the group was not only at the forefront musically, but (following Elvis's lead) it was also among the first real dynamos of product merchandising. The amount of licensed Beatles material is staggering. Moreover, the group's licensing arm, North End Music Stores, permitted hundreds of international companies to manufacture Beatles gear. Thus, there are John Lennon hangers, rubber Ringo dolls, and Beatles dresses, purses, hats, jewelry, lamps, pens, nodder dolls, jigsaw puzzles, plastic cups, and—oh, yes—records. The question is: Where does a collector start?

A good, but pricey, place might be with the material from the early 1960s, when the Beatles were beginning their career. This is the most desirable era for collectors. Photos depicting an early incarnation of the group playing in Hamburg, and the afore-mentioned posters from shows when the Beatles weren't yet a headline act (including those listing them as "The Beetles"), are

Far left: John, Paul, and the Commodore in a cel from Yellow Submarine. *Left: all four bobble-headed Beatles from the early sixties.*

valuable items. Of particular interest to American collectors is the material surrounding the group's first visit to the United States in February 1964, when "I Wanna Hold Your Hand," "She Loves You," and "Please Please Me" topped the U.S. charts and the country gathered to watch the charismatic group on *The Ed Sullivan Show.* Among exceptions to the early sixties superiority are the paraphernalia from the original release of the movie *Yellow Submarine* (1968). The cels from the extremely popular feature-length animated film are prize collectibles.

Since there was such a proliferation of Beatles merchandise, many items are still relatively affordable. Among potential good buys are mass-produced 1964 birthday cards bearing the greeting "Happy Birthday From All Of Us." (Unused cards with their original envelopes would be most collectible.) The scores of Beatles magazines that fed material to loyal fans are still eminently affordable, too, except for the various #1 issues, which sell for five times the price of any other issue. Vintage buttons featuring unfortunate puns like "I'm Bugs About The Beatles" are equally inexpensive, but their values depend somewhat on size as opposed to sentiment. The bigger the buttons get, the more expensive they become, and some of the larger ones may not lie within the reach of the wallet-conscious collector.

As for those records themselves, because millions were pressed, most are still affordable. Still there is gold amid the vinyl. Early U.K. pressings with black Parlophone labels are the most collectible, with the 1962 album *Please Please Me* leading

Among the mountains of mass-produced material, the rare one-of-a-kind piece stands out. Here, an original John Lennon drawing from 1969.

For Your Listening Pleasure

While television is the medium that transfixed baby boomers, radio was the end-all medium for the generations that preceded them. Those who collect thirties through fifties radio memorabilia remember the days when entire families gathered around a piece of furniture that, magically, talked and provided them with an unimaginable array of entertainment. Unlike television, (as its fans remind us), radio forced listeners to use their imaginations.

Collectors of radio memorabilia look for scripts, recordings, studio props (including those used for sound effects), photos of stars (particularly ones made during performances), and other mementos of that bygone era. They are interested in such programs as those listed below.

Collectors are also partial to programs that became TV series, to Lucille Ball's radio appearances, after-school serials, live shows hosted by famous band leaders, science fiction—Orson Welles's infamous 1938 broadcast *The War of the Worlds* is among the few pre-1950s sci-fi radio programs—soap operas, news reports from World War II, and *Academy Award Theater* and other programs that featured big stars in radio versions of movies (among them Humphrey Bogart in *The Maltese Falcon.*)

There are also a number of radio collectors who collect—what else?—old radios, some of which are startlingly valuable.

THE ADVENTURES OF SUPERMAN • THE AMOS 'N' ANDY • BIG TOWN • THE BOB HOPE SHOW

The Goldbergs

The Burns and Allen Show   ALDRICH FAMILY • • BOSTON BLACKIE • THE BURNS AND ALLEN SHOW • THE CHASE AND SANBORN HOUR FEATURING EDGAR BERGEN AND CHARLIE MCCARTHY • THE CISCO KID • DRAGNET • THE EDDIE CANTOR SHOW • FIBBER MCGEE AND MOLLY • THE FRED ALLEN SHOW • THE GOLDBERGS • THE GREAT GILDERSLEEVE • THE GREEN HORNET • GUNSMOKE • INNER SANCTUM • THE JACK BENNY PROGRAM • THE LIFE OF RILEY • LIGHTS OUT • THE LONE RANGER • LUX RADIO THEATRE • THE MERCURY THEATRE ON THE AIR • MR. & MRS. NORTH • THE NEW ADVENTURES OF SHERLOCK HOLMES (*particularly those starring Basil Rathbone and Nigel Bruce*) • PHILO VANCE • SGT. PRESTON OF THE YUKON • THE SHADOW • SUSPENSE • THE TALES OF THE TEXAS RANGERS • THE WALTER WINCHELL SHOW • *and* THE WHISTLER.

the pack. Monaural versions, interestingly, are frequently more valuable than their stereo cousins, perhaps because the Beatles participated in the mixing of certain mono versions and not in the mixing of the stereo ones (and, of course, because fewer of them still exist). In all cases, condition is absolutely key, except that collectors are more forgiving of dirt and scratches on the mono versions than they are on the stereo records. Ideally, album covers should show minimal wear and tear. Serious record collectors are advised to travel with a good price guide and a flashlight and magnifying glass for careful inspection for dirt and scratches in the grooves.

There are many Beatles collectibles that were intended to be disposable. Beatles bubble bath, ice cream–bar boxes, calendars, and, inimitably, Ringo Roll bread. Naturally, items that maintain all of their original contents are more desirable. It would be hard to quantify, though, how much each bite of a Ringo Roll would reduce its value.

Some Beatles items were relatively expensive even when new. Wristwatches, for example. Only three models were produced in the 1960s—by Smiths (a brooch watch), Old England UK (issued by Apple, the Beatles' recording company, as a promotional wristwatch), and Sheffield (a Yellow Submarine wristwatch). Most lamps, record players, and musical instruments picturing the Beatles are costly, as are fragile items, such as sets of glass Christmas ornaments, because few have survived intact. A bottle of the 1964 Beatles perfume, manufactured by Olive Adair of Liverpool, is currently pricier than thirty new bottles of L'Air du Temps. Cans of hairspray made by Bronson in the same year are so desirable that they have been reproduced. (Informed collectors know that the bottoms of original cans bear a stamp with an "SD" identification number.) Lunch boxes also command a premium, perhaps because they attract two different cadres of collectors, Beatles fans and lunch-box collectors, which make them "crossover" collectibles. These lunch boxes, incidentally, have reportedly risen fiftyfold in value since they were new.

For the most dedicated collectors, however, there are items that—mirabile dictu—were actually touched by John, Paul, George, and Ringo. Gold and platinum records (the gold

Both movie and rock collectors seek memorabilia associated with the Beatles' films, such as this poster for their second feature, Help!

A ticket from the Beatles' first American tour in 1964, when they played, improbably, the Indiana State Fair. It is doubtless the only Beatles ticket to include the name of a State Commissioner of Agriculture.

The Magic Box

The list below includes many of the vintage television shows that excite collector interest today. Stars from these series often appear at collectors shows to sign photographs and scripts, and a few shows that were overlooked when new have become cult classics.

THE ADDAMS FAMILY • THE ADVENTURES OF OZZIE AND HARRIET • THE ADVENTURES OF SUPERMAN • ALFRED HITCHCOCK PRESENTS • AMERICAN BANDSTAND • AMOS 'N' ANDY • THE ANDY GRIFFITH SHOW • THE AVENGERS • ALL IN THE FAMILY • BATMAN • BENNY HILL • THE BEVERLY HILLBILLIES • BEWITCHED • THE BIONIC WOMAN • THE BRADY BUNCH • CAPTAIN KANGAROO • THE CAROL BURNETT SHOW • CHEYENNE • THE COLGATE COMEDY HOUR *(with Martin and Lewis as guest hosts)* • DALLAS • DING DONG SCHOOL • DRAGNET • DR. WHO • THE ED SULLIVAN SHOW • THE ERNIE KOVACS SHOW • THE FLINTSTONES • THE FUGITIVE • THE GENE AUTRY SHOW • THE GEORGE BURNS AND GRACIE ALLEN SHOW • GEORGE OF THE JUNGLE • GET SMART • GILLIGAN'S ISLAND • THE GOLDBERGS • GREEN ACRES • GUNSMOKE • HAPPY DAYS • HAVE GUN—WILL TRAVEL • THE HONEYMOONERS • HOPALONG CASSIDY • HOWDY DOODY • HULLABALOO • I DREAM OF JEANNIE • I LOVE LUCY • THE JACK BENNY PROGRAM • THE JUDY GARLAND SHOW • KUKLA, FRAN AND OLLIE • LEAVE IT TO BEAVER • THE LONE RANGER • MAMA • THE MANY LOVES OF DOBIE GILLIS • THE MARY TYLER MOORE SHOW • M*A*S*H • MAVERICK • THE MICKEY MOUSE CLUB • THE MONKEES • MONTY PYTHON'S FLYING CIRCUS • THE MUNSTERS • MY LITTLE MARGIE • THE OUTER LIMITS • THE PARTRIDGE FAMILY • PERRY MASON • PETER GUNN • THE PHIL SILVERS SHOW/SGT. BILKO • PLAYHOUSE 90 • THE PRISONER • RAWHIDE • ROCKY AND HIS FRIENDS/THE BULLWINKLE SHOW • ROUTE 66 • THE ROY ROGERS SHOW • 77 SUNSET STRIP • SHINDIG • $64,000 QUESTION • THE SMOTHERS BROTHERS COMEDY HOUR • SONNY AND CHER • SOUPY SALES • SPACE PATROL • STARSKY AND HUTCH • STAR TREK • THE STEVE ALLEN SHOW • TEXACO STAR THEATER WITH MILTON BERLE • THREE'S COMPANY • TOM CORBETT • TWENTY-ONE • THE TWILIGHT ZONE • THE UNTOUCHABLES • THIS IS YOUR LIFE • WELCOME BACK KOTTER • THE WILD WILD WEST • WONDER WOMAN • *and* YOUR SHOW OF SHOWS.

The Brady Bunch

I Dream of Jeannie

Howdy Doody

Gilligan's Island

Captain Kangaroo

The Addams Family

The Roy Rogers Show

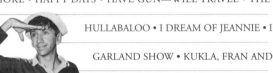

color was used for both gold and platinum awards) and awards honoring their most popular albums, such as *Sgt. Pepper's Lonely Hearts Club Band,* are particularly desirable. Way up in the stratosphere of Beatlemania are the cars owned by John Lennon. His Ferrari and his famed psychedelic Rolls Royce have fetched more than $100,000 each.

Perhaps of greater significance than cars or awards, however, are the copies of handwritten lyrics that have periodically appeared for sale. John Lennon's 1969 lyrics for "Because"—with his corrections—sold for $27,000; Paul McCartney's 1967 manuscript lyrics for "When I'm Sixty-Four" brought $55,000; and the Lennon-McCartney 1967 lyrics for "Getting Better" fetched an astronomical $250,000. Dwarfing these numbers is the amount George Michael paid in 2000 for the aforementioned upright walnut Steinway piano that once belonged to Lennon. A video exists of Lennon composing his song "Imagine" on it. Lennon bought the piano in 1970 for £1,000, and Michael bested all comers thirty years later by purchasing it for $2 million.

I Love Lucy's costume designer signed this 1951 sketch for a dress worn by the star in the 100th episode of the sitcom.

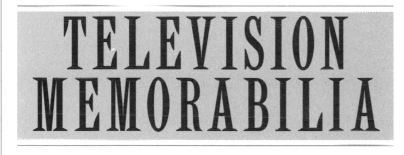

TELEVISION MEMORABILIA

Nostalgia drives collectors of television memorabilia more than it does movie collectors, for they rarely buy anything from shows they didn't watch religiously (and still watch in reruns). TV enthusiasts collect a wild assortment of material, including autographs, photos, props, scripts, toys, games, dolls, videos, costumes, theme songs, posters, magazine articles, news footage, early commercials (particularly those selling toys or featuring TV stars), *TV Guides,* kinescopes, and even old television sets.

Props from the fantasy television series of the 1960s are in high demand, with Batman props seeming to have particular appeal, and somewhere out in the Batman market is certainly a

Distinguished actor George Sanders wore this less-than-distinguished helmet to play the villainous Mr. Freeze on Batman.

A photograph of actress Yvonne Craig in her campy Batgirl costume from the 1960s hit TV series Batman.

pair of Robin's green suede shoes, complete with high-rise wings. As with so many props, Batman's hold surprises for collectors. The buyer of Batman's utility belt, for instance, has had to accept the fact that parts of it are made of cork.

Coveted TV series items from the sixties include Tina Louise's full-length beaded gown from *Gilligan's Island,* a glass genie bottle—probably empty—used in the series *I Dream of Jeannie,* and anything at all from *Star Trek* or Great Britain's *The Avengers.*

Trekkies—need it be said—are a breed unto themselves. Star Trek ran only three years on NBC, but its ever-growing cult will likely keep it in syndication until the distant future in which the series is set. When William Shatner's command jacket from *Star Trek II: The Wrath of Khan* appeared at auction, it sold for more than $10,000. Phasers (the pistol-style version, for those in the know) and communicators are somewhat less costly, although also desirable.

Chapter Eleven

COSTUME JEWELRY

Once upon a glamorous but simpler time, jewelry stores carried both fine jewelry (made from platinum, gold, and precious stones) and costume jewelry (made of base metals, plastic, and glass). The fine jewelry was displayed in the usual elegant fashion, but the costume jewelry, too, was laid out in impressive velvet boxes with gleaming satin linings. Thus, a suite of matching rhinestone necklace, bracelet, and earrings, designed and set much like the diamond suite it imitated, could achieve great retail dignity, yet be bought for a modest sum.

Rhinestone "diamonds," however, were just the tip of the iceberg. Brilliant glass "aquamarine" rings were dazzlingly convincing and desirable; "jelly belly" penguin pins with top hats, canes, and plump, translucent oval bellies were for sale in the thousands; ropes of glass bead "pearls" came in ivories and pinks. At Christmastime there were "ruby"-dotted wreaths, "emerald" trees, and enameled Santa lapel pins, all of which were as festive and fake as the icicles on the Christmas tree.

Today, enthusiastic collectors consider some vintage faux jewelry to be more stylish and sometimes even more desirable and interesting than pedestrian fine jewelry of the same period,

Top: On a rhinestone and enamel Trifari pin, a mother bird feeds her chick in a birdhouse, and right, a stylized bow brooch in rhinestones, with rhinestone pendants by Marcel Boucher, whose ads read: "conceived with imagination and wrought with exquisite finesse."

COOL JEWELS

Studio jewelry was initially hand-made by 1950s artists in their studios; hence, the name. Even when it was mass-produced in imitation of artist-crafted jewelry, its design was "arty."

Some very major artists, in fact, did produce studio jewelry; Alexander Calder was one. An unsigned brass collar attributed to Calder and resembling a sprung Slinky toy (see page 404) recently brought $31,000 at auction.

The 1950s were a very cool hot-house of free-form silver, copper, and enameled jewelry. Highly individualistic pieces were crafted by talented Scandinavian and American silversmiths. Christie Romero, an *Antiques Roadshow* expert in twentieth-century Modernist jewelry, says the work of Björn Weckström, a Finnish designer, is currently popular. Among other well-known and collectible American studio jewelers are Margaret De Patta, Art Smith, Peter Macchiarini, Betty Cooke, Sam Kramer, and Ed Wiener.

Silver jewelry tarnishes when it's not worn. So if you're not wearing your boomerang and amoeba-shaped brooches as often as you'd like and they have become extremely tarnished, try polishing them, Romero suggests, first, with a jeweler's rouge cloth. If that fails, polish them with X-Treem Metal Polish.

and it may be rarer as well. For example, a visitor to *Antiques Roadshow* in Tampa, Florida, caught the eye of expert Gloria Lieberman *not* because of the emerald beads he had driven five hours to have appraised, but because of the innovative way he displayed his collection of costume jewelry. Unable (or at least unwilling!) to wear the sparkling rhinestone brooches, bracelets, earrings, and necklaces he had inherited from his aunt in the customary fashion, the visitor had covered a plain black cap with a selection of the pieces. He explained that he wears the cap only on special occasions—among them, his visit to *Antiques Roadshow*—though he had not brought it to be appraised. Lieberman pointed out that some of the jewelry on it, such as an elegant rhinestone brooch made by Eisenberg and other pins by such top-notch companies as Kramer of New York and Fulco Di Verdura, were very desirable. She told the astonished visitor that his delightful cap was in the grand tradition of hat jewelry and that his aunt's legacy was now worth between $1,500 and $2,000. And when the Tampa *Antiques Roadshow* aired, it was the hat, not the emerald beads, that was featured!

An exotic rhinestone and enamel Thai dancer brooch manufactured by ART, a company that produced jewelry from the late forties through the sixties.

A BRIEF HISTORY

Costume jewelry is not the twentieth-century phenomenon many people consider it to be. It has a long and honorable history. Eighteenth-century women wore foil-backed paste (glass) to imitate diamonds, and, in the early nineteenth century, they wore pinchbeck (early gold plate) set with pastes. In later years, women wore jet, tortoiseshell, and Bohemian garnet and mosaic jewels that were so inexpensive in their time that they were considered costume jewelry (though they no longer are). During the Art Nouveau and Arts and Crafts periods that preceded World War I, firms like Liberty in England and Unger Brothers in the United States fashioned exceptionally well-designed pendants, brooches, and hatpins in less precious materials than gold and gemstones, frequently in silver.

Some major artists also chose to make jewelry from non-precious materials; in fact, in the 1920s, René Lalique actually preferred to make jewelry of horn, molded glass, and early experimental plastics. Later, in the mid-twentieth century, Alexander Calder created distinctive jewelry of brass and silver.

It should be noted, however, that major artistry has never been crucial to the wearer and collector of costume jewelry. Dazzle, sparkle, glitter, and flash—as well as size and large helpings of flamboyant design—are the name of this game.

ART DECO ADORNMENTS

After World War I, costume jewelry manufacturing began to come into its own. The first of the fabulous postwar fakes were Art Deco in style. Unleashed in Paris at the 1925 Exposition Internationale des Arts Décoratifs et Industriels Modernes, Art Deco design burst upon the scene beautifully proportioned, finely made, and surpassingly elegant. Most of the best Art Deco costume jewels—those pieces mounted in sterling silver or low-carat gold and set with marcasite, quartz, lapis, and the newly developed synthetic precious stones—originated in France, Austria, and Germany. Czechoslovakia, renowned for its glass, provided the beads and molded glass stones for its neighbors while also producing quantities of high-quality costume jewelry itself.

Both costume and genuine jewelry tend to parallel developments in art, architecture, and clothing design, thus these Art Deco pieces were appropriately geometric and stylized—highly successful translations of the strongly architectural into the gorgeously decorative. Earrings, necklaces, and even brooches managed to mimic gem-studded skyscrapers. They also looked amazingly like

An elegant and severely geometric marcasite and rhinestone brooch replicated precious Art Deco jewels.

COSTUME JEWELRY FROM CZECHOSLOVAKIA

Between the two world wars, Czechoslovakian jewelry makers, relying on their top-quality native glass industry, dominated the costume jewelry market. Beads and crystals combined with fine work in cold-painted enamels (those not heated in a kiln) to create a style so exceptional that, regardless of the fact that there are no known "names," collectors seek out Czech wares of this era.

the costly jewels they were imitating. From a shortish distance, you really couldn't tell if that "ruby," "emerald," and "diamond" jabot pin was a fake or Cartier. Only the fact that the fake was just a little more fabulous than the genuine might give the game away. Costume jewelry designers were a great deal more comfortable experimenting with their glass and their plastic than designers of precious jewels could ever be with unforgiving sapphires and platinum.

A HOLLYWOOD ENTRANCE

As the bubbles and baubles of the twenties hardened into Depression-era flint, geometrical styles metamorphosed from flat, two-dimensionality into sturdier, "streamlined" styles: dramatic, three-dimensional, and strong. Dramatic design is always controversial, so it's hardly surprising that there was an immediate reaction to this "soulless modernism." Almost from its inception, all that edgy jewelry provoked a simultaneous revival of softer Victorian styles.

From the late twenties until the forties, refined "cameo" and "jet" jewelry, along with floral brooches and dangly stones and "seed pearl" bits, coexisted with the streamlined pieces. The jet, of course, originally derived from the royal style of the endlessly mourning Queen Victoria; the dangly jewels were pure *Gone with the Wind*. But the fashion for neo-Victorian styles, in fact, came straight out of Hollywood.

One jewelry designer, Joseff of Hollywood (see page 418 and sidebar, page 419), is particularly associated with costume jewelry worn by movie stars both on and off the set. *Antiques Roadshow* jewelry expert Rosalie Sayyah says, "His designs were just amazing. The glitter just jumped out at you."

WARTIME SHORTAGES

The costume jewelry market flourished and grew with fashion's fads. Indeed, jewelry designers and manufacturers became increasingly successful until World War II, when most base metals, the industry lifeblood, were co-opted

This enameled Czechoslovakian necklace is a confection of curlicues, flowers, and winged lions, all tied at the neck with a chiffon ribbon.

by the military, leaving only silver for costume jewelry mountings. Czechoslovakian glass beads, too, had suddenly become unavailable, as had rhinestones (that *Rhine* prefix needed to be taken seriously, since the best were of German manufacture). Wartime costume jewelry, in response to such limitations, became chastely sculptural. Until the war's end, it was set with a single stone, perhaps, or decorated with still available enamels. Yet, it wasn't all bad news. Gilt silver (vermeil) provided a rich setting and a superior substitute, in fact, for all the brass, copper, and steel being turned into weapons.

By the early forties, skyscrapers were passé, and if any motifs could be said to typify the war years, they were those that were, touchingly, unwarlike: music, dance, mythology, and nature. Styles of this era are now called retro.

THE FABULOUS 1950S AND SWINGING 1960S

After the war, flash returned to the world and to the world of fake jewels. Suddenly, American manufacturers were busy buying rhinestones. Why not use as many as possible? Why not offer bold jewelry absolutely clotted with colors? Why confine oneself to stones, when amazing variants could now be had: Green "pearls," lilac emerald-cut glass stones, orange-and-white mottled glass cabochons? Big was back, along with bold: big pins and bracelets, statement earrings, and quantities of those boxed sets known as parures—matching earrings, bracelets, necklaces, and pins—to go with Dior's New Look. The postwar woman of the fifties was stylish, and so was her jewelry, which continued to be precisely the right accessory as her "costume" shifted to sheaths, pageboy hairdos, and white gloves.

The costume jewelry of the decade that followed was quite a contrast. The 1960s were youthful, groovy, and quite literally spacey. Outer space itself had become a motif in a culture that adorned itself with dome rings and Lucite bangles, not to mention ice-cube-shaped Lucite earrings. For the time being, the sixties mark the end of collecting interest for the costume jewelry enthusiast.

JEWELRY FOR EVERY OUTFIT

Don't assume that costume jewelry was worn only by women who couldn't afford the real thing. It was popular even with those who owned wristfuls of diamonds, because costume pieces were so variously colored, styled, and shaped that they went with any . . . well, costume.

An apocryphal legend has it that showman Florenz Ziegfeld, in ordering imitation jewelry to go with the costumes of the famous Ziegfeld girls, named it. Because costume jewelry was so affordable, it could be purchased on a whim, worn without fear on the street, and retired to the bottom of the jewel box without guilt. It could even be chucked altogether when it went out of fashion—which it did with great rapidity.

A sterling vermeil flower pin with pink "moonstone" petals by Reja, which sold its jewelry only in expensive boutiques.

In the 1950s, Trifari made this "tremblant" rhinestone pendant brooch as part of its Empress Eugenie Collection. The center stone is set on a small spring, allowing it to move with its wearer.

EVALUATING COSTUME JEWELRY

*A*ntiques Roadshow costume jewelry experts Christie Romero and Rosalie Sayyah agree that in the field of costume jewelry, condition is important. Indeed, because costume jewelry wasn't necessarily made to last, its conservation is a continuing issue for collectors. Only high-quality pieces hold up well over time. (Costume jewelry rings, for instance, can't take constant wear, which is why relatively few are around.) The least well made kind of costume jewelry, manufactured just by gluing stones to metal, comes with a fatal flaw, Sayyah says. "You can't simply stick a bunch of stones in a lump of metal and expect the thing to last."

Costume jewelry in good condition has been protected from the elements. Damp can cause the foil backing of rhinestones to deteriorate—rather like losing the silvering on the back of a mirror—warns Romero. "Once a rhinestone is dead, it's dead forever, and although it *can* be resuscitated by refoiling, that's a very expensive process."

Repairs to metal are a difficult "fix," too, because base metals show any attempt at repair. In addition, should those metal settings be damaged by corrosion or verdigris (a greenish, moldlike substance on the surface of the metal), they are usually beyond repair. (Romero, however, has a formula for the painstaking salvage of especially valuable pieces: Mix one tablespoon salt and one tablespoon white vinegar in one cup of hot water, and using a toothpick soaked in this solution, carefully scrape the corrosion off the metal, being extremely careful to avoid all "pearls.")

It seems obvious, then, that if you are considering a purchase, you should check condition carefully. Stones should be "live" and intact; metal should have no worn spots; no element should be damaged or bent; clasps, chains, and pins should work; there should be no repairs. Also, because it is more than likely that you will want to show off your purchase, rather than simply admire it, it should be comfortable to wear.

A brass Calder collar necklace from the 1940s resembles a sprung slinky toy, but it shouldn't be pulled out of shape or bent in any way other than the way the artist bent it.

CHRISTIE ROMERO'S EVALUATION BASICS

Appraiser Christie Romero has put together a list of important questions to ask yourself when you are trying to evaluate a piece of costume jewelry. They are her own appraisal criteria, and she calls them her Three C's, Two D's, and Two S's:

Condition	Are there any cracks, chips, dents, missing parts, metal corrosion, or other damages? Are all the parts original? Has the piece been repaired? (Look for evidence of lead solder on silver.)
Craftsmanship	Is the piece well made, with careful attention having been paid to details and finish?
Color	Are the colors currently popular and fashionable? If there are "gemstones," are the colors convincing? Color is especially important to costume jewelry collectors.
Design	Can the style be attributed to the period in which it was made? Can it be attributed to a particular maker? Is the piece balanced and proportioned? Does it have "eye appeal" (always a subjective evaluation)? Is it wearable?
Demand	Is the piece highly sought after? Is it currently in vogue?
Scarcity	Is this a rare item or is it commonly available?
Size	Is it a large piece or small piece? Is the size appropriate for the style? (Large-size costume jewelry is usually more desirable, but the style and proportions of the eventual wearer should be considered.)

For more information on evaluating costume jewelry, consult Romero's book, *Warman's Jewelry: Encyclopedia of Antiques and Collectibles.*

A sterling and rhinestone pin in the shape of a fly by Boucher, marked "MB." Insects have been a popular costume jewelry motif since Victorian times and continue to be desirable today.

Coro goldtone circle pin and matching earrings with colored rhinestones. Collectible costume jewelry should have no metal corrosion or missing stones.

Manufactured particularly by Trifari and its competitor, Coro, figurative "jelly belly" pins with Lucite cabochons were popular in the 1940s; this snail-shape Trifari example is unusual.

Both the materials of this brooch— marcasite and sterling—and its Art Deco style pinpoint the era of its manufacture, the late 1920s to early 1930s.

AGE

Certain design motifs are universally popular—bows, flowers, insects—so it is not always easy to tell precisely when a piece of vintage costume jewelry was created. If a manufacturer found itself with a particularly successful model, it might go on making it for years—even after its style became generally unfashionable. Nevertheless, analyzing design is perhaps the best starting point when it comes to determining age. If there are jewelry styles that you find particularly appealing, read whatever you can about them (see the Reading List, page 543), then study the actual pieces in auction catalogs, exhibitions, or stores. It will quickly become second nature for you to distinguish elegant and restrained Art Deco, for instance, from wartime retro jewelry, which is characterized by larger-than-life proportions. Or, should a piece seem distinctly Egyptian, think "twenties," a decade when the discovery of King Tutankhamen's tomb revived an interest in the art of the pharaohs. A poodle pin should immediately speak to you of the 1950s, as will anything of distinctively Parisian flavor, like a brooch made in the shape of the Eiffel Tower.

Construction is also useful in determining age. For example, clip-on earrings often reveal their age in the style of their clips. Screw-back earrings were developed before World War I, because "respectable" women stopped piercing their ears. The more comfortable spring clips became popular in the late 1930s. Ear piercing once again became fashionable for young women in the 1960s, and clip-on earrings were manufactured primarily for the "mature" customer who still considered ear piercing beyond the pale.

MATERIALS

Working without costly gold, silver, diamonds, rubies, emeralds, sapphires, and other precious metals and gemstones, manufacturers of costume jewelry have used a number of inexpensive materials to simulate them. They have also used materials that bear no likeness to *any* precious stone—Bakelite and Lucite, for example—but, nevertheless, look fabulous.

RHINESTONES AND CZECHOSLOVAKIAN GLASS: The glass "jewels" of costume jewelry descend from a long line of antique imitation stones, paste and jargoons (East Indian imitations of rose-cut diamonds) among them. Twentieth-century glassmaking technology provided clearer, brighter, more colorful "gems" than had previously been possible. "Stones" made of this twentieth-century glass, called rhinestones, are cut like gemstones and frequently coated on the back with gold- or silver-colored metal meant to increase their reflectivity. Because they *are* glass, they are easily chipped and broken, and the gilt or silver backing is easily discolored.

BASE METALS: Brass or brass alloys are the usual base-metal settings for costume jewelry. They are relatively inexpensive, generally available in quantity, and strong and malleable enough to be formed into elaborate shapes. They do discolor, however, and their very malleability makes them subject to damage.

SILVER: The least precious of the precious metals, silver was frequently used to make high-quality costume jewelry, particularly in the 1940s. Silver jewelry is less fragile and inherently more costly than base-metal jewelry, and it will almost always be marked "sterling" if it is American, or 800, if it is of European origin and produced after the Art Deco era.

MARCASITE: Jewelry that is composed of hundreds of dark, finely cut bits of crystallized iron sulfide, set usually in silver, is called marcasite. The pavé effect can almost equal that of diamonds, especially when the technique is well executed, as it was in Germany and France in the twenties and thirties. Marcasite was often the choice for strong Art Deco designs and sometimes was mixed with enamels. Pieces that reflect the Art Deco style most closely, especially those created for the American market and marked "Germany sterling" or "France sterling," are most highly sought after by collectors.

BAKELITE: Colorful pins, bracelets, rings, and necklaces made from Bakelite, an early form of plastic, were popular in the 1930s, when they provided a lighthearted and cheap replacement for the elegant baubles of the 1920s. Bakelite is a very popular collectible today—Andy Warhol had an extensive collection—and it frequently shows up on *Antiques Roadshow*.

LIBERACE: RHINESTONE REVELER

The gaudy rhinestone once had a champion named Liberace, whose rhinestone-encrusted costumes and props were a big part of his appeal.

Liberace, who probably had the largest rhinestone collection in the world, sometimes drove his "Rhinestone Roadster" across the stage to his rhinestone-sheathed Baldwin piano. His "Platinum Mink Coat and Rhinestone Costume" (that's its official name) is studded with tens of thousands of rhinestones—even the heels of his shoes sparkle with them. The "crown jewel" of Liberace's collection, now at the Liberace Museum in Las Vegas, is a 51-pound, 115,000K clear rhinestone that Swarowski of Austria gave him in 1982.

Liberace's Rhinestone Roadster.

A Plastic Worth Its Weight in Gold

Picture this Bakelite brooch from the 1930s: A brown log with three leaves. Dangling from it are a carrot, a potato, and a radish. No diamonds. No gold. No maker's label.

A fanciful Bakelite necklace with bright red raspberries and green leaves looks good enough to eat.

This brooch recently sold at auction for $5,175, and the thrilled buyer exclaimed to the world, "This is the finest vegetable pin I have ever seen. Each vegetable is twice the size of any others. It's great. It's exciting. It's folk art of the twentieth century."

Just in case you're having momentary doubts—yes, Bakelite is plastic. How can one explain such enthusiasm, except to say that Bakelite, a phenolic resin plastic invented in 1907 by chemist Leo Baekeland, is charming and frivolous, representative of its era (a given for any collectible that hopes to be taken seriously as art), and available in sufficient quantity to satisfy large numbers of potential collectors. Bakelite collectors are often as obsessed as the auction buyer mentioned above. One couple has compiled a jewelry collection of 1,250 pieces, comprising, among other rarities, "articulated people" pins, necklaces with swordfish appended from Bakelite links, and great quantities of carved and polka-dotted bracelets.

The Depression-ridden thirties, the heyday of Bakelite, was naturally the ideal moment for such cheery, colorful stuff. The public liked the upbeat style of the material, its color and whimsy, and jewelry manufacturers liked its versatility. Bakelite could be carved, ground and polished, threaded, drilled, sanded, and sliced. The variety of colors it came in—caramel, green, brown, red, blue, amber, and ivory—offered endless design possibilities. In addition, it could be fashioned into bracelets—60 percent of all Bakelite pieces are bracelets—pins, rings, and necklaces held together, in most instances, not by costly gold, silver, or even metal links, but by stretchy, elasticized strings.

This jewelry was affordable, too. When new, Bakelite bracelets cost from 5 cents to 75 cents each. Thus stacks of bracelets could be worn (and were) on each arm. Today, wide bracelets are more collectible than narrow ones, though the cornerstone of any serious Bakelite collection is the five-color hinged "Philadelphia" bracelet, known by that name since its sale at a 1984 Philadelphia show set a record price for the piece. With its red, brown, black, green, and yellow wedges, the Philadelphia bracelet is handsome and highly sought after.

The most popular Bakelite pin of the 1940s was a red heart with a key, called the MacArthur Heart (after General Douglas MacArthur), which came on a card that read: "He holds the key to my heart." Currently, the most sought-after examples are those in red and black; the least desirable are brown and green. (Oxidation has sometimes caused the colors of Bakelite to darken. For example, clear pieces have turned into a pale amber known to collectors as "apple juice." Curiously, many Bakelite collectors prefer the oxidized colors to the original colors.) Some Bakelite was carved on the reverse and painted, which gives it a three-dimensional appearance when viewed from the front. In that category are the reverse-carved aquarium motifs, which have acquired numerous fans.

Beware of imitations. One way to determine if a piece is actually made of Bakelite is to rub it with your thumb until it heats up. True Bakelite will usually give off a distinct chemical odor.

A dotted Bakelite bangle bracelet was once clear, but is now the color known as "apple juice."

LUCITE: Jewelry made from Lucite was popular in the forties and fifties, and came into its own in the sixties. This form of plastic was introduced in 1937 and began to be used in costume jewelry a few years later. Cheaper to produce than Bakelite, Lucite could easily be tinted, molded, cast, inlaid, laminated, and carved.

LABELS

Enormously important to today's collectors is the question: Who made this piece? For better or worse, the dropping of status-laden names is part of what makes so-called signed (meaning labeled with the manufacturer's name) jewelry so attractive. Owning "name" jewelry also offers a kind of club membership that people seem to find reassuring, Rosalie Sayyah observes.

Nonetheless, some of the most revered manufacturers of early French costume jewelry, Chanel among them, chose not to label their output, meaning not only that positive attribution is virtually impossible, but also that many fine and beautiful pieces—ostensibly by the best makers—come down to us completely unmarked.

It isn't until the beginning of the 1940s, in fact, that one finds more pieces that have manufacturers' labels than don't. (Designers' names, incidentally, are rarely included on the label. It is known, for example, that two of the most talented jewelry designers of the twentieth century—Fulco di Verdura and Jean Schlumberger—designed costume jewelry for Chanel and Schiaparelli, respectively, but their own ultimately famous names never appear on any of it.) To further complicate issues of attribution, many sets (parures) of costume jewelry are incompletely marked; a necklace may be labeled with the maker's name, for example, but the matching bracelet and earrings will be unmarked. If they

The mark of "Margot de Taxco," a noted Taxco jewelry designer, can be clearly seen on this screwback earring.

IS IT REALLY BAKELITE?

There is a foolproof test for verifying Bakelite, according to *Antiques Roadshow* appraiser Gloria Lieberman. To prove a guest's bright lime-green bracelet was made of this vintage plastic,

Lieberman dipped it into a bowl of steaming hot water at the Louisville, Kentucky, *Roadshow*. "Smell that?" she asked, holding it just under the visitor's nose. "Bakelite has an acrid smell. This passes the test."

"There are Bakelite price guides today," observed Lieberman, for when jewelers discovered that colors almost glowed when mixed with easily carved and shaped clear Bakelite, they quickly began to produce affordable Bakelite jewelry. Lieberman valued the Louisville bracelet at $300 to $500, not bad for a $10 plastic bracelet, but still less than carved and multicolored Bakelite pieces.

TIPS *from the experts*

"There's no right way to collect," says Christie Romero, *Antiques Roadshow* appraiser. "I tell people, 'You should try to discover what you're drawn to and see where that leads.'" Yet, to make a well-defined collection, a collector should develop what Romero calls a "unifying factor." Those who begin by picking up examples of their favorite styles—whether sixties Pop, twenties or thirties Bauhaus, or fifties studio pieces—usually uncover subspecialties. A novice attracted to Art Deco might find herself loving Egyptian revival jewelry, passing up streamlined industrial Art Deco to save money for the "scarab, pharaoh, and sarcophagus" motifs popular in the 1920s.

Styles are just one unifying factor; forms, such as necklaces, are another. Motifs are a third. One of Romero's brooch collections has a fish motif. "My students started giving me fish and now I have a school of them," she says. While Romero is reluctant to discourage any unifying category, she admits she is "wary" of collecting by name alone. Miriam Haskell, Chanel, and Eisenberg, the best manufacturers of costume jewelry, have all produced clunkers. "If you get carried away by names," she says, "you're not necessarily collecting good quality."

are sold together, fine; if over time they are separated, their manufacturer might go unrecognized.

We've illustrated this chapter with characteristic examples of the work of various designers and manufacturers. You can further familiarize yourself with a particular maker's style by reading reference books on the subject.

COLLECTING COSTUME JEWELRY

Although the current passion for the fantastic designs and imaginative subjects of vintage costume jewelry is a mere twenty or so years old, these pieces have acquired thousands upon thousands of devotees.

It takes very little money to begin to collect costume jewelry; a few dollars can buy a lot of baubles. Also, there are so many pieces around that there's hardly a tag sale that doesn't have its box (or boxes) of tangled beads, bracelets, single earrings, and ropes and ropes of imitation pearls. "But don't buy those things *just* because they're only $1 or $2," counsels Romero, although it may be hugely tempting. "If you *are* a novice, you haven't seen enough jewelry yet to be able to trust your eye. And don't—for exactly the same reason—spend more than $50 on anything. Do your homework and don't spend more than you can comfortably afford."

A genial giraffe wearing a straw boater is but one example of the lighthearted Bakelite jewelry that cheered women during the Depression. The Bakelite menagerie also included dogs, cats, flamingos, and other creatures, as well as fruits and vegetables, like the vivid cherries, above.

MANUFACTURERS

B elow, you will find a listing of the most notable costume jewelers, those whose creations range from inexpensive, "fun" novelties to elegant, high-quality adornments. While some of these companies are known especially for one style or period—for example, Kenneth Jay Lane designs summed up the sixties—many others, such as Trifari, have made jewelry in many styles over many decades. Listing chronologically would be repetitive and confusing; besides, many jewelry collectors look for the work of a particular designer or manufacturer, such as Miriam Haskell or Eisenberg. For a look at companies by style and decade, see page 415.

An owl-form brooch manufactured by ART, with rhinestone floret eyes and a body of yellow, blue, and brown enamel.

ART

Believed by some collectors to be currently undervalued, ART produced low- and medium-quality pieces from the late 1940s to the 1960s. Although the firm primarily manufactured Victorian revival styles, its polychrome, pavé figural pins are highly collectible.

McClelland Barclay

American artist McClelland Barclay began his career as a magazine illustrator in the 1930s and 1940s, moving on to design decorative household objects, such as bookends, bowls, and boxes, as well as costume jewelry. As might be expected of such an artist, Barclay's work, Art Deco–style settings mounted with rhinestones, often tended to be both beautifully crafted and sculptural. His all-sterling Arts and Crafts–style jewelry is rarer than his rhinestone jewelry and is especially sought after. Barclay designed jewelry for a relatively short period of time before he was killed in action in World War II.

Bergère

Inexpensive when new, Bergère was the jewelry trademark used by L. Erbert & Pohs and was distributed through department stores like Lord & Taylor and Marshall Field. Generally conservative and imitative of real jewelry, it was often worn on the tailored outfits of "career women." Pieces

An Art Deco–style link bracelet designed by illustrator-turned-jewelry-designer McClelland Barclay, set with rhinestones and colored stones.

(continued on page 414)

The Taxco School
(circa 1930 to 1970)

If you traveled the road from Mexico City to the resort town of Acapulco in the 1930s and 1940s, you passed through what was once the small silver-mining village of Taxco (pronounced *Tahs-co*). During those years, silver jewelry of exceptional creativity and quality was designed, made, and sold here, mainly to the tourist trade. Combining the best of Mexican, American, and European styles, this jewelry melded pre-Hispanic—and thus, indigenous—Mexican motifs with abstraction (then called modernist art). While this work is neither costume jewelry nor fine jewelry, the pieces produced in this Mexican town are avidly sought by collectors of both.

The precursor to what has come to be called the Taxco School is the jewelry of American designer Frederick W. Davis, who worked in Mexico City in the twenties and thirties. Blending native materials—among them, silver, obsidian (a dark, glassy volcanic rock), and amethyst quartz—with native motifs and contemporary American and European designs, Davis's jewelry was a departure from traditional religious or quasi-colonial Mexican pieces and set the tone for the Taxco craftspeople to come.

Matching necklace and earrings by Los Castillo, made of sterling silver set with luminous foil-backed blue glass cabochons.

Come they did, beginning with another American, architect William Spratling. In 1931, Spratling opened a small shop in Taxco to create in high-quality silver a hybrid of Mexican images with international art styles. In keeping with the aesthetic of the era, Spratling's early work is simple and, like Davis's, incorporates local stones, with occasional inclusions of rosewood. Its growing success allowed Spratling jewelry to be retailed in the United States during World War II—when silver replaced metal for costume jewelry—but this is not as popular with collectors today as those pieces that were made to sell in Mexico.

From its modest beginnings, the making of silver jewelry in Mexico has become an industry, and today more than ten thousand silversmiths work in and around Taxco. While there is a great deal of mediocre jewelry on the market, the best of Taxco School jewelry is currently considered to be on an artistic par with the work of the finest studio jewelers. The marks that will help you distinguish the wheat from the chaff can be found in books on the subject.

An early sterling pin from Los Castillo. The four Castillo brothers—Antonio, Jorge, Miguel, and Justo—held important positions in William Spratling's workshop before they opened their own Taxco shop.

Numerous Taxco artists came out of William Spratling's workshops, for Spratling was artistically generous, encouraging the most talented employees to set up shop for themselves. Among these accomplished craftspeople were the following:

HECTOR AGUILAR:

Once Spratling's shop manager. Silver jewelry from Aguilar's shop that utilizes *ranchero* motifs and doesn't incorporate stones is highly sought after.

ANTONIO PINEDA:

Another of Spratling's protégés. Pineda's work has obvious modernist antecedents. When his pieces do include stones, they are semiprecious and interesting. Imported moonstones or topaz, for example, can be combined with other stones that are native to the region.

LOS CASTILLO:

Owned by the four Castillo brothers, who specialized in the revival of ancient techniques. One of these techniques was the fusing, or "marrying," of metals. Los Castillo often combined their mixed metal settings with inlaid stone. A motif known as Parrot in Profile is perhaps Los Castillo's best-known design.

MARGOT DE TAXCO:

One of only a few women designers in Taxco. Born Margot van Voorhies Carr, she was married to one of the Castillo brothers before opening her own shop. Her gift was for combining motifs from such late-nineteenth and early-twentieth-century themes as Art Nouveau, Egyptian revival, Art Deco, and Arts and Crafts with Mexican styles. She is known for enamel work, as well.

A nautilus brooch made by William Spratling in the thirties or forties. Spratling established Taxco as a center for jewelry making by convincing local artisans to use silver from regional mines. Previously, they had considered silver to be fit only for utilitarian objects, such as candlesticks and platters.

ENRIQUE LEDESMA:

Worked for both Spratling and Los Castillo before starting his own shop. Ledesma is noted for oxidized silver jewelry and for an innovative tech-

A signed pair of bow-formed screw-back silver earrings by Margot de Taxco.

nique of simultaneously shaping both the inlaid stone and the silver in which it was mounted.

SIGI (PRONOUNCED SEEHEE) PINEDA:

Worked as a young man in Margot de Taxco's shop, but left to produce his own silver jewelry. His work, although it incorporated both Scandinavian and American influences, is distinctly Mexican. Pineda uses "Sigi" as his hallmark.

SALVADOR TERAN:

Yet another of Spratling's employees, Teran was a cousin of the Castillos and worked for them as well. Teran's jewelry tends to be more whimsical and more influenced by contemporary art than that of either of his former employers.

PIEDRA Y PLATA:

This Taxco shop (the name means stone and silver) was owned by Felipe Martinez. Its pieces can be recognized by their geometric patterns, set with indigenous Mexican stones either inlaid or bezel set—surrounded by a metal collar. There is currently a great deal of interest in this jewelry.

TIPS
from the
experts

"Costume jewelry was made to be thrown away," says *Antiques Roadshow* appraiser Christie Romero. "No one thought anyone was going to collect it." That assumption has resulted in jewelry boxes full of old costume jewelry in less than mint condition. Glass and base metals scratch easily; stones separate from glue; thin wires and chains corrode and break. To protect costume jewelry, Romero has set down some "Rhinestone Rules."

The first mistake costume jewelry owners make is to toss it willy-nilly together, where pieces can damage each other. "They need to be separated," Romero states, recommending that favorite examples be stored in small boxes or in display trays available at lapidary or jewelry supply houses. Adding a half-inch of upholstery foam provides a cushion and helps to absorb moisture, costume jewelry's worst enemy. Absorbent silica gel desiccant in packets wicks away moisture.

Moisture is not the only enemy; costume jewelry can be badly damaged by perfume and hairspray. To prevent corrosion, do your spraying *before* putting on your jewelry, and don't place perfume on your skin near your jewelry.

If your jewelry needs repair, find a jeweler experienced with costume jewelry. Often, warns Romero, unsuspecting jewelers apply high temperatures to fragile costume pieces with disastrous results.

made in the mid-1940s are harder to find than those of later production.

MARCEL BOUCHER

French-born, and apprenticed to famed jeweler Cartier, Boucher emigrated to the United States in the twenties, and made superb imitations of genuine jewelry by selecting only the best materials and carefully replicating the designs of fine jewelry. Most of Boucher's pieces are labeled "MB" over a Phrygian cap, "Boucher," or "Marboux" and bear an inventory number, making earlier pieces easy to date. After 1955, the copyright symbol was added. Pieces from the thirties and forties command a premium among costume jewelry collectors, particularly the enamels and the fantasy bird brooches.

Boucher's spectacular praying mantis pin, made in 1948 of rhinestones set in sterling silver, combines plenty of sparkle with breathtaking size.

HATTIE CARNEGIE

Stylish, Vienna-born Hattie Carnegie became a fashion designer in America. The jewelry she retailed between the 1940s and the mid-1970s was meant to accessorize her fashionable clothes. It often shows Far Eastern influences, although the company also produced pieces incorporating traditional European themes. Because Hattie Carnegie jewelry was created by various designers and changed with the whims of fashion, pieces in a wide variety of styles bear this signature.

CHANEL

The French designer Coco Chanel, in accessorizing her sporty clothing styles with beads, faux pearls, and witty bracelets, made costume jewelry fashionable and fun. Almost all jewelry designed by Coco Chanel (as well as that designed by her talented employee Fulco di Verdura) is popular with collectors,

JEWELRY MANUFACTURERS BY DECADE

Many costume jewelry manufacturers were active for years, producing jewelry that responded to changing fashions. Here's a summary of important manufacturers by decade, with brief characterizations of the prevailing modes.

THE 1930s	THE 1940s	THE 1950s	THE 1960s
Art Deco influences and styles based on real jewelry designs; white gold and clear rhinestones; conservative looks; Boucher, Hattie Carnegie, Castlecliff, Chanel, Coro, DeRosa, Leo Glass, Mazer, McClelland Barclay, Eisenberg Originals, Miriam Haskell, Hobé , Joseff of Hollywood, Pennino, Nettie Rosenstein, Schaparelli, Trifari (TKF)	A move away from imitating real jewelry; retro styles with a bolder use of color; larger pieces to go with the "New Look"; patriotic themes and Bakelite; Bergère, Bogoff, Boucher, Carnegie, Castlecliff, Coro (and Corocraft), DeRosa, Eisenberg, Hobé, Miriam Haskell, Joseff of Hollywood, McClelland Barclay, Reja, Nettie Rosenstein, Schreiner, Staret, Trifari	Gaudy colored rhinestones and aurora borealis, or more demure jewels that might have been worn by Donna Reed; matching sets (parures) of necklaces, earrings, pins, and bracelets; Art, Boucher, Carnegie, Castlecliff, Coro, DeNicola, DeRosa, Eisenberg, HAR, Stanley Hagler, Miriam Haskell, Hobé, Jomaz, Joseff of Hollywood, Pennino, Rebajes, Reja, Renoir and Matisse, Nettie Rosenstein, Schiaparelli, Schreiner, Trifari, Vogue	Flower power, especially daisies; beads; dangling earrings; jewelry for the space age; the Mod look; Art, Boucher, Coro, Hattie Carnegie, Castlecliff, DeNicola, DeRosa, Eisenberg, HAR, Stanley Hagler, Miriam Haskell, Hobé, Jomaz, Joseff of Hollywood, Kenneth Jay Lane, Les Bernard, Leo Glass, Marvella, Mazer, Nettie Rosenstein, Schiaparelli, Schreiner, Trifari

including—although to a lesser degree—the pieces still being made today. Vintage Chanel, however, is particularly highly prized, especially the earliest prewar pieces, which tend to be unsigned. Examples made after the 1960s have Byzantine and somewhat primitive motifs, and more of this jewelry comes on the market.

CORO

Coro (Cohen & Rosenberger) began manufacturing jewelry in Providence, Rhode Island, around 1920 and continued to do so until the 1970s. Coro pieces are familiar to all costume jewelry lovers, but the firm also manufactured jewelry under more different names than any other maker—Vendome, Corocraft,

A witty Coro pin with brightly enameled fingernails wears its own costume jewelry ring and bracelet.

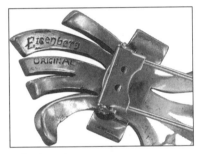

A floral DeRosa fur clip with enameled leaves, set with colored stones and a faux pearl center. DeRosa's three-dimensional compositions are unlike those of any other manufacturer.

The "Eisenberg Original" mark.

This sterling silver can-can dancer clip, with a stylized skirt set with rhinestones, jeweled shoes, and a fancy jeweled headdress, bears an "Eisenberg Original" mark on the back, confirming its manufacture between 1935 and 1945.

and Duette are just three examples. The Coro mark appeared on the more modestly priced jewelry, while Corocraft, Vendome, and François were better-quality lines with higher prices. Among the many designers responsible for the Coro style was Adolph Katz.

Although much Coro jewelry is unremarkable, both the Corocraft and Vendome subsidiaries manufactured jewelry with movable parts and dazzling enamel work, frequently set with expensive imported stones and beads. Some of Corocraft's pre-1950 jewelry in sterling silver is so desirable and highly sought after that it is only within the reach of collectors with deep pockets. Coro competed with Trifari (see below), and not infrequently, the two firms turned out virtually identical products. Lucite jelly-belly figural pins, mostly made during the war years of 1942 to 1946, are only one example.

DE ROSA

De Rosa jewelry is known for colorful translucent enameling, complexity of design, and high quality workmanship. Its designs tend to fall into one of four categories: floral, figural, retro motifs, and designs inspired by the precious jewelry. The best De Rosa pieces are made of several metal pieces fastened together to form a three-dimensional whole. Using a combination of enameling, rhinestones, artificial pearls, and good design, these sophisticated pieces are unlike those of any other costume jewelry maker.

Manufactured from the 1940s to the 1970s, De Rosa jewelry is very popular with knowledgeable collectors, and its relative rarity makes it particularly desirable. Although unsigned pieces are occasionally seen, the marks "De Rosa," "R De Rosa," and "De Rosa sterling" are found on most examples.

EISENBERG

Using only the best Swarovski crystals and colored stones in combination with careful craftsmanship, Eisenberg & Sons became a major name in costume jewelry during the 1930s and 1940s and it continued to make costume jewelry for the next seventy years. Some Eisenberg jewelry, fashioned of heavy pewter-colored metal or sterling silver, successfully replicated the genuine eighteenth-century antique pieces that the public admired in films. Such attention to detail didn't come cheap, however: During the war, when a loaf of bread cost 10 cents, an Eisenberg necklace might retail for $10 to $25. Collectors look particularly for figurals, which are the rarest form of top-level Eisenberg jewelry. They are also drawn to the dazzling clarity of the high-quality rhinestones and classic designs of the 1950s and 1960s pieces, which have a growing following.

Eisenberg marks include "EISENBERG" (1945–1958), "Eisenberg Originals" (1935–1945), and "Eisenberg Sterling" (1943–1948). Some early Eisenberg pieces are unsigned.

Collectors should be aware that early Eisenberg jewelry has been widely reproduced and that clear stones have also been replaced with colored ones in older pieces in order to increase prices. This unfortunate practice is self-defeating when these are colors that Eisenberg never used.

STANLEY HAGLER

Known for limited-edition creations in the 1950s, an era of extensive mass production, the Stanley Hagler company specialized in eccentric color combinations and bold designs. Hagler's designers were adept at creating traditional floral pieces of handwired "seed pearls" and pastes, as well as updated florals, suitable for sixties discotheque wear.

HAR

Somewhat mysterious in its origins and with some of its designs rather scarce in the market-place, HAR jewelry—manufactured by the Hargo Jewelry Company of New York in the late fifties and early sixties—often features designs with Middle Eastern or Asian motifs. The firm's cast figurals, such as dragons, cobras, genies, and fantasy themes set with unusual stones, are among the most desirable pieces.

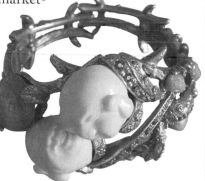

The Hargo Jewelry Company, known simply as HAR, was partial to Asian motifs, as seen in this goldtone double hinged bangle bracelet featuring Chinese heads.

THE CONTINUING ALLURE OF THE RHINESTONE

In the late forties and fifties, after the domestic austerity imposed by World War II, Americans glamorized with accessories. For many of the diamondless set, glamour meant rhinestones. Although many American buyers assumed that rhinestone jewelry of the period was imported from artistic, romantic Europe, little did they know that most jewelry in the United States was fabricated in Providence, Rhode Island, where dozens of companies employed low-paid immigrant workers to churn out rhinestone glitz.

"The rhinestone's allure is still strong," says *Antiques Roadshow* costume jewelry appraiser Rosalie Sayyah. The clients who visit her store, Rhinestone Rosie in Seattle, are frequently "women who wear suits to work, secretaries, lawyers, and even ships captains"and are looking to add a little panache to sober outfits. "Rhinestones make you smile," Sayyah says. "You put a pin on and you have a certain cachet. You wear jeans and a T shirt with a rhinestone necklace and it says, 'Look at me, I'm daring. There's a little more here than you think.'"

A gilt metal Miriam Haskell cuff bracelet, with her characteristic all-over design of clusters of three sizes of artificial pearls set among stones and beads to form a particularly intricate whole.

Costume jewelry manufacturers made more than just brooches, bracelets, necklaces, and rings. They sometimes made purse accessories, like this elegant, heavily jeweled compact set with pink, purple, and blue stones manufactured by Hobé.

MIRIAM HASKELL

Typically, Miriam Haskell jewelry made use of multiple elements, the most recognizable of which were artificial pearls in many sizes. Haskell designs are often layers and clusters of artificial pearls and seed pearls, Czech and Austrian stones and glass beads, rose montees (stones set in metal findings that can be strung side by side with others like them and then wired to a setting), and glass flowers and leaves in combination with richly plated yellow "Russian gold." It is these intricately fashioned pieces that Haskell collectors hope to find, not the more conventional simple strands of pearls and beads.

Because advertisements and artwork from the 1930s and 1940s have surfaced recently, many pieces of early unsigned Haskell jewelry can now be identified, and early Haskell has become a collectible category of its own.

A warning: Contemporary jewelry makers are reworking old Haskell elements and beads to create "Haskell" jewelry that is neither genuine Haskell nor collectible. Examine workmanship and become familiar with the way genuine pieces are assembled and finished to avoid being fooled.

HOBÉ

Hobé collectors are especially eager to own pieces created by this New York–based firm of French origins between the mid-thirties and the mid-fifties. They particularly value the sterling silver brooches incorporating glass "stones," and the unfoiled rhinestone pieces with inserts of carved faces and figures or portraits. All early Hobé jewelry exhibits elegant design and excellent workmanship. A frequent Hobé motif is the floral brooch in the form of a bouquet held together by ribbons and a bow. Hobé jewelry was manufactured by the original family from about 1927 to the mid-1990s.

JOSEFF OF HOLLYWOOD

Eugene Joseff designed the costume jewelry Joan Crawford wore in films, as well as jewel boxes–full of the antique-looking necklaces, bracelets, and rings that adorned other Hollywood celebrities. Because Joseff was also a student of genuine antique jewelry, he was able to copy the old pieces in an accurate though simplified fashion and to parlay his name and talent (not to mention his Hollywood connections) into a successful line of costume jewelry retailed by better-quality department stores.

KJL (KENNETH JAY LANE)

During the Kennedy era, Kenneth Jay Lane was the darling of the jet and Camelot sets, turning out bold and colorful, conspicuously fake jewelry for well-turned-out socialites, including Jackie herself. Lane's pieces may be recognized by the KJL hallmark and their excellent use of realistic botanical and zoological motifs. Lane's work from the 1960s is increasingly collectible.

Kenneth Jay Lane's faux pearl necklace is at once conspicuously fake and traditionally elegant.

JEWELER TO THE STARS

Vivien Leigh as Scarlett in Gone with the Wind, *dining in her grandest Joseff of Hollywood costume jewelry.*

Joseff of Hollywood designed the jewelry worn by Vivien Leigh in *Gone with the Wind,* Greta Garbo in *Camille,* Olivia De Havilland in *Robin Hood,* and many other A-list actresses in A-list movies. In the 1936 movie *The Great Ziegfeld,* for instance, actress Virginia Bruce descends a huge staircase wearing a 14-pound Joseff-designed acrylic headdress, while costar Dennis Morgan waits below singing "A Pretty Girl Is Like a Melody." "His stuff looked yummy, yummy, yummy," says *Antiques Roadshow* jewelry appraiser Rosalie Sayyah.

In addition to acrylic, Joseff used glass, tin, platinum, gold, silver, plastics, and —rarely—precious stones for his jewelry and accessories, which included cigarette cases and belt buckles. While the studios commissioned his designs for jewelry, Joseff never let them buy the creations he made for their movies. Instead, he leased his pieces to them, renting a bejeweled tiara to one celluloid princess and then modifying it to rent to another studio for a different film. Joseff was prolific, and his jewelry collection, continued by his wife after his death in 1948, is a blockbuster—currently comprising some three million pieces.

Virginia Bruce, star of The Great Ziegfeld, *wearing a 14-pound acrylic headdress designed by Joseff of Hollywood, "Jeweler to the Stars." Some say Ziegfeld coined the term "costume jewelry."*

Regardless of what you've read or seen in mystery movies, only a few designers made costume jewelry that was a direct imitation of grand, genuine pieces. Not many women ever copied their fabulous necklaces to fool thieves, let alone Cary Grant. Such replicas would have been custom work—expensive to make, expensive to buy. The vast majority of costume jewelry was mass-produced, and as trendy as fashion itself.

A modified sunburst design circle pin set with a combination of round and baguette-shaped rhinestones from Pell, a costume jewelry manufacturer known for rhinestones. Circle pins are very 1950s.

MARVELLA

Founded in Philadelphia before World War I, Marvella is best known for imitation pearls, but also for colored beads that are as opalescent and changeable as the aurora borealis. While the conservative Marvella look is not as collectible as are the larger pieces and sets, some of their jewelry is colorful, unusual, and classy—and not yet widely appreciated.

MAZER BROS. AND JOMAZ (JOSEPH MAZER)

Encouraged by Marcel Boucher (who designed jeweled shoe buckles for this firm before starting his own business) to switch from designing shoe buckles to designing jewelry (very wise advice, given what turned out to be the future of shoe buckles), Joseph and Lincoln Mazer produced jewelry until World War II. Then Joseph Mazer founded his own firm, Jomaz. Mazer Bros. continued to produce costume jewelry until the early 1950s, and Jomaz stayed in business until the 1980s. Both firms are known for their well-designed, beautifully crafted jewelry.

PELL

Beginning in 1941, Pell Jewelry Company manufactured pieces combining round and baguette-shaped clear, diamondlike rhinestones. Pell's figural pins are especially popular with collectors.

PENNINO

Working with heavy gold plate or silver and with fine-quality rhinestones and crystals, Pennino Brothers made jewelry from the late 1920s until the 1950s; the pieces produced before World War II are most popular with collectors. It is not always marked, but unlabeled Pennino pieces can sometimes be recognized by the high caliber of the workmanship.

REBAJES

The work of designer Frank Rebajes, noted designer of modernist jewelry, incorporated elements from African art, Cubism, and abstract paintings into interesting pieces fashioned of copper or of copper decorated with colored enamels and sterling. For the conservative jewelry purchaser, the work of Rebajes offered neat combinations of African and European themes. Working in the

United States from about 1932 until 1967, Rebajes eventually returned to Spain, where he continued to manufacture jewelry.

REJA

Known for elegant costume jewelry—particularly for the figural brooches of the World War II era—Reja never manufactured in large quantities. It sold its jewelry only in expensive boutiques. Originally called Deja, the name was changed to Reja in 1941 because of a name-infringement lawsuit. Most pieces are signed "Reja Reg.," "Reja," or "Reja Inc."

RENOIR AND MATISSE

A California firm with two trade names, Renoir and Matisse mass-produced inexpensive copper or copper and enameled copper jewelry from 1946 to 1964, marked with one or both names. Collectors look for pieces in pristine condition, because damage cannot be repaired.

NETTIE ROSENSTEIN

Designer of clothing and fashion jewelry, Nettie Rosenstein employed both natural silver and vermeil (gilt silver) for high-quality and expensive figural and medallion-like pins. The firm continued making jewelry and accessories for more than a decade after it ceased producing women's apparel in 1961.

SCHIAPARELLI

Schiaparelli's jewelry competed with Chanel's. Never intended to be mistaken for genuine jewelry, "fun" was the jewelry byword here (although after 1949, some collectors believe it became less witty). Because not all components of each set was marked, unsigned Schiaperelli jewelry can be found today, recognizable, perhaps, by its highly fanciful, exuberant designs.

SCHREINER

Henry Schreiner jewelry, made between 1939 and 1977, would never be termed understated. It is an explosion of colored crystals—often in fuchsias and acid greens—and high-quality rhinestones. One Schreiner specialty was rhinestones set with the pointed side facing up. During the 1960s, black-metal mountings on fantasy pins and earrings set off the stones.

A Reja-designed rhinestone pavé stylized gazelle from around 1940, with a simulated lapis lazuli belly.

When worn together, Nettie Rosenstein's royal pair of brooches seem to exchange twinkly rhinestone hearts.

JEWELRY BY SALVADOR DALÍ

At the Tampa *Antiques Roadshow,* a visitor related that, at a yard sale, he asked if the seller had any jewelry. Rummaging through the garage, he uncovered an unusual pendant and asking its price, was told, "Oh, that ugly thing. You can have that."

According to *Antiques Roadshow* appraiser Susan Florence, the pendant is the work of famous surrealist painter Salvador Dalí. "'Vegetal Vision' is what Dalí called it, and as you can see it looks like veins and leaves."

At auction, the pendant would bring between $5,000 and $7,000.

A striking 4-inch-long pin by Leo Glass, circa 1950, consists only of a swirling goldtone wire stem and a large purple rhinestone.

STARET

Highly desirable, but also obscure, Staret pieces were made throughout the 1940s, probably in Chicago. They were well designed and showy. Pieces combining painted enamel and rhinestones, depending upon their size and subject, are highly sought after by sophisticated collectors. Some of these pieces have been reproduced with original-looking "Staret" signatures, so buy carefully.

TRIFARI

The old and successful Trifari Company has been making costume jewelry since 1918. Of particular appeal to Trifari collectors are pieces with colorful demilune-shaped rhinestones and enameling, pieces with molded glass "stones" (nicknamed "fruit salads"), and pavé pieces replicating precious jewelry, as well as animal-form jelly-belly figurals. Among the most desirable are examples that imitate the craftsmanship and design of Cartier's Art Deco jewels. From 1930 to 1968, Cartier-trained Alfred Philippe was the firm's top designer.

The earliest 1920s pieces were marked "Jewels by Trifari." Pieces made circa 1935 are marked "TKF," and the firm used simply "Trifari" after World War II.

OTHER MANUFACTURERS

Because there's hardly a woman alive—young and old, rich and not so rich—who doesn't love a little sparkle, numerous manufacturers of superaffordable costume jewelry, such as B.S.K. Barclay (*not* McClelland Barclay), Cadoro, Les Bernard, Capri, DeNicola, and Vogue, made jewelry inexpensive enough to be purchased on a whim at five-and-dime stores. Serbin, Castlecliff, Judy Lee, and Leo Glass are among many others that made jewelry for this market. Emmons and Sarah Coventry costume jewelry was equally accessible, and possibly more so, since it was sold through home parties like those held by Tupperware. Bogoff is another maker of particularly good-quality inexpensive jewelry using nice-quality glass stones.

Chapter Twelve

POSTERS AND ILLUSTRATION ART

© UFS

Posters—colorful gorgeous, eye-grabbing multiples printed on paper—have attracted enthusiastic collectors since they first appeared on (gas) light poles of the nineteenth century; interestingly, the original artworks from which posters are printed are not at the heart of the hunt.

Illustration art, on the other hand, was created to be printed in multiples, and was once considered almost valueless. Today, however, a devoted coterie of serious collectors pursues these originals of paintings and drawings that have been reproduced in books, magazines, and advertisements. And, not only has original illustration art become popular, but so has its step-siblings, comic strip and comic book art. Like posters and illustration art, comic art presents itself to the public as pictures printed on paper. And although the comic books themselves have avid fans, it's those

Top: For some collectors, happiness is an original cartoon, such as Charles Schulz's Linus and his beloved blanket. Above: Derby, fedora, and homburg grace a 1938 poster by Leonetto Cappiello.

original drawings, in particular, that draw collectors. All members of this intriguing family are covered in this chapter.

POSTERS

The life of a poster is a hard one—hard, and intentionally short. Hastily pasted onto some highly public billboard, kiosk, railway station wall, or theater marquee, posters are subjected to rain, sun, snow; splashed by careless vehicles and pedestrians; defaced with mustaches and less decorous graffiti; and—in a final indignity—quickly papered over by some newer, fresher model. It's a wonder there are any left.

But there are. Posters are, after all, advertisements, and for advertisements to work, consumers have to be exposed to much more than just the occasional arresting image; they must be bombarded by them. During their golden age, from the 1860s until World War II, posters were produced in relatively large printings—usually three to five thousand. That may seem like a lot, but most did not survive. Thankfully, some posters were never put in "service" and were stored on a shelf or a bin in a printer's shop or warehouse. Many times this was due to over-runs—more were printed than had been ordered. Others were painstakingly soaked off the surface to which they had been pasted by covetous collectors. Some survived because of their popularity at the time they were created. The public had recognized posters as art long before the critics did, and its appetite for posters caused turn-of-the-twentieth-century print dealers to buy them from printers to sell to a public gripped by "postermania."

Posters were so popular at the end of the nineteenth century that a portfolio of 256 miniature French posters, *Les Maîtres de l'Affiche* (Masters of the Poster), was issued to subscribers in installments of four images a month. One complete set, in particularly good condition, turned up at the New York City *Antiques Roadshow*. It had been purchased for the visitor by

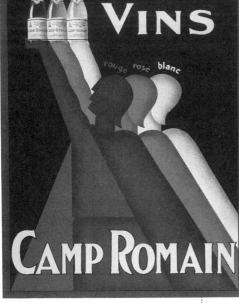

Red, white, or rosé? Stylized Roman legionnaires offer all three in Gadoud's poster for Camp Romain wines.

an art-dealer friend in Paris in 1980 for $8,000. Appraiser Nicholas Lowry told her that although her reduced-size posters were in fact reproductions—and generally, reproductions are not considered to be very collectible—sets of *Les Maîtres de l'Affiche* are popular with collectors because they were issued in the same era as the originals, between 1896 and 1900. Lowry also noted that the visitor's set was the most pristine he had ever seen: It included not only all of the posters, but also all of the sleeves that protected them and all of the original envelopes in which they had been sent to the subscriber. He told her that a lesser-quality set would sell at auction for $40,000 to $45,000. "But the condition of *this* set is absolutely incredible," he said. "It brightens up the room."

A pristine and complete set of Les Maîtres de l'Affiche *(Masters of the Poster), a portfolio of 256 miniatures of late-nineteenth-century French posters, dazzled visitors as well as the appraiser at the New York City Antiques Roadshow.*

Before Jules Cheret perfected a stone lithography process that allowed the printing of bright, multicolor posters in 1867, collecting art was a pursuit of the wealthy, inaccessible to the majority of the population. Posters democratized art, however, and made stunning images available for the first time to a large and enthusiastic audience. Their influence throughout the twentieth century should not be underestimated. Among other attributes, the poster was the medium that spread the Art Nouveau style. It was a superb propaganda vehicle to build support for World Wars I and II, and it was an effective and colorful medium for advertising the burgeoning number of products and services produced by an increasingly optimistic and muscular Industrial Age.

Because they were designed to attract the eye and to arrest attention, posters still have the power to draw us in, decades after they were produced. The well-designed poster, after all, encapsulates the spirit of its era, conveys the excitement of sport, seduces us with the glamour of a nightclub or theatrical production, captures the speed of a racing car, train, or airplane, or bears us away to exotic locales.

There is scarcely a popular subject that hasn't been represented on a poster, making this unusually fertile ground for the specialist collector. A doctor can fill his waiting-room walls with posters advertising old patent medicines. A pilot can line his den with posters of vintage airlines. A restaurateur can

Both the wine and the woman sparkle in Leonetto Cappiello's frothy 1922 poster for Contratto, an Italian liquor concern.

TIPS
from the experts

Several of the more famous and valuable posters have long been reproduced. In order to make sure you don't purchase a reproduction, you must first examine the paper on which the poster is printed, and to look at that paper unobscured. If the sheet of paper is framed under glass, and if it is possible to remove it safely, either do so yourself or take it to a competent framer.

When a potential seller contacts expert Nicholas Lowry regarding a stone lithography poster, the question he usually asks is: "Is the paper glossy like that of *Time* magazine, or is it porous like the paper of *The New York Times*?" If the paper is glossy, there's a real likelihood that the poster is a reproduction. (This rule, of course, does not apply to photo-offset posters, which were originally printed on glossy paper.) Unless you're an expert—that is, unless you're able to determine the quality of the paper yourself or evaluate the depth of color of the inks used in the stone lithography—that likelihood is about the best that you're going to get.

delight patrons with colorful images of food and wine. A classic-automobile aficionado can hang posters of streamlined racers or exotic luxury cars. Posters may actually be among the most egalitarian of art forms. There is something for nearly everyone.

The following is a brief overview of the field, with descriptions of a few of its many collecting areas. You won't find movie posters here; they are included in Entertainment Memorabilia (see page 351). Within the collecting community, there is ambiguity as to whether movie posters belong with other posters or with Hollywood memorabilia. Although they are both, they are usually considered the latter. But movie posters, in fact, have a large and dedicated following that is, for the most part, quite separate from either field.

A BRIEF HISTORY

Before the advent of the illustrated poster, most outdoor advertisements were printed broadsides; words, in other words—with no pictures. The vivid and colorful pictorial posters so avidly collected today are the result of mid-nineteenth-century advances in printing that led to lithography, a process based on the incompatibility of oil and water. In lithography, the artist draws his design on a porous, polished, flat stone with a greasy crayon, and the stone's surface is dampened with water. The water is absorbed everywhere but where the crayon has touched, so that when equally oily ink is rolled across the surface, the water repels the ink and it only adheres to the drawing. A sheet of paper laid on the stone is passed, with the stone, through a press. When the paper is peeled away, the image is revealed in one color. The process is repeated using a different stone for each color, to create the finished, full-color work.

Although there are plenty of American posters, they have nevertheless always been something of a European specialty. Perhaps the best-known artist to design posters was Henri de Toulouse-Lautrec. An established artist who lent his cachet to the poster form, Toulouse-Lautrec is known especially for theater posters, generally published in editions of not more than 3,000. (In contrast with most posters produced in the late nine-

teenth and early twentieth century, printing records have survived for Toulouse-Lautrec's work.) His masterpieces, along with posters created by his fellow artists Alphonse Mucha, Jules Cheret, Fernand Toussaint, Privat Livemont, and Theophile Alexandre Steinlen, set the standard for poster design.

Lithography remained the predominant method of printing posters through the first decades of the twentieth century. By the 1930s, however, the photo-offset process had become more widely used. Because the new process didn't use stone plates, which wear out, many more copies could be printed of each poster, allowing for real mass production. Photo-offset printing was used extensively for World War II posters promoting the war effort and war bonds. It was a particularly flexible process too, in that posters of the same image could, for the first time, be produced in different sizes. Norman Rockwell's 1943 patriotic series *Four Freedoms,* for example, was issued in three sizes. The rarest is also the largest; it is 56 inches high by 40 inches wide.

Toulouse-Lautrec's well-known poster "Divan Japonais" immortalized this fashionable Montmartre cabaret.

ROCKWELL'S FOUR FREEDOMS

A visitor brought a remarkable collection of posters to appraiser Nicholas Lowry at the Miami *Antiques Roadshow*. His father had picked up some Norman Rockwell posters used to sell war bonds at the radio station where he worked.

"In 1941, Franklin Roosevelt made a speech about America

entering into the Second World War," Lowry told the visitor, "and he told the nation that it was going to war to preserve four basic human freedoms. Rockwell portrayed these freedoms in a famous series of four posters—'Freedom of Speech,' 'Freedom to Worship,' 'Freedom from Fear,' and 'Freedom from Want'—and they were distributed all across America." Lowry noted that the posters had been folded, because they were mailed throughout the country, and told his visitor that they are especially rare in the large format. When all four in the large series appear together at auction, they bring between $4,000 and $6,000 for the set.

EVALUATING POSTERS

When evaluating posters, collectors consider the style, the subject, the image, the artist, the condition, and its rarity. They also take into account factors like trendiness, which can translate into volatile prices.

STYLE

If one were to choose a single adjective to describe the design of posters, "stylish" would do. In the most successful posters, the graphics, colors, and subjects are perfectly blended to deliver a particular message in a certain style. For the most part, the stronger the style—the more characteristic it is of its era—the more demand there is for it today. Pre–World War I Art Nouveau posters (generally awash in languorous ladies with streaming hair) have an immediately recognizable style. The best Art Deco posters are strong, bold, geometric, and chic. And photomontage Russian constructivist posters—overtly political, inspired by collage, and frequently printed in only two or three colors—have their own strong and distinctive style.

IMAGE

The best posters are a flawless combination of brilliant typography and visual image. If an automobile poster attracts your eye, for instance, that's probably because it conveys speed and style. The good travel poster, on the other hand, tempts you with a gorgeous landscape, architecture, and visions of leisure. A great poster, like other art forms, has appeal beyond its subject matter, but the subject is always among the criteria for judging it. Equally important is the design, use of color, historical content, and the skill and imagination of the artist who created it.

THE ARTIST

There are important artists known solely for the dazzling images they've created for posters; other artists are known primarily for their paintings, but also experimented with the poster format. Among the latter around the turn of the twentieth century were masters such as Gustav Klimt, Alphonse Mucha, and the aforementioned Toulouse-Lautrec; later, there was Maxfield Parrish and, even later, painter and photographer Ben Shahn created posters. But many poster artists were specialists, skilled at melding typography with a forceful visual image.

The majority of poster artists don't have famous or recognizable names; many, in fact, were anonymous commercial artists whose work went unsigned. Great poster design, however, transcends that lack of signature, and numerous posters by these anonymous artists are extremely desirable. The posters advertising Buffalo Bill's Wild West show, produced at the turn of the twentieth century, are prime examples. Although unsigned, they can command prices up to $10,000.

CONDITION

Posters are multiples; the same image has been printed hundreds or thousands of times. The example in the best condition therefore, will always be most valuable. Foxing (those little round, brownish stains), fading, tears, spotting, and discoloration—individually or in combination—are what make one poster worth less than another, undamaged, example. "Of course," says *Antiques Roadshow* appraiser Nicholas Lowry, "if the holy grail of posters happens to turn up and also happens to have a 'chip' in it, we will not turn it down." For example, a 1911 poster advertising third-class tickets on the *Titanic*'s never-taken return trip from New York to London, features a third-class cabin, dining salon, and an overall image of the ill-fated liner, and recently came up for auction. Despite the fact that it was in B condition—it had a paper split along a horizontal fold, tape on the back, tears, creases, and smudging along the right edge, plus the

Anything of the period that has to do with the ill-fated Titanic *is collectible. This White Star Line poster advertising the ship's never-to-be-made return voyage is a treasure.*

A single-color proof of an Art Nouveau style lithographed poster created for the 1904 St. Louis World's Fair by Alphonse Mucha.

A grim warning about the evils of alcohol dominates Paul Colin's poster, issued as a public service.

GRADING POSTERS

Most auction houses and poster galleries use an alphabetical system to grade posters, ranging from A (the best) to C, supplemented by + and -. Grading systems vary, so be sure you know the system and have confidence in the grader. The following are the definitions used by Swann Auction Galleries. Swann prefaces its rating scale with the following note: "Posters, for the most part, were printed in large format on the cheapest possible paper, and with an expected life of two to three months on billboards. They were ephemeral by definition and not intended to withstand the test of time. Therefore, in grading a poster's condition, the standards of the print collector cannot be used. The most important element in grading a poster's condition is defined by the lines, colors, and overall appearance."

Condition A	designates a poster in much the same state as when it was printed; colors are fresh, with no significant paper losses or tears, but there may be a slight blemish, creases, or scuffing.
Condition B	designates a poster in good condition. Some restoration (including repaired tears or slight overpainting) may have been performed, but it is not visible; there may be discoloration or fading.
Condition C	designates a poster that is showing the effects of time or heavy restoration. Fading and discoloration may be more pronounced; restoration, folds, creases, and flaking may be visible; and there may be paper loss or obvious restored losses.

A powerful roadster literally flies out of Monte Carlo in Geo Ham's poster announcing the legendary Grand Prix automobile race.

paper was tipped (glued) to mat corners—it sold for $15,000.

In the United States, posters are often mounted on linen backings to stabilize them, an archivally correct process that allows the tears or holes in the poster paper to be repaired. To discover if a poster you're interested in has been touched up (repainted) or repaired, run your hand over the paper. New paint and disguised paper-mends feel different from the original surface. Creasing and staining adversely affect value, as well. Trimmed edges, which can be the result of trying to fit a poster into a frame or trying to neaten up torn edges, also reduce value. An intact poster is unfailingly more desirable than a trimmed one. The original size is easy to research in auction catalogs, catalogues raisonnés, or on the Internet. If you think that the only way you're ever going to own a particular image that you love is if it's trimmed, however, go ahead and buy it. True love is always a collector's bottom line.

RARITY

As stated earlier, posters are multiples and it's not always known how many copies were printed. When it comes to production of late-nineteenth- and early-twentieth-century stone lithographed posters, we know that the number produced could not exceed approximately 5,000. After that the stones wore out. Fewer still were printed of many posters that did not require a large production run. But knowing how many were produced may be less important than knowing how many survived and are available to collectors today. Posters are paper, after all, and consequently disposable. This is exactly what makes surviving posters rare. If you follow auctions, examine the stock of galleries and dealers, and talk to knowledgeable collectors, that can help you learn how to determine rarity.

One extraordinarily rare poster designed by the artist Fred Spear and commissioned by the Boston Committee of Public Safety for local distribution only, is the effective and famous World War I image that appeared after the German sinking of the *Lusitania.* An underwater view depicts a drowning mother clutching her baby. The stark and simple message reads "Enlist." "This image actually caused riots and huge public outcry," says Lowry. On the other hand, certain images—although plentiful—have such widespread appeal that there are not enough of them for those who'd like to own one. One example is the classic World War II image of a Nazi officer wearing a peaked cap and a monocle. Centered in the monocle is the chilling reflection of a corpse hanging from a gibbet. The legend reads "This is the Enemy." It made enormously influential propaganda.

Occasionally, a previously unknown cache of posters is discovered. As in other fields, such finds can cause temporary price fluctuations.

SUBJECT

Posters, in arresting the eye while delivering instantaneous, punchy messages, are exceptionally well suited to convey

Karl Koehler and Victor Ancona won the 1942 National War Poster Competition—part of FDR's campaign to rouse U.S. support —with this chilling image.

Alphonse Mucha's Art Nouveau beauties have been collected for decades. On an 1899 poster, this particularly alluring maiden touts the virtues of Moët & Chandon champagne.

admonishments and commands, such as "Loose Lips Sink Ships" and "Buy War Bonds." Sex, it goes without saying, also sells. Among the posters that collectors have always coveted are those that depict pretty, provocative women drinking champagne, eating chocolates, riding horses and bicycles, smoking, and driving fast cars. In one amusing effort by Leonetto Cappiello, a master of poster design, a maiden balances on one foot on a winged wheel, sprinkles tubes of stove polish with one hand and holds a cast-iron stove aloft with the other—all (to no one's surprise, evidently) while half-naked.

POSTER SUBJECTS

The function of posters was to advertise the goods and services that were popular at the time they were issued. Late-nineteenth-century and early-twentieth-century products included items such as the above-mentioned stove polish and lamp oil, which may seem arcane to us today, along with the still-familiar bicycles, aperitifs, and candy. Early transportation posters feature ocean liners and trains rather than aircraft, but automobiles have been a constant subject throughout the twentieth century.

TRANSPORTATION

Collectors often make a distinction between transportation and travel posters. Transportation posters reflect their creator's love affairs with technology—with posh ocean liners and streamlined trains. Travel posters, in contrast, are about escape fantasies—they picture exotic destinations, distant cities, mountain vistas, and talcum powder beaches.

Technological advances abounded at the beginning of the twentieth century, particularly in the field of transportation. The automobile was replacing horse-drawn vehicles, ships of gigantic proportions were crossing the oceans, trains were becoming faster and more efficient, and airplanes and dirigibles were beginning to fill the skies. All of these new and improved forms of transport were promoted by means of posters.

OCEAN LINERS

Ocean-liner posters first appeared at the beginning of the twentieth century. Captains of industry had leisure, and they sought for themselves and their families the rounding out that travel could bring, naturally, in the first-class cabins; at the same time, immigrants hoping for a better life in the United States found passage in far less sumptuous quarters. Posters for these grand American, English, and French floating castles were produced mainly in the years before convenient air travel, between 1900 and 1950. The owners of the palatial French ship *Normandie,* the crème de la crème of passenger ships, commissioned the crème de la crème of Art Deco poster artists, Cassandre, to create their finest, most iconic poster: a brilliant, dramatic head-on rendering of the *Normandie's* monumental prow.

Poster artist William ten Broek offered a different perspective on overseas voyaging in his circa-1936 design for the Holland-America Line. Viewed from the vantage point of sea-level at the prow, an ocean liner is pictured with a tiny sloop alongside. The sloop highlights the liner's massive scale. Nearly all highly collectible ocean-liner posters are dominated by images intended to convey the hugeness of these marmmoth ships. Posters featuring famous vessels, such as the doomed *Lusitania* and *Titanic,* are, not surprisingly, enormously desirable.

Considered to be one of the finest images created by perhaps the finest of Art Deco poster artists, Cassandre's fish-eye view of the greatest luxury liner of the 1930s still dazzles.

A FREE RIDE

About a dozen years ago, a woman living in East Tennessee rescued a few dozen posters from the trash. A generous soul, she shared her curbside finds with other family members, including her brother, who brought a few of the posters to the New Orleans *Antiques Roadshow*. One depicted an ocean liner: "I was always fascinated with ships," he explained. Appraiser Nicholas Lowry told the guest that he had chosen well. "This is one of the iconic images of the twentieth century," Lowry observed. "People know this image and they don't even know why. It's so popular that you see it on refrigerator magnets." The poster was designed by Cassandre, a French graphic artist whose poster designs greatly influenced advertising art in the first half of the twentieth century. Printed in 1935, it advertised the trans-Atlantic voyage of the *Normandie,* a French ocean liner with stops in "Le Havre–Southampton–New York." The only bad news was that this poster was in less-than-perfect condition—understandable, considering where it had been found—devaluing a mint-condition price of approximately $15,000 to *only* $10,000.

RAILWAYS

In the first half of the twentieth century, posters promoting train travel were as ubiquitous as television ads are today. Advertisements for the great and famous European lines, such as the Chemin de Fer du Nord (Northern Railroad), and for well-known trains, such as *L'Oiseau Bleu* (Blue Bird), blanketed Europe. Cassandre's transportation images are recognizable even by those unfamiliar with their origins, because they have become part of our visual vernacular. Along with his *Normandie* masterpiece, Cassandre also created brilliant posters for the Nord Express railway service. The 1927 "Nord Express" poster, for example, a superb example of poster art, features an oblique view of a highly stylized locomotive speeding away from the viewer in a universal symbol of power, velocity, and modernity. Another iconic train image is the 1932 poster "Exactitude," designed by Pierre Fix-Masseau for the French national railways and featuring a locomotive pulling out of the station, its engineer leaning out of the cabin. The front of the locomotive nearly fills the foreground,

An ode to the speed and glamour of stream-lined train travel, from 1938, by American poster artist Leslie Ragan.

while the body of the train tapers to a triangular point. The train's punctuality—the poster's message—is delivered in the form of a white clock above the engineer's head.

AUTOMOBILES AND MOTORING

The automobile wasn't going to be outdone by ships and trains. Speed and luxury were more important than ever after World War I, and throughout the period, posters blazoned all the fastest, most splendid cars. The utterly dashing and luxurious Hispano-Suizas and Bugattis had their posters, but so did the

Peugeots, Fiats, and Buicks. Posters of the latter, along with those advertising Ford and Renault, are collectible but are usually less popular than those of racier, more exotic cars. Vintage car enthusiasts are interested, as well, in posters for cars that have faded from memory, such as the Suere, the Martini, the Delahaye, and the Barry.

Motoring clubs, car accessory manufacturers, tire makers, and car racing promoters all made good use of the poster. Michelin Tires were sold by Bibendum, their oversized trademark "tireman." Posters sporting his likeness, such as H. L. Roowy's 1912 "Pneu Velo Michelin," are widely collected today. The Grand Prix of Monaco, the most important automotive race of the period, issued numerous posters depicting sleek racing cars, and these are among the most valuable of racing posters. Geo Ham produced many of these dynamic designs, including posters for the 1933 to 1937 and the 1948 races. Cumulatively, they portray the thrilling Paris to Monaco race scene in bold, graphically appealing design and spectacular color.

For Peugeot, René Vincent created a poster designed to tempt post World War I speed demons back on the road.

A rare—and evidently unsuccessful—1930 poster for a long-forgotten car.

BICYCLES AND MOTORCYCLES

Somewhat less exalted forms of wheeled transport warranted posters, too. Posters for bicycling, that pre–Great War enthusiasm, are highly desirable today. Like the aforementioned stove polish saleswoman, they often relied on a kind of innocent sex appeal. One Cycles Gladiator poster, signed simply "L.W.," portrays a nude woman being pulled through the cosmos by her winged bicycle. Pal (Jean de Paleologue) designed several such bicycle posters, including one for Liberator featuring a bare-breasted Valkyrie with massive sword and shield, gripping her steedlike bicycle by the handlebars. During the cycling craze of the late nineteenth and early twentieth centuries, bicycles were seen not only as a fascinating new pastime, but also as vehicles (literally and figuratively) with which women could assert their independence. In Pal's image, a beautiful, strong woman claims the freedom that bicycle represents.

Motorcycle posters combine the attractions of risk with a sense of exhilarating speed. One poster for Motos Peugeot features a

Green sky, orange road, and a pipe-smoking Ultima motorcyclist.

ADVERTISING THE UNDERGROUND

A number of famous poster images were designed for the Underground, the London subway system. These sought to advertise the clean, safe, attractive underground train system to the fashionable traveler. The majority of London Underground advertisements illustrate attractive destinations or the advantages of subterranean travel. Emphasizing protection from the city's rainy weather, V. L. Danvers's 1924 *Where it is Bright and Warm* features a gray, misty streetscape with the splash of bright light from the Underground sign promising light and warmth. American artist Edward Kauffer McKnight also emphasized protection from the elements in his 1921 poster, "Winter Sales are best reached by Underground," depicting abstract umbrella-bearing figures battling stormy weather. Kauffer was one of the best-known designers of Underground posters. His 1922 poster advertises the London Museum as a destination and features a tiny building engulfed in a huge burst of flames. This was inspired by an illuminated model of the Great Fire of 1666, which was on display at the time.

motorcycle and rider racing obliquely toward the viewer. The text reads "Motos Peugeot," and the sense of blurring speed is imparted by blue contrails representing the rider's windswept hair and red contrails where the cycle has literally burned up the road.

AVIATION

Aviation posters of all types are always in demand. In the early decades of the twentieth century, before airplanes dominated our skies, they had serious competition from airships (also known as dirigibles)—both the blimp and, in particular, the zeppelin. By the 1930s, the Hamburg-America Line, long known for its ocean liners, was promoting an airship service. Posters, such as a circa 1930 poster for Zeppelin Fahrten by Bauer, are a reminder that until the crash of the Hindenburg, this was a promising mode of transportation.

Prior to about 1930, planes appeared on posters primarily as advertising for air shows and exhibitions, or as World War I propaganda. Wing walkers and barnstormers were common subjects and poster collectors and collectors of aeronautica like them both for their beautiful renderings of early flight and as aviation artifacts.

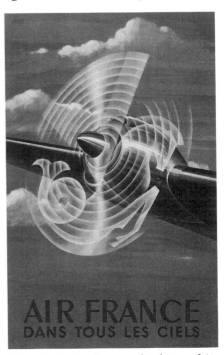

From inside the plane, a stylized view of Air France's logo is visible in the whirring propeller on one wing in this poster from 1948.

Commercial passenger airlines began flying in the late 1920s, gaining in popularity over the next three decades. Today there is growing interest in early commercial airline memorabilia and posters. Royal Dutch airlines (KLM) used the ghost ship the *Flying Dutchman* as a recurring theme. In Vincent Guerra's 1947 *Colis Postaux Avion* poster for Air France, a train and plane move in opposite directions, both connoting speed. Produced to promote the combined postal carrier service capabilities of Air

France and S.N.C.F. (the French National Railway), the text translates as "packages can be sent as quickly as letters."

TRAVEL

Travel for leisure was a glamorous, newly attainable opportunity in the 1920s, once the war was over. The realization of lifelong dreams sometimes requires encouragement, nonetheless. So the travel poster was utilized to lure people to Paris, the Mediterranean, the Rockies, or the Adirondacks with hard-to-resist images.

Travel posters were often co-opted by transportation companies, among them Norman Wilkinson's "Travel to Ireland" poster. Commissioned by the Ulster Transportation Authority, it depicts a lush Irish landscape and the Antrim Coast Road. Similarly, a series of posters for the New York Central Lines featured various attractions in the cities the railroad served. This series includes images of urban and rural landmarks, such as Manhattan's Grand Central Terminal enveloped in the steam produced by an array of sleek train engines, the Hudson River and the Palisades, West Point, and the Adirondack Mountains.

On a poster for a city not usually associated with beaches, an exuberant water-skier streaks past sunbathers in a colorful beach scene.

MERCHANDISE

The industrial giants of the early twentieth century learned quickly that poster advertising could attract new customers. Some of the first posters were for kerosene and paraffin, both used as fuel for lamps. Jules Cheret created a series of posters for the paraffin lamp fuel Saxoléine that featured beautiful women—yet again.

Clothing was another commodity that was heavily advertised. Swiss poster artist Otto Baumberger produced a series of posters for the Zurich clothier PKZ, including one from 1923 that depicts a hyper-realistic close-up of a tweed sports coat, showing only a small portion of the garment; the collar, a button, and on the bunched silk lining a label reading "Marque PKZ," the poster's only text. The texture of the wool and silkiness of the lining are so well-rendered they seem real.

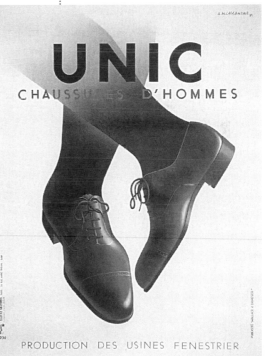

Simple yet elegant: Cassandre's 1932 image of impeccable men's footwear cleverly illustrates both the front and side views.

COGNAC GÉLAS

COGNAC
FRANCE

PAPIER à CIGARETTES

JOB

Right: A prancing satyr welcomes the cognac-drinker to the pleasures of the hedonistic life. Far right: Invoking exotic Eastern imagery, Leonetto Cappiello chose this satisfied, relaxed pasha to promote Job cigarette papers.

WINE, LIQUOR, FOOD, AND CIGARETTES

With post–World War I prosperity, luxuries such as fine liquors, chocolates, and prepared foods not only returned, but were more abundant, and their manufacturers competed for the public's attention by commissioning many posters.

A poster for chocolate by Firmin Bouisset is as popular today as it was when it was produced in 1892—so popular, in fact, that it was reused shortly after its initial issue and has been reproduced countless times since. Featuring a little girl in pigtails with a basketful of the product at her feet, the child has her back to the viewer and has stopped to scrawl "Chocolat Menier Menier" on a wall.

A true innovator in the art of the poster, Italian-born Leonetto Cappiello has been called the father of modern-day advertising. His 1903 poster for Chocolat Klaus created a sensation with its stylized image of a woman in a flowing green gown, riding sidesaddle on a stylized red horse, set against a dramatic black background. Perhaps even more shocking at the time than the color of the horse was the fact that the product did not appear anywhere on the poster. Visual shock and image association, the trademarks of Cappiello's work, became fundamental elements of twentieth-century advertising.

By the late nineteenth century—until it was banned in the second decade of the twentieth century—the potent green liqueur absinthe was the drink of choice for artists and writers in France. Absinthe was widely advertised and posters for it include Privat Livemont's classic "Absinthe Robette," in which a Greek goddess-like maiden, set against a fanciful Art Nouveau–style floral background, prayerfully lifts her (celestial-flavored) glass of absinthe.

Collectors love and pursue this fanciful poster for Chocolat Delespaul-Havez as enthusiastically as all—but one—of these bright-eyed children love their streaming cocoa.

ENTERTAINMENT

In the nineteenth century, French nightclubs commissioned hundreds of posters to promote their floor shows and stars. In 1889, Jules Cheret produced the first two posters for the Moulin Rouge. One is apparently lost, but the other, entitled "Bal au Moulin Rouge," is a classic, depicting a lissome beauty on a donkey in front of a red mill.

The reputation of Toulouse-Lautrec, already established when he began designing posters, lent artistic credibility to the form. Toulouse-Lautrec produced thirty-one posters, among them his first masterpiece, a poster for the Moulin Rouge featuring the club's headliner, La Goulue. In this composition and others, influenced by the newly popular Japanese woodblock print, he played with asymmetry and scale. Toulouse-Lautrec also designed several posters celebrating Aristide Bruant, a noted cabaret performer.

French chanteuse Mistinguett—the Madonna of her day—was portrayed on many posters by several artists, including Charles Gesmar. One of his most famous Mistinguett posters dates from 1925 and is referred to by collectors as "Jewels." It features a close-up of the singer's head and her bejeweled hand pushing away the feathery white boa that frames her doll-like face.

In 1966, pop artist Roy Lichtenstein created this eye-popping film-festival poster in his signature, comic strip–inspired style.

EASY TARGETS: WORLD WAR I POSTERS

In wartime, every nation must recruit soldiers and rally public support. During World War I, United States officials waged their public relations battles using tens of thousands of war posters in libraries, post offices, and schools across the country. Eighty years after government printing offices released these patriotic posters, they've become a collector's dream: Accessible, inexpensive, powerfully designed, brightly colored, and historically rich. "These posters were so gorgeous artistically, so compelling, and so passionate in their message that people collected them even when they were new," says *Antiques Roadshow* appraiser Nicholas Lowry. "People see them today and fall in love. I get more calls about World War I posters than any other kind of poster."

After World War II, the U.S. government broadcast its message on radio and television, but World War I propagandists concentrated on posters and their message was clear: "Contribute money, conserve food, and beware of the enemy," Lowry says. In a Navy recruitment poster, illustrator Howard Chandler Christy didn't hesitate to use seduction. He drew a winsome young woman wearing a Naval uniform and lamenting that she is unable to enlist. Her message: "Be a man and do it!" Lowry observes: "Who could turn down that kind of invitation?"

Also in 1925, a poster for the Revue Nègre by Paul Colin beckoned Parisians to the show that introduced jazz great Josephine Baker to Paris; Baker was to become a popular entertainer and poster subject.

MAGAZINES AND PERIODICALS

The poster was the perfect medium for advertising magazines, books, and newspapers. Although collectors may not consider publication posters a separate collecting field, they do pursue posters with interesting images by favorite artists. Théophile-Alexandre Steinlen's 1899 poster "La Traite Des Blanches" is an advertisement for the newspaper *Le Journal,* which was serializing the book *White Slavery.* Fernand Toussaint's "Le Sillon" is an Art Nouveau tour de force created for a small-circulation art journal. In 1893, Toulouse-Lautrec designed the poster "Reine de Joie" to promote the book *Queen of Hearts,* about a woman of easy virtue.

WAR

War posters are, unequivocally, propaganda posters. In the United States, their objective was to recruit young men, urge women to be supportive (and possibly rivet aircraft), and encourage civilians to give their all—their money, their bacon, their nylons, and their elbow grease—to the war effort. Such urgings required enlistment posters for each branch of the service, along with a variety of civilian-incentive posters. It isn't easy to keep the public stirred up against a distant enemy, which is why there are so many posters depicting whomever the current enemy happened to be in his full monstrousness (see page 431). There were also reassuring images depicting things like the Four Freedoms (which, presumably, the enemy doesn't possess), and posters exhorting everyone to "Buy War Bonds."

Charles Dana Gibson, one of the best-known illustrators of the day, was the president of the Society of Illustrators when the United States entered World War I in 1917 and he was chosen to head the Division of Pictorial Publicity of the Committee on Public Information. Gibson recruited 279 artists and 33 cartoonists to produce recruitment and propaganda posters. (The navy's recruiting bureau handled its campaign independently). Although several well-known painters such as George Bellows, Kenyon Cox, William Glackens, Joseph Pennell, and others designed posters for the committee, the majority of the images were created by commercial artists like Howard Chandler Christy and James Montgomery Flagg. Many of these posters were so well done, so effective, and so personally meaningful that at the war's end, people couldn't bring themselves to throw them away. As a result, current supply outweighs demand. Poster expert Nicholas Lowry receives at least three telephone calls a day from potential sellers of World War I posters, only a few of which have significant value. (The majority of World War I posters sell for less than $500.) Among the exceptions are some especially well known images, such as a poster by Howard Chandler Christy depicting a lovely young woman in a Marine uniform captioned "If You Want to Fight, Join the Marines." Christy's posters imply—none too subtly—that if weak, presumably helpless women want to go to war, red-blooded American boys certainly should do the same. Another exception is the most iconic of the World War I posters, one for which demand seems boundless: Good old Uncle Sam in top hat and striped suit, as envisaged by James Montgomery Flagg. He's pointing at the viewer, with the legend "I Want You." Poster collectors want him, too.

They also want rare posters, such as those that were produced locally, rather than nationally, of which Spear's devastating "Enlist" (see page 431) is a prime example. A strong image and rarity are also combined in "Destroy the Mad Brute," a poster depicting a huge gorilla in a German military helmet labeled "Militarism." With a bloody club marked *"Kultur"* in one hand and a desperate maiden, her dress artfully ripped, in the other, the slavering beast steps onto a sandy shore labeled "America." Surely it made every patriot stiffen his or her resolve that the Hun must never be allowed to invade. (Popular folklore has it that this poster was the inspiration for *King Kong*.)

If you have a World War I poster and would like to know if it is one of the rare, sought-after images, Lowry recommends consulting an expert with an established reputation—unless you have the time and resources to do the research yourself.

During World War I, Howard Chandler Christy enlisted the services of a comely girl-next-door to induce reluctant men to join the U.S. war effort.

By World War II, women also were being asked to sign up, and photography had joined drawn illustrations in the poster-design arsenal.

Tough, yet noble, a soldier, a sailor, and a civilian factory worker encourage cooperation and unity in this 1942 poster promoting the war effort.

Seen from below, a skier roars beyond the edges of this dynamic poster to publicize Dartmouth College's 1938 winter break.

Most World War II posters, printed by the photo-offset process, are even more numerous than World War I posters, and aside from the aforementioned Rockwell Four Freedoms group, to date they are even less collectible than those from "the war to end all wars."

SPORTS

Sports and sports-related themes—water sports, cycling, sledding, ice-skating, tennis, boxing, baseball, swimming, racing, and more—all have fans among poster collectors. Skiing is a current favorite, especially the very early and rare ski posters printed before World War I, and those created in the years between the wars, the period when skiing became increasingly popular as a leisure activity and resorts were first built to accommodate the sport's enthusiasts. Unquestionably, the snowscape is an ideal subject for posters. Sascha Maurer designed several ski posters, including one for the New Haven Railroad in 1938. It features a smiling man, crouched over his skis, bursting over the headline "SKI" in a cloud of fresh powder. (In order to create this image, a friend photographed Maurer, dressed in full ski outfit, balanced on a stack of telephone books.)

Two combatants face off in this poster announcing a 1941 Italian prize fight.

Golf posters, too, are popular. Given the game's many devoted enthusiasts, that should be no surprise. Golf is usually played in picturesque locales, often at grand resorts—a natural for posters.

If a poster is of Art Deco vintage, and if it touts a famous golf resort, was created by a well-known graphic artist, and depicts a golfer looking more Gatsby than Gatsby, then collectors will fight to take it home.

Fly fishing sells flying in a 1957 airline
poster by Joseph Binder.

A rare non-travel post–World War I poster by Roger
Broders encourages the French to invest in their country.

The Artists

Great poster artists worked in many European countries as well as in the United States, and many are remembered mainly for their work in this "disposable" medium. Brief biographies of some of poster art's most important practitioners follow:

OTTO BAUMBERGER
SWISS (1889–1961)

A lithographer and designer, as well as a poster artist, Baumberger produced many theater and travel posters. His works include the iconic PKZ poster (see page 437), in 1922 and a dramatic and slightly sinister poster for an international air show in Zurich in 1937.

JOSEPH BINDER
AUSTRIAN (1898–1972)

An influential graphic artist in Europe, Binder worked and taught in the United States in the 1930s. His posters include the 1923 "Milch Auf Jedem Tisch" (Milk on Every Table), a Cubist-influenced still life.

FIRMIN BOUISSET
FRENCH (1859–1925)

Known for portraits of children, Bouisset was active in painting, engraving, and illustration, as well as in creating classic posters such as "Chocolat Menier" (see page 438).

FRANK BRANGWYN
ENGLISH, B. BELGIUM (1867–1956)

Known as a painter and graphic artist, Brangwyn's works include murals, stained glass, and book illustrations, along with posters for World War I and the London Underground.

ROGER BRODERS
FRENCH (1883–1953)

One of the best known of all travel poster artists, Broders used geometric shapes and a rich palette to lure visditors to lure isitors to exotic destinations, such as India (for example, "Krishna Temple/Muttra" and "Visit India/Delhi"). He is particularly well known for French Riviera posters.

Leonetto Cappiello's poster for a Spanish mineral water tasty enough for an imperious monarch's table.

For the Etoile du Nord, Cassandre's brilliant 1927 abstraction of modernity and speed.

WIM (WILLEM FREDERIK) TEN BROEK *DUTCH* (1905–)

A painter who also designed posters, notably for the Holland-America Lines.

LEONETTO CAPPIELLO
FRENCH, B. ITALY (1875–1942)

One of the most prolific and popular creators of posters of the early twentieth century, Cappiello is recognized as a pioneer in the use of shock appeal and image association; that is, the tying of a product to an image so the consumer remembers it. His works include posters for the newspaper *Le Frou-Frou* (1899), Chocolat Klaus (1903), and the literal bull's-eye poster for Kub bouillon (1931). He produced some 1,000 posters in his forty-year career, and his work influenced a generation of poster artists, including Cassandre.

JEAN CARLU
FRENCH (1900–1997)

One of the four "Musketeers" of French poster design (with Cassandre, Colin, and Loupot), Carlu created posters in a style that evolved over the years from realism to cubism to surrealism. His work in France includes an exhibition poster, "Paris 1937," featuring the profile of a woman's head against a pattern of flags of the world. In the United States, he produced posters for the war effort, including a 1942 Cubist-influenced poster for the U.S. Division of Information, Office for Emergency Management, which depicts a black-gloved hand clutching a wrench that is turning a stylized "O" in the slogan "America's Answer! Production."

CASSANDRE (ADOLPHE MOURON)
FRENCH, B. UKRAINE (1901–1968)

Perhaps the greatest poster artist of the Art Deco period, Cassandre's bold, geometric posters were used to advertise a multitude of products, from liqueurs to records. Another of the four major poster artists known as the "Musketeers," he is particularly well known for a 1935 poster for the French Line ship *Normandie;* several railway posters, including "Etoile du Nord" and the 1927 "Nord Express"; plus a series of posters featuring Nicolas, the wine merchant.

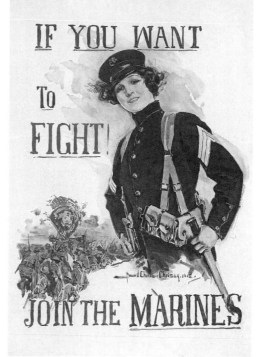

Jules Cheret's posters advertised the 1889 opening of the famed Montmartre cabaret throughout Paris.

Howard Chandler Christy's provocative recruitment poster of 1915 was issued two years before the United States entered World War I.

HENRI CASSIERS
BELGIAN *(1858–1944)*

An engraver, watercolorist, and poster artist, Cassiers is best known for posters for shipping firms, such as those for the Red Star Line.

JULES CHERET
FRENCH *(1836–1932)*

Known as the father of the poster for his improvements to the lithography process, Cheret designed some 1,000 posters, including many iconic images such as Vin Mariani (1894); several posters for Folies Bèrge, including one for dancer Loïe Fuller (1893); Papier a Cigarettes Job (1895); and Pippermint (1899).

PAUL COLIN
FRENCH *(1892–1985)*

One of the "Musketeers" of French poster artists, Colin is known for theater, ballet, and music hall posters, including a 1925 poster for the Revue Nègre.

HOWARD CHANDLER CHRISTY
AMERICAN *(1873–1952)*

Famed illustrator of books and magazines, Christy designed World War I recruitment posters, among them several for the Marines.

FREDERIC HUGO D'ALESI **FRENCH** *(1849–1906)*

Son of a French officer, d'Alesi was born in Romania and spent his first twenty-six years abroad before moving to Paris. After a few years as a landscape painter, he turned to designing posters in 1882. His first commissions were for nightclubs and theaters, but he also produced more than one hundred travel posters, mainly for railroad lines, such as the PLM (Paris-Lyons-Méditerranée) railway.

James M. Flagg's 1917 war poster seems to admonish the nation to wake up and fight.

In summer, geese and vacationers flock to northern climes in this John Held Jr. travel poster, circa 1930.

PIERRE FIX-MASSEAU
FRENCH *(1905–1994)*

A disciple of Cassandre, Fix-Masseau's works include the iconic train poster "Exactitude" (see page 434), and another for Huilles Renault (motor oil, 1934). Fix-Masseau designed posters until 1990, an astonishingly long career.

JAMES MONTGOMERY FLAGG *AMERICAN* *(1877–1960)*

A skilled painter and illustrator, Flagg produced numerous posters, including the Uncle Sam captioned "I Want You For U.S. Army." Based on a British recruitment poster, it became one of the most recognizable images of the twentieth century.

CHARLES GESMAR
FRENCH *(1900–1928)*

Gesmar created several posters and also designed the costumes for the famous Parisian nightclub singer Mistinguett.

CHARLES DANA GIBSON
AMERICAN *(1867–1944)*

Famed for creating the "Gibson Girl," a late-Victorian image of ideal American female beauty, Gibson was head of the Society of Illustrators and led the Division of Pictorial Publicity responsible for creating recruitment and propaganda posters for World War I. At least a dozen of his drawings were adapted by staff artists and used for posters.

GEO HAM (GEO HAMEL) *FRENCH* *(1900–1972)*

Known for 1930s posters of sleek motorcars for the Grand Prix of Monaco, Ham competed in the 1934 Le Mans race, and although he was forced to withdraw, he captured his racing experience in his exciting posters.

JOHN HELD JR.
AMERICAN *(1889–1958)*

Through his illustrations and cartoons in *The New Yorker, College Humor, Cosmopolitan,* and several other magazines, John Held defined the Flapper and Raccoon coat era of the 1920s. He produced streetcar posters and advertising art for Wanamaker's department

Ludwig Hohlwein's circa-1929 travel poster highlights the attractions of his native Germany.

The bucolic charms of New England, as envisioned by Edward McKnight Kauffer.

store for seed catalogues, and for numerous magazines.

LUDWIG HOHLWEIN
GERMAN *(1874–1949)*

A trained architect who specialized in exhibit and interior design, Hohlwein designed his first poster in 1906 for an exhibition of sporting guns. The poster was a great success and Hohlwein became a renowned international poster artist. Hohlwein, a master of color and line, produced propaganda posters for the German government during World War I and memorable posters for the Munich Zoo, tobacco companies, and tea companies.

EDWARD MCKNIGHT KAUFFER
AMERICAN *(1890–1954)*

Kauffer moved to London in 1914, where he created posters for the London Underground. His clients included most of the largest companies in England, among them Shell Oil. A 1935 Stonehenge poster, featuring the prehistoric site beneath a starry sky, advises "See Britain First on Shell."

PRIVAT LIVEMONT
BELGIAN *(1861–1936)*

Livemont began designing posters around 1895. Like Mucha's, the posters he produced were masterly and decorative, and usually celebrated feminine beauty. His masterworks include

"Biscuits & Chocolat Delacre" (1896), "Absinthe Robette" (1896), and "Bitter Oriental" (1897).

MAURICE LOGAN
AMERICAN *(1886–1977)*

Logan was part of the early-twentieth century California group of artists known as the Society of Six, regional impressionists known for their use of bright colors. He designed posters for the Southern Pacific Railroad and, in 1927 and 1928, created posters featuring various tourist destinations served by Southern Pacific routes, among them the Lake Tahoe region and the Alamo.

Sascha Maurer's vacationer wears sunglasses that reflect the pleasures of Atlantic City.

An elegant British luxury train hurtles into the countryside in Frank Newbould's 1935 design.

CHARLES LOUPOT

FRENCH *(1892–1962)*

A master lithographer and poster maker who started his career in Switzerland, Loupot's early work includes posters for all the usual products such as cigarettes and automobiles; he also created fashion posters. He became famous for trademark characters, such as the Valentine Man and the new Cointreau Man. One of the "Musketeers," he was also one of the cofounders, with Cassandre, of the Alliance Graphique Studio in 1930. His fine lithography and pure style is evident in posters such as those for Mira Blades and Van Heusen collars.

SASCHA MAURER

AMERICAN *(1897–1961)*

Known for travel posters, including many ski posters depicting American locations, and for Flexible Flyer wooden skis.

ALPHONSE MUCHA

CZECHOSLOVAKIAN *(1860–1939)*

Painter, designer, lithographer, author, and poster artist, Mucha's name is synonymous with flowery beauties in the Art Nouveau taste. His 1894 poster "Gismonda" for Sarah Bernhardt endeared him to the entertainer, and thereafter he designed her posters, as well as decor and costumes for her plays. Other posters include designs for champagne producers Ruinart

and Moet & Chandon, Cognac Bisquit, and Job rolling papers, and "Monaco–Monte Carlo" for the PLM (Paris-Lyons-Méditerranée) railway.

FRANK NEWBOULD

ENGLISH *(1887–1950)*

Creator of posters for the Great Western Railway, the Orient Line, and the Empire Marketing Board, Newbould designed a series of "East Coast Frolics" railway posters for the London and North Eastern Railway (L.N.E.R.), each with a line suggesting reasons to visit "The Drier Side" (the east coast of England) and advising "Travel Cheaply by L.N.E.R." Each poster features an anthropomorphic creature as the pitchman, among them

A scantily clad Valkyrie lands cycling in Pal's 1898 poster for Cycles Clément.

A very rare French version of Leslie Ragan's evocation of North America's splendors.

a dancing goose accompanied on the piano by a mouse in pointed hat, a golf-playing rabbit, a frog with a fishing pole, and a dancing fish accompanied by a banjo playing crab.

PAL (JEAN DE PALEOLOGUE)
ROMANIAN *(1860–1942)*

Painter, illustrator, and poster artist, Pal worked for the *New York Herald, Strand Magazine,* and *Vanity Fair,* as well as for the newspapers *Le Frou-Frou* and *La Plume.* His poster designs include "Cusenier Peach Brandy" (1897) and Rayon D'Or lamps (1895), along with several bicycle posters including Deesse (1898) and Falcon (1898).

MAXFIELD PARRISH
AMERICAN *(1870–1966)*

One of the most famous illustrators of the twentieth century, Parrish was a prolific producer of book illustrations, advertisements, paintings, and prints. His posters include "The Adlake Camera" (1895) and "Harper's Weekly" (1897). Parrish is enormously popular with collectors today. His work is still being reproduced.

TOM PURVIS
ENGLISH *(1888–1959)*

A marine painter whose first poster, in 1907, was for Dewar's Whisky, Purvis designed several posters for the London and Northeastern Railway (including a 1935 example entitled

"East Coast Joys" featuring a family frolicking at the beach) and the London Underground. His 1935 poster for the clothier Austin Reed of Regent Street is a sleek rendition in a distinctive pastel palette of an elegant man, overcoat slung over his arm, adjusting a flower on his lapel.

LESLIE DARRELL RAGAN
AMERICAN *(1897–1972)*

Known for cityscapes and train posters and a distinctive Art Deco style, Ragan's posters include "Rockefeller Center" (1932), "New York" (circa 1935), and "The New 20th Century Limited" (1938) for the New York Central system.

OURS...to fight for

FREEDOM FROM WANT

LINCOLN CENTER
FOR THE PERFORMING ARTS

PHILHARMONIC HALL
OPENING SEPTEMBER 23, 1962

One of the Norman Rockwell Four Freedoms poster images that defined wholesome American family life.

A graceful, angelic musician dominates Ben Shahn's 1962 poster for Lincoln Center.

NORMAN ROCKWELL
AMERICAN (1894–1978)

A prolific twentieth-century illustrator, Norman Rockwell defined the American character with his paintings and illustrations. He became nearly synonymous with the *Saturday Evening Post,* producing 324 covers. Although he was a more productive illustrator than poster artist, Rockwell did create posters for Coca-Cola, Maxwell House Coffee, the Red Cross, and the National Reserve.

WALTER SCHNACKENBERG
GERMAN (1880–1961)

The creator of many posters, among them the 1920 "Odeon Casino,"

featuring an elegant couple dancing. Schnackenberg had a way with color. In "Odeon," the man wears a monocle and is dressed in black on a black background. His form is defined only by touches of gray and his swaying dance partner's white skin, vibrant red glove, and elaborate yellow and feathered boa.

BEN SHAHN *AMERICAN,*
B. LITHUANIA (1898–1969)

Best known as a painter and photographer (see page 347), Shahn also designed posters, including a 1942 war poster featuring a group of workers, their hands up, standing before a brick wall bearing the Vichy government's official decree. The poster's message

reads: "We French workers warn you, defeat means slavery, starvation, death."

OTIS SHEPARD
AMERICAN (1893-1969)

His posters include the well-known 1930s image for Wrigley's Spearmint Gum.

THÉOPHILE-ALEXANDRE STEINLEN
FRENCH, B. SWITZERLAND (1859–1923)

In the early 1880s, Steinlen was an illustrator for the magazine *Chat Noir,* where he met Toulouse-Lautrec, Verlaine, and other notable Parisian artists. His pseudonyms include

Incongruously, a French soldier seems to leave the front to publicize a concert in a 1916 poster by Théophile Alexandre Steinlen.

The British Travel Association chose maritime artist Norman Wilkinson to create this evocative fishing poster from a series of travel posters featuring leisure-time activities.

Caillou and Petite Pierre and among his early works is "Affiche Charles Verneau" (1896). Considered one of the most important poster artists of the late nineteenth and early twentieth centuries, Steinlen created propaganda posters for the French government during World War I.

HENRI DE TOULOUSE-LAUTREC
FRENCH (1864–1901)

Son of an aristocratic family, Toulouse-Lautrec lived in the Montmartre section of Paris and frequented dance halls, cabarets, and bars, where he enjoyed the friendship of the artists, dancers, and flaneurs who defined Paris nightlife. A great painter, he also produced thirty-one posters. His classics include "Moulin Rouge" for the entertainer La Goulue, several each for performers Jane Avril and Aristide Bruant, posters advertising the book *Reine de Joie* and, quirkily, "Confetti" for a producer of that festive paper product.

FERNAND TOUSSAINT
BELGIAN (1873–1956)

Painter and poster artist, Toussaint's poster for the Brussels Commerce Fair has been reused several times over the past decades. Earlier works include the Art Nouveau–style "Le Sillon," featuring a romantic image of a delicate beauty bringing in the harvest, designed for an 1895 art journal.

RENE VINCENT
FRENCH (1879–1936)

Illustrator and painter Vincent is best known for automobile posters for Peugeot and Bugatti, as well as for posters for Shell petroleum products. For Porto Ramos-Pinto, he created a fantasy poster depicting Cupid offering a glass of port to a young couple.

NORMAN WILKINSON
ENGLISH (1878–1971)

A specialist in maritime images who designed posters for the SR, LNER, and LMS railways, among them, one example depicting St. Paul's Cathedral from the Thames.

ILLUSTRATION ART

NEWLY APPRECIATED

Magazine illustrations were once the neglected children of the art world. *Antiques Roadshow* appraiser Rudy Franchi explained to a visitor at the Louisville *Roadshow*—who had brought in an original illustration that her grandfather had painted for *Country Home* magazine in 1930—that as recently as the 1980s, many twentieth-century original illustrations created for books and magazines could be bought at auction for small sums. But recently there has been a boom in illustration art. Over the last five years, galleries featuring only illustrations have sprung up in New York City and elsewhere. "Not long ago, this might have been considered hack commercial work," Franchi said. "But it's original artwork, and it's now being taken seriously by the art community." Using the *Country Home* illustration as an example, he continued. "You're looking at a piece that only a few years ago would have sold for one hundred dollars," he said. Today, though, "something like this would sell for four or five thousand dollars."

For the cover of every *Saturday Evening Post* or *Collier's* magazine in your attic or stacked in boxes at your neighbor's yard sale; for every *Amazing Spider-Man* or *Crypt of Terror* comic book; for almost every non-photographic illustration or advertisement you've ever seen, an original painting once existed. An artist sat at his easel or drawing board, faced that blank canvas, picked up his brush, and painted what his mind's eye saw. And although that artist may have been well paid, after his work was finished and the canvas or artist's board was delivered to the magazine or advertising agency, his painting had next to no value—it was the means to a commercial end. In fact, it's been estimated that some 90 percent of

Although best known for his pre–World War I beauties, called "Gibson Girls," Charles Dana Gibson maintained his status as a superstar illustrator for many years. Here, a 1924 drawing for Life *magazine.*

all original illustration art was simply thrown away. But today, that original art for books, newspapers, magazines, calendars, comic books, posters, and other mass-produced printed items from the late nineteenth century through the twentieth has attracted thousands of collectors. There are even galleries and major auctions now devoted solely to exhibiting and selling original illustration art.

This is easy to understand, for many of these illustrations were, in fact, wonderfully well-imagined and well-executed paintings created by highly skilled artists. What's hard to comprehend is why it took so long for them to be appreciated. Certainly the publishers, magazine art directors, and advertisers who commissioned these works knew that they represented effort, imagination, and money. But their importance always seemed to be only in their use, which is why so many illustrators never even bothered to pick up their work after a project had been completed, and why they often threw out or painted over their own work—it had served its purpose and could not be reused. Not all of the material was thrown away, naturally. Sometimes, employees of advertising agencies or publishing houses took a fancy to this or that "used" illustration and rescued it from the waste bin, and sometimes the artist gave a favorite original to a friend.

Although a few of the great artists of every era illustrated magazines and books and were very well known to the public, many illustrators labored in obscurity. Most art critics considered the illustrator to be merely a commercial artist—he didn't create, he simply took direction. In recent years, however, there has been a growing recognition of illustration art as a worthwhile art form in itself, and there has never been more interest in the field than there is today. At a recent auction, the original of *Rosie the Riveter*, painted by Norman Rockwell for a *Saturday Evening Post* cover in 1943, sold for $4,959,500.

A BRIEF HISTORY

The improvements in printing and engraving in the late nineteenth century led to a revolution in illustration and publishing. For the first time, accurate reproductions of an artist's work could be produced for mass circulation. The public clamored for newspapers, magazines, and books, attracted by the pictures as well as by the text, and the advertisers soon recognized the potential of illustrated publications as an effective means to market their products.

Illustrators created hundreds of thousands of images for use inside and on the covers of books and magazines, and for advertisements. Some transcended the boundaries of commercial art to

PROVENANCE

Because so few works of illustration art come with a history of their previous ownership, or even with a history of gallery or auction sales, provenance is not often known. It is worth noting, however, that for a finished printed work, there ought to be—somewhere—a magazine cover, book jacket, or advertisement that reproduces the image. This can be worth tracking down. A painting or drawing that can be tied to a specific magazine or book gives greater weight to that piece, can help identify the artist, and can place it in the time period in which it was created.

F. X. Leyendecker, the brother of J.C., painted this fetching modern housewife riding her vacuum cleaner through the night skies for the cover of Life *magazine.*

become enormously popular. For example, illustrator Charles Dana Gibson was so influential that his work came to define the standard of beauty for his era. What pre–World War I young woman didn't want to look like a "Gibson Girl," the supermodel of her time? In the twenties, Maxfield Parrish's neoclassical beauties were "all the rage"; his lush renderings of toga-clad nymphs in prints such as *Daybreak* and *Dawn* personified the romantic

THE NATIONAL MUSEUM OF AMERICAN ILLUSTRATION

Illustration art has come into its own in recent years. Maxfield Parrish's painting *Daybreak*—reproduced more often than Leonardo Da Vinci's *Last Supper*—recently sold for $4.3 million. Norman Rockwell's iconic boys and girls were exhibited in New York City's Guggenheim Museum in 2001, and this would have been unthinkable just a decade ago. Laurence and Judy Goffman Cutler, cofounders of the National Museum of American Illustration in Newport, Rhode Island, believe that ordinary Americans have always felt comfortable with illustrations. "Illustrations are really the most American of American art," Cutler asserts. One example at the Museum is *Miss Liberty*, a 1943 Norman Rockwell *Saturday Evening Post* cover depicting a proud Miss Liberty in striped trousers and a white-starred blouse wielding tools left behind

Norman Rockwell captured the thrill of collecting for the Saturday Evening Post, *1937.*

by American soldiers. "She's one of the first images of women's liberation," Cutler says. "And this is an image that captured a pivotal moment in our history."

The Museum has in its collection some 2,000 works by American illustrators, including 124 by Norman Rockwell—along with his first paint box—and the largest collection anywhere of the original work of Maxfield Parrish.

Other important museum collections of illustration art include the Society of Illustrators Museum of American Illustration in New York, the New Britain Museum of American Art in New Britain, Connecticut, the Delaware Art Museum in Wilmington, Delaware, and the Brandywine Museum in Chadds Ford, Pennsylvania. The Library of Congress in Washington, D.C., also has important holdings.

aesthetic for the post–World War I era, and, coincidentally, provided more color prints for an adoring public than the work of any previous artist. Like most illustrators, Parrish worked in more than one field, producing posters, children's books, murals, calendar art, and advertisements. General Electric alone published more than 20 million Parrish calendars. And more than 250,000 copies of the familiar image of *Daybreak* were hung in parlors, hotels, and soda fountains throughout the country. The era of Gibson and Parrish (not to mention Howard Pyle, N. C. Wyeth, and J. C. Leyendecker) that spans from the 1880s to World War I has been called the golden age of American illustration art. In the 1930s, photography began to replace illustrations, and by the 1960s many of the magazines that were once filled with illustrations failed, having lost their audience to television.

THE PULPS

Another market for the work of illustrators were the "pulps." These inexpensive magazines and books, printed on cheap pulp paper (from which they got their name), were filled with detective, romance, western, adventure, and science fiction stories. Pulp magazines and books were published from the turn of the twentieth century to the mid-1950s, when the advent of comic books, paperback fiction, and television (yet again) displaced them.

At one time, pulp magazines were seen as cheap, disposable reads, and usually the pulps were at the bottom of the pay scale for both authors and illustrators, although in recent years, book collectors have rediscovered early works by some of the most popular and well-respected authors of the twentieth-century tucked away in pulp publications, authors like Dashiell Hammett and Isaac Asimov. This reexamination has also extended to illustrators. Growing numbers of collectors seek the original illustrations produced for western, detective, romance, and, in

In Frank R. Paul's 1940 vision of life on Pluto, as painted for the back cover of Fantastic Adventures, *bats help to harvest the planet's resources.*

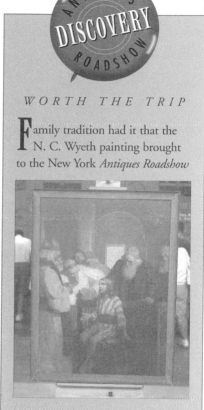

WORTH THE TRIP

Family tradition had it that the N. C. Wyeth painting brought to the New York *Antiques Roadshow* by a visitor from Ohio had been given to his grandfather by the artist. In the 1960s his aunt decided to sell it, and when the visitor learned of this he and his wife drove to Boston to recover the painting.

N. C. Wyeth, famous for his illustrations for a series of children's books, also painted western and literary scenes, landscapes, and religious subjects, explained appraiser Debra Force. This work was created to illustrate a story in *Harper's Monthly* called "The Lost Boy," by Henry van Dyke. "It's in really terrific condition," Force said. The market for Wyeth's work has gone up considerably over the past fifteen years, she observed, and the visitor-rescued family treasure might fetch as much as $250,000 today.

PAPERBACK COVER ART

Beginning with the paper-covered novels produced for the armed forces during World War II, paperback editions of classic literature became increasingly popular after the cessation of hostilities ended paper restrictions. To keep up with the new demand for paperback books, novels were written specifically for this market and, like the pulps, these soon coalesced around specialized genres—detective stories, gothic novels, love stories ("bodice rippers"), science fiction, and westerns. Providing cover illustrations for such books offered a broad new market for artists specializing in one or more of these categories. Paperback cover art is becoming increasingly collectible and may ultimately become even more important to art enthusiasts.

particular, science fiction pulps. But pulp art is not a collecting area for the impatient. Because of its rarity, collectors may have to wait months—even years—for a chance to add to their collection.

COMIC STRIPS

Comic strips were born in the late nineteenth century with the introduction of R. F. Outcault's *The Yellow Kid* in the *New York World* (see page 60). This comic strip gave such a boost to that newspaper's circulation that soon papers across the United States were looking for cartoonists to produce more and more "funnies."

Fortunately for collectors, a lot of strip art has survived. Newspaper syndicates often retained the original artwork and returned it to the artists. Frequently, fans wrote to their favorite artists and the artists sent them an original strip in return. Charles Shultz, for example, sent *Peanuts* dailies to hundreds of fans in answer to their letters. These tokens were treasured and many have survived. But there is very little strip art from before 1925, and the small amount that exists even if it is less well-known material—commands huge prices. There are thousands of strips, however, from the 1950s through the 1970s.

In the world of strip-art collecting, there are two self-explanatory terms: dailies and Sunday pages. The larger Sunday pages are more usually desirable than the more common dailies. In some cases, comic strips—and comic books—were drawn for decades, and over that period several artists may have worked on the same series. Collectors have their favorites and prices can vary from artist to artist.

A meticulously detailed panel from the 1943 Sunday pages of Hal Foster's Prince Valiant.

COMIC BOOKS

In a way, comic books are a combination of pulp books and comic strips. As Jerry Weist—an author and comic-book consultant for Sotheby's—notes, there is a link between a 1910 Tarzan of the Apes swinging from tree to tree by jungle vine in early pulps and Spider-Man, decades later, using his nets of web to swing from building to building in the concrete jungle.

From the Golden Age of comic books, a 1947 issue of Sensation Comics *featured the Amazon-like Wonder Woman.*

Comic books trace their origins to bound black and white reprints of collections of previously published comic strips that were issued as early as 1910. In 1934 the collection *Carnival of Comics* was published. It closely resembled the modern comic book—although it was bit thicker—and it was quickly followed by other collections such as *Famous Funnies* and *Comics on Parade.* Collectors consider *Action* #1 of 1939, which introduced Superman, to be the beginning of the Golden Age of comic books, which lasted until 1949. (Early reprint comics, such as *Detective Comics,* eventually incorporated original material as well; *Detective Comics* #27, issued after *Action* #1 in 1939, introduced "The Batman.")

Very little original comic book artwork survives from before 1946. Out of the hundreds of comic books produced in this era, it is believed that fewer than 250 original covers have survived. Although interior pages are also avidly sought, covers are what most collectors crave.

In recent years, mass-produced comic books have become a huge collecting area, and with this increasing popularity has come the desire by many collectors to own the original artwork. In fact, more than a dozen key issues of certain comic books have sold for more than $200,000. Some original artwork seems inexpensive by comparison.

AN ILLUSTRATOR IN THE FAMILY

Appraiser Marsha Malinowski viewed some prime examples of original children's book illustrations at the Boston *Antiques Roadshow.* A man brought in several pieces drawn by his great-aunt, Mildred Boyle, a freelance illustrator who painted for a wide assortment of greeting card manufacturers, magazines, and children's books. She collaborated, as well, with Helen Sewell on some of Laura Ingalls Wilder's classic *Little House on the Prairie* books, when Sewell was too busy to complete the work. The visitor brought in Boyle's original illustrations from other books, such as Wilder's *On the Banks of Plum Creek,* along with some first editions of books inscribed by Boyle to the visitor's younger sister. "It's not often that I see children's illustrations in such good shape," Malinowski said. "They're hard to come by." The value of these books and illustrations? "Because it's a very cohesive whole, I'd value this collection at $6,000 to $8,000," she said.

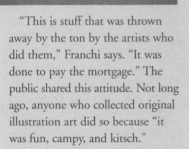

HAVE A 'GANSETT

Artists almost always signed their paintings. Illustrators, however, were less likely to do so.

"This is stuff that was thrown away by the ton by the artists who did them," Franchi says. "It was done to pay the mortgage." The public shared this attitude. Not long ago, anyone who collected original illustration art did so because "it was fun, campy, and kitsch."

Well, the ugly ducklings of the art world have grown into valuable swans. "Now it's all respectable because it's considered pop culture," Franchi explains. The changed status could be seen in an oil painting Franchi viewed at the Providence *Antiques Roadshow* that served as a maquette for a 1940s billboard. The painting depicted a man, a few Narragansett beer bottles in hand, with the caption, "Everybody's saying—'Hi neighbor, have a 'Gansett.'" What might have sold for $10 or $20 just two decades ago, now sells for what Franchi calls "high art" prices. His assessment: "I'd put a value on this piece at between $800 and $1,000."

COLLECTING ILLUSTRATION ART

Illustration art is rich in subject matter and, in its broadest sense, can include illustrations from children's books and family magazines, advertisements, pin-ups and glamour art, and pulp magazines. Collectors also covet original cartoons and comic strip and comic book art. They usually concentrate on a genre or, even more specifically, an artist, and usually refer to their area of interest by its specific name rather than generally as "illustration art."

Despite the enormous amount of original illustration art that has been lost, experts believe (and hope) that there is still a great deal of this unique Americana tucked away in basements and attics—where they also hope it's dry and cool. This means that this is a field in which there is still very fine hunting. Although important illustrators have been identified, the field is underresearched, and there are still hundreds of works of unknown, potentially great artists in those (dry, cool) attics, longing to be found.

EVALUATING ILLUSTRATION ART

The importance of an individual example of illustration art can be determined by considering a number of different elements—who the artist is, what the subject is, and other distinctive features.

ARTIST

The reputation and current desirability of a given artist are very important to an original illustration's value in the market today. Although the important names in the field are relatively few, many of the well-known artists were quite prolific, and many, as well (Dean Cornwell is one example) made several preliminary sketches before executing their final rendering.

The majority of illustration art, however, is the work of little-known or unknown artists, and in that case, other factors—such as subject, size, and color—come into play. If an unknown artist has produced a book cover for a collectible subject (e.g., Tarzan), for instance, this subject may be of more importance to collectors than the identity of the artist who painted it.

For comic-book art, a common practice is to have the page drawn in pencil and finished in pen by different artists.

SUBJECT

With the possible exception of pulp art, pictures of cheerful subjects are more popular than those of gloomy ones. Pretty girls are always especially desirable, and pretty, seductive girls—like the one pictured in the "pinup" style on Enoch Bolles's 1937 magazine cover for *Breezy Stories*—usually win hands-down. The original Bolles artwork recently sold at auction for $30,800. A baseball cartoon (two umpires arguing) by *New Yorker* cartoonist Peter Arno brought $22,000. While Arno's cartoons are sought-after, in that instance, the baseball subject was more important.

For original comic artwork, the character portrayed is extremely important, because many collectors choose comics based on their attachment to particular heroes—or villains—depicted in the strip or book. *Tarzan, Flash Gordon,* Segar's *Popeye, Buck Rogers,* and *Krazy Kat* are the strips that collectors most ardently seek. The content—the story line or theme of a

A Dean Cornwell 1947 noir illustration for the Saturday Evening Post—*a long way from Norman Rockwell.*

© UFS

He Tarzan, you collector: a 1942 Sunday strip drawn by Burne Hogarth.

An original illustration does not look like a completed canvas by Rembrandt or Van Gogh. Many pieces of illustration art will appear unfinished to the untrained eye. The blank spaces on completed illustration art are intentional; they were left blank so that a title or text could be dropped in during the printing process.

A 1965 Family Circle *magazine cover by Hilary Knight, best known as the illustrator of the* Eloise *series of children's books.*

particular piece—is also very important, because this is, after all, narrative art, and the story matters.

SIGNATURE

Perhaps because of their commercial nature, and particularly in advertising, works of illustration art are not always signed. The numbers of "rough drafts" (sketches) the artists made before starting a final rendering has much to do with this. If they were, as these craftsmen believed they were, creating disposable art, then certainly their sketches weren't worth signing.

On the other hand, much of this material *is* stamped with a company name or the publisher's name, and sometimes there are penciled notations made by the printer or designer. These can be helpful in determining the artist. The presence of a signature enhances a piece's value, but possibly even more depends on the appeal of the piece itself.

COLOR

If an illustration was to be printed in black and white in the magazine or book, it was painted en grisaille (in shades of gray). Some illustrations were painted in a second color as well (for example, blue and black). Artists were commissioned to do either color or grisaille, and they were paid more for color work. (Except for the commissions of certain advertisers, magazine covers paid most.) Collectors inevitably prefer color paintings to grisaille.

For pulp illustrations, all-color cover art is usually more desirable than interior artwork, which was often executed in black and white. There are estimated to be ten black-and-white interior illustrations for every color cover. Unsurprisingly, the artists put their best efforts into the cover, and frequently the interior illustrations were produced very quickly. Collectors should value interior artwork accordingly.

CONDITION

Unlike posters and photographs, which are multiples, original illustration art is unique. Thus the criteria for condition generally follow those used for paintings and drawings. Notations on the front or back of the piece made by the artist, the art director, or the editor, however, may actually add to the appeal of a work, provided that they do not detract from the image.

The Illustrators

The following are descriptions of some of the best-known illustration artists, with separate categories for general illustrators, children's book illustrators, comic strip artists, comic book artists, and pulp illustrators. Although the emphasis is on American artists, a few of the more collectible European illustrators are included, as well.

GENERAL ILLUSTRATORS

CHARLES ADDAMS
AMERICAN *(1912–1988)*

A witty cartoonist for the *New Yorker* magazine whose specialty was pseudo-sinister characters. If there is one word that is used most often to describe his work, it is "macabre." Although he worked mainly for the *New Yorker,* Addams also created illustrations for *TV Guide* and *Collier's* magazines and produced several books.

Classic Charles Addams: "May I ask who's doing your repair work?"

PETER ARNO
AMERICAN *(1904–1968)*

Born Curtis Arnoux Peters Jr., Arno started working for the *New Yorker* in 1925—an association that would last more than forty years. He also produced cartoons for advertisements, especially through the 1930s. His sly, sophisticated wit often lampooned New York society businessmen and "ladies who lunch."

A 1928 cover by Peter Arno, one of the New Yorker's early, defining artists.

GEORGE WESLEY BELLOWS
AMERICAN *(1882–1995)*

A painter of the Ashcan school (which took as its subject matter the rapidly expanding immigrant population of the lower East Side, entertainers, and sporting events—subjects that were outside the norm at that time), Bellows is particularly well known for his paintings and lithographs of boxers. He also created illustrations for magazines such as *The Century* and *Hearst's International.*

CHARLES LIVINGSTON BULL
AMERICAN *(1874–1932)*

Bull's expertise as a taxidermist and his work as an expert on animal and bird anatomy at the National Museum of Natural History in Washington, D.C., served him well. He specialized in illustrations of birds and animals for books and magazines in a style influenced by Japanese woodblock prints. For many years he lived near the Bronx Zoo to be close to his models.

An expertly rendered cougar by Charles Livingston Bull, 1906.

CHARLES EDWARD CHAMBERS
AMERICAN *(1883–1941)*

Produced illustrations for magazines such as *Redbook, Harper's Monthly,* and *Cosmopolitan,* and books by authors including W. Somerset Maugham, Pearl Buck, and Louis Bromfield. He also painted several billboard designs for Chesterfield cigarettes and Palmolive soap. One of Chambers' best-known commissions was a series of portraits of great musicians for the piano manufacturer Steinway & Sons.

HOWARD CHANDLER CHRISTY
AMERICAN *(1873–1952)*

Christy accompanied the U. S. troops to Cuba, and his drawings illustrated articles in *Scribner's Magazine* and *Leslie's Weekly.* He is best known for portraits of beautiful women, women who became known as "Christy girls."

Howard Chandler Christy's illustration for his World War II–era "Bill of Rights" poster.

The Rendezvous *by Dean Cornwell.*

DEAN CORNWELL AMERICAN *(1892–1960)*

Dean Cornwell's work appeared in magazines and advertisements. He also produced several large and important murals, including one for General Motors for the 1939 World's Fair. In addition to being highly prolific, he produced well-drafted preliminary sketches in preparation for his fully realized work in pencil, pastels, and oil. Many of these, fortunately, still exist.

ERIC (CARL OSCAR AUGUST ERICSON)
AMERICAN *(1891–1958)*

Eric's clients included Marshall Field in Chicago, the *Dry Goods Economist* in New York, and *Vogue* magazine in Paris, where he served as a staff illustrator. He became particularly well known for fashion illustrations, and lived in Paris until the outbreak of World War II, when he returned to the United States and worked for several American publications.

ANTON OTTO FISCHER
AMERICAN, B. GERMANY
(1881–1962)

Best known for his maritime illustrations, Fischer had a knowledge of the sea that

was born of experience. He was a sailor for eight years as a young man. For 48 years, the German-born Fischer produced illustrations for *The Saturday Evening Post;* when World War II broke out, he also worked as an artist for the U.S. Coast Guard. Among his works are illustrations for many of the adventure stories of Jack London, commissioned by *Everybody's Magazine.*

HARRISON FISHER
AMERICAN *(1875–1934)*

Son of the landscape painter Hugh Antoine Fisher. While still in his teens, he drew illustrations for the *San Francisco Call* and later for *The Examiner.* He became a staff artist for

Puck magazine and built his reputation on illustrations of beautiful women—rivaling Gibson and Christie. Fisher created covers for *Cosmopolitan* before specializing in portraits.

Harrison Fisher's illustration The Message, *from the book* Bachelor Belles *(1908).*

JAMES MONTGOMERY FLAGG *AMERICAN (1877 1960)*

Flagg is inevitably identified with the World War I poster picturing Uncle Sam (see page 441), but he was also responsible for a huge body of work that includes illustrations for books and magazines and portraits. He drew a cartoon called *Nervy Nat* and gave form to Jeeves, the prototypical butler created by P. G. Wodehouse.

A. B. FROST
AMERICAN (1851–1928)

Arthur Burdett Frost worked as an illustrator at *Harper's,* where his colleagues included Howard Pyle and Edwin Austin Abbey, and was known for illustrations of rural America. His honest, often humorous renderings connote an understanding of human nature. He is best known for illustrating the Uncle Remus stories by Joel Chandler Harris.

CHARLES DANA GIBSON
AMERICAN (1867–1944)

In addition to creating the beautiful, "modern" Gibson Girl, Gibson was a commentator and satirist of society. He was also the president of the Society of American Illustrators and the head of the Division of Pictorial Publicity that aided the war effort (see page 440).

WILLIAM J. GLACKENS
AMERICAN (1870–1938)

Glackens honed his skills sketching crowds while working for Philadelphia newspapers. Moving into magazine illustration, he gained recognition for his sketches of the Spanish-American War, produced for *McClure's* magazine. Later in his career, he concentrated on painting in the Impressionist manner. He was a member of The Eight—a group of painters that in 1908 exhibited independently from the National Academy.

William Glackens's The Wedding Guests, *for the* Saturday Evening Post, *circa 1895.*

The brilliance of Al Hirschfeld is shown in this caricature of Bing Crosby.

AL HIRSCHFELD
AMERICAN (1903–2003)

"How many Ninas?" is the question that readers of *The New York Times* asked for decades. Hirschfeld's pen-and-ink caricatures of stars of stage and screen would appear with the name of the artist's daughter, Nina, incorporated inconspicuously within the illustration, usually several times. Hirschfeld's credits are long and varied; he illustrated numerous major magazines and newspapers, worked as a theater correspondent, and designed posters for Hollywood movies. Although Hirschfeld's work is predominantly pen and ink, he also has worked extensively in color. Al Hirschfeld © The Margo Feiden Galleries Ltd. New York.

J. C. LEYENDECKER
AMERICAN, B. GERMANY
(1874–1951)

Joseph Christian Leyendecker, whose first *Saturday Evening Post* cover appeared in 1899, was Norman Rockwell's hero. Rockwell told of waiting at a New York suburban train station to catch a glimpse of his idol, and of walking behind him in the street to "inhale" what he could of Leyendecker's aura and talent. Although Leyendecker created more than 300 *Saturday Evening Post* covers in his career, his New Year's Baby series is probably most beloved. His advertising work includes the Arrow Collar Man, the 1920s quintessential dapper, handsome gentleman.

J. C. Leyendecker ushers in 1939 for the Saturday Evening Post.

ANDREW LOOMIS
AMERICAN (1891–1957)

Loomis created editorial and advertising art for *This Week* and *The Saturday Evening Post.* He also authored several books, including *Creative Illustration* and *Fun with a Pencil.*

Pierrot's Serenade, *circa 1908, by Maxfield Parrish for* Collier's *magazine.*

MAXFIELD PARRISH *AMERICAN* *(1870–1966)*

Perhaps the most successful artist of the 1920s, Parrish painted his amazingly detailed, brilliantly colored scenes with transparent pigments separated by layers of varnish, each of which dried for days between coats. He is best known for nudes and ethereal figures in imaginative fantasy-world settings of mystical landscapes. Highly prolific, he created works for magazines, children's books, and advertisements, as well as calendars, prints, and paintings. His work was so popular that magazine illustrations and calendar art were often cut out and framed. These can still be bought today at reasonable prices—less than those for his mass-produced prints, often of the same or similar themes. There are always more collectors for Parrish's work than there are prints, prompting numerous reproductions, while original paintings have soared well beyond the reach of most collectors.

HOWARD PYLE
AMERICAN (1853–1911)

A giant in the field of illustration, Pyle had a profound effect, not only with his illustrations but also through his teaching. He illustrated and wrote the classic children's books *The Adventures of Robin Hood, The Story of King Arthur and His Knights,* and *Howard Pyle's Book of Pirates,* which, along with numerous others that he illustrated, are still being read. His illustrations are superb works of art that seem as bold and exciting today as when they were created. As an educator, he taught at the Drexel Institute, in Philadelphia, and the Art Students League, in New York City, and conducted special seminars at Chadds Ford, Pennsylvania, and Wilmington, Delaware. His students include N. C. Wyeth, Jessie Willcox Smith, and Frank Schoonover.

Howard Pyle's dramatic Walking the Plank, *for* Harper's Monthly, *1887.*

ROBERT RIGGS
AMERICAN (1896–1970)

A meticulous lithographer and painter, Riggs worked primarily for the New York advertising agency N. W. Ayer. In addition to his work in illustration, he is known for lithographs of prize fighters and the circus.

NORMAN ROCKWELL
AMERICAN (1894–1978)

The dean of American illustrators, and internationally renowned, Norman Rockwell is famous for the 300-plus magazine covers he created for *The*

Saturday Evening Post. These works are pure slices of American pie, prepared with skill and served with the illustrator's wry sense of humor. Like his colleagues, he painted story illustrations for magazines, as well as advertising, calendars, books, and posters. Rockwell's original works are well beyond the pocketbook of the average collector. The 1970s saw the production of a profusion of "collectibles" based on his works, from prints to collector plates.

CHARLES M. RUSSELL
AMERICAN (1864–1926)

A self-taught artist specializing in images of the American West, Charles M. Russell lived with the Blackfoot tribe in Alberta, Canada, for several months. He produced oil paintings and bronzes as well as illustrations.

Frank Schoonover's illustration for Zane Grey's Rustlers of Silver River, *published in* The Country Gentleman, *December 1929.*

FRANK E. SCHOONOVER
AMERICAN (1877–1972)

Schoonover, a student of Howard Pyle, took adventurous trips to gain firsthand knowledge of his subjects, among them a trip to the Mississippi Bayou for the book *Lafayette, the Pirate of the*

Gulf. He illustrated several books and magazines, painted landscapes, and designed stained glass windows.

JOHN SLOAN
AMERICAN (1871–1951)

Another member of The Eight, John Sloan worked with William Glackens and George Luks at the *Philadelphia Press.* After moving to New York in 1905, he developed an interest in urban life and became known for his illustrations in radical magazines such as *The Masses* and *The Call,* although he also contributed to *McClure's, Collier's,* and *Cosmopolitan.* He eventually concentrated on painting, etching, and lithography.

JESSIE WILLCOX SMITH *AMERICAN (1863–1935)*

Smith, a kindergarten teacher, was encouraged by Howard Pyle to pursue a career in illustration. She is known for paintings of mothers and children in magazines such as Collier's *Weekly, McClure's,* and *Good Housekeeping* (nearly 200 covers), and for book illustrations of, among others, *Little Women, Heidi,* and *A Child's Garden of Verses.*

Scales, *1907, Jessie Willcox Smith's watercolor for* The Bed-Time Book.

Haddon H. Sundblom's cheerful cheese-cake for a 1950s-vintage calendar.

HADDON HUBBARD SUNDBLOM
AMERICAN *(1899–1976)*

Using a bright and lively palette, Sundblom was expert at depicting people enjoying ideally prosperous lives. In the 1920s he formed a Chicago-based studio with Howard Stevens and Edwin Henry, attracting a group of young artists such as Harry Anderson, Walter Richards, Thornton Utz, and others, often referred to as the "Sundblom Circle." He produced advertising for Palmolive soap, Proctor & Gamble, and Goodyear tires; he also created illustrations for magazine articles and calendars. Sundblom's most familiar image is the ruddy-cheeked Santa of annual Coca-Cola advertisements that he produced for more than two decades, acting in later years as his own model.

ALBERTO VARGAS
AMERICAN, B. PERU *(1896–1983)*

Alberto Vargas produced portraits of stars of the Ziegfeld Follies and similar work for Hollywood movie studios before signing with *Esquire* magazine, where his drawings of the idealized female figure frequently appeared. Although there is a wholesome glow to his beauties, Vargas girls are scantily dressed, with more than a touch of naughtiness—unlike the "proper" All-American girls of Gibson and Christy. His images fed the fantasies of the 1940s and became favorite pinups of GIs fighting World War II. Vargas images can be found on playing cards, calendars, and prints.

Gold, *a swashbuckling calendar illustration by N. C. Wyeth, 1941.*

N. C. WYETH
AMERICAN *(1882–1945)*

At the time of his death, N. C. Wyeth was among the most popular artists in America, and due to the more than 3,000 illustrations he created for magazines and books he remains so today. Particularly cherished are the illustrations of a series of some two dozen classic children's books published by Charles Scribner's Sons. Wyeth's early work emulated that of his mentor, Howard Pyle, and covered similar adventure themes such as pirates and knights. He eventually turned from illustration to painting murals, still lifes, and landscapes. Wyeth founded a dynasty of important American artists, most notably his son Andrew Wyeth and his grandson Jamie Wyeth.

CHILDREN'S BOOK ILLUSTRATORS

LUDWIG BEMELMANS
AMERICAN, B. AUSTRIA *(1898–1962)*

"In an old house in Paris. . . ." So begins Bemelmans's best-loved creation, Madeline, a series of children's books written and illustrated beginning in 1939. The Madeline books continue to be popular forty years after the artist's death. Before he wrote and illustrated books, however, Bemelmans's illustrations appeared in magazines such as the *New Yorker, Vogue,* and *Holiday.*

WALTER HARRISON CADY **AMERICAN** *(1877–1970)*

Over a long career, Harrison Cady illustrated for publications such as *The Saturday Evening Post,* and *Ladies' Home Journal.* He was an editorial artist for the *Brooklyn Eagle* and an illustrator of children's books for McLoughlin Brothers. He may be best known for illustrating *Old Mother West Wind* and for bedtime stories written by Thornton Burgess. In addition, he produced pen-and-ink political cartoons for the old *Life* magazine.

Harrison Cady's dignified duck family on the cover of the book Poor Mrs. Quack.

JEAN FRENCH *(1899–1937)* and LAURENT DE BRUNHOFF *AMERICAN, B. FRANCE (1925–)*

Babar, the elephant king, was a bedtime story created by Cecile de Brunhoff for her sons Laurent and Mathieu in 1930. Their father, Jean, created a book for the boys and then published the story with his illustrations, and followed it with more books. Jean's untimely death at the age of 37 brought an end to the series. It was, however, reestablished after World War II by his oldest son, Laurent. Jean de Brunhoff is considered to be the father of the modern children's storybook.

EDMUND DULAC

ENGLISH, B. FRANCE (1882–1953)

Dulac, one of the greatest children's-book illustrators of the early twentieth century, received a commission as a young artist to create sixty watercolors for the novels written by the Brontë sisters. The first, *Jane Eyre,* was published in 1905. Another large commission required 50 watercolor drawings to illustrate *Stories from the Arabian Nights,* which was published as a gift book in 1907; and an exhibition of the original paintings was mounted in conjunction with the release of the book. Until the outbreak of World War I, Dulac illustrated a book a year, drawing inspiration from Syrian miniatures. His style was ideal for books such as *The Rubaiyat of Omar Khayyám,* but was equally effective in such works as Nathaniel Hawthorne's *Tanglewood Tales* and *Stories from Hans Christian Andersen.*

Eastern exoticism in a 1932 magazine cover by Edmund Dulac.

A typically Seussian creature by Theodor Geisel.

THEODOR GEISEL *AMERICAN (1904–1991)*

More familiar to his adoring public as Dr. Seuss, Geisel sold his first cartoon in the late 1920s. He contributed regularly to *Judge* and also did work for the old *Life,* the old *Vanity Fair, Liberty,* and *College Humor* magazines. For many years he drew a series of comic illustrations for Flit insecticide. His first children's book, *And to Think that I Saw It on Mulberry Street,* published in 1937, was followed with a string of more than forty books filled with strange creatures and even stranger rhymes. The work of this popular author and illustrator is so desirable that even early ink drawings that have nothing to do with his books—those commissioned by magazines in the 1920s—command a premium.

HILARY KNIGHT
AMERICAN *(1926–)*

Knight's father was the book and magazine illustrator Clayton Knight, and his mother was the well-known advertising artist Katharine Sturges, who also designed fabrics and illustrated children's books. Knight has designed theater posters and illustrations for *Vanity Fair* magazine, but he is best known for his illustrations for the Eloise series of children's books, about a little girl who lives at the Plaza Hotel in New York City.

KAY NIELSEN **AMERICAN, B. DENMARK** *(1886–1957)*

Nielsen is among the greatest children's-book illustrators of the twentieth century, remarkable considering that he produced only four books of fairy tales and died in relative obscurity. His masterwork is *East of the Sun, West of the Moon,* a collection of Norwegian tales. In the 1930s he lived in California and contributed to Walt Disney's animated film *Fantasia.*

An original Kay Nielsen drawing of Bluebeard and his wife, from a 1930 collection of fairy tales.

ROSE O'NEILL
AMERICAN *(1875–1944)*

Rose O'Neill is usually remembered for her creation of the Kewpie (see page 275). So great has been the popularity of the dolls that many have forgotten that this cute character originated in stories and drawings by O'Neill for *Ladies' Home Journal* and later *Good Housekeeping.* In addition to the Kewpies, she drew illustrations for magazines such as the old *Life, Puck, McClure's,* and *Harper's.*

The best-known bunny in the world, Beatrix Potter's Peter Rabbit.

BEATRIX POTTER
ENGLISH *(1866–1943)*

Author and illustrator of the Peter Rabbit series of children's books, which have become classics. In 1893, Potter wrote a letter to a friend's sick child, and illustrated it with pictures of Flopsy, Mopsy, Cottontail, and Peter Rabbit. Seven years later she decided to turn her drawings into a book. Initially rejected by publishers, she printed the book herself with black-and-white illustrations and resubmitted it. It was

accepted and illustrated in color. She produced more than a dozen books in just thirteen years, an incredible feat. But after her marriage in 1913, she discontinued writing, with the exception of a few books based on previous work. As she later stated, "When I had nothing more to say I had the sense to stop."

A whimsical book illustration by Arthur Rackham, 1925.

ARTHUR RACKHAM
ENGLISH *(1867–1939)*

In the early 1890s, Arthur Rackham began selling illustrations to various London papers, among them *The Pall Mall Gazette, Scraps,* and *Illustrated Bits,* and he worked as a staff artist for the *Westminster Budget.* His first book illustrations were for *To the Otherside,* which dealt with travel in the United States. By the turn of the century, he had illustrated nine books, including *The Ingoldsby Legends.* In 1900 he received a commission to illustrate *The Fairy Tales of the Brothers Grimm.* The best-known edition, published in 1909, was awash in color illustrations—forty in all, with fifty-five black-and-white images as well. In 1905 he produced fifty-one watercolors to illustrate *Rip Van Winkle*. In 1906 he illustrated *Alice's Adventures in Wonderland*, going on to illustrate several books in the pre–World War I era, including J. M. Barrie's classic *Peter Pan in Kensington Gardens*. His last project was *The Wind in the Willows*, by Kenneth Grahame, in 1937.

MAURICE SENDAK
AMERICAN *(1928–)*

Maurice Sendak has illustrated books by several writers, designed sets and costumes for productions of *The Magic Flute* and *The Nutcracker*, and founded a theater company devoted to productions for children. He has written and illustrated several of his own books, including the 1963 classic *Where the Wild Things Are*. Its images are as fresh and endearing today as they where when Sendak created them.

An illustration of Maurice Sendak's fiercely lovable "Wild Thing," commissioned for a benefit auction.

PULP ILLUSTRATORS

RUDOLPH BELARSKI
AMERICAN *(1900–1983)*

Belarski was a master of the detective drama and action scene, a creator of covers that utilized color and perspective to create suspense—and draw a mass readership. His best-known works for the pulps were his aviation titles and *Operator 5*. He also created many covers for paperback books.

A fantastical Hannes Bok landscape, 1936.

HANNES BOK
AMERICAN *(1914–1964)*

Described as both the "master of macabre" and the "bad boy of science fiction," Bok—who studied under Maxfield Parrish—earned a reputation for highly stylized, almost Byzantine, figures—and for disobeying his editors. His work, which some feel was better suited to fantasy than science fiction, first debuted in *Weird Tales* in 1939.

MARGARET BRUNDAGE
AMERICAN *(1900–1976)*

Brundage was the top artist at *Weird Tales* throughout the 1930s and the lone female pulp cover artist. Brundage preferred to work with pastels, the preferred medium for women's magazines of the era. Consequently her covers appeared rich, textured, and especially lurid.

EDD (EDWARD DANIEL) CARTIER
AMERICAN *(1914–)*

Cartier did his best work during the later part of the pulp era, creating more than 800 drawings for *The Shadow*, a popular pulp that appeared from 1931 to 1949, and for John W. Campbell's *Unknown* magazine.

RAFAEL DE SOTO
AMERICAN, B. SPAIN *(1906–1992)*

De Soto's illustrations first appeared in *Wild West Weekly*, but his work for Popular Publications is probably best known, and includes more than 450 covers for titles such as *The Spider, Dime Detective, Detective Tales*, and *Black Mask*.

A lurid Raphael De Soto cover illustration from the 1940s.

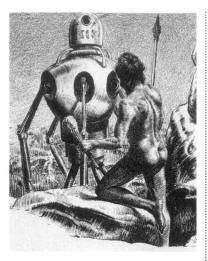

A 1938 Weird Tales *illustration from the prolific Virgil Finlay.*

VIRGIL FINLAY
AMERICAN *(1914–1971)*

Beginning in 1935, Finlay created highly detailed fantasy drawings for the interiors of *Weird Tales.* His work appeared in *Amazing Stories, Argosy, Famous Fantastic Mysteries, Fantastic Adventures, Fantastic Novels, Startling Stories, Super Science Stories,* and *Thrilling Wonder Stories.* In 1936, he produced drawings for *A Midsummer Night's Dream,* the first in a series of illustrated Shakespeare for the publishers of *Weird Tales.* Finlay is perhaps *the* most popular illustrator of science fiction and fantasy pulps and is especially known for his black-and-white work. Fortunately, a large amount of his work exists. Due to his popularity, however, it is always in demand.

FRANK R. PAUL
AMERICAN, B. AUSTRIA
(1884–1963)

Considered by many to be the father of modern science fiction illustration, Frank R. Paul's work appeared in the first issue of *Amazing Stories* (April 1926), for which he not only painted the cover but also drew the interior black-and-white artwork. He also lent his futuristic vision to such titles as *Science Wonder Stories, Air Wonder Stories, Wonder Stories,* and *Science Fiction Plus.* Paul's artwork from the twenties is extremely rare; paintings from the 1930s and 1940s are more plentiful but are avidly pursued in the market. Some 80 percent of Paul's paintings are gouache on board.

HUBERT ROGERS
AMERICAN, B. CANADA
(1898–1982)

Rogers, credited with being the driving force behind science fiction magazine design's shift away from the racy to the more serious and creative, produced paintings and pen-and-ink illustrations for such pulps as *Astounding Science Fiction.* He also worked, during the 1930s, for *Liberty* magazine.

Prospecting for gold—Hubert Rogers for Liberty *magazine, circa 1930.*

James Allen St. John's creepy cover for a 1932 issue of Weird Tales.

JAMES ALLEN ST. JOHN **AMERICAN** *(1875–1960)*

St. John is probably best known for his work on Edgar Rice Burroughs's Tarzan series. St. John's work also appeared on the covers of 1920s pulp magazines such as the *Blue Book, Green Book, Red Book,* and later series that included *The Boy's World, Amazing Stories,* and *Fantastic Adventures.* Unfortunately, many of St. John's masterworks, the cover paintings for the Edgar Rice Burroughs books, are missing, and feared lost. A collector who is lucky enough to obtain a St. John usually holds on to it. When one of his works does come on the market, it commands a premium price.

ALEX SCHOMBURG
AMERICAN *(1905–1998)*

Born in Puerto Rico, Schomburg moved to Manhattan as a teenager and, with his brothers, ran a commercial art studio. In the 1930s, he began to produce black-and-white interior illustrations and eventually moved into painting covers for Standard Publishing, which put out a series of "thrilling" pulps: *Thrilling Adventure, Thrilling Detective,* and *Thrilling Westerns.* Schomberg went on to produce covers for *Amazing Stories, Fantastic Stories,* and others, as well as for comic books. This made him one of the few commercial artists to cross over from illustrating pulps to drawing comic books.

Collectors covet original Chester Gould Dick Tracy *strips.*

CHESTER GOULD *AMERICAN* (1900–1985)

Angrily inspired by the press's love affair with Al Capone and his fellow mobsters, Gould created a good guy, Plainclothes Tracy (who would become Dick Tracy), to do battle with the mob. Prior to creating the lantern-jawed Tracy, he created such strips as *Fillum Fables* (1924) and *The Girlfriend.*

COMIC STRIP ARTISTS

MILT CANIFF
AMERICAN (1907–1988)

Nicknamed the "Rembrandt of the comic strip," Caniff created the popular forties and fifties *Terry and the Pirates, Steve Canyon,* and the World War II G.I. strip *Male Call,* featuring the provocative Miss Lace. Caniff was known for beautiful renderings and for his attention to realism, suspense, and sensuality.

Part of a World War II–era Sunday comic strip by Milton Caniff.

HAL FOSTER *AMERICAN, B. CANADA* (1892–1982)

Foster, known as the father of the adventure strip, was the original illustrator of the *Tarzan* comic strip, which debuted in 1929. His work on the strip included the epic, two-year "Egyptian" sequence, a tour de force of quality and consistency that remains unmatched today. Foster created Derek, Son of Thane, who metamorphosed into Prince Valiant, one of the most successful comic strips of all time.

GEORGE HERRIMAN
AMERICAN (1880–1944)

Herriman was the creator of *Krazy Kat,* which ran from 1916 to 1944. The strip blended artistic elements such as tone, color, and inventive inconsistency—the background location was always shifting—with Herriman's story line, which combined humor, drama, and a mix of linguistic elements from various immigrant communities.

BURNE HOGARTH
AMERICAN (1911–1996)

Hogarth was best known as the strip illustrator for *Tarzan* from 1937 to 1950, having succeeded Hal Foster, the strip's originator. Toward the end of his life, he published a number of drawing books related to sketching the human body, including *Dynamic Anatomy* (1958) and *Dynamic Figure Drawing* (1970).

A detail from the Burne Hogarth Tarzan *strip shown on page 459.*

Walt Kelly blended humor and political commentary in the ever-popular Pogo *comic trip. This example is from 1960.*

WALT KELLY *AMERICAN* *(1913–1973)*

In 1944, Kelly created the comic strip *Pogo,* an outgrowth of a character who appeared in other strips as early as 1941. *Pogo* and Kelly's editorial cartoons displayed his strong, liberal political views. His collection *We Have Met the Enemy and He is Us* highlighted how deftly he could use mere drawings and "funny" comic strips to skewer corruptions.

WINSOR MCCAY
AMERICAN, B. CANADA (1867–1934)

McCay created a number of newspaper strips, but the most famous among them were *Little Sammy Sneeze* (1904–1906) and *Dream of the Rarebit Fiend* (1904–1911). His masterpiece, however, was *Little Nemo in Slumberland* (1905), a revolutionary comic strip in which McKay broke with the prevailing formula of the time to craft a unique fantasy every week.

ALEX RAYMOND
AMERICAN (1909–1956)

Assigned in 1933 to create a science fiction strip to rival *Buck Rogers,* Raymond dreamed up *Flash Gordon,* a strip executed in Raymond's signature dry-brush, clean stroke style. Raymond also created *Rip Kirby, Jungle Jim* (with writer Don Moore), and *Secret Agent X-9* (with Dashiell Hammett).

CHARLES SCHULZ
AMERICAN (1922–2000)

Schulz created *Peanuts,* the most widely syndicated cartoon strip in history. Charlie Brown, Snoopy, and Schulz's angst-ridden gang first appeared in 1950 and were consistently drawn by Schulz until his retirement in 1999.

An early (1936) episode of Alex Raymond's Flash Gordon.

E. C. SEGAR
AMERICAN (1984–1938)

Segar created the *Thimble Theatre* series in the 1920s to follow the adventures of sister and brother Olive and Castor Oyl and their friend, Ham Gravy. The spinach-loving sailor, Popeye, joined the crew in the late 1920s, becoming its star and catapulting Segar's strip to fame.

E. C. Segar's Thimble Theatre *strip in 1933, before it was renamed* Popeye.

COMIC BOOK ARTISTS

NEAL ADAMS
AMERICAN (1941–)

Adams began at DC and Marvel comics in the late 1960s. His work on *Batman* and *X-Men* is his best known, but he also contributed to *Superman, Deadman,* and *The Green Lantern.*

CARL BARKS
AMERICAN (1901–2000)

Barks drew the adventures of Donald Duck and his nephews, Hewey, Dewey, and Lewey, from the forties through the sixties. In 1947, he created Scrooge McDuck.

In addition to creating comic books, Robert Crumb also drew the cover illustration for Big Brother and the Holding Company's classic record album, Cheap Thrills.

ROBERT CRUMB
AMERICAN (1943–)

Crumb is the weird genius behind such notorious and edgy comics as *Fritz the Cat* and *Mr. Natural.* In 1967, Crumb created the entire first issue of *Zap,* which is highly collectible.

JACK DAVIS
AMERICAN (1924–)

In the 1950s, Davis worked on the vividly horrific comics *The Vault of Horror* and *Two-Fisted Tales.* Davis also veered towards the irreverent, working at *MAD* magazine and on such comics as *Little Annie Fanny* and *Yak Yak.*

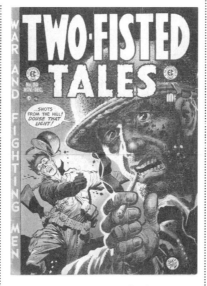

All-too-realistic G.I.'s under fire in a Jack Davis–illustrated comic book.

STEVE DITKO
AMERICAN (1927–)

Ditko was the first of the artists to work on *The Amazing Spider-Man,* and many believe that his was the definitive version of the character. Ditko also worked on such titles as *Doctor Strange, Tales of the Mysterious Traveler, Captain Atom,* and *The Question.*

Will Eisner's The Spirit *on the cover of a 1942 Sunday supplement.*

WILL EISNER
AMERICAN (1917)

Eisner created *Hawks of the Sea,* but his most famous storyline was that of *The Spirit,* a masked detective who protects Central City with little more than his wits and fists. In the late 1970s, Eisner began work on a series of graphic novels, the first and most famous of which is *A Contract with God* (1978), inspired by his experiences in the mostly Jewish Bronx tenements of the 1930s.

FRANK FRAZETTA
AMERICAN *(1928–)*

Frazetta started off drawing for numerous titles in the early 1950s, including *The Shining Knight, John Wayne Comics,* and *Li'l Abner,* on which he worked for eight or nine years. He also had a newspaper strip, *Johnny Comet.* He is best known for fantasy paperback book covers.

CARMINE INFANTINO
AMERICAN *(1925–)*

Infantino recreated *The Flash* in 1956 and continued to illustrate it for 20 years. He also drew the Adam Strange series for *Strange Adventures* and is widely credited with revitalizing *Batman* in the 1960s.

Jack Kirby is recognized as the most influential creator of super-hero and adventure comic books, such as Captain America, *seen here in its No. 1 (1941) issue.*

JACK KIRBY
AMERICAN *(1917–1994)*

"The King of the Comics," Kirby created or cocreated scores of action hero series, among them *Captain America, The Fantastic Four, The Uncanny X-Men, The Incredible Hulk, Boy Commandos, Challengers of the Unknown, Captain Victory,* and *The Mighty Thor.*

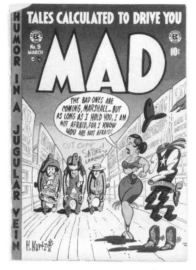

Harvey Kurtzman was not only a cartoonist, but was also the founding editor of Mad, *which switched from a comic book to a magazine format to avoid censorship in 1953.*

HARVEY KURTZMAN
AMERICAN *(1924–1993)*

Kurtzman was the irreverent editor/writer/illustrator who helped bring *MAD* magazine to prominence. Before creating *MAD*, Kurtzman founded the strip *Silver Linings* and the one-page *Hey . . . Look!* Other, later creations include the spoofs *Little Annie Fanny* and *Goodman Beaver.* Kurtzman also worked on the ghoul-and gore-filled comic book *Crypt of Terror* in the late 1940s.

JOE SHUSTER
AMERICAN, B. ***CANADA*** *(1914–1992)*

In 1938, Shuster cocreated the comic book hero Superman with Jerome Siegel. Their creation became the model for scores of comic action heroes to come. Unfortunately, the contribution of these two men was forgotten when, as the years passed, Superman and his spin-offs became big business. It has only been recently that steps have been taken to rectify this oversight.

An early Superman saves a blond aviatrix, as drawn by Joe Shuster.

Chapter Thirteen

FURNITURE

To many people, furniture seems an unlikely thing to collect. They've probably already decorated their apartment or house with pieces they like. Yet one day, at a yard sale, perhaps, they spot a chair with a style unlike anything in their fully furnished living room. It's just a quirky chair that's caught their eye, but the price is right, so they buy it. Once they get it home, they're delighted to discover that not only do they enjoy sitting in it, but because their chair is sculptural and functional, they like looking at it, too. Then, riffling through a favorite magazine, they see

it featured and become even more interested. So they go in search of another just like it (every house can use a pair of chairs), and become sufficiently enthused to begin hunting for more furniture by the same designer—and not just chairs, but tables, bookcases, and cabinets, too. And suddenly, they're redecorating that gorgeous living room with pieces that, in striking some personal aesthetic chord, really speak to them. They've become furniture collectors.

Of course, not all collections start out reflecting their current owners' taste. Every so often a collection is simply thrust upon someone, who, as the recipient of a relative's or friend's largesse, learns to love it. Take, for example, the Thomas Molesworth "frontier" furniture that showed up at *Antiques Roadshow* in Louisville. A visitor arrived with a distinctive chair that had a

Top: Dutch architect Gerrit Rietveld's ZigZag chair. Above: Danish designer Arne Jacobsen's 1957 Swan chair, which looks like a bird with outswept wings.

cowboy-in-relief wooden back and a leather seat, part of a full suite of Molesworth furniture. In the 1930s, when many furniture designers looked to machines and skyscrapers for design ideas, American furniture designer Thomas Molesworth took his inspiration from cowboys and Indians. The collection came to the visitor's family when her father bought a house filled with Molesworth furniture from Detroit Tiger catcher Mickey Cochrane. Appraiser Gary Piattoni called the made-in-Wyoming keyhole-back chair a "perfect example" of Molesworth's work. "Molesworth was the Frederic Remington of furniture makers," Piattoni continued. "He celebrated the American West and wanted to make it come alive." Molesworth's furniture has become fashionable; a collection of 318 pieces sold at auction in New York for $2.9 million in 1995. Piattoni told the delighted owner that her single chair is worth $1,500 to $2,000.

Thomas Molesworth, "the Frederic Remington of furniture," makers created furniture that celebrated the American West.

This example of Bauhaus architect Mies van der Rohe's MR chair, made of chrome-plated tubular steel with fabric panels and wooden armrests, was manufactured by Thonet, a company better known for making bentwood furniture.

A BRIEF HISTORY

It's surprising, but Americans had their first opportunity to own really well designed and fairly priced furniture only after World War I. Before the war, there was well-designed furniture—the Arts and Crafts–style work of Gustav Stickley, for example—and there was poorly designed furniture, churned out in carloads by manufacturers in Grand Rapids, Michigan, and other places in the Midwest. The impetus for combining good design with technically sophisticated mass production, and for creating beautiful things for the average home, came from a group of architects and designers working at the Bauhaus, the German design school founded in 1919 by Walter Gropius—the visionary crucible of the great twentieth-century design we call "modern."

Innovative architects who worked at the Bauhaus, such as Ludwig Mies van der Rohe and Marcel Breuer, were influenced by contemporary movements in the fine arts—especially by Cubism and the Dutch de Stijl. The Bauhaus was ardently committed to solving the problems of designing for mass manufacture while also employing the newest of materials, among them thin steel tubes. For that reason, from the early twentieth century on, hand craftsmanship would not be as important as volume and cost-effectiveness. Arts and Crafts was out, and a peacetime world, powered by the energy of the Bauhaus innovators, was gearing up to produce—amazingly—beauty.

The Bauhaus was, however, the leading edge of postwar creativity. Even as late as the 1920s, traditional and old-fashioned venues, such as design exhibitions and international fairs, were the main method by which novel ideas spread from country to country. Fairs were good advertising, as well. When the World's Fair—L'Exposition Internationale des Arts Décoratifs et Industriels Modernes—opened in Paris in 1925, visitors got their first look at a sleek, geometric, truly modern furniture style (which later took its name, Art Deco, from the exhibition; at the time, it was known as "style moderne" or "jazz moderne"). It offered a deluxe alternative to Bauhaus designs, and fairgoers were dazzled. Art Deco design was breathtakingly luxurious and extravagant, not austere or intellectual like Bauhaus design. Its slicked-back sophistication suited the effervescence of the Jazz Age, although in its most successful form it required so much hand craftsmanship that there was never any question of being able to mass produce it. Thus, two separate paths developed in twentieth-century furniture design. Art Deco looked back to a gorgeous past. The Bauhaus stepped boldly, mechanistically, into the future.

At the time, however, neither doctrine really "took" in America, nor did this country even have a display of its own at the French exhibition, despite having been invited to participate. (Due to postwar sentiment, Germany was excluded from the fair.) Secretary of Commerce Herbert Hoover quite correctly told the French fair committee that the United States had nothing legitimately "new" to exhibit. This was because any potentially interesting design trends in the United States were overridden by something a good bit more conservative. While the United States was young by European standards, the country was, at heart, a nation of traditionalists, and wholly enamored of its own history. Since the 1876 Centennial spawned the Colonial Revival, the furniture popular with the American public was, on the whole, reproductions of American Colonial and

A Suë et Mare rosewood dining table is firmly in the luxurious and extravagant tradition of post–World War I French furniture design.

Modest and squatty Colonial Revival footstools and other pieces manufactured by Wallace Nutting suited American traditionalists in the 1920s and 1930s.

FALLING INTO FURNITURE

It's said that many of the art world's great designs are happy accidents. Such was the case for a chair conceived by Finnish designer Yrjö Kukkapuro in 1946 and brought to *Antiques Roadshow* in Toronto half a century later. Appraiser Usha Subramaniam said Kukkapuro didn't come up with his design at the drafting table, but after a night of serious drinking. The story goes that he stumbled into a snowdrift after stepping out of a bar and sank into the soft snow bottom first. Afterward, Kukkapuro realized that his fall had shaped the most comfortable seat he had ever known. Back at the factory, he designed a fiberglass shell and covered it with leather. The chair turned on a cantilevered swivel on a chrome aluminum base and fiberglass foot. The woman who brought the chair to the *Antiques Roadshow* had purchased it from a colleague at her office for $150. Subramaniam estimates it might fetch about $2,000 at auction.

After World War II, "modern" materials began to appear alongside traditional materials in domestic furniture designs. One example is this maple four-drawer chest with a Formica-covered top, designed by Gilbert Rohde and manufactured by Herman Miller circa 1948.

Federal pieces. If these reproductions had been somewhat popular before World War I (a reaction to the plain tenets of the Arts and Crafts movement), they now became the American antidote to anything new and startling well into the 1930s. (Some might say that preference continues to this day.)

During the 1920s, reproduction Colonial and Federal sofas and easy chairs (popularly called wing chairs) furnished hundreds of thousands of American houses in tandem with tiny incursions of Bauhaus- or Art Deco–influenced design. By the 1930s, however, American interpretations of these new European styles—swept-back, streamlined sofas and bedroom sets made of pale woods created by newly influential American industrial designers—had settled themselves comfortably around the large, streamlined radios that were designed in a similar idiom. The maple and sycamore chests and bureaus designed by Russel Wright and Gilbert Rohde may have looked like nothing so much as sleek and rounded locomotives with drawers on fat, stumpy legs, but people liked them.

Nonetheless, most of these plump blond pieces were swept from the stage by the onset of World War II. When the smoke cleared, engineers returning to civilian duty put innovative wartime machinery and technology, those neat new plastics and alloys, to peacetime uses. Attractive furniture, some of which grew directly out of wartime experiments, was produced: Eames plywood seating, for instance, developed from wartime designs for molded plywood splints for immobilizing broken

bones (see page 494). Some postwar designs even retained a martial aesthetic. The scale of sofas and dining tables, for example, remained large, like the pieces from the thirties, but became lower and blocky, a trifle tank- or bunkerlike. Furniture design through the forties and fifties was intellectual, not emotional. Many of the designers were, after all, industrial designers. As the country developed increasing numbers of service industries, American designers even managed to insinuate office furniture design elements, such as Formica and chrome, into domestic furniture design.

An LCW (Lounge Chair Wood) designed by Charles Eames for Herman Miller, similar to the DCW (Dining Chair Wood), but lower and with a larger seat and back. The molded plywood seat—in theory, at least—made upholstery unnecessary.

In reaction to what must have been seen as a mechanistic, potentially soul-destroying trend—and there is always a reaction—many 1950s homeowners turned away from the postwar industrial look to naturalistic and craftsman-like Scandinavian Modern design. The Scandinavian designers of the 1940s and 1950s were masters of natural materials and organic forms. The romance of natural and organic furnishings in amoeba-like shapes was particularly soothing to Americans in a postwar era.

As natural, forward-looking, and modern as the United States thought itself, however, houses furnished entirely with Scandinavian Modern were relatively few. Most Americans of the 1950s, in fact, continued to buy copies of Duncan Phyfe and Queen Anne furniture, with a lone Danish Modern coffee table, perhaps, mixed in. Only the genuine trendsetters—then as now—furnished with the *really* modern.

As the fifties eased into the sixties, furniture design slid gently from Scandinavian sleek toward the zany. Employing every plastic and other artificial material (reacting, once again), designers offered chairs, sofas, and tables with such impolitic features as three-dimensional, realistic fiberglass women on all fours as supports. It was all as outlandish as Pop Art. Come the 1970s, however, there was the predictable retrenchment, with a concomitant interest in recyclable materials, for example, and in kit furniture, to be assembled at home. As for the last decades of the twentieth century, furniture manufacturers and designers seemed considerably more concerned with making

This three-legged Scandinavian Modern dining chair was designed by Hans Olsen, a Danish furniture designer active in the 1950s and 1960s. It is one of a set of four that nested perfectly around a matching round table.

MISSING MODERNS

At most gatherings of *Antiques Roadshow*, visitors line up at the glass and ceramics tables carting a wide range of twentieth-century objects. In other categories, however, attendees leave their twentieth-century possessions at home. Furniture made in the 1940s and after is largely a no-show at the *Roadshow*. There's a bit of circular logic to its absence: Viewers don't see modern furniture on the show, so they don't think to bring it. Moreover, today's buyers are just beginning to discover the virtues of vintage furniture designed in the forties, fifties, and sixties. *Antiques Roadshow* appraiser Karen Keane comments that "a set of classic plastic chairs from the 1950s can easily be thrown away at an estate sale. But," laments Keane, "we see an awful lot of twentieth-century reproductions of Victorian furniture on the *Antiques Roadshow* that people think are authentic."

affordable and good-looking "merchandise" than with anything of intrinsic value. Time will tell—very soon, most likely—if this becomes collectible.

ORIGINAL VERSUS REPRODUCTION FURNITURE

Bauhaus, Art Deco, and Scandinavian Modern furniture, as well as Molesworth pieces, chairs shaped like baseball mitts, and tables made from driftwood, are all, after their fashion, original designs. They all originated in the twentieth century; nothing at all like them (especially the baseball mitts) had ever been made before. Some designs were evolutionary dead ends. Others were invented to try out new technologies. And some of the best were the responses of influential architects to some current definition of modernity.

In one way or another, then, all these efforts pushed furniture design inexorably toward the future. They could even be quirky and—shall we say it?—uncomfortable. But they were always an imaginative corrective to everything traditional, to everything that had gone before. Some of these designs were so aesthetically groundbreaking they were selected for inclusion in museum collections. And some became so popular with the public that they were ultimately mass produced by the thousands.

What other kinds of furniture were being made from the end of World War I through the mid-1970s? In addition to the trend-setting work coming from the Bauhaus and from Art Deco designers and their followers, much of what was manufactured were reproductions of earlier styles—Early American, Louis XVI, or Jacobean, for example. Most of this was inexpensive, imitative, and of little interest to the educated collector, although some, such as the output of the Nathan Margolis Shop (see page 514) and the Wallace Nutting studio (see page 513), has begun to acquire a following. The designs of real interest to the collecting

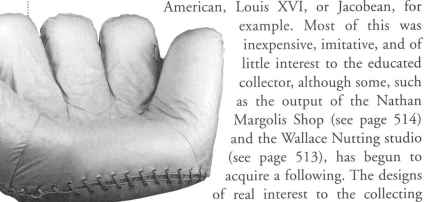

This baseball glove settee, made by the Italian manufacturer Stendis in 1972, is truly an original design of the twentieth century—one with crossover appeal for both baseball collectors and furniture collectors.

community today, however, are those that are completely original to the twentieth century: styles that are not only emblematic of their times, but are also recognized as having lasting importance in the chronology of furniture design. So while there are plenty of nice pieces of reproduction furniture for the average living room, it is the innovative styles that we'll concentrate on.

EVALUATING FURNITURE

In 1925, the same year that the groundbreaking Art Deco exhibition was held in Paris, the *House Beautiful Furniture Annual* decreed that "the secret in selecting good furniture lies in the choice of pieces, each of a form strictly true to the type it represents, not a hybrid product showing in itself the elements of several different types of period design." In other words: whether one is collecting Art Deco furniture of the twenties or streamlined styles of the thirties, the blocky, homely "retro" of the forties, or Danish Modern of the fifties, that "best" piece—and even that good piece—of original furniture ought to have internal cohesion. It ought to recognizably represent the style of the era in which it was made. It ought never be any kind of mishmash, with a bit from this period and a bit from that, because corrupted design can never be good design, and it won't hold up aesthetically or monetarily. To be considered top quality, furniture should always combine thoughtful and (usually) functional design with the best materials and craftsmanship available to its manufacturers.

The highest-quality furniture is not always easy to recognize—especially without assistance. This helps explain why so many collectors pay premiums for pieces that retain their original labels. Labels, at the least, are dependable indicators of the factories that made the furniture; at best, they identify the work of an important designer. But not all pieces of furniture, even those made by well-known designers, were originally labeled. And "suites" of furniture, such as bedroom sets, frequently have

The witty Bouloum chair designed by French furniture designer Olivier Morgue in 1968 has a cult following among collectors—as does the rest of his furniture. It is made of upholstered fiberglass.

This prototype of a side chair, designed by Charles Eames and Eero Saarinen for the Museum of Modern Art's Organic Design in Home Furnishings competition in 1940, is upholstered in its original blue fabric and bears the label of its manufacturer, Heywood-Wakefield (above).

only one or two pieces labeled at the factory. They were expected to be kept together, so chairs and side tables may have no labels at all. If you own a labeled table or bed from a set, the label may not only tell you who manufactured that piece but help you attribute other, similar pieces. The label also becomes an acceptable type of market "guarantee." Should a collector decide someday to sell that labeled piece, that stamp (or piece of paper, or metal or plastic tag) is proof to the next owner that the piece is what she claims it to be. A good example is the prototype of a side chair designed by Charles Eames and Eero Saarinen for the Museum of Modern Art's Organic Design in Home Furnishings competition in 1940. Upholstered in its original fabric and bearing the label of its manufacturer, Heywood-Wakefield, it recently sold at auction for $28,000. The identical chair, unlabeled, failed to sell.

Labels are not the only way to judge the merits of vintage furniture. Like Beethoven, even the best designers had off days, so collectible names on labels don't always guarantee importance. And sometimes superior quality and rarity are simply there for the eye to see. If it's a chest of drawers you fancy, look for drawers that are put together with dovetails instead of with nails. If the chest has a backboard, it should be made of wood, never pressboard. Plywood, on the whole, is less preferable than hardwood, although some of the best manufacturers did use it. It is absolutely integral to the work of Charles and Ray Eames and their iconoclastic colleagues. Rosewood and similar exotic woods, or woods with gorgeous grain, are generally more expensive than oak, pine, or wicker. And usefulness and comfort frequently add to value. On the whole, however, wood pieces will have more value than upholstered pieces.

Because interest in the field of twentieth-century vintage furniture is so new, there has not yet been significant fakery, although there have been reissues of popular styles, which tend to depress the market for the originals. Some styles, indeed, have never gone out of fashion and continue to be made. Perhaps the best way to determine if yours is a new or old version of an Eames chair, then, is to go to antiques shows (despite the fact that twentieth-century furniture is not yet legally antique, it does show up at antiques shows) where there are dealers who handle Eames. Many, if not most, of these dealers are also scholars of their fields, and, like *Antiques Roadshow* appraisers, are generally happy to enlighten the interested novice.

Whatever the style or decade of manufacture, regardless of the absence or presence of labels, collectors are almost always willing to wait for the piece in pristine condition, because unless the piece is one of a kind, there are untold numbers available. We are, after all, dealing here with mass-produced items.

MATERIALS

Although most of the conventional materials—wood, bronze, brass, and marble—were employed in the manufacture of furniture in the twentieth century, the tables, chairs, and cabinets of the collectible era were also a breeding ground for experimental and untried technologies. From plastics to metals to glass, if designers thought they could use it, they did.

WOODS

Wood, of course, is the most familiar traditional material. But the furniture designers after the World War I and Art Deco eras certainly didn't intend to use wood in the handmade and naturalistic way their Arts and Crafts predecessors had. Craftsmanlike simplicity was antithetical to the Art Deco aesthetic of soigné luxury, which is why its designers selected wood veneers in ebony, rosewood, amboyna, and amaranth—the most luxurious and expensive available—to emphasize the severely elegant lines of their commodes, chaise longues, and chairs. Lacquered wood surfaces were also popular for accentuating that twenties' aura of exoticism. Sleek and colorful Asian associations were particularly sought-after.

The palest woods, the maples and birches, became the signature of 1930s Hollywood high style. Filmdom's bleached and blonded finishes blended well with their owners' marcelled platinum hair and satin gowns—so artificial, so modern, so slick. Young homemakers of the Depression era fell hard for the fantasy, readily inviting it into their own homes—bedrooms, especially.

The forties was the era of molded plywood—not a brand-new technique, but one that had at last found its moment. Plywood comprises thin layers of wood glued together to make one structural board. Because all wood is weakest across the grain, the grain of one layer (or ply) is placed to run at right angles to the grain of the one above and beneath it. A many-layered sandwich is thus constructed, one in which each sheet counterbalances the weakness of the ones adjacent to it. Plywood is correspondingly strong and flexible, and can even be molded to the shape of the human body. Although it was a favorite of designer Alvar Aalto in the 1930s, it really came into its own in the next decade, when husband-and-wife design team Charles and Ray Eames thoroughly explored its three-dimensional potentialities.

In the 1950s, wood was manipulated and shaped respect-fully—even rather romantically—to show to best advantage its grain, its color, and the handsome material that it naturally is. Scandinavian designers were particularly intrigued by both their native beech and Baltic birch, but they were partial to teak, as well. In fact, teak is practically synony-mous with Danish furniture. The pendu-lum of fashion was swinging, once again, back to nature and "naturalness," so that actual tree trunks and tree branches came to be incorporated into 1950s coffee tables, desks, and chairs (see George Nakashima, page 497). (Don't try this at home. Tree trunk insects can eat through wood floors!)

One method of manipulating wood that had been developed around 1850 con-tinued through the twentieth century. Bentwood is created by subjecting treated wood rods, often copper beech, to heat and steam. They can then be placed in a form and bent into almost any shape desired, even S curves. Bentwood furniture is lightweight, durable, and con-siderably less expensive to make than either solid wood or veneered furniture.

This Art Deco–style cabinet, made in France circa 1925, has a charac-teristic geometric design and is con-structed of appropriately luxurious materials—rosewood and silvered hardware.

GLASS

Although glass has obvious drawbacks for furniture construction—not the least of which is the problem of securing tight, invisible joints—that did not discourage brilliant glass artisan René Lalique from making the attempt. One of his more dazzling experiments was a dining room table and chairs all in glass. Experiments aside, there was a definite place for glass in modern furniture design. A dark and almost eerie blue mirrored glass was fashionable throughout the 1930s, when it was much used on inexpensive geometric mirrors and for the tops of semistreamlined (and also inexpensive) wood coffee and end tables. From the 1920s until the end of the century, but particularly through the twenties and thirties, glass rod legs were applied to "modern" furniture, making it appear to hover in the air. By the late 1950s, seemingly free-floating biomorphic-shape glass tabletops were practically compulsory in any living room or den with pretensions to being modern. Glass furniture, not unexpectedly, does not always survive.

The two-piece curved wood base of Isamu Noguchi's three-piece free-form coffee table could be interlocked in any of several ways to hold the biomorphic-shape glass tabletop.

METALS

Metal, especially tubular steel, played an increasingly important role in furniture design over the course of the twentieth century.

STEEL

The steel tube was the material of choice for Bauhaus-influenced furniture: inexpensive, lightweight, and, given its lean, unembellished nature, inherently chic. Tubular steel was the future and embodiment of modern design; so much so, that it is almost impossible to envision the furniture of the twentieth century without its often chromed, sometimes brushed, quintessentially modern tubular steel components.

ALUMINUM

A light, malleable, silvery white metal that resists corrosion, aluminum has been used for furniture since the 1920s. Because it can be incorporated into furnishings in sheet, structural, tube, and extruded forms, it held a special attraction for the industrial

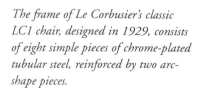

The frame of Le Corbusier's classic LC1 chair, designed in 1929, consists of eight simple pieces of chrome-plated tubular steel, reinforced by two arc-shape pieces.

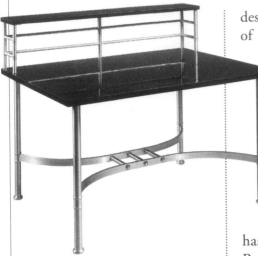

A 1930s aluminum and formica desk from the library of the State of Virginia, designed and manufactured by Warren McArthur, a pioneer in the use of aluminum in furniture.

designers of the thirties. Cool and pale, it was the very essence of "streamlined." What is more, aluminum resists corrosion and is gratifyingly lightweight and flexible. While this material, used extensively during World War II, was most popular for furnishings in the forties, in the 1950s, near the end of his career, Frank Lloyd Wright designed upholstered aluminum armchairs.

WROUGHT IRON

The word "wrought," in this context, means shaping metal by hammering or beating it; wrought iron is crafted by heating and bending iron rods into shape and has been employed for architectural details since the Renaissance. Wrought-iron furniture in the twentieth century was primarily made for porch or terrace use, although it was dazzlingly fashionable for living and dining rooms during the Art Deco era. Today, the term "wrought iron" has come to cover a multitude of different metals and techniques, including cast aluminum.

Wicker and Wrought Iron

In the first decades of the twentieth century, living spaces appeared that were new to the middle-class American home: Outdoor terraces, enclosed porches and sun rooms, sleeping porches (once the last word in health), and breakfast rooms. These transitional areas were the perfect spots for wicker, undeniably the perfect material for transitional furniture. Wicker was easy to move. It could stand getting wet. It could be painted. It was affordable.

The firm that rode to success on its founder's discovery that wicker furniture could be created from hitherto discarded rattan packing material was Heywood-Wakefield (which later successfully produced wood furniture; see page 505). By the twentieth century, as the result of acquiring the Lloyd Manufacturing Company—a producer of woven fiber products, primarily baby carriages—Heywood-Wakefield was weaving a vast line of wicker sofas, chairs, tables, rockers, and even lamps on giant power looms. There was also wrapped-wire wicker, made by the Lloyd division of Heywood-Wakefield, an even more durable product. Numerous other firms made wicker, as well, and by the 1920s, a less expensive version of an already inexpensive commodity arrived: this was a paper-wrapped reed imitation, recognizable by its paper-wrapped reed braided legs.

The designs of all these furnishings followed the styles of furniture design faithfully. A handsome, tailored 1912 rocker was a dignified Edwardian chair with a high, solidly woven upper back, and open scrollwork in the lumbar region, for instance. It cost $12.

Art Deco wicker frequently incorporated small, colored diamond shapes or other geometric motifs into a back or a chair apron. The taste for wicker lasted until the late 1930s, at which

PLASTICS

Unquestionably, "plastic" is one of the catchwords of the twentieth century. Plastic, a synthetic material with a polymeric structure that molds easily when soft, also hardens to whatever shape or configuration is required. From its beginnings as celluloid, the earliest "plastic," each incarnation of the material has been refined and improved upon to become stronger, more durable, and lighter (or heavier) than its predecessor. All plastics are relatively inexpensive and uniquely hard wearing, but certain varieties have been used with particular success for furniture.

BAKELITE

A resin first developed in 1907 by Dr. L. H. Backcland (the source of the name), Bakelite was an improvement over its plastic predecessors in that it could not be softened once it had set. Its use in furniture is usually restricted to decorative details such as inlays and drawer fittings, but it also appeared in chair frames and, in France, for example, as one-piece tabletops.

From the late sixties, a "mod" and stylish molded plastic cabinet on wheels.

time a commentator wrote, "Such perfection of weaving and comfortable springing is now found in this woven fiber furniture that it is in the most constant use in the most fashionable households, liners, cinemas, lounges, and dance halls." Such pervasiveness has guaranteed us plenty of collectible wicker today.

Although wrought-iron furniture had to be lightweight, bravely resistant to all kinds of weather, and generally less expensive than its wood counterpart, it still managed to reflect the current aesthetic. So, for the most part, it was

This wrought-iron dining table, with a stylized floral motif, was manufactured by John Salterini.

a stripped-down version of indoor furniture. In the 1950s, the Russell Woodard firm of New York produced organic, body-conforming wire seating, while Woodward and Sons of Michigan (don't confuse the two), which is still in business today, produced graceful wrought-iron pieces.

Russell Woodard's work from the thirties and forties is deemed particularly fine and collectible.

John Salterini, also of New York, created outdoor wrought-iron garden furniture that was surprisingly comfortable, for metal. It often reproduced the forms of indoor furniture—for example, sectional sofas and glass topped coffee tables. Salterini wrought iron can often be recognized by its distinctive, hammered "snake head" tips.

Florentine Craftsmen, Inc., has manufactured wrought-iron furniture since 1918, and specializes in botanically ornamented outdoor furniture, awash in leaves, vines, and berries—all hand-forged. It is increasingly collectible.

CARETAKERS ALL

Most people assume that dealers are collectors, but that's not always true. David Rago, an *Antiques Roadshow* appraiser, isn't in the business of buying for himself. "I don't want to compete with my customers," says Rago, a specialist in Arts and Crafts–style decorative arts and furnishings. "My 'collection' is what I handle. I don't have to pay for it, I don't have to insure it, and I don't have to worry about it. But I get to visit it.

"I'm just a caretaker," he adds. "Nobody really owns anything, and we're all just caretakers. I see my job as trying to make sure the people who are buying what I sell will understand what it is and take good care of it."

This black and white fiberglass and steel chair was designed by George Nelson Associates and manufactured by Herman Miller in 1959.

LUCITE

Also known as Plexiglas, Lucite is a trade name for a very stable polymer created by Dupont in the 1930s. It is transparent, tough, and resistant to weathering. (In Britain, it is called Lexan.)

FORMICA

First patented in the 1920s, Formica, also a trade name, is a plastic laminate, manufactured by pressing synthetic resin into specially impregnated paper and allowing it to harden.

OTHER FURNITURE MATERIALS

The fact is, there's scarcely a malleable material that hasn't been converted to furniture, and several are familiar and enormously successful.

FIBERGLASS

When used for furniture manufacture, fiberglass, which is spun, molten glass, is often mixed with polymers. Fiberglass has proved to be the ideal material for creating formed chair seats.

LEATHER

Whether treated with softeners or made as stiff and unyielding as wood, leather is a natural material that has seldom been out of style. From Bauhaus-designed furniture to that iconic upholstered Eames lounge chair, leather is a favorite choice for both upholstery and semistructural elements in the twentieth century. It wears particularly well.

RATTAN

The pliant and strong stems of enormously tall, climbing palms, rattan in great bundles was originally used to keep cargo from shifting on ships. It remained mere dunnage until it was discovered to be useful in furniture manufacture.

WICKER

Today, wicker is woven rattan. Before the nineteenth century, however, it was made from long, pliable willow twigs and had been used for making furniture and other household necessities since time immemorial. Lightweight, versatile, and intrinsically air-conditioned, wicker is currently considered to be an informal material, appropriate for the porch or beach houses. At one time, however, wicker furniture was intended solely for indoor use.

REED

Some wickerlike furniture is woven from the stalks of various perennial aquatic grasses called reeds. Reed furniture is frequently used for porches and sunrooms because it doesn't tolerate weather as well as twentieth-century wicker does.

COLLECTING VINTAGE FURNITURE

These days, twentieth-century furniture is most abundant in shops, at yard sales, and at auctions, rather than at flea markets. This is because it's cumbersome to carry sofas and sideboards to a one- or two-day outdoor fair. You can expect to find plenty of small things there, however—including chairs, tables, and stools.

The collecting of original furniture requires of the collector a bit more aesthetic daring and risk taking than does acquiring a houseful of reproductions of eighteenth- and nineteenth-century pieces. But whatever and wherever you buy, you will discover that furniture is one of the most gratifying of collectibles. Even if you make a mistake (definition of a mistake: the piece is not by the designer you thought it was; the upholstery isn't original; an arm or a leg has been previously—perhaps deviously—replaced), you will still have a perfectly usable chair, table, or chest, and one that you like. You like it because you've adhered to the great collectors' maxim: Buy Only Those Things You Like.

The hard part about making a mistake, however, is that unlike other categories of collectibles—dolls or posters or ceramics, for instance—a bad buy in furniture often takes up an inordinate amount of room. This is another reason why, regardless of your style preferences, you should always try to collect only those pieces that really speak to you. You'll find that a chest

A turn-of-the-nineteenth-century wicker settee made by Heywood-Wakefield shows the flights of fancy made possible by this pliable material.

of drawers you bought primarily because it was a bargain takes up a great deal more room, somehow, than a chest of the same size that you absolutely love.

To learn which pieces of twentieth-century furniture are collectible, what materials they're made of, who the designers were, and where to look for their labels, read on. And while this is unquestionably an enormous field, if you look around your living room right now, you may very well find that you've already made a start. After all, everyone owns some furniture.

Because the field breathes hot on contemporary heels (furniture of the 1980s has already begun to creep into the ranks of the collectible), assembling a satisfying collection can mean doing primary research, such as tracking down manufacturers' trade catalogues or original advertisements. To avoid treading on the toes of "future" collectibles, we are limiting our focus here to the years between 1920 and 1970.

IMPORTANT DESIGNERS

Furniture that is neither a reproduction of an earlier style nor designed by committee can be called "original." Some original furniture of the twentieth century was one-of-a-kind, but much of it was mass-manufactured under the supervision of its designer, who was ensuring the quality of the workmanship. Some of the choicest twentieth-century furniture falls into this category. Here are several of the most highly respected designers.

ALVAR AALTO

One of the century's most prolific designers, Finnish architect Alvar Aalto worked with solid birch, laminated birch plywood, and lacquered woods to create a Scandinavian version of Bauhaus design. Uncluttered, bearing his trademark ripples, there was nothing remotely cold or standoffish in Aalto's aesthetically accessible designs. As a result, during the late twenties and thirties, Aalto-designed furniture met with far more popular success than did its clinical, tubular steel counterparts in

Alvar Aalto's 1932 Paimio chair—originally created for an Aalto-designed tuberculosis sanatorium in southwestern Finland—consists of a molded birch plywood seat suspended within a continuous laminated wood frame. The angle of the chair's back was intended to help patients breathe more easily.

Germany and France. Most Aalto pieces have a metal label with a model number and are stamped in ink. Those made in the 1930s may have an identifying plastic tag.

HARRY BERTOIA

Harry Bertoia came to the United States from Italy in 1930, when he was fifteen. A contemporary (and eventually an associate) of Charles Eames, Bertoia always preferred working with wire to working in wood. It seems appropriate, therefore, that he is best known for his Diamond chair, a diamond-shape grid of hand-bent steel wire on steel rod legs supporting a thin cushion. Bertoia himself described his creation as being made "mainly of air," and his chair, designed for the Knoll Furniture Company in 1952, didn't become the classic it is today until the 1960s. From that time on, the Diamond chair—in wire, plastic-coated wire, or molded plastic versions—has been ubiquitous and seemingly indispensable to America's lobbies, airline terminals, and offices.

Although Bertoia claimed that his wire chair was composed "mainly of air," its metal back makes sitting in it for any length of time a far cry from floating on a cloud.

EDGAR BRANDT

Ferrobrandt, the Paris firm of Edgar Brandt, also maintained a Manhattan outlet. In both locations, Brandt dealt in a broad array of immensely stylish Art Deco decorative ironwork that contrasted silvered bronze and wrought iron with textured, hammered surfaces, often decorated with stylized scrollwork flowers and animals. A measure of Brandt's artistry was that the screws and bolts on his furniture were virtually invisible. Brandt's metalwork—which included screens, console tables, pedestals, lamps, and even radiator grilles—is stamped with his name.

"The more you learn, the greater your awareness of how little you really know," says *Antiques Roadshow* twentieth-century furniture expert Chris Kennedy. "The problem with a lot of twentieth-century crafted furniture, even Nakashima, is that it was never labeled. Nakashima frequently put his clients' names, not his own, on his designs, so collectors see, for example, the name Schwartz on furniture that looks like—and turns out to be—Nakashima. If you knew his work and that he didn't sign his own name to it, it would lessen the confusion."

Kennedy suggests that beginning collectors not buy furniture designed by someone whose name has become overly familiar. Early Eames furniture, which was meant to be affordable, has had so much recent press that now it isn't. "If you keep hearing a name," he says, "it's already too late." Instead, look for pieces that seem better than the ordinary, but are priced like run-of-the-mill used furniture. For example, if you find a bureau, desk, or bookcase that you like, look at how the back is put on. If it's screwed on, that's better than if it's nailed on, which in turn is better than if it's stapled on.

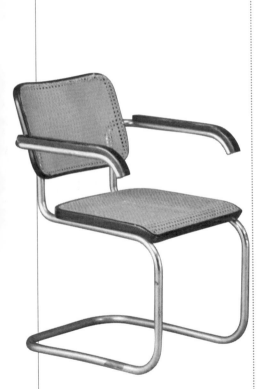

Marcel Breuer's Cesca armchair—the most frequently reproduced piece of modern furniture—features a cane seat and back, black lacquered bentwood trim, a chrome-plated tubular steel frame, and a cantilevered base.

MARCEL BREUER

Hungarian architect Marcel Breuer produced some of the best known of Bauhaus furniture designs. The most familiar of these is possibly the Wassily chair, created at the Bauhaus for artist Wassily Kandinsky. The Wassily chair was the first large-scale-production piece ever to be made in standard-strength tubular steel, and the first to be designed for residential use. (An interesting sidelight on this chair is the fact that the venerable Thonet company—see page 506—was its Viennese manufacturer). Breuer's cane-seat Cesca chair is the most reproduced piece of modern furniture in the world.

Breuer emigrated to England from Germany, where he had managed the Bauhaus carpentry shop during the mid-1920s. In the 1930s, in England, he gave up his work in metal and turned to designing highly sculptural, organic furniture in plywood for the Isokon firm. He moved to the United States in 1937.

LE CORBUSIER

Charles-Edouard Jeanneret, the Swiss architect universally known as Le Corbusier, was among the most influential figures in shaping what was to become the International style in architecture and design. He was the leading exponent of the Modernist movement and an early minimalist. It was Le Corbusier who famously dubbed the modern house "a machine for living in." Le Corbusier employed the tubular steel frame in the furniture he designed with Charlotte Perriand and Pierre Jeanneret, and most spectacularly for his cubical Grand Confort chair, in which the leather upholstery left most of the basic structure exposed (a technique quite unlike the upholstering of the traditional chair, in which the intent is to hide the frame). The rather small amount of furniture Le Corbusier designed was carefully engineered to be mass manufactured under his supervision; a great deal of his work began to be reproduced after World War II and is still being made today.

DONALD DESKEY

Deskey, who hoped to produce great designs for the multitudes, turned out to be a bit too expensive for the common man. Consequently, the majority of his sleek and geometric Art Deco–style furniture, designed for his own company, AMODEC (American Modern Decoration), could be found in the residences of the wealthy. (Deskey also designed several pieces for the American manufacturers Schmieg & Kotzian and Widdicomb.) Deskey decorated the public area of Radio City Music Hall in Manhattan and often incorporated Bakelite into his work—a highly practical idea in an era in which both alcohol and tobacco (equally ruinous to furniture) were heavily consumed. Deskey furniture is often recognized by its contrasting stripes in bold reds, yellows, and blues.

WHO'S WHO

Many of the best furniture designers were employed or commissioned by some of America's most far-seeing and innovative furniture manufacturers. For collectors who find a super-looking piece bearing a manufacturer's label but no designer's name, here are some of the leading manufacturers and the designers they worked with:

MANUFACTURER	DESIGNER(S)
Baker	Donald Deskey, Finn Juhl, T. H. Robsjohn-Gibbings, Kem Webber
Conant Ball	Russel Wright
Dunbar	Edward Wormley
Herman Miller	Charles Eames, Paul Laszlo, George Nelson, Isamu Noguchi, Verner Panton, Gilbert Rohde
Heywood-Wakefield	Alfons Bach, Alexis de Sakhnoffsky, Leo Jiranek, Gilbert Rohde, Russel Wright
Knoll	Harry Bertoia, Marcel Breuer, Ludwig Mies van der Rohe, Isamu Noguchi, Eero Saarinen
Schmieg & Kotzian	Donald Deskey
Widdicomb Furniture Company	Donald Deskey, George Nakashima, T. H. Robsjohn-Gibbings, Kem Weber

Antiques Roadshow furniture expert J. Michael Flanigan offers some advice to budding furniture enthusiasts to help them keep their living rooms from becoming warehouses:

For those interested in collecting modern furniture, Flanigan states that, technically and aesthetically, the chair is a woodworker's greatest challenge, and the rarest type of woodworker is one who is a great chair maker. Novices in collecting furniture could do worse than to assemble a collection of original, or even one-of-a-kind, vintage chairs.

An Art Deco–style five-drawer bureau—designed by Donald Deskey and manufactured by Widdicomb—with black lacquer top and side, burl veneer front, curved side panel, and chrome drawer pulls.

EAMES PROTOTYPES

Husband and wife Charles and Ray Eames, the American design team, were the envy of European furniture designers because they mass-produced their own designs. The Eameses mass-produced molded plywood and molded plastic furniture and may have set a standard for postwar design, but today, it is the prototypes (original models) of their creations that have exceptional value. Ray's sculptural wood leg splints and stretchers for carrying the World War II wounded are far more art than appliance and are valued as such.

The distinction between rare Eames and medium-rare Eames merits illustration. A 1950s storage unit composed of 250 parts was usually shipped assembled as customers couldn't do it themselves. But the manufacturers eventually realized that shipping it in one piece was too costly, and the design was altered for easier shipping. Recently, one of those first models (recognizable by its lack of doweled legs and the presence of angled uprights) brought $70,000 at auction.

Similarly, the 1946 DCW side chair (the acronym stands for "Dining Chair Wood"), is especially rare and valuable when covered in slunkskin (variegated calfskin) over foam rubber. Later examples are less highly valued.

CHARLES AND RAY EAMES

Charles and Ray Eames were the all-American husband-and-wife design team of the forties, the fifties—in fact, of the century. Together, they designed many pieces of furniture made of fiberglass and other materials, but they were particularly noted for their work in plywood. Eames plywood chairs conformed exactly to the shape of the body seated upon them—in theory making upholstery unnecessary. Of course, the truth about the classic molded fiberglass chair, not to mention the famous plywood chair—both still found in offices and doctors' waiting rooms nationwide—is that they were as uncomfortable as they looked. They were, as one contemporary wag noted, "thirty-minute chairs."

All Eames chairs, plus other Eames seating, owed much to industrial design—to the tractor seat in particular. But while Eames designs are mildly unsittable, and certainly not without their detractors (one of whom tellingly observed that "Eames furnishings will always be well designed and badly executed"), they are undeniably attractive, and they were possibly the first American furniture to carry the message of the Bauhaus successfully into the middle-

An icon of 1950s American furniture design, the Eames lounge chair and ottoman, manufactured by Herman Miller. This example in rosewood veneer has its original black Naugahyde upholstery.

class home. The Eameses also produced embossed plywood, aluminum, and Masonite storage units that were light, practical, and witty. The undulant Eames folding screen is a marvel of molded plywood, and their rosewood and leather lounge chair and ottoman are a status symbol even today.

JEAN-MICHEL FRANK

Jean-Michel Frank, a French interior designer, managed to combine severity of design with surrealism, and his spare, yet elegant furniture was one progenitor of American Art Moderne. Bizarre and exotic materials—vellum (lamb-, calf-, or goatskin parchment) and shagreen (sharkskin)—were among Frank's favorite embellishments on pure and basic shapes. The designer's Mouth settee, modeled after a Dali painting of Mae West's lips, was a distinct and witty departure.

Jean-Michel Frank's elegant Louis XVI–inspired black lacquer, gilt wood, and gilt brass coffee table, from about 1930.

PAUL FRANKL

The Viennese architect Paul Frankl emigrated to the United States after World War I. He designed one-of-a-kind furniture throughout the 1920s and 1930s, although some of his later designs were mass-produced. In his best-known works, he synthesized the Jazz Age: a series of bookcases, cabinets, and desks that simulate, in wood, the potent image of the jagged setbacks of Manhattan skyscrapers. Frankl-designed seating includes an enormous upholstered lounge chair with cork hand rests, as well as a red-lacquer "puzzle" desk in which an integral stool fits precisely into the desk's kneehole opening. His early work is quite rare.

ALBERTO AND DIEGO GIACOMETTI

Swiss-born sculptor Alberto Giacometti worked in bronze and was particularly influenced by the work of Romanian artist Constantin Brancusi. Although Giacometti's sculpted bronze figures from the 1920s to the 1960s are museum standards, he also designed furnishings, often in collaboration with his brother Diego, who specialized in furniture. The work of the Giacomettis typically employs droll mythological references, verging on the surreal. Beaten-bronze human and animal figures make this work easily recognizable. Giacometti lamps and tables are perhaps best known, and these often incorporate human heads and birds.

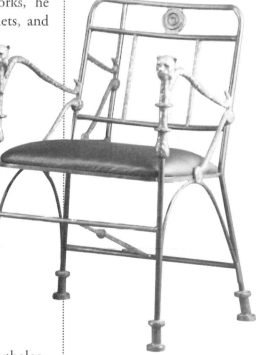

A classically inspired iron and bronze armchair designed by Diego Giacometti, with decorative circular medallions, arms terminating in lions' heads, and a black leather upholstered seat.

Danish designer Arne Jacobsen is best known for his 1952 three-legged Ant Chair, accompanied here by its matching table. He also created a four-legged version of the chair, but it wasn't manufactured until after his death in 1971.

EILEEN GRAY

Eileen Gray was an Irish designer who established her workshop in Paris in the 1920s. Gray's shiny lacquer furnishings, with their cool, Japonesque aesthetic, epitomized the best and most sophisticated of Art Deco design. She is probably best known, however, for her small, adjustable side table, the E-1027 ("E" for Eileen), an ingenious composition in tubular steel and glass that has become a classic of modern design. The adjustability of the E-1027 was originally intended to facilitate having breakfast in bed, a function it no doubt seldom serves today.

ARNE JACOBSEN

Noted for the three-legged, molded plywood Ant chair of 1952, Danish designer Arne Jacobsen was also the creator of the amusing Egg chair of 1957—the essence, in the fifties and sixties, of enveloping, swiveling, all-empowering biomorphism. These triumphs, like Jacobsen's Swan chair (also 1957; see page 475), are among the most avidly collected of mid-century seat furniture. (All three chairs were manufactured by Fritz Hansen.) Throughout the 1960s, this designer also worked in laminated teak, rosewood, and oak.

LUDWIG MIES VAN DER ROHE

As director of the famous Bauhaus school in the early 1930s, renowned German architect Ludwig Mies van der Rohe famously stated (apropos of making handmade things look machined) that "God is in the details." Mies's greatest furniture design is the luxurious, hand-detailed Barcelona chair that was intended as a "throne" for the king of Spain during the inaugural ceremony of the Mies-designed German Pavilion at the 1929 International Exhibition at Barcelona. With its padded leather upholstery and crossed chrome stretchers, this celebrated chair is both an homage to antique Greek and Neo-Classic furniture and a brilliant emblem of

Designed as a "throne" for the King of Spain during the inaugural ceremony of the German Pavilion at the 1929 International Exhibition at Barcelona, the Barcelona Chair is the most celebrated piece of furniture designed by Ludwig Mies van der Rohe.

modernity. Mies created mass-market furniture as well, working in his favorite media: glass, tubular steel, padded leather, and raffia. His cantilevered tubular steel furniture, especially the MR chair of 1926, is still the epitome of elegance. The original models of the MR chair, produced by the firm of Berliner Metallgewerbe for two years only, are exceptionally rare. Since the late 1940s, however, reproductions of several of Mies most popular styles have been produced by Knoll and other manufacturers (see page 506), and are fairly commonplace.

THOMAS MOLESWORTH

In 1931, Thomas Molesworth, who had studied at the Art Institute of Chicago, settled in Cody, Wyoming, and started the Shoshone Furniture Company. There he produced the "cowboy style" furniture that captured the romance of the frontier, furniture that was particularly suited to Western lodges, dude ranches, and rustic vacation retreats. Utilizing tree-trunk posts, leather panels, and antlers, Molesworth created chairs, sofas, tables, and other furnishings, some upholstered in Indian-patterned woven fabrics. He furnished Dwight Eisenhower's den, the Rockefeller Ranch in Wyoming, and several large Western hotels. His highly individual furniture is very collectible today.

CARLO MOLLINO

Influenced by Charles Eames, Italian architect Carlo Mollino was a major force in post–World War II Italian design. Unlike Eames's fairly down-to-earth work, however, Mollino's idiosyncratic furniture managed to combine the erotic with the surreal. Mollino himself termed it "fantastic," although his curvilinear style simply continued the long and venerable tradition of flamboyant Italian furniture. Mollino's Arabesque table, for example, is a playful whiplash of biomorphic asymmetrically pierced wood (shades of the Eames splints), almost coincidentally supporting two levels of asymmetrical glass. Most of Mollino's work was specially commissioned.

GEORGE NAKASHIMA

American George Nakashima was a twentieth-century craftsman of the old school. While being held in a Japanese internment camp during World War II, he apprenticed himself to a Japanese

One of a set of eight custom-made side chairs from the Casa de Sole, an apartment complex in an Italian ski resort that was designed by Carlo Mollino between 1947 and 1955. The chairs are made of oak with hexagonal brass bolts and brass screws.

A SECOND LIFE

*A*ntiques Roadshow appraiser David Rago considers himself lucky to live only a few minutes from the New Hope, Pennsylvania, compound where furniture designer George Nakashima constructed his twentieth-century masterpieces, and where many are still on display. "It's a very intimate place," Rago says of the compound, which is open to the public by appointment. Operating the museum since Nakashima's death in 1990 are his widow, Marion, his son, Kevin, and his daughter, Mira, a furniture maker herself. "Most museums aren't run by people who have helped make the material and lived with the designer," notes Rago.

Nakashima trained as an architect, but while visiting Japan, the land of his parents' birth, he decided to make furniture. He made only wood furniture. "In his best pieces, he lets the wood become decoration by doing nothing more than polishing it," says Rago.

Nakashima once wrote: "It is an art and soul-satisfying adventure to walk the forests of the world, to commune with trees . . . to bring this living material to the work bench, ultimately to give it a second life."

George Nakashima used a slab of dramatically edged and fissured walnut mounted on a tripod support, to make this one-of-a-kind coffee table in 1972. Unlike much of his work, this piece is signed.

carpenter, and there he may have developed the organic approach to furniture design for which he is known—an aesthetic in which the top of a table may be just a step away from the tree trunk from which it is fashioned. Influenced by the Shakers' simple approach to design and by American eighteenth- and nineteenth-century furniture, Nakashima's idiosyncratic work employs traditional construction techniques, hand workmanship, and an agreeable harmony between the materials and the object they've become. Nakashima's Windsor chairs are often created from the walnut timbers he himself selected and cut to incorporate "the soul of the tree."

GEORGE NELSON

George Nelson, who became head designer for Herman Miller (see page 505) in 1945, was an important Modernist interior, industrial, and exhibition designer. At Herman Miller, with which he was associated for nearly fifty years, he developed an

A pair of birch four-drawer chests, designed by George Nelson Associates in the 1950s and manufactured by Herman Miller.

innovative line of his own furniture while commissioning important designs from Isamu Noguchi and Charles and Ray Eames. His marshmallow sofa, of which only a few hundred were made during his lifetime, is a whimsical study in tubular steel and vinyl-coated "marshmallow" cushions (in fact, standard bar-stool seats). Nelson's innovative Storagewall is an infinitely variable construct of poles and storage components, rearrangeable to suit its owner's taste.

ISAMU NOGUCHI

Noguchi, an American artist and sculptor, is noted for the 1940s free-form coffee tables produced by the Herman Miller Furniture Company. In his "do-it-yourself" sculpture/furniture, two curved pieces of walnut or ebonized walnut could be interlocked in any of several combinations to form a base for a biomorphic-shape glass top. Cherry bases on Noguchi tables were made only in the first year of manufacture (1948), whereas tables with birch bases were manufactured between 1948 and 1955. Around 1950, Miller also produced, for a limited time, a Noguchi-designed "rudder" dining table with a single, massive parabolic wood leg and two wire legs, accompanied by four stools.

In addition to a "rudder" dining table, Isamu Noguchi also designed a similar but smaller "rudder" coffee table. It too featured one wood and two aluminum wire legs.

VERNER PANTON

A Danish designer, Panton originally worked with fellow Dane and exponent of modern design Arne Jacobsen. After establishing his own firm in 1955, Panton developed techniques for crafting furniture in man-made materials—especially plastic. In preferring plastics, he differed from other Scandinavian designers, most of whom had chosen to work with wood and other all-natural materials. Panton determinedly pursued the ideal of a single-form chair. A revolving Cone chair was one solution, but he succeeded best with a futuristic, all-in-one-piece cantilevered plastic S chair, available in several colors from the Herman Miller Furniture Company in the United States and Vitra in Europe. The first series of Panton's injection-molded chairs dates from 1968 to 1970. A second series, less desirable than its predecessors, has a wider seat, and can be recognized by a series of strengthening, molded "gills" on the underside of its curved

Breaking with the Scandinavian tradition of wooden furniture, Verner Panton introduced his revolutionary S chair, the first chair to be produced from a single piece of molded plastic, in the mid-1960s.

A CLASSIC FROM 1952

A visitor to the Boston *Antiques Roadshow* brought in a sleek, functional desk that she had purchased for $500 in 1952, when it was the latest thing. She had lived happily with it for fifty years. "When we bought it," she said, "we loved the idea of it being modern, cutting edge, and up-to-date."

Manufactured by Herman Miller, the desk was designed by George Nelson, the company's design director. The forward-thinking Nelson was interested in ergonomics. "He cared about you sitting at your desk and wanted to be sure you had everything you needed within reach," said appraiser Karen Keane.

"Ten years ago, you could have found a George Nelson desk left on a Manhattan street corner," Keane said. "Only in the past ten years has this furniture really been looked at in the context of American design."

Because of a recent surge in interest, Herman Miller has resurrected old designs and begun manufacturing them again. While the desks' reissue does affect the value of the visitor's desk, hers remains an original and a classic, with a value of $6,000 to $8,000.

back. In addition to these, Panton also designed a Heart Cone chair and a Peacock chair—all eminently desirable at the moment.

GIO PONTI

Architect Gio Ponti is regarded as one of the most important Italian designers of the twentieth century. Along with elegant furniture, he designed plumbing fixtures, kitchen equipment, and glassware. Ponti is particularly celebrated for his post–World War II chairs, especially a lightweight ash model with a woven rush seat, called "Superleggera" (Superlight). Mass-produced in numerous colors and also made in chrome-plated steel, the chair was an updated version of an Italian fisherman's chair.

GERRIT RIETVELD

The Dutch were among the most influential of post–World War I designers, especially those associated with the movement known as de Stijl, and one member, Utrecht architect Gerrit Rietveld, designed one of the first pieces of truly avant-garde furniture, the Red Blue chair. This chair's construction required no joinery. This would, theoretically, have made it inexpensive to

Gio Ponti's Superleggera *chairs were designed to be so light that a child could lift one with one finger. These examples are made of chromed steel, with black and white woven vinyl-coated rope seats.*

mass-produce. Rietveld also designed the ZigZag chair (see page 475), which gives the impression of being made from one piece of wood (actually an impossibility). None of Reitveld's furniture was ever commercially manufactured however, perhaps because, like the famous Red Blue chair, it was usually both unstable and uncomfortable. If, stability notwithstanding, you hope to add the Red Blue chair to your collection, note that post-1923 examples are painted in bright primary colors and black. Chairs made before that date are stained, limed, or varnished.

GILBERT ROHDE

In 1930, Heywood-Wakefield (see page 505) hired furniture designer Gilbert Rohde to create a line of contemporary furniture. He capitalized on that invitation to invent a real dazzler: the first commercially made modular and sectional furniture. Gilbert Rohde's furniture was actually a translation of the metallic Bauhaus ideal into wood. Comprising interrelated bookcases and chests that could be endlessly rearranged and recombined to suit any room configuration—at the time, a new idea—his furniture designs were instantly successful. Many of Rohde's pieces for Heywood-Wakefield employed straight-grain American walnut veneers, although eventually his work became equally well known for its bentwood-style construction.

In the "Design for Living" house at the 1933 World's Fair (the Century of Progress exposition) in Chicago, Rohde was given space in which to display the full scope of his creativity. The main floor of the house was furnished with his designs for Heywood-Wakefield and its Lloyd division; the bedrooms were decorated with pieces Rohde had executed for Herman Miller, for whom he had become design director (see page 505).

EMILE-JACQUES RUHLMANN

Emile-Jacques Ruhlmann's luxurious aesthetic was about as far from the strict Bauhaus theory as it was possible to get—at least in the streamlined twentieth century. Last in a long line of great

Gilbert Rohde's bow-front six-drawer chest with semicircular pulls, burl walnut veneer, and an aluminum vertical divider was manufactured by Herman Miller.

A circa-1930 pedestal table in oak by Jacques-Emile Ruhlmann bears the distinctive (and indecipherable) "Ruhlmann" brand on the underside.

French cabinetmakers stretching back to the seventeenth century, his emblematic Art Deco designs incorporated rare and costly woods inlaid in floral motifs with ivory and other natural materials, creating a riff on Modern classicism that owed far more to Louis XV than to Louis Armstrong. The elegant Ruhlmann hallmark leg was tapered both top and bottom, and his furniture, like that of his predecessors, was stamped with his name.

Eero Saarinen's rhythmic Grasshopper chair has a bentwood frame with an upholstered molded plywood seat.

EERO SAARINEN

A leading architect of the 1940s and 1950s, Saarinen pursued the personal grail of a wholly organic chair. His rhythmic Grasshopper chair and Womb chair were both results of that pursuit.

The 1946 Womb chair, an enveloping capsule of molded plastic, cupped the sitter within a large upholstered shell, while its fabric cover had a dual purpose: Along with the obvious aesthetic one, the covering hid the unattractive plastic fibers that reinforced the fiberglass shell. Saarinen's elegant pedestal table, a slice of marble or Formica on a slender aluminum pedestal, became a symbol of the fifties, as did the related and remarkably graceful Tulip chair, produced from 1956 on. Saarinen's furniture was manufactured by Knoll (see page 506).

LOUIS SUË AND ANDRÉ MARE

Working in the traditionalist mode, the firm of Louis Suë and André Mare designed handsome commodes, desks, and chairs for the Compagnie des Arts Français; all were updated versions of classical Empire furniture. Massive, stylized, and distinctly exotic, the furniture of Suë et Mare was a virtual symphony of rich woods, gilt, and inlay, in concert with traditional bronze mounts and marble.

Kem Weber, a European émigré Modernist working in California, produced sleek furniture designs as well as film sets. This 1930s occasional table, manufactured by Lloyd, is made of chromium-plated steel and silvered and lacquered wood.

KEM WEBER

Karl Emanuel Martin (Kem) Weber, one of only a few Modernists working in 1930s California, found diverse and interesting employment in Hollywood, where he designed not only furniture but film sets. His goal was "to make the practical more beautiful, and the beautiful more practical." Greatly influenced by the Bauhaus, Weber's sleek work frequently incorporated experimental laminated woods or sprung steel. Although he is best known for his private commissions for residential furniture, some of his designs were mass-produced by the Lloyd Manufacturing Co. (the same firm that manufactured wicker and baby carriages and was ultimately acquired by Heywood-Wakefield) and bear their label. Other companies that produced Weber furniture include Widdicomb, Baker, and Berkey & Gay.

Along with his contemporaries' work, custom-designed Weber furniture has become increasingly collectible. A small wood, leather, and aluminum stool designed for a San Francisco shoe store brought $8,500 at auction in 2000.

HANS WEGNER

The tiny country of Denmark was the midcentury design Pied Piper, for its products represented all those things the era valued. The furniture made in Denmark was organic, natural, and humane, in the sense of being uniquely suited to the body's ease. It was as far from steel and aluminum—those materials of weaponry—as postwar society could get. The Piper incarnate was cabinetmaker Hans Wegner, a masterly craftsman who shaped exotic, expensive woods such as rosewood and teak (and, very rarely, plywood) into comfortable seating. Wegner's peaceful naturalism was particularly apparent in the flowing lines and sinuous curves of the chairs and tables manufactured by Fritz Hansen of Copenhagen and also by Johannes Hansen. His furniture generally bears their labels. Wegner's 1949 wood armchair is today considered the acme of Danish Modernism, and more than twenty museums worldwide include Wegner chairs in their collections.

EDWARD WORMLEY

Edward Wormley was the design director for Indiana's Dunbar Corporation, a former buggy manufacturer that, from the thirties through the fifties, factory-produced affordable, traditionally

This molded teak chair by Hans Wegner, known for his elegant and comfortable chairs, was manufactured by Fritz Hansen of Copenhagen.

Edward Wormley's walnut coffee table with a six-sided top, manufactured by Dunbar, is inset with Tiffany Favrile glass tiles. The base features relatively delicate cross-stretchers.

This armchair with a bentwood frame and loose upholstered cushions is from Russel Wright's American Modern furniture line; the furniture was successful, but never as successful as his dinnerware of the same name.

inspired modern furniture. Many of the Scandinavian-influenced, Wormley-designed pieces were constructed of unusually rich materials, including mahogany and cherry, or were embellished with brass fittings. They owed a genuine debt to classic Shaker design. Wormley is known for his prolific output. His conservative adaptations of modern design were a popular success, perhaps because, as one contemporary put it, Wormley's furniture had "good manners."

RUSSEL WRIGHT

Industrial designer Russel Wright, usually remembered for his innovative ceramic tableware (see page 15), also developed an affordable line of commercial blond wood furniture in the 1950s that he called "Easier Living." While forthrightly chunky in design, the furniture was indeed "easier" to live with because individual pieces were often cunningly multipurpose. Chair arms, for example, opened out to become magazine racks; coffee-table tops slid open to reveal niches meant to hold food and beverages. But clever as his designs were, and affordable (in 1936, the most expensive dining room piece, a maple buffet, was only $40.50), the Easier Living furniture was ultimately unsuccessful. Poorly marketed, it was just too practical, perhaps too foursquare—postwar America apparently preferred its prosperity to show.

Wright also designed furniture for retailing giants (Sears, Roebuck & Company and others) and for Conant Ball of Gardner, Massachusetts. For the latter, he created a fifty-piece line of considerably more successful solid maple furniture called "American Modern."

IMPORTANT MANUFACTURERS

A few American furniture manufacturers made important contributions to the field of twentieth-century furniture, nurturing designers as well as building chairs, tables, and other pieces.

HERMAN MILLER, INC.

Founded early in the century by D. J. DePree, a former clerk at the Star Furniture Company of Zeeland, Michigan, and his father-in-law, Herman Miller, the Herman Miller Furniture Company, as it was then called, originally manufactured reproductions of earlier styles. With the hiring of designer Gilbert Rohde in 1930, DePree, a highly religious and moral man, allowed himself to be convinced that making reproduction furniture was basically dishonest—the pieces were, after all, knock-offs—and the firm began to work exclusively with modern designers. Ultimately, Herman Miller, Inc. introduced designs by Modernist luminaries such as George Nelson, Isamu Noguchi, Verner Panton, and particularly Charles and Ray Eames, and the company developed into one of the leading exponents of American postwar design.

HEYWOOD-WAKEFIELD

The Heywood-Wakefield Company was founded in the nineteenth century to manufacture rattan wicker, at which it was successful beyond all expectations (see page 486). By 1935, an advertisement for its Streamline Maple line, heralding the firm's venture into marketing wood, read: "Its clean, simple lines are in perfect decorative harmony with quaint Colonial interiors, as well as sophisticated apartment settings." From quaint to sophisticated is something of a decorative stretch, but it may be as good an explanation as any for the immediate and lasting success of Heywood-Wakefield's suites of sturdy

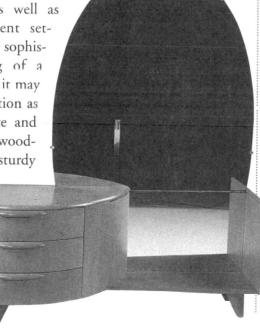

The lines and champagne finish of this 1955 Heywood-Wakefield vanity complemented pieces the company manufactured in 1935.

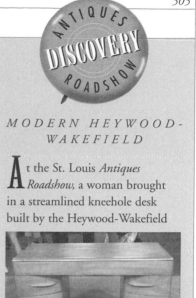

MODERN HEYWOOD-WAKEFIELD

At the St. Louis *Antiques Roadshow,* a woman brought in a streamlined kneehole desk built by the Heywood-Wakefield Company and purchased by her mother in 1940. Appraiser Chris Kennedy told her that her birch desk, a honey-colored finish, was designed by Alexis de Sakhnoffsky, a noted designer of automobiles and radios sometimes referred to as the father of American streamlining. Kennedy defined streamlining as "the art of making things look like they're in motion."

The desk exhibited excellent craftsmanship, especially in the dovetailed construction of the drawers. Because it was manufactured before the company adopted its trademark in 1946, it lacks the identifying eagle mark of later furniture. "But it is definitely Heywood-Wakefield," noted Kennedy, and is worth between $1,200 and $1,500.

blond wood furniture. With their airflow design, these sets sum up the spirit of the thirties. During the Depression era, the unthreateningly rounded corners of the style combined with real affordability to make Heywood-Wakefield's blocky, homely sofas, dressing tables, easy chairs, and dining room sets the friendly face of the modern American interior. For a full 30 years thereafter, the company continued to produce—as it had promised the buyers of its furniture it would—assorted complements to the 1930s designs that were wholly harmonious in design and finish with the originals of a generation earlier.

KNOLL

The firm that began as H. G. Knoll Furniture Company in 1938 became synonymous with "modern" mainly because its owners, Hans and Florence Knoll, were farsighted enough to employ artists such as Harry Bertoia, Hans Wegner, George Nakashima (see page 497), and Eero Saarinen (see page 502). Knoll also had the good sense to offer royalties to its illustrious stable of top designers, a novelty at the time. Many of the firm's classic designs continue to be manufactured.

THONET

A bentwood rocker from the turn of the twentieth century. Michael Thonet began making bentwood furniture in the 1840s, and the style became enormously popular in the 1870s. The furniture is very collectible today.

Michael Thonet (*tone*-it), owner of a furniture factory in Vienna, first became interested in creating furniture made of softened and bent beechwood poles in the 1840s. At the Philadelphia Centennial Exhibition of 1876, his invention—lightweight, graceful, and affordable bentwood furniture—was an immediate success and was quickly taken up by every level of society. It wasn't long before hundreds of manufacturers discovered bentwood. Along with useful hat racks and hall stands, Thonet and his sons manufactured thousands of stools, chairs, settees, and large sinuous rockers—many with decorative impressed seats—for use in public buildings and offices and on shipboard. The furniture was shipped in pieces from Austria, then assembled by the retailer at its destination. By 1930, the firm had sold a stunning 50 million of its No. 14 bentwood chairs. Thonet furniture is a precursor of Bauhaus design, appearing frequently in museum exhibitions, and is eagerly collected by twentieth-century furniture enthusiasts. Thonet pieces are often labeled.

DECORATOR-DESIGNED FURNITURE

Furniture designers and architects are not alone in designing furniture. Interior decorators also design special pieces for their clients. Vintage decorator-designed furniture was custom-made furniture and, as such, definitely a luxury item. But it was a vanity field too, for both client and designer; if the client needed a certain size bookcase for the living room, for instance, it would naturally be less expensive to find a usable example in a furniture store than it would be to have a special piece designed and built. Many decorators, however, yearned then as they do now to create their own furniture—it is, after all, their only chance to do "couture." And some clients seem to have rather enjoyed paying for the privilege of owning the one-of-a-kind furnishings designed and made only for them.

Collectors today believe that the best decorator-designed pieces were made between the 1920s and the 1960s (some pieces made in the fifties, inspired by eighteenth-century French furniture, in fact, merit comparison with eighteenth-century originals). Although sometimes such custom-made pieces were labeled, many were not.

French designer Jacques Adnet is known today for his leather furniture. Even the rockers of this circa-1950 rocking chair, manufactured in association with Hermès, are sheathed in leather.

JACQUES ADNET

Jacques Adnet advocated French Modernism during the 1950s, creating inventive pieces in walnut and leather. He worked particularly with Hermès of Paris to create leather chairs and tables.

ELSIE DE WOLFE

Elsie De Wolfe, the New York interior designer who claimed to have invented the decorating profession, was known for employing hints of surrealism in her designs, and for whimsies such as white palm trees. She also designed furniture that was carefully traditional in most respects, as she did for her first important commission, the Colony Club, a private women's club in New York.

DOROTHY DRAPER

An American decorator known primarily for large-scale and vividly colored furnishings, Dorothy Draper designed custom work that tends, amazingly, to seem neo-Baroque, neo-Victorian, and forties Hollywood—all at the same time.

WILLIAM HAINES

Billy Haines, once a movie star, later transformed himself into a successful Hollywood interior designer. His most notable furniture design was the "hostess chair," first used in the house of director George Cukor. Other clients included Lionel Barrymore, Claudette Colbert, and Joan Crawford. Haines furniture with a Hollywood provenance is much sought-after.

Actor-turned-designer William Haines was famous for his "hostess chair," a modified slipper chair with short legs and a comfortable upholstered seat and back.

JANSEN

The Jansen firm, headed by Stephane Boudin, had offices in Paris and New York, and assisted the young Jackie Kennedy when she redecorated the White House in the early 1960s. Boudin had great range, and because he created furniture for both maids' rooms and the Duke and Duchess of Windsor, there's quite a lot available, although it is of mixed quality.

PAUL LASZLO

Launched on his career as an industrial designer by a 1929 commission to redesign a duplicating machine, Hungarian Paul Laszlo ran the metalworking shop at the Bauhaus for five years. He emigrated to the United States in 1937, and promptly found work in Beverly Hills, where he attracted several clients with major star power, Cary Grant and Elizabeth Taylor among them. Although Laszlo created custom furniture for these and other notables, he also turned out a commercial line of upholstered pieces and tables for Herman Miller in the late 1940s.

A soigné club chair designed by Paul Laszlo, circa 1941, with ebony-stained wood armrests and leather upholstery.

JULES LELEU

Jules Leleu was an exhibitor in the seminal 1925 Paris Art Deco exhibition. His classically inspired stools, commodes, and desks always reveal their traditional French antecedents, and his work often incorporates period details such as bronze mounts and inlaid flowers, often in mother of pearl. Because Leleu worked into the 1960s, his pieces are relatively plentiful in the market.

Jules Leleu's bronze-mounted mahogany, silver-leaf, and glass-topped side table, from about 1930, shows his familiarity with the emerging Art Deco idiom as well as with its classical French antecedents.

T. H. ROBSJOHN-GIBBINGS

Furniture designer T. H. Robsjohn-Gibbings had his own shop on Madison Avenue, but he also designed for the Widdicomb Company and for Baker. Ultimately, he is better remembered for the furniture he designed and manufactured himself than he is for the work he did for mass manufacturers, particularly for such pieces as coolly elegant Klismos chairs, modeled after the Greek originals. Both playful and stylish, Robsjohn-Gibbings's furniture, especially an Art Deco series executed in blond woods, is also highly sculptural.

JEAN ROYERE

A French designer of the 1950s, Jean Royère was partial to amoebalike forms and long, horizontal lines. He is known particularly for upholstered seating, sculptural furniture, and wood pieces incorporating cane.

This elegant gilt bronze and marble console table, designed by Jean Royère, a French designer fond of biomorphic forms, combines luxe materials with up-to-the-minute style in 1948.

REPRODUCTION FURNITURE

However enthusiastic design critics may be, the general furniture-buying public is resistant to the new. Consequently, many well-known furniture manufacturers of the twentieth century established their reputations by reproducing beautiful and authentic-looking examples of antique furniture. These pieces are not fakes. Instead, they constitute a

For those who choose to collect reproductions, *Antiques Roadshow* appraiser Kerry Shrives says that the big advantage to buying a vintage reproduction of a Williamsburg secretary made by a top-quality manufacturer—Kittinger, for example—is that you can often purchase a used piece in the secondary market (at an auction gallery or a vintage furniture store) for a fraction of what it cost when new. Or what it would cost if made today, in fact. She strongly recommends, however, that before you buy anything, you do your homework. This means reading everything you can find on the styles you're interested in, including books, auction catalogs, and, if you can locate them, sales brochures. (For twentieth-century objects, they are not very hard to find.) Many books and catalogs are available on the Web or in libraries. Copies of sales brochures can sometimes be obtained from the original manufacturer, and originals can occasionally be found at flea markets.

This reproduction Sheraton-style mahogany bow-front chest, made by the Nathan Margolis Shop of Hartford, Connecticut, has somewhat awkward, provincial-style legs.

genuine homage to the styles of the past. And because the market for this traditional furniture has always been so much larger than that for modern furniture, much more of it is available today.

When examining any piece of reproduction furniture, keep in mind that the better it replicates the antique original, the better its quality is likely to be. If a chair, for example, has carving, look for it to be deep and crisp, and with a back that is as carefully executed as the front. If a piece has an elaborately painted finish, the subject of the painted reserves (flowers, pastoral scenes, stenciled patterns) and the condition of the paint should always be a factor in your evaluation.

When examining anything unlabeled, teach yourself to spot pieces that have good design. Begin by looking at pictures of the original Chippendale, Hepplewhite, Federal, or Jacobean chairs, tables, or whatever form you're interested in, and then weigh the genuine antique, in your mind's eye, against the twentieth-century copy. The reproduction should measure up in several ways: The proportions should be close to those of the original; the carving should be deep, as mentioned above, and preferably, done by hand. Carved elements, if there are any, should not be glued on. If the piece is veneered, look for carefully matched veneers. If it isn't veneered, it shouldn't be made of "sow's ear" wood, stained to look like a mahogany silk purse. The well-made piece might have expensive details, as well, such as actual inlay, not just painted-on design pretending to be inlay. And if the piece is supposed to look like one in use in 1776, the form should be

a form that actually existed. There was never such a thing as a Chippendale coffee table, for example. That ubiquitous "Martha Washington" sewing table so popular in the teens and twenties—the one with the lift-up top and D-shape side compartments—is a perfect example of "invented" Colonial design, as is the "Hepplewhite" phonograph cabinet. Neither piece of furniture is in danger of being of value to the collecting community. (The phonograph inside that cabinet might be another story.)

Until the last decade of the twentieth century, very few collectors bought reproduction furniture, especially if they could find the much more desirable original antique. Then, a few scholars and curators (like those at the Metropolitan Museum) began to look more closely at the Colonial Revival furniture the scholarly community had formerly ignored. Following that lead, dealers in vintage furniture began to reevaluate the bedroom, living room, and dining room suites that had been stamped out in quantities by some of the better manufacturers, Biggs or Margolis, for example, with a trickle-down effect extending to such lesser-known Grand Rapids makers as the Phoenix Furniture Company and Nelson, Matter & Company. Pieces manufactured by Kittinger of Buffalo, New York, and Baker of Allegan, Michigan, especially, find ready buyers today, as these companies produced "nicely made, clean copies" of American Colonial furniture. The latter two, along with the John Widdicomb Company (not the same as the Widdicomb Furniture

A 1930s effort at a mahogany Chippendale-style chest on stand (frequently called a "highboy"), with a full-bonnet pediment top, betrays its non-period origins by its proportions.

PAINTED SHERATON-STYLE REPRODUCTIONS

In recent years, beautifully painted reproductions of eighteenth-century English Adam and Sheraton furniture have become very attractive to fans of these delicate traditional styles who might be unwilling or unable to pay the truly astounding prices being asked for originals. Made in the first decades of the twentieth century and into the thirties and forties by numerous high-end furniture manufacturers—many of them, like Gillow, British—these paint-decorated tables and cabinets are actively sought after by collectors who appreciate their decorative appeal, provided their competently rendered decorations of garlands, musical instruments, and romantic vignettes are not faded (or "buffed" away by overenthusiastic housecleaning or alcohol spills). The better examples exhibit very fine quality hand painting.

"NEWPORT" FURNITURE

"Newport" furniture, which has just recently become collectible, is the furniture associated with the era of Edith Wharton. Edwardian in spirit—that is, delicate and French influenced—it is not veneered in expensive marquetry or trimmed in bronze. It was usually painted the palest gray or creamy white. By today's standards, it was brilliantly carved, with spiraling or finely reeded arms and legs, and dainty, carved rosebud crests and crisp corner rosettes. Such furniture was generally found, in the teens and twenties, in the guest rooms of elegant hotels or in summer cottages by the sea, the most prominent examples of which could be seen at Newport—thus, the name.

Company), are among the manufacturers still in business. There is a growing market for their vintage products.

There is a market, as well, for certain Boston manufacturers such as Irving and Casson, Charak Furniture Co., A. H. Davenport, and the Paine Furniture Company, as well as for the work of Meier & Hagen of New York. *Antiques Roadshow* appraiser Kerry Shrives notes that today, in the Northeast particularly, vintage twentieth-century reproductions of the Queen Anne style can do as well at auction as early-nineteenth-century French furniture, which is genuinely antique! What follows is a selection of notable manufacturers of reproduction furniture.

NOTABLE MANUFACTURERS OF REPRODUCTION FURNITURE

BERKEY & GAY

In the 1920s, the Berkey & Gay Company, with some 2,800 employees and thirty acres of factories, showrooms, and warehouses, led the industry in producing mid-priced Colonial and Jacobean styles. (The fashion for Jacobean was inspired, to some extent, by its association with great and new American wealth, such as the collection of period antiques amassed by that grand acquisitor of the pre–World War I era, J. P. Morgan.) The firm, which originated in the 1860s, specialized in manufacturing "suites" of furniture for living rooms, dining rooms, bedrooms, libraries, and halls. It declared bankruptcy in 1931, but was successfully revived three years later, continuing in business until 1948.

BIGGS AND H. C. VALENTINE

Some rather fine reproduction furniture was made by Biggs of Richmond, Virginia. In the 1930s, Biggs sold genuine antiques and also did a thriving mail-order business in "Fine Colonial Reproductions" (presumably copied from its own antique stock). Biggs was eventually acquired by Kittinger.

Another Richmond firm, H. C. Valentine & Co., advertised that each one of the seven coats of finish on its furniture was hand-applied and hand-rubbed. Such quality would be well worth looking for today—and a far cry from the spray varnishes of some reproduction furniture of current manufacture.

WALLACE NUTTING

Between World War I and the 1930s, Wallace Nutting, a retired Congregational minister, ran a single-minded campaign to convince his fellow Americans that reproductions of their own colonial-era furnishings were not only worth owning, but were homier, more functional, and more appropriate than any of the steel and glass furniture coming out of Europe. Nutting wrote lengthily on the subject and took extensive photographs of recreated early American interiors, extant early American houses, and landscapes. In his Framingham, Massachusetts, shop, his workmen crafted exceptionally high-quality, largely handmade reproduction furniture, particularly reproductions of Windsor chairs. (His catalog contained more than 100 styles of Windsor chair.)

Nutting's furniture was not inexpensive. In an era when a commercially made desk might cost $100 to $150, the Nutting desk was $300. Although his patriotism was commendable, and his insistence on quality was admirable, he wasn't a purist, certainly not by today's standards. He reworked original proportions, adding, narrowing, or enlarging

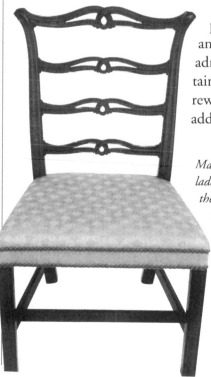

Many reproductions of Chippendale-style ladderback side chairs were produced in the United States during the first half of the twentieth century; this one, made of carved mahogany, came from the workshop of Wallace Nutting.

A knuckle-armed, fan-backed Windsor chair from Wallace Nutting's shop is a well-produced reproduction of a Colonial example.

PSEUDO PHYFE

The cabinetmaker Ernest Hagen apprenticed as a young man in the workshop of early New York furniture designer Duncan Phyfe. For much of the twentieth century, Hagen's nineteenth-century reproductions of Phyfe's work were sufficiently well executed to fool museum curators. Today, these excellent copies have become collectible in and of themselves.

TABLES FROM GOOD STOCK

During the twentieth century, few sources of interesting, furniture-worthy materials were overlooked. In the 1920s, for example, when the renowned War of 1812 battleship *Constitution* was being restored in Boston, the Berkey & Gay Company of Grand Rapids, Michigan, purchased the discarded timbers from one of its lower decks to use in a special series of "Old Ironsides" tables. These tables were designed for the firm by the famed traditional furniture expert Wallace Nutting; each table of this "special edition" was embellished with carvings of eagles.

This Philadelphia-style mahogany Chippendale dressing table (or "lowboy") is a decently proportioned and fairly well carved reproduction made by the Nathan Margolis Shop.

on antiques if he deemed their aesthetics imperfect, giving his output a distinctive "Nutting" style. The tidal wave of his all-too-successful proselytizing bore in its backwash an oppressive detritus: furniture stores full of ersatz Colonial-style "accents," such as cutesy cobbler's-bench coffee tables, high-backed rocking chairs, and scaled-down spinning wheels. Most Nutting furniture is either labeled or numbered.

NATHAN MARGOLIS

During the first and second quarter of the twentieth century, the peak years of Colonial Revival furniture's popularity, the Nathan Margolis Shop of Hartford, Connecticut, manufactured fine-quality handmade reproductions of eighteenth-century American furniture priced for the upper-middle-class household. In one twenty-five-year period, some 7,400 individual pieces of Colonial-style reproduction furniture were offered for sale, including sideboards, high chests, and Chippendale-style chairs, as America's appetite for its proper English products seemed insatiable. The quality of Margolis's craftsmanship may have been mainly due to its employing highly skilled émigré

artisans. Only very recently, beginning in the 1990s, have such pieces been sought by collectors.

Chapter Fourteen

AN EXPERTS' ROUNDTABLE

Now that you've made your way through this book, you know a good deal about the current collectibles market. You've read about twentieth-century ceramics, glass, costume jewelry, toys, dolls, fashion, furniture, advertising memorabilia, and many other collecting areas. You've learned a little about their history, about who made them and when, and you've learned a bit about how to examine them, how to evaluate them, and where to go for more information. But you probably still have questions and would definitely like to

know, for instance, where the experts think the collectibles market is going and what they'd suggest for your collection.

Antiques Roadshow appraisers are frequently asked this question. Matchbox cars? Yo-yos? Bricks? Eight-track tapes? Lava lamps? Smurfs? So many beginning, and even experienced, collectors seem to want direction; of course, the best answer—some say the only answer—and the one that the experts offer first, is: Collect What You Love. People who are "born collectors" understand this instinctively; their passion for owning the

Top: Cast-iron mechanical banks, like this elephant, were collected only a few decades after they were manufactured. Right: Lava lamps—trash or treasure?

Who'd have dreamed these rare Bride and Groom Pez dispensers would ever be worth $3,000 to devoted collectors?

things they collect is matched by their passion for acquiring them, and they happily spend their time finding, learning about, obtaining, and showing off their collections. Nevertheless, some people love everything; some people haven't yet come across their true (inanimate) love; some, confronted with a house, apartment, or office with empty tabletops, shelves, and cabinets, simply hope to fill them with objects that will illuminate otherwise unapparent depths of their personalities. No appraiser ever suggests that collectibles be bought primarily for investment. All, in fact, place that at the bottom of their lists of reasons to collect. Still, many sensible people have come to view the collectibles market as a kind of user-friendly stock market. So when people who haven't yet found their collecting passion ask *Antiques Roadshow* experts what to collect, what these potential collectors—people who enjoy a bit of a gamble—*really* want to know is: "Are there types of collectibles that will be fun to collect, be a reasonable investment for me, and a nice legacy, perhaps, for my grandchildren? What can you recommend for me now that will increase the likelihood of my descendants making an appearance on the *Antiques Roadshow* of 2103?"

That's a difficult and provocative question, but a group of *Antiques Roadshow* collectibles experts agreed to take it on, along with a few other aspects of twenty-first-century collecting, as well as give their necessarily distilled impressions of the current collectibles market. Their observations here highlight the interesting and important place that collectibles occupy in America's cultural panorama. For just beyond pop culture, fads, aesthetics, and Mickey Mouse lie sociology and history. If entire societies can be summed up in their artifacts, then those who possess considerable knowledge of and experience with certain of those arifacts may be able to offer a special insight into our lives and times. So these *Antiques Roadshow* experts have given serious thought to questions such as "Which, if any, of the items we think of as 'collectibles' will become the 'antiques' of tomorrow—will be treasured and valued the way Chippendale chairs and Sèvres porcelain are today." They also offered—with enthusiasm, reservations, ambivalence, and various explanations—their opinions on what may be the most interesting element in the world of collecting today: the impact the Internet has had on twentieth-century collectibles. The discussion ultimately led to the $64,000 question: "What can the average person collect today that will retain its collectibility (value) beyond our own era; beyond the generation that grew up with it?"

Their answers, of course, were as varied and idiosyncratic as the appraisers are themselves. Although each knows his or her specialty thoroughly, many were cautious—as anyone but Nostradamus, perhaps, would be—when asked to predict the future. Fortunetelling, all were careful to explain, isn't usually part of an appraiser's job description. Nevertheless, each *Antiques Roadshow* expert quoted here was willing, for the edification (and perhaps amusement) of future enthusiasts, to stick his or her neck way, way out. So you'll find below well considered, intelligent, really "insider" suggestions as to what things you should think of looking at twice. Pick and choose among their opinions and these objects, but remember to take them with the proverbial grain of salt—all the while refraining from retroactive blame, legal recourse, and audible laughter.

And don't forget to come to the 2103 *Antiques Roadshow*!

His burning eyes, on this 1920s poster, promise clairvoyance. But every collector could use an Alexander.

THE GROWING INTEREST IN COLLECTIBLES

"America is a collecting nation and I like that," says Noel Barrett. "I think it's healthy." He notes that collecting in the United States really started in the 1950s, when the average person first began to accumulate some disposable income. "Unlike European countries, however, the United States has a short past," he continues, "and because change is so rapid here, things start to look 'quaint' fairly quickly. In fact, in 1926, the first mechanical bank appeared on the cover of *Antiques* magazine. It was only thirty or so years old, then, and it was already considered 'antique.'"

David Lackey says, "Collectibles capture history, nostalgia, sentiment, and fantasy. And—significantly—the more exposure things get (who knew there would ever be a television show about antiques?), the more scholarship improves." He thinks the best thing about the scope of the current collectibles market is that it represents practically every social, intellectual, and financial level and makes everything available. "The field used to be narrower and more rigorous," he says, "but today, if you only want to collect objects relating to motorcycles or the military, for instance, there's a world of items to choose from."

The Roundtable Participants

ERIC ALBERTA

Alberta heads an independent advisory service specializing in antique toys and artifacts of popular culture, that provides appraisals, cataloguing, and acquisition and dispersal services to clients including auction houses, museums, dealers, and collectors. He was formerly vice president of the collectibles department at Sotheby's in New York. He has extensive experience in the collectibles marketplace, having begun his career as a dealer in upstate New York when he was thirteen years old.

NOEL BARRETT

The owner of Noel Barrett Antiques & Auctions Ltd. in Carversville, Pennsylvania, Barrett is an antiques dealer specializing in vintage toys and advertising memorabilia who also produces two to three specialized auctions annually. He is a noted lecturer and consultant in the field of antique toys.

LEILA DUNBAR

Dunbar is senior vice president, director of the collectibles department, and global director of online collectibles

auctions at Sotheby's in New York. Previously, she assisted in expanding her family's business, Dunbar's Gallery in Milford, Massachusetts, which specializes in toys, automotive and motorcycle memorabilia, and sports, advertising, and folk art, into international arenas.

KEN FARMER

Farmer is owner of Ken Farmer Auctions & Appraisals in Radford, Virginia, and is an expert in many areas of antiques and collectibles, including Southern material culture, American furniture, folk art, decorative arts, and selected musical instruments.

J. MICHAEL FLANIGAN

A private antiques dealer in Baltimore, Maryland, Flanigan has worked with American furniture for more than twenty years. He learned about furniture from the inside out by spending seven years repairing and restoring furniture for a noted antique dealer.

RUDI FRANCHI

With his wife, Barbara, Franchi owns The Nostalgia Factory in Boston,

Massachusetts. He deals in a wide variety of collectibles and ephemera, specializing in entertainment memorabilia, original vintage advertising, travel and war posters, and other forms of vintage graphic art. For the last several years, Franchi has focused entirely on selling original movie posters and related film advertising over the Internet.

CHRISTOPHER KENNEDY

A dealer in twentieth-century furniture, Kennedy became interested in modern design when he was studying American history at the University of Massachusetts–Amherst. After completing his studies, he opened an antiques store in Northampton, Massachusetts, specializing in items from the Victorian age to the present. Since 1981, he has concentrated on modern design.

DAVID LACKEY

Owner of David Lackey Antiques in Houston, Texas, Lackey has been collecting since he was six years old and dealing since he was twelve. He has specialized in ceramics since 1986, although his company also sells

Ken Farmer thinks the urge to collect is in the genes. "The acquisition of favorite objects—and for my age group, these seem to combine childhood sentiment with affordability—probably satisfies some basic hunter-gatherer urge," he says. "We don't have to hunt and gather expensive things, either. The vast majority of collectibles changing hands today are valued at less than $500."

Christie Romero agrees with Farmer. "It's human nature to collect," she says. "Even kids collect." Concerning the diversity

eighteenth- and nineteenth-century furniture and decorative arts, along with regional art of the twentieth century.

TIM LUKE

Cofounder of TreasureQuest Auction Galleries in Jupiter, Florida, Luke specializes in antique toys, dolls, bears, and pop-culture collectibles. He was formerly the director of the collectibles department at Christie's in New York.

PHILIP J. MERRILL

An expert in black memorabilia and material culture, Merrill is the founder of Nanny Jack & Company, named after Mr. Merrill's great-grandmother. His specialties include African-American historical research, oral history interviewing techniques, as well as collecting and interpreting artifacts. Merrill coauthored the book *Baltimore*, which documents the everyday life of the city's African-American citizens before and after desegregation. He has also written *The Art of Collecting Black Memorabilia*, a guide to collecting African-American material culture.

DAVID RAGO

Owner of David Rago Auctions, Ltd., in Lambertville, New Jersey, Rago is a specialist in American and European Arts and Crafts–style decorative arts and furnishings. His auctions focus on twentieth-century decorative art from Mission furniture and art pottery to art glass and Modernist furniture. He also conducts specialty auctions featuring Roseville pottery.

CHRISTIE ROMERO

Director of the Center for Jewelry Studies and the West Coast Antique and Period Jewelry Seminar, Romero is an antique jewelry historian, lecturer, instructor, consultant, and collector. She is the author of *Warman's Jewelry*, and is a member of the faculty of the gemology department at Santiago Canyon College in Orange, California, near her home in Anaheim.

GARY SOHMERS

Operator of Wex Rex Collectibles, a retail and Internet collectibles business in Framingham, Massachusetts, Sohmers has thirty years of experience as a retailer and consultant to collectors and investors. He also produces an annual "Collectibles Extravaganza,"

for which he organizes cast reunions of old television programs such as *Lost in Space* and *The Munsters*.

USHA SUBRAMANIAM

The founder of Icon20, a web site devoted to twentieth-century design and decorative arts, Subramaniam has extensive experience in the auction business, having worked at Christie's and Phillip's, New York, where she founded the twentieth-century decorative arts department.

RICHARD WRIGHT

Owner of Richard Wright Antiques in Birchrunville, Pennsylvania, Wright is an antiques dealer with particular expertise in dolls from the eighteenth through the mid-twentieth centuries. His shop also features antique toys, Art Nouveau and Art Deco glass, pottery, and bronzes, furniture, and Victoriana.

NECKLACE OR SCULPTURE?

When appraiser Gloria Lieberman met a woman with a magnificent piece of jewelry hanging around her neck at the Boston *Antiques Roadshow,* she

asked the owner if she regularly wore the piece. The visitor said that her mother, the original owner, preferred to hang it on the wall. The visitor's mother had purchased the necklace in New York City's Greenwich Village in the late fifties or early sixties. Lieberman told her that the necklace was clearly made by a famous African-American jeweler of that period, Art Smith, who set up shop in Greenwich Village. Smith was a studio jeweler who, along with others such as Sam Kramer and Ed Wiener, helped bring the Modernist and abstract sensibility into the world of jewelry. "Smith liked to make things that reminded him of tribal art," Lieberman said. Her appraisal: between $5,000 and $10,000.

of current collecting fields, she says, "These days, everything is collectible. This may be because it's a pleasant diversion, but it may also be because it gives people more of an identity."

Rudy Franchi thinks it has to do with the prevalence of leisure time. "The great early collectors were very wealthy; by the fifties, collecting had spread to the middle class, to ordinary people who unexpectedly found themselves with enough time and money to 'curate' collections," he says. "Today, collecting is something like cultivating a green lawn. Everyone does it. Moreover, as Americans travel more, the hobby of 'collecting' gives them something to look for on their travels."

Chris Kennedy thinks that there may be a kind of group collecting psychology that makes some people want to "keep up with the Joneses." But, he says, "Most people enjoy a challenge and the satisfaction of having done all their homework to the extent of being able to say, 'Hey, I remember when you could buy—insert your own collectible here—for a song.'"

"The reasons for collecting are as endless as the range of collectibles," notes Eric Alberta. "There is passion, there is nostalgia, and there is culture. The baby-boomer generation was brought up collecting things, which may be partly due to the influence of Andy Warhol. He legitimized the ordinary—things like cookie jars—making it okay to collect it." Speaking of baby boomers, Richard Wright says, "Probably the majority of collectors today are baby boomers, and they are buying back the things they had as kids—toys and dolls from late fifties into the early eighties. These days, too, more and more people are beginning to realize that the stock market isn't necessarily the best place to put their money. They'd rather own something they can look at."

"The range of collectibles is wider than it ever has been," says Leila Dunbar, "primarily because there is more information and greater awareness of the field. It used to be that only small groups collected, and the

Conventional costume jewelry is always collectible: a rhinestone and "emerald" lizard pin.

information they shared was purely anecdotal. Now, there's a ripple effect: the more people know, the more they collect."

And collecting areas are growing ever wider. "Sports and toys, of course, have been collected seriously for thirty years," says Dunbar. "Hollywood and Rock and Roll are newer—they've only been popular since the early eighties. Now we live in a celebrity culture, and so, if you fell in love with Audrey Hepburn in *Breakfast at Tiffany's*, you might want to own that poster. Such things used to be hard to find, but these days the studios realize that props and costumes can all be collectible and they're making them available to the public almost as soon as their films are released. Sports collectibles, too, are celebrity driven. Today, Wall Streeters like having a Michael Jordan basketball in their offices."

On the subject of the expanding collectibles universe, Gary Sohmers goes even further. "The range of collectibles available today is absolutely *infinite*," he says. "Among some two hundred to five hundred macro-niches, each has at least one thousand micro-micro niches."

Tim Luke thinks collecting is therapeutic. "People want to collect things that can transport them to another time," he says, "and collecting is always an outgrowth of nostalgia and disposable income. There is something for everyone out there, too, something that's a combination of fantasy and whatever brings it home for you. You don't get that from buying a brand-new couch."

Phillip Merrill thinks collecting is educational, social, *and* therapeutic. "The *Antiques Roadshow* itself has inspired other 'appraisal fairs,'" he notes, "thereby causing people to examine more carefully the objects of their own social and cultural history. This in turn produces more and more collectibles, so that now there are even McDonald's collector's conventions. Does this mean we're all crazy? Well, collecting has become a way of life."

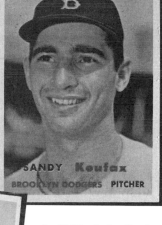

Costume jewelry with personality: a 1950s silver bracelet by studio jeweler Sam Kramer named "Taxidermology."

In 1957, pitcher Sandy Koufax smiled shyly on a Topps card; Jackie Robinson, on a Topps card from 1955, slammed one.

Collectibles Micro-niches

Most experts advise being a focused collector, and for those who want to take that advice to its extreme, *Antiques Roadshow* appraiser Gary Sohmers, an expert in pop culture, has supplied this "partial" list of subcategories within the universe of collecting.

ADVERTISING, AUTOGRAPHS & EPHEMERA

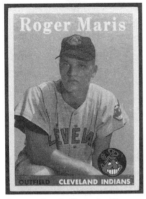

Serious baseball-card collectors look for serious Roger Maris on Topps cards from 1958.

Advertising Dolls; Airline; Alcohol; Anime; Auction Catalogs; Autographs *(Historical, Performing Arts, Political, Radio, Sports, Movies & Television)*; Bakery; Biscuit Tins; Borden's/Elsie; Burger King; Bus; Business Cards; Calendars; Campbell Soup; Candy *(Hershey, Nestle, Willie Wonka, Other)*; Cards *(Non-Sports Trading, Sports Trading, Food Premiums, Gum, Tobacco)*; Catalogs *(Wholesale, Mail Order)*; Cereal *(Boxes, Premiums)*; Checks; Chewing Gum Wrappers; Clocks; Coca-Cola; Coffee; Comic Characters; Comics *(Premiums, Newspaper, Books)*; Country Store; Cracker Jack; Daguerreotypes; Dairy; Deeds; Displays; Dr. Pepper; Documents; Drug Store; Esso; Fast Food *(McDonald's, Burger King, Ads, Premiums, Other)*; Forestry; Gasoline; Giveaways; Greeting Cards; Hires; Household; Illuminated Manuscripts; Illustrations; Insurance Companies; Labels; Magazine Advertisements; Magazines; Magic; Maps/Charts; Matchcovers; Menus; Mirrors; Misprints; Money; Moxie; Newspapers; Paper Dolls; Passports; Patent Drawings; Pepsi-Cola; Photographs; Place Cards; Planters Peanuts; Playbills; Photographs; Playing Cards; Political; Posters *(Art, Concert, Circus, Travel, Magic, Performing Arts, Movies, Television)*; Premiums *(Radio, Food, Drinks, Other)*; Produce Box Labels; Promotional Glasses; Radio *(Surveys, Ads, Premiums)*; Railroad; Restaurant *(General, Howard Johnson's)*; Seed and Feed; Shoes; Signs; Sinclair; Smokey the Bear; Soap; Soda; Soup; Stocks and Bonds; Tea; Telephone; Television; Texaco; Theater Programs; Thermometers; Timetables; Tires; Tins *(Food, Other, Tobacco)*; Tobaccoiana; Trade Cards; Travel Brochures; Trays; Truck Lines; TV Guides; Utilities; Valentines; Victoriana; Visiting Cards

AROUND THE HOUSE

Accessories; Animal Licenses; Architectural Artifacts

A Roseville Apple Blossom vase from 1948 is of interest to collectors of Roseville as well as household ceramics.

(Backbars, Mantels, Beveled Glass, Moldings, Decorative, Stained Glass, Doorknobs, Plumbing, Doors, Windows, Fences, Garden); Art Deco; Art Noveau; Arts and Crafts; Bathroom; Bookends; Boxes; Brass; Cast Iron; Charge Plates; Chase Chrome; Copper; Doorstops; Early American; Faberware; Fans; Fireplace; Hammered Aluminum; Ink Wells; Iron Implements; Irons; Jointed Boxes; Keys and Locks; Kitchen and Bar *(Agateware, Apple Peelers, Baskets, Boxes, Butter Pats, Butter Churns, Butter Molds, Candy Molds, Cast-Iron Cookware, Chocolate Molds, Cocktail Shakers, Coffee Grinders, Cookie Cutters, Cookie Jars, Cooking Utensils, Corkscrews, Crocks, Dinnerware, Egg Beaters, Electric Appliances—Pre-1950, Electric Appliances—Post-1950s, Electric Appliances—Toasters, Electric Appliances—Mixers, Electric Appliances—Other Chrome, Enamelware, Food Molds, Fruit Jars, Graniteware, Home Canning, Ice Cream Scoops, Iron Cookware, Jugs, Match Holders, Melmac, Nutcrackers, Nutmeg Grinders, Oak Ice Cabinets, Pie Birds, Pie Crimpers,*

523

Reamers, Refrigerator Magnets, Rolling Pins, Salt and Pepper Shakers, Spoons, String Holders, Sugar Packets, Swizzle Sticks, Tea Caddies, Toasters, Toothpick Holders); Lead; Letter Openers; Locks and Keys; Matchsafes; Mirrors; Napkin Rings; Oriental; Pewter; Pewter Molds; Picture Frames; Pocket Knives; Radios (Transistors, Cathedral, Wooden, Ham, Shortwave, Catalin and Bakelite, Novelty, Character); Rug Beaters; Sadirons; Sewing machines; Scales; Shaving (Razors, Mirrors, Other); Sheffield Plate; Silver (Boxes, Flatware, Holloware, English, Sterling Service); Silverplate (Flatware, Holloware); Spittoons; Stoves; Telephones (pre–World War II, post–World War II, Character/Novelty); Television Sets (pre–World War II, 1950s, post–1950s); Tin and Tole; Toiletry; Tools (Garden, Planes, Metalworking, Rulers, Stanley, Woodworking, Wrenches); Treen Ware; Trivets; Trunks; Victorian Design; Washboards; Wrought Iron

MEMORABILIA

Amusement Park; Associations (Rotary, Lions Club, Kiwanis, Masonic, Other); Aviation; Boats; British Royalty; Buddhism; Buildings; Bus; Casino; Celebrity; Centennial Exposition; Christianity; Civil War; College; Colombian Exposition; Commemorative; Dance; Dinosaur; Exploration; Exposition; Fire; Floating Pens; Fraternal Group; Gas Station; Gold Rush; Hotel; Howard Johnson's; Industrial; John F. Kennedy; Judaica; License Plates; Lindbergh; Lottery; Mardi Gras; Martin Luther King Jr.; Medical; Miss America; Motion Picture; Ocean Liner; Olympic Games; Police; Political; Presidential; Princess Diana; Prohibition; Railroad; Resort; Salvation Army; Scouting (Boy Scouts, Girl Scouts, Brownies, Other); Souvenir; Souvenir Buildings; States (East Coast, Midwest, South, Rockies, West Coast, Other); Statue of Liberty; Telegraph; Tokens; Trade Union; Train; Travel; Trolley; Wedding/Baptism; World's Fair; Zeppelin.

MOVIES, MUSIC, RADIO & TELEVISION

Advertising; Amplifiers: (pre–1970, post–1970); Beatles (1960s Memorabilia, Records, Magazines and Paper, Autographs, Yellow Submarine, Limited Editions); Blues (Records, Posters, Paper and Memorabilia); Brass Instruments; Cassettes; Classical; Country (Records, Posters Paper and Memorabilia); Drums and Percussion Instruments; Edison; Eight-Track Tapes; Elvis Presley; Guitar Amplifiers; Guitar Effects; Guitars (Acoustic, Electric); Harmonicas; Jazz (Records, Posters, Paper and Memorabilia); Lobby Cards; Mandolins; Music Boxes; Other Musical Instruments; Opera Memorabilia; Phonographs (Cylinder Disc, 78 rpm, Horn, 1950s–1960s); Photographs (Lobby Stills, Promotional, Candid, Music, Television, Radio, Other Media); Player Pianos and Rolls; Posters (Concert, Performing Arts, Movies, Television, Radio, Other Media); Radios (Transistors, Cathedral, Wooden, Ham, Shortwave, Catalin and Bakelite, Novelty, Character); Records (78s, LPs [33⅓ rpm] 45s, Children's, by Artist, by Musical Style, by Label, Soundtracks and Show Tunes, Personalities); Saxophones; Set Designs; Sheet Music; Television Memorabilia: (pre–1960s, post–1960s); Television Sets (pre–World War II, 1950s, post–1950s); Victrolas; Violins; Woodwinds

As dated today as those Gibson Girls: Jane Fonda as Barbarella in 1968.

*Always a winner:
Cracked and cleat-
marked, this Mickey
Mantle 1955 All-
Star bat smashed
Mick's three-run
homer to center field.*

COLLECTIBLES
AND ANTIQUES

*(In 2050, will your Fiesta ware be "antique"
like your tiger maple highboy?)*

Michael Flanigan notes that there are really *three* types of "collectibles." There are artistic and historical treasures that are currently less than one hundred years old, like Tiffany lamps, that are almost certain to remain valuable after they become actual "antiques," because they *are* artistic and historical treasures that measure up in terms of quality to the things we consider to be antiques today. Then there are mass-produced objects with little or no artistic merit—such as Hummel figurines and Pokemon cards—that weren't manufactured in response to some overwhelming artistic urge. These things, basically, were made to be sold as "collectibles," and the chance of these items retaining desirability in the future is slim. There are also items that have interesting associations, such as that Marilyn Monroe birthday dress or a Mickey Mantle bat. When these kinds of collectibles reach "antique" age, they will retain their value only if their associations still make them desirable to collectors. Buying things from this third group, according to Flanigan, is very much a betting game.

Leila Dunbar agrees, saying, "Some things are already so 'very vintage' as to be almost antiques—early tin toys, thirties wind-up toys, and even the mechanical banks made in the twenties (see Noel Barrett's comment about *Antiques* magazine, page 517). But I have to say that even when the first Barbies get to be one hundred years old and actually *are* antiques, they'll never have the weight or substance of that antique Chippendale chair."

Gary Sohmers takes a slightly broader view. He says, "Tin keywind toys, especially those made by Lehmann [see page 214], will be considered antiques when they reach the appropriate age. Erector sets will, too. The 1956 to 1972 Beatles and Elvis material will become antiques someday, and, yes, the original Barbie will certainly be considered an antique."

Like many of the other appraisers, Chris Kennedy thinks that there are distinctions that need to be made among the different types of collectibles. He says, "Before the United States bicentennial in 1976, items like eagle-stenciled milk cans were thought to be iconic antiques. Now, they're almost valueless. Knoll and Herman Miller furniture won't share that fate, nor will the furniture of Edward Wormley and T. H. Robsjohn-Gibbings [see pages 503 and 509]. All these were innovative and original conceptions and will probably outlast their current collectibility to become the antiques of the future."

David Lackey has a different approach. He said, "In the future, our term 'collectibles' may actually become the accepted label for all twentieth-century antiques. This current appellation, in other words, will simply stick." But he is in complete agreement with Leila Dunbar. "Shirley Temple dolls, nevertheless, will never quite be the equal of Chippendale chairs."

> # "America is a collecting nation and I like that. I think it's healthy."
> ## —NOEL BARRETT—

Rudy Franchi's definition of what collectibles are is more limited than that of some of the other appraisers—and indeed, more limited than the definition used in this book—although it is shared by some. He says, "Most collectibles are artifacts of pop culture, rather than furnishings, and probably will never be 'antique.' As with antiques, however, this is a market moved by fads." Tim Luke responds, "Actually, every collecting group seems to have its own definition of the word. Doll people, for instance, know what 'antique' connotes to them, although maybe furniture collectors would disagree. Although people are already using the word 'collectibles' somewhat freely on eBay now, I do think that the careful use of the word will add clarity to young collecting fields."

Eric Alberta, however, speculates, "Perhaps the things we call 'collectibles' become 'antiques' when they reach a certain *value*, as well as a certain age." Phillip Merrill agrees, saying, "Absolutely yes! We never value what's right in front of us, but for things that represent the beginning of a movement—like rap, or hip-hop, in contemporary African-American music—prices are already

THE ISSUE OF ORIGINALS

With much midcentury modern furniture being reproduced, will these reproductions have an effect on the value of the original, vintage pieces? Not if the McCoy was virtually one of a kind, say the experts, for rarity is important to serious collectors. But it is also true that the more Eames lounge chairs are reproduced, the less special even those first examples will become. People like exclusivity.

Fiesta ware pitchers hold lemonade, ice tea, or water—and their value.

going up, and today's African-American decorative arts will certainly be antiques."

Noel Barrett thinks that many objects that are collectibles today will probably never become valued antiques, because, as he says, "ultimately, quality will rear its ugly head. In the past, stardom has only accrued to those things that were made with care. This is not to say that 'antique' Beanie Babies won't hold up, in *some* way, simply as items that bespeak their time. Toys with a 'collecting history' ought to retain their current value, but I wonder: When—and how—does simple nostalgia become something more permanent?"

How do torn cushion straps and a Knoll Associates factory tag affect the market for this classic Mies van der Rohe daybed?

THE IMPACT OF THE INTERNET

"If you're dedicated and smart, too," David Lackey claims, "and you can read between the lines, it's possible today to put together a world-class collection just sitting at your computer." Online dealers, eBay, and other auction sites have revolutionized the buying and selling of almost everything in the last decade. "One of the phenomenal things about the Internet," says Phillip Merrill, "is that even if you don't own a computer, from a keyboard at a public library you can buy something halfway around the world, or just surf a hundred years of history. There are, at any given time, some 3,500 to 4,500 items of black memorabilia available on eBay. Even museums buy and deaccession online, and you can shop 24/7. But as a result, there are fewer good things to be found in stores."

Leila Dunbar thinks that the Internet should be considered an enormous tool for collectors, because there are more collectibles and more information available on them than has ever been available before. "There's always someone who knows more than you do," she says. "On the flip side, you'll also find a lot of misinformation."

Unlikely as it seems, Pez dispensers such as this Fireman and Vucko Wolf inspired the creation of eBay.

Tim Luke notes that eBay was created to make the buying and selling of collectibles easier. It was conceived by a man whose wife was a devoted Pez collector. In a casual conversation between them, she had commented that it would be great to be able to buy and sell them—and to connect with other collectors—over the Internet. The rest is online history.

"The trading of Pez dispensers is responsible for the birth of eBay, and now it's *the* global marketplace, perhaps because the Internet embodies the essence of the true auction," Luke observes. On eBay, prices start out reasonably and end only at the price the market decides upon. And the attendance in this auction saleroom is preselected—the only people there are the people who want to buy your doll or toy or poster. "Perhaps the only drawback to selling on the Internet," he says, "is that there is a big learning curve for novices."

Ken Farmer goes as far as to say that the Internet has *defined* twentieth-century collectibles. "It has made it so much easier to collect what used to be obscure," he says. "I have a customer who collects comic-book character rings, for example, and since the advent of Internet shopping, the size of his collection has quadrupled."

"The influence of the Internet has been dramatic, most particularly for twentieth-century items," continues Lackey. But to use the Internet efficiently, focusing on a specific manufacturer, designer, pop-culture icon, or artist is the key to finding what you want, notes Lackey. Fortunately, you are more likely to have, and to be able to locate, information about twentieth-century objects than you would about many earlier ones. Lackey also thinks that the Internet has changed the way things are priced, with the rarest things increasing in value.

Farmer believes the Internet has caused other important changes in the marketplace. "Listings on the Internet encourage objective, rather than subjective, descriptions, which is a really good thing," he notes. "It's also exploded myths about rarity. Finally, for me as an auctioneer, it's been a blessing. I now do only digital auction catalogues instead of paper ones."

Find it on the Internet: George Nelson's chrome and leather Sling sofa for Herman Miller.

Fornasetti was for the sophisticated buyer. His classical borrowings became midcentury objects, among them the pair of cabinets shown on this spread, that will be our future collectibles.

Rudy Franchi has also found that the Internet has altered the way he does business. "I no longer deal with the public at all," he says, "and—after all these years—I take Sundays off. Why stay open, and why bother to exhibit at expensive shows, when you can sell on the Internet?" He notes that the prices he achieves on eBay are the same as those in the sale room, so there is no advantage to holding a traditional auction.

Chris Kennedy thinks the Internet's effect on the collecting of twentieth-century objects has been both good and bad. "One positive effect of the Internet," he says, "is the speed with which you can find your heart's desire. It used to take days, months, even years to visit every little shop, read the trade papers, attend the shows and auctions. Now, in a flash, you can find just the Herman Miller table you've been looking for—even if it's in Mexico or France. And while you may not buy it, it gives you hope, because you know that things are out there." And as Kennedy also says "If you want to sell something, you can hold your very own auction with millions of eyes in the sale room." But on the downside, he notes, there's the fact that you can all-too-quickly discover how common some things are, which may mean that the price of an object you once paid dearly for unexpectedly drops.

Christie Romero has also found that the impact of the Internet has been phenomenal, but not without drawbacks. "It's made the collectibles market both global and easily accessible," she says. "There are tens of thousands of pieces of costume jewelry on eBay, for example, but the mediocre things just sit there, because the market finds its own level." Still, she has some reservations about it. She finds, for example, that the Internet can be tricky for beginners. "Things often look different on a computer screen than they do in reality, and beginners often don't know the right questions to ask." And perhaps most importantly, she believes there is one broadly negative aspect to collecting on the Internet. "I do think," she insists, "that the Internet has taken some of the fun out of collecting. People miss the hands-on aspect and the immediacy."

Eric Alberta also has reservations. "I don't think the Internet has ruined the collectibles market, but it has changed it," he says. "In fact, it's kind of like the Wild West out there, and the jury is still out on whether this is a good thing. On the one hand, it's democratizing; everyone can own a you-name-it. On the other hand, the amount of misinformation can be scary. As time goes on, however, I think it will be filtered better."

Noel Barrett points out that the Internet has softened prices for many things in the collectibles market, because people can almost instantly discover that what they own isn't especially rare. And while Rudi Franchi claims, "The only people still buying at auction are technophobes—people who don't use computers," Barrett doesn't think it's time to say goodbye to traditional dealers and auction houses yet. "Many collectors—both new and old—are coming around to the conviction that it's better to buy from a knowledgeable professional," he says. "You can often count on getting a complete and scholarly description of an item from them, or answers to questions that many eBay buyers, being fairly unsophisticated, don't even know to ask. You may not get a bargain from a professional," he observes, "but you'll get better value."

"The Internet doesn't replace the marketplace," Lackey observes. "I would never buy furniture on the Internet, for instance, because, for me, this is always a sensual purchase. I want to see and touch." Richard Wright agrees with him. "I actually think that interest in the Internet may be leveling off now," he says, "perhaps because if you're going to spend a lot of money on something, you really want to see it, to have the item right in front of you. I know I do. Nevertheless, the Internet has become an easy and useful means of finding other collectors who share your interests."

> "It takes three things to create a great collectible. It must connect to our past, be emblematic of its era, and be a great object."
>
> — ERIC ALBERTA —

INTO THE FUTURE

"**I** BELIEVE IN COLLECTING OBJECTS that are the essence of their period," says ceramics specialist David Lackey. "Elvis, for example, will always be iconic because he was the essence of rock and roll. And the very best Italian glass of the fifties perfectly represents, it seems to me, the artistic aspect of that era. Great quality, of course, is always collectible, so you should look twice at things by well-known designers branching out into other areas. And, on the other hand, be aware of the fact that contrived collectibles such as Lladro figures and Beanie Babies can only be curiosities of their period.

"In ceramics, I like Versace and Fornasetti china. Not many people were venturesome enough to buy Fornasetti when it was new. Keep in mind that people who say they have a rare set of Fiesta ware, on the other hand—don't. There are millions of sets out there.

"Personally, I collect what I love, which is English ceramics, especially shell-shape serving dishes."

"IT TAKES THREE THINGS to create a great collectible," says toy and Hollywood memorabilia expert Eric Alberta. "First, the item must have a connection with our past. Second, it must be emblematic of its era. And third, it must be—all other considerations aside—just a great object in itself. Mickey Mouse has iconographic status, but although E.T. and Willy Wonka are popular now, they may not endure the way Mickey, or Dorothy's ruby slippers, will. Television and rock and roll made a huge impact on the twentieth century, which is why I think some of these collectibles will become iconic. And while Elvis key chains may not last, the guitars will."

Will this tin-litho 1938 Marx Lone Ranger hold his value? Or in years to come, will he ride—Hiyo, Silver— away?

"I BELIEVE THAT HANDMADE, high-quality, limited production furniture, glass, and ceramics," says auctioneer and generalist Ken Farmer, "will hold their value. Iconic images, like Coke or the Lone Ranger memorabilia (there's something forever exciting about cowboys) will always be top collectibles, but run-of-the-mill Elvis, I think, will fall by the wayside. Perfectly preserved toys are good collectibles (although no unplayed-with toys ever made it out of my family!), as are things that required the skill of an artisan to make, rather than a machine.

"My personal collection includes Watt Ware from the thirties, forties, and fifties."

"POP CULTURE THINGS are all junk, and won't last," declares entertainment memorabilia specialist Rudy Franchi, "and in the field of movie posters, the silent movie posters won't hold up, although thirty or forty years ago, people were buying them all. Now, the only people interested in silent posters are serious film enthusiasts.

"For the future," he predicts, "look to collect the things that technology will obliterate. The touch system will eliminate credit cards, for instance, so 'affinity' credit cards—those that donate a percentage of your purchase to the National Trust for Historic Preservation or Yale University, for instance—will become collectibles. There are collectors today, in fact, for paper Diner's Club cards from the forties. Press kits will become collectibles, as will relics of the big old companies that once were icons (AT&T, anyone?). Keep an eye out, too, for items that mark major changes in packaging, like those from Coke."

"WE'RE TALKING CRYSTAL-BALL time," says jewelry expert Christie Romero, "but generally speaking, quality and scarcity should always prevail for things that are representative of their era. Maybe sentiment will keep certain types of collectibles popular, too. Kids might love a thing because Mom did, though it seems to me that the things that will hold up in the future will be the things that have been written about. Still, in the field of costume jewelry, there's already been a shaking out. My vote today goes to the work of studio jewelers Sam Kramer, Ed Wiener, Margaret de Patta, Art Smith, and Peter Macchiarini [see page 400], who died recently and has just been 'discovered,' along with James Parker, an obscure California artist."

"IN AFRICAN-AMERICAN collectibles," says Phillip Merrill, "the sky's the limit, because the field is so large and so full of crossover appeal. Nevertheless, I think there are three categories with big potential. The first is the artifacts and memorabilia of early African-American businesses, such as stock certificates from Madame C. J. Walker's hair products, or early UNIA (United Negro Improvement Association) paperwork.

"The second is African-American militaria, an ideal example of which would be the uniform of a decorated veteran, his I.D.

In the collectibles market, as on this 1964 Asahi Space Station carousel, what goes around, comes around.

substantiated by accompanying photographs and dog tags, such as the uniform of a First World War Buffalo soldier with a medal attached—perhaps a Croix de Guerre. The third is memorabilia of black education, which would include diplomas from historically black colleges and universities. The most important aspect of each of these future treasures is that each has a true connection to history."

"MY FIRST RULE for evaluating collectibles," says toy expert Tim Luke, "is to see if a piece was hugely mass-produced. That's a no-no. It should be rare, have a definite decorative element, and be in good condition. I recommend tin keywind toys from the thirties and forties, particularly comic keywinds and the ones made by Lehmann [see page 214]. Teddy bears—even if you've paid $10,000 for one—have the added value of being comforting. And battery-operated animals might be another good category. Over the past fifteen years, however, cast-iron mechanical banks have been like blue-chip stocks, possibly because they are true early Americana. In other words—and this might be a clue to gauging the future potential of other collectibles—they were not made in any other country."

"THE FUTURE IS A LONG ROAD with many hills and valleys," says furniture expert Chris Kennedy, "but that said, I personally like the midcentury furniture of Milo Baughman and Glenn of California, along with that made by Drexel; furniture designed by architect Ralph Rapson for Knoll; and furniture by Allan Gould, who designed for Raymor, Herman Miller, and his own label as well.

"I am also partial to bowls, plates, and vases in turned wood by Rudy Osolnick, and by John May Sr., James Prestini, Arthur Espenet Carpenter, and Sam Maloof, an artist who is mainly associated with furniture."

"I'D BET ON THE FURNITURE of Wharton Esherick and Sam Maloof, although Esherick's work can be unnerving, because it doesn't adhere to classical principals of

In contemporary chair design, form sometimes follows fashion: witness Jordan Mozer's Bell Bottom chair.

COMFY CHAIRS

"Chairs are the iconic furniture of the twentieth century," says *Antiques Roadshow* appraiser Usha Subramaniam without hesitation. Despite modern designers' obsession with the chair, comfort sometimes took a back seat to style. The list of most uncomfortable twentieth-century chairs "could go on and on and on," Subramaniam notes. A more manageable list is her three most comfortable chairs of the twentieth century. But she is quick to say, "I'm only recommending the ones I've sat in."

SHIRO KURAMATA

"HOW HIGH THE MOON" CHAIR

Shiro Kuramata was an innovative and eccentric Japanese designer of the late twentieth century who used all kinds of materials in his designs—he once placed artificial flowers in a clear Lucite Miss Blanche chair. Says Subramaniam of the Moon chair, designed in 1986: "It looks like he turned a fence into a chair, but when you sit in it, it's absolutely fabulous."

CARLO BUGATTI

COBRA CHAIR

Italian furniture designer Carlo Bugatti constructed a chair in 1902 for the Exhibition of Modern Decorative Arts in Turin. The exhibition sought entries with innovative designs free of historical precedent, and Bugatti delivered. "It's his most famous design," Subramaniam says of the chair, which is a continuous wooden form covered in vellum, painted with stylized flowers, dragonflies, and geometric shapes. "It looks like a cobra about to attack."

HARRY BERTOIA

DIAMOND CHAIR

This inexpensive chair, invented by furniture designer Harry Bertoia in the early 1950s (see page 491), has a special place with Subramaniam: at home. She bought her vinyl-covered version about ten years ago at an auction; you can also buy them with wool and leather coverings or in plain mesh metal. "It is extremely comfortable," Subramaniam says.

symmetry," says Michael Flanigan, also an expert on furniture. "Maloof uses black walnut, cypress, rosewood, ebony, and teak and has made what many call the perfect rocker."

"I LIKE THE WHIMSICAL FURNITURE of Jordan Mozer," says David Rago, a specialist in both ceramics and furniture, "which is found today in restaurants and offices. Like new cars, however, as soon as someone sits in a piece of new furniture, its price drops significantly. But in years to come, if the quality is there, prices will reflect that quality and rise again."

"TWENTIETH-CENTURY DESIGNERS were obsessed with chair design," says Usha Subramaniam, another furniture authority. "But if you're collecting for comfort, in my opinion,

DON'T THROW AWAY THOSE LPS!

In the seventies and eighties—until the advent of the compact disk—millions of vinyl record albums were produced. Record albums are now on the wane, and today's music is available only on CDs and tapes. Yet young people are becoming interested in older music, electronics companies are again making turntables, and rare vinyl rock and roll records are being collected by 20-somethings. "These collectors like fifties do-wop recordings, of which there are very few because the small record companies that produced them couldn't afford to manufacture many copies," says *Antiques Roadshow* appraiser Gary Sohmers. "The records of Larry Williams and Ruth Brown are very collectible now—but only in perfect condition. Classic rock and roll—the original recording by the original artist, before Paul Anka did his version of it—is popular, too."

From the 1960s, he notes that collectors look for rhythm and blues and obscure psychedelic groups, like the Chocolate Watchband and 13th Floor Elevator. These and other bands made a small number of pressings for small labels, so they're somewhat rare. "People are also collecting Punk Rock, like the Ramones, from the 1970s," says Sohmers. "Rap, which marks the end of vinyl, will be collectible soon."

three of the best are Shiro Kurmata's "How High the Moon" chair, Carlo Bugatti's Cobra chair, and Harry Bertoia's inexpensive Diamond chair. They are easy to sit in, and you will probably not go wrong with seating that's easy to sit in."

> ## "Pick from among the very best. No one beats Marilyn, James Dean, and Elvis."
> —LEILA DUNBAR—

"THE BEST OF THE BEST will always retain its value, while the rest goes up and down," says general collectibles expert Leila Dunbar. "If I were advising a new sports collector," she continues, "I'd say to mix vintage with contemporary. Take the early blue-chip sports figures Ty Cobb, Babe Ruth, and Lou Gehrig, and combine them with later greats Joe Dimaggio, Mickey Mantle, and Ted Williams, then add some modern ones, such as Barry Bonds, Roger Clemens, and Nolan Ryan, perhaps.

"If that new collector loves movies, for instance, I'd advise him or her, again, to pick from among the very best and buy the collectibles belonging to its stars, because this market is about star power. But for Hollywood memorabilia, it's not just the star, but the performance, too. You want to own things relating to the greatest stars in their greatest roles and iconic is the name of the game. For instance, in vintage, your blue chips are Valentino, Mary Pickford, and of course, Charlie Chaplin. Add some midcentury Errol Flynn, Jimmy Cagney, Elizabeth Taylor, and Clark Gable and contemporary stars like Tom Hanks, Tom Cruise, Harrison Ford, and Julia Roberts, and you have a solid collec-

Great stars in great roles: Bette Davis and Anne Baxter in an All About Eve *publicity still.*

tion," she continues. "Of course, you'll want Cagney in *Yankee Doodle Dandy* and Gable in *Gone With the Wind*. That said, no one beats Marilyn, James Dean, and Elvis!"

"THERE WILL BE PEAKS AND VALLEYS in collectibles in the future," says toy expert Noel Barrett, "as well as *long* flat spots. Barbed wire and glass telephone insulators spoke to a couple of generations, for example, but now they're just curios.

"Today we've become self-conscious about our collecting, buying, say, one toy to play with and one to put away. This means that down the road, there will probably be an overwhelming supply of those 'put-away' toys. But I would advise new collectors that whether it's a Snoopy music box or a Garfield telephone, whatever you collect should be something you want to live with. I buy only what I have room to display."

"FOR THE FUTURE," says doll specialist Richard Wright, "I would collect good American composition dolls from the 1930s and forties, particularly those that have Hollywood associations. This, of course, means Shirley Temple, Deanna Durban, and Shirley's nemesis, Jane Withers [see page 284].

"All the dolls from this era need to have their original wigs, shoes, and dresses, however, to be desirable."

"BECAUSE OF ITS HUGE nostalgia factor," predicts popular culture guru Gary Sohmers, "I believe that fifty years from now the big collectible thing will be television. Each TV generation has had its favorites. There are even a few generations that have never seen the *Wizard of Oz* anywhere but on television. *I Love Lucy, Bonanza, The Man from U.N.C.L.E., M*A*S*H*, The Brady Bunch*—all define different eras of television watchers. I predict that TV collectibles are the future.

"Rock and roll, however, has suddenly arrived at a place where three generations all have loved it. In 2003, there are a lot of people walking around whose grandparents loved rock and roll."

Defining mid-sixties television: Ilya Kuriakin and Napoleon Solo, The Man—*or men—from* U.N.C.L.E. *Will artifacts associated with this once-popular TV show become sought after collectibles?*

ANTIQUES ROADSHOW APPRAISERS

Uluiaipou Aiono
Nanny Jack and Co.
5100 Edmondson Avenue
Baltimore, MD 21229-2333

Eric Alberta
440 East 79th Street, #16K
New York, NY 10021

Sally Ambrose
Ambrose Appraisal Service
P.O. Box 536
Leavenworth, WA 98826-
0536

Caroline Ashleigh
Caroline Ashleigh Associates,
Inc.
800 East Lincoln
Birmingham, MI 48009

Richard Austin
327 West 21st Street, #1E
New York, NY 10011

Kathleen Bailey
160 NW Gilman Boulevard,
Suite #1
Issaquah, WA 98027

Noel Barrett
Noel Barrett Antiques &
Auctions Ltd.
P.O. Box 300
Carversville, PA 18913

Dianne Batista
Dior Fine Jewelry
17 East 57th Street
New York, NY 10022

C. Jeanenne Bell
Jewelry Box Antiques, Inc.
7325 Quivira Road
Suite #238
Shawnee, KS 66216

Max Bernheimer
Christie's
20 Rockefeller Plaza
New York, NY 10020

Bill Bertoia
Bill Bertoia Auctions
2141 DeMarco Drive
Vineland, NJ 08360

David Bonsey
Skinner, Inc.
357 Main Street
Bolton, MA 01740

Frank Boos
Frank H. Boos Auctioneers
& Appraisers
420 Enterprise Court
Bloomfield Hills, MI 48302

Ron Bourgeault
Northeast Auctions
93 Pleasant Street
Portsmouth, NH 03801

Andrew Brunck
Christie's
20 Rockefeller Plaza
New York, NY 10020

Hugh Bulmer
Maynards Fine Art
Auctioneers and
Appraisers
415 West 2nd Avenue
Vancouver, British Columbia
Canada

John A. Buxton
BAACS
6717 Spring Valley Road
Dallas, TX 75254

Joan Caballero
Joan Caballero Appraisals
P.O. Box 822
Santa Fe, NM 87504

Cathy Calhoun
Calhoun Zenker Jewelers
340 Main Street
Royersford, PA 19468

Jim Callahan
Skinner, Inc.
357 Main Street
Bolton, MA 01740

Judy L. Campbell
Judy Campbell Appraisal
Services
5500 Summerset Drive
Midland, MI 48640

Karen Cangelosi
Ivey-Selkirk
7447 Forsythe Boulevard
St. Louis, MO 63105

Frank Castle
Castle Fine Arts, Inc.
P.O. Box 557
San Ramon, CA 94583

Nan Chisholm
Sotheby's
1334 York Avenue
New York, NY 10021

Margot Chvatal
Christie's
20 Rockefeller Plaza
New York, NY 10020

LaCheryl Cillie
Premiere Estate and Auction
Service
P.O. Box 28233
Birmingham, AL 35228

Gordon Converse
Spread Eagle Village
503 W. Lancaster Avenue
Strafford, PA 19087

Chris Coover
Christie's
20 Rockefeller Plaza
New York, NY 1002

C. Wesley Cowan
Cowan's Historic Americana
747 Park Avenue
Terrace Park, OH 45174

Donald Cresswell
Philadelphia Print Shop
8441 Germantown Avenue
Philadelphia, PA 19118

Carl Crossman
Northeast Auctions
93 Pleasant Street
Portsmouth, NH 03801

Peter Curran
Peter Curran Antiques &
Appraisals
P.O. Box 7395
Wilton, CT 06897

Nicholas Dawes
67 East 11th Street
New York, NY 10003

Wyatt Day
Swann Galleries
104 East 25th Street
New York, NY 10010

Doug Deihl
Skinner, Inc.
357 Main Street
Bolton, MA 01740

Andrew Dipper
Givens Violins
1004 Marquette Avenue
Minneapolis, MN 55403

Linda Donahue
Doyle New York
175 East 87th Street
New York, NY 10128

Nancy Druckman
Sotheby's
1334 York Avenue
New York, NY 10021

Ernest DuMouchelle
DuMouchelles Gallery
409 E. Jefferson Avenue
Detroit, MI 48226

Lawrence DuMouchelle
DuMouchelles Gallery
409 E. Jefferson Avenue
Detroit, MI 48226

Robert DuMouchelle
DuMouchelles Gallery
409 E. Jefferson Avenue
Detroit, MI 48226

Leila Dunbar
Sotheby's
1334 York Avenue
New York, NY 10021

Linda Dyer
P.O. Box 1104
Franklin, TN 37065-1104

Rafael Eledge
Shiloh's Civil War Relics
4730 Hwy. 22
Shiloh, TN 38376

Ian Ehling
Christie's
20 Rockefeller Plaza
New York, NY 10020

Donald Ellis
Donald Ellis Gallery
1002 Mineral Springs Road,
    RR#3
Dundas Ontario
Canada

Jerome Eisenberg
Royal-Athena Galleries
153 East 57th Street
New York, NY 10022

Dean Failey
Christie's
20 Rockefeller Plaza
New York, NY 10020

Peter Fairbanks
Montgomery Gallery
353 Sutter Street
San Francisco, CA 94108

Ken Farmer
Ken Farmer Auction, LLC
105A Harrison Street
Radford, VA 24141

Virginia Farrell
Goose Lane Antiques
47 Court Street
Westfield, MA 01085

Alan Fausel
Doyle New York
175 East 87th Street
New York, NY 10128

Colleene Fesko
Skinner, Inc.
357 Main Street
Bolton, MA 01740

James Ffrench
Beauvais Carpets
201 East 57th Street
New York, NY 10022

Tara Ana Finley
1042 Sorolla Avenue
Coral Gables, FL 33134

Andrea Fiuczynski
Christie's
360 North Camden Drive
Beverly Hills, CA 90210

J. Michael Flanigan
J. M. Flanigan American
    Antiques
1607 Park Avenue
Baltimore, MD 21217

Stephen Fletcher
Skinner, Inc.
357 Main Street
Bolton, MA 01740

Susan Florence
Christie's
216 Newbury Street
Boston, MA 02116

Debra J. Force
Debra Force Fine Art, Inc.
14 East 73rd Street, #4B
New York, NY 10021

Barbara Franchi
Rudy Franchi
The Nostalgia Factory
51 North Margin Street
Boston, MA 0211

Andrea Blunck Frost
Doyle New York
175 East 87th Street
New York, NY 10128

Wendell Garrett
Sotheby's
1334 York Avenue
New York, NY 10021

Mona Gavigan
Gallery Affrica
2010 R Street, NW
Washington, D.C. 20009

Claire Givens
Givens Violins
1004 Marquette Avenue
Suite #205
Minneapolis, MN 55403

George Glastris
Skinner, Inc.
357 Main Street
Bolton, MA 01740

Ken Gloss
Brattle Book Shop
9 West Street
Boston, MA 02111

Dessa Goddard
Bonhams & Butterfields
220 San Bruno Avenue
San Francisco, CA 94103

Michael Grogan
Grogan & Co
22 Harris Street
Dedham, MA 02026

William Guthman
Guthman Americana
P.O. Box 392
Westport, CT 06881

Kathleen Guzman
200 East End Avenue
New York, NY 10128

Reyne Haines
JustGlass.com
405 Lafayette Ave
Cincinnati, OH 45220

Titi Halle
Cora Ginsburg, Inc.
19 East 74th Street
New York, NY 10021

Martha Hamilton
Skinner, Inc.
357 Main Street
Bolton, MA 01740

Christopher Hartop
Pudding Norton Hall
Fakenham, Norfolk
NR21 7NB
England

Kathleen Harwood
Harwood Fine Arts, Inc.
P.O. Box 380
Montrose, PA 18801

Ann G. Hays
Ken S. Hays
120 South Spring Street
Louisville, KY 40206

John Hays
Christie's
20 Rockefeller Plaza
New York, NY 10020

Bruce Herman
P.O. Box 195
Pasadena, CA 91102-0195

Vivian Highberg
Hilding & Larson Appraisals
473 Carnegie Drive
Pittsburgh, PA 15243

Mark O. Howald
Ivey-Selkirk
7447 Forsythe Boulevard
St. Louis, MO 63105

Riley Humler
Cincinnati Art Galleries
225 East 6th Street
Cincinnati, OH 45202

Anne Igelbrink
Christie's
20 Rockefeller Plaza
New York, NY 10020

Susan Kaplan Jacobson
Leo Kaplan, Ltd
967 Madison Ave
New York, NY 10021

Don L. Jensen
Cotswold Appraisal Service
7216 Soundview Drive
Edmonds, WA 98026

Joyce Jonas
Joyce Jonas & Associates
215 East 80th Street
New York NY 10021

Alan Kaplan
Leo Kaplan, Ltd.
114 East 57th Street
New York, NY 10022

Daile Kaplan
Swann Galleries
104 East 25th Street
New York, NY 10010

Karen Keane
Skinner, Inc.
357 Main Street
Bolton, MA 01740

Kerry Keane
Christie's
20 Rockefeller Plaza
New York, NY 10020

Mary Beth Keene
Wayne Pratt, Inc.
346 Main Street South
Woodbury, CT 06798

Chris Kennedy
e-modern, Vintage Modern
Design
3 Olive Street
Northampton, MA
01060-4215

Richard Kennedy
The Gun Room, Inc.
2468 Spring Road
Smyrna, GA 30080

Leigh Keno
Leigh Keno American
Antiques
127 East 69th Street
New York, NY 10021

Leslie Keno
Sotheby's
1334 York Avenue
New York, NY 10021

Selby Kiffer
Sotheby's
1334 York Avenue
New York, NY 10021

Susan Kleckner
P.O. Box 877
Grand Central Station
New York, NY 10163

Lea Koonce-Ogundiran
Christie's
550 Biltmore Way, Ste. 1270
Coral Gables, FL 33134

Jo Kris
Skinner, Inc.
357 Main Street
Bolton, MA 01740

David Lackey
David Lackey Antiques
2311 Westheimer
Houston, TX 77098

Christopher Lane
Philadelphia Print Shop
8441 Germantown Avenue
Philadelphia, PA 19118

Thomas Lecky
Christie's
20 Rockefeller Plaza
New York, NY 10020

Catherine Leonhard
Christie's
360 North Camden Drive
Beverly Hills, CA 90210

Gloria Lieberman
Skinner, Inc.
357 Main Street
Bolton, MA 01740

Molly Morse Limmer
Christie's
20 Rockefeller Plaza
New York, NY 10020

Simeon Lipman
P.O. Box 1181
New York, NY 10028

Martin Lorber
Doyle New York
175 East 87th Street
New York, NY 10128

Karen Lorene
Facere Jewelry Art Gallery
1420 Fifth Avenue #108
Seattle, WA 98101

Peter Loughrey
Bonhams & Butterfields
220 San Bruno Avenue
San Francisco, CA 94103

Nicholas D. Lowry
Swann Galleries
104 East 25th Street
New York, NY 10010

Timothy Luke
Treasure Quest Auction
Galleries, Inc.
2581 Jupiter Park Drive,
Suite #E-5
Jupiter, FL 33458

Louise Luther
Skinner, Inc.
357 Main Street
Bolton, MA 01740

Richard Madley
Hamptons Auctioneers
93 High Street
Godalming, Surrey
GU7 1AL
United Kingdom

Marsha Malinowski
Sotheby's
1334 York Avenue
New York, NY 10021

Jeremy Markowitz
Swann Galleries
104 East 25th Street
New York, NY 10010

Elyse Luray Marx
Luray & Marx
11 Pennsylvania Plaza,
2nd Floor
New York, NY 10001

Stephen Massey
108 East 81st Street
New York, NY 10028

Lark Mason
Sotheby's
1334 York Avenue
New York, NY 10021

David McCarron
Frank H. Boos Auctioneers &
Appraisers
420 Enterprise Court
Bloomfield Hills, MI 48302

Milly McGehee
P.O. Box 666
Riderwood, MD 21139-0666

Dorothy McGonagle
Skinner, Inc.
357 Main Street
Bolton, MA 01740

Philip Merrill
Nanny Jack & Co., Inc.
5100 Edmondson Avenue
Baltimore, MD 21229-2333

Gary Metzner
Sotheby's
188 East Walton Place
Chicago, IL 60611

Gregory L. Minuskin
Time On Your Hands
P.O. Box 538
Tustin, CA 92781-0538

Christopher Mitchell
J. Christopher Mitchell
    American Antiques
    & Militaria
P.O. Box 9
Point Clear, AL 36564

Alasdair Nichol
Freeman's Fine Art
    Auctioneers
1808 Chestnut Street
Philadelphia, PA 19103

Juliet Nusser
Pudding Norton Hall
Fakenham, Norfolk
    NR21 7NB
England

Fred Oster
Vintage Instruments, Inc.
1529 Pine Street
Philadelphia, PA 19102

Andy Ourant
The Village Doll & Toy Shop
8 N. Village Circle
Reinholds, PA 17569

Peter Pap
Peter Pap Oriental Rugs Inc.
P.O. Box 286
Dublin, NH 03444

Adam Patrick
A La Vieille Russie
781 Fifth Avenue
New York, NY 10022

Jerry Patterson
Doyle New York
175 East 87th Street
New York, NY 10128

Suzanne Perrault
David Rago Auctions
333 N. Main Street
Lambertville, NJ 08530

Ron Peterson
Ron Peterson Antiques, Inc.
4418 Central Ave. SE
Albuquerque, NM 87108

Gary Piattoni
Gary Piattoni Decorative
    Arts, Inc.
1114 Dobson Street
Evanston, IL 60202

Elisabeth Poole
Christie's
20 Rockefeller Plaza
New York, NY 10020

Wayne Pratt
Wayne Pratt, Inc.
346 Main Street South
Woodbury, CT 06798

Sarah Shinn Pratt
LeBaron Antiques Trading
358 Main Street South
Woodbury, CT 06798

Jane Prentiss
Skinner, Inc.
357 Main Street
Bolton, MA 01740

Marley Rabstenek
216 Grand Street
Brooklyn, NY 11211

David Rago
David Rago Auctions, Ltd.
333 N. Main Street
Lambertville, NJ 08530

Carolyn Remmey
Carolyn Remmey Antiques &
    Fine Art
P.O. Box 197
New Vernon, NJ 07976-0197

Lee Richmond
The Best Things
299 Herndon Parkway,
    Suite #210
Herndon, VA 20170

Letitia Roberts
200 East 72nd Street
    Apt. 10E
New York, NY 10021-4540

Christie Romero
Center For Jewelry Studies
P.O. Box 424
Anaheim, CA 92815

Trudy Rosato
Trudy Rosato Fine Art
39 Great Jones Street
New York, NY 10012

Margot Rosenberg
Christie's
20 Rockefeller Plaza
New York, NY 10020

Albert Sack
Northeast Auctions
93 Pleasant Street
Portsmouth, NH 03801

Virginia Salem
New York, NY
virginsalem@aol.com

Rosalie Sayyah
Rhinestone Rosie
606 West Crockett
Seattle, WA 98119

Mark Schaffer
Peter L. Schaffer
A La Vieille Russie
781 Fifth Avenue
New York, NY 10022

John E. Schulman
Caliban Books
410 South Craig Street
Pittsburgh, PA 15213

Frank M. Sellers
151 Crane Brook Road
Alstead, NH 03602

Bruce Shackelford
P.O. Box 15707
San Antonio, TX 78212

Peter W. Shaw
Amati Violin Shop, Inc.
2315 University Boulevard
Houston, TX 77005

Peter J. Shemonsky
Bonhams & Butterfields
220 San Bruno Avenue
San Francisco, CA 94103

Sig Shonholtz
Second Time Around
8840 Beverly Boulevard W.
Hollywood, CA 90048

Kerry Shrives
Skinner, Inc.
357 Main Street
Bolton, MA 01740

Eric Silver
Lillian Nassau Ltd.
220 East 57th Street
New York, NY 10022

Leonard Sipiora
Leonard Sipiora Fine Art
    & Antiques
1012 Blanchard Street
El Paso, TX 79902-2727

Stuart Slavid
Skinner, Inc.
357 Main Street
Bolton, MA 01740

Anthony Slayter-Ralph
P.O. Box 61
Santa Barbara, CA 93102

Jeffrey T. Smith
Bonhams & Butterfields
220 San Bruno Avenue
San Francisco, CA 94103

Jonathan Snellenburg
Jonathan Snellenburg
    Antiques Inc.
594 Broadway, Ste. 507
New York, NY 10012

Gary Sohmers
"Wex Rex" Collectibles
WexRex@aol.com

Marvin Sokolow
425 West Fairy Chasm Road
Bayside, WI 53217

Daniel Buck Soules
ArtFact, Inc.
1130 Ten Rod Road
    Suite #D202
North Kingstown, RI 02852

Gary Stradling
The Stradlings
1225 Park Avenue
New York, NY 10128-1758

Usha Subramaniam
Mt. Kisco, NY
ushas@att.net

Arlie Sulka
Lillian Nassau Ltd.
220 East 57th Street
New York, NY 10022

Beth Szescila
Szescila Appraisal Service
224 Birdsall
Houston, TX 77007

Gerald Tomlin
Gerald Tomlin Antiques
54 Highland Park Village
Dallas, TX 75205

Mark Topalian
Doyle New York
175 East 87th Street
New York, NY 10128

Nick Vandekar
17 Cypress Lane
Berwyn, PA 19312

Christine Vining
34 Manataug Trail
Marblehead, MA 01945

Francis Wahlgren
Christie's
20 Rockefeller Plaza
New York, NY 10020

Barry Weber
Edith Weber & Associates
994 Madison Avenue
New York, NY 10021

John S. Weschler
Weschler's Auctioneers and
    Appraisers
905 E Street NW
Washington, D.C. 20004

William P. Weschler
Weschler's Auctioneers and
    Appraisers
905 E Street NW
Washington, D.C. 20004

Todd Weyman
Swann Galleries
104 East 25th Street
New York, NY 10010

Stuart Whitehurst
Skinner, Inc.
357 Main Street
Bolton, MA 01740

Catherine Williamson
Bonhams & Butterfields
220 San Bruno Avenue
San Francisco, CA 94103

Jody Wilkie
Christie's
20 Rockefeller Plaza
New York, NY 10020

Brad Witherell
Brian Witherell
Witherell's Americana
    Auctions
9290 Yorkship Court
Elk Grove, CA 95758

Richard Wright
Richard Wright Antiques
    & Dolls
P.O. Box 227
Birchrunville, PA 19421

Berj Zavian
Doyle New York
175 East 87th Street
New York, NY 10128

Kevin Zavian
Cluster Jewelry
48 West 48th Street,
    Suite #1501
New York, NY 10036

AUCTION HOUSES

Bonhams & Butterfields
220 San Bruno Ave
San Francisco, CA 94103
Tel. (415) 861-7500
Fax (415) 861-8951

Christie's
20 Rockefeller Plaza
New York, NY 10020
Tel. (212) 636-2000
Fax (212) 636-2399

David Rago Auctions, Ltd.
333 N. Main Street
Lambertville, NJ 08530
Tel. (609) 397-9374
Fax (609) 397-9377

Doyle New York
175 East 87th Street
New York, NY 10128
Tel. (212) 427-2730
Fax (212) 369-0892

Frank Boos Gallery
420 Enterprise Court
Bloomfield Hills, MI 48302
Tel. (248) 332-1500
Fax (248) 332-6370

Northeast Auctions
93 Pleasant Street
Portsmouth, NH 03801
Tel. (800) 260-0230 or
(603) 433-8400
Fax (603) 433-0415

**Phillips-Selkirk Fine Art
Auctioneers & Appraisers**
7447 Forsyth Boulevard
Clayton, MO 63105
Tel. (314) 726-5515
Fax (314) 726-9908

Skinner, Inc.
357 Main Street
Bolton, MA 01740
Tel. (978) 779-6241
Fax (978) 779-5144

63 Park Plaza
Boston, MA 02116
Tel. (617) 350-5400
Fax (617) 3505429

Sotheby's
1334 York Avenue
New York, NY 10021
Tel. (212) 606-7000
Fax (212) 606-7107

Swann Galleries
104 East 25th Street
New York, NY 10010
Tel. (212) 254-4710
Fax (212) 979-1017

**Weschler's Auctioneers
and Appraisers**
905 E Street NW
Washington, D.C. 20004
Tel. (202) 628-1281

**Witherell's Americana
Auctions**
9290 Yorkship Court
Elk Grove, CA 95758
Tel. & Fax (916) 683-3266

APPRAISAL ORGANIZATIONS

**American Society of
Appraisers**
232 Madison Avenue,
    Suite #600
New York, NY 10016
Tel. (212) 953-7272
Fax (212) 683-1076

**Appraisers Association of
America, Inc.**
386 Park Avenue South,
    Suite #2000
New York, NY 10016
Tel. (212) 889-5404
Fax (212) 889-5503

**International Society of
Appraisers**
16040 Christensen Road,
    Suite #102
Seattle, WA 98188
Tel. (206) 241-0359 or
    (888) 472-5587
Fax (206) 241-0359

READING LIST & BIBLIOGRAPHY

This book could not have been written without the help of many experts in the various subject areas covered, who agreed to be interviewed or who read the manuscript at different stages and answered questions whenever asked. They are all listed in our Acknowledgments. The following published sources and Web sites were also invaluable in preparing this volume and should help readers interested in more information on specific subjects.

GENERAL

Buster, Larry. *The Art and History of Black Memorabilia*. New York: Clarkson Potter, 2000.

Christie's. *Masterworks 1900–2000 Catalog*. New York: June 2000.

Hayward, Helena. *The Connoisseur's Handbook of Antique Collecting: A Dictionary of Furniture, Silver, Ceramics, Glass, Fine Art, etc.* New York: Galahad Books, 1960.

Johnson, J. Stewart. *American Modern: 1925–1940: Design for a New Age*. New York: Harry N. Abrams Inc., 2000.

Kovel, Ralph, and Terry Kovel. *Kovels' Know Your Collectibles: The Comprehensive Guide to the Antiques of the Future by America's Foremost Experts in the Field*. New York: Three Rivers Press, 1981.

Lanmon, Dwight P. *Evaluating Your Collection: The 14 Points of Connoisseurship (Winterthur Decorative Arts Series)*. Hanover, NH: University Press of New England, 1999.

Lucie-Smith, Edward. *The Thames and Hudson Dictionary of Art Terms*. New York: Thames & Hudson, 1988.

Marsh, Madeleine. *Miller's Collectibles Price Guide 1996–97 (Serial)*. London: Mitchell Beazley, 1997.

——. *Miller's Collecting the 1950s*. London: Mitchell Beazley, 1997.

McAlpine, Alistair, and Cathy Giangrande. *The Essential Guide to Collectibles: A Source Book of Public Collections in Europe and the U.S.A.* New York: Viking Press, 2001.

Muensterberger, Werner. *Collecting: An Unruly Passion: Psychological Perspectives*. New York: Harvest Books, 1995.

Rinker, Harry L. *The Official Price Guide to Collectibles*, 2nd ed. New York: House of Collectibles, 1998.

Rosson, Joe L., and Helaine Fendelman. *Treasures in Your Attic*. New York: HarperResource, 2001.

Rozakis, Laurie. *The Complete Idiot's Guide to Buying and Selling Collectibles*, 2nd ed. Indianapolis: Alpha Books, 2000.

Tambini, Michael. *The Look of the Century: Design Icons of the 20th Century*. New York: DK Publishing, 1999.

CERAMICS

Huxford, Bob, and Sharon Huxford. *Collectors Encyclopedia of Fiesta: Plus Harlequin, Riviera, and Kitchen Kraft*. Paducah, KY: Collector Books, 2000.

Kerr, Ann. *Collectors Encyclopedia of Russel Wright: Identification & Values*, 3rd ed. Paducah, KY: Collector Books, 1998.

Ketchum, William C. Jr., and Elizabeth von Habsburg. *American Pottery and Porcelain*. New York: Black Dog & Leventhal, 2000.

Levin, Elaine. *The History of American Ceramics, 1607 to the Present: From Pipkins and Bean Pots to Contemporary Forms*. New York: Harry N. Abrams, Inc., 1998.

Venable, Charles, editor. *China and Glass in America: 1880–1980, From Tabletop to T.V. Tray*. New York: Harry N. Abrams Inc., 2000.

ADVERTISING

Anderson, Scott. *Check the Oil: Gas Station Collectibles with Prices*. Radnor, PA: Wallace-Homestead Book Company, 1986.

Bertoia Auctions.

Bruce, Scott. *Cereal Box Bonanza, the 1950's: Identification and Values.* Paducah, KY: Collector Books, 1995.

"Cigarettes: The Ad Machine in Action: Cigarettes and Art in Advertising." <http://xroads.virginia.edu/~UG00/3on1/tobaccoads>

Clark, Hyla. *The Tin Can Book.* New York: New American Library, 1977.

"Coca-Cola History and Collecting." <www2.netdoor.com/~davidroy/cocacola.html>.

Cracker Jack Collectors Association. <www.collectoronline.com/CJCA>

Dotz, Warren. *Advertising Character Collectibles: An Identification and Value Guide.* Paducah, KY: Collector Books, 1993.

Enes, Bill. *Silent Salesmen: An Encyclopedia of Collectible Gum, Candy, and Nut Machines, with Price Guide.* Lenexa, KS: Enes Publishing, 1987.

Forbes, Robert, and Terrance R. Mitchell. *American Tobacco Cards: A Price Guide and Checklist.* Iola, WI: Antique Trader, 2000.

Goodrum, Charles, and Helen Dalrymple. *Advertising in America, The First Two Hundred Years.* New York: Harry N. Abrams, Inc., 1990.

Griffith, David. *Decorative Printed Tins: The Golden Age of Printed Tin Packaging.* New York: Studio Vista, 1979.

Hake, Ted. *Hake's Guide to Advertising Collectibles: 100 Years of Advertising from 100 Famous Companies.* Radnor, PA: Wallace-Homestead Book Co., 1992.

———. *Hake's Price Guide to Character Toys,* 4th ed. New York: House of Collectibles, 2002.

———. *Hake's Price Guide to Character Toy Premiums,* 2nd ed. New York: Avon Books, 1998.

———. *Hake's Guide to Advertising Collectibles.* Radnor, PA: Wallace-Homestead Book Company, 1996.

———. *Overstreet Presents: Hake's Price Guide to Character Toy Premiums: Including Comic, Cereal, TV, Movies, Radio & Related Store Bought Items.* Paducah, KY: Collector Books, 1996.

Heide, Robert, John Gilman, and Timothy Bissell. *Cartoon Collectibles: Fifty Years of Dime-Store Memorabilia.* New York: Doubleday, 1984.

Huffman, Carol, and Tom Hoder. *Tomart's Price Guide to Character & Promotional Glasses,* 3rd ed. Dayton, OH: Tomart Publications, 2000.

Husfloen, Kyle, ed. *Antique Trader Advertising Price Guide.* Iola, WI: Antique Trader, 2001.

Huxford, Sharon, Bob Huxford, and Rich Penn. *Huxford's Collectible Advertising: An Illustrated Value Guide,* 4th ed. Paducah, KY: Collector Books, 1998.

Jaramillo, Alex. *Cracker Jack Prizes.* New York: Abbeville Press, 1989.

Klug, Ray. *Antique Advertising Encyclopedia,* 3rd ed. (vol. 2). Atglen, PA: Schiffer Publishing, 2001.

Lesser, Robert. *A Celebration of Comic Art and Memorabilia.* New York: Hawthorn Books, 1975.

Longest, David. *Cartoon Toys & Collectibles: Identification and Value Guide.* Paducah, KY: Collector Books, 1998.

———. *Character Toys & Collectibles (Second Series).* Paducah, KY: Collector Books, 1989.

Mugrage, Bill. *The Official Price Guide to Beer Cans,* 5th ed. New York: House of Collectibles, 1993.

Munsey, Cecil. *Disneyana: Walt Disney Collectibles.* New York: Dutton, 1974.

The Official Web Site for the National Association of Collectors and the Association of Collecting Clubs. <http://collectors.org/index.asp>

Overstreet, Robert M. *The Overstreet Toy Ring Price Guide,* 2nd ed. Paducah, KY: Collector Books, 1996.

Pettretti, Allan. *Pettretti's Coca-Cola Collectibles and Price Guide,* 11th ed. Iola, WI: Antique Trader Books, 2001.

———. *Pettretti's Soda Pop Collectibles Price Guide: The Encyclopedia of Soda Pop Collectibles,* 2nd ed. Iola, WI: Antique Trader Books, 1996.

Pina, Ravi. *Cracker Jack Collectibles: With Price Guide.* Atglen, PA: Schiffer Publishing, 1997.

Olson, Richard D. "The R. F. Outcault Society's Yellow Kid Site." <www.neponset.com/yellowkid/history.htm>

Randy Inman Auctions Inc. <www.inmanauctions.com>

Shimizu, Yukio, and Teruhisa Kitahara, eds. *Motion Display.* Los Angeles: Books Nippan, 1989.

Soda Museum. <www.sodamuseum.com>

Stern, Michael. *Stern's Guide to Disney Collectibles (Second Series).* Paducah, KY: Collector Books, 1995.

Straub, Gary I. *Collectible Beer Trays.* Atglen, PA: Schiffer Publishing, Ltd., 1997.

Summers, B. J. *Value Guide to Advertising Memorabilia,* 2nd ed. Paducah, KY: Collector Books, 1998.

Terranova, Jerry, and Douglas Cogdon-Martin. *Great Cigar Stuff for Collectors.* Atglen, PA: Schiffer Publishing Ltd., 1997.

Tombush, Tom. *Tomart's Illustrated Disneyana Catalog and Price Guide* (vols. 1-4). Dayton, OH: Tomart Publications, 1985.

——. *Tomart's Price Guide to Radio Premiums and Cereal Box Collectibles.* Radnor, PA: Wallace-Homestead Book Company, 1991.

Wells, Stuart, III. *A Universe of Star Wars Collectibles,* 2nd ed. Iola, WI: Antique Trader, 2002.

Witherell, Bradley L., and Brian L. Witherell. *California's Best: Old West Art & Antiques.* Atglen, PA: Schiffer Publishing, Ltd., 1999.

Young, David, and Micki Young. *Campbell's Soup Collectibles: A Price and Identification Guide.* Iola, WI: Krause Publications, 1998.

Zimmerman, David. *Encyclopedia of Advertising Tins,* 2nd ed. (vol. II). Paducah, KY: Collector Books, 1998.

GLASS

Battie, David, and Simon Cottle, eds. *Sotheby's Concise Encyclopedia of Glass.* Wappingers Falls, NY: Antique Collectors Club, 1995.

Bredehoft, Tom, and Neila M. Bredehoft. *50 Years of Collectible Glass, 1920–1970: Easy Identification and Price Guide: Stemware, Decorations, Decorative Accessories,* 2nd ed. Dubuque, IA: Antique Trader Books, 2000.

Fairbanks, Jonathan L. et al. *Collecting American Decorative Arts and Sculpture, 1971–1991.* Boston: Museum of Fine Arts, 1991.

Florence, Gene. *Collectible Glassware from the 40s, 50s, and 60s,* 6th ed. Paducah, KY: Collector Books, 2002.

Liberty's. "Marks from French Glass Makers." <www.libertys.com>

Whitehouse, David. *Glass: A Pocket Dictionary of Terms Commonly Used to Describe Glass and Glassmaking.* Corning, NY: The Corning Museum of Glass, 1993.

SPORTS COLLECTIBLES

GENERAL

Mortenson, Tom. *Warman's Sports Collectibles: A Value & Identification Guide.* Iola, WI: Krause Publications, 2001.

BASEBALL

Baseball Think Factory. <www.baseball-reference.com>

Beckett, James. *The Official 2002 Price Guide to Baseball Cards,* 11th ed. New York: House of Collectibles, 2001.

Price Guide Editors of Sports Collectors. *2001 Baseball Card Price Guide,* 15th ed. Iola, WI: DBI Books, 2001.

Raycraft, Don, and Michael Raycraft. *Collectibles 101: Baseball.* Atglen, PA: Schiffer Publishing, Ltd., 1999.

Reichler, Joseph L., ed. *The Baseball Encyclopedia: The Complete and Definitive Record of Major League Baseball,* 8th ed. New York: Hungry Minds, Inc., 1990.

Seymour, Harold. *Baseball: The Early Years.* New York: Oxford University Press, 1989.

Sports Market Report, April 2002. *PSA Grading Scale,* pp. 50–51.

Thorn, John et al., eds. *Total Baseball: The Official Encyclopedia of Major League Baseball,* 7th ed. Kingston, NY: Total Sports Publishing, 2001.

Zoss, Joel, and John Bowman. *Diamonds in the Rough.* New York: Macmillan Publishing Company, 1989.

GOLF

Campbell, Malcolm. *The New Encyclopedia of Golf: The Definitive Guide to the World of Golf—Courses, Champions, Characters, Traditions.* New York: DK Publishing, 2001.

Dey, Joseph C., Jr. "Golf." *Microsoft Encarta Encyclopedia,* 2000.

Ellis, Jeffery B. *The Golf Club: 400 Years of the Good, the Beautiful & the Creative.* Oak Harbor, WA: Zephyr Productions, Inc., 2003.

Farino, Bob. *Golf Club Collectors Handbook,* 1996.

Furjanic, Chuck. *Antique Golf Collectibles: A Price and Reference Guide,* 2nd ed. Iola, WI: Krause Publications, 2000.

——. *Antique Golf Clubs: A Price and Reference Guide,* 2nd ed. Iola, WI: Krause Publications, 2000.

Jeff Ellis Golf Collectibles. <www.antiqueclubs.com>

John, Ronald O. *The Vintage Era of Golf Club Collectibles: Identification & Value Guide.* Paducah, KY: Collector Books, 2001.

Kelly, Leo M., Jr. *Antique Golf Ball Reference & Price Guide.* Richton Park, IL: Old Chicago Golf Shop, 1993.

McGimpsey, Kevin, and David Neech. *Golf: Implements and Memorabilia—Eighteen Holes of Golf History.* London: Philip Wilson Publishers Ltd., 2000.

Olman, Morton W., and John Olman. *The Encyclopedia of Golf Collectibles: A Collector's Identification and Value Guide.* Florence, AL: Books Americana, 1985.

Olman, John M., and Morton W. Olman. *Olman's Golf Antiques & Other Treasures of the Game.* Cincinnati: Market Street Press, 1993.

Schwartz, Gary H. *The Art of Golf, 1754–1940: Timeless, Enchanting Illustrations and Narrative of Golf's Formative Years.* Tiburon, CA: Wood River Publishing, 1991.

F I S H I N G

"A History of Fly Fishing." <www.flyfishinghistory.com>

"Antique Lures." <www.antiquelures.com>

Campbell, A. J. *Classic and Antique Fly Fishing Tackle: A Guide for Collectors and Anglers.* Guilford, CT: The Lyons Press, 2002.

Coykendall, Ralph. *Coykendall's Complete Guide to Sporting Collectibles.* Radnor, PA: Wallace-Homestead Book Co., 1996.

Francis, Austin McK. *Land of Little Rivers: A Story in Photos of Catskill Fly Fishing.* New York: The Beaverkill Press, 1999.

Homel, Daniel B. *Antique Fly Reels: A History & Value Guide.* Bellingham, WA: Forest Park Publishers, 1998.

Lewis, Russell E. *Modern Fishing Lure Collectibles: Identification & Value Guide.* Paducah, KY: Collector Books, 2002.

Luckey, Carl F. *Old Fishing Lures and Tackle: Identification and Value Guide,* 6th ed. Iola, WI: Krause Publications, 2002.

Antique Fishing Lures and Boxes. <www.mrlurebox.com>

Murphy, Dudley, and Rick Edmisten. *Fishing Lure Collectibles,* 2nd ed. Paducah, KY: Collector Books, 2000.

The National Fishing Lure Collectors Club. <www.nflcc.com>

Schultz, Ken. *Ken Schultz's Fishing Encyclopedia.* New York: John Wiley & Sons, 1999.

Tonelli, Donna. *Top of the Line Fishing Collectibles.* Atglen, PA: Schiffer Publishing Ltd., 2000.

TOYS

Ackerman, Evelyn, and Frederick E. Keller. *Under the Bigtop with Schoenhut's Humpty Dumpty Circus.* Los Angeles: Gold Horse Publishing, 1996.

Alberta, Eric, and Art Maier. *Official Price Guide to Antiques and Collectibles,* 15th ed. New York: House of Collectibles, 1998.

Barenholtz, Bernard. *American Antique Toys, 1830–1900.* New York: Harry N. Abrams, 1980.

Bertoia Auctions. <www.bertoiaauctions.com>

Bertoia, Rich. *Antique Motorcycle Toys.* Atglen, PA: Schiffer Publishing, Ltd., 1999.

Boogaerts, Pierre. *Robot.* Paris: Futureopolis, 1978.

Burlington Toys. <www.burlingtontoys.com>

Buser, Elaine M., and Dan Buser. *M. Elaine and Dan Buser's Guide to Schoenhut's Dolls, Toys and Circus (1872–1976).* Paducah, KY: Collector Books, 1976.

Carlson, Pierce. *Toy Trains, A History.* New York: HarperCollins, 1989.

Cieslik, Jurgen, and Marianne Cieslik. *Lehmann Toys: The History of E.P. Lehmann, 1881–1981.* Atglen, PA: Schiffer Publishing, Ltd., 1983.

Clark, Jack, and Robert P. Wicker. *Hot Wheels: The Ultimate Redline Guide, Identification and Values, 1968–1977.* Paducah, KY: Collector Books, 2002.

Claytor, W. Graham, Jr., Paul A. Doyle, and Carlton Norris McKenney. *Greenberg's Guide to Early American Toy Trains.* Sykesville, MD: Greenberg Publishing Co. Inc., 1993.

Club Diecast. <http://clubdiecast.com>

DeSalle, Don, and Barb DeSalle. *Collectors Guide to Tonka Trucks, 1947–1963.* Marion, IN: L-W Book Sales, 1996.

——. *Smith-Miller & Doepke Trucks, with Prices.* Marion, IN: L-W Book Sales, 1997.

Dunbar, Leila. *Motorcycle Collectibles with Values.* Atglen, PA: Schiffer Publishing Ltd., 1997.

Emchowicz, Antoni, and Paul Nunneley. *Future Toys: Robots, Astronauts, Spaceships, Ray Guns.* London: New Cavendish Books, 2000.

Fawdry, Marguerite. *British Tin Toys.* London: New Cavendish Books, 1990.

Freed, Joe, and Sharon Freed. *Collector's Guide to American Transportation Toys, 1895–1941.* Raleigh: Freedom Publishing Inc., 1995.

Frey, Tom. *Toy Bop: Kid Classics of the 50's & 60's.* Murrysville, PA: Fuzzy Dice Productions Inc., 1994.

Gallagher, William C. *Japanese Toys, Amusing Playthings from the Past.* Atglen, PA: Schiffer Publishing Ltd., 2000.

Gottschalk, Lillian. *American Toy Cars and Trucks 1894–1942.* New York: Abbeville Press, 1986.

Greenberg, Bruce C. *Greenberg's Guide to Lionel Trains 1901–1942.* (vol 1). Sykesville, MD: Greenberg Books, 1994.

Hake, Ted, ed. *Hake's Guide to TV Collectibles, An Illustrated Price Guide.* Radnor, PA: Wallace-Homestead Book Co., 1990.

Hillier, Bevis, and Bernard C. Shine. *Walt Disney's Mickey Mouse Memorabilia: The Vintage Years, 1928–1938.* New York: Harry N. Abrams, Inc., 1990.

Horowitz, Jay, Gary Linden, and Charles Marx. *Marx Western Playsets: The Authorized Guide.* Sykesville, MD: Greenberg Publishing Company, Inc., 1992.

Huxford, Sharon, and Bob Huxford. *Schroeder's Collectible Toys, Antique to Modern Price Guide,* 8th ed. Paducah, KY: Collector Books, 2001.

Jaffe, Alan J. *Chein & Co., A Collector's Guide to an American Toymaker.* Atglen, PA: Schiffer Publishing Ltd., 2000.

James D. Julia Inc. <www.juliaauctions.com>

Johnson, Dana. *Collectors Guide to Diecast Toys and Scale Models: Identification & Values,* 2nd ed. Paducah, KY: Collector Books, 1998.

——. *Matchbox Toys 1947–1998,* 3rd ed. Paducah, KY: Collector Books, 1999.

——. *Toy Car Collector's Guide.* Paducah, KY: Collector Books, 2002.

Joplin, Norman. *The Great Book of Hollow-Cast Figures.* London: New Cavendish Books, 2000.

Kaonis, Keith, and Andrew Yaffee. *Schoenhut Toy Price Guide.* Englewood Cliffs, NJ: Self-published, 2000.

Kelley, Dale. *Collecting the Tin Toy Car, 1950–1970.* Atglen, PA: Schiffer Publishing Ltd., 1984.

Kelly, Douglas R. *The Die Cast Price Guide: Post-War: 1946 to Present.* Dubuque, IA: Antique Trader Books.

Kitahara, Teruhisa. *Robots: Tin Toy Dreams.* San Francisco: Chronicle Books, 1985.

——. *Yesterday's Toys: 734 Tin and Celluloid Amusements From Days Gone By.* New York: Black Dog & Leventhal, 1997.

——. *Yesterday's Toys: Robots, Spaceships and Monsters.* San Francisco: Chronicle Books, 1989.

Korbeck, Sharon, and Dan Stearns, eds. *Toys & Prices 2003,* 10th ed. Iola, WI: Krause Publications, 2003.

Kurtz, Henry I., and Burtt R. Ehrlich. *The Art of the Toy Soldier.* New York: Abbeville Press, 1990.

Lesser, Robert. *A Celebration of Comic Art and Memorabilia.* New York: Hawthorn Books, Inc., 1975.

Levitt, Jeffrey L. *The World of Antique Toys.* New York: Mint & Boxed, 1990.

Levy, Allen. *Tri-Ang Toys, 1937/38 Golden Era Catalogue.* New York: PEI International, 1994.

Luke, Tim, and Lita Solis-Cohen. *Miller's American Insider's Guide to Toys & Games.* London: Mitchell Beazley, 2002.

Marchand, Frédéric. *Avions-Jouets des Origines à 1945.* Paris: Maeght Éditeur, 1993.

——. *The History of Martin Mechanical Toys.* Paris: Editions l'Automobiliste, 1987.

Mark Bergin Toys. <www.bergintoys.com>

Marsella, Anthony R. *Toys from Occupied Japan, With Price Guide.* Atglen, PA: Schiffer Publishing Ltd., 1995.

Massucci, Edoardo. *Cars for Kids.* New York: Rizzoli, 1983.

McComas, Tom, and James Tuohy. *Lionel Collector's Guide and History, Postwar, Vol. II,* 4th ed. St. Paul: Motorbooks International, 1998.

McCollough, Albert W. *The New Book of Buddy "L" Toys,* 2nd ed. Sykesville, MD: Greenberg Publishing Company, 1997.

Milet, Jacques, and Robert Forbes. *Toy Boats 1870–1955, a Pictorial History from the Forbes Magazine Collection.* New York: Scribner, 1979.

Moran, Brian. *Battery Toys, The Modern Automota.* Atglen, PA: Schiffer Publishing Ltd., 1999.

Munsey, Cecil. *Disneyana: Walt Disney Collectibles.* New York: Dutton, 1974.

Murray, John J., and Bruce R. Fox. *Fisher-Price: A Historical, Rarity, and Value Guide, 1931 to Present,* 3rd ed. Iola, WI: Krause Publications, 2002.

National TCA Book Committee. *Lionel Trains, Standard of the World 1900–1943.* Strasburg, PA: Train Collectors Association, 1989.

Noel Barrett Vintage Toys @ Auction. <www.noelbarrett.com>

O'Brien, Richard. *The Story of American Toys: From Puritans to the Present.* New York: Artabras Publishers, 1992.

Ottenheimer, Peter. *Toy Autos 1890–1939.* London: New Cavendish Books, 1995.

Outwater, Myra Yellin, et al. *Cast Iron Automotive Toys.* Atglen, PA: Schiffer Publishing Ltd., 2000.

Ozzie's Robots, Toys & Collectibles. <www.ozziesrobots.com>

Parry-Crooke, Charlotte. *Märklin: 1895–1914.* London: New Cavendish Books, 1995.

Phil Weiss Auctions. <www.philipweissauctions.com>

Pinsky, Maxine A., et al. *Greenberg's Guide to Marx Toys, Volume 1: 1923–1950.* Sykesville, MD: Greenberg Publishing Company, Inc., 1995.

Ponzol, Dan. *Lionel: A Century of Timeless Toy Trains.* New York: Friedman/Fairfax Publishing, 2000.

Pressland, David. *The Art of the Tin Toy.* Atglen, PA: Schiffer Publishing, Ltd., 1992.

———. *The Book of Penny Toys.* New York: Pincushion Press, 1999.

———. *Pressland's Great Book of Tin Toys.* New York: Pincushion Press, 1995.

Randall, Peter. *The Products of Binns Road: A General Survey (The Hornby Companion Series).* New York: Pincushion Press, 1995.

Remise, Jac. *Carriages, Cars, and Cycles.* Atglen, PA: Schiffer Publishing Ltd., 1984.

Rich, Mark. *Toys A to Z: A Guide and Dictionary for Collectors, Antique Dealers and Enthusiasts.* Iola, WI: Krause Publications, 2001.

Richardson, Mike, and Sue Richardson. *The Great Book of Dinky Toys.* London: New Cavendish Books, 2000.

Riddle, Peter H. *America's Standard Gauge Electric Trains.* Iola, WI: Antique Trader Books, 1998.

Sagendorf, Bud. *Popeye, the First Fifty Years.* New York: Workman Publishing, 1979.

Singer, Leslie. *Zap! Ray Gun Classics.* San Francisco: Chronicle Books, 1991.

Sotheby's. *The Hegarty Collection of Antique Toys* (auction catalog). New York: October 2001.

Souter, Gerry, and Janet Souter. *Classic Toy Trains.* St. Paul: MBI Publishing Company, 2002.

———. *Lionel: America's Favorite Toy Trains.* St. Paul: MBI Publishing Company, 2000.

Stephan, Elizabeth. *O'Brien's Collecting Toys: Identification and Value Guide,* 10th ed. Iola, WI: Krause Publications: 2001.

———, ed. *O'Brien's Collecting Toy Trains, Identification and Value Guide,* 5th ed. Iola, WI: Krause Publications, 1999.

———. *Collecting Toy Trains: Identification and Value Guide.* Iola, WI: Krause Publications, 1999.

Strauss, Michael Thomas. *Tomart's Price Guide to Hotwheels Collectibles.* Dayton, OH: Tomart Publications, 2002.

TreasureQuest Auction Galleries. <www.tqag.com>

Wallis, Joe. *Regiments of All Nations: Britains Ltd. Lead Soldiers, 1946–1966.* Rev. ed. Washington, D.C.: Joe Wallis, 1992.

Whitehill, Bruce. *Games: American Boxed Games and their Makers 1822–1992, with Values.* Radnor, PA: Wallace-Homestead Book Company, 1992.

Wieland, James, and Edward Force. *Corgi Toys: The Ones with Windows.* Osceola, WI: Motorbooks International, 1981.

———. *Tootsietoys, World's First Diecast Models.* Osceola, WI: Motorbooks International, 1980.

Wood, Neil S., ed. *Evolution of the Pedal Car.* (vol. 5). Marion, IN: L-W Booksales, 1999.

———. *Evolution of the Pedal Car and Other Riding Toys, 1884–1970's, with Prices.* Marion, IN: L-W Booksales, 1989.

World Collectors Net. <www.worldcollectorsnet.com>

FASHION & TEXTILES

Bardey, Catherine. *Wearing Vintage.* New York: Black Dog & Leventhal, 2002.

Brownstein, Jerry, and Kathy Brownstein. *Beacon Blankets: Make Warm Friends.* Atglen, PA: Schiffer Publishing, Ltd., 2001.

Bruton, LaRee Johnson. *Ladies' Vintage Accessories: Identification and Value Guide.* Paducah, KY: Collector Books, 2000.

Dolan, Maryanne. *Vintage Clothing 1880–1980: Identification and Value Guide,* 3rd ed. Florence, KY: Books Americana, 1995.

Friedman, Barry. *Chasing Rainbows: Collecting American Indian Trade & Camp Blankets.* New York: Bulfinch Press, 2003.

Frost, Patricia. *Miller's Collecting Textiles.* London: Mitchell Beazley, 2000.

Horn, Richard. *Fifties Style.* New York: Friedman/Fairfax Publishing, 1995.

Johnson, Anna. *Handbags: The Power of the Purse.* New York: Workman Publishing, 2002.

Johnson, Frances. *Collecting Antique Linen, Lace and Needlework.* Radnor, PA: Wallace-Homestead Book Co., 1991.

Kapoun, Robert W. *Language of the Robe: American Indian Trade Blankets.* Layton, Utah: Gibbs Smith Publisher, 1992.

Tolkien, Tracy. *Handbags: A Collectors Guide (Miller's Collector's Guides).* London: Mitchell Beazley, 2001.

DOLLS & DOLL ACCESSORIES

Foulke, Jan, Ralph Kovel, and Terry Kovel. *Insider's Guide to Doll Buying & Selling: Antique to Modern.* Grantsville: Hobby House Press, 1995.

Handler, Ruth. *Dream Doll: The Ruth Handler Story.* Stamford, CT: Longmeadow Press, 1994.

Herlocher, Dawn T. *200 Years of Dolls: Identification and Price Guide.* Dubuque, IA: Antique Trader Books, 2002.

Herron, R. Lane. *Warman's Dolls: A Value and Identification Guide.* Iola, WI: Krause Publications, 1998.

Lavitt, Wendy. *Dolls: The Knopf Collector's Guide to American Antiques.* New York: Alfred A. Knopf, 1983.

Smith, Patricia. *Doll Values, Antique to Modern (7th Series).* Paducah, KY: Collector Books, 1992.

WRISTWATCHES

Braun, Peter, editor. *Wristwatch Annual 2003: The Catalogue of Producers, Models, and Specifications.* New York: Abbeville Press, Inc., 2002.

Brunner, Gisbert, and Christian Pfeiffer-Belli. S*wiss Wristwatches: Chronology of Worldwide Success; Swiss Watch Design in Old Advertisements and Catalogs.* Atglen, PA: Schiffer Publishing, Ltd., 1991.

Faber, Edward, and Stewart Unger. *American Wristwatches: Five Decades of Style and Design.* Atglen, PA: Schiffer Publishing, Ltd., 2000.

Kahlert, Helmut, Richard Mühe, and Gisbert L. Brunner. *Wristwatches: History of a Century's Development,* 4th ed. Atglen, PA: Schiffer Publishing, Ltd., 1999.

Liebe, Frankie. *Watches: A Collector's Guide (Miller's Collector's Guides).* London: Mitchell Beazley, 1999.

Second Time Around Watch Co. <www.secondtimearound watchco.com>

PHOTOGRAPHY

The American Museum of Photography. <www.photographymuseum.com>

American Photo: The Joy of Collecting issue, March 1995.

The Artchive. <www.artchive.com>

Auer, Michèle, and Michel Auer. *Photographers Encyclopedia International, 1839 to Present.* Geneva: Camera Obscura, 1985.

Baldwin, George. *Looking at Photographs: A Guide to Technical Terms.* Los Angeles: J. Paul Getty Museum Publications, 1991.

Blodgett, Richard E. *Photographs: A Collector's Guide.* New York: Ballantine Books, 1979.

Browne, Turner. *Macmillan Biographical Encyclopedia of Photographic Artists and Innovators.* New York: Macmillan Publishing Company, 1987.

"Conservation of Photographs & Works on Paper: Resources." <www.paulmessier.com>

The J. Paul Getty Trust. <www.getty.edu>

George Eastman House International Museum of Photography and Film. <www.eastman.org>

Jagger, Todd. "The Dye Transfer Process." <www.jagger.com/dyetrans.html>

Johnson, William S., Mark Rice, and Carla Williams. *Photography from 1839 to Today: George Eastman House, Rochester, NY.* Los Angeles: TASCHEN America, 2000.

Kingston, Rodger. *Walker Evans in Print: The Kingston Collection: An Illustrated Bibliography.* Belmont, MA: R.P. Kingston Photographs, 1995.

Krehbiel, D. *"Making Black & White Photographic Images: A Journey Through the Opto-Chemical Era into the Digital Age."* <www.slonet.org/~mhd

Landt, Dennis. *Collecting Photographs: A Guide to the New Art Boom.* New York: E.P. Dutton: 1977.

Leggat, Robert. "A History of Photography: From its Beginnings til the 1920s." <http://rleggat.com/photohistory>

The Library of Congress, Prints and Photographs: Online Catalog. <http://memory.loc.gov/pp>

Luis Nadeau's Online Printing, Photographic and Photomechanical Processor Museum. <www.photoconservation.com>

Masters of Photography. <www.masters-of-photography.com>

Newhall, Beaumont. *History of Photography from 1839 to the Present Day,* 5th ed. New York: New York Graphic Society, 1982.

Photo Techniques. <www.phototechmag.com>

Pitnick, Richard. "ABC of Collecting: Part 2 Assembling a Collection." *Black and White Magazine,* August 2002, no. 20.

Rosenblum, Naomi. *A World History of Photography.* New York: Abbeville Press, 1997.

Roth, Andrew, ed. *The Book of 101 Books: Seminal Photographic Books of the Twentieth Century.* New York: Roth Horowitz LLC, 2001.

Walker Art Center. <www.walkerart.org>

Weinstein, Robert A., and Larry Booth. *Collection, Use, and Care of Historical Photographs.* Nashville: American Association for State and Local History, 1977.

ENTERTAINMENT MEMORABILIA

Brooks, Tim, and Earle Marsh. *The Complete Directory to Prime Time Network and Cable T.V. Shows.* New York: Ballantine, 1999.

Franchi, Rudy, and Barbara Franchi. *Miller's Movie Collectibles.* London: Mitchell Beazley, 2002.

Hilton, Joe, and Greg Moore. *Rock-N-Roll Treasures: Identification & Value Guide.* Paducah, KY: Collector Books, 1999.

Martin, Kevin. *The Official Autograph Collector Price Guide.* Corona, CA: Odyssey Publications, 2001.

Neely, Tim, ed. *Goldmine Records & Prices.* Iola, WI: Krause Publications, 2002.

Pareles, Jon, and Patricia Romanowski, eds., *The Rolling Stone Encyclopedia of Rock & Roll.* New York: Rolling Stone Press/Summit Books, 1983.

Thompson, Dave. *The Music Lover's Guide to Record Collecting.* San Francisco: Backbeat Books, 2002.

COSTUME JEWELRY

Ball, Joanne Dubbs. *Costume Jewelers: The Golden Age of Design,* 3rd ed. Atglen, PA: Schiffer Publishing Ltd., 2000.

Bennett, David, and Daniela Mascetti. *Understanding Jewelry.* Wappingers Falls, NY: Antique Collectors Club, 2000.

Kelley, Lyngerda, and Nancy Schiffer. *Costume Jewelry, The Great Pretenders.* Atglen, PA: Schiffer Publishing Ltd., 1998.

Morning Glory Antiques & Jewelry. <www.morninggloryantiques.com>

Rezazdeh, Fred. *Costume Jewelry.* Paducah, KY: Collector Books, 1997.

Tolkien, Tracy, and Henrietta Wilkinson. *A Collectors Guide to Costume Jewelry: Key Styles and How to Recognize Them.* Toronto: Firefly Books Ltd., 1997.

POSTERS AND ILLUSTRATION ART

POSTERS

Ades, Dawn, and Richard Peterson. *The 20th-Century Poster, Design of the Avant-Garde.* New York: Abbeville Press, 1985.

Artfact. <www.artfact.com>

Artnet. <www.artnet.com>

AskART. <www.askart.com>

Barnicoat, John. *Posters, A Concise History.* New York: Thames & Hudson, 1985.

Bernstein, David. *The Shell Poster Book.* Boston: David R. Godine, 1993.

Broido, Lucy. *The Posters of Jules Cheret.* Mineola, NY: Dover Publications, 1992.

Feinblatt, Ebria. *Toulouse-Lautrec and His Contemporaries: Posters of the Belle Epoque from the Wagner Collection.* New York: Harry N. Abrams, Inc., 1986.

Franciscono, Marcel. *The Modern Dutch Poster: The First Fifty Years, 1890–1940.* Cambridge: MIT Press, 1987.

Gleeson, Janet. *Miller's Collecting Prints and Posters.* Wappingers Falls, NY: Antique Collectors Club, 1997.

Green, Oliver. *Underground Art: London Transport Posters, 1908 to the Present,* 2nd ed. London: Laurence King Publishing, 2001.

Heyman, Therese Thau. *Posters, American Style.* New York: Abradale Press, 2000.

Hillier, Bevis. *Travel Posters.* New York: Dutton, 1976.

Howard Lowery Gallery. *Vintage Hollywood Posters.* Burbank, CA: 1999.

The International Vintage Posters Dealers Association. <www.ivpda.com>

Macy, Laura, ed. Groveart.com. <www.groveart.com>

Margadant, Bruno. *The Swiss Poster, 1900–1983.* Geneva: Birkhauser, 1984.

The Metropolitan Museum of Art. *American Posters of the 1890s in the Metropolitan Museum of Art, Including the Leonard A. Lauder Collection.* New York: Metropolitan Museum of Art, 1987.

Rawls, Walton. *Wake Up America: World War I and the American Poster.* New York: Abbeville Press, 2001.

Rennert. Jack. *100 Years of Bicycle Posters.* London: Hert-Davis Mac Gibbon, 1973.

——. *Posters of the Belle Epoque: The Wine Spectator Collection.* New York: Posters Please, 2003.

Weill, Alain. *L'Invitation au Voyage: L'Affiche de tourisme dans le monde.* Paris: Editions Somogy, 1994.

——. *One Hundred Years of Posters of the Folies-Bergere & Music Halls of Paris.* Oakland, CA: Bookpeople, 1977.

——. *The Poster: A Worldwide Survey and History.* Woodbridge, CT: G.K. Hall & Co., 1985.

Wrede, Stuart. *The Modern Poster.* New York: Harry N. Abrams, 1991.

Yount, Sylvia. *Maxfield Parrish, 1870–1966.* New York: Abradale Press, 2003.

ILLUSTRATION ART

Adventure House. <www.adventurehouse.com>

The American Center for Artists. <www.americanartists.org>

Bud Plant Illustrated Books. <www.bpib.com>

Charles M. Schulz Museum and Research Center. <www. schulzmuseum.org>

Comic Art & Graffix Gallery. <www.comic-art.com>

Don Markstein's Toonopedia. <www.toonopedia.com>

Eloise Web site. <www.eloisewebsite.com>

Illustration House. <www.illustration-house.com>

International Center for the Study of Children's Literature. <www.ricochet-jeunes.org/eng>

International Museum of Cartoon Art. <http://cartoon.org/fame.htm>

Juddery, Mark. "Burne Hogarth." *The Australian,* February 16, 1996. <www.markjuddery.com>

Kingman, Lee. *Illustrators of Children's Books 1957–1966.* Boston: The Horn Book, Inc., 1968.

Lambiek Comic Shop. <www.lambiek.com>

Lesser, Robert, and Robert Reed. *Pulp Art: Original Paintings.* New York: Random House Value Publishing, 1997.

"Live Foreverett: Blake Bell's Web site on Three Comic Book Greats: Bill Everett, Alex Schomburg, and Syd Shores." <www.ess.comics.org>

MacCloskey, Ron. "Charles Addams." <www.westfieldnj.com/addams/>

Meyer, Susan E. *A Treasury of The Great Children's Book Illustrators.* New York: Abradale Press, 1987.

Overstreet, Robert M. *The Official Overstreet Comic Book Price Guide,* 32nd ed. New York: House Of Collectibles, 2002.

Reed, Walt. *The Illustrator in America: 1860–2000.* New York: The Society of Illustrators, 2001.

The Best in Science Fiction and Fantasy. <www.sfsite.com>

Smithsonian American Art Museum. "Metropolitan Lives: The Ashcan Artists and their New York." <www.nmaa.si.edu/collections/exhibits/metlives>

Steve Ditko. <www.geocities.com/Hollywood/7941>

Swenson, Rich. "Hannes Bok." <http://ebbs.english.vt.edu/20th/etudes/swenson/bok.html>

Taylor, Judy, ed. *Beatrix Potter, 1866–1943: The Artist and Her World.* New York: Viking Press, 1988.

Weist, Jerry. *The Comic Art Price Guide: With Pulp, U.G. Comix and Monster Magazine Price Guides,* 2nd ed. Gloucester, MA: Arcturian Books, 2000.

Weber, Nicholas Fox. *The Art of Babar, the Work of Jean and Laurent deBrunhoff.* New York: Harry N. Abrams, Inc., 1989.

Will Eisner. <http://willeisner.tripod.com>

Wu, Frank. "The House of Crunchy Art: Award-winning Sci-Fi & Fantasy Art by Frank Wu." <www.frankwu.com>

FURNITURE

Battersby, Martin. *The Decorative Thirties.* New York: Whitney Library of Design, 1988.

Bishop, Robert Charles. *Centuries and Styles of the American Chair 1640–1970.* New York: Dutton, 1972.

Boyce, Charles, ed. *Dictionary of Furniture,* 2nd ed. New York: Checkmark Books, 2000.

Brunhammer, Yvonne. *Art Deco Style.* New York: St. Martin's Press, 1984.

Christie's New York. *Important 20th-Century Decorative Arts, Including Arts & Crafts and Architectural Designs Catalog.* New York: June 2000.

Clark, Robert Judson, et al. *Design in America: The Cranbrook Vision, 1925–1950.* New York: Harry N. Abrams, 1983.

Collector's Compass, ed. *50's Decor.* Woodinville, WA: Martingale & Company, 2000.

Dormer, Peter. *Design Since 1945 (World of Art).* London: Thames & Hudson, 1993.

Dubrow, Eileen, and Richard Dubrow. *Styles of American Furniture 1860–1960.* Atglen, PA: Schiffer Publishing Co. Ltd., 2000.

Duncan, Alastair. *Modernism: Modernist Design 1880–1940: The Norwest Collection.* Wappingers Falls, NY: Antique Collectors Club, 1998.

Eidelberg, Martin, ed. *Design 1935–1965: What Modern Was.* New York: Harry N. Abrams, 2001.

Fehrman, Cherie, and Kenneth Fehrman. *Postwar Interior Design, 1945–1960.* New York: Van Nostrand Reinhold, 1987.

Fiell, Charlotte, and Peter Fiell. *Design of the 20th Century.* Los Angeles: TASCHEN America, 2001.

Fitzgerald, Oscar P. *Four Centuries of American Furniture.* Radnor, PA: Wallace-Homestead Book Co., 1995.

Gallagher, Fiona. *Christie's Art Deco.* New York: Watson-Guptill Publications, 2000.

Gaston, Mary Frank. *Collectors Guide to Art Deco: Identification and Values,* 2nd ed. Paducah, KY: Collector Books, 1997.

Greenberg, Cara. *Op to Pop: Furniture of the 1960s.* Boston: Bulfinch Press, 1999.

Hanks, David A., and Whitney Museum of Art. *High Styles: Twentieth-Century American Design.* New York: Summit Books, 1985.

Heisinger, Kathryn, and George H. Marcus. *Antiquespeak: A Guide to the Styles, Techniques, and Materials of the Decorative Arts, from the Renaissance to Art Deco* (Speak Series). New York: Abbeville Press, 1997.

Hillier, Bevis. *The Style of the Century: 1900–1980.* Chicago: New Amsterdam Books, 1990.

Jenkins, Emyl. *Emyl Jenkins' Reproduction Furniture: Antiques for the Next Generation.* New York: Crown Publishers, 1995.

Julier, Guy. *The Thames & Hudson Dictionary of 20th-Century Design and Designers* (World of Art). London: Thames & Hudson, 1993.

Kras, Reyer, and Jonathan M. Woodham, eds. *Icons of Design: The 20th-Century.* New York: Prestel USA, 2000.

Lindquist, David P., and Caroline C. Warren. *Colonial Revival Furniture, with Prices.* Radnor, PA: Wallace-Homestead Book Co., 1993.

McConnell, Kevin. *Collecting Art Deco.* Atglen, PA: Schiffer Publishing Ltd., 1997.

Meadmore, Clement. *The Modern Chair: Classics in Production.* New York: Van Nostrand Reinhold, 1975.

Miller, R. Craig. *Modern Design in the Metropolitan Museum of Art, 1890–1990.* New York: Harry N. Abrams, Inc. 1990.

Naeve, Milo M. *Identifying American Furniture: A Pictorial Guide to Styles and Terms, Colonial to Contemporary.* New York: W.W. Norton & Company, 1998.

Pile, John F. *The Dictionary of 20th-Century Design.* New York: Da Capo Press, 1994.

Pina, Leslie. *Classic Herman Miller.* Atglen, PA: Schiffer Publishing Ltd., 1998.

——. *Fifties Furniture.* Atglen, PA: Schiffer Publishing Ltd., 1996.

Rouland, Steve, and Roger Rouland. *Haywood-Wakefield Modern Furniture.* Paducah, KY: Collector Books, 1994.

Society of Industrial Designers. *Industrial Design in America.* New York; Farrar, Straus & Giroux, Inc, 1954.

Sparke, Penny, et al. *The New Design Source Book.* New York: Knickerbocker Press, 1997.

Terraroli, Valerio. *Skira Dictionary of Modern Decorative Arts: 1851–1942.* Milan: Skira, 2001.

Trench, Lucy. *Materials and Techniques in the Decorative Arts.* Chicago: The University of Chicago Press, 2000.

Yates, Simon, Mark Bridge, and Constance Eileen King. *Encyclopedia of Furniture.* San Diego, CA: Thunder Bay Press, 1999.

Zaczek, Iain. *Essential Art Deco.* Bath, England: Parragon Publishing, 2000.

PHOTOGRAPHY CREDITS

Unless otherwise specified, copyright on the works reproduced lies with the respective photographers, illustrators, agencies, and museums. Despite extensive research, it has not always been possible to establish copyright ownership. Where this is the case, we would appreciate notification.

COVER

American Toys, www.american-toys.com: bottom middle.

Antiques Roadshow: middle upper left, bottom right.

Courtesy Louis and Susan Meisel Collection: top right, spine.

Courtesy McMasters Harris Auction Company: bottom left.

Morning Glory Antiques & Jewelry: middle right.

Courtesy Phillips, de Pury & Luxembourg: top left.

Photos Ron Gast, http://home.cfl.rr.com/rkgast/: middle lower left.

BACK COVER

Eric Boman: (author picture) bottom right.

Christie's Images: middle left.

Courtesy Sotheby's: top right.

CONTENTS

Aaron Faber Gallery, photo by Stan Schnier: page xiv top right.

American Toys, www.american-toys.com: page xiii top right.

Antiques Roadshow: pages xi middle left, xii top, xiii middle left, bottom right, xiv bottom right.

Courtesy Barry Halper Baseball Archives: page xii bottom.

Courtesy Doyle New York: page xv bottom left.

Gary Metz's Muddy River Trading Co.: page xi bottom right.

Lelands.com: page xiv left.

Courtesy Phillips, de Pury & Luxembourg: xv middle right.

Courtesy Swann Auction Galleries: xv top left.

COLLECTING 101

Adamstown Antique Gallery: page xxi bottom, xxix bottom.

The Advertising Archives: page xxxi top.

American Toys, www.american-toys.com: pages xix center right, xxvii top, xxxv top.

Antiques Roadshow: page xxi top.

Courtesy Barry Halper Baseball Archives: pages xx, xxxvi bottom, xxxvii middle left.

Christie's Images: pages xix center left, xxxv bottom, xxxviii bottom.

Bettmann/Corbis: page xxxiii.

Courtesy Doyle New York: page xxvi.

Duke Homestead Museum: page xxiii middle left.

Eri Morita Photography: page xxxvi top.

Irving Solero/ The Museum at the Fashion Institute of Technology, New York: page xxxiv top.

Michael J. Hipple/Gasoline Alley Antiques: page xxxi bottom.

Photos Ron Gast, http://home.cfl.rr.com/rkgast/: page xxxii bottom.

Courtesy The Glass Cupboard, www.trocadero.com/cupboard3, photo by Stan Schnier: xxvii bottom.

LIONEL L.L.C.: page xxix top.

©MastroNet, Inc: xxiii bottom right, xxxiv bottom. Pictured items were sold in a MastroNet, Inc. division auction.

Courtesy Phillips, de Pury & Luxembourg: page xix left.

Rago Modern Auctions, Lambertville, NJ: xxii, xxx top, bottom.

Richard Gutman: pages xxxvii top.

Richard Opfer Auctioneering, Inc.: xix right, xxiv top.

Courtesy Skinner, Inc.: xxxii top, xxxviii top.

Courtesy Toledo Museum of Art: xxviii.

Private collection of Rosemary Trietsch, photos by Stan Schnier: xix bottom center.

Courtesy Joe and Donna Tonelli, photos by James Krancic: page xxiv bottom.

Courtesy Steve Whitney, redsgolf1@aol.com: xix center.

CHAPTER 1

CERAMICS

Courtesy of Antik: pages 7 top, bottom, 24 top right, 27 top left.

Antiques Roadshow: pages 2, 21, 26 right and left, 30 left, 32 bottom left.

The California Connection: page 14 top.

Christie's Images: pages 18 top, bottom, 19, 29 top right, 30 middle, 32 top.

Courtesy of Jane Kahan Gallery: page 25 top.

My Glass Duchess: pages 11 top, 12 top left, 13 top, 16 top.

Collection of the Newark Museum: pages 11 bottom, 20 bottom.

Courtesy of Marjorie E. Parker: page 8.

Rago Modern Auctions, Lambertville, NJ: pages 3 top, 4, 5, 9 left, 13 bottom, 14 bottom, 15 bottom, 20 top, 22 top left, 23 middle, 24 top left, bottom left, 25 bottom, 27 bottom, 28 top left, middle left, bottom left, 29 bottom right, 30 top right, 31 top and bottom, 32 bottom right.

Replacements, Ltd.: pages 9 top right, 10, 12 top right, bottom right, 16 bottom, 17.

Courtesy Skinner, Inc.: pages 1 top, bottom, 3 bottom, 6 top, bottom, 22 right, 23 top right, 15 top.

CHAPTER 2

ADVERTISING

The Advertising Archives: page 45.

Antiques Roadshow: pages 34 top, 51 right, 60 top right, 63, 64 left, 67 bottom.

Barker Animation Art Gallery: pages 36, 37 top, 50, 58 bottom, 60 bottom right, 61 all, 65 top, bottom, 69 bottom, 70.

Buffalo Bay Auction Co: pages 49 bottom left, 56 left, 59 top.

Corbis: page 56 bottom all.

Dan Morean's Breweriana.Com: pages 51 left, 52-53 all.

John A. Daniel: page 62 top.

Duke Homestead Museum: pages 57 top, left, 59 bottom.

Gary Metz's Muddy River Trading Co.: pages 33 all, 37 bottom, 39 top, 46 top, 47 middle, 48 bottom, 49 top all, 62 bottom, 67 middle, 69 top.

Rick Grossman/Collection of Pam Budzinski: page 40 left, 42 bottom, 43 top, bottom right.

Michael J. Hipple/Gasoline Alley Antiques: pages 46 bottom, 64 top right, 65 middle, 66 top, bottom.

Tony Hyman: pages 55 top left, top right, 58 top.

Iowa Gas Swap: page 47 top, bottom.

New York Public Library: page 54.

Richard Opfer Auctioneering, Inc.: pages 34 bottom, 35, 38, 39 bottom, 40 middle, right, 41, 42 top, 43 bottom left, 44 bottom, 48 top, 60 bottom left.

Courtesy Skinner Inc.: pages 44 top, middle, 69 middle.

Larry White: page 68 all.

CHAPTER 3

GLASS

Antiques Roadshow: pages 72 top, 76 top left, 98 left, 102 top left, 105 right, 108 top left.

Barry Friedman Ltd.: page 106 top.

Courtesy Doyle New York: pages 73, 98 right, 105 left.

Courtesy The Glass Cupboard, www.trocadero.com/cupboard3; photos by Stan Schnier: pages 71 bottom, 75 top, 78 top, bottom, 80 bottom, 81, 83, 84 bottom left, 84 middle left, 85 bottom, 89 bottom, 90 bottom, 93 top, 96 bottom.

Private collection of Joseph F. Muratore, M.D.; photos by Stan Schnier: pages 72 bottom, 82 bottom, 84 bottom right, 87 middle, 96 top.

Rago Modern Auctions, Lambertville, NJ: pages 71 top, 74, 76 bottom right, 77, 87 top, 99 bottom, 99 top, 100 bottom, 101, 104 top, 106 bottom, 107 bottom, 108 bottom right, 109 top.

Reyne Gallery: page 80 top.

Courtesy Royal Leerdam Crystal: page 109 bottom.

Courtesy Skinner, Inc.: pages 92 bottom left, 97 top, 102 bottom right, 103 top, bottom, 107 top, 110 top, bottom.

Private collection of Rosemary Trietsch; photos by Stan Schnier: pages 75 bottom, 84 top left, 85 top, 87 bottom, 88, 89 top, 90 top, 91, 92 bottom right, top left, 93 bottom, 94 bottom left, 94 top right, 95 bottom. Toledo Museum of Art: pages 79 right and left, 82 top, 94 top left, 95 top, 97 bottom, 100 top, 104 bottom.

CHAPTER 4

SPORTS COLLECTIBLES

Antiques Roadshow: page 166 middle left.

Courtesy Barry Halper Baseball Archives: pages 111 top, bottom right, 112 top, bottom, 115 bottom, 116 top and bottom, 117, 118, 119 right, 122, 124, 125, 126 top and bottom, 128 top left, bottom, top right, 129, 131 bottom left all, 132 top, bottom, 133 top and bottom, 134 top right, 134 top left, 135 top and bottom; additional permission.

Topps Company, Inc.: pages 119 middle, left, 121 top and bottom 123.

Christie's Images: pages 137 top, 141 bottom, 149 top left, bottom right, 148 bottom, 150 bottom right, bottom left.

Courtesy The Complete Sportsman, photos Paul Schmookler: pages 164, 165 bottom right, top right, left.

Photos ©Enrico Ferorelli 1999, Land of Little Rivers: pages 156 left, 157 right, 159 right, 159 top, 160, 161 bottom, 162 top right, top left.

Photos Ron Gast, http:/home.cfl.rr.com/ rkgast/: pages 154 middle, 154 top, 157 top left, 161 top, 166 top, bottom, 167 bottom, 168 top.

Images from THE GOLF CLUB by Jeffrey Ellis ©Zephyr Productions, Inc. 2003: pages 113, 137 bottom, 139, 140 top right, top middle, top left, 141 top, 142 all, 143 top, bottom, 144 top, middle, bottom, 146 top, middle left, bottom right, 147 top, bottom.

Courtesy H. Leonard Rod Company: pages 155 bottom, 156 bottom right.

©MastroNet, Inc.: pages 115 top, 120, 127, 130, 131 right, top right. Pictured items were sold in a MastroNet, Inc. division auction.

Courtesy Sotheby's: pages 136 top, bottom, 138 top, bottom, 148 top 150 top left, 151, 152 top.

Courtesy Joe and Donna Tonelli, photos James Krancic: pages 154 bottom, 157 top right, 158, 162 bottom left, 163 top, bottom, 167 top, 168 middle, bottom.

Courtesy Steve Whitney, redsgolf1@aol.com: pages 149 top right, 155 top, 152 bottom, 153 bottom right, top all.

CHAPTER 5

TOYS

Adamstown Antique Gallery: pages 176 bottom, 177 top, 179, 180, 181 bottom, 181 top, 182, 183 top, bottom, 185 bottom, 187 bottom, 191 top, middle right, bottom right, 194 bottom, 195, 199, 200 bottom, 207 top, 211 top right, top middle, 214 top.

American Toys, www.american-toys.com: pages 169 top, bottom, 170 bottom, 171 bottom, 172 top, bottom, 173 top, 174 top, bottom, 175, 176 top, 184 top, bottom, 186 top, bottom, 187 top, 188, 189 top, 190 top, bottom, 192, 196 top, 197 top left, 200 top, 201 top, bottom, 202 top, 204 top, bottom, 206 top left, bottom left, bottom right, 207 bottom right, 208 top, bottom, 209, 211 top left, 212, 213 top, bottom, 214 bottom, 216, 217 top, bottom, 218 top, bottom.

Antiques Roadshow: pages 170 top, 171 top, 173 bottom, 185 top, 189 bottom.

Barker Animation Art Gallery: page 210.

Christie's Images: pages 202 bottom, 207 bottom left.

Dietrich Gehring: pages 177 bottom, 178 top, bottom, 193 top left, top right, bottom, 194 top, 196 bottom.

LIONEL L.L.C.: page 198 top.

Robot Hut: pages 203, 205 top, bottom.

Courtesy Skinner, Inc.: pages 198 bottom, 215.

CHAPTER 6

FASHION AND TEXTILES

Antiques Roadshow: pages 222, 238 left, 254.

Bettmann/Corbis: pages 226, 227 bottom, top, 231 top, 237.

Hulton-Deutsch Collection/Corbis: pages 225 left, 225 right, 231 bottom.

Courtesy Doyle New York: pages 219 bottom, 221, 229 right, middle, 232, 234, 238 right, 239 top right, left, bottom right, 240, 241 top, 243 right, left, 248 top, bottom, 249 top, 251 all.

ENOKIWORLD.COM: page 252 top.

Eri Morita Photography: page 219 top, 249 bottom, 250.

Irving Solero/ The Museum at the Fashion Institute of Technology, New York: pages 228, 229 left, 230, 231 top, 233 left, right, 236, 241 bottom, 242 bottom, right.

Quentin Bertoux/Hermès: pages 247 top.

Courtesy Karen Augusta Antique Lace and Fashion: page 253 right, bottom right.

Eri Morita Photography/Laura Fisher Antiques: pages 259 both, 260.

Laura Fisher Antiques: pages 255 both, 256, 257 both, 261 both, 262 both.

Swann Auction Galleries: 247 bottom.

Courtesy Vintage Textile.com: pages 224, 231 bottom, 244, 245, 252 bottom, 253 top right.

Vintage Trends.com: page 223.

CHAPTER 7

DOLLS AND DOLL ACCESSORIES

Antiques Roadshow: pages 265 right, 277, 285, 288 left, 292 top.

Courtesy Dollworks: pages 264 bottom, 271 bottom, 272 bottom, 276 top, 279 top, 283 top, 284 all.

Courtesy Doyle New York: page 280.

Courtesy McMasters Harris Auction Company: pages 263 bottom, 264 top, 265 bottom, 266 top, bottom, 267, 269, 270 top, bottom, 271 top, 272 top, 274, 275 top, 276 bottom, 278 top, bottom, 279 bottom, 281 top, bottom, 282, 287 bottom, 287 top, 288 right, 289 bottom, 289 top, 290, 291 bottom, top, 292 bottom, 293.

Mid-Ohio Historical Museum, Inc.: page 275 bottom.

Rosalie Whyel Museum of Doll Art, Photo by Charles Backus: page 268.

Courtesy Skinner, Inc.: pages 294, 296.

Courtesy Treasure Quest Auction Galleries: pages 263 top, 273, 283 bottom, 295 all.

CHAPTER 8

WRISTWATCHES

2nd Time Around Watches: pages 304 top, 314 top, middle, 315 top, bottom, 317 left, 318 right, middle, 319 middle, left, 320.

Aaron Faber Gallery: pages 298, 299 left, 304 bottom, 306 right, 310.

Aaron Faber Gallery, photos by Stan Schnier: pages 297, 298, 299 right, 307 right, 308 bottom, 315 middle, 316 left 318 left, 301 middle, bottom left, 302, 303 middle, 306 middle, left, 311 top, bottom.

Antiques Roadshow: pages 313, 317 bottom, 319 right.

Courtesy Lisa and David Hellerstein: page 312.

Movado Museum: page 316 right.

Courtesy Phillips, de Pury & Luxembourg: pages 297 bottom, 300 left, right, 301 right, 303 left, right, 305 top, bottom, 307 middle, left, 308 top, 314 bottom.

Corp, all rights reserved, page 470 right, ©Al Hirschfeld/Margo Feiden Galleries Ltd., New York, www.alhirschfeld.com page 463 top right, ©The New Yorker Magazine, 1928, Peter Arno, www.cartoonbank.com, page 461 middle; printed by permission of the Norman Rockwell Family Agency ©2003 The Norman Rockwell Family Entities, page 454; courtesy Maurice Sendak page 469 left; ©Dr. Seuss Enterprises, Lk.P. 2003, all rights reserved, page 467 top right; Tribune Media Services, Inc. all rights reserved, reprinted with permission, page 471 top right; Linus reproduced with Permission from UFS, Inc. PEANUTS ©UFS page 423 top; TARZAN reprinted by permission of United Feature Syndicate, Inc. pages 459 bottom, 471 bottom right.

Courtesy Swann Auction Galleries: pages 424, 427, 432, 433, 434, 436, 423 bottom, 425 bottom, 429 top right, bottom left, 430 top, bottom, 431, 435 top right, middle, bottom right, 437 top right, bottom right, 438 top right, top left, 439 top, 441 top, bottom, 442 top left, middle right, bottom left, 443 top right, top left, 444 top right, top left, 445 top right, top left, 446 top right, top left, 447 top right, top left, 448 top right, top left, 449 top right, top left, 451 top right, top left; ©Estate of Roy Lichtenstein page 439 bottom right; printed by permission of the Norman Rockwell Family Agency ©2003 The Norman Rockwell Family Entities page 450 top left; courtesy Ben Shahn Estate page 450 top right.

CHAPTER 13

FURNITURE

Antiques Roadshow: pages 476 top, 505 top.

The Colonial Furniture Company: page 510.

Donzella Ltd.: page 508 top, bottom.

Courtesy Doyle New York: pages 475 bottom, 479 bottom, 481, 487 top, 496 top, 503 top.

Nadeau's Auction Gallery Inc.: page 514.

Courtesy Phillips, de Pury & Luxembourg: 475 top, 476 bottom, pages 482 top, bottom, 486, 488, 495 top, 497, 498 top, bottom, 499 top, 501 bottom inset, 501 bottom, 502 bottom, 507.

Rago Modern Auctions, Lambertville, NJ: pages 479 top, 480, 487 bottom, 491, 492, 493, 495 bottom, 499 bottom, 501 top, 502 top, 503 bottom, 504, 506.

Courtesy Skinner, Inc.: pages 478, 484, 485 top, 489, 490, 494, 496 bottom, 500, 505 bottom.

Courtesy Sotheby's: pages 477 top, 485 bottom, 509 both.

www.wallacenuttingfurniture.com: pages 477 bottom, 511, 513 both.

CHAPTER 14

AN EXPERTS' ROUNDTABLE

Adamstown Antique Gallery: page 515 top.

American Toys, www.american-toys.com: pages 530 and 531.

Antiques Roadshow: page 520.

Courtesy Barry Halper Baseball Archives. (Additional Permission Topps Company, Inc.): pages 521 bottom both, 522 top.

Courtesy Burlingame Museum of Pez Memorabilia: pages 516 both, 526 bottom both.

Courtesy Doyle New York: pages 520, 528, 529.

Courstey Mark Mcdonald/330: page 521 top left.

L.A. Finders Keepers: page 522 bottom.

Jordan Mazer: page 532.

©MastroNet, Inc: page 524. Pictured items were sold in a MastroNet, Inc. division auction.

Photofest: pages 534, 535.

Rago Modern Auctions, Lambertville, NJ: pages 525, 526 top, 527.

Courtesy Swann Auction Galleries: page 517.

COLOR SECTION:

COLOR CERAMICS

Antik: page c1 middle left.

Courtesy The California Connection: page c2 bottom all.

Christie's Images: pages c1 bottom all, c2 upper middle right, c3 top left, middle left, middle right.

Courtesy Jane Kahan Gallery: page c3 bottom right.

Courtesy Louis and Susan Meisel Collection: page c1 top right.

Courtesy Phillips, de Pury & Luxembourg: page c3 middle center left.

David Rago Art Dealer: pages c1 top left, center, middle right, c2 top right, middle right, middle left, upper middle, c3 top middle, top right, middle right, bottom center left.

Replacements, Ltd.: page c2 middle left.

Courtesy Skinner, Inc.: pages c2 middle, c3 bottom left.

Courtesy Sotheby's: page c3 bottom center right.

COLOR ADVERTISING

Barker Animation Art Gallery: pages c5 bottom left, c7 top right, bottom left.

John A. Daniel: page c7 bottom right.

Duke Homestead Museum: pages c5 top right, c6 bottom left.

Gary Metz's Muddy River Trading Co.: pages c4 right, top left, c6 top right, top left.

Michael J. Hipple/Gasoline Alley Antiques: page c4 middle left.

Richard Gutman: page c4 bottom.

Iowa Gas Swap: page c6 bottom right.

Richard Opfer Auctioneering, Inc.: pages c5 bottom right, center, c6 middle right.

The New York Public Library: page c7 top left.

Larry White: pages c5 top right, middle left both.

COLOR GLASS

Courtesy Antik: page c9 bottom left.

Courtesy Doyle New York: pages c8 top left, bottom left, c9 bottom right.

Private collection of Joseph F. Muratore, M.D.; photos by Stan Schnier: pages c8 middle right, c9 top all.

Rago Modern Auctions, Lambertville, NJ: pages c8 middle left, bottom middle left, c9 bottom center, bottom middle right.

Courtesy Skinner, Inc.: pages c8 bottom middle, bottom middle right, c9 bottom middle left.

Courtesy Toledo Museum of Art: page c8 top right.

Private collection of Rosemary Trietsch, photos by Stan Schnier: pages c8 bottom right, c9 top all.

COLOR SPORTS

Courtesy Barry Halper Baseball Archives: pages c10–c11 all except c10 far right.

Christie's Images: page c12 top right, middle right.

Courtesy The Complete Sportsman, photos Paul Schmookler: page C13 top all.

Photos © Enrico Ferorelli 1999, Land of Little Rivers: page c13 middle right, middle center right.

Photos Ron Gast, http://home.cfl.rr.com/rkgast/: page c13 middle left, bottom all.

Images from THE GOLF CLUB by Jeffrey Ellis ©Zephyr Productions 2003: page c12 middle both, bottom all.

©MastroNet, Inc.: page c10 far right. Pictured item was sold in a MastroNet, Inc. division auction.

Courtesy Joe and Donna Tonelli, photos James Krancic: page c13 middle center.

Courtesy Steve Whitney, redsgolf1@aol.com: c12 top left, top middle, middle left.

COLOR TOYS

Adamstown Antique Gallery: pages c16 top left, c17 bottom left.

American Toys, www.american-toys.com: pages c14 top left, middle, bottom right, c15 all, c16 top right, top middle, middle left, bottom right and bottom left, c17 top both, middle both, bottom right.

Dietrich Gehring: pages c14 top right, bottom left, c16 middle right.

COLOR FASHION AND TEXTILES

Courtesy Doyle New York: pages c18 top left insert, middle left, c19 all except bottom middle.

ENOKIWORLD.COM: page c18 top left.

Courtesy Karen Augusta: page c18 middle.

Laura Fisher Antiques: c18 bottom left, bottom right.

Levi Strauss & Co.: page c18 middle right.

Courtesy Vintage Textile.co: pages c18 top right, c19 bottom middle.

COLOR DOLLS AND DOLL ACCESSORIES

Courtesy Doyle New York: page c20 bottom right.

Courtesy McMasters Harris Auction Company: page c20 top right, top left, middle right, middle left, bottom left.

Courtesy Treasure Quest Auction Galleries: page c20 middle.

COLOR WRISTWATCHES

Stan Schnier/Aaron Faber Gallery: page c21 all.

COLOR ENTERTAINMENT

Christie's Images: pages c22 top right, bottom left, bottom middle, c23 bottom left and bottom middle.

Courtesy Hard Rock Café: c23 bottom right.

Courtesy Skinner, Inc.: pages c22 top middle, c23 top right, bottom middle right.

Courtesy Sotheby's: pages c22 middle, bottom right, c23 top middle, top left.

COLOR JEWELRY

Courtesy Doyle New York: pages c24 top right, middle center, bottom right, bottom middle right, bottom left, c25 top right, center, middle left, bottom center.

Courtesy Mark Mcdonald/330: page c24 middle right.

Morning Glory Antiques & Jewelry: pages c24 top left, bottom middle left, c25 bottom middle left and bottom right.

Rhinestone Rosie: pages c24 middle left, c25 bottom left.

Sparklz Vintage Jewelry: pages c24 bottom center.

COLOR POSTERS AND ILLUSTRATION ART

Photos Courtesy Illustration House: pages c28 bottom left, c29 middle, middle right, middle left, bottom left; printed by permission of the Norman Rockwell Family Agency–©2003 The Norman Rockwell Family Entities, page c28 bottom right.

Courtesy Swann Auction Galleries: pages c26 top left, bottom left, c27 all, c28 top right, top middle, top left, c29 top right, top left; courtesy Milton Glaser: page c26 bottom right.

COLOR FURNITURE

Courtesy Doyle New York: page c30 middle.

Courtesy Phillips, de Pury & Luxembourg: pages c30 bottom left, c31 bottom left, c32 top left, middle left.

Rago Modern Auctions, Lambertville, NJ: page c30 top left, c31 top, bottom right, c32 top middle, bottom.

Courtesy Skinner, Inc.: page c30 bottom right.

Courtesy Sotheby's: page c32 top right.

INDEX

R